❧ The New Encyclopedia of Wine

Alexis Bespaloff has been the wine columnist for *New York* magazine since 1975, is a regular contributor to *Elle*, and has written about wine for *Food & Wine*, *Connoisseur*, and *House & Garden*. He is the author of *The New Signet Book of Wine*, a paperback guide that is the best-selling wine book in America, with more than 800,000 copies in print, and edited *The Fireside Book of Wine*, a literary anthology.

Frank Schoonmaker, who had his own wine importing firm, was considered one of the world's greatest wine experts. He pioneered the widespread use of varietal names and informative back labels for American wine in the 1940s, published the first edition of his *Encyclopedia* in 1964, and remained a leading figure in the wine industry until his death in 1976.

The New Encyclopedia of Wine

ALEXIS BESPALOFF
from the Classic Work by
FRANK SCHOONMAKER

**A Jill Norman Book
Century**

First published in 1990 by Century,
an imprint of the Random Century Group Ltd,
20 Vauxhall Bridge Road, London SW1V 2SA

Random Century (Australia) Pty Ltd,
20 Alfred Street, Milsons Point, Sydney,
New South Wales 2061, Australia

Random Century New Zealand Ltd, PO Box 40-086,
Glenfield, Auckland 10, New Zealand

Random Century South Africa (Pty) Ltd,
PO Box 337, Bergvlei, 2012 South Africa

British Library Cataloguing in Publication Data
Bespaloff, Alexis
   The wine encyclopaedia.
   1. Wines
   I. Title
   II. Schoonmaker, Frank, *1905-1976*. Encyclopedia of wine
   641.22

   ISBN 0-7126-3940-3

Cover photograph by Mick Rock
Design by Gillian Riley
Typeset in Garamond Original by SX Composing Ltd, Rayleigh, Essex
Printed and bound in Great Britain by Mackays of Chatham

🎔 Contents

❧ *List of Maps*

Alphabetical Encyclopedia

❧ A

Abboccato An Italian word that, when applied to wine, means "sweet" or "semisweet". The equivalent of the French *moelleux*, it is used particularly with the wines of Orvieto, which are customarily classified as either *secco* (dry) or *abboccato*.

Abfüllung German for "bottling". See Erzeugerabfüllung.

Abocado Spanish for "semisweet".

Abruzzi A mountainous region (Abruzzo in Italian) on the mid-Adriatic coast of Italy, producing about 40 million cases annually, its best-known wines, both DOC, are Montepulciano d'Abruzzo and Trebbiano d'Abruzzo.

Achaea A Greek province forming the southern shore of the Gulf of Corinth in the Peloponnesus; it produces a considerable quantity of red and white wine, particularly in the neighbourhood of Patras.

Acid A natural and essential component of wine, acidity contributes zest and liveliness (as a squeeze of lemon does to a drink or a dish) and is especially important in a white wine, whose crisp, refreshing taste is often its most important characteristic. Acidity also plays a role in the longevity of white wines, which lack the tannic structure of reds. A wine with too much acidity, such as one made from unripe grapes, will taste tart or sharp; one with too little acidity, from a very warm region or an unusually hot year, will taste flat, flabby, and lifeless. Sweet and semisweet white wines, in particular, have a cloying taste if they lack balancing acidity. And the acidity in such diverse wines as Riesling from the Moselle, California Sauvignon Blanc, and red Bordeaux makes them more compatible with food; the right amount of mouthwatering acidity stimulates the appetite, cuts across rich foods, and refreshes the palate. *Acetic acid*, also known as volatile acidity, is present in all wines in trace amounts, but a wine that tastes sour betrays an excess of acetic acid, the result of bacterial spoilage. (Although the word *vinegar* is derived from *vin aigre*, or "sour wine", the vinegary smell that is sometimes encountered in a defective wine is attributable to ethyl acetate, a volatile and disagreeable ester.) Technical terms that define a wine's acidity include *total acidity*, which refers to all of the acids derived from grapes, both volatile and fixed; *volatile acidity*, which refers to the acids that become volatile and evaporate from wine when it is boiled; *fixed acidity*, which refers to the acids that remain after the volatile acidity boils off (a combination of tartaric, malic, citric, lactic, and succinic acid, the first being the principal acid of grapes); and *pH*, which is related to the intensity of a wine's acidity.

Adega Portuguese for a wine warehouse or cellar, generally above ground; the equivalent of a *chai* in France or a *bodega* in Spain.

Adige An important river of northern Italy, draining the picturesque and interesting vineyard districts of Alto Adige and Trentino as well as Valpolicella, running through Verona, and emptying into the Adriatic south of Venice.

Adulterated Wine A wine that has been treated with unauthorized material or with an excessive amount of a permitted substance.

Aestivalis, Vitis A native American vine species widespread through the central southern states; Cynthiana, also called Norton, is one of its best-known grape varieties.

Affentaler A German wine from the Black Forest foothills in the Baden region made from the Spätburgunder (Pinot Noir) grape, light in colour, almost a rosé, and whose quality is hardly more than passable. Its odd name has nevertheless given it a certain notoriety, like Zeller Schwarze Katz and Kröver Nacktarsh: *Affental* means "monkey valley", and the wine is therefore marketed in a bottle embossed with a monkey.

Africa This vast continent produces wine only in its northern and southern extremities, in the temperate zone. *See* Algeria, Morocco, Tunisia, South Africa.

Aftertaste The sensation that remains in the mouth after swallowing or

– at a professional tasting – expectorating wine; also known as the finish. *See* Caudalie.

Agassac, Château d' A *cru bourgeois exceptionnel* in the commune of Ludon, entitled to the appellation Haut-Médoc; its 85 acres produce about 15,000 cases.

Aging All wines age to some extent, first in the cellar (in barrel, cask, vat or tank) and then in the bottle, and many wines, if properly stored, improve somewhat with aging. It's well to remember, however, that 90 percent of the wine produced in the world is as good when six months old as it is ever likely to be, and most of those wines will deteriorate, not improve, after their second birthday. Although wine is often described as a "living thing", our enjoyment should not be diminished by accepting the more prosaic fact that wine is a combination of natural components – primarily water, alcohols, acids, and tannins – that interact during aging, a process that will eventually result in decay; for many fine wines, of course, the interaction will improve the wine's flavour for a number of years. In practice, all rosés and most white wines are bottled within months of the harvest and are best consumed young, while they retain the freshness, fruit, and charm that is their main appeal. Many light reds, too, are bottled within six or eight months of the harvest and are best consumed within a year or eighteen months. Many fine red and white wines are aged in small oak barrels or larger casks, where they evolve in the presence of limited, but necessary, amounts of oxygen. Although most wines are ready to drink when bottled, or within six months, some improve with additional bottle age; such wines as fine red Bordeaux, the best California Cabernet Sauvignon, Barolo and Brunello di Montalcino from Italy, vintage port, and certain sweet white wines need five years or more to develop the qualities for which they are known. Bottle aging, which occurs without the further absorption of oxygen and is therefore a different and slower process than wood aging, softens the initial vigour and harshness of certain red wines and enriches the taste of a number of dry and sweet white wines. There has perhaps been too much emphasis placed on age, as if age itself were a virtue. It can be, but often is not, and it's likely that more wine has been drunk too old than too young. See Barrel Aging, Bottle Aging.

Aglianico del Vulture A remarkable red wine, made from the Aglianico grape in the Italian region of Basilicata. The better vineyards are planted entirely on the volcanic soil of Monte Vulture, about 80 miles east of Naples; in this isolated and rather backward district, well-equipped cellars are few, and genuine, well-made Aglianico del Vulture is not easy to come by. The excellent Taurasi, produced in the adjoining region of Campania, is also made from the Aglianico grape.

Agrafe A metal clip used to secure the temporary cork during bottle fermentation of champagne, now almost entirely replaced by the less expensive and more easily manipulated crown cap.

Ahr A small river in western Germany that joins the Rhine north of Koblenz and gives its name to the second smallest of the eleven Anbaugebiete, or specified wine regions. Its hillside vineyards, the northernmost in Germany, are planted largely with Spätburgunder (Pinot Noir) and Portugieser, and red wines account for about two thirds of the region's production, most of which is consumed locally. Riesling and Müller-Thurgau make up nearly a third of the Ahr's 1,000 planted acres, whose wines are marketed with one Bereich, one Grosslage, and about 40 Einzellagen. The principal wine-producing towns are Ahrweiler, Bad Neuenahr, and Walporzheim.

Aigle A village in the Chablais district, in the canton of Vaud, in western Switzerland, producing fine, dry white wines from the Chasselas grape, known locally as Dorin.

Airén Curiously enough, this is the most widely planted grape variety in the world; virtually all of the acreage is found in central Spain, however, in the La Mancha and Valdepeñas regions, where the grape produces relatively undistinguished white wine (much of which is distilled into brandy) and is also used to lighten the local red wines.

Aisne A French *département* with about 3,700 acres of vineyards, almost all planted with Pinot Meunier, which are included within the Champagne appellation; the vineyards, situated north of the Marne River, produce wines that are not of first-rate quality.

Aix *See* Coteaux d'Aix-en-Provence

Ajaccio An *Appellation Contrôlée* for red, white, and rosé wines produced in the hills around that city, on the west coast of the island of Corsica.

Alameda A county in northern California, east of San Francisco Bay, whose principal vineyards are in the Livermore Valley. Most of the county's 1,800 acres are planted with white varieties, including Chardonnay, Sauvignon Blanc, Sémillon, and Grey Riesling; the principal red varieties are Cabernet Sauvignon and Petite Sirah.

Alba An important town south of Turin, in the Italian region of Piedmont, famous for its white truffles, and one of the principal centres of fine wine production in northern Italy. Barbaresco is some four miles to the east, Barolo about eight miles to the southwest.

Albana di Romagna An attractive dry white wine produced from the Albana grape in Italy's Emilia-Romagna region, elevated from DOC to DOCG in 1988; the delimited production zone, which includes 23 communes in the provinces of Forli, Ravenna, and Bologna, overlaps those for the DOCs Sangiovese di Romagna and Trebbiano di Romagna and extends from Bologna to Rimini, on the Adriatic coast. Some semi-sweet *amabile* is also made, as well as *spumante*, or sparkling wine; potential production amounts to more than 400,000 cases a year, but only 50,000 cases are marketed as DOCG.

Albano *See* Colli Albani

Albariño A Spanish white-wine grape cultivated in the northwest corner of the country, in the region of Galicia; identical to the Alvarinho of Portugal, grown on the other side of the Miño River, it produces similar wines – fresh, crisp, and light-bodied.

Albariza The extraordinary white soil, containing a high proportion of water-retaining chalk, found in the vineyards round Jerez de la Frontera, in southern Spain; the finest sherries are produced from the Palomino grape grown in *albariza*.

Alcamo A dry white wine, also called Bianco d'Alcamo, from a DOC zone round the village of that name, in the western part of Sicily; it is made primarily from the local Catarratto grape.

Alcohol The colourless, volatile spirit ethyl alcohol (C_2H_6O, also known as ethanol), is formed by the activity of enzymes secreted by living micro-organisms known as yeast cells. These convert the sugar in grape juice into approximately equal parts of alcohol and carbon-dioxide gas by the process of fermentation; in practice, 55 or even 60 percent of the sugar may be converted to alcohol by modern vinification techniques, so that grape juice containing 22 percent sugar can result in wine with 13.2 percent alcohol. Fermentation may produce wines with as much as 16 percent alcohol, and some wines contain no more that 7 or 8 percent alcohol, but most table wines contain between 11 and 14 percent. Fortified wines, to which alcohol in the form of brandy or high-proof neutral spirits has been added, generally contain from 17 to 22 percent alcohol. Although alcohol is often described as flavourless, it has a slightly sweet taste; and wines high in alcohol are characterized by a sensation often described as warm, hot, or even biting.

Alcoholic A term applied to a wine that has too much alcohol for its body and weight, making it unbalanced; an excess of alcohol is revealed by a burning or biting sensation.

Aleatico An Italian grape that produces a sweet red wine with a pronounced flavour reminiscent of Muscat. Two versions have achieved DOC status – Aleatico di Puglia and Aleatico di Gradoli – and a well-known Aleatico comes from the island of Elba, near the town of Portoferraio.

Alella A village just north of Barcelona, in Spain's Catalonia region, known for its agreeable red, white, and rosé wines. More than three quarters of the production consists of dry and semisweet white wines made primarily from Xarello and Garnacha Blanca grapes; most of this comes from the local co-operative cellar and is marketed under the brand name Marfil. Once one of the most popular wines of the region, Alella now comes from fewer than 1,000 acres of vineyards.

Alexander Valley A viticultural area in northern Sonoma County that extends along the Russian River from a point near Healdsburg north past Geyserville, Asti, and Cloverdale to the Mendocino County border. Named after Cyrus Alexander, who settled there in the 1840s, the area now contains more than 6,000 acres of vineyards; perhaps best known for its relatively rich Chardonnay and supple Cabernet Sauvignon and Merlot, the area also produces Gewürztraminer and Johannisberg Riesling in the cooler parts of the valley, and Zinfandel in the warmer, northern section. Simi, Jordan, Alexander Valley Vineyards, Chateau Souverain, and Geyser Peak are some of the wineries situated in the Alexander Valley.

Algarve A district along the southern coast of Portugal perhaps better known as a tourist attraction than for its agreeable red, white, and rosé wines; an aperitif wine, similar to a dry sherry, is also made.

Algeria A former French colony, now an independent country on the Mediterranean coast of North Africa, bounded on the east by Tunisia and on the west by Morocco. Beginning about a hundred years ago, vast areas were planted with vineyards by French settlers, nearly 900,000 acres in all; at the time of independence, in 1962, annual production was the equivalent of 160 million cases, and nearly a third of the Algerian labour force (largely Mohammedan and therefore not wine-drinking) was engaged in grape growing and winemaking. Most of the production was rather common red table wine made primarily from such grape varieties as Cinsault, Carignane, Alicante-Bouschet, Morrastel, and Aramon. Two thirds of Algeria's huge output was regularly shipped to France (it then accounted for about six times the total volume of all French wine exports put together); blended with the wines of the Midi, it formed the base of France's *vin ordinaire*. In addition, enormous quantities of *mistelle* were produced and shipped to France as a base for vermouth and aperitif wines.

When Algeria gained independence, many of the French landowners and technicians left the country, and today there are about 300,000 acres producing fewer than 15 million cases of wine. Although many of the high-yielding, low-quality vineyards on the plains have been replanted to other agricultural products, Algeria's best vineyards continue to produce good wines. They are situated in mountainous country, generally 30 to 50 miles from the coast, at altitudes ranging from 1,500 to 2,500 feet, and they include a dozen districts that had previously been given VDQS status by the French. Grenache, Mourvèdre, Syrah, and even Cabernet

Sauvignon are planted in some sites, along with Cinsault, Carignane, and Alicante-Bouschet. A little white wine is also made, primarily from Ugni Blanc and Clairette. Algeria's fine wine districts are Aïn-Bessem Bouira, Medea, and Côtes du Zaccar, in the region of Alger; and in the Oran region, which accounts for most of the country's vineyards, the best districts are Mostagenem, Mostagenem-Kenenda, Mascara, Coteaux du Mascara, Haut Dahra, Monts du Tessalah, and Coteaux du Tlemcen.

Alicante A province south of Valencia, on the Mediterranean coast of Spain, most of whose wines are sturdy, full-flavoured reds made primarily from the Monastrell grape; some sweet Moscatel is also made.

Alicante-Bouschet One of a number of heavy-bearing, rather common red-wine grapes developed in the nineteenth century by Louis Bouschet and his son, Henri, who were seeking a hybrid with deep colour and a high sugar content for the production of cheap bulk wine in the Midi region of France and in Algeria. Unlike almost all other red-wine varieties, it has red juice, being a cross of Teinturier du Cher × Aramon × Grenache. Widely planted in California during the Prohibition years as a juice grape for home wine-makers – its thick skin made it easy to ship – it now accounts for only 2,300 acres, all of them in the hot San Joaquin Valley. (This variety should not be confused with Bouchet, the local name for Cabernet Franc in the Saint-Emilion district of Bordeaux.)

Aligoté A productive white-wine grape of secondary quality, widely grown in Burgundy, where it yields an undistinguished, short-lived white wine that is nevertheless very agreeable if drunk young. White burgundies made from the Aligoté grape must be so labelled, as Bourgogne Aligoté; the village of Bouzeron, in the Côte Chalonnaise, is known for its Aligoté and, in fact, has its own AOC, Bourgogne Aligoté de Bouzeron. Recent vintages have produced 500,000 to 900,000 cases of Bourgogne Aligoté, but little is exported.

Aloxe-Corton A famous wine-producing village of the Côte d'Or, in France's Burgundy region. Located in the northern part of the Côte de Beaune district, Aloxe-Corton is unusual in that its red and white wines are almost equally celebrated, although the best of these – from *grand cru* vineyards – do not carry the name Aloxe at all and are labelled Corton-Charlemagne, Corton, Corton Clos du Roi, Corton Bressandes, etc. The wines from certain plots situated in two nearby villages, Ladoix-Serrigny and Pernand-Vergelesses, are also legally entitled to these vineyard names, as they are produced on adjacent portions of the same impressive, steep, vine-covered hill of Corton. All of the red wines must come exclusively from Pinot Noir, the whites from Chardonnay. The red Cortons of great years are probably the best, certainly the longest-lived wines of the Côte de Beaune; they are magnificent Burgundies of wonderful breed and texture, silky, well balanced, and fine. The white Corton-Charlemagne is fully the equal of the best wines of Meursault and Puligny-Montrachet and, in the opinion of many experts, may be even better. Wines marked as Aloxe-Corton (with or without the name of a specific vineyard) are delicate and attractive, but lighter in body and quicker to mature than those from Corton itself.

Alsace An ancient French province (although many of its inhabitants speak a dialect of German among themselves) bordering the Rhine north of Switzerland and comprising the modern *départements* of Haut-Rhin and Bas-Rhin. The vineyards, which are about 20 miles west of the Rhine, extend for about 70 miles along the lower slopes of the Vosges Mountains from Strasbourg on the north past Colmar to Mulhouse; they are among the most beautiful in the world, and the small vineyard towns are exceedingly picturesque. About 10 million cases of wine are produced from 31,000 acres, virtually all of it white, although a small amount of rosé and light red is made from the Pinot Noir grape. About 80 percent of Alsace's acreage is planted with four varieties – Riesling, Gewürztraminer, Sylvaner, and Pinot Blanc. Other varieties cultivated include Pinot Gris (also known as Tokay d'Alsace), Muscat, and Chasselas.

The *Appellation Contrôlée* Alsace or Vins d'Alsace was established in 1962 and includes more than 90 villages, among them Barr, Eguisheim, Guebwiller, Kayserberg, Ribeauvillé, Riquewihr, Thann, and Turckheim, but these names rarely appear on labels; Alsace wines are usually marketed with the name of the grape from which each is made (the wine must contain 100 percent of the named variety). The term *Edelzwicker*, which means "noble blend", is actually used for wines made from lesser varieties, such as

Chasselas and Sylvaner. In 1983, after years of discussion, the appellation Alsace Grand Cru was officially established for wines that come from 25 specific *lieux-dits* or vineyard sites, whose names may appear on a label. Only wines made from Riesling, Gewürztraminer, Pinot Gris, or Muscat are eligible for *grand cru* status, and the regulations also specify minimum alcohol levels, maximum production per acre, and other aspects that affect quality. Another 20-odd vineyard sites have been be added to the original list, but wines entitled to the *grand cru* designation account for less than 5 percent of the total crop. Phrases such as *Grande Réserve* or *Réserve Personnelle* are used at the discretion of individual producers.

Two designations used for Alsace late-harvest wines were officially recognized in 1983 – *Vendange Tardive* and *Sélection de Grains Nobles*; the appellation Crémant d'Alsace is used for sparkling wines produced by the *méthode champenoise*.

The wines of Alsace, shipped in tall green bottles and labelled with the names of grape varieties associated with Germany, are often confused with the delicate, slightly sweet wines produced in that country. Alsace wines are, in fact, completely dry, intensely flavoured, and more assertive than those of Germany, and fully deserve the popularity they are beginning to achieve.

Alsheim   A wine village situated between Worms and Oppenheim, in Germany's Rheinhessen region, with about 1,000 acres of vineyards; its best-known sites are Frühmesse and Sonnenberg.

Altesse   A white-wine grape cultivated in the Savoie region of eastern France, where it is also known as Roussette; it is used to make the AOC Seyssel, and its crisp, dry wines are also entitled to the regional appellation Roussette de Savoie.

Alto Adige   The upper portion of the Adige River Basin, the northernmost part of Italy, forming the modern province of Bolzano and extending to the present Austrian frontier. The fertile valleys and hillsides of this mountainous country, known to its large German-speaking population as Südtirol, or South Tyrol, have been famous for their wines since the days of Rome, and they produce today 6 to 7 million cases of wine from 14,000 acres of vineyards; more than three quarters of this consists of DOC wines, a remarkably high proportion. About 80 percent of the wines made in Alto Adige are red, and most of this comes from the native Schiava grape (Vernatsch in Germany); other red varieties include the native Lagrein, Pinot Nero (Blauburgunder), Cabernet, and Merlot; white grapes include Chardonnay, Pinot Bianco (Weissburgunder), Pinot Grigio (Ruländer) Sylvaner, Müller-Thurgau, and Traminer. (The latter grape is believed to have originated south of Bolzano in the village of Termeno, whose German name is Tramin.) The basic DOC for the province is Alto Adige (Südtiroler), whose name is joined to that of the appropriate varietal name, as Pinot Grigio dell' Alto Adige, or Südtiroler Ruländer. The most important DOC in terms of volume, however, is Caldaro, or Lago di Caldaro (Kalterersee), one of the biggest DOC zones in Italy, with an annual production of 2.5 million cases; this pleasant red wine, light in colour and body, is made from Schiava. Other reds made from Schiava are Santa Maddalena (St. Magdalener); Colli di Bolzano (Bozner Leiten) from the hills around Bolzano; and Meranese di Collina (Meraner Hugel), from the hills around Merano. White wines are produced in the DOC zones Terlano (Terlaner) and Valle Isarco (Eisacktaler). In addition, fine sparkling wines are now being produced from Chardonnay, Pinot Bianco, and Pinot Nero grapes, much of it by the *méthode champenoise*.

Alto Douro The classic zone of port-wine production; the mountainous area north and south of the Douro River upstream and east of Oporto, in northern Portugal.

Alvarinho A Portuguese white wine named after the grape variety from which it is made, in limited quantities, in the Monção district of the Vinho Verde region.

Amabile An Italian word used to describe a semisweet wine that is likely to be somewhat sweeter than one labelled *abboccato*.

Amador A California county situated east of Sacramento, along the foothills of the Sierra Nevada Mountains, and part of the more extensive region sometimes referred to as the Sierra Foothills. The Gold Rush of 1849 brought many new settlers to the region, vineyards were extensively planted in Amador, and wine was produced there until Prohibition. In the late 1960s and early 1970s, when there was only one winery left in the county, a number of California wineries began to make rich, intensely flavoured Zinfandels from Amador county grapes, and the region has since enjoyed a revival; more than a dozen new wineries have been established, and there are about 1,500 acres of vineyards. Zinfandel accounts for two thirds of this, and much of the rest is Sauvignon Blanc, but a number of other varieties are also planted, including Chardonnay, Cabernet Sauvignon, and Chenin Blanc. There are two viticultural areas in Amador – Shenandoah Valley and the adjoining Fiddletown; wineries include Monteviña, Karly, and Shenandoah Vineyards.

Amarone An unusual, heady red wine from Italy's Valpolicella district, near Verona; its full name is Recioto della Valpolicella Amarone. The wine is made from especially ripe bunches of grapes (primarily Corvina Veronese) that are spread out on trays and stored indoors for three or four months in cool dry, well-ventilated rooms until the grapes are partially shrivelled and dehydrated, which increases the proportion of sugar in the juice and concentrates various elements that affect flavour. The grapes, which lose 25 to 30 percent of their weight, are also affected by the beneficial mould, *Botrytis cinerea*. When the grapes are crushed and fermented, usually in January or February, the resulting wine is likely to have 14 or 15 percent alcohol and a ripe, intense, grapey taste very different from those marketed simply as Valpolicella. Although Amarone is always fermented until it is completely dry (Amarone is derived from amaro, "bitter") and aged for several years in cask, its richness sometimes gives a slightly sweet impression on the palate; it is among the most powerful of Italy's reds.

Amboise A picturesque little town and celebrated Renaissance château on the Loire River near Tours whose vineyards produce fresh, fruity, and engaging wines entitled to the appellation Touraine-Amboise. The whites, which resemble Vouvray, are made from the Chenin Blanc grape; the reds and rosés come from Malbec (known locally as Cot), Gamay, and occasionally Cabernet Franc. About 75,000 to 100,000 cases are produced, most of it consumed locally.

Ambonnay One of the best wine-producing villages of the Montagne de Reims, in France's Champagne region. Its vineyards, planted with Pinot Noir, are rated at 100 percent.

Amelioration A winemaker's term, often too broadly used, to cover certain cellar practices, some of which are entirely necessary and some of which are illegal; these include the addition of sugar to the must during fermentation, the addition of water to the must to reduce acidity or to compensate for overripe grapes, adjusting the acidity of must or wine, and so on. Strict laws cover such matters in most wine-producing countries. See Chaptalization, Gallisation, Water.

American Wine *See* United States

Amontillado A type of Spanish sherry whose name is derived from the Montilla district south of Cordoba, whose wines amontillado supposedly resembled at one time. Technically, an amontillado is a fino that has aged in such a way as to acquire a deeper colour, more body and flavour, and a characteristic nutty taste. The wine is completely dry as it ages in barrel, but rarely bottled as such; most sherries labelled amontillado are medium-sweet wines and, truth to tell, are likely to be sweetened blends of fino and oloroso rather than true amontillados.

Amoroso A Spanish term, seldom seen today, which refers to a sweet oloroso sherry; similar to cream sherry.

Ampelography The study and classification of vines and grapes; also, the publication of such studies with text and illustrations.

Amphora An ancient earthenware container for wine or oil, usually with two handles and a pointed end.

Amtliche Prüfungsnummer A qualification number, usually abbreviated to A.P. Nr., which must appear on German Qualitätswein labels to indicate that the wine has been analyzed and approved by a tasting panel. There are five sets of numbers (which may or may not be separated by spaces), and they signify the following: the control centre where the wines are tested and tasted; the place of bottling; the producer's own identification number; the number assigned to that particular lot of wine; and the year of examination (not the wine's vintage year).

Anbaugebiet The term, established by the 1971 German wine laws, for a specified region whose wines are entitled to Qualitätswein or Qualitätswein mit Prädikat status. There are eleven such regions: Ahr, Mosel-Saar-Ruwer, Mittelrhein, Rheingau, Nahe, Rheinhessen, Rheinpfalz, Hessiche Bergstrasse, Franken, Württemberg, and Baden. The appropriate regional name must always appear on the label of a quality wine, thus giving the consumer an indication of the wine's origin. Each Anbaugebiet has subdivisions: Bereich (district), Grosslage (general site), and Einzellage (individual site, or vineyard). Individual entries will be found for all of these names and terms.

Andalusia A famous, fertile, and beautiful region, comprising most of the southernmost fourth of Spain; its best-known wines are sherry, Málaga, and Montilla.

Anderson Valley A viticultural area west of Ukiah, in Mendocino County, which follows the Navarro River, a tributary of the Russian River; the vineyards, which were first planted in the late 1960s, begin about ten miles from the coast and continue for a dozen miles from Navarro to Boonville. The district's cool climate has been especially successful for such white varieties as Gewürztraminer and Johannisberg Riesling, and for *méthode champenoise* sparkling wines made from Chardonnay and Pinot Noir. Husch and Navarro are known for their white wines, Scharffenberger for sparkling wines; the French champagne firm of Louis Roederer has established vineyards in this area.

Añejo Spanish for "old" or "aged", but without legal definition for wines.

Angelica Rarely seen today, this was one of the poorest and cheapest of American fortified wines, often little more than a blend of grape juice and high-proof brandy; said to take its name from the city of Los Angeles.

Angélus, Château l' One of the better-known, and largest, *grands crus classés* of Saint-Emilion; its 60 acres produce about 12,000 cases a year of soft, pleasant red wine.

Anghelu Ruju A sweet, red, fortified proprietary wine (the name means "red angel") produced by Sella & Mosca on the island of Sardinia; reminiscent of port, it is made from semi-dried

Cannonau grapes.

Angludet, Château d' An excellent vineyard in the commune of Margaux, in the Médoc, whose 75 acres produce about 12,000 cases a year; a second label, Baury, was introduced with the 1985 vintage. The property was acquired in 1961 by Peter Allan Sichel, a Bordeaux *négociant* of British origin, and its supple, well-structured wines fully merit their popularity.

Anjou Historically, a province in west-central France, now contained within the *département* of Maine-et-Loire, on both sides of the Loire River. Its best-known cities are Angers, situated about halfway between Nantes and Tours, and Saumur; indeed, for AOC purposes, the region is referred to as Anjou-Saumur. The production of AOC wines varies from 7 to 12 million cases, two thirds of it rosé and red. The white wines are made from the Chenin Blanc grape (also called Pineau de la Loire, although it is not a pinot), and they include some of the best sweet wines of France; Cabernet Franc is the principal red-wine grape; others include Malbec (known locally as Cot), Gamay, and Groslot. Rosé d'Anjou and Cabernet d'Anjou, the latter a rosé made from Cabernet Franc, are the principal appellations; there is also a great deal of red and white wine entitled only to the basic name Anjou – these three appellations account for almost two thirds of all the AOC wines of the region.

Other white-wine appellations include Anjou-Coteaux de la Loire, which contains the better-known Savennières; Roches aux Moines and Coulée de Serrant are its most famous vineyards. Two tributaries of the Loire give their names to white-wine appellations – Coteaux de l'Aubance and the more highly reputed Coteaux du Layon, which can produce sweet, honeyed wines in favourable vintages; its best-known vineyards are Quarts de Chaume and Bonnezeaux. The appellation Saumur may be used for red or white wines, and a certain amount of rosé is sold as Cabernet de Saumur. The best red wines of the Anjou-Saumur region are produced from Cabernet Franc near the village of Champigny and labelled Saumur Champigny. Most of the white wines of the Saumur district are transformed into sparkling wines, many of them made by the *méthode champenoise*.

AOC *See* Appellation Contrôlée

A.P. Nr. *See* Amtliche Prüfungsnummer

Aperitif A French word now used in a very general way to describe almost any alcoholic beverage consumed before a meal to whet the appetite. A cocktail is an aperitif, as is a glass of white wine, if so consumed. Vermouth, both sweet and dry, is a popular aperitif, as are a number of fortified and flavoured wines sold under proprietary names, such as Dubonnet, Lillet, St. Raphaël, and Byrrh. National preferences vary; the French often choose a sweet aperitif, such as tawny port or an anise-flavoured drink such as Pernod or Ricard; many Italians prefer such bitter drinks as Campari and Punt e Mes; and in England sherry and gin-and-tonic are enjoyed. From the wine-drinker's perhaps biased point of view, the best aperitifs stimulate the appetite and are neither too alcoholic nor too sweet; good choices include champagne or sparkling wine, dry sherry, and white wine.

Appellation Contrôlée Two words that now appear, often in small type, on virtually all of France's best wines. The phrase, often abbreviated to AOC (from *Appellation d'Origine Contrôlée*), means controlled place name and is the consumer's best guide to the origin and authenticity of any wine whose label bears these words. The laws specify the geographical limits of each appellation, whether a region, such as Anjou or Beaujolais; a village, such as Pommard or Sancerre; or even a specific vineyard, such as Chambertin or Montrachet. The AOC laws also take into account other factors besides a wine's place of origin that affect its quality; the grape varieties from which it may be made, the minimum amount of alcohol the wine must contain (to assure an adequate level of ripeness in the grapes), the maximum production permitted per acre, and certain aspects of viticulture and vinification that must conform to traditional practices in the region. The AOC laws were originally established, in 1935, to protect growers in the best-known vineyard areas against the unscrupulous use of famous wine names for inferior bottlings, and it must be added that just because a wine is genuine does not necessarily mean that it is good – some winemakers are more skilled and conscientious than others. Nevertheless, the AOC system is a very useful one indeed. There are now about 250 appellations (many of which apply to both red and white wines and, in some cases, to rosés), and their combined production accounts for the top 20 to 30 percent or so of all French wines, the equivalent in recent vintages of 140 to 230 million cases, of which about one third is white.

Almost every AOC wine has its own entry, and a complete list can be found on page 523.

Appellation d'Origine French term referring to a wine's place of origin, whether a region, a village, or a single plot of vines. Wines have been known by their place of origin since Greek and Roman times, and most modern wine-labelling laws are based on this traditional practice, including those of France, the *Denominazione di Origine Controllata* laws of Italy, and the *Denominación de Origen* laws of Spain, among others; the United States, too, has now established viticultural areas. There have, of course, been many abuses, and there still are, but regulations on the whole are far more strict than they were in the last century, or even twenty years ago.

In France, *Appellation d'Origine Contrôlée* laws have been established for three categories, officially regulated by an admirable organization called the Institut National des Appellations d'Origine (INAO). The highest rank is *Appellation Contrôlée*, which includes practically all of the famous wines of France. A second category is known as *Vins Délimités de Qualité Supérieure* (VDQS); its wines are also strictly regulated, and these include a number of good, if less famous, wines produced throughout France. In 1973 the third category, *Appellation d'Origin Simple* was discontinued to bring French law into line with the regulations of the European Common Market. The replacement category is *vins de pays*, whose wines must come from specified, though more broadly defined, areas.

At the bottom of the ladder is a vast quantity of wines with no geographical appellation at all, once known as *Vins de Consommation Courante* and now as *Vins de Table*. These may be blends of anything not found objectionable under the French pure food laws, and they need not be French wines at all unless they bear the words *Product of France* or the equivalent. There is nothing inherently objectionable about them (they are all cheap and some quite passable) providing consumers know just what they are getting.

Apre French for "harsh"; most often used to describe rough, young red wines of high tannin content.

Aprilia A DOC zone south of Rome and the Castelli Romani district that produces pleasant if undistinguished red and white wines labelled with the name of the grape variety from which each is made: Merlot di Aprilia, Sangiovese di Aprilia, and Trebbiano di Aprilia.

Apulia A region in southeast Italy (Puglia in Italian) that is often first in wine production among that country's twenty regions: 110 to 130 million cases, about 15 percent of all Italian wines. Most of this is common blending wine, with deep colour, high alcohol, and low acid. The table wines have improved in recent years, however, and include such noteworthy ones as Alezio, Salento, Castel del Monte, the dry white Locorotondo, the pink Rosa del Golfo, the red Primitivo di Gioia, and those of the Torre Quarto estate. Excellent wines from such varieties as Pinot Bianco, Chardonnay, Cabernet Franc, and Pinot Nero are produced by Attilio Simonini and marketed under the Favonio label.

Aquileia A DOC zone south of Udine in the Friuli-Venezia Giulia region of Italy. Merlot is the most widely planted grape; others include the indigenous Refosco, Tocai Friulano, and Verduzzo Friulano, as well as Cabernet and Pinot Grigio.

Aramon A common and immensely productive grape, once widely planted in the French Midi and in Algeria. The red wine it yields is deficient in colour and generally of poor quality.

Arbois A village and wine district in eastern France, near the Swiss border, forming part of the Côtes du Jura, in the ancient province of Franche-Comté. AOC red and rosé wines are produced from Poulsard, Trousseau, and Pinot Noir; dry white wines from Sauvagnin and Chardonnay.

Arche, Château d' A classed growth in the Sauternes district, situated between Châteaux Guiraud and La Tour Blanche; its 90 acres produce about 8,000 cases a year of an excellent, well-balanced sweet wine. Château d'Arche-Lafaurie is another property under the same ownership, and the name was previously used as a second label for the wines of Chateau d'Arche.

Arena Spanish for "sand", the term is applied to certain sherry-producing vineyards around Jerez de la Frontera whose wines are generally coarser than those from *albariza* and *barro* soils.

Argentina In terms of volume, the most important wine-producing country of South America; about 200 million cases a year come from 700,000 acres of vineyards. Exporting very little and importing even less, Argentina drinks her own wines at the rate of some 75 bottles per capita. Most of this is sound, inexpensive, and quite ordinary, the red better than the rosé or white. The vineyards are planted along the foothills of the Andes, about 600 miles west of Buenos Aires, not far from the Chilean border. Three quarters of the acreage is in the state of Mendoza, with additional plantings in San Juan and a limited amount in Rio Negro. The Criolla grape is still the most widely planted variety, but there are extensive plantings of French varieties, first introduced in the mid-nineteenth century, including more than 75,000 acres of Malbec, about 18,000 acres of Cabernet Sauvignon and Merlot, and lesser amounts of Chenin Blanc, Chardonnay, and Pinot Noir.

Arneis An Italian grape variety cultivated in the Roeri hills of the Piedmont region, north of Alba; it produces limited quantities of an excellent dry white wine.

Aroma Very different from bouquet, the aroma of a wine is more pronounced and more distinctive when the wine is young, being more directly related to the odour of the fresh grape. Certain varieties of grape (Gewürztraminer, Muscat, and Concord, to cite a few extreme examples) have particularly distinctive aromas, but they are diminished during fermentation and tend to fade further as bouquet takes its place in a mature wine.

Arrière-goût French for "aftertaste".

Arrières-Côtes The name given to a series of slopes in Burgundy, west of and roughly parallel to the Côte d'Or proper; vineyards planted in Aligoté and Gamay produce wines sold as Bourgogne Aligoté and Bourgogne Passe-tout-grains, but an increasing amount of Pinot Noir and Chardonnay has been planted here, and the attractive red and white wines they make are marketed as Bourgogne-Hautes Côtes de Beaune and Bourgogne-Hautes Côtes de Nuits.

Arroba A Spanish measure of approximately 16 litres – or just over three and a half gallons, and equivalent to 25 pounds of grapes.

Arrope Grape concentrate, used in Spain as a sweetening and colouring agent in sherries. It is produced by boiling down unfermented grape juice to its quintessence, or one fifth of its volume, whereby it acquires a deep brown colour and a burnt-sugar, or caramel, flavour.

Arroyo Grande Valley A small district between the Edna Valley and Santa Maria districts, 12 miles southeast of the town of San Luis Obispo, whose cool, foggy climate is suitable for Chardonnay, Pinot Noir, and Pinot Blanc grapes vinified to produce sparkling wines; Deutz, a French champagne firm, has established vineyards and a winery there.

Arroyo Seco A viticultural area in Monterey County, on the western side of the Salinas Valley, whose vineyards are planted on the foothills of a canyon formed by the Arroyo Seco River; this district, somewhat shielded from the cool ocean breezes, is best known for wines made from Chardonnay, Cabernet Sauvignon, Sauvignon Blanc, and Johannisberg Riesling, and as a source of grapes for fine sparkling wines.

Arsac A wine-producing commune of the Haut-Médoc, in the Bordeaux region, now entitled to the appellation Margaux; it contains one classed growth, Château du Tertre, plus several *crus bourgeois*.

Asciutto An Italian word which, when applied to wine, means "dry".

Asprino A dry, light Italian white wine produced just north of Naples.

Assemblage French for "assembling", as for a blend. The term has a specific, and important, meaning in Bordeaux, where the *assemblage* takes place at most châteaux in the first two or three months of the year following the vintage. The proprietor and cellar master taste each individual lot of wine from the most recent vintage – representing different grape varieties, different days of picking, and different plots within the vineyard, some of them with young vines – to determine which ones will be assembled and eventually bottled with the château name; the lesser lots are sold off in bulk or bottled under a second label. A conscientious proprietor is likely to set aside 15 to 30 percent of his crop in most years, and the severity with which the wines for the final *assem-*

blage are selected plays an important role in the quality and reputation of each château.

Assmannshausen A village on the Rhine just north of Rüdesheim, producing what may be the best and is certainly the most famous red wine of Germany; made from the Pinot Noir grape (known in Germany as Spätburgunder), it is perhaps comparable to a light, mediocre Burgundy, and is often somewhat sweet.

Asti An important wine-producing village south of Turin, in the Piedmont region of Italy, especially famous for its sweet sparkling wine, Asti Spumante. The village gives its name to an extended area that produces much red wine of good quality from Barbera, Dolcetto, Freisa, and Grignolino grapes; those that qualify for DOC status may add the name of the region, as Barbera d'Asti, Dolcetto d'Asti.

Asti Spumante Italy's best-known sparkling wine, made from Moscato di Canelli grapes (identical to the Muscat de Frontignan of France) planted on 23,000 acres in an extensive district just south of the village of Asti, in the Piedmont region. After the harvest, the grapes are pressed and the filtered juice stored at 32 degrees F. so that fermentation can take place weeks or months later. Virtually all of the 5 to 7 million cases of Asti Spumante produced annually is made by the *autoclave*, or Charmat process of tank fermentation from the still wine entitled to the DOC Moscato d'Asti. Unlike most sparkling wines, which are made in two steps – first the wine is fermented dry, then the still wine undergoes a second fermentation to produce the bubbles – Asti Spumante is made directly from the juice, which is transformed into a sparkling wine without first being made into a still wine. The finished wine, which is sweet and intensely grapey in taste, must contain between 7.5 and 9 percent alcohol and between 7.5 and 9 percent residual sugar.

Astringent A wine-taster's term applied to wines that make the mouth pucker, generally because of an excess of tannin. Many excellent red wines are astringent when young; providing they are not bitter, this is not a serious flaw, for they will soften and mellow with age. In a young red wine, astringency is often, but not invariably, an indication that the wine will be long-lived.

Aszú   A Hungarian term that refers to grapes affected by *Botrytis cinerea*, the mould that is sometimes called noble rot; these are crushed into a paste and added to the regular wine to produce the scarce and unusual sweet wines labelled Tokaji Aszú. *See* Tokay.

Atesino   An Italian term occasionally seen on labels to describe a wine produced along the Adige River, that is, in the Trentino-Alto Adige region.

Attica   An extensive vineyard region in Greece, near Athens, most of whose production is made into Retsina.

Aubance   *See* Coteaux de l'Aubance.

Aube   A French *département* with about 9,000 acres of vineyards entitled to the Champagne appellation; the vineyards, planted with Pinot Noir, Chardonnay, and some Pinot Meunier, are situated about 60 miles south of Epernay and the main Champagne districts.

Aude   A French *département*, second only to the Hérault in total wine production, with some 270,000 acres of vineyards producing 80 to 100 million cases, almost all of it red. Part of the Languedoc-Roussillon, also known as the Midi, its most important towns are Carcassonne and Narbonne; most of what it produces is simply *vin ordinaire*, but three districts, Corbières, Fitou, and the Minervois (the last partly in the Hérault), yield what are among the best of the common table wines of France. The sparkling Blanquette de Limoux is also produced there.

Aurora   A French-American hybrid (whose official name is Seibel 5279), the most widely planted hybrid in the Finger Lakes district of New York State; also known as Aurore, it makes good-quality white table and sparkling wines.

Aus Eigenem Lesegut   German for "Grower's own harvest", equivalent to estate-bottled, although not widely used. *See* Erzeugerab-füllung.

Ausbruch   A term used in Austria for sweet white wines made, mostly in the Burgenland region, from grapes affected by *Botrytis cinerea*. The minimum sugar content of the grapes at the time of harvest has been officially established as being between that required for a Beerenauslese and a Trockenbeerenauslese.

Auslese A German term that means "selected picking"; one of the designations within the category Qualitätswein mit Prädikat. Whether a wine labelled Auslese comes from the Moselle, the Rhine, or elsewhere in Germany, it is a special and superior sort, considerably sweeter and more expensive than those labelled Spätlese or Kabinett. At the time of the Lese, or harvest, especially ripe bunches, which may even be affected by *Botrytis cinerea*, or *Edelfäule*, are put aside and pressed separately. An Auslese must be made from grapes that contain specified minimum amounts of natural grape sugar – about 20 to 24 percent – depending on the grape variety and region. The bottled wine is likely to contain 4 to 7 percent sugar and is properly classified as a dessert wine, or one that is best enjoyed after a meal, rather than with food, although some oenophiles enjoy these wines with rich dishes. Auslesen from the Rhine, especially the Rheinpfalz and Rheinhessen, are richer and sweeter than those from the Moselle. The amount of Auslesen produced in Germany rarely exceeds 5 percent of the crop, even in favourable vintages, and in some regions such wines are produced in only one or two years out of ten.

Ausone, Château A celebrated *premier grand cru classé* in the Saint-Emilion district of Bordeaux that ranks with Château Cheval Blanc as one of the two best vineyards of the district. Its 17 acres, planted with almost equal parts of Merlot and Cabernet Franc, produce an average of fewer than 2,500 cases a year, which makes it the smallest of all the first growths of Bordeaux. The vineyard suffered a decline in the 1960s and early 1970s, but as a result of new management in the mid-1970s, the wines have re-established themselves in the top rank. Ausone takes its name from the fourth-century Latin poet and wine lover Ausonius, who had an estate and vineyard somewhere in the neighbourhood, although almost certainly not on the actual site of Château Ausone.

Australia Few countries have made their mark on the international wine scene as quickly and dramatically as did Australia in the mid-1980s, primarily with its range of varietal wines, including Chardonnay, Cabernet Sauvignon, Sauvignon Blanc (sometimes labelled Fumé Blanc), Shiraz (the Syrah of France's northern Rhône Valley), Sémillon, Rhine Riesling, and Muscat (vinified as a delicate, off-dry table wine or fortified to produce a rich, sweet dessert wine). The country also produces such unusual varietal blends as Cabernet-Shiraz and Sémillon-Chardonnay, as well as the more traditional Cabernet-Merlot and Sémillon-Sauvignon Blanc.

There are no indigenous native wines in Australia (whose history of viticulture and winemaking closely parallels that of the United States, especially of California). The first grapes were planted near Sydney in 1788 and commercial winemaking was established in the 1820s and 1830s in several regions throughout the country. At that time, the Scottish-born James Busby brought back cuttings of superior grape varieties from Europe, wrote treatises on viticulture, and planted the first vineyard in the Hunter Valley. Fortified wines such as port and sherry accounted for three quarters of wine consumption as recently as the 1960s; today, table wines – 80 percent of them white – make up more than three quarters of the wines drunk in Australia (where per capita consumption is nearly twice that of the United Kingdom, albeit based on a population of 16 million). About 40 million cases are produced by more than 550 wineries, and the diversity of Australian wines is such that it is not unusual for more than 2,000 different wines to be entered at each of the many annual wine competitions held there. As in most wine-producing countries, of course, fine wines represent only a small proportion of the total crop. About 60 percent of the country's wines go to market as cask, or bag-in-the-box wines, in cartons containing four litres or more, lined with inert and impermeable materials that collapse as the wine is drawn out (through a spigot) to prevent oxidation of the remaining wine.

Most inexpensive Australian wines are labelled with such generic names as Chablis, White Burgundy, Hock, Sauterne, Moselle, and Claret; fine wines are usually marketed with a full range of varietal names. Proprietary names are also widely used, and often combined with generic names, as in Ben Ean Moselle and Jacob's Creek Claret, or with varietal names, as in Siegersdorf Rhine Riesling and Yellow Label Cabernet Sauvignon.

Although Australia has achieved particular success with its Chardonnay, Cabernet Sauvignon, and Sauvignon Blanc, those varieties were virtually nonexistent in the mid-1960s, and most of the plantings have occurred in the past ten years. (As recently as 1981, there were fewer than 1,700 bearing acres of Chardonnay and Sauvignon Blanc combined; eight years later, however, these two varieties accounted for more than 11,000 acres and Cabernet Sauvignon for nearly 10,000 acres.) The most widely planted grape in Australia is Sultana, used mostly for raisins; Muscat Gordo Blanco (Muscat of Alexandria), also called Lexia, is extensively cultivated as well, and these two varieties, plus Palomino and Doradillo, account for more than a third of Australia's 140,000 acres of vineyards. Until quite recently, the two most widely planted white-wine grapes were Rhine Riesling (as the true Riesling of Germany is known in Australia) and Sémillon, but both have now been overtaken by Chardonnay. The most widely planted red-wine grape is the Syrah of the northern Rhône, known in Australia as Shiraz, and sometimes as Hermitage. There are also large plantings of Grenache, used mostly for inexpensive reds and port-style wines. Sauvignon Blanc, Merlot, Gewürztraminer, Chenin Blanc, and Pinot Noir are also cultivated. A varietally labelled wine must contain a minimum of 80 percent of the named variety. However, it is traditional in Australia to market wines that are blended from two or more varieties. Cabernet-Shiraz and Shiraz-Cabernet are frequently seen (the varieties must be listed in order of their importance in the blend), as is Sémillon-Chardonnay. (Shiraz softens the tannic intensity of Cabernet, as Merlot does in California and Bordeaux; and Chardonnay, playing the role of Sauvignon Blanc, contributes acidity to Sémillon.) Similarly, it is not unusual for wines to be blended from grapes grown hundreds of miles apart; indeed, most of the major wine firms – Penfolds, Lindemans, Orlando, Seppelts, McWilliam's, Hardy, and Smith's Yalumba – have vineyards and wineries in several different regions. The Australian tradition of blending wines from different varieties and different regions, which gives the winemaker greater flexibility in achieving quality or maintaining a particular style, may decline as exports increase, since the expectations of many consumers is for varietal wines made primarily from a single variety and from a single appellation.

The principal wine regions of Australia extend throughout much of the southern quarter of that vast continent, from the Hunter Valley, north of Sydney, to the Margaret River district, south of Perth, 2,000 miles away. The state of

South Australia produces about 60 percent of the country's wines; major districts include the Barossa Valley, Clare/ Watervale, Coonawarra, Padthaway, Langhorne Creek, and the Southern Vales region, which includes McLaren Vale. New South Wales accounts for a quarter of the total; the Hunter Valley is its most famous district, but Mudgee is becoming known as well. There are vineyards throughout the state of Victoria, including the Yarra Valley, near the capital city of Melbourne; to the northeast are the Corowa-Rutherglen and Milawa-Glenrowan districts; the Goulburn Valley, which includes Tabilk, is north of Melbourne; and to the northwest are the Pyrenees and Great Western districts. The first vineyards of Western Australia were established in the Swan Valley near the capital city of Perth; more recently, the cool Margaret River area and the even cooler Mount Barker/Frankland region have become known for their fine varietal wines. There are also vineyards in the state of Queensland, on a plateau southwest of Brisbane, north of

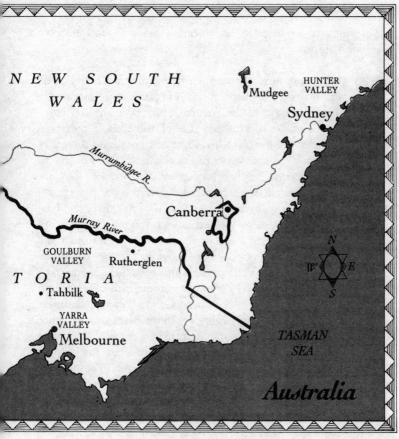

the Hunter Valley; and vineyards have been established on Tasmania. During the past twenty years, Australian growers have extensively replanted existing vineyards with such varieties as Chardonnay, Cabernet Sauvignon, and Sauvignon Blanc, and have also created vineyards in new districts with cooler microclimates, such as the Margaret River and Tasmania, and at higher elevations within established regions, such as northeast Victoria and the Barossa Valley.

About three quarters of Australia's grape crop, including virtually all of those used for inexpensive wines, comes from an area that overlaps three states. The Murrumbidgee River flows through an irrigated region in New South Wales known as Riverina and as MIA (Murrumbidgee Irrigation Area), centred around the town of Griffith, 400 miles west of Sydney; the Riverland district, in South Australia, about 150 miles northeast of Adelaide, is situated along the Murray River, near the towns of Renmark and Berri; and that river continues into northwest Victoria, where most of that state's

wines are produced in the Sunraysia region around the town
of Mildura.

Austria To a far greater extent than Germany, Austria is by tradition
a wine-drinking country; it was, of course, even more so in
the high old days of the Austro-Hungarian Empire, when
the best vintages of Hungary, Czechoslovakia, Yugoslavia,
and of what is now the Alto Adige of Italy found their way
to Vienna. Even today, per capita consumption is nearly 50
bottles a year. More than 80 percent of Austrian wines are
white, and most of them can be described as fruity, refreshing, dry or off-dry wines with lively acidity, and best
drunk young; perhaps the best known and most popular are
the *Heurigen*, a term that refers both to new wines and to the
taverns and cafés around Vienna in which they are copiously
consumed. Grüner Veltliner accounts for a third of Austria's
acreage, other white varieties include Müller-Thurgau,
Rheinriesling, Ruländer (Pinot Gris), Gewürztraminer,
Welschriesling, Weissburgunder (Pinot Blanc), Zierfandler
(also known as Spätrot), Rotgipfler, and Neuburger.
Austria's light-bodied, pleasant red wines are made from
such varieties as Blauburgunder (Pinot Noir), Portugieser,
Blaufrankisch, Zweigelt, and Saint-Laurent. As in Germany, the wines may bear such designations of ripeness as
Qualitätswein, Kabinett, Spätlese, and Auslese.

Many of Austria's most agreeable wines are produced just
west of Vienna in the celebrated Vienna Woods, in such villages as Grinzing and Nussberg. Gumpoldskirchen, a village
some 15 miles south of Vienna, enjoys an even higher rating;
Gumpoldskirchner (the suffix er is added to a village or district name when it appears on a label) is made primarily from
Zierfandler and Rotgipfler. Farther south is the village of
Vöslau, best known for its reds made from Portugieser; and
the well-known wine village of Klosterneuberg is situated
just north of Vienna. About 40 miles northwest of Vienna,
along the north bank of the Danube River, is the extensive
Wachau district, whose best-known villages are Dürnstein
and Loiben; and just east of the Wachau are the equally
famous districts of Krems and Langenlois. Falkenstein and
Poysdorf are villages in an extensive district north of Vienna
known as the Weinviertel; the small Styria district is situated
in the southeast corner of the country, near the Yugoslav
border. The Burgenland district, southeast of Vienna, is
unusual among Austria's wine regions in that it is best

known for sweet wines. The mist that rises off the Neu-siedlersee, a long narrow lake, permits the development of *Botrytis cinerea*, also known as "noble rot", in most years, and results in Auslese, Beerenauslese, and Trockenbeeren-auslese wines, most of them made from Weissburgunder, Müller-Thurgau, and Neuburger rather than the more tradi-tional Riesling. Rust and Apetlon are the most famous wine villages of Burgenland, and the best known of the region's sweet wines is probably Ruster Ausbruch, the latter term used for wines that are even sweeter than a Beerenauslese. (In 1985 a number of Austrian producers were found guilty of adding diethylene glycol to certain wines; this potentially harmful chemical contributed a rich, viscous texture to wines that were also sweetened and then passed off as ex-pensive, late-harvest, botrytised wines. Strict new laws were passed in 1986.) Austrian wines may be labelled with the name of a grape variety, with that of the village or district of origin, or with a combination of both, such as Kremser Grüner Veltliner, Dürnsteiner Rheinriesling, and Apetloner Weissburgunder. The popular Schluck (which means "sip") is a proprietary name for a light white wine produced by the firm of Lenz Moser.

Autoclave The Italian equivalent of the Charmat process of bulk fer-mentation, a technique used to make sparkling wines, notably Asti Spumante and most Lambrusco.

Autolysis A reaction that occurs when wine is aged *sur lie*, that is, on the lees, the residue of dead yeast cells left after fermentation is complete. The yeast cells decompose and slowly release amino acids and organic compounds into the wine, which adds flavour and aroma, enriches the wine's texture, and re-sults in greater complexity. Autolysis is especially important in the production of *méthode champenoise* sparkling wines, and in the Champagne region contact with the lees after the second fermentation is completed in the bottle may continue for several years before the wines are disgorged. The benefi-cial effects of autolysis may also be incorporated in the pro-duction of still white wines, such as a barrel-fermented white Burgundy or California Chardonnay, which may be aged *sur lie* for several months before being racked off the lees into a clean container.

Auvergne A famous old province in central France, near the headwaters of the Loire. Although of ancient reputation, its vineyards are of little consequence today, and names such as Chanturgues, Châteaugay, and Corent are hardly wine names at all (and are, in any case, now included in the VDQS Côtes d'Auvergne). These wines are made primarily from Gamay, plus Pinot Noir and Pinot Blanc. Other VDQS appellations from the Auvergne are Côtes du Forez, Côtes Roannaises, and Saint-Pourçain-sur-Sioule.

Auxerrois A white-wine grape cultivated in France's Alsace region and erroneously thought to be related to Pinot Blanc; Auxerrois is also, and confusingly, the local name for the red Malbec grape in the Cahors district, east of Bordeaux.

Auxey-Duresses One of the good, secondary wine-producing villages of the Côte de Beaune, in Burgundy situated in a little side-valley northwest of Meursault. Both white and red wines of good quality are produced, from Chardonnay and Pinot Noir; the former is comparable to the lesser Meursaults, the latter not unlike Volnays, albeit without as much body and class. Being little known, they are often good value.

Avellino *See* Fiano di Avellino

Avelsbach A village in the Ruwer region of Germany whose vineyards are now incorporated into those of Trier; Altenberg, Herrenberg, and Hammerstein are its best-known sites.

Avignon A historic and interesting little city on the Rhône River, in southern France, seat of the Papacy from 1309 to 1377. An important centre of the trade in the wines of the lower Rhône Valley – Côtes-du-Rhône, Châteauneuf-du-Pape, Tavel, Lirac, Gigondas.

Avize A major wine-producing village in the Champagne region of France, south of Epernay and the Marne, whose vineyards are rated 100 percent in the official classification. It is, with Cramant one of the two most important communes of the Côtes des Blancs, and its wines, produced entirely from the Chardonnay grape, have extraordinary finesse and class.

Ay A village in the Champagne region of France, near Epernay, on the north bank of the Marne; its admirable hillside vineyards, planted almost entirely with Pinot Noir, have an official rating of 100 percent.

Ayl An important wine-producing village on the Saar, in Germany; Kupp and Herrenberger are the best vineyards.

Azay-le-Rideau A charming little town and lovely Renaissance château southwest of Tours in France's Loire region; also a pleasant, fruity white wine, somewhat like Vouvray, produced there from the Chenin Blanc grape, and legally entitled to the appellation Touraine-Azay-le-Rideau, as are a red and rosé made from Groslot.

Azienda An Italian term for "firm": *azienda vinicola* refers to a winery; *azienda agricola* may be used on a label only if the grapes were grown and vinified at the estate.

❧ B

Bacchus Another name for Dionysus, the Greek and Roman god of wine. Also: A new German white-wine variety, a cross based on Riesling, Sylvaner, and Müller-Thurgau, producing wines relatively low in acid and with a Muscat-like bouquet; introduced in the 1960s, plantings now amount to nearly 9,000 acres, more than half in Rheinhessen.

Bacharach A small and picturesque town of the Mittelrhein, between Bingen and Koblenz. Once an important centre of the German wine trade, it still produces a certain number of Rhine wines of second quality, of which Bacharacher Posten and Bacharacher Wolfshöhle are perhaps the best known.

Baco The French hybridizer Maurice Baco has given his name (plus the appropriate serial number) to several successful hybrids developed at the turn of the century. Baco 1 is a red-wine grape grown in the eastern United States under the name Baco Noir. Baco 22A, a white grape also known as Baco Blanc, is extensively planted in the Armagnac region of France, and its wine may legally be distilled to produce that brandy, although it is not considered as good as the traditional Ugni Blanc; both hybrids are based on the Folle Blanche grape.

Bad Dürkheim A small resort town in the Rheinpfalz region that is one of the largest wine-producing townships in all Germany, with 2,000 acres of vineyards. Some excellent white wine is produced from Riesling, as well as less distinguished whites and reds, much of the latter from the Portugieser grape. The wines are labelled without Bad (which refers to the town's mineral springs) – Dürkheimer Feuerberg is a Grosslage; individual sites include Herrenmorgen, Spielberg, and Nonnengarten.

Bad Kreuznach   A German town, with mineral springs and some modest local fame as a watering place, which is the centre of the Nahe wine region; it lies some ten miles up this lesser stream from Bingen, where the Nahe joins the Rhine. The Kreuznacher wines, as they are labelled, rank with those of Schlossböckelheim, a village further up the Nahe, as the best of the region, especially those from such top vineyards as Kahlenberg and Brückes. The village also gives its name to Bereich Kreuznach, which encompasses the northern part of the Nahe region, and to the Grosslage Kreuznacher Kronenberg. There is an important wine school and experimental vineyard in Bad Kreuznach, and the filters manufactured by the celebrated local firm of Seitz are gratefully used by vintners all over the world.

Badacsonyi   A celebrated Hungarian appellation of origin that derives its name from Mount Badacsony, an extinct volcano on the north shore of Lake Balaton. Some of Hungary's finest white wines are produced here, from such native grapes as Kéknyelü, Szürkebarat, and Furmint.

Baden   A large province in southwestern Germany, bounded on the south by Switzerland and on the west by France's Alsace region. Baden is the southernmost of Germany's eleven Anbaugebiete, or specified wine regions, and most of its 35,000 acres of vineyards extend south along the Rhine from the old university city of Heidelberg past the famous spa town of Baden-Baden to a point opposite Basel: much of this is planted along the foothills of the Black Forest, the region's most important physical feature. The Baden appellation also includes vineyards near Bodensee, better-known as Lake Constance, and some that adjoin those of Franconia, in the north. More than a third of Baden's total acreage consists of Müller-Thurgau, another third of Spätburgunder (Pinot Noir) and Ruländer (Pinot Gris); in fact, Baden's nearly

7,000 acres of Spätburgunder account for three quarters of Germany's total plantings of that red variety. Co-operative cellars produce about 85 percent of Baden's wines, of which the whites are somewhat broader in taste than those of other regions, with less acid and more alcohol; an unusual rosé, Badisch Rotgold, is made from a mixture of Ruländer and Spätburgunder grapes. There are seven specified districts, or Bereiche, in Baden, the best known of which are Kaiserstuhl-Tuniberg, named after the two hills that dominate the district, and whose volcanic soil gives its wines a special tang; Ortenau, where Riesling (known locally as Klingelberger) is a widely cultivated variety; Markgräflerland, planted principally with Gutedel (Chasselas); and Bodensee, where Weissherbst, a mild, somewhat sweet rosé, is made from Spätburgunder. In the seven Bereiche are 16 Grosslagen and over 300 Einzellagen.

Badisch Rotgold A rosé that is a speciality of the German region of Baden; it is a blend of two grape varieties, Ruländer (Pinot Gris) and Spätburgunder (Pinot Noir), which are pressed and fermented together.

Bairrada A region in northern Portugal, between the Dão district and the Atlantic coast, which derives its name from its clay soils (*barro* means "clay"). About 5 million cases are produced annually, nine tenths of it rich, intense, tannic red wines, made primarily from the Baga grape; they must be aged for a minimum of eighteen months in wood and six months in bottle. A certain amount of dry white wine is also produced, much of it transformed into sparkling wine.

Baking A process used on the island of Madeira to transform wine into Madeira (*see* Estufa, Maderized); also used by some wineries in America and other countries as a less expensive alternative to the *flor* process to approximate the taste of sherry.

Balanced A wine-taster's term; a well-balanced wine is one in which all the components – especially acid, sugar, alcohol, and extract – are in harmony, with nothing in excess, and no striking deficiency. If light, it will have appropriate delicacy; if full-bodied, it will have a corresponding measure of flavour and character. Although a well-balanced wine may not be great, it should be exactly of its type and class, since the term is high praise.

Balaton The biggest lake in Europe, located in western Hungary, whose shores are extensively planted with vineyards. The overall appellation appears on labels as Balatoni; specific districts situated on the north shore of the lake include Badacsony, Balatonfüred, and Csopak.

Balestard-La-Tonelle, Château One of the better *grands crus classés* of Saint-Emilion, sturdy, but with considerable breed; the 28-acre estate produces about 5,000 cases a year. It is famous above all for a poem in its praise written five hundred years ago by François Villon, who described the wine as *"ce divin nectar, Qui porte nom de Balestard"*. The complete poem now appears on the label.

Balling *See* Brix

Balthazar An oversize champagne bottle, holding sixteen ordinary bottles.

Bandol An appellation for red, white, and rosé wines produced in the hills behind the village of Bandol, just west of Toulon, along the Mediterranean coast of France. Annual production averages more than 300,000 cases, 95 percent of it red and rosé, and it is the red, made primarily from Mourvèdre, plus Grenache and Cinsault, that has given these wines more than local fame. The red wine of Bandol must be aged in wood a minimum of eighteen months, which makes it one of the very few French wines subject to minimum wood-aging requirements (Fitou is another). Domaine Tempier is the best-known property of Bandol; others include Moulin des Costes, Château de Pibarnon, Château Romasson, and Château Vannières.

Banyuls An unusual French dessert wine, somewhat comparable to a light tawny port; it is classified either as a *vin doux naturel* (a misleading name, since it is fortified) or, more correctly, as a *vin de liqueur*. By law, it must have at least 15 percent alcohol, but often runs much higher; it is russet-brown in colour, quite sweet, and with age acquires a special bouquet and flavour known as *rancio*. Banyuls is made largely from the Grenache grape in a picturesque little district known as the Côte Vermeille, where the Pyrenées come down to the

Mediterranean along the Spanish border. The tiny fishing port of Banyuls is the centre of the trade, and the other villages of the zone, beloved of artists and summer tourists, are Collioure, Port-Vendres, and Cerbère. The vineyards are terraced on steep, sun-drenched hillsides, and the grapes are picked late; even if unfortified, the wine would tend to be strong and sweet, but it receives the addition, during fermentation, of from 5 to 10 percent of high-proof spirits. About 20 percent of the crop, which generally varies from 400,000 to 500,000 cases, is entitled to the higher AOC Banyuls Grand Cru.

Barbacarlo   A lightly sparkling Italian red wine of good quality, from the Oltrepò Pavese district in Lombardy. Like two other oddly named wines from the same district, Buttafuoco and Sangue di Giuda, it is produced from various grape varieties, including Bonarda, Barbera, and Croatina.

Barbaresco   One of the finest red wines of Italy, made from the Nebbiolo grape in the Piedmont region, around the village of Barbaresco, just east of Alba. Most of the district's 1,300 acres of vineyards, which produce 150,00 to 250,000 cases a year, are situated in the communes of Barbaresco and Neive; the wine must be aged a minimum of two years, one in wood and, according to the DOCG laws established for Barbaresco in 1981, a Riserva must be aged for four years, one of which in wood. Although similar to Barolo, produced only a few miles away, Barbaresco is generally more elegant and not as long-lived; many Piedmont producers make both Barolo and Barbaresco, however, and their personal styles may override the traditional distinctions between wines from these two neighbouring appellations. As in Barolo, a number of producers of Barbaresco now prefer to age their wines in wood for a shorter time than in the past, and some now use small French oak barrels rather than the traditional large casks. Specific vineyard sites may appear on labels of Barbaresco, among them Bricco Asili, Gallina, Martinenga, Santo Stefano, and Sorí Tildin.

Barbera   A red-wine grape of Italian origin that produces sturdy, tannic wines capable of aging. Barbera is widely planted in Italy's Piedmont region, where it accounts for half the total acreage; most of this production, which can amount to as much as 25 million cases, is sold simply as Barbera del

Piemonte, but about a quarter of the total is entitled to DOC status, including Barbera d'Alba and Barbera d'Asti. Barbera is also found in the Oltrepò Pavese area of Lombardy, the Colli Bolognesi district of Emilia-Romagna, and is the principal variety in such wines as Botticino and Buttafuoco.

Barberone A name used occasionally and unofficially on labels of inexpensive California red wines that are likely to be full-bodied and slightly sweet.

Bardolino An attractive light red wine produced around the village of that name, on the eastern shore of Lake Garda, in Italy's Veneto region. Like the fuller-bodied Valpolicella, which is grown on a very different soil some ten miles to the east, Bardolino is made mostly from Corvina Veronese, Rondinella, Molinara, and Negrara grapes; more often the colour of a dark rosé, relatively low in alcohol, fruity, charming, never great but often delightful, it is at its best within two years of the harvest. The district's 7,500 acres produce 2 million cases or so a year, about half of which come from the inner *classico* zone and may be so labelled; a rosé version of Bardolino may be sold as Chiaretto.

Barolo One of the finest red wines of Italy, full-bodied, richly textured, complex, and long-lived, with a distinctive bouquet and taste often described as reminiscent of tar, truffles, and faded roses. It is made from the Nebbiolo grape in Piedmont, just south of Alba, in a small, strictly delimited, hilly district of which the village of Barolo is the centre, and which includes eleven communes, among them Castiglione Falletto, La Morra, Serralunga d'Alba, and Monforte. Three thousand acres of vineyards produce between 400,000 and 600,000 cases a year; the wine must be aged a minimum of three years, two of them in wood, and the DOCG laws, which were established for Barolo in 1981, specify that a wine labelled Riserva must be aged five years, two of which in wood. Because Barolo is a powerful, tannic wine, with a minimum alcohol content of 13 percent, it has long been the practice to age the wine in large casks for more than the two years required by law, and five or six years is not uncommon; as a result, many non-Italian consumers find a traditional Barolo excessively woody and faded in taste. In recent years, a number of producers have altered their vinification techniques and reduced wood aging to a minimum to emphasize fruit rather than tannic extract; there are, consequently, many styles of Barolo to be found. Also, some producers have begun to draw attention to specific vineyard sites, or *crus*, within the Barolo district, and such names as Annunziata, Brunate, Cannubi, Cerequio, Rocche, and Rocchette now appear on labels.

Barossa Valley An important Australian wine district about 35 miles northeast of Adelaide, in the state of South Australia, whose vineyards were established in the 1840s. Rhine Riesling, Shiraz, and Grenache account for almost half the district's 13,000 acres, but there are now nearly 2,000 acres of Cabernet Sauvignon and Chardonnay as well; most of the acreage is on the broad flatlands, but successful new vineyards have been established in the cooler climate of the hills to the east, especially around Eden Valley and Springton. Leading wineries include Wolf Blass, Kaiser Stuhl, Krondorf, Peter Lehmann, Penfolds, Orlando, Seppelts, Tollana, and Yalumba (Hill-Smith Estate).

Barrel As far as the wine trade is concerned, a wooden container of any size, preferably made of oak, in which wine is stored, aged, and sometimes shipped. A barrel is readily movable; a cask, in many cases, is not. *See* Cask.

Barrel Aging Although most of the world's wines are bottled within months of the vintage, with only a brief period of time spent in large vats or tanks to rid them of impurities and prepare them for bottling, a number of red and white wines are aged in small oak barrels or larger casks to mature them and improve their taste. Sturdy reds, in particular, undergo barrel aging to soften their initial tannic harshness, and both red and white wines acquire complexity and certain flavour elements from contact with oak, especially new oak. The tannin in oak barrels also imparts structure to wines, especially white wines, which normally contain considerably less tannin than reds. Although proper cellar technique calls for minimal exposure to air (except for such wines as sherry and Madeira, which owe part of their special tastes to deliberate oxidation); barrel aging is a process that takes place in the presence of oxygen; the evaporation of wine that inevitably occurs in barrels contributes to this, as do the rackings from one container to another that aerate the wine, as well as separating it from its lees, or sediment. In recent years, there has been a movement away from extensive barrel aging, which can result in wines that are dried out, withered, and faded in colour and taste; contemporary winemaking practices favour red wines with more fruit and vigour, and a richer style. In Bordeaux, for example, many of the finest properties now age their wines in small barrels for only twelve or fourteen months instead of two years; in Italy and Spain, the minimum wood aging required by law for a number of wines has been reduced, and in regions where wines were traditionally kept in barrel or cask for four to six years, eighteen to twenty-four months is now the norm.

Barrel Fermentation A technique used in the production of some white wines, including fine Burgundies and a number of California Chardonnays, whereby the wine is fermented in small oak barrels rather than in large, temperature-controlled tanks. Fermentation may take place at a higher temperature than in tanks, the must is more exposed to air, and it comes into contact with oak; the resulting wine usually has less fruit, but acquires richer, more complex flavours. The technique is not without its problems, however, as fermentation is more difficult to control in barrels than in large containers, and more expensive.

Barrique One of many French words meaning "barrel", used particularly in the Bordeaux region to designate the oak casks of 225 litres (approximately 50 gallons) in which wines are commonly stored there; a *barrique* yields 25 cases, or 300 bottles, of finished wine. (The Burgundian equivalent is a *pièce*.)

Barro A Spanish word that refers to clay soil, used particularly in connection with the sherry-producing vineyards around Jerez de la Frontera; wines from this soil do not have the finesse of those from the chalky *albariza* vineyards.

Barsac The northernmost and, after Sauternes itself, the most famous of the five townships that make up the Sauternes district; it is some 25 miles southeast of the city of Bordeaux, and its vineyards are on low, rolling hills that overlook the Garonne River. All Barsacs are, legally, Sauternes, made by the same methods and from the same grape varieties; its producers are permitted to call their wines by either name, however, and the fame of Barsac is such that most vineyard owners use that more specific name on their labels. Barsacs are sweet, luscious wines, of course, but some connoisseurs claim that they have slightly more fruit, delicacy, and acidity than other wines from the Sauternes district. Châteaux Climens and Coutet are the outstanding vineyards of Barsac, but there are many others, including Doisy-Védrines, Doisy-Daëne, Broustet, and Nairac.

Basilicata A region in southern Italy producing about 4 or 5 million cases of relatively undistinguished wine, with the exception of its single, but famous, DOC: Aglianico del Vulture.

Basket *See* Cradle

Bas-Médoc *See* Médoc

Bassermann-Jordan A distinguished 100-acre estate at Deidesheim, in Germany's Rheinpfalz region; planted almost entirely with Riesling, it encompasses important holdings in several villages, and includes most of the famed Forster Jesuitengarten vineyard. Among wine lovers, the name is one of the most respected in Germany, and the label one of the most familiar. The late Dr. Friedrich von Bassermann-Jordan was considered the dean of German wine producers; he was the author of a number of scholarly books on the history of the vine and created a remarkable museum on his estate.

Bastard A sweet wine from the Iberian Peninsula, popular in England in Elizabethan days and mentioned by Shakespeare; its name was presumably derived from the Bastardo grape, once a principal variety in Madeira and still widely cultivated in Portugal along the Douro and in the Dão region.

Basto A Spanish term meaning "coarse" or "common", the opposite of *fino*; applied to a sherry of no breed and poor quality.

Batailley, Château A Fifth Classed Growth of Pauillac, in the Médoc, divided into two properties in 1942 (the other is Château Haut-Batailley); this 135-acre vineyard produces about 25,000 cases a year.

Bâtard-Montrachet One of the best and most celebrated white-wine vineyards of Burgundy, whose 29 acres – which adjoin those of the great Montrachet vineyard – are almost evenly divided between the villages of Puligny-Montrachet and Chassagne-Montrachet; average annual production is about 5,000 cases. Generally ranked third among the Montrachet vineyards – after Montrachet itself and Chevalier-Montrachet – it often produces better wines than its reputed superiors. Made exclusively from the Chardonnay grape, the wines are pale gold in colour, comparatively rich in alcohol, dry without being excessively so, and have a quite extraordinary wealth of bouquet and flavour.

Baumé A scale of expressing the specific gravity of liquids, used to measure the sugar content of juice or wine, especially in the sherry and port districts. In the case of grape juice, 1 degree Baumé is equivalent to a potential degree of alcohol, and is therefore equal to about 17 or 18 grams of sugar per litre; thus, grape juice with 10 degrees Baumé would ferment out into wine with about 10 percent alcohol. In the case of wine, however, especially sweet, fortified wines, the density of the solution affects the result; thus, port with 3 degrees Baumé contains about 90 grams per litre of sugar, or 9 percent, and cream sherry with 6 degrees Baumé contains about 14 percent sugar.

Béarn An appellation for red, white, and rosé wines produced in several districts in southwest France, primarily in vineyards situated east of Bayonne and Biarritz; red and rosé wines, produced from the native Tannat grape plus Cabernet Sauvignon and Cabernet Franc, account for 95 percent of the annual production of about 100,000 cases, and the dry, agreeable Rosé de Béarn is the most frequently encountered wine from this appellation. The Béarn region also includes the appellations Jurançon, Madiran, Irouléguy, and Pacherenc du Vic-Bilh.

Beaujeu A small town on the western edge of the Beaujolais region, still the capital of the Beaujolais-Villages district, but today far overshadowed in commercial importance by Villefranche-sur-Saône. The Hospices de Beaujeu is a charity hospital organized somewhat along the lines of the Hospices de Beaune in that a large part of its endowment consists of vineyards.

Beaujolais One of the most popular and best-loved wines of France,

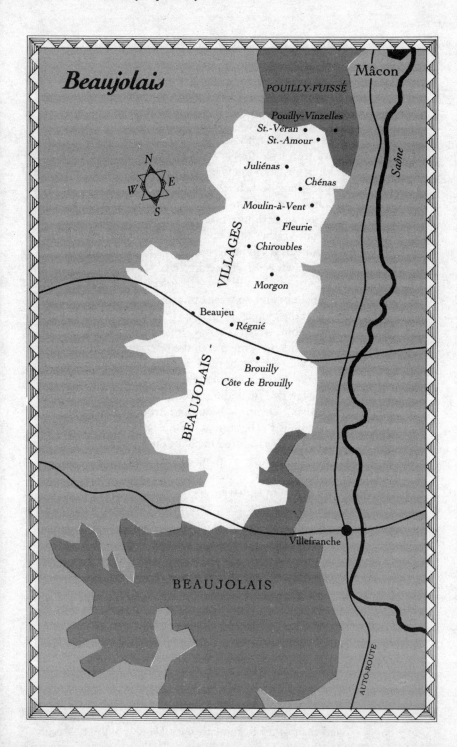

Beaujolais

Mâcon

POUILLY-FUISSÉ

Pouilly-Vinzelles
St.-Véran •
St.-Amour •

Juliénas •

Chénas •

Moulin-à-Vent •

Fleurie •

Chiroubles •

Morgon •

Beaujeu •
• Régnié

Brouilly •
Côte de Brouilly

VILLAGES

BEAUJOLAIS -

Saône

Villefranche

BEAUJOLAIS

AUTO-ROUTE

N
W E
S

nearly always red, produced in the Beaujolais district, in southern Burgundy. (An insignificant amount of white and rosé is also made, less than 1 percent of the average crop of 11 to 14 million cases.) The vineyards make up a rather small, compact area of vine-covered hills west of the main Paris-Riviera autoroute, and extend from Mâcon to a few miles north of Lyon. Although traditionally part of Burgundy, its wines are very different from those of the great Côte d'Or, being made from the Gamay grape rather than Pinot Noir; its prevailing soil, furthermore, is clay and granite rather than limestone; and most of the wines are vinified by a local variation of carbonic maceration, which emphasizes fruit and charm rather than body and longevity.

Beaujolais is a light, agreeable, fruity, eminently drinkable red wine whose lively acidity enables it to complement a variety of foods; the best examples have a special, almost spicy flavour and no trace of harshness. The wine is usually served at the temperature of the cellar rather than that of the dining room, which is to say, it is one of the few red wines that benefits by being put in the refrigerator for an hour or so. The wines of the Beaujolais district are generally divided into three basic categories: Beaujolais, Beaujolais-Villages, and the ten *crus* (including Régnié, officially recognized as a *cru* in 1988). Ordinary Beaujolais, from the southern half of the region, is the lightest and simplest of the three; Beaujolais-Villages is produced in about three dozen villages in the northern half of the region, and these wines generally have more distinction. (The appellation Beaujolais Supérieur, whose wines must have 1 degree more alcohol than Beaujolais, does not indicate superior quality and is rarely used.) Wines labelled Beaujolais and Beaujolais-Villages account for about three quarters of the crop; the rest comes from ten *crus* situated within the Beaujolais-Villages area whose wines, considered the best of all, are entitled to their own appellations: Brouilly, Chénas, Chiroubles, Côte de Brouilly, Fleurie, Juliénas, Morgon, Moulin-à-Vent, Régnié, and Saint-Amour. These wines combine character and intensity of flavour with the fruit and suppleness that makes all Beaujolais so appealing, and any one of these names on a bottle of Beaujolais is an indication of superior quality. Although the wines from the *crus* are legally entitled to be sold with the AOC Bourgogne, they rarely are, as they are more saleable under their own names. The *crus* are longer-lived than other Beaujolais, with Moulin-à-Vent, Morgon, and Chénas considered the sturdiest; as to quantity, Brouilly, Morgon, Moulin-à-Vent, and Fleurie account for more than half the production of these ten appellations (each has its own entry).

A special category of wines known as Beaujolais *nouveau* or *primeur* (the terms are interchangeable) has become very popular in the past twenty years or so. These are especially light and fruity wines that may legally be released for sale within weeks of the harvest; the traditional date was November 15, but in 1985 this was changed to the third Thursday in November. In recent years nearly half the crop of Beaujolais and Beaujolais-Villages has been sold as *nouveau*. Such wines are at their best within two or three months of being bottled and, for that matter, almost all Beaujolais is best consumed within a year or eighteen months of the harvest. Exceptional bottles of Beaujolais *crus* from great years may improve after their third birthday, but most enthusiasts prefer the wines of this region when their age can still be counted in months, not years.

Beaumes-de-Venise A village in the southern part of the Rhône Valley whose red wines are entitled to the appellation Côtes-du-Rhône-Villages; it is best known, however, for a sweet Muscat wine. *See* Muscat de Beaumes-de-Venise.

Beaune The centre of the Burgundy wine trade, a picturesque little city of some 20,000 inhabitants that is famous both for its wines and its ancient buildings, among them the Hôtel-Dieu of the Hospices de Beaune, an extraordinary charity hospital dating from 1443. Beaune has given its name to the Côte de Beaune, the southern half of the Côte d'Or, as well as to the wines, almost all red, produced by its own 1,600 acres of hillside vineyards west of the town. Annual production of Beaune, which sometimes exceeds 200,000 cases, is second only to Gevrey-Chambertin among the red-wine villages of the Côte d'Or, and about the same as for Pommard and Santenay. The best of the Beaune wines are of extremely high quality, remarkable for their distinction, balance, and grace, and comparable to the better wines of Pommard, the village that adjoins Beaune on the south. There are nearly three dozen *premier cru* vineyards within the Beaune appellation, among them Les Grèves, Les Fèves, Les Cent Vignes, Bressandes, Marconnets, Clos des Mouches, Clos de la Mousse, Clos du Roi, Boucherottes, and Les Teurons. The vineyards of Beaune also produce a few thousand cases of white wine; the most famous comes from that part of the Clos des Mouches vineyard owned by the firm of Joseph Drouhin. *See* Côte de Beaune, Côte de Beaune-Villages.

Beaunois Another name, rarely used today, for the Chardonnay grape.

Beauregard, Château A well-known vineyard of Pomerol noted for its handsome eighteenth-century château; its 32 acres of vines produce about 5,000 cases a year. There is also a Clos Beauregard, whose ten acres were once part of the original estate.

Beauséjour, Château A vineyard in the Saint-Emilion district of Bordeaux that was divided in 1869, both parts retaining the name Beauséjour; in the 1955 classification of the wines of Saint-Emilion, both were classed as *premiers grands crus classés*. The Château Beauséjour that is also labelled with the name Duffau-Lagarrosse consists of 17 acres and produces about 4,000 cases, much of it sold within France. The other Château Beauséjour was associated with the name Fagouet until 1968, when it was acquired by Michel Bécot, and in the 1970s its name was changed to Château Beau-Séjour-Bécot. Two adjoining properties owned by Bécot, Châteaux La Carte and Trois-Moulins, were combined with his part of the original Beauséjour vineyard, and the total amounts to 37 acres producing about 8,000 cases a year; in the Saint-Emilion reclassification of 1985, this property was demoted to *grand cru classé*.

Beau-Site, Château A *cru bourgeois exceptionnel* in Saint-Estèphe, in the Médoc, under the same ownership as Châteaux, Batailley and Lynch-Moussas; its 85 acres produce about 15,000 cases.

Beerenauslese A German term that means "selected berry picking"; one of the designations within the category Qualitätswein mit Prädikat. Wines labelled Beerenauslese, exceedingly rare, special, and expensive, are made from individual berries selected for their overripeness at the time of the *Lese*, or harvest, cut from the bunches with tiny scissors, and pressed separately. Beerenauslesen are produced, for the most part, from Riesling grapes by the leading growers in the best districts; only in the very best years, perhaps once or twice a decade; and in very limited quantities – an estate that produces a total of 250,000 bottles might, in a favourable year, make 1,000 bottles of such a wine. The grapes must contain a minimum of 125 degrees Oechsle in the Rhine (slightly less in the Moselle), the equivalent of about 30 percent sugar, with a potential alcohol content of nearly 18 percent. In practice, of course, the bottled wines contain only 6 to 8 percent alcohol and 10 to 12 percent residual sugar. Beerenauslesen are usually, but not always, made from grapes that have been shrivelled by *Edelfäule*, or "noble rot"; they are quite sweet, but not cloying, because of their balancing acidity, with an almost indescribable wealth of bouquet, fruit, and flavour. Properly served on their own, after dinner, they are among the most remarkable white wines in the world, and fully worth the fabulously high prices they bring.

Beeswing A light, translucent sediment, sometimes floating, found occasionally in very old bottles of port; the name comes from its appearance.

Bégadan An important wine-producing commune in the northern Médoc where several well-known *crus bourgeois* are located, including Châteaux Patache d'Aux, La Tour de By, and Greysac.

Belair, Château One of the best *premiers grands crus classés* of Saint-Emilion, directly adjoining Château Ausone, long owned by the same family, and still under the same direction, although the two wines are vinified and aged separately; its 32 acres, planted almost entirely with Merlot and Cabernet Franc, produce about 5,000 cases a year. There also exist, in the Bordeaux region, a number of other wine-producing properties called Château Bel-Air (and so spelled), and these should not be confused with the one in Saint-Emilion. There is, in addition, a *cru bourgeois* in the Margaux district of the Médoc called Château Bel-Air-Marquis d'Aligre.

Belgrave, Château A Fifth Classed Growth of the Médoc, in Bordeaux, situated in the commune of Saint-Laurent and entitled to the appellation Haut-Médoc; the 130-acre property, recently renovated by new owners, produces about 23,000 cases a year.

Bellet A small and rarely encountered appellation for red, white, and rosé wines produced in the hills behind Nice, along the French Riviera; annual production varies from 10,000 to

20,000 cases, two thirds of it red and rosé, and virtually all of this is promptly and happily consumed by the Niçois and by thirsty tourists.

Benicarló A village on the Mediterranean cost of Spain, north of Valencia, once known for its heavy, deep-coloured wines, but of little importance today; in the late eighteenth century, the wines of Benecarló and Alicante were often used to add colour and body to the lighter wines of Bordeaux.

Bentonite A type of clay used in powdered or granulated form to clarify wines by absorption. *See* Fining.

Bereich German for "region" or "area", and specifically defined by the 1971 German wine laws as a subregion within an Anbaugebiet, or specified wine region; there are 34 Bereiche within the eleven Anbaugebiete. A Bereich encompasses many wine-producing villages in a given region and covers extensive vineyard areas. Bereich Johannisberg, for example, includes the entire Rheingau region; Bereich Bernkastel includes more than 60 villages in the Mittelmosel district of the Mosel-Saar-Ruwer region, about 19,000 acres in all; and Bereich Nierstein includes 25,000 acres of vineyards within the Rheinhessen region. A Bereich wine, which never carries a vineyard name, generally corresponds in quality to a French regional wine, such as one labelled simply Saint-Emilion, Anjou, or Côtes-du-Rhône. Wines marketed with a Bereich name are usually of perfectly satisfactory quality, as are the regional wines of France, but neither category attains the distinction of a single-vineyard wine from a superior district. A list of the principal Bereiche will be found on page 553.

Bergerac A town on the Dordogne River, about 60 miles east of Bordeaux, which gives its name to an extensive region that includes the AOCs Bergerac, Monbazillac, Montravel, Saussignac, Rosette, and Pécharmant; the total AOC production of this region, also known as the Dordogne, is 4 or 5 million cases a year. The specific *Appellation Contrôlée* Bergerac, however, refers to red and white wines similar in style to those of Bordeaux, and made from the same grape varieties – Merlot and Cabernet for the reds, Sémillon, Sauvignon Blanc, and Muscadelle for the whites. Red wines marketed as Côtes de Bergerac are somewhat better, and the appellation

Côtes de Bergerac Moelleux is reserved for semisweet white wines.

Berliquet, Château A vineyard in Saint-Emilion, situated near the town itself, which was promoted to *grand cru classé* status in 1985; its 21 acres produce about 5,000 cases a year.

Bernkastel A wonderfully picturesque and world-famous little wine village situated along a bend of the Moselle, in the heart of Germany's Mosel-Saar-Ruwer region. Its finest wines, estate bottlings from such individual vineyards as Doctor, Lay, Bratenhöfchen, and Graben, have always been rightfully considered among the best of all Germany and are certainly among the most expensive, especially those from the eight-acre Doctor site. Confusingly, the village name is also used for a Bereich and two Grosslagen. Bereich Bernkastel corresponds to what is often called the Mittelmosel, a stretch of the river that includes more than sixty villages and 19,000 acres of vineyards whose production amounts to 60 percent or so of the entire Mosel-Saar-Ruwer region. The Grosslage Bernkasteler Badstube is reserved for the top vineyards of Bernkastel itself; the name Bernkasteler Kurfürstlay, however, may be used for wines from about a dozen villages.

Bestes Fass A German term that means, literally, "the best barrel". The term was sparingly and traditionally used by the estates of the Rhine to designate the very best cask of a given vintage; the equivalent on the Moselle was *Bestes Fuder*. These phrases, which appeared on the labels of wines so designated, were prohibited by the German wine laws of 1971.

Beychevelle, Château One of the best-known vineyards of the Médoc district of Bordeaux, situated in the commune of Saint-Julien; officially classified as a Fourth Classed Growth, its wines now bring higher prices than many Second Growths and are notable for their texture, delicacy, and breed. The 175-acre vineyard produces about 25,000 cases a year, plus an additional amount marketed under a second label, Amiral de Beychevelle (a reference to the Duc d'Epernon, onetime owner of the property and grand admiral of the French fleet); the 600-acre estate is dominated by an elaborate château, one of the most beautiful of the Médoc, that dates from 1757.

Bianco Italian for "white"; any white wine may be called *vino* *bianco*, but the word is incorporated into certain DOC names, such as Bianco di Custoza and Bianco di Pitigliano.

Bianco della Lega A dry white wine from the Chianti Classico zone of Tuscany made primarily from Trebbiano and Malvasia grapes; the name was created by the Chianti Classico *consorzio* to help its members market the excess production of white wines in the district.

Bianco di Custoza An attractive dry white wine produced southeast of Lake Garda in Italy's Veneto region. The wine is made from Trebbiano, Garganega, and Tocai grapes in a zone that partially overlaps the one for Bardolino; similar to Soave, and long overshadowed by that more famous neighbour, Bianco di Custoza is now achieving success on its own.

Bienvenues-Bâtard-Montrachet A *grand cru* vineyard in Burgundy's Côte d'Or, situated in the village of Puligny-Montrachet. Its nine acres, which produce about 1,700 cases of dry white wine a year, are actually carved out of a corner of the larger Bâtard-Montrachet vineyard, and its wines were once entitled to be marketed with the better-known appellation. Not surprisingly, the wines are among the best of Burgundy and, to most palates, indistinguishable from those of Bâtard-Montrachet.

Big A term applied to a wine with more than the average amount of body, alcohol, and flavour, but not necessarily fine or great; quite possibly a wine without much distinction.

Bikavér *See* Egri Bikavér

Bingen An important wine town, in Germany's Rheinhessen region, that overlooks the confluence of the Rhine and the Nahe and is directly across the Rhine from Rüdesheim. Its best wines, produced from the Riesling grape, are of excellent quality and are surpassed within Rheinhessen only by those from the villages of Nierstein and, perhaps, Nackenheim and Oppenheim. Bingen's best-known vineyard is the 87-acre Scharlachberg, or scarlet hill, although the colour of its soil is more dark brick-red than scarlet; other vineyards are Kirchberg, Kapellenberg, and Rosengarten. The village also lends its name to the regional appellation Bereich Bingen, which includes the northwestern part of

Rheinhessen. Corkscrews are sometimes jokingly referred to as Bingen pencils in Germany, on the assumption that the citizens of Bingen are more likely to have corkscrews than pencils in their pockets.

Binning The laying away of bottled wine for aging; table wines, sparkling wines, and such fortified wines as vintage port should invariably be stored lying on their sides so that the wine is in contact with the cork, thus preventing it from drying out, shrinking, and allowing air to get at the maturing wine. *See* Aging, Bottle Aging, Cellar.

Bischöflichen Weingüter An important estate in Trier, on the Moselle, that now includes more than 250 acres of vineyards along the Moselle, Saar and Ruwer, almost all of them planted with Riesling. The estate was created in 1966 by uniting three well-known charitable institutions that were already famous for their vineyard holdings – the Bischöfliches Konvikt, the Bischöfliches Priesterseminar, and the Hohe Domkirche.

Bischöfliches Konvikt A Catholic refectory for students at Trier, on the Moselle, a large part of whose endowment is in the form of vineyards, most of them on the Saar and Ruwer; now part of the Bischöflichen Weingüter.

Bischöfliches Priesterseminar A Catholic seminary at Trier, on the Moselle, with important holdings in many of the better vineyards of the Moselle, Saar, and Ruwer; now part of the Bischöflichen Weingüter.

Bishop One of the many versions of mulled wine, and not the best. Most recipes call for a bottle of port, an unpeeled orange stuck with cloves and halved, and a few spoonfuls of sugar, all heated together in a saucepan.

Bitter A wine-taster's term; bitterness, which is not the same as astringency, is generally perceptible only in the finish, or aftertaste, of a wine. Although a desirable element in certain beverages, such as tonic water and sweet vermouth, it is considered a fault in wine; bitterness may be due to the variety of grape, the climate (an overly dry year, in most cases), or careless cellar work, and is much more likely to be found in red wines than white. The palate quickly ceases to register bitterness, however, and a slightly bitter finish in a wine is often unnoticeable after one or two sips.

Black Rot   A fungus disease to which grape vines are subject, particularly in moist areas and in periods of exceptional humidity. It attacks both the leaves and the grapes themselves, and copper sulphate is commonly used as a preventive.

Blagny   A tiny hilltop hamlet in Burgundy's Côte de Beaune district that sits on the border of Meursault and Puligny-Montrachet and has vines in both villages. Although the Blagny vineyards produce both red and white wines, only the former are entitled to the appellation Blagny, which amounts to about 2,000 cases a year of fine, sturdy red; the whites are marketed either as Puligny-Montrachet or as Meursault, the latter sometimes as Meursault-Blagny.

Blanc de Blancs   A term that refers to a white wine made from white grapes, originally and properly used in the Champagne district of France to describe wines made entirely from the Chardonnay grape. Since most champagne is made from a combination of Chardonnay and the black varieties Pinot Noir and Pinot Meunier (the latter two accounting for nearly three quarters of the total Champagne acreage), the term *blanc de blancs* has a very specific meaning and suggests that any wine so labelled will be lighter-bodied and more delicate than a traditional champagne. The term is now widely used on the labels of still white wines from other parts of France and from many other countries as well, where it is entirely meaningless, since virtually all of the world's white wines are made from white grapes.

Blanc de Noirs   A term applied to a white wine made from black grapes. Since the colour of red wines comes from pigments inside the grape skin (which is why red wines are fermented in contact with the skins), a *blanc de noirs* can be produced by pressing the grapes quickly and separating the clear juice from the skins before they can impart any colour. When used for champagne and certain other fine sparkling wines, the term almost always means that the wine was made entirely from Pinot Noir grapes, without the use of Chardonnay. *Blanc de noirs* also refers to still white wines made from such red grapes as Zinfandel, Pinot Noir, and Cabernet Sauvignon, especially in California; in practice, however, such wines are rarely white, or colourless, but are more likely to be pale salmon or pink. *See* Blush Wine.

Blanc-Fumé   The name given to the Sauvignon Blanc grape in and around the town of Pouilly-sur-Loire. A Blanc-Fumé de Pouilly-sur-Loire, more often labelled simply Pouilly-Fumé, is therefore a wine made from the Sauvignon Blanc grape in this district, and thus distinguished from the common wines, made from the Chasselas grape, labelled Pouilly-sur-Loire. The origin of the name Blanc-Fumé (literally, "smoked white") is uncertain.

Blanchots   One of the seven *grand cru* vineyards of Chablis, whose 29 acres adjoin Les Clos.

Blanquefort   The southernmost commune of the Médoc; its little tidal stream, the Jalle de Blanquefort, forms the official boundary between the Médoc district and that of Graves.

Blanquette de Limoux   A sparkling white wine produced around the town of Limoux, near Carcassonne, in southern France; the principal grape variety is Mauzac (known locally as Blanquette), and Chenin Blanc and Chardonnay are also permitted.

Blau   German for "blue"; when used in connection with grapes, however, it refers to those that produce red wines, as Blauer Spätburgunder and Blauer Portugieser.

Blauer Portugieser   *See* Portugieser

Blaufrankisch   A grape widely planted in Austria, where it produces agreeable light red wines marked by acidity; this variety is also cultivated in the Württemberg region of Germany, where it is known as Blauer Limberger.

Blaye   A town and large wine-producing district in the Bordeaux region, north of Bourg and opposite the Médoc, on the east bank of the Gironde estuary; its vineyards produce about 1.5 million cases a year, about 80 percent of it red. The reds, which are sold as Premières Côtes de Blaye, are variable in quality, but the best are fruity and full-bodied; the whites, usually marketed as Blaye, Blayais, or Côtes de Blaye, are for the most part undistinguished.

Blending   The practice of mixing wines from different grape varieties, geographical origins, or vintages, or similar wines with somewhat different characteristics. Most champagnes and ports are blended from different grapes, vineyards, and vintages, and sherry is produced by a well-established and carefully controlled process of fractional blending; the producers of such wines would insist that the final blend is better than any of its component parts. Many fine wines, on the other hand, are the unique product of a single vineyard, including find Bordeaux and estate-bottled wines from Burgundy, Italy, California, and elsewhere. A purist might point out that even a château-bottled red Bordeaux from the Médoc or an estate-bottled Napa Valley Cabernet Sauvignon is likely to be a blend of Cabernet Sauvignon with such complementary grapes as Merlot and Cabernet Franc. Then, too, a Burgundy shipper's bottling from a specific vineyard such as Chambertin, Corton, or Montrachet may be a blend of wines from the named vineyard but from different growers. On a less exalted level, virtually all inexpensive and moderately priced generic wines (California Burgundy, Australian Claret) and regional wines (Liebfraumilch, Beaujolais, Chianti) are blended to produce a wine of consistent quality and character, year after year, which a consumer can buy with confidence under a familiar name or label. Most varietal wines (Sonoma Chardonnay, Australian Shiraz, Chilean Cabernet Sauvignon) are likely to be blended from different vineyards and may also contain, quite legally a proportion of wine from a grape other than the one on the label; this is often done when the producer believes that blending in a complementary variety will improve the wine's taste and balance. Blending is perfectly legitimate, often necessary, and frequently desirable, and there can be no objection to blended wines, providing, of course, that the final product is honestly labelled, does not pretend to a vintage that is not its own, nor to be a wine from a specific region or grape variety when it is not.

Blush Wine   A term used informally to describe a category of wines whose colour varies from pale salmon to pink, and which are usually simple, light-bodied, and slightly sweet. First produced in California, these wines were originally *blanc de noirs*, that is, white wines made from such black grapes as Zinfandel, Pinot Noir, and Cabernet Sauvignon, and labelled with such varietal names as White Zinfandel, Blanc de Pinot Noir, and Cabernet Blanc. They were created in response to the increasing demand for white wines and also to make use of the surplus of red grapes planted in California. In the early 1980s, White Zinfandel, in particular, became tremendously popular, and the term *blush wine* was adopted to describe these wines, which were, in practice, not really "white", or colourless, but pale pink. (The word *blush* was first used on a label by Mill Creek Vineyards in Sonoma County for a 1976 Cabernet Blush released in 1977.) The success of these wines, and of the description blush wines (which avoids the less desirable "rosé"), was such that a number of producers around the world began to market light rosés, some made by mixing red and white wines, as blush wines.

Boal Once one of the leading grape varieties cultivated on the island of Madeira; now used to describe a medium-sweet style of wine. The name Bual, which also appears on labels, is the Anglicized version of this variety.

Boca A dry red DOC wine produced in the Novara Hills, just north of Gattinara, in Italy's Piedmont region; the 30 acres of vineyards are planted with Nebbiolo, Vespolina, and Bonarda grapes.

Bocksbeutel The squat, flat-sided, green flagon used for Qualitätswein and Qualitätswein mit Prädikat from Germany's Franken, or Franconia region, as well as for certain wines from the northern part of Baden, known as Badisches Frankenland. This distinctive bottle presumably gets its name from its fancied resemblance to a goat's scrotum; a somewhat similar bottle is widely used in Chile and Portugal.

Bodega Spanish for a wine warehouse or storage area, usually above ground; also, a winery.

Boden German for "soil". Certain wines are noted for a distinctive taste that may be unpleasantly earthy or may simply reflect the particular soil in which they are produced; this characteristic is known as *Bodengeschmack* or *Bodenton*, both of which mean "taste of the soil", similar to the French *goût de terroir*.

Body A wine-taster's term, often misused – body means substance. A full-bodied wine is not necessarily high in alcohol, but it is the opposite of watery or thin; it gives an impression of weight, rather than lightness. Full body is not a virtue in itself; in excess it can be a fault, but in the best wines it is always balanced by elegance, finesse, and distinction.

Bolgheri A DOC zone established in 1984 along the coast of Tuscany, southeast of Livorno; its dry rosés from Sangiovese and Canaiolo grapes have already achieved a reputation, its whites are less familiar.

Bon Pasteur, Château le A small estate in the Pomerol district of Bordeaux producing about 2,500 cases a year of supple, well-structured wine.

Bonarda An Italian red-wine grape planted in the Piedmont region, especially in the Novara-Vercelli hills, near Gattinara; the name Bonarda dell'Oltrepò Pavese, however, actually refers to the Croatina grape.

Bonnes Mares A celebrated Burgundian vineyard that produces what is unquestionably one of the dozen finest red wines of the Côte d'Or. It consists of 37 acres of vines, of which 33.5 acres are in the commune of Chambolle-Musigny, the remaining 3.5 acres in Morey-Saint-Denis; its average production is about 5,000 cases. Situated halfway between Chambertin and Musigny, its wine has some of the characteristics of each of its illustrious neighbours – the power and great class of Chambertin, somewhat attenuated; the incomparable finesse of Musigny, though to a less remarkable degree.

Bonnezeaux A small appellation within the Coteaux du Layon district, itself within the large Anjou region of France's Loire Valley. The village of Bonnezeaux is situated on the north bank of the Layon, a tributary of the Loire, and its 325 acres of vineyards, granted *grand cru* status in 1951, produce about 13,000 cases a year of sweet, fruity, elegant wines made from the Chenin Blanc grape and similar in style to Quarts de Chaume, produced only a few miles away.

Bontemps A shallow wooden bowl traditionally utilized in the Bordeaux region for beating egg whites used for fining; as such it has become the emblem of a well-known wine fraternity, the Commanderie des Bontemps du Médoc et des Graves.

Bordeaux A seaport and city of 225,000 on the Garonne River in

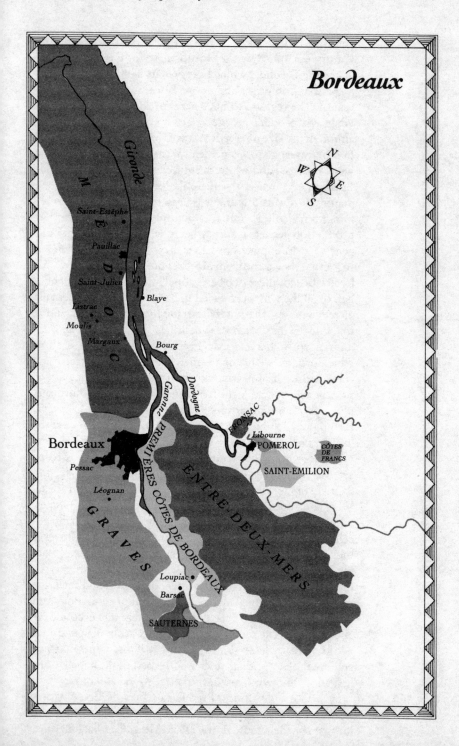

Bordeaux

southwestern France. A few miles north of the city, the Garonne is joined by the Dordogne to form the broad estuary of the Gironde, which has given its name to the *département* that comprises the entire Bordeaux wine-producing region. The region's 215,000 acres of *Appellation Contrôlée* vineyards produce an average of 35 million cases of wine, although the size of recent vintages has varied from 22 to 60 million cases; about 75 percent of the total is red. All of this wine, both red and white, is entitled to the basic appellation Bordeaux, which is the region's lowest common denominator; Bordeaux Supérieur is very little better – the wine's minimum alcohol content is slightly higher, and maximum production per acre is somewhat lower. Both wines may and generally do come from lesser areas within the Bordeaux region – if they came from more reputed districts they would be so labelled; these two basic appellations account for about half of all the wines produced in Bordeaux. There are, in all, 25 red-wine appellations within the Bordeaux region, and 18 for white wines, each of which has been defined and delimited with characteristic French precision, and each of which produces wine of a somewhat different character and class. Most consumers are likely to recognize only a dozen names, which include the five principal districts of Bordeaux plus a few communal appellations. Thus, north of the city, forming the left or west bank of the Gironde estuary are the low, gravelly hills of the incomparable Médoc, whose red wines are among the greatest in the world; within the Médoc are the communes of Margaux, Saint-Julien, Pauillac, and Saint-Estèphe, plus the lesser known Moulis and Listrac. West and south of Bordeaux is the wide district of Graves, which produces dry and semidry white wines and many excellent reds. Enclosed within the southern part of Graves is the Sauternes district, which includes the commune of Barsac, and whose sweet white wines are world famous. Across the Garonne, and beyond the intervening hills and the Dordogne, are the vineyards of Saint-Emilion and Pomerol, which produce red wines only. These districts account for about 20 percent of the total Bordeaux crop. There are, in addition, many lesser-known districts whose wines may not achieve the exceptional quality of the best of the appellations just cited, but which are nevertheless sound and moderately priced. Côtes de Bourg, Premières Côtes de Blaye, Côtes de Francs, Fronsac, and Montagne-Saint-Emilion are known for their reds, Entre-Deux-Mers, Cadillac, Cérons,

Loupiac, and Sainte-Croix-du-Mont for their whites.

The red wines of Bordeaux, which are usually referred to as claret by British connoisseurs (the term is not officially defined and is not used in France), are made primarily from Cabernet Sauvignon, Cabernet Franc, and Merlot grapes, plus lesser amounts of Malbec and Petit Verdot. The Cabernets, which predominate in the Médoc and Graves, contribute backbone, character, and longevity; Merlot, more widely planted in Saint-Emilion and Pomerol, produces softer, more supple, and quick-maturing wines. (Although Cabernet Sauvignon is the grape traditionally associated with red Bordeaux, Merlot actually accounts for about half the red-wine acreage.) Red Bordeaux is comparatively light in alcohol – about 12 percent – with a deep colour, mouth-puckering tannins when young, and an agreeable, brisk acidity; the wines are among the longest-lived in the world, and fine vintages from the nineteenth century are still enjoyable. White Bordeaux is made primarily from Sémillon and Sauvignon Blanc, plus smaller amounts of Muscadelle, Colombard, and Ugni Blanc. Sémillon contributes body, richness, and longevity, and is also susceptible to *Botrytis cinerea*, the so-called noble rot that is responsible for the luscious taste of Sauternes and Barsac and, to a lesser extent, the semisweet taste of Loupiac and Sainte-Croix-du-Mont. Sauvignon Blanc is characterized by a herbaceous taste and lively acidity, and a number of Bordeaux producers now bottle crisp, dry wines made from this grape alone.

Although one or another of the Bordeaux appellations appears on the label of every AOC wine from this extensive region, the finest wines carry the name of a specific château, or vineyard. The best vineyards of the Médoc, Graves, Saint-Emilion, and Sauternes have been classified, and these classifications will be found on page 537. There are nearly 200 of these *crus classés*, or classed growths – *cru*, or "growth", is synonymous with vineyard or château – and they include most of the finest vineyards of Bordeaux (the vineyards of Pomerol have never been classified). There are, in addition, more than a hundred *crus bourgeois* in the Médoc, and a number of lesser properties throughout the Bordeaux region, the latter referred to as *petits châteaux*, whose wines go to market labelled with the name of a specific château. Note, however, that there are about 7,000 châteaux (that is, individually named vineyards) in Bordeaux, and the fact that a wine is château-bottled and bears a château name is no guarantee of quality. Apart from the extensive range of château-bottled wines, from the finest classed growths of the Médoc to inexpensive Bordeaux Supérieur, there are also regional wines, which are blended from different properties within a particular appellation and are labelled with the name of that appellation, as Médoc, Margaux, Saint-Emilion, Graves, or Sauternes. In recent years, such regional wines from various Bordeaux shippers have been largely replaced either by château-bottled wines from the same appellation or by proprietary brands; the latter are blends – usually of Bordeaux or Bordeaux Supérieur – that are marketed with a brand name, such as Mouton-Cadet.

Bordeaux Mixture   Our name for what the French call *bouillie bordelaise*, a fungicide spray made of copper sulphate and slaked lime, widely used in Europe against oidium and mildew. It is this – or some quite similar, related product, that so often gives the French and German vineyards their characteristic blue-green tinge in summertime.

Bota   The Spanish term for "butt", or "cask"; also, a leather wine pouch.

Bottle   A bottle's shape and its colour offer useful but by no means infallible clues to a wine's origin and type. The straight-sided, high-shouldered Bordeaux bottle is used, in dark green glass, for all red Bordeaux, and in clear glass for nearly all white Bordeaux, but the same or a very similar bottle is used in almost all other wine-producing countries, and sometimes for very dissimilar wines. The slope-shouldered Burgundy bottle is also that of the Rhône Valley, of many Italian and Spanish wines, of a number of California wines, and, in a somewhat heavier version, that of Champagne and other sparkling wines. The slender, tapering Rhine bottle is brown on the Rhine, but green in Alsace and on the Moselle, and a colourless *flûte* in nearly the same form serves for many rosés. The straw-coloured *fiasco* of Italy is still encountered on occasion, and both Germany and Chile have their stumpy flagons, known as a bocksbeutel. Actually, the form of the bottle makes no difference at all, providing that it can be easily binned, that is, put on its side for extended storage and aging. All wines, however, age more quickly in small bottles than in large, and a half-bottle of a given wine will always be readier than a full bottle, and both readier than a magnum. All wines are adversely affected by light, and all last longer, except under absolutely ideal conditions, when in green or brown bottles. The standard bottle, according to EC regulations, contains 75cl (750ml); a half bottle 37.5cl (375ml). Certain wines, most often Champagne and Bordeaux, are sometimes marketed in oversize bottles, the best known of which are the magnum (equal to two standard bottles), double magnum (four bottles), jeroboam (four bottles in Champagne, six in Bordeaux), Imperial or Methusalem (eight bottles), Salmanazar (twelve bottles), Balthazar (sixteen bottles), and Nebuchadnezzar (twenty bottles).

Bottle Aging   A term that describes the development of wine after bottling. Contrary to popular belief, the various interactions that occur in bottled wine do so without the continuous absorption of oxygen, as the air trapped in the headspace between the cork and the wine is absorbed by the wine within months of bottling; in fact, in many modern wineries the air in the empty bottles is replaced with inert gas just before they are filled with wine so that there is virtually no oxygen in the headspace. Furthermore, bottles with dried or loose corks, which permit air to come into contact with the wine, invariably result in wines that are oxidized or otherwise spoiled. Rosés, most white wines, many light reds, and even fino sherry are at their best when bottled, and only a small proportion of the world's wines improve beyond two years in bottle (bearing in mind that many of them have already been matured in wood). A number of red wines, notably vintage port, fine red Bordeaux, certain California Cabernet Sauvignons, and such Italian wines as Barolo and Brunello di Montalcino need some years of bottle age to soften their tannic harshness and to develop complex nuances of taste; fine dry white wines, such as those from Burgundy and the best California Chardonnays, take on richness and complexity with bottle age, as do such sweet wines as Sauternes and late-harvest Rieslings from Germany and California. Although some consumers believe that each wine has a particular peak at which it tastes best, even long-lived wines that benefit from bottle age are likely to achieve a plateau of maturity that lasts for several years, during which changes occur very slowly, and then to gradually deteriorate in quality.

Bottle Sickness   A condition that affects many wines immediately after bottling, characterized by a flat, lifeless taste. Wines may be numbed by the handling they receive as part of the bottling process, or, in some cases, by the oxygen they absorb when bottled; sound wines invariably recover from bottle sickness after a few weeks.

Botrytis Cinerea A beneficial mould known as *pourriture noble* in France and *Edelfäule* in Germany; both terms mean "noble rot". *Botrytis* is responsible for the special taste of such wines as Sauternes, from the Bordeaux district of France; Beerenauslese and Trockenbeerenauslese from Germany's Rhine and Moselle districts; Tokay Aszú from Hungary; and a number of late-harvest wines from California. The mould forms on the skins of ripe grapes under specific conditions – humidity alternating with dry heat – and sends filaments into the grapes, perforating the skin. This shrivels the grapes and reduces their liquid content, which is mostly water, and the remaining juice is thus especially rich in sugar (and also retains its acidity, which prevents the wines from being cloying). When the juice is transformed into wine, not all of the sugar is fermented into alcohol, and the resulting wine contains quite a bit of residual sugar. *Botrytis* not only concentrates the sugar content of the juice, however; it also transforms the taste of the resulting wine, which is honeyed, complex, intense, and luscious. (If the same mould infects unripe or damaged grapes, however, it results in *pourriture grise*, or "grey rot", which deteriorates the grapes.) The range of *botrytis*-affected wines varies enormously. Sauternes is made primarily from Sémillon, and the wine contains 13 to 14 percent alcohol and 8 to 10 percent residual sugar. German examples are usually made from Riesling and are likely to contain 7 to 9 percent alcohol; Auslesen usually contains 6 to 8 percent residual sugar, Beerenauslesen contain 10 to 12 percent, and Trockenbeerenauslesen contain 15 to 20 percent residual sugar. Most California late-harvest wines, usually Riesling, contain 8 to 10 percent alcohol and 5 to 25 percent residual sugar. Sweet wines, including Sauternes and even Trockenbeerenauslesen, can be made without *botrytis*, but the result is a sweet wine without the honeyed complexity and concentration that is the particular contribution of the noble rot. Botrytised wines are also made along the Loire from Chenin Blanc; from Weissburgunder (Pinot Blanc) in the Burgenland district of Austria; from Gewürztraminer, Scheurebe, Optima, Ortega, and Huxelrebe in Germany; from Gewürztraminer, Sauvignon Blanc, Sémillon, and Chenin Blanc in California; from Riesling and Sémillon in Australia; and, of course, from Furmint and Harslevelü in the Tokay district of Hungary.

Bouchet   A name sometimes used for Cabernet Franc in the Saint-Emilion and Pomerol districts of Bordeaux.

Bouchonné   French for "corked", from *bouchon*, "cork".

Bougros   One of the seven *grand cru* vineyards of Chablis, whose 39 acres adjoin Les Preuses.

Bouquet   This can be defined, quite simply, as the way a wine smells. The term is also used, more specifically, to describe the complex of diverse odours that a good, mature wine develops with bottle age, primarily from the interaction of alcohols and acids. Bottle bouquet is one of a fine wine's greatest attractions and greatest charms. (In this context, aroma is properly applied to young wines, and refers to simple, fruity odours related to the grape variety.) Amateur and professional tasters alike recognize the importance of smell in evaluating a wine and appreciating its qualities. Indeed, on the basis of smell alone, many experts can determine a wine's origin, the grape variety from which it is made, its approximate age, its overall condition, and its value. The fact is that smell accounts for most of what we think of as taste; when we recognize the taste of duck, salmon, or an apple, it is the olfactory nerves, situated in the upper part of the nose, that are doing most of the work. Also, most people have a better sense memory for smells than for taste, which is why wine tasters always devote a few moments to a wine's smell before tasting it. One does not have to be any sort of expert to appreciate the bouquet of a fine wine.

Bourg   A village about 20 miles north of the city of Bordeaux, on the right bank of the Garonne, directly across from the southern Médoc; its 9,000 acres of vineyards produce 1.5 million cases of red wine in abundant vintages, and they are entitled to the appellation Côtes de Bourg. There are a number of *petits châteaux* in this district, and their wines, made primarily from Merlot, can be quite appealing examples of moderately priced red Bordeaux.

Bourgeois   *See* Cru Bourgeois

Bourgogne   French for the province of Burgundy and its wines; although any wine so labelled must be made from Pinot Noir or Chardonnay, the AOC Bourgogne refers to regional red and white wines that are much less distinguished than those bearing village or vineyard names. (Note that the *crus* of Beaujolais, although made from the Gamay grape, are entitled to the appellation Bourgogne.)

Bourgogne Aligoté *See* Aligoté

Bourgogne Grand Ordinaire   AOC for red and white wines produced in less-distinguished districts of France's Burgundy region; the reds are more likely to be made from Gamay than Pinot Noir, the whites from Chardonnay. Despite the name, the wines are anything but grand, and actually lower on the quality scale than those labelled simply Bourgogne.

Bourgogne-Hautes Côtes de Beaune   An AOC for red (and a little bit of white) wines produced in the southern part of the Arrierès-Côtes, the hills west of the Côte d'Or, from Pinot Noir (and Chardonnay). As plantings of Pinot Noir have increased in the Arrières-Côtes, production of red wines in the Hautes Côtes de Beaune and adjoining Hautes Côtes de Nuits have exceeded 400,000 cases in some recent vintages; lighter and less concentrated than those of the Côtes d'Or, the wines are nevertheless attractive red Burgundies and, often, good value.

Bourgogne-Hautes Côtes de Nuits   An AOC for red (and a small amount of white) wines produced in the northern part of the Arrières-Côtes, the hills west of the Côte d'Or, from Pinot Noir (and Chardonnay).

Bourgogne Mousseux   An AOC for white (and, until 1986, red) sparkling wines from France's Burgundy region; this appellation has been almost entirely replaced by the more recent AOC Crémant de Bourgogne.

Bourgogne Passe-tout-grains   An AOC for lesser red wines (and some rosé) from the Burgundy region produced from Gamay and at least one third Pinot Noir grapes fermented together; most Passe-tout-grains comes from the Côte Chalonnaise and the Arrières-Côtes, rather than from the Côte d'Or.

Bourgueil   A village in the region of Touraine, in the Loire Valley, long famous for its red wines, made from the Cabernet Franc grape (known locally as the Breton). One of the most agreeable lesser red wines of France, Bourgueil should be drunk fairly young and preferably at cellar temperature; it is rather light and fruity, with a berrylike aroma, and combines charm and character, as do the similar wines produced nearby at Saint-Nicolas-de-Bourgueil and Chinon. Production amounts to more than half a million cases a year.

Bouscaut, Château One of the biggest of the *grands crus classés* of the Graves district, producing about 20,000 cases a year of both red and white wines from 110 acres of vineyard, three quarters of which are planted with red-wine grapes.

Bouzeron A village just northwest of Rully, in the Côte Chalonnaise region of Burgundy, known for its Aligoté; in fact, there is now an AOC Bourgogne Aligoté de Bouzeron.

Bouzy An important wine-producing village in France's Champagne region whose vineyards, planted with Pinot Noir, are rated 100 percent. Although most of its wines are transformed into champagne, a certain amount of still red wine from Bouzy is bottled and marketed as such.

Boyd-Cantenac, Château A Third Classed Growth of the Médoc district of Bordeaux, situated in the commune of Cantenac, within the Margaux appellation; its 45 acres produce about 8,000 cases a year of a relatively firm, slow-maturing wine. The property, originally known simply as Château Boyd was split up into two parts, Boyd-Cantenac and Cantenac-Brown, in 1860.

Brachetto An Italian grape cultivated in the Piedmont region, where it produces a light red wine that is likely to be slightly sweet and fizzy; Brachetto d'Acqui is a DOC from a zone just east of Alba.

Bramaterra A small district just west of Gattinara, in Italy's Piedmont region, whose vineyards, planted primarily with Nebbiolo, were granted DOC status in 1979.

Branaire Ducru, Château A Fourth Classed Growth of Saint-Julien, in the Médoc district of Bordeaux, directly adjoining Château Beychevelle; its 120 acres of vines produce some 20,000 cases a year of concentrated, well-balanced wine whose quality has improved considerably when it came under the same direction as Château Giscours. The label actually reads Château Branaire (Duluc-Ducru), a reference to the change in ownership from the Duluc to the Ducru family in 1860, but the vineyard is always referred to as Branaire Ducru.

Brane-Cantenac, Château A Second Classed Growth of Margaux, in the Médoc district of Bordeaux; its 200 acres of vines produce about 32,000 cases a year of supple, fruity, and elegant wine (some of which goes to market under the second label Château Notton). The vineyard, situated in the commune of Cantenac and originally known as Gorse-Cantenac, was acquired in 1835 by the Baron de Brane, who had previously owned Brane-Mouton (now Mouton-Rothschild); it was acquired by the Lurton family in 1925, and the 750-acre estate is now the residence of Lucien Lurton, who also owns Châteaux Durfort-Vivens and Desmirail in the Médoc, Climens in Sauternes, and Bouscaut in Graves.

Brauneberg A famous village on the Moselle, in Germany, situated between Bernkastel and Piesport; its wines were long considered, even by such a discerning taster as Thomas Jefferson, as the best of the region. Today the Braunebergers are less fashionable but no less admirable, full-bodied, fine, and rich, and comparable to those of Wehlen and Zeltingen; its best-known vineyard is the 76-acre Juffer.

Brazil The world's most important producer of coffee, oranges, and bananas, Brazil is not yet famous for its wines. Most of this country's vineyards are planted in the southernmost state of Rio Grande do Sul, which is sufficiently far from the equator and temperate enough in climate for the vine to flourish. Nevertheless, for most of this century, almost all of Brazil's wines were produced from such native American grapes as Isabella and Niagara, and from French-American hybrids. In recent years, new vineyards have been planted with such *vinifera* varieties as Cabernet Sauvignon, Merlot, Nebbiolo, Barbera, Chardonnay, Riesling, Sémillon, and Pinot Blanc. About 30 million cases are produced annually, almost all of it consumed locally.

Breathing Even the most casual wine drinker has learned that a bottle of red wine is supposed, somehow, to improve if it is uncorked thirty minutes or an hour before it is to be served, and this practice is what most people understand by the term *breathing*. Actually, the term more properly applies to the aeration of wine, almost always red, before it is served, and common sense suggests that simply uncorking a bottle is the least effective way to aerate it – the surface of wine exposed to air in the neck of a bottle is so small as to have no effect on its taste, even after an hour or more. The most effective way to aerate wine is to pour it into a decanter or other clean container; the act of pouring will aerate the contents of the bottle, and if the wine is left in the decanter for a period of time, the surface of wine exposed to air will continue the aeration process. In situations where decanting may be impractical, as in some restaurants, simply have the red wine poured into large glasses as soon as possible, and let it stand until needed to accompany the food; here again, the surface of wine exposed to air in each glass is considerably greater than if the wine is simply uncorked, and, of course, the wine can also be swirled in its glass to further aerate it. All that being said, there is some controversy as to whether aeration actually improves the taste of red wines: decanting may soften some of the tannic harshness of young wines, but they also lose some of their fruit and flavour and may be somewhat less appealing than if simply poured from the bottle, with no more aeration than occurs in the glass. Certainly older wines should be decanted to separate them from their sediment, but it may be best to decant them just before serving and let them develop their qualities in the glass, rather than risk the possibility of having a fifteen- or twenty-year-old wine fade in the decanter. In the end, of course, personal preference, based on experience, is the determining factor in deciding whether wines should be aerated, and for how long.

Breed   A word used for wines of high quality, with elegance, refinement, and finesse.

Breganze   A DOC zone north of Vicenza in Italy's Veneto region. Breganze Rosso is made primarily from Merlot, the most widely planted variety in this zone, and Breganze Bianco primarily from Tocai Friulano; a number of varietally labelled wines are also made from Cabernet, Pinot Bianco, Pinot Grigio, Pinot Nero, and the native white Vespaiolo.

Brescia   A wine-producing province situated west of Lake Garda, in

Italy's Lombardy region; among the DOC zones within its borders are Franciacorta, Lugana, and Riviera del Garda Bresciano; less familiar DOCs include the reds of Botticino and Cellatica, the reds and whites of Capriano del Colle, and the white Tocai di San Martino della Battaglia.

Bricco In the dialect of Italy's Piedmont region, this refers to the top of a hill, whose exposure presumably results in riper grapes and finer wines; the term is found on labels of Barolo and Barbaresco, as Bricco Bussia and Bricco Asili.

Brilliant A term applied to a wine that is impeccably clear, as all good wines should be.

Bristol Cream A well-known proprietary brand of Spanish sherry marketed by Harveys of Bristol; this sweet wine is the most popular sherry sold in the United States.

Brix A hydrometer and scale used for measuring the sugar content of unfermented grape juice, and therefore the probable alcoholic content of the finished wine. The Brix scale, which has pretty much replaced the earlier and similar Balling scale, measures the dissolved solids in the juice – primarily glucose and fructose – and expresses this in terms of grams of sugar per 100 grams of juice. In general, the Brix reading multiplied by .55 will give the wine's future alcoholic content by volume: juice of 22 degrees should give a 12 percent wine. The conversion factor for white wines fermented slowly at low temperatures, however, is closer to .60. *See* also Oechsle.

Brochon A village directly north of Gevrey-Chambertin, on Burgundy's Côte d'Or; about half the wines – all of them red – from its 230 acres of vineyards are entitled to the appellation Gevrey-Chambertin, and almost all the rest is marketed as Côte de Nuits-Villages.

Brouilly One of the best and most famous wine-producing districts in France's Beaujolais region. The vineyards of this extensive zone are situated in five communes, and consequently there is somewhat more variation in the taste of Brouilly than in other Beaujolais *crus*. Nevertheless, the wine is one of the most attractive of all Beaujolais, especially when young – fruity, supple, full-flavoured yet soon ready, it is among the most agreeable red wines in the world.

Broustet, Château A classed growth in the Sauternes district, in the commune of Barsac; its 40 acres produce some 4,000 cases a year of a white wine that is perhaps a little less sweet than most Barsacs, but with considerable distinction and breed.

Brunello di Montalcino One of Italy's finest red wines, deep-coloured, intense, powerful, tannic, and exceptionally long-lived; it is produced entirely from the Brunello grape, a variant of Sangiovese, around the town of Montalcino, 25 miles southeast of Siena, in southern Tuscany. The wine was created in the late nineteenth century by Ferruccio Biondi-Santi, who isolated this strain of Sangiovese and produced a sturdy wine unusual for the region in that it contained no other grape varieties. The rapid development of this wine's fame may be measured by the fact that as recently as the late 1960s there were fewer than 200 acres of vineyards within the Montalcino zone; today there are more than 2,000, producing 300,000 to 400,000 cases a year, although not all of this wine is bottled as Brunello di Montalcino. The DOC regulations stipulated a minimum of four years of wood aging for Brunello, which many producers believed was too long a period, especially for lighter vintages. The DOCG law, established in 1980, states that although the wines may not be released until four years after the vintage, minimum wood aging is reduced to three and a half years. The alternative DOC Rosso di Montalcino was established in 1983 for wines that may be sold a year after the harvest; producers may decide whether to designate a particular lot of wine as Rosso di Montalcino (for which no wood aging is required) or to age the wine as stipulated and market it as Brunello di Montalcino.

Brut A French term applied to the driest champagnes and other sparkling wines, drier than those labelled Extra Dry. Common Market regulations limit the amount of sweetness to 1.5 percent, but most Brut champagnes are likely to contain only .8 to 1.2 percent sugar. Extra Brut indicates a champagne or sparkling wine with no more than .6 percent sugar and replaces such terms as *Brut Absolu, Brut Zéro,* and *Brut Intégral,* previously used for wines to which no *dosage,* or sweetening, was added.

Bual *See* Boal

Bucelas A full-bodied, dry white Portuguese wine, often wood aged, produced a few miles north of Lisbon in a small district set back from the Tagus, along the Trancao River; production of this wine, which is also labelled Bucellas, is limited.

Bugey A little district in the *département* of Ain, northeast of Lyons, producing a variety of light but agreeable red, white, and rosé wines entitled to the VDQS Vins de Bugey; the whites made from the Altesse grape, known locally as Roussette, may be marketed as Roussette de Bugey.

Buhl, Reichsrat von An important estate in Germany's Rheinpfalz region whose 235 acres include important vineyard holdings in Forst, Ruppertsberg, Wachenheim, and Deidesheim, planted, for the most part, with Riesling.

Bulgaria Situated in eastern Europe between the Black Sea and Yugoslavia, and separated from Romania on the north by the Danube River, Bulgaria is part of ancient Thrace, whose wines were celebrated by Homer more than 2,700 years ago. Today, 375,000 acres of vineyards produce 45 to 55 million cases of wine a year, almost all of it made in state-controlled wineries; about 80 percent of this is exported, primarily to Russia and other Eastern bloc countries, but increasingly to the West as well. Until the 1950s, Bulgaria's vineyards were planted almost exclusively with such native grapes as the red Gamza (the Kadarka of Hungary), Mavrud, and Pamid, and the white Dimiat, Misket, and Rkatsiteli, the latter still the most widely planted white variety. Classic European varieties now account for more than half the total acreage, and the 88,000 acres of Cabernet Sauvignon make it Bulgaria's principal red variety, with Merlot second. Other varieties that are increasingly found in Bulgaria include a small amount of Pinot Noir and, among the whites, Chardonnay, Italian Riesling, Rhine Riesling, Sauvignon Blanc, Gewürztraminer, Pinot Gris, and Aligoté.

The principal wine-producing regions of Bulgaria are Shumen, in the northeast, known for its white wines; Suhindol, in the centre of the country and north of the Balkan Mountains, whose best-known varieties are Cabernet Sauvignon and Gamza; Haskovo, south of the Balkan Mountains, planted with Merlot, Cabernet Sauvignon, and Mavrud (the Strandja district, known for its Cabernet Sauvignon, is situated within Haskovo); and the Sungulare

Valley, south of Shumen, where the native Misket is the most widely cultivated variety. The village of Melnik, in the southwest corner of the country, gives its name to an acclaimed red wine made fom the Mavrud grape. The wines of Bulgaria are divided into three principal categories – the inexpensive generic and blended wines that make up about 90 percent of the total crop; wines from about 40 broadly defined geographical regions; and, at the top of the pyramid, about 20 wines from individual varieties and specific districts of origin. The latter category, sometimes referred to as Controliran and first defined in 1978, corresponds to the appellation of origin wines of France and Italy, and includes Chardonnay from Novi Pazar, Cabernet from Svishtov, Merlot from Sakar, Traminer from Khan Kroum, Misket from Sungulare, and Mavrud from Assenovgrad. In recent years, Vinprom, the government agency responsible for the production and marketing of most of Bulgaria's wines, has created specific brand names for generic and varietal wines exported to western countries; these include Trakia (Bulgarian for Thrace), and Sophia, used in Canada since 1983. Bulgarian reds, especially Cabernet Sauvignon and Merlot, provide good value; of the native varieties, the sturdy, long-lived Mavrud is the most interesting.

Bulk Process *See* Charmat Process

Burger A white-wine grape grown in California, where almost all of the 2,500 acres planted are in the San Joaquin Valley; long thought to be identical to the Elbling of Germany, the California variety may be the Monbadon of southern France. Note, however, that Burger is the name used for Elbling in Alsace and Switzerland.

Burgunder *See* Spätburgunder

Burgundy An extensive region in France that includes Chablis, the Côte d'Or, the Côte Chalonnaise (also known as the Région de Mercurey), Mâcon (which includes Pouilly-Fuissé), and Beaujolais. Chablis, somewhat isolated from the rest of Burgundy, is situated 90 miles southeast of Paris; the other districts stretch from just below Dijon almost to Lyons. The average annual production of Burgundy is 20 to 22 million cases a year, about 3 percent of all French wines and 15 percent or so of all AOC wines, but Beaujolais alone accounts

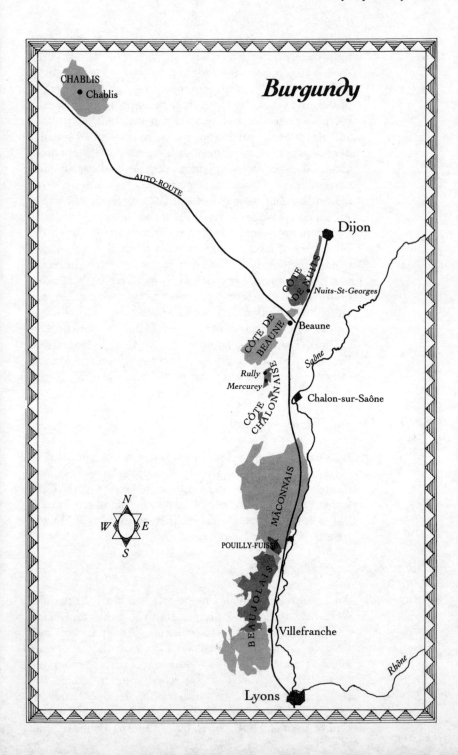

for 50 or 60 percent of the total. Indeed, when oenophiles discuss fine Burgundy, they are usually referring to the relatively limited amount of red and white wines – about 10 percent of the total Burgundy crop – produced along the Côte d'Or, or Golden Slope, made up of the Côte de Nuits and the Côte de Beaune. It is here that the classic Chardonnay and Pinot Noir grapes produce some of the world's most remarkable wines, including those from the vineyards of Chambertin, Musigny, Romanée-Conti, Corton, Corton-Charlemagne, and Montrachet, and from such villages as Vosne-Romanée, Nuits-Saint-Georges, Beaune, Volnay, Pommard, and Meursault.

Curiously enough, the French AOC Bourgogne is the lowest appellation within the region we refer to as Burgundy, since red and white wines of any distinction would be labelled with a more specific appellation of origin, such as Chablis, Pouilly-Fuissé, Mâcon-Villages, Mercurey, or a village or vineyard name such as the ones cited above. Nevertheless, wines labelled Bourgogne Rouge must be made entirely from Pinot Noir (with the exception of the Beaujolais *crus*, such as Morgon, Brouilly, and Moulin-à-Vent, which are made from Gamay, but entitled to be sold as Bourgogne); and those labelled Bourgogne Blanc must be made entirely from Chardonnay and Pinot Blanc (although in practice there is virtually no Pinot Blanc left in Burgundy). There are, in addition, three lesser Burgundy appellations, more fully described elsewhere – Bourgogne Aligoté, a light white wine made from the Aligoté grape; Bourgogne Passe-tout-grains, a light red made from Gamay and at least a third Pinot Noir vinified together; and Bourgogne Grand Ordinaire, red and white wines that, despite the name, are blends of lower standing than wines labelled simply Bourgogne. A complete listing of all the Burgundy appellations will be found on page 530, and the principal vineyards of the Côte d'Or will be found on page 545.

In many countries, including the United States, the word *Burgundy* is considered a generic term applicable to any red wine, however and wherever produced; most wines so labelled are inexpensive, and some may even be slightly sweet.

Bürklin-Wolf A famous 270-acre estate in Wachenheim, in Germany's Rheinpfalz, or Palatinate, with important holdings in the four major wine villages of the region – Forst, Ruppertsberg,

Wachenheim, and Deidesheim. The wines, which range from the drier Trocken styles to remarkable Beerenauslesen and Trockenbeerenauslesen, are noted for their elegance, balance, and breed.

Butt A large barrel or cask, especially of the sort and size in which sherry is traditionally aged and shipped; it holds 500 litres (about 110 gallons).

Buttafuoco An Italian red wine whose name means "spatters like fire"; one of three oddly named reds produced in the Oltrepò Pavese district of the Lombardy region – the others are Barbacarlo and Sangue di Giuda – each of which is likely to be slightly sparkling and semisweet.

Butyric A rancid odour sometimes found in certain spoiled wines.

Buzet A district in the Lot-et-Garonne *département* of southwest France, 60 miles southeast of Bordeaux, producing about 600,000 cases a year from 3,000 acres; the appellation was elevated from VDQS to AOC in 1973, and changed from Côtes de Buzet to Buzet in 1985. The red wines, which amount for almost all the production, are made from about 40 percent Merlot and 30 percent each of Cabernet Franc and Cabernet Sauvignon; the whites are made almost entirely from Sémillon, with some Sauvignon Blanc and even less Muscadelle; 95 percent of the crop is vinified and marketed by the local co-operative cellar.

❧ C

Cabardès A VDQS for red wines produced north of Carcassonne in the Aude *département* of the Languedoc-Roussillon region of southern France.

Cabernet d'Anjou An appellation for rosé wines made from the Cabernet Franc grape in the Anjou region of France's Loire Valley; production averages about 1.5 million cases a year. The semidry wine is pleasant, moderately priced, and more distinctive than Rosé d'Anjou, made primarily from the Groslot grape.

Cabernet Franc An excellent red-wine grape most often associated with the wines of Bordeaux; it is widely planted in Pomerol and Saint-Emilion (where it is also known as Bouchet), and is also cultivated in the Médoc and Graves districts. It produces wines similar in style to the more famous Cabernet Sauvignon, but lighter bodied, with less tannin and perhaps more aroma. Cabernet Franc is also extensively planted in the central Loire, where it is used to make such appealing red wines as Chinon, Bourgueil, Saumur-Champigny, and Cabernet de Touraine, as well as the popular rosé known as Cabernet d'Anjou; vinified to produce a white wine, it is often blended with Chenin Blanc in the production of sparkling Loire wines. The grape is also widely planted in northern Italy, in the Veneto, Friuli, and Trentino-Alto Adige, where the light, attractive wines labelled simply Cabernet are likely to be Cabernet Franc; of the more than 20,000 acres of Cabernet planted in Italy, 80 percent are Cabernet Franc. In California, about 1,300 acres have been planted in the past decade to provide wines that can be blended with Cabernet Sauvignon, as is done in Bordeaux.

Cabernet di Pramaggiore *See* Pramaggiore

Cabernet Sauvignon A superb red-wine grape responsible in large part for the great wines of Bordeaux, for California's finest red wines, and for outstanding wines from many other countries as well. Tannic and puckerish when young, the best examples are well-structured, complex, and among the longest-lived of all wines. Although Cabernet Sauvignon is considered the premier grape of Bordeaux, it accounts for only a quarter of the red-grape acreage (Merlot makes up half the total); it is the dominant variety in the well-drained, gravelly soils of the Médoc and Graves districts, however, where it represents 60 to 90 percent of the acreage of most top vineyards (the rest being made up primarily of Merlot and Cabernet Franc). The variety is less extensively planted in the Saint-Emilion and Pomerol districts, whose clay soils and cooler growing conditions do not always permit Cabernet Sauvignon to ripen. Cabernet Sauvignon is also planted in the Bergerac district, east of Bordeaux; along the middle Loire, where it adds substance to the Cabernet Franc-based wines of Chinon and Bourgueil; and is successfully cultivated in selected sites in the Midi region. In California, Cabernet Sauvignon has long been associated with the Napa Valley; there are extensive plantings in Sonoma County as well, and Napa and Sonoma counties account for half of the acreage in California, which has increased from 2,600 acres in 1966 to more than 29,000 acres. Cabernet Sauvignon is also planted in Mendocino, Lake, Monterey, San Luis Obispo, and Santa Barbara counties. Most California versions of this wine were originally made with 100 percent of the variety, and some still are, including such notable examples as Heitz Martha's Vineyard and the Georges de Latour Private Reserve of Beaulieu Vineyard. In recent years many producers have blended in a proportion of Merlot and, increasingly, Cabernet Franc; a few producers have even planted such less familiar Bordeaux varieties as Malbec and Petit Verdot to create a more complex Cabernet-based wine. Because a California wine labelled as Cabernet Sauvignon must contain a minimum of 75 percent of that variety, a number of wineries have removed the varietal name from their labels and market their Cabernet-based blends with proprietary names. (*See* Meritage.) Fine Cabernets are also made in other parts of the United States from Washington's Columbia Valley to New York's Long Island. A wide range of excellent Cabernet Sauvignon wines is now produced in Australia, where this variety hardly existed in the late 1960s; the grape has achieved particular success in the Coonawarra district. Many Australian producers also market blends of Cabernet and Shiraz (the Syrah of France's Rhône Valley); the latter softens the tannic austerity of Cabernet, as Merlot does in France and California, and adds richness to the blend. Cabernet Sauvignon is not as widely planted as Cabernet Franc in northern Italy, but it has been successfully cultivated in Tuscany, where it adds structure and complexity to wines made with the traditional Sangiovese. Cabernet Sauvignon is a hardy grape that also thrives in many other countries, including Chile and Argentina, parts of Spain and Portugal, and Bulgaria and Romania; in fact, both Chile and Bulgaria now have more acreage of Cabernet Sauvignon than does California.

Cabinet A German term used on labels until 1971 to indicate a wine considered by its producer to be superior to his regular bottling; it has now been replaced by the term *Kabinett*, whose use is strictly defined.

Cadillac A picturesque little town in the Premières Côtes de Bordeaux district, facing Cérons and Barsac across the Garonne

River, which gives its name to semisweet white wines produced in a number of neighbouring villages; white wines so labelled must contain a minimum of 1.8 percent sugar.

Cahors An interesting and sometimes excellent red wine produced around the old city of that name, in southwest France, about 120 miles east of Bordeaux. Years ago, Cahors achieved a legendary status as a deeply coloured, tannic, and long-lived wine produced in very limited quantities. Phylloxera destroyed the vineyards in the late nineteenth century, and recovery was very slow – as recently as 1960 there were only 500 acres of vineyards. Today, there are 4,500 acres planted on both banks of the Lot River, and production in recent years has varied from about 800,000 cases to as much as 1.7 million. Cahors, originally a VDQS wine, was granted AOC status in 1971. The principal grape, which accounts for about 70 percent of the total, is Malbec (known locally as Auxerrois); others are Merlot, Tannat (which produces the wines of Madiran), and Jurançon Rouge (known locally as Dame Noire). The once-famous "black wine" of Cahors came from hillside vineyards and was enriched with concentrated must, which added colour and body. Many of the new vineyards are planted on the valley floor, vinification techniques have changed, and about half the district's production now comes from an efficient co-operative cellar – as a result, many of the wines from Cahors are likely to be pleasant, but relatively light, reds. A number of individual domains, however, do produce solid, well-structured wines.

Caillou, Château A classed growth of the Sauternes district, adjoining Château Climens in the commune of Barsac; its 37 acres produce 3,500 cases a year of elegant sweet wine, most of which is sold directly to consumers and restaurants in France. There is also a Château Le Caillou in Pomerol.

Cairanne A village north of Avignon whose wines are entitled to the superior appellation Côtes-du-Rhône-Villages; the fame of Cairanne's sturdy red wines is such that the village name usually appears on labels as well.

Calabria The toe of the Italian boot, this mountainous region produces 10 to 13 million cases a year, most of it undistinguished, from abut 70,000 acres of vineyards; the region's best-known wines come from the village of Cirò.

Calcium Alginate Beads The key element in a new technique developed by
Moët & Chandon in France's Champagne region. The yeasts
needed for the second fermentation in the bottle are en-
capsulated in small calcium alginate beads about one tenth of
an inch in diameter. (The process is also referred to as *en-
capsulated yeasts*.) The yeasts, which are trapped in the
beads, perform their traditional function without clouding
the wine, and when the time comes to disgorge the beads, the
bottles are placed upside down *sur pointe*, and the beads fall
to the bottom in a few moments; this technique thus elim-
inates the time-consuming riddling, or *rémuage*, process.

Caldaro An Italian red wine, also known as Lago di Caldaro (and, in
German-speaking markets, as Kalterersee), which takes its
name from the lake southwest of Bolzano, in the Alto Adige
region. Its nearly 6,000 acres of vineyards make Caldaro one
of the biggest DOC zones in Italy, with an annual production of 2.5 million cases of light, agreeable wine made from
the native Schiava grape.

California America's major vineyard region, producing more than 90
percent of the wines made in the United States, and about 70
percent of the wines consumed in the country (the rest is
made up of imports and wines from other states). There are
700,000 acres under vines, producing an annual crop of
about 5 million tons of grapes. About 60 percent of this is
made into wine by 600-plus wineries that produce an average of 200 million cases of wine a year; the rest of the crop is
marketed as table grapes or raisins.

The emergence of California as one of the world's finest
wine-producing regions has occurred in a remarkably short
period of time. As recently as the 1950s, three quarters of
California's production consisted of such fortified wines as
sherry, port, angelica, and muscatel, and it was not until 1968
that table wines – red, white, and pink – accounted for even
half the total; today, table wines represent three quarters of
the wines made, fortified wines less than 10 percent. Even
more important than the shift to table wines has been the remarkable improvement in the quality of California wines,
the result of the greater availability of quality grapes, as well
as new technology and changing cellar practices. An
example of technology is the widespread use of temperature-
controlled tanks, which enabled winemakers to ferment
white wines slowly at low temperatures, to retain their fruit

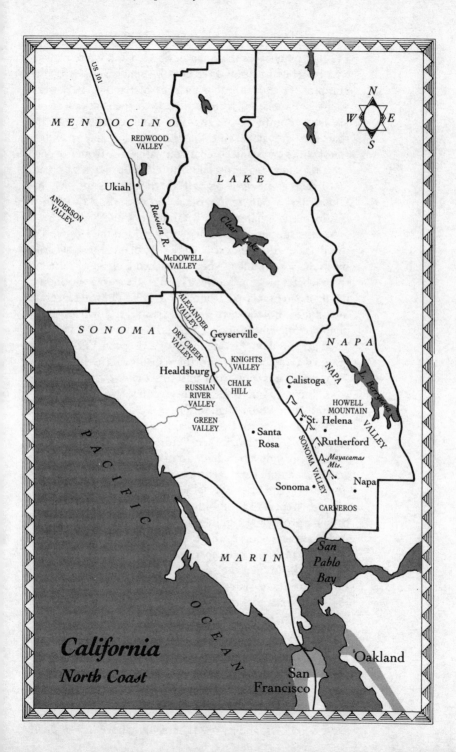

California
North Coast

and delicacy and prevent oxidation and spoilage; an example of cellar practices is the aging of fine red and white wines in small barrels made of French oak, which adds structure, complexity, and desirable nuances of flavour. Because of such techniques, and many others, less expensive table wines are now soundly made, appealing, and, on average, better than the equivalent wines of France, Italy, and Spain; the finest wines can stand comparison with those from Europe's greatest vineyards, especially those California wines made from such grape varieties as Cabernet Sauvignon, Merlot, Chardonnay, Sauvignon Blanc, and Riesling (known in California as Johannisberg Riesling or White Riesling).

Several species of grapevine grow wild in the area west of the Rockies, but vineyards were first planted in California by Franciscan monks, who established a chain of missions from what is now the Mexican border all the way to Sonoma, north of San Francisco, from 1769 to 1823. The original grape introduced, now known as the Mission, is a hardy variety giving on the whole poor wine, and accounts for fewer than 1,400 acres today. A wide range of European *Vitis vinifera* grapes was introduced to northern California in the 1860s by Agoston Haraszthy from cuttings that he brought back from Europe, but several other pioneer winemakers, including Jean-Louis Vignes, Pierre Pellier, Louis Prevost, Antoine Delmas, and A. P. Smith, had introduced *vinifera* varieties to California even before Haraszthy. The California wine industry, which flourished in many parts of the state in the nineteenth century, was dealt a severe blow by phylloxera and then virtually wiped out by Prohibition. After the repeal of Prohibition in 1933, there was a shortage of wine-producing facilities and of trained winemakers; to make matters worse, there were very few quality wine grapes available, since most vineyards had been replanted with thick-skinned high-yield red varieties that could be shipped to other states for home winemaking. In the early 1940s, for example, there were only 200 acres of Cabernet Sauvignon in California, and almost no Chardonnay. It is not an exaggeration to claim that the California wine industry is less than sixty years old and, in fact, most of the activity has taken place in the past thirty years. In 1959 there were only 80,000 acres of wine grapes in the state, and half of that consisted of Zinfandel, Carignane, and Grenache. Extensive plantings of new vineyards occurred in the late 1960s and early 1970s, and by 1974 there were more than 300,000 acres of wine grapes; some of this acreage was later uprooted or abandoned, much of it was converted from one grape variety to another, and new plantings have also taken place, raising the total to 330,000 acres. The increase in fine varieties over the past twenty-five years has been especially dramatic: Cabernet Sauvignon has increased from 630 acres to 29,000, Chardonnay from 231 acres to 48,000, Merlot from two acres to 5,500, and there are now 14,000 acres of Sauvignon Blanc, about 9,000 acres of Pinot Noir, 6,000 of Johannisberg Riesling, 2,000 of Gewürztraminer, and 2,500 of Semillon. (Zinfandel, a grape of European origin that is indigenous to California, is the most widely planted red-wine grape.) These changes must be seen within the larger context of the California wine industry; just as plantings of top varieties increased, so did those of other varieties, especially in the hot, fertile, irrigated San Joaquin Valley – also known as the Central Valley – which stretches for more than 250 miles from Lodi to Bakersfield. More than 80 percent of California wine comes from the San Joaquin Valley and finds its way into inexpensive jug wines, fortified wines, and brandy. (California produces virtually all of the brandy made in the United States.) And despite the fame of the wines made from Cabernet Sauvignon and Chardonnay, French Colombard and Chenin Blanc account for almost three quarters of the total white-wine crop, and more than half the red-wine crop is made up of such varieties as Barbera, Carignan, Grenache, Rubired, and Ruby Cabernet (the last two are relatively new varieties developed by the University of California at Davis). In effect, the wines produced from the best grapes in the best wine regions account for less than 15 percent of California's production, which is about the same proportion of fine wines as is found in France, Italy, and other wine-producing countries.

With a few exceptions, the finest California wines come from cool valleys that open to the maritime influence of the Pacific Ocean. In the coastal counties that stretch from Mendocino south to Santa Barbara, acreage has increased from only 24,000 acres in 1959 to 175,000, much of it in areas not previously known for wines. These include the Anderson Valley in Mendocino, the Russian River Valley in Sonoma, the Salinas Valley in Monterey, the Edna Valley in San Luis Obispo, and the Santa Maria and Santa Ynez valleys in Santa Barbara. The coastal counties are usually divided into the North Coast, north of San Francisco, which includes Napa,

California

Central Coast

Sonoma, Mendocino, Lake, and Solano counties; and the Central Coast, between San Francisco and Santa Barbara, which encompasses Alameda, Contra Costa, Santa Clara, Santa Cruz, Monterey, San Benito, San Luis Obispo, and Santa Barbara counties. (The area sometimes known as the South Coast includes the vineyards south of Los Angeles, including Temecula. In addition, excellent wines, especially Zinfandel and Sauvignon Blanc, are made from vineyards in the Sierra Foothills, east of Sacramento, which include Amador, El Dorado, and Calaveras counties.) Unlike the great wine regions of Europe, each of which is known for a particular kind of wine produced from specific grape varieties, California has a great many districts that are capable of producing fine wines from several different grape varieties; that is, a particular grape variety may produce fine wines in several different districts, and a given district may produce fine wines from several varieties. This is possible because most of California's coastal valleys run east-west or northwest-southeast, and within a given district, the cooler section nearest the ocean is often best suited for Chardonnay, Pinot Noir, Johannisberg Riesling, and Gewürztraminer; the warmer inland section is likely to produce fine Cabernet Sauvignon, Merlot, Sauvignon Blanc, and Zinfandel. Thus the cool climate best suited to Pinot Noir and Chardonnay grapes to be used for elegant *méthode champenoise* sparkling wines can be found in the Anderson Valley and also 400 miles to the south in the Santa Maria Valley. Growing conditions are also affected by whether grapes are planted along the warm valley floor or on cooler hillside vineyards. Some years ago, a system known as degree-days, or heat summation, was devised in California to measure the climatic conditions of a given area to determine which grapes would be most likely to produce the best wines. Beginning in the early 1980s, officially defined viticultural areas were established for wine-producing regions throughout the United States, and more than fifty such areas have been recognized in California. Although viticultural areas define the geographical boundaries of a given region, not the grapes grown there, this attempt at appellations of origin has focused more attention on matching a particular district with the grapes best suited to its soil and climate. *See* Degree-Days, Viticultural Area.

In general, the less expensive California wines for sale in

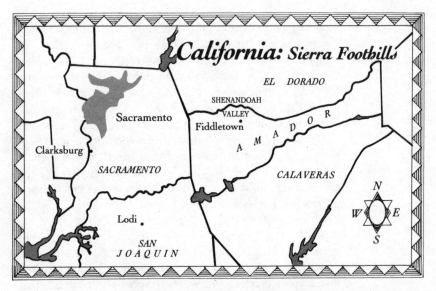

the United States are labelled with such generic names as Chablis, Burgundy, Claret, and Rhine Wine, which are not defined in any way; many wineries prefer not to trade on European place names, and label such wines Red Table Wine, Vintage White, Premium White, and so on. Many of the better California wines, and almost all the best ones, are marketed with varietal names, that is, with the name of the grape variety from which the wine is primarily or entirely made; at least 75 percent of a varietally labelled wine is made with the named grape. Yet another way of labelling a wine is with a proprietary name created by the winery; Hearty Burgundy, Spiceling, and Emerald Dry are some moderately priced examples. Recently, a number of wineries have also begun to market expensive wines, most often those made from Cabernet Sauvignon, with proprietary names, examples include Opus One and Dominus. At least 75 percent of a wine labelled with a county name – Sonoma, Mendocino, Santa Barbara – must come from that county; the minimum is 85 percent for a wine labelled with a designated viticultural area, such as Napa Valley, Sonoma Valley, Sonoma Mountain, Anderson Valley, Carneros, Arroyo Seco, Santa Ynez Valley, or Temecula. At least 95 percent of a vintage-dated wine must come from the indicated vintage, and if a wine is labelled with the name of a specific vineyard, 95 percent of the wine must come from that vineyard. Many wineries now label selected lots of wine, especially those made from Cabernet Sauvignon and Chardonnay, as Reserve, Private Reserve, Special Reserve, or Proprietor's Reserve; although some of California's finest wines are so labelled, such terms have no official meaning.

The range and quality of California sparkling wines has increased tremendously since the mid-1970s. Although many such wines, which may be labelled "champagne", continue to be made from neutral grapes by the Charmat process of bulk fermentation, a number of producers now make their sparkling wines as in France's Champagne region, from Pinot Noir and Chardonnay grapes, and use the traditional *méthode champenoise*. None of these wines is entitled to the name "champagne" within the EC. There are other categories of California wines as well: Special Natural Wines are flavoured wines which may be fortified, like Thunderbird, or lower in alcohol, like Boone's Farm. Wine coolers, first marketed in 1981, accounted for about a quarter of California's wine sales five years later but have since declined in importance; these wine products, which contain 4 to 6 percent alcohol, are a mixture of wine, water, carbon dioxide, sugar, and various flavours, most often fruit. Blush wine is the unofficial name of a category that became very popular in the mid-1980s; these pale pink and slightly sweet wines are made from red grapes and marketed with such names as White Zinfandel, White Cabernet, Cabernet Blanc, and Gamay Blanc.

For all the acclaim that California wines have already achieved, it is well to remember that many wines are still being made from vineyards that are not yet mature and that many producers are just beginning to discover which varieties are best suited to the newer districts. Also, the style of many California wines is still being refined. Throughout the 1970s, there was particular emphasis on ripeness, concentration, and intense varietal character as winemakers attempted to extract the maximum flavour from the grapes and added additional flavours by extended barrel aging; consequently, many wines were powerful, oaky, and relatively high in alcohol. More recently, the focus has been on restraint, balance, and elegance as many winemakers have tried to scale back their wines, which are now marked by less alcohol and more lively acidity. It is more than likely, therefore, that California wines will continue to improve in quality, that distinct regional styles will emerge based on new appellations of origin, and that the wines will be even more appealing than in the past.

Calon-Ségur, Château A Third Classed Growth of Saint-Estèphe, in the
Médoc district, its 116 acres of vines produce about 18,000
cases a year of a well-balanced, relatively earthy wine. The
vineyard is under the direction of the Capbern-Gasqueton
family, also owners of Châteaux du Tertre and the aptly
named Capbern-Gasqueton.

Calories These come almost entirely from the alcohol in wine and, in
the case of sweet wines, from the sugar as well. Generally
speaking, a five-ounce glass of dry table wine – whether red,
white, or sparkling – contains between 100 and 110 calories.
White wines do not have fewer calories than red; in fact, a
rich, heady Chardonnay contains more calories than a light,
delicate Beaujolais or Valpolicella. The sugar in semisweet
wines adds fifteen or twenty calories per glass, but such
wines usually contain less alcohol, so their calorie content is
about the same as for dry wines. Sweet, fortified wines such
as port and cream sherry, which have higher amounts of
both alcohol and sugar, contain 200 calories or more per
glass.

Caluso Passito An unusual sweet white wine made from the Erbaluce grape
near the town of Caluso, north of Turin, in Italy's Piedmont
region. The wine is made from grapes that have been left to
dehydrate before being crushed, thus increasing the proportion of sugar in the juice, and the resulting wine must be aged
a minimum of five years. If the wine is fortified to a minimum of 16 percent alcohol by the addition of spirits, it may
be marketed as Caluso Passito *liquoroso*.

Camensac, Château de A Fifth Classed Growth in the commune of Saint-
Laurent, adjoining Châteaux Belgrave and La Tour Carnet,
and entitled to the appellation Haut-Médoc; its 160 acres of
vineyards produce about 30,000 cases a year of a supple,
appealing wine.

Campania A region in southern Italy whose capital is Naples and
whose attractions include Mount Vesuvius, Pompeii, the
Amalfi coast, and the islands of Capri and Ischia. Annual
production amounts to more than 30 million cases, but less
than 1 percent of that, from only 2,300 acres, is DOC.
Nevertheless, some fine wines are produced in this region,
the best of them in the province of Avellino, about 30 miles
east of Naples, from such unusual varieties as Greco, Fiano,

and Aglianico, which are used to make, respectively, the white Greco di Tufo and Fiano di Avellino and the red Taurasi. Red, white, and rosé wines from vineyards at the foot of Mount Vesuvius are entitled to the DOC Vesuvio or the superior DOC Lacryma Christi del Vesuvio; red and white wines are made on the islands of Capri and Ischia, which face each other across the Bay of Naples; and some attractive wines are made around the village of Ravello.

Caña A small, slender tumbler with a heavy bottom out of which manzanilla sherry is often drunk in southern Spain. The *venencias*, or long-handled little dippers, used for taking samples of manzanilla out of the cask in Sanlúcar de Barrameda were originally made of caña, or bamboo (instead of whalebone and silver, as in Jerez), and these probably gave the glass both its unusual shape and its name.

Canada As recently as the 1960s, most of Canada's wine production consisted of such fortified wines as port and sherry; today, table wines, including wine coolers, account for more than three quarters of the total. Almost 90 percent of Canada's wines are produced in the province of Ontario, primarily in the Niagara Peninsula, situated between Lake Ontario and Lake Erie, west of Niagara Falls; it is therefore not surprising that the history of winemaking in Canada is similar to that of adjoining New York State. Even today, about half of the 24,000 acres in the Niagara Peninsula consists of such native American varieties as Concord, Elvira, Niagara, and Catawba, but most of this crop is now used for grape juice and for wine coolers, fortified wines, and inexpensive sparkling wines rather than for table wines. Almost all of the Peninsula's other vineyards are planted with such French-American hybrids as DeChaunac, Seyval Blanc, Maréchal Foch, and Vidal 256. In addition, about 1,500 acres of *vinifera* grapes, mostly Chardonnay and Johannisberg Riesling, have been planted since the late 1970s; there are also limited amounts of Gamay, Gewürztraminer, and Pinot Noir. Ontario producers recently formed the Vintners Quality Alliance (VQA) and established their own appellation laws. Wines labelled Ontario may be made only from European *vinifera* and French-American hybrid grapes. Those produced in one of the three new viticultural areas – Niagara Peninsula, Pelee Island, and Lake Erie North Shore – and so labelled, may be made only from *vinifera*.

The other important wine-producing region of Canada is the Okanagan Valley in British Columbia, just north of the state of Washington; most of its 3,200 acres are planted with French-American hybrids and *vinifera* varieties. Canadian firms are permitted to add a proportion of wine made from imported grapes to their own production; most of these grapes come from California, with lesser amounts from Chile and Spain, and they find their way primarily into inexpensive white-wine blends. Canadian wines are marketed with generic names, varietal names, and with such proprietary names as Hochtaler, Schloss Laderheim, Alpenweiss, and Bambino. There has been much improvement in the overall quality of Canadian table wines in recent years, especially those made from French-American hybrids and *vinifera* varieties.

Canaiolo   An Italian red-wine grape cultivated in Tuscany and Umbria, where it is blended with Sangiovese to soften and round out the latter's tannic astringency. The DOCG laws established for Chianti in 1984 have reduced Canaiolo's role, previously 10 to 30 percent, to less than 10 percent; the grape was particularly suitable for the *governo* process, little practised today.

Canary   Wines from the Canary Islands, a part of Spain, were celebrated in England in Elizabethan times, and Shakespeare described "canaries" as "a marvellous searching wine, and it perfumes the blood ere one can say, What's this?" In the nineteenth century the vineyards were devastated by insects and fungus diseases brought in from overseas, and although 700,000 cases or so of red and white wines are made today, primarily for local consumption, the once-famed Canary Sack is a thing of the past.

Cannonau   An Italian grape widely grown in Sardinia, producing red wines that may be dry or sweet, natural or fortified, as well as some rosés; those entitled to DOC status must have a minimum of 13.5 percent alcohol and one year of wood aging, but a number of lighter, well-balanced, attractive non-DOC reds are now being made from this variety as well.

Canon, Château   One of the best of the *premiers grands crus classés* vineyards of Saint-Emilion; its 45 acres of vineyards, planted almost entirely with Merlot and Cabernet Franc, produce an average of 7,500 cases a year of sturdy, full-bodied, generally long-lived red wine.

Canon-Fronsac *See* Fronsac

Canon-La Gaffelière, Château A *grand cru classé* in the Saint-Emilion district of Bordeaux producing about 10,000 cases a year of supple and dependable red wine.

Cantemerle, Château A Fifth Classed Growth situated in the commune of Macau, just south of Margaux, and entitled to the appellation Haut-Médoc; the vineyard, which came under the direction of the Cordier firm in 1981, was expanded to 130 acres, with an annual production of about 20,,000 cases of a very good wine notable for its suppleness and structure.

Cantenac An important wine-producing commune in the Médoc district of Bordeaux whose wines are officially entitled to the appellation Margaux; leading vineyards within this commune include Château Brane-Cantenac, d'Issan, Cantenac-Brown, Kirwan, Palmer, Boyd-Cantenac, and Prieuré-Lichine.

Cantenac-Brown, Château A Third Classed Growth of Margaux, in the Médoc district, situated in the commune of Cantenac; its 115 acres of vines produce about 22,000 cases a year. The property, originally known as Château Boyd, was divided into Châteaux Boyd-Cantenac and Cantenac-Brown in 1860.

Cantina Italian for "cellar"; a *cantina sociale* is a "co-operative cellar".

Cap The solid parts of grapes – skins, pips, stems – that rise to the top of the must during red-wine fermentation; known in French as *chapeau*. Red wines extract colour and tannin from this mass, and to promote interaction between the cap and the must, the cap may be broken up at regular intervals during fermentation, the must may be pumped over the cap from time to time, or the cap may be kept immersed below the surface of the must by a grid.

Capbern-Gasqueton, Château A *cru bourgeois* of Saint-Estèphe, in the

Médoc, under the same ownership as Château Calon-Ségur.

Capiteaux A French term meaning "heady", applied to a wine that is high in alcohol and likely to be intoxicating.

Capri An island in the Gulf of Naples producing some red and white DOC wines whose appeal owes as much to their attractive place of origin as to their inherent quality.

Carafe A clear-glass container used to serve wine at table; young, inexpensive wines are generally served *en carafe* in France, and a *vin de carafe* is any wine of this sort, so served. Carafes may also be used for decanting old red wines that have thrown sediment in the bottle, although the more elaborate containers used for fine wines are usually called decanters.

Caramino A fine red wine produced from Nebbiolo, Croatina, and Vespolina grapes planted on a hillside in the Fara district, in Italy's Piedmont region.

Carbonated This refers to wines that are made sparkling, like club soda and soft drinks, by the addition, under pressure, of carbon dioxide (CO_2), rather than by the classic *méthode champenoise* or the faster Charmat method of tank fermentation. Such wines, which have to be labelled carbonated in the United States and *gazéifié* in France, have large, coarse bubbles and tend to lose their sparkle rapidly. There are no good sparkling wines produced in this way, although there are some moderately priced table wines that are lightly carbonated to give them a refreshing crackling, or *pétillant*, character.

Carbonic Maceration A fermentation technique used for certain red wines, notably Beaujolais, which results in suppler, more aromatic wines with less acidity and tannin than if made in the traditional manner. Instead of crushing the grapes and letting the yeast ferment the juice in the presence of air, whole bunches of grapes are put into tanks that also contain carbon dioxide gas; a different and partial fermentation then occurs within the individual berries (the technique is known in California as whole-berry fermentation). Inevitably, the weight of the bunches crushes the grapes at the bottom of the tank, which then ferment in the usual way, and in any case the must is usually drawn off before fermentation is complete, and fermentation then continues in the presence of air; in practice, wines produced by carbonic maceration are actually a mix of both methods. For all their appeal, such wines are not long-lived and are meant to be consumed young.

Carbonnieux, Château The largest of the *grands crus classés* of the Graves district of Bordeaux, whose 175 acres of vineyard produce about 35,000 cases a year, almost evenly divided between red and white wines; it is the pale, dry, racy white which first established the reputation of this vineyard. According to a possibly apocryphal story, the Benedictine monks who owned the property in the eighteenth century shipped the white wine to the court of the Sultan of Turkey (where the consumption of wine was prohibited) as *eau minerale de Carbonnieux*, or "Carbonnieux mineral water".

Carcavelos A sweet, fortified, deep-coloured Portuguese white wine produced in limited quantities just west of Lisbon, near the resort of Estoril.

Cardonne, Château La A *cru bourgeois* in the northern Médoc producing 30,000 cases or so of dependable wine; until 1990 it was under the same ownership as Château Lafite-Rothschild.

Carema A fine, elegant DOC red wine made from the Nebbiolo grape in Italy's Piedmont region. The Carema district is situated north of Turin, near the border of Valle d'Aosta, and its 100 acres of hillside vineyards yield about 10,000 cases a year; the wine must be aged for four years, two of them in wood.

Carignan A very productive red-wine grape that yields ordinary wine noted for its deep colour, high alcohol content, and tannic astringency. It is the most widely planted grape in France, where most of the acreage is in the extensive Languedoc-Roussillon region, also known as the Midi; the wines made from Carignan are often blended with those made from Cinsault and Grenache. In California, the acreage of Carignane (as it is spelled there) rose to 30,000 acres in the mid-1970s, making it the state's top red grape; the acreage, most of which is in the San Joaquin Valley, has since diminished to about 12,000 acres. Carignan has long been a principal variety in Israel and is still found in Spain, where it originally acquired its name, from the town of Cariñena.

Cariñena   A district in northern Spain, in the Aragón region, producing copious quantities of everyday wine, primarily from the
red Garnacha grape and the white Viura. Curiously enough,
although the Cariñena, or Carignan grape – widely planted
in Catalonia, southern France, and California – originally
came from this district, little of this variety is now found in
its place of origin.

Carmel Valley   A small viticultural area in Monterey County, west of the
Salinas Valley and the Santa Lucia Mountains, best known
for its rich Cabernet Sauvignon; about 300 acres are planted
there at an elevation of 1,200 feet, half of them belonging to
the Durney Vineyard.

Carmenère   A grape variety of the Bordeaux area, widely planted in the
nineteenth century, but rarely encountered today; also
known as Vidure and Carmenet.

Carmes Haut-Brion, Château Les   A small vineyard near Château Haut-
Brion, but unrelated to it, producing about 1,000 cases a year
of red wine.

Carmignano   A small DOC zone ten miles west of Florence situated
within the larger Chianti Montalbano district. Wines entitled to the Carmignano DOC, established in 1975, are
made primarily from Sangiovese with 10 percent Cabernet
Sauvignon and are likely to have 18 to 24 months of wood
aging; the result is a wine richer, sturdier, and more complex
than Chianti. Villa di Capezzana of Count Contini-Bona-
cossi is the leading estate and accounts for about half of Carmignano's annual 25,000-case production; the estate also
bottles a younger version of Carmignano, not entitled to the
DOC, and labelled Barco Reale.

Carnelian   A cross of Carignane, Cabernet Sauvignon, and Grenache
developed in California and first planted in the San Joaquin
Valley in 1973; there are only 1,400 acres in production.

Carneros   A large and increasingly famous viticultural area situated in
Napa and Sonoma counties; it extends from the southern
foothills of the Mayacamas Mountains, below the towns of
Napa and Sonoma, down to San Pablo Bay (as the northern
part of San Francisco Bay is called), and from the Napa River
on the east to the Sonoma River on the west. There are about

9,000 acres planted in Carneros (which means "sheep", in tribute to its earlier fame as a shepherding region); about three fifths of this is planted in Napa and also entitled to the Napa Valley appellation, the rest is in Sonoma and also entitled to the Sonoma Valley and Sonoma County appellations. More than 80 percent of the acreage in this especially cool region is planted with Chardonnay and Pinot Noir, which have established the reputation of Carneros; Cabernet Sauvignon is also planted, as are Merlot, Johannisberg Riesling, Gewürztraminer, and Sauvignon Blanc. Such Napa Valley wineries as Beaulieu Vineyard, Charles Krug, and Louis Martini established vineyards here some time ago, as have Cuvaison, Domaine Chandon, and Clos Du Val more recently, and in 1986 the 175-acre Winery Lane vineyard, established by René di Rosa, was acquired by Sterling Vineyards; the first winery established on the Napa side of Carneros was Carneros Creek, in 1972, and others now include Acacia, Château Bouchaine, Domaine Carneros, and Saintsbury. Buena Vista is the best-known winery on the Sonoma side of Carneros, and Gloria Ferrer is also situated there.

Carruades de Lafite-Rothschild *See* Lafite-Rothschild, Château

Carso A small new DOC district in the Friuli-Venezia Giulia region of Italy that encompasses three wines: Carso, a red made primarily from Refosco; Carso Terrano, also made from Refosco, but from a delimited inner zone; and Carso Malvasia, a white wine.

Cartizze A sparkling white wine, also known as Superiore di Cartizze, made primarily from the Prosecco grape in a small district within the DOC zone that produces Prosecco di Conegliano-Valdobbiadene.

Cascade The popular name for Seibel 13053, an early ripening hybrid variety that produces agreeable red and rosé wines.

Case Production figures in this volume are expressed in cases, the equivalent of twelve bottles of 75 centilitres, or 25.6 ounces; a case equals nine litres.

Cask A wooden container, generally with round or oval heads, in which wine is matured, stored, and sometimes shipped; oak is by all odds the best wood, chestnut (in Europe) and redwood (in California) being barely passable substitutes. Casks of widely varying shapes and sizes are associated with the wines of different regions, and the following list includes the most important. Note, however, that in certain instances the traditional cask of a region is now more likely to be used as a measure of volume for trading purposes than for actual wine storage; most of the wines produced today in Chablis and along the Rhine and Moselle, for example, are no longer aged in wood.

District	Name	Litres	U.S. Gallons	U.K. Gallons	Cases*
Chablis	Feuillette	136	36	30	15
California	Barrel	188	50	41	21
Champagne	Queue	216	57	48	24
Beaujolais	Pièce	216	57	48	24
Bordeaux	Barrique†	225	59	49	25
Burgundy	Pièce‡	228	60	50	25
Sherry	Butt	500	132	110	55
Port	Pipe	534	141	118	59
Rhine	Halbstück	600	158	132	67
Moselle	Fuder	1,000	264	220	111

* Approximate cases of twelve bottles each.
† A *tonneau*, in Bordeaux, is the equivalent of four *barriques*, but there is no cask of this size; in today's commerce, a *tonneau* represents 100 cases.
‡ A *queue*, in Burgundy, is the equivalent of two *pièces*.

Cassis A picturesque fishing village on the Mediterranean coast of France, some 20 miles east of Marseilles; its vineyards produce about 60,000 cases a year of red, white, and rosé wines, but Cassis is unusual among the wine villages of Provence in that it is best known for its pale gold, dry, fragrant white wine, made primarily from the Ugni Blanc grape, which accounts for two thirds of the crop. The wines from this Provençal village should not be confused with *crème de cassis*, a sweet, red-purple liqueur made from blackcurrants and widely used in combination with white wine to produce the popular aperitif known as kir.

Castel del Monte A DOC for red, white, and rosé wines produced in the hills west of Bari, a few miles inland from the Adriatic, in Italy's Apulia region. The attractive rosé, made from Bombino Nero grapes, accounts for about half of the total annual production of 500,000 cases; the red is made from Uva di

Troia, the white from Pampanuto.

Castell A wine-producing village east of Würzburg in Germany's Franken, or Franconia, region; its best-known vineyards are Schlossberg and Bausch.

Casteller A DOC zone in Italy's Trentino region that extends along both sides of the Adige River from north of Trento down to the adjoining Veneto region; its undistinguished light red wines are made from an unusual combination of Schiava, Merlot, and Lambrusco grapes.

Castelli di Jesi *See* Verdicchio

Castelli Romani A series of hills southeast of Rome, on whose slopes are produced the popular, inexpensive, and often quite agreeable table wines of that city's restaurants. Almost all of those wines are white, made from local clones of Malvasia and Trebbiano; the best known come from specific DOC zones within 20 miles or so of Rome, including Frascati, Marino, Colli Albani, and Colli Lanuvini. Velletri is the one DOC within this district that encompasses both red and white wines.

Castillon *See* Côtes de Castillon

Catalonia An extensive region in northeastern Spain whose principal city is Barcelona; bounded on the north by France and on the east by the Mediterranean, Catalonia comprises the principal provinces in which Catalan is spoken: Barcelona, Gerona, Lérida, and Tarragona. The 250,000 acres of vineyards in Catalonia – in Spanish, Cataluña – produce 30 to 37 million cases a year, two thirds of it white wine. There are seven *Denominación de Origen* districts in Catalonia – Alella, known primarily for its dry and medium-dry whites; Ampurdán-Costa Brava, along the French border, whose production consists mostly of rosé, but which may be best known for Perelada sparkling wine; Priorato and Tarragona, traditional areas for sweet, fortified wines and full-bodied reds; Terra Alta, most of whose production consists of relatively high-alcohol whites from Garnacha Blanca and Macabeo; Costers de Segre, north of Lérida, where the Raimat firm (owned by Codorníu) has planted 2,500 acres, including 2,000 acres of Chardonnay and Cabernet Sauvignon; and

Penedès, by far the most important in terms of volume and quality. It is in the Penedès district that most of Spain's sparkling wines are made.

Catarratto An Italian white-wine grape widely planted in Sicily, where it is a component of such wines as Marsala, Alcamo, and Etna.

Catawba A native American grape of somewhat uncertain origin, believed to be an accidental hybrid of wild, indigenous varieties (it is of the species *labrusca*) probably first found growing in the woods along the Catawba River, in the Carolinas. In the 1820s it was being cultivated in Maryland and in the District of Columbia, where it found a champion in Major John Ludlum, who once hopefully stated that "in bringing this grape into public notice, I have rendered my country a greater service than I could have done had I paid off the national debt". Time has perhaps proved him wrong, but for the better part of a century Catawba was the leading wine grape of America. It was the basis of Nicholas Longworth's famous sparkling wine, produced along the banks of the Ohio, near Cincinnati, and it is still widely grown in Ohio and in the Finger Lakes district of New York, where it is second in acreage only to Concord. Catawba is a light red grape, highly productive, giving a wine with a pronounced native or grapey flavour; it has long been used in New York State sparkling wine and is also marketed as a still wine, especially the version labelled Pink Catawba. Nevertheless, few people today would agree with what Longfellow once wrote about sparkling Catawba: "Very good in its way/Is the Verzenay,/Or the Sillery, soft and creamy;/But Catawba wine/ Has a taste more divine,/More dulcet, delicious, and dreamy."

Caudalie A French technical term that measures the persistence of aromatic flavours after tasting, that is, the length of a wine's aftertaste; one caudalie = one second of persistence.

Cava Spanish for "cellar"; when used in connection with sparkling wines, however, *cava* refers specifically to those made by the *méthode champenoise*. These attractive dry wines, most of them moderately priced, have become enormously popular in the United States in recent years. Virtually all *cava* wines are produced in the Penedès region, near

Barcelona; in fact, the region accounts for 90 percent of all Spanish sparkling wines, including those made by the *granvas*, or Charmat process, but more than 80 percent of the total Penedès production is made by the *méthode champenoise*. Production of *cava* wines from Penedès, centred round the town of San Sadurní de Noya, has increased from about 12 million bottles a year in the late 1960s to more than 130 million bottles, compared to an average of 200 million bottles in France's Champagne region; two Spanish firms, Codorníu and Freixenet, each produce more bottles of *méthode champenoise* wines than the biggest firm in Champagne and account for more than 85 percent of all *cava* wines between them. Most of these wines are made from a combination of three grape varieties: Xarello, which provides body; Macabeo (the Viura of Rioja), known for its balance and elegance; and Parellada, which contributes aroma. Chardonnay has been planted in the region and is now used for some *cava* wines. The wines must be aged in bottle for a minimum of nine months before being disgorged. It was in Penedès that the efficient riddling machine called a *girasol* was first used to prepare bottles for disgorging.

Cave The French word for "cellar". This can mean, as in English, an underground storage space, or simply a collection of bottles. On a French wine label, the word is just as meaningless as in English, unless a good deal of sound information follows it directly; thus, *mis en bouteille dans nos caves* does *not* mean estate-bottled.

Cayuga White A new white-wine hybrid variety developed by the experiment station at Geneva, New York, and first planted commercially in the 1970s.

Cellar Storage space for wine and, by inference, the wine it contains; traditionally, but by no means necessarily, below ground. There are few underground cellars in the Bordeaux region, few in California, almost none in Spain. Whether underground or not, a wine cellar should be cool, with as even a temperature as possible throughout the year, free from vibration, and dark. A somewhat damp cellar is likely to be cooler than one absolutely dry; some ventilation is essential. The ideal cellar temperature is between 55 and 60 degrees, with 45 and 70 degrees as perhaps permissible extremes; within these limits, the cooler the cellar, the more slowly wines will develop and the longer they will live. Bottles should be stored horizontally, of course, so that the wine is in contact with the cork, preventing it from drying out and shrinking.

Apart from one's current requirements, the wines that should be laid away in a cellar are those most likely to increase in value or improve with age; most wines do neither. A carefully kept cellar book, or record of any kind, is a very useful guide to the contents of even a modest cellar and makes it easier to choose wines that are ready to drink, most suitable for certain menus, or appropriate for special occasions.

Central Coast A California appellation that was officially defined in 1985 to include all the coastal counties from San Francisco to Los Angeles: Alameda, Contra Costa, Santa Clara, Santa Cruz, Monterey, San Benito, San Luis Obispo, and Santa Barbara. Several of these counties have only recently become an important source of fine wines: in the mid-1960s there were only 8,000 acres planted, most of them in Santa Clara and San Benito; today, there are 50,000 acres of vineyards, more than half of that in Monterey, most of the rest in San Luis Obispo and Santa Barbara.

Central Valley The hot, interior valley of California, also known as the San Joaquin Valley, which extends for about 300 miles from Lodi south to Bakersfield, and whose 540,000 acres of grapes are planted in the fertile, irrigated soils of San Joaquin, Stanislaus, Merced, Madera, Fresno, Tulare, Kings, and Kern counties. (Properly speaking, the Central Valley also includes the Sacramento Valley, north of Sacramento, but the terms Central Valley and San Joaquin Valley are often used interchangeably, as in this volume.) More than 80 percent of the grapes crushed to make wine in California come from the Central Valley, which produces almost all of the state's inexpensive jug wines, virtually all of its fortified wines, and all the wines distilled into brandy. Although most of the vineyards consist of table and raisin grapes, primarily Thompson Seedless, the 200,000-plus acres of wine grapes account for more than 60 percent of the state total and, as a result of high yields, produce about 75 percent of all California table wines. The Central Valley vineyards account for two thirds or more of the wines made from such varieties as Chenin Blanc, French Colombard, Barbera, Carignane,

Grenache, Ruby Cabernet, Carnelian, and Zinfandel.

Centurion A cross of Carignane, Cabernet Sauvignon, and Grenache developed in California and first planted in the Central Valley in 1974; current plantings amount to fewer than 1,000 acres.

Cépage A variety of grapevine; thus one may say that Pinot Noir and Chardonnay are the leading *cépages* of France's Burgundy region. *Cep* means an individual vine or vine stock.

Cerasuolo Italian for "cherry-coloured"; the word is used to describe several dark rosés, such as Montepulciano d'Abruzzo Cerasuolo and Cerasuolo di Vittoria.

Cérons A small village and district in the Bordeaux region; it adjoins Barsac and is enclosed within the much larger Graves district. The Cérons appellation, which includes the townships of Illats and Podensac, applies to sweet white wines similar to a light Sauternes; the dry wines from this region are entitled to the Graves appellation, and in recent years the production of sweet Cérons has declined considerably as local growers have chosen to make dry wines instead.

Certan-Giraud, Château A small vineyard in the Pomerol district situated near Vieux-Château-Certan and Château Certan-de-May, producing about 3,000 cases a year.

Certan-de-May, Château A small vineyard in the Pomerol district situated between Château Pétrus and Vieux-Château-Certan; its 12 acres produce about 2,000 cases a year of a rich, concentrated, widely acclaimed red wine.

Cesanese An Italian red-wine grape cultivated about 25 miles east of Rome.

Chablais A wine district in the canton of Vaud, in eastern Switzerland; the vineyards, planted with the Chasselas grape (known there as Dorin), extend from Villeneuve, at the eastern tip of Lake Geneva, southeast along the upper Rhône Valley. The wines are all white, fairly full-bodied, and some of them, from the villages of Yvorne and Aigle, rank among the best Swiss wines.

Chablis A little town of 2,500 inhabitants 110 miles southeast of

Paris, in the *département* of the Yonne, whose surrounding vineyards produce one of the world's most famous wines. As is the case for all white Burgundies, Chablis may be made only from the Chardonnay grape, and the district entitled to the name is strictly delimited, comprising certain areas of chalky soils in a total of 20 small communes. As recently as the 1950s, the average annual production of Chablis was 115,000 cases, but thanks to the introduction of frost-control devices in the early 1960s, new vineyards have been planted and production per acre has increased; today, there are more than 5,000 acres of vineyards around Chablis, and crops of 1.2 to 1.5 million cases are not unusual, although severe spring frosts can still reduce that total by half. Most of the Chablis crop is labelled with the name alone, but there are three other appellations for the region. Wines from the seven finest vineyards of all may be labelled Chablis Grand Cru; the vineyards, which are all situated on a single slope over-looking the Serein River, are Vaudésir, Les Clos, Gre-nouilles, Valmur, Blanchots, Les Preuses, and Bougros. (La Moutonne is the proprietary name of a 5.8-acre plot that straddles Vaudésir and Les Preuses.) There are only 240 acres entitled to the *grand cru* appellation, and they produce no more than 60,000 cases or so. Another thirty vineyards, clustered throughout the region, are entitled to the appella-tion Chablis Premier Cru, but since 1967 those with less familiar names may be labelled with the name of a better-known neighbour, such as Montée de Tonnerre, Vaulorent, Mont de Milieu, Vaucoupin, Fourchaume, Vaillons, and Montmains; Vaudevey is a new *premier cru* whose first crop was in 1983. Wines labelled Petit Chablis come from lesser plots within the region and are usually lighter and shorter-lived; the appellation accounts for less than 10 percent of the total Chablis crop. Although Chablis is a Burgundy, the vineyards are actually closer to Champagne than to the Côte d'Or, and as a result of this northerly location, the quality of Chablis varies enormously from one vintage to the next. At its best it is a dry, almost austere wine with lively acidity, pale straw in colour (sometimes with a hint of green), with a delicate, fleeting bouquet, and is remarkably clean on the palate. In poor years, the acidity dominates, and the wines can be disagreeably thin and tart; in unusually hot years, the wines may be rich and full, but lack the balancing acidity and nerve that characterize fine Chablis. There has been some controversy among Chablis producers, in recent years, over the traditional use of oak barrels to age Chablis; many wine-makers now ferment and age their wines only in stainless-steel or glass-lined concrete tanks in order to preserve fruit and freshness; others continue to age all their wines, or at least the *premiers crus* and *grands crus*, in oak to enhance their flavour and complexity.

The name *Chablis* has long been used in other countries, notably the United States and Australia, to denote any white wine, usually inexpensive and not always dry; such wines have nothing in common with the Chablis of France, of course, except their colour (and not always that – some California wineries market a Pink Chablis).

Chai A building used for wine storage in France, generally above ground, as distinguished from a *cave*, or true cellar. (In Bordeaux, most châteaux and shippers store their wines in ground-level *chais*; in Burgundy, underground *caves* are the rule.) Commercially, the two terms are largely interchangeable.

Chalk Hill A viticultural area in Sonoma County that is contained within the larger Russian River Valley appellation and adjoins both the Alexander Valley and Knights Valley areas. The small district, which gets its name from the white volcanic ash found in its soil, contains nearly 1,000 acres, planted primarily with Chardonnay and Sauvignon Blanc. The Balverne and Chalk Hill wineries are situated there.

Chalon *See* Côte Chalonnaise

Chambertin One of the most famous vineyards in the world, situated in the commune of Gevrey-Chambertin, in Burgundy's Côte d'Or region. Its 32 acres of Pinot Noir vines produce an average of 5,500 cases a year of a remarkable red wine, powerful, long-lived, and with astonishing class and breed. The wines from the adjoining Clos de Bèze vineyard, whose 38 acres produce an average of 5,000 cases a year, are also entitled to the name Chambertin, although they are more often sold as Chambertin-Clos de Bèze. (That is, the wines from Clos de Bèze may be sold as Chambertin, but those from Chambertin may not be sold as Clos de Bèze.) The Clos de Bèze vineyard was first planted in the seventh century by monks from the nearby Abbey of Bèze, and its fame was such that, according to the story, an enterprising peasant named Bertin planted an adjoining vineyard in the twelfth century; the latter was known as the *Champ de Bertin*, "Bertin's field", and eventually as Chambertin. The wine was a favourite of Napoleon's, and Alexandre Dumas once wrote that "nothing makes the future look so rosy as to contemplate it through a glass of Chambertin". The 70 acres of vines are divided among more than two dozen owners, and consequently wines labelled Chambertin and Chambertin-Clos de Bèze will vary somewhat in style and quality; indeed, the differences between the two *grand cru* appellations are more likely to be based on who produces the wine than on which vineyard it comes from. There are seven other *grand cru* vineyards whose names include Chambertin – Chapelle-Chambertin, Charmes-Chambertin, Griotte-Chambertin, Latricières-Chambertin, Mazis-Chambertin, Mazoyères-Chambertin, and Ruchottes-Chambertin; wines labelled with the village appellation Gevrey-Chambertin, however, come from vineyards that lie anywhere within the commune and should not be confused with those from the *grands crus*, whose names appear alone on a label.

Chambolle-Musigny A celebrated wine-producing village in the Côte de Nuits district of Burgundy's Côte d'Or; like many another Burgundian village, it has added the name of its most famous vineyard, Musigny, to its own. There are some 550 acres under vines, all – except for a tiny portion of Musigny – producing red wines only, and they are among the most charming, delicate, and fragrant of all Burgundy. Musigny and almost all of Bonnes Mares are the two *grand cru* vineyards associated with Chambolle-Musigny, and the best known of its *premiers crus* are Les Amoureuses and Les Charmes; wines labelled simply with the village name are often a bit lighter, but generally make up in finesse what they may lack in body.

Chambourcin A French-American hybrid whose official name is Joannes-Seyve 26205; widely planted in France's Loire Valley and to some extent in the eastern United States, it produces a good-quality red wine.

Chambrer To bring a red wine up to room temperature, presumably from the cooler temperature of a cellar; from *chambre*, French for "room". The only proper way to do this is to bring the bottle to the dining room an hour or two ahead of time, and let it stand. (No wine worth drinking should be set near a radiator or plunged into hot water.) Bear in mind, however, that the custom originated when cellars were cold and dining rooms cool; today, when many dining rooms are likely to be too warm, it often makes more sense to serve red wines at a temperature slightly cooler than that of the room.

Champagne An extensive, but strictly delimited region about 90 miles northeast of Paris, and the sparkling wine produced there by a process known the world over as the *méthode champenoise*. Most of the Champagne region's 71,000 acres of vineyards (which includes more than 10,000 acres planted in the 1980s) are in the *département* of the Marne, with some portions in the Aube and the Aisne; they produce an average of 200 million bottles a year, although the northerly climate is so uncertain that production in recent years has varied from 80 to 300 million bottles. Only three grape varieties are permitted in the production of champagne – Chardonnay, which accounts for about 25 percent of the total acreage; Pinot Noir, which accounts for 35 percent; and Pinot Meunier, which makes up the remaining 40 percent. The better vineyards are planted in three principal districts – the Montagne de Reims, south of that old cathedral city, and made up primarily of Pinot Noir, plus Pinot Meunier in the western part of the district; the Vallée de la Marne, where Pinot Noir and Pinot Meunier are planted on slopes overlooking that river; and the Côte des Blancs, which extends south of Epernay and consists almost entirely of Chardonnay. There are about 270 villages and communes in the Champagne region, each of which has been officially rated from 80 to 100 percent, based on the quality of the wines they produce; seventeen villages have been rated 100 percent, among them Ambonnay, Avize, Ay, Bouzy, Cramant, Le Mesnil, Sillery, and Verzenay, and another fifty villages are rated 90 to 99 percent. Every year, just before the harvest, the vineyard owners and the large champagne firms – which account for about 70 percent of production, but own a much smaller proportion of the vineyards – negotiate a base price per kilo of grapes for that year's crop, and the combination of that price and the percentage rating determines what the growers get for their grapes.

The many steps needed to produce champagne begin with the harvest. Because almost three quarters of the vineyards are planted with black grapes, they must be pressed as quickly and as gently as possible so that their clear juice does not pick up any colour from the skins. The traditional batch of 4,000 kilos (8,800 pounds) of grapes produces the equivalent of thirteen barrels of 205 litres each; today, modern presses can handle 6,000 kilos or more at a time, and, with one or two exceptions, all the firms ferment the wines in large stainless-steel or glass-lined tanks, not in barrels, but the following proportions still apply. The first 2,050 litres of juice, the equivalent of ten barrels, produce what is known as the *vin de cuvée*, and popularly referred to as the first press-

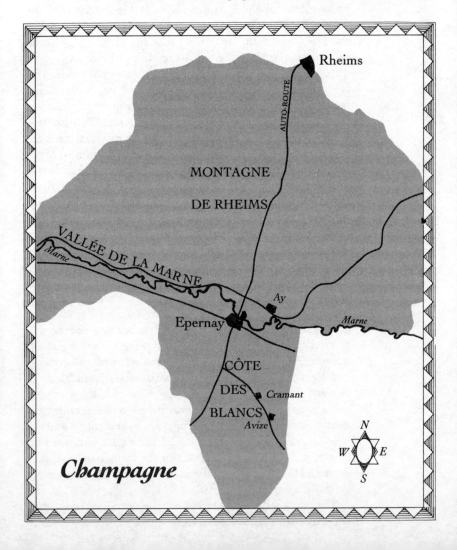

Champagne

ing, although it actually takes several pressings to produce that amount of juice. The next two barrels are known as the *première taille*, and worth less than the *vin de cuvée*, and the last barrel, worth considerably less, is called the *deuxième taille*; many firms do not use the *tailles*, and sell them off in bulk. The Champagne region produces wines that are light, low in alcohol, and relatively acid. (The still wines of the region – known in the past as Champagne Nature or Vin Nature de la Champagne and, since 1974, as Coteaux Champenois – are sometimes bottled and sold as such, but very little still wine is available these days.) In the January or February after the harvest, each firm assembles a trial *cuvée*, or blend, of still wines selected from among all the lots of that vintage; in the case of non-vintage wines (which make up about 80 percent of the total champagne market), 15 to 30 percent of reserve wines kept back from previous vintages are also used to maintain a continuity of style. In certain years, a firm may decide that the quality and personality of its wines is such that a part of the crop will be set aside and bottled as a vintage-dated champagne. There are no official vintage years, and the years declared by one firm may not correspond to those of another; one firm may produce two or three vintage champagnes in a decade, another firm may produce six or seven. Nor are there any official regulations prohibiting the use of reserve wines in vintage-dated champagnes, and some firms use these judiciously to maintain their overall house style. In any case, the resulting *cuvée*, which is usually made up of from twelve to forty different lots, represents each firm's particular style, the one its customers have come to expect, and once it has been decided on, the wines in stock are blended in the same proportions and bottled, usually in the spring and early summer following the harvest. Before bottling, however, the still wines are mixed with the *liqueur de tirage*, made up of wine, sugar, and yeast. This mixture causes a second fermentation – which lasts for 6 to 12 weeks – to occur in each bottle; its most important result is that the carbon-dioxide gas that is a by-product of fermentation is trapped in the bottle and dissolved in the wine, thus transforming the still wine into sparkling wine. (Another result is that the wine's alcohol content increases about 1 percent, which is why the base wine for champagne rarely has more than 11 percent alcohol.) The bottles of newly sparkling wine are stored on their sides in the vast and cool underground cellars of Champagne, which usually contain between 400 and 600 million bottles. The wine is now aging *sur lie*, on the lees, which consist primarily of dead yeast cells; they enrich the wine's texture and add complexity to its bouquet by a process known as autolysis. The amount of time that champagne is permitted to age *sur lie* is an important factor in its eventual quality. Non-vintage champagne must be aged at least a year in the bottle before being released for sale, and the bottling cannot occur until January 1 of the year following the harvest. Vintage champagne cannot be marketed until three years after the harvest, which means it can actually be sold after only 2.5 years *sur lie*. In practice, most major firms age their non-vintage champagne for two or three years, their vintage for three to five years.

Before bottle-fermented sparkling wines can be sold, the lees must be removed from each bottle without a loss of bubbles. The first step is this process is *rémuage*, or riddling. Each bottle is placed at a slight downward angle in a *pupitre*, or riddling rack, an A-shaped device with rows of holes; the *rémueurs*, or riddlers, give each bottle a slight shake to loosen the sediment and then a downward turn; after about six weeks of riddling, each bottle is *sur pointe*, that is, upside down, and all the sediment has collected next to the cork. This necessary, but time-consuming process has largely been replaced today by the use of *gyropalettes*, large metal frames in the shape of a cube that hold 500 or more bottles and that can be manipulated, either by hand or by a computerized programme, to duplicate the work of the *rémueurs* in a week or ten days. (*See also* Calcium Alginate Beads.) Once the bottles are *sur pointe*, they may remain that way for additional aging, or they may immediately undergo the next step, which is *dégorgement*, or disgorging. First, the upside-down bottles are placed in a brine solution that freezes the sediment against the temporary crown cork, then they are disgorged – each bottle is uncorked and the frozen plug of sediment expelled. The bottle is then topped up with wine that contains *liqueur d'expédition*, also known as *dosage*, and then recorked with the traditional champagne cork. It is the *dosage*, a mixture of wine and sugar, that determines the relative sweetness of champagne. With few exceptions, the driest champagnes are labelled Brut, and contain no more than 1.5 percent sugar; in practice, most contain .8 to 1.2 percent. Extra Dry contains 1.2 to 2 percent sugar; Sec, 1.7 to 3.5 percent; Démi-Sec, 3.3 to 5 percent; and Doux, more than 5 percent. Occasionally, a firm will market a champagne without any *dosage*, and such bone-dry, austere wines have been labelled Brut Absolu, Brut Intégral, or Brut Zéro; today, the official term for champagne with less than .6 percent of sugar is Extra Brut.

Although the most frequently encountered champagnes are non-vintage Brut, Extra Dry, and vintage Brut, a few other terms are sometimes seen on labels. *Blanc de blancs*, which means a white wine made from white grapes, refers to a champagne made entirely from Chardonnay, which is likely to be lighter bodied and more elegant than the traditional style. A *blanc de noirs*, a white wine made from black grapes, refers to a champagne made entirely from Pinot Noir and/or Pinot Meunier, without Chardonnay, and is likely to be comparatively rich and full bodied. Crémant, or creaming, refers to delicate wines with less effervescence than champagne (3 to 4 atmospheres rather than 6); this term should not be confused with Cramant, which is the name of a village in the Côte des Blancs. There has been a renewed interest in rosé champagnes in recent years; these pink wines are made, for the most part, by creating a *cuvée* of still wines that includes 5 to 15 percent red wine, usually from the villages of Bouzy or Cumières. The result is a wine with more body and flavour than usual, and with a colour that varies from pale salmon to pink-orange. The term *cuvée spéciale* refers to a firm's most expensive wine, usually marketed in a specially designed bottle. The best known of these prestige *cuvées* is Dom Pérignon of Moët & Chandon; others include Bollinger R. D., Krug Grande Cuvée, Laurent Perrier Grand Siècle, Louis Roederer Cristal, Perrier-Jouët Belle Epoque, and Taittinger Comtes de Champagne. (A list of *cuvées spéciales* will be found on page 550.) Some champagnes are referred to as *grandes marques*, a term that has not been officially defined, but which encompasses virtually all of the most prestigious champagne firms.

Champagne is a blend of wines from different grape varieties, different villages and districts within the region, and for the most part, different vintages; it is thus one of the very few wines – perhaps the only fine French wine – for which the name of the producer is more important than that of a vineyard, district, or even vintage.

The label of each shipper bears – in very small type – a code number preceded by the letters NM, for *Négociant-Manipulant*, indicating that they are shippers who produce their own wines; there are more than 100 such firms, and they account for two thirds of all champagne sales and about 95 percent of exports. The letters RM on a label, infrequently seen outside France, stand for *Récoltant-Manipulant*, a grower who sells champagne made from his own vineyards. CM stands for *Cooperative-Manipulant*, or cooperative cellar, and is found on such widely distributed labels as Jacquart and Nicholas Feuillatte. MA means *Marque d'Acheteur*, or buyer's own brand, and indicates that the name on the label is a proprietary brand created by a restaurant, retailer, or importer, and is not that of the firm that produced the champagne.

French sparkling wines other than champagne are known as *mousseux*, and many of them, especially those made by the *méthode champenoise* along the Loire, in Burgundy, and Alsace, can be very good. Spanish sparkling wines labelled *cava* are made by the *méthode champenoise*, as are some German *Sekt* and Italian Brut *spumante*; most German and Italian sparklers, however, are produced by the Charmat method of bulk fermentation. Most countries recognize that Champagne is an appellation of origin, and that the use of the name is restricted to the wines produced in that region of France. In the United States, however, any sparkling wine may be labelled champagne, although the word must be preceded by some indication of geographical origin, such as American, California, or New York State. Most American sparkling wines are made by the Charmat method or the transfer method, but in recent years an increasing number of California wineries, some of them established by French champagne firms, are producing excellent *méthode champenoise* sparkling wines from Chardonnay and Pinot Noir grapes.

Champagne Nature *See* Coteaux Champenois

Champigny A village southeast of Saumur, in the Loire Valley, which gives its name to the appellation Saumur-Champigny, restricted to red wines made from the Cabernet Franc grape in a delimited district on the left bank of the Loire; the light, fragrant wines, somewhat resembling Chinon, are properly considered the best reds of the Anjou-Saumur region.

Chancellor The popular name for the French-American hybrid Seibel 7053, which produces relatively full-bodied red wines in the eastern United States.

Chantepleure A rather fanciful name given to the spigot of a wine barrel, generally made of boxwood and inclined to squeak when opened; thus it "sings" (*chante*) and "weeps" (*pleure*) as the wine runs out. The wine fraternity of Vouvray, one of many in France, is known as the Confrèrie de la Chantepleure.

Chapeau *See* Cap

Chapelle-Chambertin A *grand cru* vineyard in the Burgundy village of Gevrey-Chambertin; its 13 acres, which adjoin the Clos de Bèze vineyard, produce about 2,200 cases a year of excellent red wine that is perhaps less powerful than that of its more illustrious neighbour.

Chapitre French for "chapter house"; a name often given in France to a vineyard adjoining, or connected with, an important church, as Clos du Chapitre.

Chaptalization The special process of adding sugar to must, or grape juice, before or during fermentation in order to increase the alcohol content of the resulting wine. Widely decried but often helpful and, in some instances, necessary in winemaking, it takes its name from J. A. Chaptal, Napoleon's minister of agriculture, who suggested the idea at the beginning of the nineteenth century (although honey, for precisely the same reason, has been used in winemaking for centuries). Chaptalization does not make a wine sweeter, of course, since the sugar is converted into alcohol. It is properly resorted to in cool wine regions, as well as in many other regions in poor years, when the grapes do not have enough natural sugar to produce wines with an acceptable level of alcohol (which has a stabilizing effect on wine, and also affects its weight and texture). In the Bordeaux, Burgundy, and Beaujolais regions of France, for example, where the natural alcohol content of the wines is often no more than 10 percent or so, chaptalization is frequently practised to raise the alcohol level by 1 or 2 percent; in Germany, where poor vintages would produce wines with only 6 or 7 percent alcohol, chaptalization may be used for wines labelled Qualitätswein, although never for those labelled Qualitätswein mit Prädikat (Kabinett, Spätlese, etc.). It should perhaps be added that chaptalization can also be used to compensate for excessively high yields, which produce weak, low-alcohol wines. Chaptalization is prohibited in California and in Italy, although the use of grape concentrate is permitted to achieve similar results; chaptalization is permitted in Oregon and in several eastern states, including New York, where both sugar and water may be added to the must (a process known as amelioration or Gallisation). Apart from its principal purpose, chaptalization often makes fermentation easier and produces wines that are fuller, richer, and more appealing when young; when overdone, however, it results in wines that are out of balance, too alcoholic, and that do not age gracefully.

Character A wine-taster's term for a wine, whether passable, good, or outstanding, that has definite and unmistakable qualities; these may be due to its geographical origin, its grape variety, or something else, such as the nature of the vintage or the way it was made. A wine without character is likely to be dull and uninteresting.

Charbono A grape of uncertain origin – it may be related to the Corbeau of France – which produces an agreeable, full-bodied red wine in California; less than 100 acres are planted, almost all of them in Napa.

Chardonnay The very finest of all white-wine grapes, rivalled only by the best examples of true Riesling; fashionable as well as popular, Chardonnay is now widely planted throughout the world. Although the wines it produces are not as distinctive as those made from Riesling or Sauvignon Blanc, they have an unmistakable class and an appealing balance of fruit, acidity, and texture; some tasters associate Chardonnay with apples, ripe figs, or melon, while others describe the wines as creamy or buttery. Winemakers play a particularly important role in the style of Chardonnay, which can range from clean, crisp bottlings with a hint of varietal fruit to rich, complex, oak-aged examples that need several years of bottle age to fully display their qualities; the grape also produces fine sparkling wines. In France, which may be considered its homeland (there is, in fact, a small village named Chardonnay in the Mâcon district), this grape produces all the white Burgundies, from Chablis to such Côte d'Or wines as Meursault, Montrachet, and Corton-Charlemagne, to the wines of Mâcon and Pouilly-Fuissé; Chardonnay also accounts for a quarter of the acreage in the extensive Champagne region.

In California, Chardonnay plantings have increased from fewer than 1,000 acres in 1965 to 48,000, more than twice as much as in all of Burgundy; half the plantings are in Napa and Sonoma counties, but this grape has also achieved success – for both still and sparkling wines – in such relatively new districts as the Anderson Valley in Mendocino, the Edna Valley in San Luis Obispo, and the Santa Maria Valley in Santa Barbara. Oregon and Washington have produced fine Chardonnays, as has New York, whose 1,000 acres of Chardonnay represent half the state's total acreage of *vinifera* varieties. Chardonnay is extensively planted in northeast Italy, where it was confused with Pinot Bianco (Pinot Blanc) until a few years ago; the variety is now harvested and vinified separately in Trentino-Alto Adige, Friuli, and the Veneto, and often marketed as a varietal wine, most examples of which are relatively light and crisp. Richer, oak-aged Chardonnays are produced in other parts of Italy, including Piedmont, Tuscany, and Umbria. In Australia, most of the Chardonnay vineyards have been planted since the early 1970s, and as recently as 1981 there were only 1,200 bearing acres in that country; there are now more than 9,000 acres, and they produce some of the world's finest examples. The popularity of Chardonnay is such that this variety is now planted, at least on an experimental basis, in just about every wine-producing country. Although the grape has long been called Pinot Chardonnay, most ampelographers are now certain that it is not a Pinot, and not related to Pinot Blanc or Pinot Noir.

Charente A district north of Bordeaux that encompasses the *départements* of Charente and Charente-Maritime; its 200,000 acres of vineyard, planted almost entirely with Ugni Blanc (known locally as Saint-Emilion), produce 12 to 15 percent of the total French wine crop. Most of these light, acid, low-alcohol white wines are distilled to make cognac; some are used to provide zest to inexpensive blends.

Charlemagne King of the Franks and, from 800 to his death in 814, emperor of the West. He is said to have been responsible for the planting of the first vines around what is now Schloss Johannisberg after observing, from his palace at Ingelheim, across the Rhine, that snow melted on this slope earlier than elsewhere; he seems also to have had a vineyard at Aloxe-Corton, in Burgundy, with which his name is still associated – Corton-

Charlemagne.

In addition, the name Charlemagne is officially recognized as a *grand cru* appellation for white wines from a vineyard whose boundaries are very similar to those of Corton-Charlemagne. The name was used for those parts of the vineyard planted with the inferior Aligoté grape, but they have now been replaced with Chardonnay, and the wines are entitled to be marketed as Corton-Charlemagne; the Charlemagne appellation has not been used for twenty years or so.

Charmat Process A technique developed by Eugène Charmat in the early years of this century whereby the second fermentation that transforms still wines into sparkling wines takes place in large tanks rather than in individual bottles, as in the classic *méthode champenoise*. After the second fermentation is completed, the wines are filtered, the appropriate *dosage* is added, and the wines are bottled. (In the case of such wines as Asti Spumante and Lambrusco, the wines are filtered and bottled when the desired balance between sparkle and residual sugar has been achieved.) The tanks may be small or large enough to hold the equivalent of more than 200,000 bottles, and the process may take less than a month; in some regions, however, the wines are left *sur lie* for several months before being bottled, to acquire additional complexity. The technique, also known as the bulk process of tank fermentation, is called *cuve close* in France, *autoclave* in Italy, and *granvas* in Spain. Most Italian sparkling wines are made this way, as are almost all German *Sekt*. The process is widely used in the United States, and such wines must be labelled Charmat Process or Bulk Process.

Charmes-Chambertin A *grand cru* vineyard in the village of Gevrey-Chambertin, in Burgundy's Côte d'Or. The 76-acre vineyard produces about 11,000 cases a year of an admirable red wine, only slightly inferior in body and distinction to that of Chambertin itself. The vineyard consists of two contiguous parts – Les Charmes, which adjoins Chambertin, and Mazoyères, which adjoins Latricières-Chambertin; wines from any part of the vineyard may be labelled either Charmes-Chambertin or Mazoyères-Chambertin, but the latter name, which is less familiar to consumers, is almost never used.

Charnu A French term for a wine that is fleshy, rich in substance, full-bodied.

Charpenté A French term for a wine that is well-structured.

Charta An association of estates in Germany's Rheingau region, formed in 1983, whose aim is to produce Riesling wines that are rich but dry, rather than light, soft, and sweet. Wines eligible to bear the Charta symbol must be estate bottled, made entirely from Riesling, and may have no more than 18 grams (1.8 percent) of residual sugar, balanced by a minimum of .75 acidity.

Chassagne-Montrachet An important wine-producing village near the southern end of the Côte de Beaune, in Burgundy's Côte d'Or. There are some 1,100 acres of vineyard, and the average annual production is about 120,000 cases, 40 percent of it white wine of extremely high quality, the balance red, often very good but rarely of absolutely top class. About half of the *grand cru* vineyards Montrachet and Bâtard-Montrachet lie within the communal limits of Chassagne-Montrachet, as does all of Criots-Bâtard-Montrachet; wines from these great vineyards do not carry the name Chassagne-Montrachet on their labels and are sold simply under the vineyard name alone. (The unfortunate, but understandable confusion between the village name and that of the top individual vineyard is caused by the fact that in the late nineteenth century Chassagne, like many other Burgundian villages, appended the name of its most famous vineyard to its own.) Of almost equal excellence are those from *premier cru* vineyards in Chassagne-Montrachet, such as Les Ruchottes, Cailleret, Les Chenevottes, Morgeot, and a few others; and even whites labelled simply with the village name are almost always good. Many of the lesser red Chassagne-Montrachets have an easily recognizable and not unpleasant earthy taste, or *goût de terroir*; the finer ones carry on their labels the names of such *premier cru* vineyards as Clos St. Jean, La Boudriotte, La Maltroie, and Morgeot.

Chasselas A productive and hardy white grape of which many subvarieties exist; several of these are justly famous as table grapes, but none can be considered a truly superior wine grape since, except in very cool regions, their wines have a tendency to be low in acid, flat, and short-lived. Nevertheless, in Switzerland, where it is also known as Fendant and Dorin, the

Chasselas is the leading wine grape, as it is in Markgräfler-land, in the southern Baden region of Germany, where it is known as Gutedel. Chasselas is also cultivated in France in the Haute-Savoie, in Alsace, and around Pouilly-sur-Loire.

Chasse-Spleen, Château A *cru bourgeois exceptionnel* in the commune of Moulis, in the Médoc district; its 185 acres produce about 25,000 cases a year of a generous, well-structured wine that some experts consider finer than many of the lesser classed growths of the Médoc. The vineyard also markets a second wine as L'Ermitage de Chasse-Spleen. The château's name, which may be freely translated as "dispels melancholy", is attributed both to a remark of Lord Byron's and to a work by Baudelaire titled *Spleen et idéal*.

Château When used in reference to French wines, and especially those of Bordeaux, the word *château* is synonymous with vineyard. There are a number of properties, especially in the Médoc district, that are adorned with structures that fully merit the name château, but more often than not, the house attached to a specific vineyard, especially in the less-renowned parts of the Bordeaux region, may be nothing more than a simple country home or small farmhouse whose owners cultivate their own vines and make their own wine. According to French law, the word *château* may not appear on a label, as part of the name of a wine, unless a *bona fide* vineyard exists, has produced it, and has some traditional right to the name. (As it happens, it is legal for co-operative cellars to label a wine with a château name if they have vinified the grapes from that particular property separately.)

The châteaux, or vineyards, described in this volume will be found listed alphabetically under their own names. The exceptions that follow are those for which the word *château* forms an integral part of the name.

Château Bottled A wine bottled on the property that produced it, by the vineyard owner, especially in the Bordeaux region. (The equivalent in most other regions is estate bottled.) Château bottling is practised by the vast majority of owners of better vineyards in Bordeaux and became compulsory for the classed growths of the Médoc in 1972. It is a definite guarantee of authenticity, to a much lesser extent of quality. Château-bottled wines are invariably so labelled, most often with the phrase *Mis en bouteille au château*, although *Mise* *du château* is equally valid; in addition, the corks of such wines are usually branded with the name of the château and the vintage. Note that wines from co-operative cellars may also carry the name of a château and the phrase, unusual for Bordeaux, *Mis en bouteille a la propriété.*

Château-Châlon An unusual and rare white wine from France's Jura region, which is not, despite its name, the product of a specific vineyard, but of a tiny, hilltop village that bears this name. Much closer in character to an unfortified sherry from Spain than to any other French wine, Château-Châlon is made from the Savagnin grape. It is the only French wine – except Fitou and Bandol – that must be kept in cask for a specified period (in this instance, six years), and it has its own special bottle, the *clavelin*. It is a sort of accidental French version of sherry, and it matures in casks that are not kept full, under a layer of *flor* yeast, just as fino sherry does. Higher in acid than sherry, and lower in alcohol (the legal minimum is 12 percent), it is less good; its fame is based as much on its uniqueness as on its quality.

Château-Grillet A famous, tiny vineyard on the west bank of the Rhône River, about eight miles south of Vienne, owned by the Neyret-Gachet family since 1820. The vineyard, which has been expanded from 4 to 7.5 acres in the past twenty years, is planted entirely with the Viognier grape and produces, at its best, golden, rich, full-bodied dry wines with nuances reminiscent of apricots, peaches, and honey; annual production now averages about 1,200 cases and has varied in recent years from 345 cases to 1,500 or so. Château-Grillet has often been called the smallest vineyard in France with its own *Appellation Contrôlée* by those who forget that each of the *grand crus* of Burgundy also has its own *Appellation Contrôlée*; thus, the 2-acre La Romanée merits that particular distinction, and Criots-Bâtard-Montrachet (3.9 acres), Romanée-Conti (4.5 acres), and Griotte-Chambertin (6.7 acres) are all smaller than Château-Grillet.

Châteaumeillant A VDQS for light reds and pale rosés made from the Gamay grape in a small district in the Cher *département*, whose best-known wine is Sancerre.

Châteauneuf-du-Pape A celebrated, sturdy red wine of the Rhône region, from the village of that name, situated about a dozen miles north of the old papal city of Avignon, in southern France. The *château neuf*, or "new castle", now a ruin, was the summer home of the Avignon popes in the fourteenth century; the vineyards are planted on an extraordinary, high, stony tableland that dominates the Rhône and the surrounding fertile plain; the soil consists of the coarsest sort of gravel and small boulders on which it seems impossible that vines should grow, but which retain and reflect the heat of the day well into the evening. As a district, Châteauneuf-du-Pape is the most important of the Rhône, some four miles by five in extent, and its annual production is about 1 million cases, 97 percent of it red. Thirteen different red and white grape varieties are permitted in this district, but in practice most estates are planted with 60 to 75 percent Grenache, which provides body and alcohol, but does not age well, plus varying amounts of Syrah, for colour and bouquet; Mourvèdre, for tannin and structure; and Cinsault, for body and softness. (The full-bodied white is made from such varieties as Grenache Blanc, Clairette, Roussanne, and Bourboulenc.) Traditionally, the red is deep crimson in colour, generously flavoured, and fairly high in alcohol – the wine must have at least 12.5 percent alcohol, the highest such minimum in France; it is softer and matures more quickly than Hermitage and Côte Rôtie, from the northern Rhône, and is often at its best between the ages of five and ten. In recent years, many producers have begun to make somewhat lighter wines, less tannic and robust, and sooner ready to drink; consequently, there is quite a range of styles of Châteauneuf-du-Pape available today. Estate-bottled wines are entitled to be marketed in a special bottle on which is embossed the papal coat of arms, featuring a mitre and crossed keys, and the legend "Châteauneuf-du-Pape Contrôlée", although, as it happens, co-operative cellars are also entitled to use this bottle.

Chatillon-en-Diois An appellation established in 1975 for red, white and rosé wines produced along the eastern edge of the Rhône Valley, near the village of Die; unlike Clairette de Die, these wines are not sparkling, and most of the production – about 25,000 cases a year – is consumed locally.

Chaucé Gris *See* Grey Riesling

Chavignol One of the better communes of the district of Sancerre, in the upper Loire Valley of France; the village is also famous for its small, round cheeses made of goat's milk, known as *crottins de Chavignol*.

Cheilly-les-Maranges A village south of Santenay, at the extreme southern end of the Côte d'Or in Burgundy, whose undistinguished red wines are now marketed as Maranges.

Chelois A French-American hybrid whose official name is Seibel 10878; cultivated in the Finger Lakes and elsewhere, it produces light red wine.

Chénas A village in France's Beaujolais region whose wines are relatively sturdy and long-lived. Part of its vineyards fall within the appellation Moulin-à-Vent; consequently, Chénas is one of the smallest and least familiar of the ten Beaujolais *crus*.

Chenin Blanc An excellent grape capable of producing white wines that range from clean, crisp, and fruity to rich, sweet, honeyed, and exceptionally long-lived; it is also known as Pineau de la Loire, but it bears no relation to the true Pinots. Chenin Blanc is the predominant variety in the central Loire, in the Anjou and Touraine regions, and is responsible for such wines as Vouvray, Montlouis, Anjou, and Saumur, as well as for a great deal of sparking wine; depending on the year, the still wines may be dry, medium-sweet, or sweet. Other examples of Chenin Blanc from the Loire include the dry wines produced in Savennières and the sweet wines of the Coteaux du Layon, which encompass the appellations Quarts de Chaume and Bonnezeaux. There are more than 35,000 acres of Chenin Blanc planted in California, mostly in the Central Valley, and this variety accounts for nearly a quarter of the white wine crop. Slow, cool fermentation enables California winemakers to produce clean, delicate, fruity wines, most of which are blended with French Colombard and bottled as jug wines. A number of wineries market Chenin Blanc as a varietal wine; some examples are fairly dry, most are semisweet. The most extensive plantings of this variety are in South Africa, where it is known as Steen.

Cheval Blanc, Château A celebrated and remarkable *premier grand cru classé* vineyard in the Saint-Emilion district, ranked with Château Ausone as one of the two best of the district. Its 90-

odd acres, planted two thirds with Cabernet Franc and one third with Merlot, are situated on the gravelly plateau adjoining the Pomerol district, rather than on the slopes near the town of Saint-Emilion itself; its production of 12,000 to 14,000 cases a year makes it one of the biggest of the top properties of Saint-Emilion. In great years its wines have extraordinary distinction and are among the finest of all Bordeaux, although they mature perhaps more quickly than the finest wines of the Médoc.

Chevalier, Domaine de One of the most celebrated of the *grand crus classés* of the Graves district of Bordeaux; its 35 acres produce about 5,000 cases a year of red and white wines. The white is something of a rarity – its annual production amounts to 1,000 cases or less – but it has long been considered perhaps the finest of dry white Graves; the red is also excellent and often sells for a price only slightly below that of the first growths.

Chevalier-Montrachet A *grand cru* vineyard in Burgundy's Côte d'Or, in the village of Puligny-Montrachet; its 18 acres of sloping and stony soil produce some 2,000 to 3,500 cases a year of one of the very best dry white wines of France. It lies directly west of, and uphill from, the great Montrachet vineyard, and its wine, as might be expected, is a great rarity, expensive, but of memorable quality.

Chevaliers du Tastevin A wine fraternity founded in 1934 to promote the wines of Burgundy and named after the shallow silver tasting cup still used in the region. The organization holds a number of convivial dinners every year at the Château de Vougeot, the most famous of which occurs in November, on the eve of the Hospices de Beaune wine auction.

Cheverny A VDQS for red, white, and rosé wines produced along the Loire, near the village of Blois.

Chevrier Another name for the Sémillon grape, occasionally seen on California labels.

Chianti A wonderfully agreeable and, in some cases, quite distinguished Italian red wine from Tuscany. Although annual production has decreased from 12 to 15 million cases a year to about 10 million cases, Chianti is still the most important of Italy's DOC and DOCG wines, and accounts for about 12 percent of the total. Much of Chianti's worldwide fame is undoubtedly due to the attractive and distinctive straw-covered *fiasco* in which it was shipped for so many years. Weaving the straw by hand became so expensive, however, that in recent years the *fiasco* often cost more than the wine it contained. The *fiasco* has virtually disappeared today, to the relief of Chianti producers, since it perpetuated an image of Chianti as a cheap wine of indifferent quality. Admittedly, most Chianti is drunk young, often as a carafe wine, in the restaurants of Florence; inexpensive, refreshing, tart, and sprightly (and, in the past, containing a slight tingle caused by a traditional technique known as *governo alla toscana*), it goes admirably with Italian food. But there are other styles of Chianti as well, and those admired by connoisseurs are richer, more complex, wood-aged wines that can develop in bottle for many years. Many of these come from the de-limited Chianti Classico zone, and all are likely to be labelled Riserva, indicating that they have been aged for a minimum of three years (although not necessarily in wood); they are among the finest wines of Italy.

The traditional blend of grapes for Chianti, established by Baron Bettino Ricasoli in the mid-nineteenth century, con-sisted of Sangiovese with some Canaiolo, plus 5 percent of the white Malvasia grape to add lightness to those wines meant to be consumed young. When the DOC laws for Chianti were established in 1967, the formula was codified as 50 to 80 percent Sangiovese, 10 to 30 percent Canaiolo, and 10 to 30 percent white Trebbiano and Malvasia grapes. A number of producers complained that the use of white grapes in a red wine might be acceptable for a carafe wine, but the 10 percent minimum made it impossible to produce truly fine, long-lived reds; some even went on to create wines made entirely from red grapes which, of course, could not legally be called Chianti – the most famous of these is Tignanello of Antinori. When Chianti was elevated to DOCG, in 1984, the regulations were changed: today, San-giovese accounts for 75 to 90 percent, Canaiolo has been re-duced to 5 to 10 percent, and white grapes are restricted to 5 to 10 percent (only 2 to 5 percent in the Classico zone). In addition, the new law permits the use of up to 10 percent of non-traditional varieties in the Chianti blend, an acknow-ledgement of the increasing use of Cabernet Sauvignon in the district. The DOCG law has also reduced the permitted yield from Chianti vineyards by about 20 percent.

There are seven inner zones within the extensive Chianti district. The most famous is Chianti Classico, situated between Florence and Siena, which contains many, but certainly not all, of the best-known estates. Members of the Chianti Classico *consorzio*, a voluntary growers' association, may use the familiar *gallo nero*, or "black rooster", seal on their bottles. The six other zones are Chianti Montalbano, west of Florence, which contains the DOC zone Carmignano; Chianti Rufina, which contains the DOC Pomino; Chianti Colli Senesi, which extends in an arch south of the Classico zone and encompasses the DOCs Brunello di Montalcino and Vino Nobile di Montepulciano; and Chianti Aretini, Chianti Colli Fiorentini, and Chianti Colline Pisani. The *consorzio* for these six regions has adopted as its symbol the *putto*, or cherub, and its seal consists of a pink cherub on a blue ground.

Chianti Classico Situated between Florence and Siena, this classic, inner zone within Tuscany's extensive Chianti district was first delimited in the thirteenth century. It consists of the four townships of Greve, Radda, Castellina, and Gaiole, plus portions of six others. Production now varies from 2.7 to 3.5 million cases a year, about 25 to 33 percent of the total production of Chianti. Most of the best and best-known producers of Chianti are situated in the Classico zone, whose firm, well-balanced wines have a deserved reputation for excellence. It must be added, however, that extensive new plantings in the 1960s and 1970s have resulted in many wines labelled Chianti Classico that are not up to the standards of the best producers. Because the name Chianti has long been used for wines produced throughout central Tuscany, a number of producers established a *consorzio*, or growers' association, in 1924, to define the Classico zone, establish quality controls, and oversee production. The Chianti Classico *consorzio* adopted the *gallo nero*, or "black rooster", neck seal to identify its wines. Although DOC laws for Chianti Classico were established in 1967, the *consorzio* is still active: its requirements are somewhat stricter than the DOCG ones, and it continues to monitor the quality of its members' wines and promote sales. Nevertheless, not all Chianti Classico producers belong to the *consorzio*; some prefer to rely on a combination of the DOCG laws and their own reputations.

Chiaretto An Italian term for certain rosés produced along the south-ern and eastern shores of Lake Garda, in the DOC zones that produce Bardolino and Riviera del Garda Bresciano; light, pale, fresh, low in alcohol, and best consumed young, Chiaretto is, in effect, the pink version of those red wines.

Chile Although this country's annual production of 60 to 70 million cases is only one quarter that of Argentina's, Chile's best wines – especially those made from Cabernet Sauvignon and Sauvignon Blanc – are generally ranked as the finest of South America and often represent good value as well. The first vines, known as Pais, were planted in Chile in the mid-sixteenth century; similar to the Mission grape of California, this variety still accounts for about half the country's acreage. The modern history of wine in Chile dates from 1851, when French vintners were first brought over, along with French grape varieties, primarily the Cabernet Sauvig-non, Malbec, Sauvignon Blanc, and Sémillon of Bordeaux; these are still the most widely planted European varieties, with Cabernet Sauvignon and Sémillon making up about one quarter of Chile's vineyards. At present, Chile has more Cabernet acreage than California and two thirds as much as Bordeaux. Amusingly enough, about twenty years ago, when Chile first began to export its wines, the inexpensive bottles labelled Burgundy were made primarily from Caber-net, and those marketed as Riesling and Rhine Wine from Sémillon. In recent years, the emphasis has been on varietal wines, and there have been new plantings of Cabernet, Chardonnay, and Sauvignon Blanc, as well as Merlot, Pinot Noir, Riesling, and Gewürztraminer. The current interest in Chilean wines has also been sparked by a few notable foreign investors: Miguel Torres, best known for the wines he pro-duces in Spain's Penedès region, established a vineyard in the Curicó district in 1979; Agustin Huneeus, the Chilean born co-owner of Napa Valley's Franciscan Vineyards, recently created the Caliterra label; and in 1988 that branch of the Rothschilds that owns Lafite bought a half-interest in the Los Vasco winery. One result has been the introduction of such techniques as the cool fermentation of white wines to retain their fruit, and the aging of red wines in small oak bar-rels. Chile extends for 2,800 miles between the Andes Mountains and the Pacific Ocean, but its vineyards are sit-uated in the central, temperate zone north and south of Santiago; most are planted along the foothills of the Andes, on irrigated plains, and along valleys formed by rivers flowing west from the Andes to the ocean. The best vineyards are found between the Aconcagua River, about 45 miles north of Santiago, and the Curicó region, about 125 miles south of that city; the famous Maipo district is just southwest of Santiago. Because Chile is so well protected by mountains and the ocean, its vineyards were never attacked by phylloxera and are among the very few in the world planted on their own rootstocks.

Chill *See* Ice Bucket, Temperature

China Although vineyards were first planted more than 2,000 years ago, wine has never played an important part in China's economy and is consumed only on special occasions; even today, most of the country's extensive vineyard acreage produces table grapes, and much of the 20 million cases of wine made are sweet and high in alcohol. In recent years, however, the government has entered into joint ventures with outside investors, who have introduced modern technology, planted new vineyards, and begun to produce light, medium-dry table wines that are consumed by foreign tourists and shipped to Western markets. Among the results of these ventures are Dynasty, a white wine produced near Tianjin, about 100 miles south of Beijing, primarily from Muscat Hamburg and the Dimiat grape of Bulgaria; Spring Moon, an off-dry white wine produced at the Heavenly Palace winery, also near Tianjin; and a winery near Qingdao, on the Shandong Peninsula, which produces wines from Italian Riesling and, in limited quantities, from Chardonnay.

Chinon A picturesque and historic little town situated on the Vienne River, a tributary of the Loire, in the Touraine region; it is the birthplace of Rabelais, and it was here that Joan of Arc first met the Dauphin, later crowned king of France. The red wine produced here, made entirely from the Cabernet Franc grape, is fruity and agreeable, with enough backbone and structure to make it one of the most interesting of France's lesser wines. Its production of 600,000 to 700,000 cases a year is somewhat larger than that of Bourgueil and Saint-Nicolas-de-Bourgueil, similar wines made nearby.

Chiroubles A village in France's Beaujolais region whose excellent red wines are fruity, charming, and elegant; in the opinion of many connoisseurs, Chiroubles is the most appealing and immediately accessible of all Beaujolais *crus*.

Chorey-les-Beaune A wine-producing village in Burgundy's Côte d'Or district, directly north of Beaune; its 400 acres of vineyards produce red wines sold under its own name or as Côte de Beaune-Villages.

Chusclan A village northwest of Avignon whose wines are entitled to the superior appellation Côtes-du-Rhône-Villages; Chusclan is best known for its excellent rosés.

Cinqueterre An Italian white wine produced in five villages (hence, presumably, its name) on the Ligurian coast east of Genoa, near La Spezia. The wine, made primarily from Bosco grapes, plus Vermentino and Albarola, cultivated in steep vineyards that overlook the Mediterranean, is of greater historic than current interest.

Cinsault A red-wine grape capable of giving a full-bodied, deep coloured wine of definite character, but the vines are usually pruned for maximum productivity, which results in a lighter, less distinguished wine. Cinsault (also spelled Cinsaut) is extensively planted in France's Midi region, where it is usually combined with Grenache and Carignan, and also plays a role in the Rhône vineyards of Châteauneuf-du-Pape and Tavel. It was once the most important variety in South Africa, where it was known as Hermitage, and is still widely planted today.

Cirò A DOC district in Italy's Calabria region producing attractive red and rosé wines from the Gaglioppo grape and lesser amounts of white from Greco Bianco.

Cissac, Château A *cru bourgeois* situated west of Pauillac and entitled to the appellation Haut-Médoc; it produces about 18,000 cases a year of a wine admired by British connoisseurs.

Citran, Château A *cru bourgeois exceptionnel* entitled to the appellation Haut-Médoc, and one of the larger such properties; its 200 acres produce about 35,000 cases a year.

Clairet An old French term – from which the English word *claret* is derived – applied centuries ago to the then rather light red wine of Bordeaux. Revived in recent years, it is now the name given to certain specially vinified light red Bordeaux, without much colour or tannin and soon ready to drink, that resemble full-bodied rosés, although deeper in colour; they are usually served cool, and may be agreeable or even quite good.

Clairette   A white-wine grape, widely grown in southern France, that produces rather neutral wines, low in acid and short-lived. It is one of the varieties used for white Côtes-du-Rhône and Châteauneuf-du-Pape, and its wines have been granted AOC status in two districts of the Languedoc-Roussillon region: Clairette du Languedoc comes from vineyards between Montpellier and Béziers, in the Hérault *département*; and Clairette de Bellegarde is produced about 20 miles southwest of Avignon. The variety is also cultivated in South Africa, where it is known as Clairette Blanche; and to a limited extent in Australia, where it is called Blanquette.

Clairette de Die   A French sparkling wine produced around the town of Die, southeast of Valence, along the eastern edge of the Rhône Valley; a local co-operative cellar now accounts for most of the production, which often amounts to more than 600,000 cases a year. There are actually two styles of sparkling wine produced there: one is a *méthode champenoise* wine made from the Clairette grape; the other is a fragrant wine made primarily from Muscat by the traditional *méthode dioise*. The latter consists of stopping the original fermentation by refrigerating the must and bottling the incompletely fermented wine, which then continues to ferment in the bottle. The sparkling wine is then decanted, filtered and rebottled.

Clape, La   A village east of Narbonne, along the Mediterranean coast of France, whose red, white, and rosé wines are included within the regional appellation Coteaux du Languedoc, but which are more often marketed as La Clape.

Clare Valley   An excellent Australian wine district about 75 miles north of Adelaide in the state of South Australia, sometimes referred to as Clare/Watervale after its two principal towns. The district is particularly famous for its fine Rhine Riesling and, more recently, for its Cabernet Sauvignon and Chardonnay; the name Clare Riesling, rarely used today, refers to a lesser grape known in France as Crouchen. Wineries situated there include Tim Knappstein, Quelltaler, and Stanley Leasingham.

Claret A loosely and widely used term meaning, in most countries other than England, a light red wine. Thus, in the United States, any red table wine may be labelled claret, whatever its origin, character, or type; the name has no meaning or legal status in France, nor has *clarete* in Spain or Chile. In England, however, the word traditionally refers to red Bordeaux (as *hock* means Rhine wines), and a number of British wine merchants market their basic red Bordeaux as Claret.

Clarete A term traditionally used in Spain, especially in the Rioja district, to describe any red wine that is comparatively light in colour and body; the word has no official status, however.

Clarke, Château A notable *cru bourgeois* in the commune of Listrac, in the Médoc district, acquired in 1973 by Baron Edmond de Rothschild, one of the owners of Lafite; more than 300 acres of the 400-acre property have been planted in vines, the first crop was 1978, and the vineyard now produces more than 40,000 cases a year of a dependable, well-balanced wine that merits its newfound popularity.

Clarksburg A viticultural area south of Sacramento, in the Sacramento River delta, which includes the smaller districts of Merritt Island and Mandeville Island; it is best known for Chenin Blanc, although Chardonnay and Cabernet Sauvignon are also planted.

Classed Growth The English equivalent of the French *cru classé*, used to designate a vineyard that has been officially classed, or classified; the first such official grading was the famous Bordeaux Classification of 1855, which focused on the vineyards of the Médoc and Sauternes, and almost all references to classed growths in this volume are based on this listing. *See* Classification of 1855, Cru Classé.

Classico Italian for "classic". The term refers to an inner district within the overall zone of production defined by DOC laws, often the original area first cultivated in vines; wines so labelled are likely to be the best of that appellation. The most famous *classico* district is that in the Chianti zone, which accounts for 25 to 30 percent of the total production of Chianti; many other DOC zones contain a *classico* district, including Orvieto, Soave, and Valpolicella.

Classification of 1855 In preparation for the *Exposition Universelle* held in Paris in 1855, a committee of wine brokers submitted a classification of the leading wines of two great Bordeaux districts, the Médoc and Sauternes, basing their ratings almost entirely on the prices at which the wines were then being sold; the wines of Saint-Emilion, Pomerol, and Graves (with the exception of Château Haut-Brion) were not yet celebrated enough to be included. Although a number of unofficial classifications had been established throughout the eighteenth century, and as recently as 1848, the one published in 1855 achieved a permanent status and is still referred to today. The 60 wines of the Médoc (plus Haut-Brion from Graves) were grouped into five categories, from *premiers crus*, or "first growths", to *cinquièmes crus* or "fifth growths", but the differences were gradual, with the second growths selling for only 15 percent less than the first growths, and the fifth growths for about half the price of the firsts. Today, the first growths (Châteaux Lafite-Rothschild, Latour, Margaux, and Haut-Brion, plus Mouton-Rothschild, which was elevated from second to first in 1973) usually sell for two, three, or even four times that of the other châteaux; indeed, it is now common practice within the wine trade to divide all of the classified wines into just two groups, the *premiers crus*, or "first growths", and the *crus classés*, or "classed growths", the latter term referring to all the other châteaux, irrespective of their official ranking. (The wines of Sauternes, which were considerably more fashionable in 1855 than in recent years, were divided into just two categories, *premiers crus* and *deuxièmes crus*, with the incomparable Château d'Yquem in a category of its own.) There have been many changes in ownership since 1855, a number of vineyards have been reduced or expanded, some have been divided, and a few have disappeared entirely, but, except for the elevation of Mouton, the classification has remained unchanged for more than 130 years. In practice, many fourth and fifth growths now sell for more than some seconds and thirds, and both the Bordeaux trade and informed consumers know that the exact ranking established by the classification is not to be taken too literally. Nevertheless, the list, reproduced on page 537, still remains a useful guide to the top wines of the Médoc and Sauternes. In 1953, a classification was created for the best red wines of Graves, and this was expanded in 1959 to include the best white wines as well. The châteaux of Saint-Emilion were classified in 1955, and this list was revised in 1969 and again in 1985. The wines of Pomerol have never been classified.

Clavelin A special sort of stumpy bottle, holding 62 centilitres, or about 20 ounces, used in the Jura district of France for Château-Châlon and other *vins jaunes*.

Clean A wine-taster's term applied to a sound wine, one that is palatable, agreeable, and without any off odour or taste; the word can be used to describe a young, inexpensive wine as well as a fine, old one. A wine that is not clean is bad, and generally not fit to drink.

Clear Lake A viticultural area in Lake County that takes its name from the largest lake in California; the vineyards, situated along the western shore of the lake, are planted primarily with Sauvignon Blanc and Cabernet Sauvignon.

Clerc Milon, Château A Fifth Classed Growth of Pauillac, known for many years as Clerc Milon Mondon until its acquisition in 1970 by Baron Philippe de Rothschild, owner of Château Mouton-Rothschild; its 70 acres produce about 12,000 cases a year.

Climat French for "climate", but when used in connection with wine, especially in Burgundy, it means a specific, named vineyard; its implications are similar to those conveyed by the English word *microclimate*.

Climens, Château A classed growth of the Sauternes district, situated in the commune of Barsac, and one of the latter's two finest vineyards (the other being Château Coutet); its 75 acres, planted 98 percent with Sémillon, produce 4,000 to 6,000 cases a year of a sweet, luscious, golden wine noted for its elegance and breed, and considered by many connoisseurs to be second only to Château d'Yquem. The property incorporates the ten acres of Château Doisy-Dubroca, and that name has become a second label for the wines of Climens.

Clinet, Château A vineyard in the Pomerol district producing about 4,000 cases a year.

Clone   A plant reproduced asexually, and therefore retaining the genetic characteristics of the parent. There are, however, many different clones for a specific variety, such as Cabernet Sauvignon or Chardonnay, each of which has its particular characteristics – greater resistance to rot, higher yield, the ability to ripen in a cool climate, and so on. The process of clonal selection is being pursued in various wine regions to improve quality and yield and to overcome specific growing conditions.

Clos   A French term originally used for a walled or otherwise enclosed vineyard, as Clos de Vougeot. The term is much more widely used today, but may not appear on a French wine label, as part of the name of a wine, unless the *clos*, or vineyard, actually exists and produces the wine in question.

Clos, Les   A celebrated *grand cru* vineyard of Chablis, one of the best of the seven so classified; its 64 acres also make it the biggest of the *grand crus*, and the one most frequently encountered.

Clos de Bèze   *See* Chambertin

Clos l'Eglise   A vineyard in the Pomerol district whose 15 acres produce about 2,500 cases a year of fine red wines.

Clos Fourtet   A *premier grand cru classé* of Saint-Emilion whose vineyard actually adjoins the town itself, and whose impressive cellars are tunnels carved out of the chalky hillside; its 40 acres produce an average of 7,000 cases a year of firm, slow-maturing red wine.

Clos des Jacobins   A *grand cru classé* of Saint-Emilion that produces about 4,000 cases a year of sound, agreeable red wine.

Clos des Lambrays   A red-wine vineyard in the village of Morey-Saint-Denis, in Burgundy's Côte d'Or; its 22 acres, which adjoin the famous Clos de Tart vineyard, were acquired by new owners in 1979, and the vineyard elevated to *grand cru* status in 1981. As a result of extensive replanting, production was negligible until 1983, when about 2,300 cases were made, and recent vintages have averaged around 3,000 cases.

Clos des Mouches   A well-known vineyard in Beaune, in Burgundy's Côte d'Or, whose 62 acres produce an attractive, fine-textured red and, curiously enough, an even better white. The latter, Beaune's only white wine of any consequence and comparable to a fine Meursault, is a speciality of the firm of Joseph Drouhin, which owns more than half the Clos des Mouches vineyard.

Clos René   A vineyard in the Pomerol district whose 25 acres produce about 5,000 cases a year of an appealing, well-made red wine, some of which is marketed under the label Château Moulinet-Lasserre.

Clos de la Roche   A distinguished *grand cru* vineyard in the commune of Morey-Saint-Denis, in Burgundy's Côte d'Or. Its 42 acres produce about 6,000 cases a year of a red wine that, at its best, is one of the truly great Burgundies, quite the equal in power and depth, if not always in class and breed, of Chambertin.

Clos Saint-Denis   A *grand cru* vineyard situated in the commune of Morey-Saint-Denis, in Burgundy's Côte d'Or. Its 16 acres, which are almost surrounded by the larger Clos de la Roche vineyard, produce about 2,200 cases a year of a particularly sturdy, well-knit red wine that is long-lived and slow to mature.

Clos de Tart   A celebrated *grand cru* vineyard in the village of Morey-Saint-Denis, in Burgundy's Côte d'Or. One of the few top Burgundy vineyards under a single ownership, it was acquired by the Mommessin family in 1932. Its 19 acres, which adjoin the Bonnes Mares vineyard, produce an average of 2,500 cases a year of a wine that is richly textured, elegant, and long-lived.

Clos de Vougeot   A world-famous Burgundian vineyard whose 125 acres make it the largest of the Côte d'Or. It was first planted in the twelfth century by Cistercian monks on what had been, until then, wasteland, and the present vineyard was completed two centuries later. The average annual production of this *grand cru* vineyard is about 17,000 cases, but production has varied in recent vintages from 8,000 to 28,000 cases. There are about 65 owners of this vineyard, and consequently there are dozens of different wines marketed each year under the name Clos de Vougeot (or simply Clos Vougeot); the quality of these wines is bound to vary considerably. Traditionally, the finest wines come from the upper part of the vineyard, which is bounded by the *grand cru* vineyards of Musigny and Grands-Echézeaux, but almost the entire Clos is capable of producing red Burgundy of classic quality, distinguished perhaps more for its breed and bouquet than for its body and power. A limited amount of a pleasant red Burgundy is also produced around the village of Vougeot, and labelled as such, and about 600 cases a year of a distinctive white wine are made in a plot that adjoins Clos De Vougeot and sold as Clos Blanc de Vougeot. The picturesque and venerable Château de Vougeot – parts of which date from the late sixteenth century, and whose massive, ancient wooden wine presses are a popular tourist attraction – is now the property of the Burgundian wine fraternity, the Chevaliers du Tastevin. For map, *see* Vosne-Romaneé.

Cloudy A wine that is not clear or brilliant. No good, sound wine is ever cloudy, but the term should not be applied to a clear wine that has thrown a sediment in the bottle.

Cloying A wine-taster's term applied to a sweet wine that lacks the lively acidity necessary to make it balanced and attractive.

Coarse A wine lacking in finesse; common, heavy, with plenty of body and not much else. Many cheap wines, especially those from warm regions, are coarse.

Colares An interesting Portuguese red wine produced a dozen miles northwest of Lisbon along the dunes and sandy foothills of the Atlantic coast. It is made from the Ramisco grape planted in ditches or pits in the clay subsoil that underlies ten feet or more of sand; because the phylloxera louse cannot exist in sand, these are among the very few vines of Europe that were not affected by that epidemic. Tannic and well-structured, somewhat lacking in subtlety but improving with age, Colares has definite character, but so little is now produced that it must be ranked as a curiosity.

Cold Duck Theoretically a mixture of champagne and sparkling Burgundy, it is actually a pink sparkling wine that can be made by any method. The name is a translation of the German *Kalte Ente*, or "cold duck", which is a corruption of *Kalte Ende*, or "cold end", which refers to a mixture of the unused open wine at the termination of a banquet, saved for subsequent drinking. Pink sparkling wines produced in America and labelled Cold Duck were wildly successful in the late 1960s and served as an introduction to wine for many beginners; the name is infrequently encountered today.

Colheita Portuguese for "vintage" or "harvest"; its appearance on a table-wine label may indicate a superior bottling. On a port label, however, the term has the specific meaning that the wine is a port of the vintage; that is, a tawny from the vintage shown on the label that has been aged in wood for at least seven years, usually longer; such a wine is emphatically *not* a vintage port.

Collage *See* Fining

Colli Albani A DOC zone about 20 miles south of Rome, near Lake Albano, which produces pleasant dry white wines frm Malvasia and Trebbiano grapes; it is part of the Castelli Romani district.

Colli Berici A DOC zone south of Vicenza, in the central part of Italy's Veneto region, which produces a number of varietal wines. The native white Garganega is the most widely planted grape, followed by Merlot; others include Pinot Bianco, Cabernet, and the unusual red Tocai Rosso.

Colli Bolognesi A DOC zone in the foothills of the Apennines, southwest of Bologna, in Italy's Emilia-Romagna region. A number of different varieties are planted there, including such red grapes as Barbera, Cabernet Sauvignon, and Merlot, and such whites as Sauvignon, Riesling Italico, and Pinot Bianco; the wines may be labelled with the names of two subdivisions, Monte San Pietro and Castelli Medioevali.

Colli Euganei A DOC zone southwest of Padua, in the Euganean Hills of Italy's Veneto region, where Petrarch is said to have owned a vineyard in the fourteenth century; Merlot is by far the most widely planted grape here, although varietal wines are also made from Cabernet, Moscato, Pinot Bianco, and Tocai Italico.

Colli Lanuvini A DOC zone south of Rome and below Lake Albano that produces attractive white wines, from Malvasia and Trebbiano grapes, that are considered among the best from the Castelli Romani district.

Colli Orientali del Friuli A DOC zone – its name means the "eastern hills of Friuli" – situated in that region, in northeast Italy. A full range of varietal wines are produced there, of which Merlot and Tocai Friulano are the most important; the most unusual is Picolit, a sweet white dessert wine made, in very limited quantities, from partially shrivelled grapes.

Colli Piacentini A recently established DOC zone around Piacenza, in the western part of Italy's Emilia-Romagna region. Several different varieties are cultivated there, among them the red Barbera, Bonarda, and Pinot Nero, and the white Pinot Grigio, Sauvignon, and Ortrugo, the latter a local grape.

Collio A DOC zone, also known as Collio Goriziano, in the northeast corner of Italy, in the Friuli-Venezia Giulia region. With the exception of the white wine labelled simply Collio, made from Ribolla, Malvasia, and Tocai Friulano, all of the Collio wines are marketed with varietal names; the best known include Pinot Grigio, Pinot Bianco, Tocai Friulano, Merlot, and Cabernet Franc. In 1990, Chardonnay, Ribolla Gialla, Riesling Renano, and Cabernet Sauvignon were admitted to the DOC Collio. About 3,500 acres of vineyards produce 600,000 to 800,000 cases a year, 85 percent of it white. This impressive range of elegant, well-balanced varietal wines includes some of the very best white wines of Italy.

Collioure A village along France's Mediterranean coast, only a few miles from the Spanish border, which gives its name to a small AOC zone producing full-bodied red wines; part of the vineyards around Collioure are entitled to the appellation Banyuls.

Colombard A productive, good-quality white-wine grape that is the most widely planted wine grape in California, where it is known as French Colombard; acreage has tripled in a decade, and the 65,000 acres – almost all of which are in the Central Valley – account for half of California's white-wine crop. The wine, pale, fresh, and tart, is usually blended with Chenin Blanc to make California "Chablis" and the lesser grades of sparkling wine. Once extensively planted in the Cognac region of France, this variety has been almost entirely replaced there by Saint-Emilion (the local name for Ugni Blanc). It is still cultivated in Bordeaux, however, where, surprisingly enough, it is more widely planted than Sauvignon Blanc; most of the acreage is in Bourg and Blaye.

Colour A wine's appearance can quickly reveal much about its quality and evolution, especially if it is examined in a clear glass, tilted against a white cloth or background. A good wine should be clear and brilliant. The intensity of its colour will convey some idea of its character – a pale, watery white is likely to have less body than one that is medium-gold; a pale red wine will probably have less power than one that is deeply coloured. As they age, white wines get darker and acquire a trace of amber or brown; red wines lose their original purple or deep red colour and gradually become pale brick-red or reddish brown. These changes provide a useful guide to a wine's evolution, irrespective of the year on its label – a year-old white that is already browning, or a two-year-old red that is faded are showing premature signs of age, and each is likely to be disappointing; a brick-red colour in a ten-year-old Bordeaux or California Cabernet Sauvignon, however, would be appropriate.

Coltura Promiscua Italian for "promiscuous cultivation", this refers to the traditional method of growing grapes with other crops whereby vines are interplanted with potatoes, attached to trees, or strung over random pergolas. This old-fashioned system has been largely replaced by modern vineyards but still accounts for 20 percent of Italy's grape acreage.

Columbia Valley A viticultural area in south central Washington, east of the Cascade Mountains, which encompasses almost all of the state's vineyards; the Columbia River flows through this region, as do its two tributaries, the Yakima and Snake rivers. This extensive district, which is actually an irrigated desert with long sunny days and cool nights, has proven to be an excellent source of *vinifera* wine grapes. Two other viticultural areas, the Yakima Valley and the Walla Walla Valley, are situated in the Columbia Valley appellation, which extends south of the Columbia River into northern Oregon.

Comblanchien A tiny Burgundian village, at the southern end of the Côte de Nuits, more famous for its marble quarries – which supplied much of the stone for the Paris Opera and Orly airport – than for its red wines, which are marketed as Côte de Nuits-Villages.

Common   A wine-taster's term applied to a wine that may be sound and clean, but is nevertheless ordinary and without distinction; nothing that can be called fine.

Commune   A French word meaning a "township" – a small administrative unit consisting of a village and its surrounding land. Although often used interchangeably with village, as for Meursault, Pauillac, or Brouilly, *commune* is the more accurate term because it encompasses more of the adjoining land (including vineyards) than does the word *village*.

Concentrate   In its simplest form, this is grape juice that has been boiled down to a very sweet syrup; the more water is removed from the juice, the sweeter the concentrate. It can now be produced by sophisticated means that involve heating under vacuum at a temperature below boiling, and the resulting concentrate may contain 60 to 70 percent sugar. It can be added to fermenting must to increase the alcohol content of the resulting wine, and is thus an alternative to chaptalization (the addition of sugar) in such places as Italy and California, where chaptalization is prohibited. Because concentrate contains not only sugar, but also acids and other flavour elements present in the juice, it is considered less neutral than sugar as a means of increasing alcohol. Concentrate may also be used to sweeten a wine just before bottling.

Concord   A blue-black, slip-skin American grape of the *labrusca* species, by far the most widely planted of the native varieties and probably the second most extensively planted grape in the United States, after the Thompson Seedless of California. It takes its name from Concord, Massachusetts, where it appeared as a seedling in the garden of Ephraim Bull in 1843. It is doubtless a cross of two *labrusca* varieties, perhaps one of them Catawba; hardy and productive, a good table grape, and a wholly satisfactory variety for jelly and unfermented grape juice, it rapidly became both popular and famous. It still accounts for 60 percent of the vineyard acreage in New York, 90 percent in Michigan, and about two thirds of the vineyards of Washington. It has little to recommend it as a true wine grape, however; it can hardly be made into wine at all unless heavily sugared, and the wines are marked by a pungent, grapey aroma and taste. As it happens, most of the crop is marketed as table grapes or as grape juice; in New York, where about a quarter of the crop is made into wine, much of that is used for sweet kosher wines, wine coolers, and fortified wines.

Condrieu An interesting, unusual, and scarce white wine of the northern Rhône, produced on steeply terraced hillsides situated between Côte Rôtie and Château Grillet; the vineyard, planted entirely with the Viognier grape, produces between 4,000 and 10,000 cases a year, much of it consumed locally. Golden in colour, fruity, and intense, the wine is dry but rich, and its bouquet and taste often evoke peaches and apricots.

Conegliano A small city about 35 miles north of Venice, in the Veneto region, known for its important wine school and viticultural station, but even more for its white wines; these include the light, delicate Verdiso, and the sparkling wines made from the Prosecco grape and entitled to the appellation Prosecco di Conegliano-Valdobbiadene.

Cònero *See* Rosso Cònero

Conseillante, Château La One of the best vineyards of the Pomerol district, owned by the Nicolas family for over a century; its 30 acres of vines, which produce about 5,000 cases a year, are situated on the eastern edge of Pomerol, just across a narrow road from Saint-Emilion and Château Cheval Blanc. The vineyard contains only 50 percent Merlot, and a higher proportion of Cabernet Franc and Malbec than is usual in Pomerol, and consequently its excellent wines are perhaps less opulent than those of its neighbours, but display more finesse and structure.

Consorzio Italian for "consortium"; in practice, a voluntary growers' association, established within a specific wine-producing area, that sets minimum standards for the wines of its members, monitors quality, and promotes the wines. Many were created before the DOC laws, notably Chianti Classico, but continue to function with self-imposed regulations that may be even stricter than those imposed by DOC. Wines that have been approved by a particular *consorzio* are entitled to display a neck seal decorated with the association's emblem; the *gallo nero*, or "black rooster", of the Chianti Classico *consorzio* is the most famous.

Constance   One of the largest lakes of western Europe, bounded on the south by Switzerland, on the east by Austria, and on the north by Germany. The Rhine, rising in Switzerland, empties into and runs out of Lake Constance, just as does the Rhône into and out of Lake Geneva. Lake Constance is known in German as the Bodensee, and a few wines, almost all of them consumed locally are produced along its northern shore and known as Seeweine. Of these, the Ruländer, or Pinot Gris, is perhaps the best, but there is also an interesting oddity known as Weissherbst, a pale rosé made from Spätburgunder, or Pinot Noir.

Constantia   A legendary wine produced near Cape Town, South Africa, that achieved extraordinary fame in Europe during the nineteenth century and was reputed to be a favourite of Napoleon. It came from an estate called Groot Constantia, originally planted by the Dutch governor Simon van der Stel around 1700; Constantia, which was a sweet, fortified Muscat wine, was first produced in the late eighteenth century and was in vogue for about a century, until phylloxera destroyed the vineyard. The estate, purchased by the government in 1885, now produces a range of excellent red and white table wines.

Cooked   The flavour resulting from must or wine having been heated; more pronounced when heated in the presence of air, which also results in oxidation.

Cooking Wine   An inexcusable term, since it leads one to believe that something not good enough to drink could be good enough to eat. In practice, the two major elements that good and bad wines have in common – water and alcohol – are largely dissipated in cooking by evaporation (the alcohol, being more volatile, almost completely), and what remains is the flavour; quality is no less important in the saucepan than in the wine glass. It is not necessary to use the finest and most expensive wines for cooking, but certainly nothing less than a sound, well-made wine; whether the wine is rich and full-flavoured or lighter-bodied will depend on the dish being prepared. Note that leftover wine (if there is no sediment) can certainly be kept overnight and used for cooking the next day or even, if kept in the refrigerator, two or three days later. A wine so kept will lose its bouquet and may pick up a little volatile acidity, but this is no disadvantage in cooking since the bouquet is evanescent anyway, and volatile acidity, within reason, is an asset in the kitchen. A product called cooking wine can be found in supermarkets, especially in states that prohibit the sale of wine in food stores; it consists of inexpensive wine plus enough salt to make the wine unpalatable as a beverage.

Cooler *See* Wine Cooler, Ice Bucket

Coonawarra A district considered by many experts to be the finest red-wine area in Australia, situated about 270 miles southeast of Adelaide in the state of South Australia. About nine miles long and no more than a mile wide, Coonawarra (the name is derived from the aboriginal word for wild honeysuckle) is noted for its cool climate and unusual red soil, actually a layer of red loam on a bed of limestone. First planted in the 1890s, the district began to achieve its present reputation only in the late 1950s, first for Shiraz and, since the late 1960s, for Cabernet Sauvignon; vineyards have increased from about 400 acres in the mid-1960s to more than 6,000 today. Shiraz and Cabernet Sauvignon are the most widely planted red varieties, along with Merlot, Cabernet Franc and some Pinot Noir; the leading white varieties were Rhine Riesling and Sémillon, but Chardonnay (used primarily for sparkling wines) is now first. Wineries include Lindemans, Mildara, Rouge Homme, and Wynn's.

Cooperage A term applied to the totality of wooden casks, vats, or barrels (that is, those made by a cooper) used for storage in a given cellar or winery. Thus 100,000 gallons of cooperage means a storage capacity of 100,000 gallons, whether all the containers are actually in use or not; new cooperage refers to unused casks or barrels. Because so many of the world's wines are now stored in stainless-steel or glass-lined concrete tanks, the term *storage capacity* is often used instead of cooperage.

Co-operative A winery or cellar owned and operated jointly by a number of small producers; there are hundreds of such in Europe and a good many in California, some of quite modest size and others that rank among the largest wineries and cellars in the world. They have come into being primarily because the small grower, except in districts of famous and expensive wines, cannot afford alone the machinery and cellar equipment he needs to properly vinify his own wine. Furthermore, large co-operative cellars can afford to invest in the latest technology, especially important in making clean, sound white wines; indeed, co-operative cellars account for a significant proportion of the wines produced in the Alsace, Champagne, and Mâcon regions of France (where a co-operative cellar is called a *cave cooperative*), throughout Germany (*Winzergenossenschaft*), and in Italy (*cantina sociale*).

Corbières   A district of vineyard-covered, rolling hills, southeast of Carcassonne, in the Languedoc-Roussillon region of France, also known as the Midi. This is, in general, the home of *vin ordinaire*, but Corbières, while produced on a large scale – crops of 6 or 7 million cases are not uncommon – belongs in a somewhat higher category and, in fact, was raised from VDQS to *Appellation Contrôlée* status in 1986. A small amount of white wine, and some rosé, is produced, but it is the red, made primarily from Carignan, plus Cinsault, and Grenache, that is by all odds the best.

Corgoloin   The southernmost village of the Côte de Nuits, in Burgundy; its wines, of secondary quality, are used in such regional appellations as Côte de Nuits-Villages and Bourgogne.

Corkage   A fee paid to a restaurant for the privilege of having one's own wine, purchased elsewhere, served there with a meal or for a party. If not too high, this is a legitimate charge; if corkage is not charged, one has been done a favour, and that should be taken into account when tipping.

Corked   A corked wine is one that has the definite and disagreeable odour and flavour of a bad cork; the odour, reminiscent of damp cardboard, mould, or of wet earth, is due to an invisible flaw in what appears to be a perfect cork. Such bottles come along occasionally, even from the best of cellars, but fortunately they arrive much less frequently than many consumers imagine. A wine so affected is clearly unpleasant, and even casual wine drinkers are likely to recognize this defect.

The word *corky* is sometimes used to describe this flaw.

Corks Flexible, airtight, chemically inert, and stable at extremes of temperature, corks are considered indispensable and irreplaceable for wines capable of aging and improvement in bottle. A natural vegetable tissue, cork is made from the bark of *Quercus suber*, the cork oak, and its structure is such that a 1¾ inch cork contains 800 million cells; about three quarters of all the corks produced come from Portugal and Spain. A cork's length and its quality should be in relation to the expected life span of the wine it is supposed to protect, for longer corks last longer; thus a Beaujolais or Moselle may legitimately have a shorter cork than a great Bordeaux, Burgundy or Barolo. Even the best corks have a life span of about twenty-five years, although a fine cork may last fifty years or more under proper storage conditions. Bottles are stored on their sides so that the cork will remain wet and expanded, providing an airtight seal. A cork that is loose in its bottle indicates that the wine has been poorly stored; a cork that is dry and hard to pull usually means that the wine has been kept in too dry a cellar, but has nothing to do with its quality. That the top of a cork, beneath its capsule, should be moist or even black with mould means nothing at all. A defective cork may render a wine corky, but this is impossible to determine until the cork is pulled and the wine smelled or tasted.

Agglomerate, or composite, corks, made from cork granules bound with an adhesive, are widely used for inexpensive wines meant to be consumed young. Plastic corks are increasingly used for inexpensive sparkling wines, though rarely for table wines. Metal screw-top closures with an airtight and inert liner between the metal and the wine are also widely used today for inexpensive wines and for many ports and sherries. Most of the world's wine is made to be consumed soon after bottling, and providing its closure is sanitary, cheap, and gives no bad taste to the wine, there can be no objection to the use of materials other than cork; such containers are certainly better than the goatskins, leather flasks, re-used bottles, and other picturesque paraphernalia of the last century. Actually, some metal closures have proved to be more effective than cork, even for bottle-aged wines, but the association of cork with fine wine is such that it is unlikely that corks will be replaced in the near future.

Corkscrew A device for pulling corks; in its simplest, traditional form, a wire spiral attached to some sort of handle, but there are literally hundreds of diverse and ingenious modifications to this basic form, some admirably efficient, some wholly worthless. A wine drinker, in choosing a corkscrew, should keep in mind that the screw itself – the worm, or bore – is far more important than all the elaborately designed devices that are supposed to bring out the cork with a minimum of effort; all are pretentious and ridiculous unless the screw itself is properly designed. A good one is easy to recognize: it is not a gimlet, but an open spiral in which one can easily insert an old-fashioned kitchen match. The screw should be thin and tapered, with a sharp point that follows the spiral and is not centred; under no circumstances should a corkscrew have a sharp cutting edge on the outer side of its spiral. If it is to be used for fine wines, which contain especially long corks, it is essential that the screw be at least two inches long, preferably 2½ inches. Such a corkscrew, with a long, open spiral, will fully penetrate and grip a long, fragile cork, rather than simply boring a hole in it. This said, a wine lover may suit his or her fancy, but it is certainly a fact that a corkscrew with some sort of leverage or double screw arrangement is far preferable to a simple T-shaped device that requires the cork to be tugged out by force.

Another popular type of cork-puller consists of two thin, flexible, parallel blades attached to a handle and separated by about the diameter of a wine cork. Inserted into the neck of the bottle, between the cork and the glass, this device permits one, after a bit of twisting, to lift out the cork unpierced. Although some find this device difficult to use, others prefer it to the conventional corkscrew as being quicker and less likely to break the cork. In recent years, a new corkscrew has come on the market: called Screwpull, it has a plastic frame that fits over the neck of the bottle and a separate handle attached to a long, open spiral coated with an anti-friction substance for easy insertion into the cork; as the handle is twisted continuously in one direction, the cork climbs the bore without having to be pulled out.

Cornas A small district in the northern Rhône, opposite Valence, that produces about 20,000 cases a year of a sturdy, tannic wine that is capable of aging well; it is made from the Syrah grape, as is the better-known Hermitage, situated about a dozen miles south, on the opposite bank of the Rhône.

Corsé A French adjective meaning "full bodied", "robust", from the noun *corps*, which means "body".

Corsica A large Mediterranean island, one of the *départements* of France, which produces a great deal of sturdy, full-bodied red, white, and rosé, most of it *vin ordinaire* or *vin de pays*; about 800,000 cases a year are entitled to *Appellation Contrôlée* status, more than 90 percent of it red and rosé. The Patrimonio district, near the northern end of the island, was the first AOC of Corsica, and the Ajaccio district, along the west coast, is another, but most of the island's wines are marketed with the appellation Vin de Corse, sometimes combined with the name of a particular district, such as Calvi, Figari, or Sartène.

Cortaillod A village along Lake Neuchâtel, in Switzerland, that gives its name to an agreeable, fruity wine, pale red or rosé, made from Pinot Noir.

Cortese An Italian white-wine grape of superior quality grown mostly in southeastern Piedmont. Cortese yields a pale, fresh, light, eminently agreeable wine whose production now amounts to more than a million cases a year; most of this is sold simply as Cortese del Piemonte, but the better examples are sold under the DOC names Cortese dell'Alto Monferrato and Gavi. The word *cortese*, incidentally, means "courteous" in Italian, just as *soave* means "suave".

Corton Generally and rightly regarded as the greatest red wine of the Côte de Beaune, the southern half of Burgundy's Côte d'Or. Most of the sloping vineyards entitled to the *grand cru* appellation Corton – nearly 400 acres in all – are situated in the village of Aloxe-Corton, but parts of the appellation extend into the neighbouring communes of Ladoix-Serrigny and Pernand-Vergelesses. The hill of Corton produces about 30,000 cases of outstanding red wine a year, but not all of it is labelled simply Corton; many producers prefer to add the name of the specific plot from which the wine comes, as Corton-Bressandes, Corton-Clos du Roi, Corton-Maréchaudes, or Corton-Renardes. This may create confusion in the minds of consumers because some parts of the named plots are entitled to only *premier cru* status; thus Corton-Maréchaudes is part of the *grand cru* Corton (and can be labelled Corton or Corton-Maréchaudes), but a wine labelled Aloxe-Corton, Les Maréchaudes comes from the *premier cru* part of that plot. Only the *grand cru* wines have names beginning with Corton; as is the case throughout the Côte d'Or; if the name of a *premier cru* vineyard appears on the label, it must be preceded by that of the village in which it is situated, in this case Aloxe-Corton. (Château Corton-Grancey is a proprietary name used by the firm of Louis Latour for wines from its own vineyards within the Corton appellation.) A few hundred cases a year of white wine are produced within the appellation Corton, but the great white wines of this vineyard are marketed as Corton-Charlemagne.

Corton-Charlemagne A celebrated and outstanding white Burgundy produced on the hill of Corton, in the Côte de Beaune district of the Côte d'Or. There are 178 acres of vineyards entitled to the *grand cru* appellation Corton-Charlemagne, most of them situated within the village of Aloxe-Corton, but some in Ladoix-Serrigny and Pernand-Vergelesses; average annual production is about 13,000 cases. The wine comes from the upper part of the hill of Corton, where the chalky soil is suited to the Chardonnay grape, just as the red Corton comes from lower down the slope, where the richer soils are more appropriate for Pinot Noir. This distinctive, richly textured wine is comparatively long-lived and, in fact, needs a few years of bottle age to fully display its qualities.

Corvina Veronese An Italian red-wine grape widely planted in the Veneto region, where it is the principal variety in Valpolicella and Bardolino.

Cos d'Estournel, Château An outstanding vineyard of Saint-Estèphe, in the Médoc district, and one of the best of the Second Classed Growths; its 160 acres of vines produce about 25,000 cases a year sold as Cos d'Estournel, and the rest of the larger total crop is marketed under the second label Château de Marbuzet. The wine, which has been made under the direction of Bruno Prats since the early 1970s, is consistently excellent – concentrated, well-structured, elegant, and long-lived. In the early nineteenth century the property was owned by Louis Gaspard d'Estournel (*cos* is the Gascon word for "hill"), who constructed cellars decorated with turrets in the style of a Chinese pagoda; the massive wooden doors that once belonged to the Sultan of Zanzibar were installed in the 1970s.

Cos Labory, Château A Fifth Classed Growth of Saint-Estèphe, in the Médoc district; its 30-odd acres produce about 7,000 cases a year.

Cosecha Spanish for "vintage".

Costières de Nîmes Formerly called Costières du Gard, this extensive district, elevated from VDQS to *Appellation Contrôlée* in 1986, is situated about 20 miles southwest of Avignon, in the Aude *département*. About 2 million cases a year of agreeable red and rosé wines are produced, plus a small amount of white.

Cot *See* Malbec

Côte, La A large wine district in Switzerland, along the steep northern shore of Lake Geneva, between Geneva and Lausanne, in the canton of Vaud. The wines, all white and made from the Chasselas grape (known locally as Dorin), are light, fresh, and agreeable.

Côte de Beaune The southern half of the celebrated Burgundian Côte d'Or, the long, narrow strip of hillside vineyards that is responsible for almost all of the greatest Burgundies. Unlike the northern half, known as the Côte de Nuits, the Côte de Beaune produces white wines fully as famous as its reds. The latter come from such villages as Aloxe-Corton, Beaune, Pommard, and Volnay, as well as from the *grand cru* vineyard of Corton; for all their wonderful refinement, softness, and charm, the reds of the Côte de Beaune are less extraordinary than those of the Côte de Nuits, which are generally richer and longer-lived. The whites, however, are among the greatest in the world; they come primarily from the villages of Meursault, Puligny-Montrachet, and Chassagne-Montrachet (although the latter usually produces slightly more red wine than white), and from such *grand cru* vineyards as Montrachet, Bâtard-Montrachet, Chevalier-Montrachet, and Corton-Charlemagne.

    The specific appellation of Côte de Beaune, not often seen, includes the vineyards of Beaune (whose wines are invariably marketed with that more desirable appellation) plus 125 acres that produce a few thousand cases a year of red and white wines. A wine that carries the appellation Côte de Beaune preceded by that of a specific village, as Santenay-Côte de Beaune, must come from that village. The much more familiar appellation Côte de Beaune-Villages may be used for wines that come from one or more villages of the Côte de Beaune other than Beaune, Aloxe-Corton, Pommard, or Volnay.

Côte de Beaune-Villages An appellation widely used for certain red wines from the Côte de Beaune, the southern half of the famed Côte d'Or region of Burgundy. A wine so labelled may come from one or more of sixteen villages, excluding Beaune itself, as well as Aloxe-Corton, Volnay, Pommard, but including the less familiar Blagny, Cheilly-les-Maranges, Chorey-les-Beaune, and Ladoix, among others. The appellation thus permits Burgundy shippers to blend together wines primarily from lesser-known villages and market them with a more recognizable name. Although Côte de Beaune-Villages may be considered a regional appellation, the wines are, of course, made from Pinot Noir in the heart of Burgundy, and often provide good value.

Côte des Blancs One of the three principal districts within France's Champagne region, it is situated south of Epernay and includes such highly rated villages as Avize, Cramant, Le Mesnil-sur-Oger, Oger, and Vertus. The Côte des Blancs is planted almost entirely with Chardonnay – hence its name – and its wines are noted for their delicacy and finesse.

Côte de Brouilly An excellent district in France's Beaujolais region whose vineyards are situated on the slopes of Mont Brouilly, site of an annual pilgrimage to the chapel at the top of the hill, aptly named Notre Dame du Raisin. The wines, while typical of Beaujolais, have more character and concentration than those of Brouilly, whose vineyards are at the foot of the hill.

Côte Chalonnaise A vineyard district in Burgundy, south of the Côte d'Or, that begins just about where the Côte de Beaune ends; it takes its name from the industrial city Chalon-sur-Saône, east of the vineyards, but is sometimes referred to as the Région de Mercurey, after its most famous wine commune. As in the Côte d'Or, the reds are made from Pinot Noir, the whites from Chardonnay, and many are quite good Burgundies. The best-known appellations are Mercurey, Givry, Montagny, and Rully.

Côte de Nuits The northern half of Burgundy's Côte d'Or (whose southern half is the Côte de Beaune); arguably the greatest red wine district of France, perhaps of the world, its only rival in France being the Médoc district of Bordeaux. The area takes its name from Nuits-Saint-Georges, its principal town, and extends from Fixin on the north to Corgoloin on the south, a distance of only a dozen miles. It is here, along a narrow strip of hillside vineyards no more than a mile wide, that most of the red wines responsible for Burgundy's worldwide reputation are produced. The principal wine-producing villages include Gevrey-Chambertin, Morey-Saint-Denis, Chambolle-Musigny, and Vosne-Romanée, and such illustrious *grand cru* vineyards as Chambertin, Clos de la Roche, Musigny, Bonnes Mares, Clos de Vougeot, Grands Echézeaux, Romanée-Conti, La Tâche, and Richebourg. (A very limited amount of white wine is produced in Musigny, as well as in the villages of Vougeot, Nuits-Saint-Georges, and Morey-Saint-Denis.) The name Côte de Nuits does not appear on labels, but the regional appellation Côte de Nuits-Villages does.

Côte de Nuits-Villages   An appellation for red wines (and a very small amount of white) produced in any of five villages in the Côte de Nuits district of Burgundy's Côte d'Or. The villages are Brochon, Comblanchein, Corgoloin, part of Fixin, and a few acres in Prémeaux, most of whose wines are sold as Nuits-Saint-Georges.

Côte d'Or   French for "golden slope"; a *département* in the heart of the old province of Burgundy, southeast of Paris, that takes its name from a vineyard-covered hillside that produces some of the world's greatest red and white wines. With a handful of exceptions – Chablis, perhaps Pouilly-Fuissé, and a few outstanding Beaujolais *crus* – all of the wines that have made Burgundy's international and enduring fame come from this extraordinary Golden Slope, which extends south from near Dijon past Beaune to Santenay. The slope faces east or southeast over the wide, flat valley of the Saône River, and parallels for some 35 miles the main railway line and one of the main roads from Paris to Lyons, Marseilles, and the Riviera; the vineyards form a band, never more than a mile wide, along the hillside, between the rocky outcroppings and trees near the crest and the fertile farmland below. When both genuine and well made (and unfortunately, despite all the controls, there are some Burgundies that are neither), the

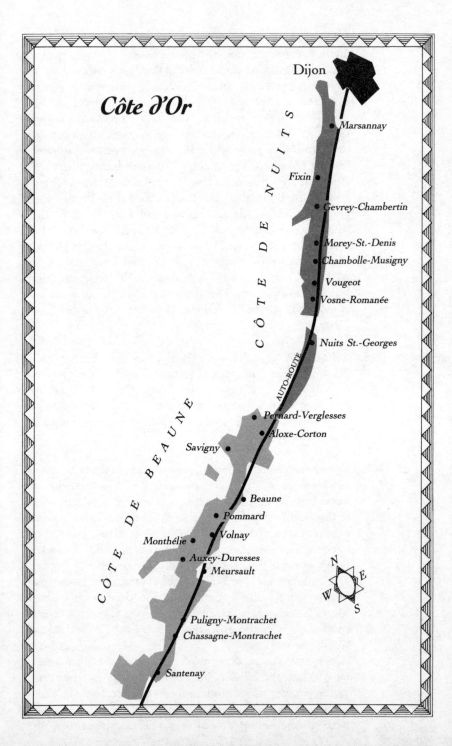

wines are remarkable; the reds, made from Pinot Noir, have warmth, fruit, and vigour, and combine power and finesse in a unique way; the whites, made from Chardonnay, display an impressive balance of fruit and depth of flavour, elegance and richness of texture.

The Côte d'Or, divided into the Côte de Nuits and the Côte de Beaune, produces about 2 million cases of wine a year, 80 percent of it red; this is only a tenth of the total production of Burgundy (which includes Beaujolais, Chablis, and Mâcon), and only half as much as the Médoc district of Bordeaux. This limited production, and the fact that good vintages occur less frequently in Burgundy than in Bordeaux, means that fine Burgundy will always be scarce and expensive. The basic appellation for the wines of this district is Bourgogne, but the fame of Burgundy derives from the wines that come from specific villages and vineyards, and so labelled. There are more than 20 wine-producing villages, or communes, along the Côte d'Or whose names may appear on labels, among them Gevrey-Chambertin, Chambolle-Musigny, Vosne-Romanée, Nuits-Saint-Georges (which gives its name to the Côte de Nuits), Aloxe-Corton, Pommard, Volnay, Beaune (the principal town of the Côte de Beaune), Meursault, Puligny-Montrachet, and Chassagne-Montrachet. There are also, along the Côte d'Or, about 30 vineyards defined as *grand crus* by the AOC laws, and their names may appear alone on a label, without that of the particular village within which each *grand cru* is situated; the best known of these include Chambertin, Clos de Tart, Bonnes Mares, Musigny, Clos de Vougeot, Romanée-Conti, La Tâche, Corton, Corton-Charlemagne, Montrachet, and Bâtard-Montrachet. The confusion that sometimes occurs between village and vineyard names is due to the fact that, over the years, a number of villages have added the name of their most famous vineyard to their own; thus, Gevrey became Gevrey-Chambertin, Chambolle became Chambolle-Musigny, and so on. Because *grand cru* wines are likely to be better, and certainly more expensive, than the nevertheless excellent village appellations, a Burgundy drinker will want to distinguish between the two. There are, in addition, several hundred *premier cru* vineyards whose names on a label must be preceded by that of their villages of origin; the vineyard name may be joined to that of the village, as Meursault-Perrières or Pommard-Epenots, or follow it, as Vosne-Romanée, Les Suchots or Beaune, Clos des Mouches. The appellations Côte de Nuits-Villages and Côte de Beaune-Villages, which encompass wines from lesser-known villages, are described elsewhere, as are Bourgogne-Hautes Côte de Nuits and Bourgogne-Hautes Côtes de Beaune, which refer to wines from the hills west of the Côte d'Or itself. (A complete list of Burgundy appellations will be found on page 524, and a listing of *grands crus* and the most important *premiers crus* of the Côte d'Or will be found on page 545.)

The number of villages and vineyards along the Côte d'Or makes it more difficult to buy, and to understand, fine Burgundy than fine Bordeaux, but there are two other factors that play a role as well – the multiple ownership of most Burgundy vineyards, and the distinction between estate-bottled wines and those bottled by *négociants*, or shippers. Whereas many top Bordeaux vineyards are 100 to 200 acres in size and have a single ownership (thus each produces relatively large quantities of a single wine), most of the *grands crus* and *premiers crus* of Burgundy are smaller than 30 acres and are in turn split up among a number of different owners, each of whom produces a somewhat different wine from his part of the vineyard. The most famous example is Clos de Vougeot, whose 125 acres are divided among more than 65 owners; the 26 acres of Musigny belong to more than a dozen growers, and the 20 acres of Montrachet have 17 owners. Consequently, the informed consumer of Burgundy must be familiar not only with the names of specific villages and vineyards, but with the reputation of individual producers as well.

In Bordeaux, virtually every fine wine is château-bottled, that is, bottled at the vineyard by the proprietor. In Burgundy's Côte d'Or, an increasing proportion of the crop is estate-bottled by growers in their own cellars, but even more is marketed by *négociants* who buy wine from a number of growers, then age and bottle it in their own cellars. (A number of leading *négociants* now buy grapes and vinify the wines themselves.) Some consumers prefer estate-bottled wines (which bear the phrase *mis en bouteille au domaine* or *mis en bouteille a la propriété*) as being more authentic and distinctive, others recognize that the leading Burgundy shippers bottle a wide range of excellent wines; furthermore, a number of *négociants* are themselves among the biggest vineyard owners in the Côte d'Or.

Côte Rôtie A celebrated red wine of the northern Rhône, produced near Vienne, some 20 miles south of Lyon. The vineyards, which overlook a great bend in the river and face southeast (the name means "roasted slope"), are incredibly steep, and consist really of a series of narrow terraces held up by retaining walls, and of necessity worked by hand. In the late 1970s the vineyard was extended from 250 acres to 300 by including the flat part on top of the hill, and production now amounts to 40,000 to 50,000 cases a year. There are 52 officially listed *quartiers*, or vineyard areas, but the two main divisions are the Côte Brune and the Côte Blonde, so named, according to legend, because long ago a noble lord of the district bequeathed one slope to his blond daughter, the other to her dark-haired sister. The truth is more prosaic – the two slopes acquired their names because of the colour of the soil, and while there may be subtle differences in the wines from each slope, most examples of Côte Rôtie are blends of the two *côtes*. The principal grape is Syrah, but the vineyard is interplanted with 5 percent or so of the white Viognier, and the two are harvested and vinified together; the Viognier contributes acidity and enhances the wine's bouquet. A fine Côte Rôtie of a great year is a truly admirable wine – spicy, deep-coloured, opulent, and long-lived; it has been famous since the days of Rome.

Coteaux d'Aix-en-Provence An appellation for red, white, and rosé wines produced around the fine old university city of Aix-en-Provence, 20 miles north of Marseilles, in southern France. About 95 percent of the million cases produced annually are red and rosé, made primarily from Grenache, Carignan, and Cinsault, although Syrah, Mourvèdre, and Cabernet Sauvignon are also planted. Among the best-known wines from this region – which was promoted from VDQS to *Appellation Contrôlée* at the end of 1985 – are Château Vignelaure, Château de Fonscolombe, Château de Beaulieu, and Commanderie de la Bargemonne.

Coteaux d'Ancenis A VDQS for wines, mostly light reds made from the Gamay grape, produced northeast of Nantes, along the Loire River.

Coteaux de l'Aubance The Aubance is a tributary of the Loire, in the French region of Anjou. The adjoining hillsides, entitled to the AOC Coteaux de L'Aubance, produce a limited amount of semidry white wines from the Chenin Blanc grape.

Coteaux des Baux An appellation in France's Provence region – elevated from VDQS to AOC in 1986 – for red and rosé wines (and a minuscule amount of white) produced round the village of Les Baux, about 20 miles south of Avignon; annual production is about 100,000 cases.

Coteaux Champenois A still wine from the Champagne region of France; such wines, usually white but occasionally red, are produced in limited quantities by a few champagne firms. Before 1974, such wines were known officially as Vin Nature de la Champagne and were often referred to inaccurately as Champagne Nature. Coteaux Champenois became more widely available in the late 1970s, but since then there have been several small crops and a steadily increasing demand for champagne; as a result, almost all of the region's production is transformed into sparkling wine, and very little is left to be bottled as a still wine.

Coteaux du Languedoc A relatively new appellation (established as a VDQS in 1980 and elevated to *Appellation Contrôlée* five years later) for wines produced on hillside vineyards in nearly 100 communes situated in the Languedoc region of southern France, also known as the Midi. The red wines and rosés, which account for virtually all of the 2 to 3 million cases produced annually, are made primarily from Carignan, Grenache, and Cinsault, and a number of them go to market with the name of the village of origin, such as Saint-Saturnin, Quatourze, La Clape, and Cabrières.

Coteaux du Layon The Layon is a small river that flows into the Loire, and the vineyards cultivated along its banks make up, in both quantity and quality, the most important wine-producing district in the region of Anjou. Red and white wines entitled to the appellation Anjou are produced there, as well as rosés marketed either as Rosé d'Anjou or Cabernet d'Anjou. Only a part of the total acreage, however, is entitled to the specific *Appellation Contrôlée* Coteaux du Layon, which applies only to white wines made from the Chenin Blanc grape. They range from fairly dry to very sweet, depending on the vineyard and the year; at their best they are rich, golden wines of excellent texture and breed. The two most famous vineyard areas, each with its own appellation, are

Bonnezeaux and Quarts de Chaume.

Coteaux du Loir A minor wine-producing district north of Tours, in France. Not to be confused with the Loire, of which it is a tributary, the Loir runs westward along the extreme northern limit of the cultivation of the vine; there are some 1,500 acres of vineyard, largely Pinot Noir and Chenin Blanc, which yield red and white wines of quite remarkable quality, although only in exceptionally good years. The most celebrated wine is that of Jasnières.

Coteaux de la Loire Literally, the Loire hillsides, and, in general, the wines produced along the Loire River, in France; legally and specifically, however, the name is associated with two AOC wines, one produced directly south of the city of Angers, capital of the old province of Anjou, the other farther west, round the town of Ancenis, near Nantes. Wines from the latter zone are made from the Melon, or Muscadet, grape and sold as Muscadet des Coteaux de la Loire. Wines from the former, produced in limited quantities from the Chenin Blanc grape, are labelled Anjou-Coteaux de la Loire; if harvested very late, they are rather sweet white wines of excellent quality. Savennières is the district's most important wine-producing village.

Coteaux du Lyonnais An AOC, promoted from VDQS in 1984, for wines produced round Lyons; almost all of the annual production of 100,000 cases consists of light reds made from the Gamay grape and similar in style to those from the nearby Beaujolais district.

Coteaux de Pierrevert A VDQS in France's Provence region for wines produced in a small zone situated in the hills behind the extensive Côtes de Provence district; red wines and rosés account for about 90 percent of the annual production of 120,000 cases.

Coteaux du Tricastin An extensive region in the south of France, situated east of the Rhône River and about 35 miles north of Avignon; the vineyards, which adjoin those entitled to the appellation Côtes-du-Rhône, are planted with similar varieties – primarily Grenache, plus Cinsault, Syrah, and Mourvèdre – and produce 700,000 to 1 million cases a year of agreeable red wine, as well as a minuscule amount of white. The region was granted VDQS status in 1964 and elevated to AOC in 1974.

Coteaux Varois A VDQS created in 1984 for light and agreeable red and rosé wines produced in the *département* of the Var, within the more extensive Côtes de Provence district.

Côtes d'Agly A district in France's Roussillon region, not far from the Spanish border, producing sweet, full-bodied fortified wines; as in nearby Rivesaltes and Banyuls, the principal varieties are Grenache, Muscat, and Malvoisie, and the wines, known as *vins doux naturels*, must contain a minimum of 15 percent alcohol.

Côtes d'Auvergne A VDQS established in 1977 for light reds and rosés made from Gamay grape in a district near Clermont-Ferrand, in central France.

Côtes de Blaye *See* Blaye

Côtes de Bordeaux A name given unofficially to two adjoining districts in the Bordeaux region, both on the rather steep right bank of the Garonne River, east and southeast of the city of Bordeaux; the northern and more important of the two has the appellation Premières Côtes de Bordeaux, the smaller southern area is correctly called Côtes de Bordeaux-Saint Macaire.

Côtes de Bourg *See* Bourg

Côtes de Brulhois A VDQS established in 1984 for red and rosé wines produced along both banks of the Garonne River, in a district that adjoins that of Buzet, in southwest France.

Côtes de Buzet *See* Buzet

Côtes de Castillon A secondary Bordeaux district situated east of Saint-Emilion, producing well over 1 million cases a year of simple red wines; previously marketed with the appellation Bordeaux (or more often Bordeaux Supérieur) Côtes de Castillon, now simply labelled Côtes de Castillon. It was at the battle of Castillon, in 1453, that the French army defeated the English and Gascon forces led by General Talbot, thus ending the 300-year English domination of Aquitaine, the region that includes all the vineyards of Bordeaux.

Côtes de Duras An AOC for dry red and both dry and semisweet white wines produced east of Bordeaux, in France's Lot-et-Garonne *département*.

Côtes du Forez A VDQS for red and rosé wines made from the Gamay grape near the headwaters of the Loire River, southwest of Lyons.

Côtes de Francs A small Bordeaux district northeast of Saint-Emilion producing about 100,000 cases a year of red wine, most of it sold simply as Bordeaux; there has recently been a revival of interest in this area, vineyards have been replanted, and some attractive château-bottled wines can occasionally be found.

Côtes du Frontonnais An AOC for red and rosé wines produced just north of Toulouse, in southwestern France; the principal grape is the indigenous Negrette.

Côtes du Jura Literally, the Jura hillsides; the regional AOC name under which most Jura wines – other than Château-Châlon, Arbois, and L'Etoile – are sold. The vineyards, due east of Burgundy's Côte d'Or, and not far from the Swiss frontier, are planted along the foothills and lower slopes of the Jura Mountains. The Côtes du Jura appellation consists primarily of white wines, but red, rosé, and some sparkling wines, too, are produced; very little is exported.

Côtes du Lubéron An appellation, elevated from VDQS to AOC in 1988, for red, rosé, and white wines produced in southern France, in a region southeast of Avignon and just south of the better-known Côtes du Ventoux district; the agreeable reds and rosés, which account for about 85 percent of the 1.2 million cases produced annually, are made from Grenache, Cinsault, and Carignan and resemble those of the Côtes-du-Rhône.

Côtes de Malepère A VDQS established in 1983 for red and rosé wines produced southwest of Carcassonne, in the Aude *département* of the Languedoc-Roussillon region.

Côtes du Marmandais A VDQS for red and some white wines, primarily of local interest, produced around the town of Marmande, on the Garonne River, in southwestern France. The reds are made from local varieties such as Grappu (also known as

Bouchales) and, increasingly, Cabernet Franc and Merlot; the whites, from Sémillon and Sauvignon Blanc.

Côtes de Provence An extensive region situated along the Mediterranean coast of France – from Marseilles east past Saint-Tropez and Saint-Raphael almost to Nice – best known for its fresh, agreeable, dry rosés, which have long been popular with visitors to the Riviera. The rosés, generally sold in amphora-like bottles, make up about 60 percent of an annual production of 7 to 8 million cases; the light, pleasant red wines account for about 30 percent of the total; the dry whites for less than 10 percent. The reds and rosés are made primarily from Carignan, Grenache, and Cinsault, although Syrah, Mourvèdre, and even Cabernet Sauvignon are also planted; Ugni Blanc and Clairette are the principal white-wine varieties. The wines, most of which come from the *département* of the Var, were promoted from VDQS to *Appellation Contrôlée* in 1977. Château de Selle, from the Domaines Ott, is probably the best-known wine of the region; other labels include Castel Rubine, L'Estandon, Pradel, and Château Minuty.

Côtes Roannaises A VDQS for light red and rosé wines made from the Gamay grape round the city of Roanne, northwest of Lyon.

Côtes de Saint-Mont A VDQS established in 1981 for wines, primarily sturdy reds made from the Tannat grape, produced in a district adjoining that of Madiran, in southwest France.

Côtes de Toul A VDQS for light reds made from Pinot Noir and pale rosés made from Gamay in the ancient French province of Lorraine; the village of Toul is situated about halfway between the Champagne and Alsace regions.

Côtes-du-Rhône The general name given to all the wines produced in the Rhône Valley between Vienne, south of Lyon, and Avignon, a distance of 120 miles; also a specific *Appellation Contrôlée* for wines produced in an extensive area north of Avignon. The best of the Rhône wines are marketed under specific vineyard, village, and district names, of course, which are, from north to south: Côte Rôtie and part of Condrieu in the *département* of the Rhône; Château-Grillet and the rest of Condrieu in the *département* of the Loire; Hermitage and Crozes-Hermitage in the Drôme; Cornas, Saint-Péray, and

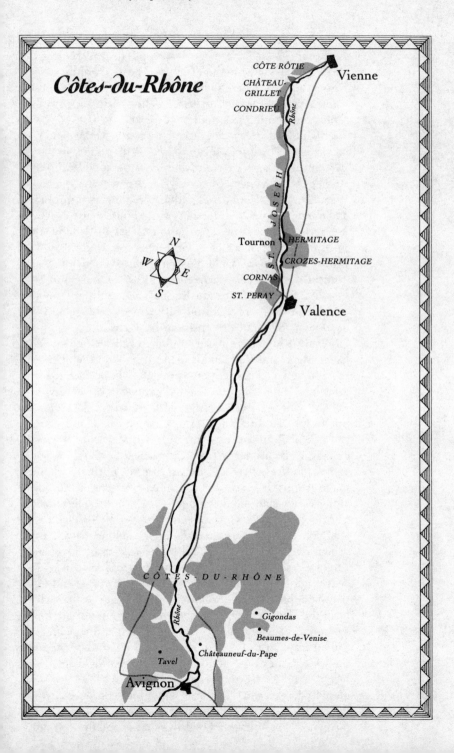

Côtes-du-Rhône

Saint-Joseph in the Ardèche; Tavel and Lirac in the Gard; Châteauneuf-du-Pape, Gigondas, Rasteau, and Muscat de Beaumes-de-Venise in the Vaucluse. The total production of Rhône wines now amounts to between 20 and 27 million cases a year, almost all of it red. The specific appellation Côtes-du-Rhône accounts for 80 percent of that, all of it from vineyards in the southern part of the Rhône, and the superior appellation Côtes-du-Rhône-Villages for another 5 percent; 17 villages are entitled to the latter appellation, and some of their names occasionally appear on labels, among them Cairanne, Chusclan, Laudun, Vacqueyras, Vinsobres, and Visan. About 20 different red and white grape varieties are authorized for the appellation Côtes-du-Rhône, the most important of which is Grenache, followed by Syrah, Mourvèdre, and Cinsault, plus such white varieties as Marsanne, Roussanne, Grenache Blanc, Clairette, and Bourboulenc. The basic red Côtes-du-Rhône is a pleasant, soft, moderately priced wine, sound but without any claim to greatness; the light, dry rosé can be agreeable; and white Côtes-du-Rhône, produced in limited quantities generally lacks finesse and fruit, and is the least good of the three.

Although the description Côtes-du-Rhône includes all the wines of the Rhône, a distinction must be made between the red wines produced in the southern part of the region – not only Côtes-du-Rhône and Côtes-du-Rhône-Villages, but also Châteauneuf-du-Pape and Gigondas (both of which are also made primarily from Grenache, plus Syrah, Mourvèdre, and Cinsault) – and the wines of the northern Rhône, made from the Syrah grape planted on terraced hillsides along either side of the Rhône – Côte Rôtie, Hermitage, Crozes-Hermitage, Cornas, and Saint-Joseph – which have a different style and are generally finer and longer-lived. Excellent dry rosés are produced in the villages of Tavel and Lirac, and although white wines account for less than 2 percent of all Rhône wines, they include such scarce and distinctive appellations as Condrieu and Château-Grillet, made from the Viognier grape; the full-bodied whites of Hermitage and Crozes-Hermitage, and the crisp sparkling wines of Saint-Péray, all made from Marsanne and Roussanne; and the white Côtes-du-Rhône and Châteauneuf-du-Pape.

Côtes du Roussillon Red, rosé, and (very little) white wines produced in the Pyrenées-Orientales; the better reds can be labelled Côtes du Roussillon-Villages. Total production of these wines, promoted from VDQS to *Appellation Contrôlée* in 1977, is about 3 million cases.

Côtes du Ventoux An extensive region in France's Vaucluse *département*, east of Avignon, which was granted AOC status in 1974; the vineyards are spread out to the west and south of the aptly named Mont Ventoux (which means "windy mountain") and are planted with the same varieties as in the nearby Côtes-du-Rhône – Grenache, Cinsault, Carignan, Mourvèdre, and Syrah. The region produces 2 to 2.5 million cases of wine, 99 percent of it red or *vin de café*, a dark rosé; the reds are generally somewhat lighter than those of the Côtes-du-Rhône.

Côtes du Vivarais A VDQS for wines produced in the Rhône Valley, in the *département* of the Ardèche; annual production is about 400,000 cases, 90 percent of it red and rosé.

Cotnari A sweet white wine produced in the northeast corner of Romania from grapes affected by *Botrytis cinerea*; this famous wine, once known as "the pearl of Moldavia", is made primarily from Fetească and Grasă grapes, thought to be, respectively, the Leányka and Furmint of Hungary.

Couderc A french hybridizer who created a number of crossings at the time of the phylloxera epidemic; the best-known of these varieties, now known as French-American hybrids, is Couderc Noir, still grown in the south of France.

Coufran, Château A *cru bourgeois* in the Haut-Médoc whose 160 acres produce about 32,000 cases a year; the vineyard is unusual among those of the Médoc in that it is planted 85 percent with Merlot, and the wine tends to be softer and more supple than those of its neighbours.

Couhins, Château A *grand cru classé* in the Graves district of Bordeaux, well known for its dry white wines; the main portion of the vineyard, planted with equal parts of Sémillon and Sauvignon Blanc, belongs to the French government and is used as a viticultural research centre. A part of the vineyard was acquired by André Lurton in the late 1970s, and this now consists of about 15 acres, planted only with Sauvignon Blanc, whose wines are marketed as Château Couhins-Lurton.

Coulant   French for "flowing", as of a stream of water; applied to wine, it means easy to drink, and is used to describe light, fresh wines that are low in tannin and alcohol.

Coulée de Serrant   A famous Loire vineyard in the Savennières district, in France's Anjou region. The 17 acres of Coulée de Serrant are planted with the Chenin Blanc grape and produce what some connoisseurs consider to be the finest dry white wine of the Loire. The property has been owned by the Joly family since 1962.

Coulure   The disastrous result of persistent rain or very cold weather during the flowering season of the vine – some blossoms are never properly pollinated, or the embryo grapes never develop and eventually drop off; this has no effect on the quality, but may reduce the crop by as much as half. A similar problem is called *millerandage*, or shot berries.

Coupé   French for "cut"; when applied to wine, it means blended or diluted. A *vin de coupage* is a "blending wine".

Courtier   French wine broker; *courtiers* are local expert intermediaries between the numerous small growers who sell their wine in barrel and the shippers, who assemble many small lots of wine to be aged and bottled in their own cellars. In Bordeaux, the sales of virtually all château-bottled wines, as well, are handled by *courtiers*, some of whose firms were founded in the eighteenth century.

Coutet, Château   A classed growth of the Sauternes district and one of the two finest vineyards in the commune of Barsac (Château Climens being the other); its 90-odd acres produce about 8,000 cases a year of classic Barsac – golden in colour, rich, but not cloyingly sweet, racy, elegant, and distinctive. The design of the Coutet label is almost identical to that of Château Filhot and dates to a time when both properties were owned by the Lur-Saluces family of Château d'Yquem. Part of the property lies within the Graves district, and a dry wine with that appellation is marketed as Vin Sec du Château Coutet.

Couvent des Jacobins   A *grand cru classé* of Saint-Emilion situated on the gravelly part of the district that adjoins Pomerol; its 23 acres produce about 4,000 cases a year of sound red wine.

Crackling   A term meaning slightly sparkling, whether natural, induced, or pumped in, and similar to the French *pétillant* and the Italian *frizzante*. If pressure does not exceed 1 atmosphere (15 lb per square inch, compared to 6 atmospheres for champagne) and the wine is not packaged as a sparkling wine, the lower, table-wine taxes apply. A number of moderately priced red, white, and rosé wines are bottled with just a little carbon-dioxide gas to give them a refreshing quality; the best-known examples are Italian Lambrusco and certain Portuguese rosés.

Cradle   A wire, wicker, or straw basket made to hold a mature bottle of red wine in nearly the same horizontal position it occupied in the cellar, thus permitting it to be brought from storage to a place where the wine will be opened and decanted without disturbing the sediment. Using a cradle to serve a wine that has no sediment at all is unnecessary; putting a wine with sediment into a cradle *after* it has been brought from its resting place and the sediment shaken up, as is sometimes done in restaurants, is pointless.

Cramant   An important wine-producing village in France's Champagne region, situated south of Epernay, in the Côte des Blancs. Its vineyards, all planted with the Chardonnay grape, are rated 100 percent, and the wines are noted for their delicacy, bouquet, and breed. The wines of Cramant are among the rare champagnes that are sometimes sold unblended under the village name.

Cream Sherry   A generic name for a smooth sweet sherry; most contain about 19 percent alcohol and between 12 and 14 percent sugar.

Crémant   A French term, which literally means "creaming", applied to wines that are mildly sparkling – between *pétillant* and *mousseux* – with about 3.5 to 4 atmospheres of pressure, compared to 6 for champagne. (It should not be confused with Cramant, which is a village in the Champagne region and, in fact, a Crémant de Cramant exists). Crémant has also been incorporated into three AOCs established in the mid-1970s for French sparkling wines made by the *méthode champenoise* – Crémant d'Alsace, Crémant de Bourgogne, and Crémant de Loire – whose production is more carefully controlled as to grape varieties, production per acre, and minimum bottle aging than other *mousseux.*

Crémant d'Alsace Increasingly popular dry sparkling wines made by the traditional *méthode champenoise* from wines – primarily Pinot Blanc and Sylvaner – that qualify for AOC; the wines must be aged in the bottle for a minimum of nine months.

Crémant de Bourgogne A dry sparkling wine produced by the *méthode champenoise* in France's Burgundy region; several grape varieties are permitted, but the base wine must contain at least 30 percent Chardonnay, Pinot Blanc, Pinot Noir, and/or Pinot Gris, and the wine must be aged in bottle a minimum of nine months.

Crémant de Loire A dry sparkling wine produced by the *méthode champenoise* in the Anjou, Saumur, and Touraine districts of France's Loire region. Chenin Blanc is the principal grape variety, but others may also be used, including Chardonnay and Cabernet Franc; the wine must be aged in bottle a minimum of twelve months.

Crépy A pleasant, dry white wine produced in the Savoie region of eastern France, not far from the southern shore of Lake Geneva. It is made from the Chasselas grape, known as Fendant in Switzerland, and much resembles that country's light white wines; annual production is about 40,000 cases.

Criadera Literally, in Spanish, a "nursery"; as applied to wine, its use is confined to the sherry district, where wines are aged and blended in *soleras*. The *criadera*, in Jerez, is the section in which young wines are cared for and evaluated before being assigned to a specific *solera*; the term may also be used, quite correctly, to describe all the stages, or scales, of a *solera* except the final one.

Crianza A Spanish term that refers to aging in oak casks. A wine labelled *con crianza* or *vino de crianza* has been aged in wood a minimum of a year; one labelled *sin crianza* has been bottled without wood aging.

Criots-Bâtard-Montrachet A *grand cru* vineyard in Burgundy's Côte d'Or, situated in the village of Chassagne-Montrachet. The 3.9-acre vineyard, which produces about 600 cases a year of superlative white wine, consists of a small prolongation, to the south, of the Bâtard-Montrachet vineyard. The wines from these two adjoining vineyards are both of very high quality and can hardly be told apart, even by an expert.

Crisp A wine-taster's term applied to a white wine with lively, refreshing acidity.

Croix de Gay, Château La A vineyard in the Pomerol district whose 30 acres produce about 6,000 cases a year; the wine from a 2.5-acre plot within this vineyard is marketed as Château La Fleur de Gay.

Croizet-Bages, Château A Fifth Classed Growth of Pauillac, in the Médoc district, producing about 10,000 cases a year; it is under the same ownership as Château Rauzan-Gassies.

Cross A term that refers to cross-pollination within the same species, as *vinifera* × *vinifera*; also known as crossing and *métis*. Müller-Thurgau is perhaps the best-known cross, and many of the varieties developed in this century, such as Ruby Cabernet and Carnelian in California, and Bacchus, Optima, and Ortega in Germany are, technically speaking, crosses, although commonly referred to as hybrids. *See* Hybrid.

Crouchen An obscure grape variety from southwest France capable of producing agreeable white wine; of interest because it is the grape that was until recently known as Clare Riesling in Australia and Paarl or Cape Riesling in South Africa.

Crozes-Hermitage An appellation of the northern Rhône established in 1952 to designate the red and white wines produced in eleven townships north, east, and south of the one extraordinary hillside that alone yields Hermitage. Until then, many of the better red wines of this district had been sold as Crozes and some excellent whites as Mercurol, village names both, and both now part of the Crozes-Hermitage appellation. The reds are made exclusively from the Syrah grape and the whites primarily from Marsanne, with some Roussanne; total production usually varies from 400,000 to 500,000 cases, of which the white accounts for about 10 percent. The wines are not unlike those of Hermitage, but on a smaller scale, without their richness, concentration, and longevity.

Cru A French word meaning "growth"; when applied to wine, it refers to a specific vineyard and, by implication, one of superior quality, as in the *grand crus* and *premiers crus* of Burgundy, the *grand crus* of Alsace, and the *crus classés* of Bordeaux. Notable exceptions to the rule that *cru* means vineyard occur in the Beaujolais region, where the ten top communes are referred to as *crus*, and in the Champagne region, where individual villages are ranked as *grand crus* and *premiers crus*.

Cru Bourgeois A term that specifically refers to châteaux, or vineyards, in the Médoc district of Bordeaux that rank just below the *crus classés*, or classed growths. The Bordeaux Chamber of Commerce drew up a list of *cru bourgeois* in 1932, and the list was revised in 1966 and again in 1978 by the Syndicat des Crus Bourgeois, and limited to its members. There are about 240 *crus bourgeois* altogether, and they account for 40 percent of the total production of the Médoc; the *cru bourgeois* association, established in 1962, includes about 150 châteaux, each with a minimum of 7.5 hectares of vineyards (about 18 acres). Most *crus bourgeois* are entitled only to the appellation Médoc or Haut-Médoc, a few to the more specific appellations Saint-Estèphe, Margaux, Listrac, Moulis, etc. A number of these properties produce wines considered on a par with some of the *crus classés*, and most of them provide good examples of Médoc at moderate prices. The category *cru bourgeois exceptionnel* includes only those châteaux situated in that part of the Haut-Médoc from which the *crus classés* of the 1855 classification were drawn; there were eighteen such châteaux in the 1978 revision, and although Common Market regulations do not permit the word *exceptionnel* to appear on labels, the term is used in this volume where appropriate. A partial list of *crus bourgeois* will be found on page 539, and their labels are worth looking for. Some of the better-known *crus bourgeois* include Châteaux Chasse-Spleen, Citran, Coufran, Fourcas-Dupré, Fourcas-Hosten, Loudenne, Marbuzet, Meyney, Patache d'Aux, Phélan-Ségur, Potensac, and La Tour de By. Note, however, that several excellent Médoc châteaux have chosen not to join the association of *crus bourgeois*, among them Châteaux d'Angludet, Gloria, Lanessan, de Pez, Siran, and La Tour De Mons.

Cru Classé French for "classed growth"; that is, a vineyard, almost invariably in the Bordeaux region, that has been classified, either in the famous Classification of 1855 (which focused on the wines of the Médoc and Sauternes), or in subsequent classifications of Graves and Saint-Emilion. All such wines are referred to as *crus classés*, or "classed growths", but there are notable differences in the way each classification has been established. In the 1855 classification of the Médoc, the 60 wines are ranked from *premier cru*, or "first growth", to *cinquième cru*, or "fifth growth". There are now five first growths entitled to put the phrase *premier grand cru classé* on their labels – Châteaux Lafite, Latour, Margaux, Mouton-Rothschild (elevated from second to first in 1973), and Haut-Brion (the only Graves included) – although neither Lafite nor Mouton does so; almost all the other *crus classés* of the Médoc are labelled Grand Cru Classé. The Sauternes classification is divided into *premiers crus* and *deuxièmes crus*, with Château d'Yquem in a class of its own; whereas the Yquem label makes no reference to its rank, all the châteaux in the first group are labelled 1er Grand Cru Classé, the others simply Grand Cru Classé. There is no ranking in the Graves classification of 1953, simply an alphabetical list of *crus classés* that includes the leading châteaux, almost all of whom label their wines Grand Cru Classé. The 1953 classification of Saint-Emilion (revised in 1969 and 1985) is more generous and more confusing; eleven châteaux are now ranked as *premiers grands crus classés*, and although most experts agree that only Châteaux Ausone and Cheval Blanc are really entitled to *premier cru* status by Médoc standards, all of those châteaux label themselves 1er Grand Cru Classé. Another 60-odd châteaux are classified as *grands crus classés*, and so labelled, although only some of them produce wines equivalent in quality to the *grands crus classés* of the Médoc. The wines of Pomerol have never been classified. *See* First Growth.

Crush   As used in California (and a few other areas), this word is synonymous with harvest or vintage; because much of California's vineyards are planted with table and raisin grapes, only a part of the grape harvest is actually crushed to produce wine, hence the term.

Crusted Port   A term applied to a style of port that is a blend of two or three vintages aged in wood for about four years; it is, in effect, a kind of ruby port that will improve in bottle, and which throws a deposit, or crust, as it ages, hence its name.

This style of port has been almost entirely superseded in the marketplace by Late Bottled Vintage ports, which do not throw a deposit.

Cultivar   A cultivated variety; a vine selected for planting from thousands of wild varieties and hybrids. In some countries the word *cultivar* is used in preference to the term *grape variety*.

Cuvaison   The practice, essential in the making of red wine, of allowing the juice and skins to ferment together; this enables the fermenting must to extract colour, tannin, and aroma from the skins. *Cuvage*, also known as maceration, is the length of time this process lasts, a matter of hours in the case of rosés, about four or five days for light-bodied reds such as Beaujolais, two weeks or more for such sturdy, long-lived reds as fine Bordeaux, California Cabernet Sauvignon, and Barolo.

Cuve Close   *See* Charmat Process

Cuvée   From the French *cuve*, a "vat" or "tank", especially a large one in which wines are fermented or blended; therefore, a specific lot, or blend, of a given wine. The term is often loosely used on labels to denote a special blend, as Cuvée Réservée; the phrase Tête de Cuvée was once used in Burgundy to indicate the best lot of a given vintage. The term is most often associated with the wines of the Champagne region, where, in the months following the vintage, each firm makes up one or more *cuvées*, or "blends", that conform to its traditional house style, from all the wines in its inventory; each *cuvée* is then bottled and transformed into sparkling wine. *Vin de Cuvée* also has a specific meaning in the Champagne region – it refers to the first 2,050 litres of wine extracted from the press, often called the first pressing (although it actually takes several pressings to obtain that quantity of juice). The term *cuvée spéciale* refers to the deluxe champagnes marketed by many firms, usually in specially designed bottles. *See* page 550.

Cyprus   This Mediterranean island has more than 80,000 acres of vineyards, almost entirely planted with native varieties. The Mavron grape, which produces full-bodied reds, accounts for more than 80 percent of the acreage, and most of the rest is planted with Xynisteri, which makes neutral white wines; a small amount of Muscat of Alexandria is also grown. Long known for its sherry-style wines, Cyprus also produces a range of red, white and rosé table wines. The island's most famous wine is Commandaria, a sweet red or amber-coloured wine that has been admired since the twelfth century; it is traditionally made from dried, raisined grapes, and while most available examples are simply sweet, the best bottlings are rich, intense, and concentrated.

Czechoslovakia Perhaps better known for its beer than for its wine, this country has about 100,000 acres of vineyards producing 15 million cases a year. Two thirds of the acreage is in the province of Slovakia, and most of the rest in Moravia, near the city of Brno. With Germany, Austria and Hungary as its neighbours, it comes as no surprise that most of Czechoslovakia's production consists of light white wines, almost all of it consumed locally.

❧ D

Dame Jeanne The French term from which the English *demijohn* is derived; literally "Lady Joan", it means about the same thing as in English, an oversize bottle of no fixed capacity that may be covered with straw or wicker, or set in a wooden frame.

Dão A hilly district in north-central Portugal, south of the Douro River, which fans out from the city of Viseu; the vineyards produce 5 to 6 million cases of red and white wine a year, but only 15 percent or so are entitled to the appellation Dão. The reds, deep-coloured and rather full-bodied, must be aged for at least eighteen months in wood; the dry whites are less frequently seen.

Dassault, Château One of the biggest and best known of the *grands crus classés* of Saint-Emilion, whose nearly 60 acres of vineyards produce about 10,000 cases a year.

Dauzac, Château A Fifth Classed Growth of Margaux, in the Médoc district; under new ownership since 1978, the property has been restored and the vineyards expanded to 125 acres producing about 22,000 cases a year.

Débourbage A practice, highly beneficial in the making of white wine, of delaying the fermentation of the freshly pressed juice for twelve to twenty-four hours, until various impurities such as pulp, bits of grape skin, stems and seeds (called *bourbe* in French) can fall to the bottom of the tank, thus ridding the juice of its coarse sediment; this is also known as settling. To accomplish this worthy end, fermentation must be inhibited, usually by keeping the juice at a very low temperature. Many modern wineries now accomplish this clarification more quickly by centrifuging the juice or by light filtration.

Debröi Hárslevelü One of Hungary's best-known wines, this semisweet white is produced in the Debrö district, in the northeast part of the country, from the indigenous Hárslevelü grape, whose name means "lime-leaf".

Decant To transfer a wine – almost always an older red – from its original bottle to another vessel – carafe, bottle, or decanter. The purpose of decanting is to separate the clear wine from any sediment that may have formed in the bottle so that the unattractive and bitter-tasting sediment will not spoil the appearance and taste of the wine in the glass. Wines may be decanted in the cellar by placing the bottle as gently as possible in a cradle, or basket, without disturbing the sediment; those without cellars or cradles may simply stand up the bottle (which has presumably been stored on its side) for 30 minutes or an hour, to let the sediment slide to the bottom, and then proceed with decanting. This consists of pouring the wine out slowly, in one continuous motion, into another container against a candle, upright flashlight, or other source of light, until the first signs of sediment appear in the shoulder of the bottle. Some wine drinkers also decant young, tannic red wines and some whites to let them breathe, or aerate. *See* Breathing.

Decanter A glass carafe into which old wines are decanted, and in which young, inexpensive wines are sometimes served. Also, the rather more elaborate containers, usually of cut crystal, in which sherry, port, amd Madeira are sometimes kept on the sideboard.

DeChaunac A widely planted red hybrid grape in the eastern United States; most of the acreage of this variety, known officially as Seibel 9549, is in the Finger Lakes district of New York, and much of the crop is now used to produce neutral wines for sherry and wine coolers. About 2,000 acres are planted in Canada, in the province of Ontario; the French chemist Adhemar de Chaunac introduced this grape to Ontario in the 1950s with such success that it was subsequently renamed in his honour.

Dégorgement *See* Disgorging

Degree-Days
A technique, also known as the heat summation method, created in the 1930s at the University of California at Davis to classify California vineyards based on the average daily temperature during the growing season. The grape does not mature when the air temperature is below 50 degrees F., so by determining the average number of degrees above this base for every day of the growing season (the 200-plus days from April to October), one can evaluate the suitability of a given region for grape growing. Thus, if the average temperature for a given day is 60 degrees F., that would yield 10 degree-days (60 degrees less 50 degrees), also known as heat summation units; the total of units or degree-days for the growing season yields the appropriate figure for that region. California was divided into five theoretical climatic regions: Region I, the coolest, includes any areas with fewer than 2,500 degree-days, Region II includes any areas with 2,501 to 3,000 degree-days, and so on to Region V, with over 4,000 degree-days. This method proved useful in determining which new areas were suitable for vineyards, and the specific varieties to be planted in both new and existing areas; early ripening varieties, for example, would be suitable for cool regions with short growing seasons. Despite its past influence, however, the degree-days technique has certain limitations, and its use is declining. Average temperature is not the same as maximum and minimum temperatures, which affect the rate of growth; no reference is made to the amount of sunlight per day, which affects photosynthesis; there is no consideration of night temperatures, which, if cool, help grapes retain their acidity; and, of course, such factors as wind, rain, and humidity are not included in the calculations.

Deidesheim
A famous and picturesque little town in Germany's Rheinpfalz, or Palatinate region; with the adjoining villages of Forst, Ruppertsberg, and Wachenheim, it produces the best of the Palatinate's white wines. The village is quaint and

charming, with fine old patrician houses in red sandstone, a venerable Rathaus, or town hall, and dozens of winding narrow streets and walled gardens green in summer with apricot and fig trees. There are nearly a thousand hillside acres under vines, more than half of them planted with Riesling; the leading vineyard sites are Hohenmorgen, Grainhubel, Kieselberg, Leinhöhle, Paradiesgarten, Nonnenstück, Herrgottsacker, Maushöhle, and Langenmorgen. Curiously, with the exception of Nonnenstück, all these sites are within the Grosslage Forster Mariengarten, and often marketed as such. The much larger Grosslage Deidesheimer Hofstück, however, encompasses nine villages and 3,000 acres, and only the Nonnenstück site is from Deidesheim itself. The best wines of Deidesheim are full-bodied, with great bouquet, and range all the way from dry to very sweet; they have remarkable distinction, especially the Rieslings, and fully deserve their reputation.

Deinhard *See* Wegeler-Deinhard

Delaware One of the best native American varieties, unusual in that it yields excellent table grapes that are also very good for wine; its precise ancestry and origin are unknown. It was first noted in 1850 in a vineyard at Frenchtown, New Jersey, whence it was transplanted to Delaware, Ohio, and it therefore takes its name from this town, rather than from the river or the state. A pink grape, it yields a fresh, pale white wine, well-balanced but rather high in acid, with the definite but not too oppressive native-grape aroma and flavour of its *labrusca* ancestors. It was once widely used in Eastern sparkling wines and can also produce appealing white table wines in New York, where there are more than 1,000 acres of this variety.

Delicate A wine-taster's term applicable to wines that are light, rather than full or big; subtle, rather than coarse or sturdy; fine and elegant, rather than great.

Demi, Demie These, in French, are the masculine and feminine forms of the same words, and both mean "half".

Demijohn A large, squat, round bottle or jug, often wicker-covered, holding anywhere from one to ten gallons; in French it is called a *bonbonne* or *Dame Jeanne*.

Demi-Sec French for "half-dry", but when applied to champagne or other sparkling wines it indicates a relatively sweet wine. Now that it is no longer fashionable to label champagnes, even the sweetest of them, *doux*, the *demi-sec* wines are about the sweetest on the market, and contain 3.5 to 5 per-cent of sugar, the result of the *dosage* or *liqueur d'expédition* that is added to each bottle just before the shipping cork is inserted. The term is rarely used for still wines and has no precise meaning in this connection, although it suggests a wine that is slightly sweet.

Denominación de Origen Spanish for "appellation of origin", often abbre-viated as DO. The first such laws were established for Rioja in 1926, Jerez in 1933, and Málaga in 1937. More recently, two dozen appellations were defined in the mid-1970s, and several more since then. Similar to the *Appellation Contrôlée* laws of France and the *Denominazione di Origine Con-trollata* laws of Italy, the Spanish DO laws define the geo-graphical boundaries of each district, permitted grape vari-eties, minimum alcohol content, maximum yield, minimum aging requirements in wood and in bottle, and other factors that affect quality. One aspect of these laws that may be con-fusing is that the names of some of the new demarcated *denominación* zones are often the same as that of the overall area; that is, the DO Mancha is a limited zone within the ex-tensive area known as La Mancha, the DO Valdepeñas in-cludes only a part of the region commonly known as Valde-peñas, and so on. Another element that may confuse those unfamiliar with Spanish wines is that, as in Italy, a specific DO may apply to table wines, *vinos generosos*, with 14 per-cent or more alcohol, or even fortified wines. *Denominación de Origen* wines described elsewhere include Alella, Ali-cante, Cariñena, Cava, La Mancha, Ribera del Duero, Málaga, Manzanilla, Montilla, Navarra, Penedès, Priorato, Ribeiro, Ribera del Duero, Rioja, Rueda, Tarragona, and Valdepeñas; the *denominación* Jerez-Xérès-Sherry is, of course, listed under Sherry. A complete list of DO wines will be found on page 563.

Denominazione di Origine Controllata The Italian wine laws, usually abbreviated as DOC (and pronounced by the Italians as "dock"). Modelled to some extent on the *Appellation Con-trôlée* laws of France, DOC was established in 1963 and went into effect in 1967, when 14 DOC wines accounted for about

12 million cases of wine. Today, more than 210 DOC zones have been established, and they produce 75 to 110 million cases annually, or 10 to 12 percent of Italy's total crop. The DOC laws specify the geographical limits to each zone, the grape varieties that may be used, minimum alcohol levels (to assure sufficiently ripe grapes), the maximum yield per acre, and other factors that affect quality. The DOC laws differ from the AOC laws of France in two important respects: to qualify for DOC, many Italian wines must be aged in wooden casks for a minimum amount of time (which may be as much as four years for certain reds), whereas there are virtually no such aging requirements for French wines, not even for the finest Bordeaux; the other difference is that the DOC laws make no reference to specific vineyards, as do the French (and German) laws. A DOC wine may be labelled with the name of the place from which it comes or the grape variety from which it is made, but even varietal wines must be anchored to a specific production zone, as Nebbiolo d'Alba, Cabernet del Piave, or Barbera dell'Oltrepò Pavese. Actually, because some DOC names apply to both red and white wines, and because a number of DOC zones produce a dozen or more varietal wines, the total number of DOC wines probably exceeds 600. (The more recent, and stricter, category *Denominazione di Origine Controllata e Garantita* is described in the following entry.)

Although the DOC laws defined and enforced minumum standards and established more coherent labelling, they have been criticized by some innovative producers as too confining. In effect, the laws codified the situation that existed within each zone in the late 1960s and early 1970s, especially in terms of permitted grape varieties and minimum wood aging. Since then, many producers have planted nonauthorized varieties, especially Cabernet Sauvignon and Chardonnay, and prefer to age their wines in wood for less than the established minimums. Rather than restrict themselves to the existing laws, these producers have created wines that are marketed with proprietary names; although some of them are considered among the best in Italy, they must be labelled *vino da tavola*, or "table wine", since they are not eligible for DOC. *See* Classico, Riserva, Superiore.

Denominazione di Origine Controllata e Garantita An Italian wine law, usually abbreviated to DOCG, which is stricter than DOC. Wines that have been elevated from DOC to DOCG include

Brunello di Montalcino, Barolo, Barbaresco, Vino Nobile di Montepulciano, Chianti, and Albana di Romagna. The first DOCG bottlings appeared on the market in the mid-1980s. The "guaranteed" aspect of this law indicates that the wines have been tasted by an official panel and that each approved bottle must display a government-issued strip, pasted over the cork, to guarantee authenticity. Although DOCG wines are more carefully controlled than DOC, the new laws are more flexible in certain respects. For example, the minimum wood-aging requirement for Brunello di Montalcino was reduced from four years to three and a half, and the relative percentages of grape varieties permitted for Chianti were drastically altered.

Département An administrative unit in France, more or less the equivalent of an American county; there are 95 of them. The term is often used in this volume to give the location of certain villages and vineyards.

Deposée French for "registered"; *marque deposée* means "registered trademark".

Deposit The sediment that many red wines and some whites tend to throw in the course of their normal evolution in the bottle. *See* Sediment.

Desmirail, Château A Third Classed Growth of Margaux, in the Médoc district, this vineyard disappeared in the late 1930s, when it was split up and sold; a part was purchased by Château Palmer, which occasionally used the name as a second label for its own wines. The vineyard was reconstituted by Lucien Lurton, owner of Châteaux Brane-Cantenac and Durfort-Vivens, who eventually re-purchased the last parcel of vines, and the name, from Palmer, and produced his first vintage of Château Desmirail in 1981; the replanted vineyard has a potential production of about 8,000 cases.

Dessert Wine A somewhat confusing term, since it is used in different senses. In the more common usage, the term refers to sweet wines that are properly served with dessert, or after a meal; these include Sauternes, Beerenauslesen and Trockenbeerenauslesen from the Rhine and their California equivalents, late-harvest Rieslings, Vins Doux Naturels, as well as ports and cream sherries.

Destemming   A process, essential in the making of all good wine, of removing the stems from the grapes prior to fermentation; known in French as *égrappage*. Because the stems contain bitter tannins, their presence during fermentation may result in harsher wines, and their removal produces wines that are comparatively more supple and delicate.

Deutscher Sekt   This term, which means "German sparkling wine", may be used only if the base wine is made entirely from grapes grown in Germany; until 1986, the term could also be used for sparkling wines produced in Germany from imported wines. *See* Sekt.

Deutscher Tafelwein   This term, which means "German table wine", has been officially defined by the Common Market and refers to a category of wine below Qualitätswein. On average, less than 6 percent of the total German wine crop falls into this lowest category, although the percentage has varied in recent years from 1.5 to 13. Such wines must have a minimum alcohol content of 8.5 percent (after chaptalization) and may be labelled only with one of four rather broad regional names – Bayern, Neckar, Oberrhein, and Rhein-Mosel. Wines labelled Deutscher Tafelwein may contain only German wine; those labelled Tafelwein contain neutral wine from outside Germany, and the country or countries of origin must be shown on the label. *See* Landwein.

Dézaley   One of the best dry white wines of Switzerland, produced on steep, terraced vineyards overlooking Lake Geneva, east of Lausanne in the canton of Vaud; although made from the Chasselas grape, it has considerable distinction, and its reputation on the whole is deserved.

Dezize-les-Maranges   A village south of Santenay, at the extreme southern end of Burgundy's Côte d'Or, whose limited production of red wine was marketed as Côte de Beaune-Villages and is now entitled to the appellation Maranges.

Dhron   A wine-producing town on the Moselle, between Trittenheim and Piesport, whose attractive wines are linked with those of the adjoining village of Neumagen; Hofberger is its best vineyard.

Die   *See* Clairette de Die

Dienheim   An important wine-producing town in Germany's Rhein-hessen region, situated along the Rhine south of Nierstein and Oppenheim, where the escarpment of the Rheinterrasse falls away to the alluvial plain toward Worms. The Dien-heimer wines, from 1,200 acres of vines, are soft and plea-sant, but a bit common; its best vineyards are Falkenberg, Tafelstein, and Herrengarten, but much of its wines are mar-keted with the Grosslage Oppenheimer Krötenbrun.

Dionysus   In Greek mythology, a nature god, especially of the vine and wine; the son of Zeus and Semele, the earth goddess. He was also called Bacchus, and his symbol was the thyrsus, a staff wreathed with ivy and grape leaves and surmounted by a pinecone.

Disgorging   One of the essential, final steps in the production of spar-kling wines by the *méthode champenoise*, by which the sedi-ment is removed from each bottle before it receives its *dosage*, or sweetening, and its final cork; known in French as *dégorgement*.

Distinguished   When used by a wine expert, this is the highest sort of praise, reserved for wines of exceptional balance and class; the qual-ity of such wines is immediately obvious, even to a beginner.

Dizy   One of the better wine-producing villages of France's Champagne region, situated directly across the Marne from Epernay; its vineyards, almost entirely planted with Pinot Noir, are officially rated 95 percent.

DOC   *See* Denominazione di Origine Controllata

DOCG   *See* Denominazione di Origine Controllata e Garantita

Doctor   A world-renowned vineyard in the village of Bernkastel, on the Moselle, which has been rated as the most valuable agri-cultural land in Germany. In 1984, the boundaries of the vineyard, which is planted entirely with Riesling, were fixed at 3.26 hectares, or 8 acres; Bernkasteler Doctor is thus one of only two Einzellagen, or individual vineyards, that are smaller than the 5-hectare (12.35-acre) minimum established by the 1971 German wine laws. The principal owners are Thanisch, Deinhard, and Lauerburg.

Doisy-Daëne, Château   A *cru classé* of the Sauternes district of Bordeaux, in the commune of Barsac; it is part of what was originally known simply as Château Doisy (and owned by a Monsieur Daëne), later divided into three parcels. Its 35 acres produce about 3,000 cases a year of an excellent, elegant sweet wine made entirely from Sémillon; the estate is also known for a light, racy, dry white wine labelled Doisy-Daëne Sec.

Doisy-Dubroca Château This 10-acre section of the original Château Doisy has long been under the same ownership as Château Climens, and the name has become the second label of that better-known property.

Doisy-Védrines Château A *cru classé* of the Sauternes district, in the commune of Barsac; originally part of Château Doisy, it produces about 5,000 cases a year. The owners of this property also produce a popular red and a white Bordeaux under the proprietary name Chevalier Védrines, but those wines do not come from Doisy-Védrines.

Dolceacqua An attractive Italian red DOC wine produced in the Liguria region, near the French border; made from the Rossese grape, it is also entitled to the name Rossese di Dolceacqua.

Dolcetto An Italian red-wine grape of good quality, widely grown in Piedmont, where it accounts for about 15 percent of the total acreage. The grape derives its name from the sweetness of the juice at the time of harvest; the wine itself is always dry, and its soft, lush, supple qualities make it a very appealing red, at its best within two or three years of the harvest. There are seven DOC names based on Dolcetto, but they account for less than 20 percent of the large Dolcetto crop; the best-known DOCs are Dolcetto d'Alba and Dolcetto d'Asti.

Dôle Generally considered the best red wine of Switzerland, Dôle is produced in the high, rocky, upper valley of the Rhône, in the canton of Valais; made from a combination of Pinot Noir and Gamay, it somewhat resembles a light Burgundy. Lesser examples of this wine may be sold as Goron.

Dom Pérignon The cellar master at the Abbey of Hautvillers, in France's Champagne region, from 1668 to 1715 and, according to well-publicized tradition, the man who invented champagne. Actually, no one invented champagne, and the old monk never claimed to have done so. He noted, as had many others, that in the spring following the harvest, the wines stored in barrel became lightly sparkling; the winter cold had stopped the original fermentation from continuing until all the sugar had been transformed into alcohol, and the bubbles were the result of the carbon-dioxide gas that was given off by the refermenting wine. Dom Pérignon did not invent these bubbles, and in fact the process of fermentation was not fully understood until Pasteur's experiments in the nineteenth century. But Dom Pérignon apparently discovered that by blending grapes from different vineyards, he could improve the quality of the sparkling wine produced the following spring. And it's likely that he experimented with putting the incompletely fermented wine in bottles and sealing them with cork stoppers (rather than the less effective wooden pegs then in use), so that the second stage of fermentation would occur in the bottle, thus trapping the bubbles in the wine; this technique is known as the *méthode rurale*, or "rural method". The monk certainly did not employ what is now known as the *méthode champenoise*, which consists of first fermenting the wine out completely, then bottling the still, dry wine with a measured amount of sugar and yeast to induce a second fermentation in the bottle. In any event, the wine producers of the Champagne region were not even permitted to ship their wines in bottle until 1728.

The Abbey of Hautvillers is a singularly gracious old building that commands an incomparable view of the vineyards and of the Marne Valley; it is now the property of Moët & Chandon, and a statue of Dom Pérignon has been set up in the courtyard. In the 1920s Moët & Chandon began to use the name Dom Pérignon for their best and most expensive wine, shipped in a distinctive, slender-necked black bottle, and it is still the best known of the *cuvées speciales*, the deluxe champagnes now produced by many firms and marketed in specially designed bottles. (A list of such wines will be found on page 550).

Domaine French for "estate", most often used in Burgundy, where it refers to all the vineyards making up a single property, although they may be in different villages; such wines will be labelled with the appropriate village or vineyard appellation, with the name of the *domaine* appearing only as the producer. Many *domaine* wines are estate-bottled, although by no means all; those that are carry on their labels the phrase

Mise du domaine, Mis en bouteille au domaine, or *Mis en bouteille a la propriété*. The term *domaine* is used quite differently in other regions of France, where it means a single vineyard, as Domaine de Chevalier in Bordeaux.

Domäne German for "domain" or "estate"; the term is used almost exclusively for the state-owned vineyards, which are justly famous, and for a very few privately owned estates whose owners had at one time achieved a certain official status. *See* Staatsweingüter.

Dominique, Château La A *grand cru classé* of Saint-Emilion whose 45 acres of vineyards produce about 9,000 cases a year of well-balanced, distinctive red wines.

Dominus The proprietary name for a red wine produced in the Napa Valley from part of the 124-acre Napanook vineyard that belonged to the late John Daniel, the former owner of Inglenook; the wine, made under the supervision of Christian Moueix, director of Château Pétrus in Bordeaux, consists primarily of Cabernet Sauvignon, with about 25 percent of Merlot and Cabernet Franc. (About 75 acres of Napanook are planted with these varieties.) The wine was first produced in 1983, but the 1984 vintage was the first one released for sale, in early 1988; production is about 6,000 cases a year. A second wine from the property is labelled Daniel Estate.

Domkirche *Dom* is German for "cathedral", and the Hohe Domkirche is the Cathedral of Trier, on the Moselle, which has some important vineyards as part of its endowment; the finest include a 19-acre portion of the Scharzhofberg in Wiltingen, and the entire 24-acre Avelsbacher Altenberg. The estate is now part of the Bischöflichen Weingüter.

Donnaz A light red wine made primarily from the Nebbiolo grape in Italy's Valle d'Aosta region; the hillside vineyards are adjacent to those of Carema, in the adjoining Piedmont region.

Dordogne An important river of southwestern France, joining the Garonne just north of Bordeaux to form the tidal estuary of the Gironde; also the name of a *département* just east of the Bordeaux region whose wines include Bergerac, Monbazillac, Montravel, and Pécharmant.

Dosage The second fermentation that creates the bubbles in champagne and other sparkling wines leaves the wine completely dry. After the sediment is removed (in the case of bottle-fermented wines, by riddling and disgorging; in the case of transfer method and Charmat process wines, by filtration), and before the cork is inserted, the wine receives what is known as *dosage* or *liqueur d'expédition*, a mixture of wine and sugar that determines whether wine is Brut, Extra Dry, Sec, or Demi-Sec.

Double Magnum An oversize bottle holding the equivalent of four regular bottles.

Douro One of Portugal's three great rivers, all of which rise in Spain and change their spelling and their nationality before they empty into the Atlantic: the Tajo becomes the Tejo; the Duero, the Douro; and the northernmost is the Spanish Miño on its northern bank and the Portuguese Minho on its southern. For wine lovers, all three are relatively undistinguished in Spain, but once the Douro crosses the border, it becomes the spinal column (and was, in the past, the principal highway) of one of the world's great wine regions. *See* Port.

Doux French for "sweet", but its meaning becomes more complicated when applied to wine. Good, semisweet white wines, such as certain Graves or Vouvrays, are more properly described as *moelleux*; naturally sweet wines such as Sauternes are called *liquoreux*. A *vin doux* is generally a wine possessing a sweetness not entirely normal, such as the so-called *vins doux naturels*, the sweet fortified wines that include Banyuls and Muscat de Frontignan; or the very sweetest, and infrequently encountered, wines of Champagne. The term, in brief, is one rarely applied to good, let alone outstanding, wine. When *Doux* appears on the label of a champagne or sparkling wine, the wine contains at least 5 percent sugar.

Dry As far as wine is concerned, the opposite of sweet is not sour, but dry; practically all of the world's table wines are dry rather than sweet. An oenologist would define as dry a wine that contains no more than 2 grams of sugar (equivalent to two tenths of 1 percent), although many people cannot perceive sweetness until the sugar level is increased to 5 grams (½ of 1 percent). Of course, there are many popular wines that are by no means dry, including Liebfraumilch, Portuguese rosés, California White Zinfandels, and Italian Lambruscos.

Dry Creek Valley A viticultural area in northern Sonoma County that extends for about a dozen miles northwest of Healdsburg, approximately parallel to the Alexander Valley; nearly 6,000 acres of vineyards are planted. The area, which gets its name from Dry Creek, a tributary of the Russian River, has long been known for its intense Zinfandel, much of it produced from old, hillside vineyards; more recently, Cabernet Sauvignon, Chardonnay, and especially Sauvignon Blanc have been cultivated with great success. Dry Creek Vineyard, Pedroncelli, Preston, Robert Stemmler, Lambert Bridge, and Domaine Michel are located in this district.

Dry Sauterne Sauternes is a legally defined district in France's Bordeaux region that by law may produce only sweet wines; the name was appropriated (without the final "s") in the nineteenth century for dry white wines made in the United States. Fortunately, the name is rarely used these days, although a number of American firms still market inexpensive, semidry white wines as Sauterne.

Ducru-Beaucaillou, Château A Second Classed Growth of Saint-Julien, in the Médoc district; its 123 acres produce about 20,000 cases a year of an exceptionally fine wine – subtle, elegant, beautifully balanced, and displaying both structure and finesse – which has for many years been considered one of the dozen top red wines of Bordeaux. The property was once owned by the Ducru family (*beau caillou* means "beautiful pebble", a reference to the vineyard's gravelly soil), and was acquired in 1942 by the Borie family, who also own Châteaux Haut-Batailley and Grand-Puy-Lacoste.

Duhart-Milon-Rothschild, Château A Fourth Classed Growth of Pauillac, in the Médoc district, adjoining Châteaux Lafite-Rothschild and Mouton-Rothschild; the property, previously known as Château Duhart-Milon, was acquired by the owners of Lafite-Rothschild in 1962, who expanded the vineyard to more than 100 acres, which now produce about 20,000 cases a year. As of the 1983 vintage, the label has been changed back to Château Duhart-Milon.

Dulce Spanish for "sweet". The term also refers to a sweetening agent, made in several different ways, added to certain sherries at the time of bottling.

Dull A dull wine is like a dull person – perhaps honourable and sound, but not very interesting and certainly not much fun. Such a wine may be full-bodied and have other qualities, but it lacks distinction and individuality, and should certainly not be expensive.

Dumb A wine-taster's term for a wine with potential, but not yet developed enough to show its character.

Duras *See* Côtes de Duras

Durfort-Vivens, Château A Second Classed Growth of Margaux, in the Médoc district, with an annual production of about 8,000 cases. This vineyard was owned by the Durfort family in the fifteenth century and, in the nineteenth century, by the Vicomte de Vivens; in 1961 it was acquired by Lucien Lurton, owner of two other châteaux in Margaux, Brane-Cantenac and Desmirail.

Durif *See* Petite Sirah

Dürkheim *See* Bad Dürkheim

Dutchess An American hybrid variety that produces white wines of good quality, like Delaware, but scarcer and more difficult to grow.

❦ E

Earthy This is perhaps the best English translation of what the French call *goût de terroir* and the Germans *Bodengeschmack*, a rather odd special flavour that certain soils tend to give to the wines they yield. It is typical and desirable in certain wines, but disagreeable if too pronounced, when it is the mark of a coarse wine produced on heavy, alluvial soil. It is easy to recognize, almost impossible to describe.

Echézeaux An important *grand cru* vineyard in Burgundy's Cote de Nuits whose 93 acres produce about 11,000 cases a year of an excellent red wine. Technically in the commune of Flagey-

Echézeux, Echézeaux is contiguous to the Les Suchots vineyard of Vosne-Romanée and, in fact, its wines may also be sold as Vosne-Romanée Premier Cru. More remarkable for subtlety than power, rather light in colour and body, but racy and fine, the wines of Echézeaux are generally considered not quite as good as those from the adjoining Grands Echézeaux vineyard.

Edel A German word meaning "noble" or, in a wider sense, "fine" or "superior". Thus, *Edelfäule* means "noble rot", and *Edeltraube* refers to superior grape varieties.

Edelfäule A German term meaning "noble rot" and identical to the French *pourriture noble*. *See* Botrytis Cinerea.

Edelzwicker An Alsace wine term meaning "noble blend", but now that the lesser designation Zwicker has been abolished, Edelzwicker is used for what is, in effect, a simple white carafe wine made from less distinguished varieties such as Chasselas, Sylvaner, and perhaps Pinot Blanc and Auxerrois. In some cases the wine is a field blend, that is, the grapes are actually harvested and vinified together. The term is rarely seen in labels because a producer would be more likely to market such a blend with a proprietary name.

Edna Valley A relatively cool viticultural area just south of the city of San Luis Obispo, between the Santa Lucia Mountains and the San Lucas Range; this district has achieved particular acclaim for its Chardonnay, Pinot Noir, and Sauvignon Blanc. Edna Valley Vineyards, Chamisal, and Corbett Canyon are situated there.

Eglise, Domaine de L' A vineyard in the Pomerol district – its full name is Château du Domaine de L'Eglise – whose 17 acres produce about 3,500 cases a year; Clos L'Eglise and Château L'Eglise-Clinet are neighbouring properties (*église* means "church").

Eglise-Clinet Château L' A vineyard in the Pomerol district whose 10 acres produce about 2,000 cases of supple and distinctive red wine.

Egrappage *See* Destemming

Egri Bikavér The most famous red wine of Hungary (as Tokay is its most famous white wine), produced around the village of Eger, situated in mountainous country about 120 miles northeast of Budapest. Egri Bikavér, which means "bull's blood from Eger", is said to have acquired its colourful name in the sixteenth century, when Eger was successfully defended against an attack by the Turks, presumably because the Hungarian soldiers were fortified with copius amounts of this wine. Once made primarily from the Kadarka grape, it is now produced from Kékfrankos, to which such varieties as Pinot Noir, Merlot, Gamay, and Cabernet Sauvignon may be added. Traditionally sturdy, full-bodied, and long-lived, today's bottlings are more often made in a lighter style.

Ehrenfelser A new German variety, a cross of Riesling and Sylvaner, that displays some of the characteristics of the former; about 1,300 acres are planted, half of that in the Rheinpfalz.

Einzellage The German term for a single vineyard, as defined by the 1971 wine laws, which reduced the number of existing vineyards in that country from more than 25,000 to about 2,600 Einzellagen with strictly defined boundaries and a legally approved name; only Qualitätswein and Qualitätswein mit Prädikat may be labelled with vineyard names. The minimum size of the Einzellage - with a very few exceptions – is 5 hectares (about 12.5 acres), so many small vineyards were absorbed into that of a more famous neighbour, and a number of large, well-known vineyards were made even larger. Consequently, there are many vineyards in Germany that are 100 to 250 acres in size, and Einzellagen that extend for 400 to 600 acres are not uncommon. As in France's Burgundy region, most vineyards are divided among many different growers. Vineyard names are invariably preceded, on the label, by that of the village in which the vineyard is situated, as Piesporter Goldtröpfchen, Rauenthaler Baiken, and Forster Jesuitengarten. (Notable exceptions to this rule include the vineyards Schloss Johannisberg, Schloss Vollrads, Steinberg, and Scharzhofberg.) As it happens, wines marketed with the considerably more inclusive Grosslagen names are similarly labelled. A list of the top Einzellagen will be found on page 553.

Eiswein A German word that means "ice wine" and refers to wines made from frozen grapes; in 1982 Eiswein became one of the six designations within the category Qualitätswein mit

Prädikat, and wines so labelled must now be made from grapes that have the same minimum percentage of natural grape sugar as a Beerenauslese (125 degrees Oechsle, equivalent to about 30 percent sugar). To make Eiswein, ripe, healthy grapes are deliberately left on the vine past the normal harvest in the hope that the temperature will drop below 20 degrees F.; this freezes most of the water in the grapes, leaving sugar, acid and flavour extracts unfrozen. If the frozen grapes are quickly pressed, the resulting juice will produce sweet, elegant, and distinctive wines marked by a relatively high acidity, and very different in style from such wines as Auslese, Beerenauslese, and Trockenbeerenauslese. The grapes for Eiswein are not affected by *botrytis*, or *Edelfäule*, because if such grapes were left on the vine indefinitely in anticipation of a freeze, they would simply rot. The sweetness of an Eiswein is the result of the freeze, which more than doubles the proportion of sugar in the unfrozen portion of the juice, and also increases the proportion of acid. Thus, Eiswein is made in years that are not noted for *botrytis*, and the finest vintages for this speciality are not always the same as those for Beerenauslese and Trockenbeerenauslese. Sometimes the grapes for an Eiswein are picked as late as January following the normal harvest, but such wines are nevertheless labelled with the year in which the grapes were grown.

Eitelsbach A tiny town on the Ruwer, a tributary of the Moselle, known for a single estate, the Karthäuserhofberg. The steep, splendid vineyards belonged to a Carthusian monastery for nearly five centuries (the name means "Carthusians' Hill"), but since the early nineteenth century has been owned by the Rautenstrauch (now Tyrell) family. The vineyard's 50 acres are divided into five plots, the biggest of which are Burgberg, Kronenberg, and Sang, and these names, too, appeared on the crowded little label, which consists simply of a collar around the bottle's neck; there is no main label, which has led to the amusing observation that the German wine with the longest name has the smallest label. Since the 1985 vintage, however, the individual vineyard names are no longer used, and the wines are labelled Eitelsbacher Karthäuserhofberger. The wine is among the very best of the Mosel-Saar-Ruwer region, especially in good vintages – very light, rather austere, with a bouquet of incredible floweriness and distinction, it is unquestionably one of the two finest wines of the Ruwer, the other being Maximin Grünhäuser.

El Dorado A county that adjoins Amador in the Sierra Foothills region of California; its 500 acres, situated at an elevation of 1,200 to 3,000 feet, are planted primarily with Zinfandel, Sauvignon Blanc, and Cabernet Sauvignon. The region was first settled by gold miners in the 1850s, and its principal town, Placerville, was once known as Hangtown; wineries include Boeger and Sierra Vista.

Elba An island off the coast of Tuscany whose wines have been granted DOC status; the red is based on Sangiovese, the white on a variant of Trebbiano known locally as Procanico.

Elbling A productive white-wine variety of no particular distinction cultivated in Germany; virtually all of the acreage is in the upper Moselle Valley, and the wines are often used to make inexpensive sparkling wine.

Elegant A wine-taster's term applied to well-balanced wines that have finesse and breed.

Eleveur From the French for "raising", or "bringing up"; in the wine trade, an *éleveur* is someone who buys new wine and cares for it during maturation, then bottles and ships it. Thus, many shippers use the phrase *négociant-éleveur* on their labels.

Eltville A major wine-producing town of Germany's Rheingau region, with 600 acres of vineyards giving wines that are rarely remarkable, but consistently sound and good. The Grosslage is Eltviller Steinmächer, and the individual vineyards include Taubenberg, Langenstück, Sonnenberg, and Sandgrub. A number of famous producers have their cellars in Eltville, including Langwerth von Simmern and the Staatsweingüter, or Hessian State Domain.

Elvira One of the better-known native grapes, closely resembling and perhaps identical to what is called the Missouri Riesling, it is not a Riesling at all, but was first noted and popularized by Jacob Rommel in Missouri in 1869. Its wine, especially from the Finger Lakes district, is fresh and attractive, despite a rather pronounced grapey, or *labrusca*, aroma.

Emerald Riesling A cross of Riesling and Muscadelle developed in California and introduced in 1948; there are about 1,500 acres planted, mostly in the Central Valley. This light, pleasant white wine usually goes into blends, but is occasionally marketed as a semidry varietal wine.

Emilia-Romagna An Italian region, north of Tuscany, whose capital is Bologna; known for its gastronomy, for such local products as Parmesan cheese and Parma ham, and for tourist attractions that include the mosaics at Ravenna and the resort town of Rimini, on the Adriatic coast. The region produces between 100 and 140 million cases a year, even more, in some vintages, than Sicily and Apulia. Its most famous wine is Lambrusco, produced around Modena; Albana di Romagna, Trebbiano di Romagna, and Sangiovese di Romagna come from an extensive area between Bologna and Rimini; and a variety of red and white wines is produced in the DOC zones Colli Bolognesi, southwest of Bologna, and Colli Piacentini, at the western end of the region.

Enfer d'Arvier An acclaimed but rarely encountered DOC red wine produced from the Petit Rouge grape on steep, south-facing slopes across the Dora Baltea River from the village of Arvier, in Italy's Valle d'Aosta region; fewer than 2,000 cases a year are made.

England Vines may have been planted in southern England by the Romans, and historical documents indicate that more than three dozen vineyards existed in the eleventh century; but when Henry VIII broke up the monasteries, which were then England's most important vine growers, domestic wine production virtually ceased. Modern English winemaking dates from an acre planted in Hampshire in 1952; there are now 1,000 acres of vineyards, and about 200 commercial growers, plus many amateurs who cultivate an acre or two. (A distinction must be made between English wines from English vineyards and a product called British wine, which is made from imported must or concentrate.) Because of England's short, cool, rainy summers, growers prefer early-ripening varieties, especially Müller-Thurgau, as well as Scheurebe, Reichensteiner, and the French-American hybrid Seyval Blanc; varieties such as Pinot Noir and Chardonnay are also planted in limited quantities. The wines, virtually all white, can be hard and acid, but good examples are light, fresh, and clean; some producers add *Süssreserve*, unfermented juice, just before bottling, as is done in Germany, to round out, and slightly sweeten, their wines.

Enkirch A little wine-producing village on the Moselle, just downstream from Traben-Trarbach.

Enoteca Italian for a place where wines may be sampled and purchased; *enotecas*, some of them quite elaborate, have been established in many of the best-known wine regions of Italy.

Entre-Deux-Mers A large district in the Bordeaux wine region situated on lovely, rolling hills between the two confluent rivers, the Dordogne and the Garonne; the somewhat grandiose name literally means "between two seas", and should perhaps more logically be changed to Entre-Deux-Fleuves. The district produces 1 to 2 million cases a year of inexpensive white wine, and until recently, they were generally somewhat sweet, and in fact much of the crop was sold simply as Bordeaux Blanc. Faced with a declining demand, the growers – most of whom belong to the local co-operative cellars – made the decision to sell dry wines exclusively, and adopted the amusing slogan *"Entre deux huitres* [between two oysters] – *Entre-Deux-Mers"*. The quality of the wines has improved, and they are today good value in their price class, although hardly distinguished.

L'Eperon, Château A vineyard near Fronsac, in the Bordeaux region, whose 75 acres produce about 7,000 cases of sound red wine.

Epluchage A French term for the operation of picking over, by hand, the newly harvested grapes before they are crushed or pressed, so as to eliminate defective bunches and berries. This is an expensive procedure, but will obviously result in finer wines, and is especially important in the production of delicate white wines, such as champagne.

Equilibré A French taster's term for a well-balanced wine all of whose elements are in harmony.

Erbach A justly famous little village in Germany's Rheingau, producing some of the region's most distinguished wines. Although part of the incomparable Marcobrunn vineyard is in adjoining Hattenheim, all of its wines are labelled Erbacher Marcobrunn; other celebrated plots include

Steinmorgen, Honigberg, Siegelsberg, Hohenrain, Schlossberg, and Michelmark, all yielding rather hard, firm wines,
long-lived, and of great class.

Erbaluce di Caluso A light, dry white wine made from the Erbaluce grape
near the town of Caluso, north of Turin, in Italy's Piedmont
region. If the grapes are left to dry before being pressed, they
produce an unusual sweet wine called Caluso Passito.

Erben A German term, often found on wine labels, that means
"heirs" or "successors".

Erden A small wine-producing village on the Moselle, near Zeltingen, whose spicy, delicate wines are among the best of the
region. Its vineyards are especially steep, as the name of one
of them – Treppchen, or "little stairway" – would indicate;
other top sites are Prälat and Herrenberg.

Ermitage A variant spelling, rarely encountered today, of Hermitage,
the famous vineyard of the northern Rhône. Also, a white
wine from the canton of Valais, in Switzerland, made from
the Marsanne grape.

Erzeugerabfüllung A German term meaning "bottled by the proprietor",
similar to estate bottled, although the term may also be used
by co-operative cellars. Prior to the 1971 German wine law,
the most widely used term was Originalabfüllung.

Escherndorf An important wine town in the German region of Franken,
or Franconia, the quality of whose wines is second only to
those of Würzburg; the best vineyards are Lump, Fursten-
berg, and Berg.

Espumoso Spanish for "sparkling"; if made by the *méthode champenoise*, the wines are labelled *cava*.

Essencia A very rare, extremely sweet, and particularly expensive
style of Hungarian Tokay. *See* Tokay.

Est! Est!! Est!!! di Montefiascone A light, dry, and for the most part, undistinguished white wine produced around Lake Bolsena,
about 50 miles north of Rome, from Trebbiano and Malvasia
grapes. The wine owes its curious name, and what fame it
still has, to the often-told story of the wine-loving German

bishop who, on his way to Rome in the twelfth century, sent his servant ahead as a scout and taster. The latter was instructed to write the word *Est* (Latin for "it is") on the side of every tavern where he found the wine especially good. On reaching Montefiascone he wrote, *Est! Est!! Est!!!* and, according to the legend, the bishop concurred so heartily with this assessment of the local wine that he stopped his journey and spent the rest of his days in that town.

Estate Bottling The practice whereby vineyard owners bottle the product of their own vines in their own cellars. Like château bottling in Bordeaux and Erzeugerabfüllung in Germany, which are virtually the same thing, estate bottling is always a guarantee of authenticity and to some extent of superior quality. In France, the practice has become increasingly general in Burgundy, the Côtes-du-Rhône, the Loire Valley, and elsewhere. The labels of estate-bottled wines will carry the phrase *Mise du domaine, Mis en bouteille au domaine*, or *Mis en bouteille a la propriété*, and the producer's name will be followed by the word *propriétaire* (vineyard owner), *récoltant* (a grower who harvests his own crop), *viticulteur* or *vigneron* (both of which refer to someone who cultivates his own vines).

Some wines appear to be estate bottled when they are not and carry phrases that might confuse the unwary. *Mis en bouteille dans nos caves* and *Mis en bouteille dans nos chais* simply mean "bottled in our cellars", and the name of the producer is likely to be followed by the word *négoçiant* or "shipper". *Mise d'origine* means "bottled in the region of production", as does the more specific *Mis en bouteille à Beaune* (or Nuits-Saints-Georges, etc.). *Produced and bottled by*, in English, on a French label, has no legal meaning.

In the United States, the term *estate bottled* has been redefined and can be used by a winery in California, or elsewhere, only for wines that come from its own vineyards, or from vineyards leased by the winery on a long-term basis, and if the vineyards and the winery are both located within the appellation of origin shown on the label.

Esters Formed by a combination of acids and alcohol – during both fermentation and aging – esters contribute a fruity, flowery, sweetish element to a wine's bouquet; ethyl acetate is the most important of the esters.

Estufa Portuguese for "hot house"; a term used in the production of Madeira to describe the specially heated rooms where casks of wine are baked, thus transforming them into pungent wines with a distinctive and desirable burnt taste. Today, most Madeira is produced by being heated in large cement tanks, also called *estufas*.

Etna A DOC zone situated on the lower slopes of Mount Etna, a famous volcano on the eastern end of Sicily. Most of the wines from this district are red and rosé, from the local Nerello Mascalese grape; a limited amount of white is also made.

Etoile A village in the Jura district of France that produces about 90,000 cases a year of AOC white wines, some of which are transformed into the unusual *vin jaune*.

L'Evangile, Château One of the finest vineyards of the Pomerol district, situated near the border of Saint-Emilion, and equidistant from Châteaux Pétrus and Cheval Blanc; its 35 acres produce about 6,000 cases a year of a rich, supple, and elegant wine.

Extra Dry A term used for sparkling wines that are not as dry as those labelled Brut; Common Market regulations specify that an Extra Dry sparkling wine may contain between 1.2 and 2 percent sugar.

Extract To the oenologist, extract refers to the nonvolatile and nonsoluble substances in wine; to the taster, it indicates the presence of elements that add flavour and character. Thus, a Médoc is likely to have more extract than a Beaujolais, a Barolo more than a Bardolino, and ripe Riesling from the Rheingau more than a Muscadet from the Loire.

❧ F

Faber A new German variety, a cross of Weissburgunder (Pinot Blanc) and Müller-Thurgau, which ripens well and also retains balancing acidity; nonexistent in the 1960s, this variety now accounts for 5,600 acres, three quarters of that in Rheinhessen.

Factory House A splendid granite mansion in Oporto, in northern Portugal; it was built in the late eighteenth century by the British Association and is still used by the British port shippers for weekly luncheons and occasional festive dinners. The building is famous for its duplicate dining rooms, each of which seats about forty people at a long oval table; at the end of formal dinners, the guests move from the first room, set with a damask tablecloth, to the second, whose table is bare, to enjoy their port. The name is derived from the definition of a factory as a foreign trading station (just as a factor is an agent or merchant).

Faded A term applied to a wine that has lost its character and definition, usually through age, and that tastes flat and insipid.

Faible A French term that means "weak", lacking character, anaemic.

Falerno The most celebrated wine of ancient Rome was Falernian, extravagantly praised by Pliny, Virgil, and Horace, and considered "immortal" in its ability to age for a century or more. Falernian, or Falernum, was produced near Formia, along the coast north of Naples, on the border of what are now the regions of Latium and Campania; the identical hillsides are planted in vines today and the wines marketed as Falerno. The reds, made primarily from Aglianico, are sound, the whites perhaps less interesting: they have nothing in common with the legendary Falernian of antiquity except their geographical origin and their name.

Fara A dry red DOC wine produced from Nebbiolo, Vespolina, and Bonarda grapes in the Novara Hills, just southeast of Gattinara, in Italy's Piedmont region.

Fargues One of the five townships within the Sauternes district of Bordeaux. There is also a Château de Fargues, owned by the Lur-Saluces family of Château d'Yquem since 1472; its 30 acres produce not much more than 700 cases of an excellent, concentrated sweet wine.

Farm Winery Laws Since the early 1970s, legislation has been passed in more than twenty American states to encourage local wine production. These laws usually lower the licence fees for small wineries and permit them to sell their wines directly to consumers at the winery, without the trouble and expense of wholesalers and distributors; in some instances, taxes are reduced considerably for wines produced from locally grown grapes. This has enabled grape growers to become winemakers, and has encouraged many others to start their own wineries. In New York State, for example, more than seventy wineries have been created since the passage of the Farm Winery Bill in 1976, and similar laws have encouraged grape growing and wine production in Pennsylvania, Connecticut, Massachusetts, Virginia, and elsewhere.

Faro A DOC zone for red wine, produced in very limited quantities, around the village of that name, on the northeastern tip of Sicily.

Fass German word for "wooden cask", or "barrel".

Fat A taster's name for a wine with much substance, one that is rich and supple rather than firm; it may be applied to a dry red wine as well as a sweet white wine.

Fatigué A French term meaning "tired". Even fine wines are *fatigué* just after bottling and travelling, and recover; older wines eventually become *fatigué*, losing their sprightliness and verve.

Fattoria An Italian term traditionally used in Tuscany to describe an estate; its use implies, but does not guarantee, estate bottling.

Faugères A decent and sturdy red wine – elevated from VDQS to AOC in 1982 – produced near Béziers, not far from the Mediterranean coast, in the Hérault *département* of southern France; more than 500,000 cases a year are made, primarily from Carignan, Grenache, and Cinsault.

Favorita An unusual Italian white-wine grape, cultivated near Alba in the Piedmont region, that produces light, crisp wines.

Feeble A term applied to a wine lacking character, colour, and distinction, usually the result of an indifferent vintage.

Feine, Feinste German for "fine" and "finest"; these words are no longer permitted on labels under the 1971 wine laws.

Fendant The name given in Switzerland to the Chasselas grape, which is by a wide margin the leading variety in this small, thirsty country. It is, on the whole, a far from remarkable grape for wine, but in the cantons of the Valais, the Vaud (where it is known as Dorin), and around Geneva (where is it known as Perlan), it yields fresh, often fine, and almost invariably agreeable white wines.

Ferme A French term for a firm wine, one that is likely to improve with age.

Fermentation The process by which sugar is transformed into alcohol and carbon-dioxide gas, and by which grape juice becomes wine. Although fermentation had been observed since the dawn of history, it was thought to be a wholly spontaneous phenomenon until Pasteur, in 1857, showed it to be the work of living organisms – more specifically, of wine yeasts; it is now understood that fermentation is caused, not by the yeast itself, but by numerous enzymes, called zymase, secreted by the yeast. Modern technical knowledge goes much further, and oenologists know that fermentation creates many byproducts, such as glycerol, acetaldehydes, higher alcohols, and a number of different acids, all of which affect the taste and quality of wine. In the production of red wines, the grapes are crushed and the juice fermented in contact with the skins to extract colour, tannin, and flavour elements; for white wines, the grapes are pressed and the juice fermented away from the skins. Since the 1950s, fermentation temperatures have been more carefully controlled to obtain maximum quality, especially for white wines, which are usually fermented slowly at low temperatures to retain more fruit aroma and delicacy. Other common practices involve inhibiting the wild yeasts in the juice with sulphur and the introduction of special strains of cultured yeast to obtain a more controlled fermentation. Fermentation normally continues until all, or practically all, of the grape sugar has been converted, and most table wines contain 9 to 14 percent alcohol; if enough sugar is present, however, and if the proper yeast is used, fermentation can continue until 15 or 16 percent alcohol is attained. Fermentation can be stopped at any time, as in the making of port, by the addition of high-proof spirits. To produce semisweet table wines that retain some of their original grape sugar, the yeast population can be reduced and fermentation stopped by adding sulphur dioxide, their activity can be inhibited by chilling the must, or they may be removed by centrifuging the wine or filtering it.

Ferrande, Château A large estate in the Graves district of Bordeaux whose 105 acres produce about 25,000 cases a year of well-made and appealing red and white wines. There is also a Château de Ferrand in Saint-Emilion.

Ferrière, Château A Third Classed Growth of Margaux, in the Médoc district; for many years it 10 acres of vines, producing about 1,500 cases a year, have been farmed by Château Lascombes.

Feuillette A small oak barrel of 136-litre capacity (about 30 gallons) traditionally used in France's Chablis region. These barrels were largely replaced by the conventional Burgundy *pièce* of 228 litres, but today most of the wines of Chablis are stored in large stainless-steel tanks or glass-lined concrete vats and never come into contact with wood.

Feytit-Clinet, Château A small vineyard in the Pomerol district producing about 2,500 cases a year.

Fiano di Avellino An unusual and excellent DOC white wine produced from the indigenous Fiano grape around the village of Avellino, east of Naples, in the Campania region.

Fiasco Italian for "flask"; the plural is *fiaschi*. The *fiasco* that established the fame of Chianti, once hand-blown, is round bottomed, thin and light; it would be extremely fragile without its straw covering and, of course, would not stand upright on a table. The straw had to be woven around each flask by hand, and eventually the cost of labour made these special bottles, which could not be stored on their sides, too expensive to use for the cheap wines they usually contained. *Fiaschi* have virtually disappeared today, except for tourist shops within the Chianti region itself.

Fiddletown A small viticultural area in California's Amador County known primarily for its rich Zinfandels.

Fiefs Vendéens A VDQS established in 1984 for red, white, and rosé wines produced in the Vendee *département*, south of Nantes.

Fieuzal, Château de A *grand cru classé* of the Graves district of Bordeaux;

its 80 acres of vineyards produce about 10,000 cases a year, almost all of it red.

Figeac, Château An excellent vineyard in Saint-Emilion, whose 90 acres and average annual production of about 14,000 cases make it one of the biggest of the *premiers grands crus classés* of that district; it is unusual among top Saint-Emilions (most of which are planted primarily with Merlot) in that it is planted 70 percent with Cabernet Sauvignon and Cabernet Franc, and only 30 percent with Merlot, the result of its situation on a gravelly plateau that adjoins the Pomerol district, rather than on the predominantly clay and limestone soils near the town of Saint-Emilion itself. The wines have a distinct style, combining firmness and finesse, and rival those of its neighbour, Château Cheval Blanc, which was created from a part of the original Figeac vineyard in the 1830s. Several other vineyards, all good but somewhat less famous, were also once part of the extensive Figeac property, and they still carry that name, but in a combined form, as Châteaux La Tour-Figeac, La Tour-du-Pin Figeac (now divided in two), Yon-Figeac, and Petit-Figeac.

Filhot, Château A classed growth in the Sauternes district situated within an estate of 750 acres dominated by an elegant eighteenth-century château; the 130 acres of vineyard produce about 10,000 cases a year of a stylish and elegant Sauternes that is vinified so as to be slightly less sweet than most, but with perhaps more finesse. A dry white wine is also made, labelled Grand Vin Sec de Château Filhot. The property was acquired by the Lur-Saluces family of Château d'Yquem in the early nineteenth century and was more recently owned by the Comtesse Durieu de Lacarelle, herself a member of that family, hence the phrase that dominates the label: Comtesse Durieu de Lacarelle née Lur-Saluces.

Fillette Literally, in French, a "young girl"; the word is also used informally in the Loire Valley, and elsewhere, to mean a half-bottle of wine.

Filtering The clarifying of a wine, prior to bottling, by passing it through one of the many different types of filter, including cellulose fibres, diatomaceous earth, or fine membrane filers. Too heavy or severe a filtration can numb a wine and remove some of its flavour and character; consequently, many of the world's best wines are filtered lightly, a few not at all. Filtering is a necessity for most wines, however, especially for a public that prefers wines that are absolutely brilliant and have a minimum of sediment, or none at all. Many white wines are now sterile-filtered, a process that removes all yeast and thus permits earlier bottling and fresher, fruitier wines; filtering is especially important for sweet and semisweet white wines, since the combination of yeast and sugar might result in a second fermentation in the bottle. Most modern wineries both fine and filter their wines.

Fine A wine-taster's term, rather loosely used and, indeed, overused. It is properly applied to any wine that has an inherent, unmistakable superiority.

Finesse A term, difficult to define, applied to a wine that has breed, class, and distinction, qualities that raise it well out of the ordinary.

Finger Lakes The principal wine-producing region of New York State; although its 14,000 acres of vineyards account for only a third of the state's total acreage, its 40-odd wineries produce 80 to 90 percent of the wines. There are about a dozen lakes in this area, southeast of Rochester and about 300 miles northwest of New York City, but the four principal ones, Canandaigua, Keuka, Seneca, and Cayuga, elongated and roughly parallel, look like the imprint made by a giant hand, whence the name. The first grapes were planted in Hammondsport in 1829, and the first commercial winery was established in 1860. Until recently, almost all of the vineyards were planted with native Eastern varieties such as Catawba, Niagara, and Delaware, as well as Concord, and these were used not only for sweet, grapey red, white and rosé table wines, but also for sparkling wines and such fortified wines as sherry and port. Since the 1940s, such French-American hybrids as Aurora, Seyval Blanc, Baco Noir, Chelois, and De Chaunac have been planted (of which the first two are now the most important). Chardonnay, Johannisberg Riesling, and other European *vinifera* varieties were grafted on to native rootstocks in the 1950s by Dr. Konstantin Frank for Charles Fournier of Gold Seal, the first successful cultivation of these varieties in New York State, and most Finger Lakes wineries now produce at least some wines from *vinifera* grapes. Although the vineyards and wineries established in the nineteenth century were situated along Keuka and Canandaigua lakes, most of the wineries created in the past dozen years are located along Seneca and Cayuga lakes, whose moderating influence on the harsh winter climate has encouraged the cultivation of hybrid and *vinifera* varieties. The better-known wineries include Glenora, Heron Hill, Plane's Cayuga, Taylor (which also produces Gold Seal and Great Western wines), Wagner, Widmer, Hermann J. Wiemer, and Vinifera Wine Cellars, established by Dr. Frank.

Fining A traditional method of clarifying wine whereby certain substances are added to the wine in barrel, vat, or tank and gradually settle to the bottom, carrying down suspended particles in the form of sediment, and leaving the wine clear. The substances are usually proteins that coagulate and entrap the particles, or clays that work by adsorption; egg whites, whole milk, isinglass (from the bladders of sturgeon), and fresh or powdered blood have all been used as fining agents, but the most commonly used products today are gelatin, fresh or frozen egg whites, albumen (derived from egg whites), and casein (derived from milk), as well as Bentonite (aluminium silicate), a clay from Wyoming.

Finish *See* Aftertaste

Fino A type of sherry – pale, light-bodied, and dry, it has a wholly distinctive and memorable bouquet, the result of the *flor* under which it passes a good deal of its life in cask. Like any white wine, it should be served chilled, and is one of the best and most versatile of aperitifs; it is also, despite its 17 percent alcohol, one of the most delicate of all wines, and once a bottle is opened, the wine should be consumed within a few days. La Ina and Tio Pepe are the best-known brands of fino sherry.

Fiorano A proprietary name for unusual, and very fine red and white wines produced just south of Rome, in limited quantities, by Boncampagni Ludovisi. The red is made from Merlot and Cabernet Sauvignon, the white from Malvasia di Candia.

First Growth The English equivalent of the French *premier cru*; although there are *premier cru* vineyards in Burgundy and Champagne, the English phrase almost always refers to the top vineyards of Bordeaux. The first growths of Bordeaux, as understood by the wine trade and consumers alike, are Châteaux Lafite-Rothschild, Latour, Margaux, and Mouton-Rothschild in the Médoc; Haut-Brion in Graves; Ausone and Cheval Blanc in Saint-Emilion; and Pétrus in Pomerol. All have been officially classified as *premiers crus* except Pétrus – the wines of Pomerol have never been classified – but its quality, fame, and price entitle it to first-growth status. Château d'Yquem, the great wine of Sauternes, has also been classified as a *premier cru*, of course, but the term *first growths* usually refers to the eight top red wines.

Fitou An AOC red wine produced along the Mediterranean coast of France, in the Aude *département*, which is part of the Languedoc-Roussillon, or Midi, region. The Fitou appellation is actually within the much larger Corbières district, and the wine, made from Grenache and Carignan, is one of the very few in France that must be aged in wood for a minimum period, in this case nine months.

Fixin The northernmost village of the Côte de Nuits, in Burgundy, whose red wines, too little known, are often among the best value in fine Burgundy. Some of the wines from Fixin go to market as Côte de Nuits-Villages, some as Fixin, but those produced in the *premier cru* vineyards are often comparable in quality and character to the wines of Gevrey-Chambertin; these include Clos de la Perrière, Clos du Chapitre, Clos Napoléon, Les Arvelets, and Les Hervelets.

Flagey-Echézeaux A village just north of Vosne-Romanée, in the Côte de Nuits district of Burgundy's Côte d'Or, which contains two *grand cru* vineyards, Echézeaux and Grands Echézeaux. Those wines are invariably sold under their own names, and the other red wines produced within the commune are entitled to the appellation Vosne-Romanée, so Flagey-Echézeaux is, in practice, a wine-producing village whose name never appears on a label.

Flasche German for "bottle".

Flat When applied to a sparkling wine, one that has lost its sparkle; to still wines, one too low in acid, neutral, dull.

Flavoured Wine The Greeks and Romans often flavoured their wines to disguise flaws, and there is also a long history of medicinal wines flavoured with herbs, spices, and a variety of plants. Today, vermouth is the best known of the flavoured wines, and Retsina, a Greek wine flavoured with pine resin, is another. In the United States, a category known as Special Natural Wines is made up of flavoured wines, as are the more recently introduced wine coolers.

Fleshy A wine of substance, a proper mouthful harmoniously combining flavour and suppleness.

Fleurie A little village in the very heart of France's Beaujolais region, whose attractive, fruity, and fragrant wines are one of Beaujolais's best, and best-known, *crus*.

La Fleur-Pétrus, Château A small vineyard in the Pomerol district situated near Châteaux Pétrus and Lafleur, and whose distinctive label displays a red flag; its 18 acres produce about 3,000 cases a year of an opulent and distinguished wine.

Fliers Small tasteless particles that float in wine; they are harmless and, if produced by exposure to cold, will ordinarily disappear in time.

Flinty A wine-taster's term used to describe a dry, clean, hard, almost austere white wine – such as certain examples of Chablis and Muscadet – that has a special bouquet recalling the smell of flint struck with steel. The French call it *pierre-à-fusil*, which is the same thing.

Floc de Gascogne A sweet, aromatic aperitif produced in the Armagnac region of France and similar to the Pineau des Charentes produced in the Cognac region; it consists of unfermented grape juice and young Armagnac brandy, and contains about 18 percent alcohol.

Flor The Spanish word for "flower"; in connection with wine, it refers to an unusual and special yeast most often associated with the production of sherry. After fermentation is completed in the wineries around Jerez de la Frontera, in southern Spain, the dry white wines selected to become finos and manzanillas are put into barrels that are not completely filled, and this deliberate exposure to air permits the formation of *flor*, a white film that appears on the surface of the wine and gradually forms a layer that somewhat resembles cottage cheese. The *flor* radically affects the bouquet and flavour of these wines while preventing the spoilage and oxidation that would normally occur when wines are exposed to air. The *flor* is also native to the Montilla district of Spain and to the Château-Chalon district of France; in addition, the producers of the best sherry-style wines in California, Australia, and South Africa now inoculate their wines with *flor*, and this has greatly improved the quality of those wines.

Flora A cross of Sémillon and Gewürztraminer developed in California and released in 1958; fewer that 100 acres are planted.

Floraison The French term for "flowering".

Flowering Like all fruit-bearers, grapevines have flowers; these are a good deal less spectacular than those of the cherry or the peach, but they are no less necessary antecedents to the fruit. A succession of rainy days or a period of cold weather during the blossoming season, in late May or June, can and often does bring about disaster; *coulure* is a particular problem, and may reduce the potential crop by half. The critical flowering period, called *floraison* in French, lasts for a week or two and results in the appearance of small green berries.

Flowery A term of high praise applied to the bouquet of certain white wines that recall the scent of flowers. The finer Moselles have this quality to a pronounced degree, but a few other wines, particularly those produced from the Riesling grape in cool districts, share this special quality.

Flurbereinigung A German term that refers to the ongoing project of reconstructing that country's vineyards by changing the existing landscape – especially where the terrain was difficult to farm – and reallocating vineyards among local growers, so that a given area may be cultivated more easily and yield a bigger and more consistent crop; more than half of Germany's vineyard acreage has already undergone such a transformation.

Flûte The French name for a tall, slender bottle like that used in Alsace and on the Rhine; many rosés are now shipped in clear-glass flutes as well. A flûte is also an attractive glass, often used for champagne, in the shape of a slender, elongated V.

Foch   *See* Maréchal Foch

Folle Blanche A white-wine grape, once widely grown in France, especially in the Cognac and Armagnac districts; fairly productive, it gives a pale, light wine, not distinguished but fresh,
and very high in acid. It is an excellent grape for distillation
into brandy, but its tightly packed bunches are vulnerable to
mildew and mould, and since phylloxera, when it has had to
be grafted on to American rootstock, it has not done well in
the calcerous soil of the Cognac district. Folle Blanche has
been supplanted by Ugni Blanc in Cognac, and by Baco 22A
in Armagnac. Most of France's acreage is now around
Nantes, at the mouth of the Loire, where it is known as Gros
Plant and produces the light, tart VDQS wine Gros Plant du
Pays Nantais. There were 250 acres of Folle Blanche in California in the 1970s, but this has since diminished to fewer
than 100 acres.

Fombrauge, Château One of the largest vineyards in Saint-Emilion whose
120 acres of vineyards produce more than 25,000 case of
appealing red wine entitled to the *grand cru* appellation.

Fonreaud, Château A *cru bourgeois* in Listrac, in the Médoc district, under
the same ownership as Château Lestage; its 120 acres pro-
duce about 30,000 cases.

Forst A justly celebrated little town, of well under a thousand inhabitants and some 500 acres of vines, which produces what
are certainly among the best white wines of Germany's
Rheinpfalz region. The vineyards have a high proportion of
Riesling grapes, and the wines, while quite full-bodied, have
extraordinary elegance and bouquet, said to be due to outcroppings of a special sort of black basalt in the soil. All of
the leading Palatinate producers have acreage in Forst,
whose most famous vineyard is the 15-acre Jesuitengarten;
others include Kirchenstück, Ungeheuer, and Pechstein.
The Grosslage Forster Mariengarten, which also includes
vineyards situated in Wachenheim and Deidesheim, is often
seen, and wines so labelled are likely to be of a very high
quality.

Fortified Wines A category of wines to which brandy or, more accurately, neutral wine spirits have been added somewhere between the vineyard and the bottle; the best-known examples are port, sherry, Madeira, and Marsala. These wines generally contain between 17 and 21 percent alcohol, which makes them more stable than table wines, and less likely to spoil once opened. The wine spirits are not added simply to increase alcoholic strength, of course, but as a necessary step in the creation of different and distinctive types of wine.

Foudre A French term for a large wooden cask of indefinite size.

Fourcas Dupré, Château A *cru bourgeois exceptionnel* in the commune of Listrac, in the Médoc district; its 110 acres produce about 18,000 cases a year.

Fourcas Hosten, Château A well-known *cru bourgeois exceptionnel* in the commune of Listrac, in the Médoc district, acquired in 1971 by a French-American group that has renovated and expanded the vineyards; its 100 acres produce about 20,000 cases a year of a charming wine that combines fruit and structure.

Fourtet *See* Clos Fourtet

Foxy Foxes have had to do with vineyards since biblical days, generally as consumers, but many of the early settlers in America called the wild, native grape the Fox grape. The pronounced aroma - often called foxy – of native *labrusca* varieties, notably Concord, is unmistakable, whether as grape juice, grape jelly, or wine, and has been traced to the presence of methyl anthranilate. The French, who began to import American grape cuttings at the time of the phylloxera, and who were the first hybridizers of American and European varieties, called this aroma *queue de renard*, or "fox's tail", for no well-established reason. Wines having this wholly American grape-juice-like tang are usually found either delicious or undrinkable by those who taste them for the first time, but this is entirely a matter of personal preference.

Fragrant A term applied to a wine that has an especially pronounced and agreeable aroma or bouquet.

Frais French for "fresh"; it also means "cool", however, and *servir très frais* on a French wine label means "serve well chilled".

France This country has been called the world's vineyard. One fifth of all the wines of the world are produced in France, and French wine has long been the universal standard by which wine is judged. In recent years, of course, the finest wines of California, Italy, and now Australia have been widely acclaimed, and justifiably so, but French wines have been the prototypes for many of the top wines produced throughout the world. These include the reds of Bordeaux, made primarily from Cabernet Sauvignon and Merlot; the sweet white wines of Sauternes, from Sémillon and Sauvignon Blanc; the red and white wines of Burgundy, from Pinot Noir and Chardonnay; the whites of the Loire, from Chenin Blanc and Sauvignon Blanc; the reds of the northern Rhône, from Syrah; the rosés of Tavel and the reds of Châteauneuf-du-Pape, made primarily from Grenache; the wines of Beaujolais, from Gamay; the sweet Muscats produced along the Mediterranean Coast; and, of course, the sparkling wines of Champagne, made primarily from Pinot Noir and Chardonnay. (It should perhaps be added that Riesling attains its greatest distinction in Germany, Nebbiolo and Sangiovese in Italy, Zinfandel in California, and Palomino in the sherry district of Spain, but France's contribution to the roster of wines made from the best, and best-known, grape varieties is clear.) Nevertheless, out of an annual production of some 750 million cases, less than 20 percent has any real claim to superior quality; in fact, 40 to 50 percent of the crop is nameless – marketed simply as *vin rouge, vin blanc,* or *vin rosé,* it is a staple, like potatoes or milk. The French drink it with their meals not because the water in France is bad, but because this sort of wine is cheap, goes well with food, is cheering and pleasant; they like it better than coffee, tea, or sweet carbonated drinks, and in the opinion of many doctors (including, of course, Pasteur), it is a healthier mealtime beverage for adults than milk. Per capita consumption in France is about 100 bottles a year, compared with 15 bottles in the UK and 11 in the US, although admittedly French consumption has decreased by more than 20 percent in a decade, just as France's vineyard acreage has been reduced from more than 3 million acres to about 2.4 million; as a result of increased regional specialization and more efficient agricultural methods, however, total production is about the same

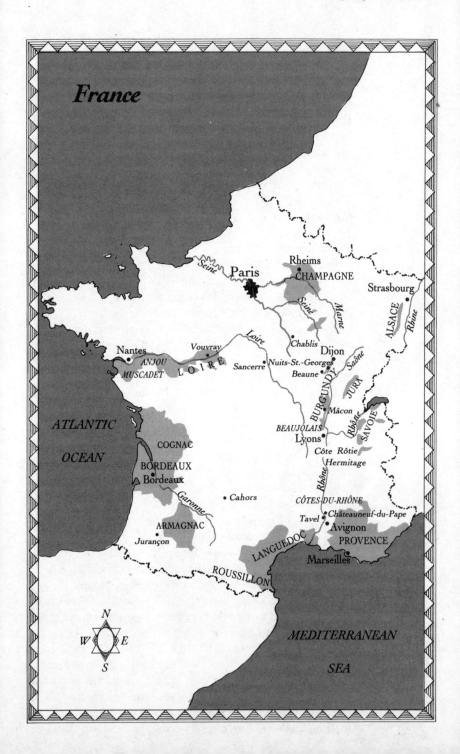

as in the recent past.

Nearly a third of France lies beyond the northern limit of commercial viticulture, its climate too sunless and cold, and too rainy and undependable for grape growing. The line has been clearly drawn by a dozen centuries of trial and error; it begins on the Atlantic Coast near Nantes, in southern Brittany, parallels the Loire some 50 miles to the north, sweeps up to include the Champagne region east to Paris, and runs on east to the border of Luxembourg on the Moselle. South of this line, except in a few mountainous districts, it is safe to say that there is hardly a French farm on which the vine has not been planted at one time or another and where wine has not been made. About two thirds of the 95 *départements* of France produce wine commercially.

France is a country of small vineyards rather than large, and the average holding of its 600,000 *vignerons* is only slightly more than 4 acres; there are few vineyards that comprise as much as 500 acres under one ownership. Although most French wine has traditionally been produced by peasant farmers, modern co-operatives have become increasingly important in France, especially in such regions as Alsace, Champagne, the Mâconnais and Beaujolais, the southern Rhône, and in the Languedoc-Roussillon region, also known as the Midi; co-operatives now account for nearly half the total crop. (It should be added that about 15 percent of the wine crop, from vineyards in the Charente and Charente-Maritime *départements*, is distilled to produce cognac.)

In no other country is wine produced according to such strict rules as in France, and there exists, in addition, a precise and immensely complicated classification of districts, villages, and *crus*, or individual vineyards. Clear lines of demarcation have been drawn, with the accord of all concerned, between great wines, good wines, decent, well-made wines, and *vins ordinaires*. Virtually all of the best French wines are entitled to the designation *Appellation Contrôlée*, and these words always appear on the label of such wines (except in the case of champagne, where they are considered unnecessary). The phrase means that the French government guarantees the origin of such wines, and their right to the name they bear; these words are also, to some degree, an assurance of quality, since they may appear only on wines made in delimited districts, from specified, superior grape varieties, and according to rules that control yield per acre, vinification, and other practices that affect quality. *Appellation Contrôlée* wines, which accounted for 10 to 15 percent of the crop in the 1960s, now account for 20 to 30 percent of the total. In all, there are about 250 appellations of origin, but as many of these apply to both red and white wines (and, in some cases, rosés as well), the total number of different wines is closer to 400. The appellations range from individual vineyards, such as Montrachet and Chambertin, to extensive districts, such as Alsace, Beaujolais, Côtes de Provence, and Côtes-du-Rhône. About twenty *vins mousseux*, or sparkling wines, have been accorded *Appellation Contrôlée* status, including Crémant d'Alsace, Blanquette de Limoux, Clairette de Die, Gaillac, Seyssel, and the *mousseux* of Saumur and Vouvray. A number of sweet, fortified wines are also accorded this rank, including Muscat de Beaumes de Venise, from the southern Rhône, and Muscat de Frontignan, Banyuls, and Rivesaltes, produced along the Mediterranean coast. The rest are table wines, and they include all of the best and practically all of the well-known wines of France: Bordeaux and its principal districts – Médoc, Saint-Emilion, Pomerol, Graves, and Sauternes; the wines of Burgundy, including Chablis, Nuits-Saint-Georges, Vosne-Romanée, Beaune, Pommard, Meursault, Puligny-Montrachet, Beaujolais, and Pouilly-Fuissé; such Loire wines as Muscadet, Vouvray, Sancerre, Pouilly-Fumé, and Rosé d'Anjou; Côte Rôtie, Hermitage, and Châteauneuf-du-Pape from the Rhône; the white wines of Alsace, the rosés of Provence, and many more. A complete list will be found beginning on page 529.

Below these in rank come about 35 others, officially known as VDQS, *Vins Délimités de Qualité Supérieure*. These (listed on page 536) are also controlled, though perhaps less stringently, and their labels carry the VDQS seal, which looks rather like a postage stamp. This category is less important than it once was because most of its best-known appellations have been elevated to *Appellation Contrôlée*, including Cahors, Corbières, Côtes de Provence, and Côtes du Ventoux; the remaining wines, including Gros Plant du Pays Nantais and Sauvignon de Saint-Bris, account for only 1 percent of the French crop. *Vins de pays* make up a still lower category established in 1973; these are country wines from specific, if somewhat broadly defined, districts – Vin de Pays d'Oc, Coteaux d'Ardèche -and they now account for 10 to 15 percent of the total crop. (*Vin de pays*, which is an official designation, should not be confused with *vin du pays*, which simply means a local wine.) The lowest grade of all, of course, is *vin de table*, sometimes referred to as *vin ordinaire*, which must be marked with its alcoholic content, but which may not carry a designation or origin; almost always a blended wine, it it controlled by the French equivalent of the pure food regulations. When sold under a proprietary brand name, it is known as a *vin de marque*.

If most French wine is admittedly common or mediocre, the best can be superb. Of all the fruits of nature and man's skill that have, over the centuries, given delight and comfort to people of good taste in all countries, the wines of France are easily first, and by a wide margin.

Franciacorta A DOC zone just northwest of the city of Brescia in Italy's Lombardy region. The red is made from Cabernet Franc, Barbera, Nebbiolo, and Merlot, the white from Pinot Bianco; the region is becoming best known for its fine sparkling wines, produced by the *méthode champenoise*, from various combinations of Pinot Bianco, Pinot Grigio, Pinot Nero, and Chardonnay.

Franconia English for Franken

Franken One of the eleven Anbaugebiete, or specified wine regions, of Germany, located southeast of Frankfurt along an extensive W-shaped portion of the Main River and on the western slopes of the Steigerwald mountains. The 13,000 acres of vineyards in this region, known in English as Franconia, produce about 4 percent of the total German crop, an average of 4 million cases a year, almost all of it white. About half the acreage is planted with Müller-Thurgau, and Sylvaner, which once accounted for more than half the plantings and now represents about 20 percent; nevertheless, it is Sylvaner that has achieved a particular reputation in Franken, and the name Franken Riesling, used in other parts of the world, actually refers to Sylvaner. Such new varieties as Bacchus, Kerner, and Scheurebe are also planted, while Riesling accounts for only 2 percent. Franken wines are unusual among those of Germany in that they are typically dry and flavourful, rather than delicate, flowery, and semisweet, and often marked by a particular earthy taste; most of them are marketed in a distinctive, flat-sided flagon known as a Bocksbeutel. There are three Bereiche in

Franken – Mainviereck, Maindreieck, and Steigerwald. The most important wine town is Würzburg, the capital of Franken, and as famous for its beer as its wine. Its most famous vineyard is the 210-acre Stein, and in the past most Franken wines were referred to as Steinwein; since 1971, only the wines from the Würzburger Stein vineyard may be so labelled. Other important wine towns in Franken are Randersacker, Escherndorf, Thüngersheim, Iphofen, and Castell. Although about half of the Franken wines are produced by co-operative cellars, the region includes three of the largest estates in Germany, all situated in Würzburg – Juliusspital, Bürgerspital, and the Staatlicher Hofkeller, or Bavarian State Domain – with a combined total of nearly 1,200 acres of vineyards; father east is the famed Fürstlich Castell'sches Domänenamt of the Princes of Castell.

Franken Riesling *See* Sylvaner

Frappé When used of a wine, this French term means "very cold"; a liqueur served *frappé*, however, is poured over shaved ice.

Frascati Long considered the traditional house wine of the *trattorie* of Rome, this agreeable dry white is now widely exported as well. It is produced around the village of Frascati, a dozen miles southeast of Rome, in the Alban Hills, also known as the Castelli Romani; the average annual production of this wine, made from Malvasia and Trebbiano grapes, is about 2 million cases.

Frecciarossa A well-known estate, whose name means "red arrow", situated near Casteggio in the Oltrepò Pavese district of Italy's Lombardy region; its red and white wines are now marketed under the DOC Oltrepò Pavese.

Free Run Applied to juice, it is that part of the juice that runs out freely from white-wine grapes after crushing but before pressing; the crushed grapes are then pressed to yield additional juice. Red wines are fermented in contact with the skins, and free-run wine is that part of the total that flows freely off the skins out of the fermentation tanks; the skins are then pressed to yield press wine, which may or may not be recombined with the free-run wine.

Freiherr German for "baron", as in Freiherr Langwerth von Simmern.

Freisa An Italian red-wine grape cultivated in Piedmont, where it produces two quite different wines; the one more likely to appeal to the average wine drinker is a dry red wine, fruity and berry-like, often a little tart and rough when young, but quite ready to drink; even more popular in Italy, but rarely exported, is the Freisa that is both *abboccato* and *frizzante* – this slightly sweet and sparkling wine is not one that will please all palates. A part of the total production of Freisa is entitled to the DOCs Freisa di Chieri and Freisa d'Asti.

French-American Hybrids In the late nineteenth century, when French vineyards were devastated by phylloxera, such hybridizers as Baco, Kuhlmann, Ravat, Seibel, and Seyve-Villard created hybrids, or crosses, of European *vinifera* grape varieties and phylloxera-resistant native American varieties in an attempt to produce plants that would have the sturdiness and resistance to disease of the American parent, yet produce wines with the quality of the French parent. These new varieties, known as French-American hybrids, have never achieved the quality of such classic *vinifera* varities as Chardonnay or Cabernet Sauvignon, but many of them produce attractive and appealing wines, and at one time there were more than a million acres planted in France. When grafting *vinifera* scions to phylloxera-resistant American rootstock was adopted as the best solution to that scourge, most growers lost interest in the new hybrid varieties, also known as *producteurs directes*, or "direct producers", because they can be planted on their own roots. Then, in the 1930s, Philip Wagner, who later founded Boordy Vineyards, experimented with French-American hybrids in his Maryland vineyard as an alternative to such native grapes as Concord, Catawba, Delaware, and Niagara, which were then believed to be the only varieties capable of surviving the cold winters and humid summers of the eastern United States, but whose pungent, grapey wines were not to everyone's taste; much of the credit for the success of these new varieties goes to Wagner, who did much to popularize the better hybrids in America. Charles Fournier of Gold Seal was the first to plant a commercial vineyard with French-American hybrids – in the 1940s in the Finger Lakes – but these varieties were not widely planted in the East until the 1960s. Many wineries east of the Rockies now make wine from these grapes, which are known by such names as Aurora, Baco Noir, Cascade,

Chelois, DeChaunac, Maréchal Foch, Seyval Blanc, and Vidal-Blanc. A more complete list is on page 566. *See* Hybrid, Native American Grapes.

French Colombard *See* Colombard

Fresh Although many people have been led to believe that an old wine is necessarily better than a younger one, this is by no means the case – the majority of wines are at their best when young. Most white wines, all rosés, and a good many lighter reds have an engaging freshness in their youth that they tend to lose after their first birthday. A fresh wine is one that has not lost this early charm.

Freidrich-Wilhelm-Gymnasium A famous secondary school in Trier, on the Moselle, founded in the sixteenth century; its endowments include extensive vineyard acreage in many of the best villages of the Moselle and the Saar, including Bernkastel, Graach, Trittenheim, Zeltingen, and Ockfen.

Friuli-Venezia Giulia A region in the northeast corner of Italy, adjoining Yugoslavia and Austria; its capital is Trieste. Although not one of Italy's most important regions in terms of volume, about one third of its wines are DOC, and these 4 to 5 million cases represent a tremendous range of excellent wines. Virtually all of the wines, which are produced in the Friuli part of the region, are marketed with varietal names; these come from such familiar French and German white grapes as Pinot Grigio (Pinot Gris), Pinot Bianco (Pinot Blanc), Chardonnay, Sauvignon, Traminer, Müller-Thurgau, and Riesling Renano (the true Rhine Riesling), and such red grapes as Merlot, Cabernet Franc, Cabernet Sauvignon, and Pinot Nero (Pinot Noir). In addition, white wines are produced from such native varieties as Tocai Friulano, Verduzzo, Ribolla, Malvasia, and Picolit; Refosco is an indigenous red grape. Although the region is best known for its whites, Merlot is by far the most widely planted variety; Tocai Friulano is next in volume. Most, but not all, of these varieties are planted in each of the DOC zones of Friuli, which include Grave del Friuli (which accounts for more than half the wines of the entire region), Collio, Colli Orientali del Friuli, Aquileia, Latisana, and Isonzo.

Frizzante An Italian term meaning "slightly sparkling", equivalent to the French *pétillant*. Many Italian wines, red and white, are bottled in both a still and *frizzante* version, the latter often slightly sweet as well. They foam up briefly when poured and their prickly or crackling taste makes them appealing to many comsumers. Lambrusco is the best-known example of a *frizzante* wine.

Fronsac A small red-wine district in the Bordeaux region that deserves to be better known that it is. The little town of Fronsac is on the Dordogne River, just west of Saint-Emilion and Libourne, and the vineyards are on steep hills overlooking the verdant and singularly beautiful valley. There are actually two appellations around Fronsac – one is simply Fronsac (formerly Côtes de Fronsac), the other is Canon-Fronsac (formerly Côtes de Canon-Fronsac); the two appellations produce more than 500,000 cases of wine in abundant vintages, with Fronsac accounting for three quarters of the total. Canon-Fronsac is traditionally considered a somewhat finer wine, but the vineyards within both appellations are based primarily on Cabernet Franc, and produce firm, deep-coloured, distinctive wines whose overall quality has improved in recent years.

Frontignan A town on the Mediterranean coast of France, between Sète and Montpellier, famous for its sweet, golden wine from the grape variety known as Muscat de Frontignan. The wine, labelled Muscat de Frontignan (to distinguish it from Muscat de Rivesaltes, Muscat de Lunel, and others, which are made from the less fine Muscat of Alexandria), is the best of the category known as *Vins Doux Naturels*, which are actually fortified to contain a minimum of 15 percent alcohol and 11 percent residual sugar; production averages 200,000 cases.

Frost Of the many anxieties that beset the vintner and cause him sleepless nights, few are as bad as frost. And since most of the best still and sparkling wines of the world are produced fairly close to the northern limit of the vine, frost is a worry shared by most wine growers; even California is not exempt, especially those vineyards situated on a valley floor, where cold air accumulates. Theoretically, the danger exists in French and German vineyards for about six weeks, from early April to mid-May. The vines are safely dormant during the winter, but once the shoots begin to grow, they are vulnerable to frost, which can considerably reduce the year's crop. In some cases the damage is more lasting, and can affect the following year's vintage as well; in extreme cases, the vines are destroyed and have to be replanted.

Progressive growers in some of the northern districts, notably Champagne, Chablis, and the Moselle, now set out little fuel-oil or gas stoves in the vineyards, and these have proved enormously helpful. Other antifrost measures have been no less successful, both in America and abroad; these include infrared heaters overhead, enormous fans to mix the warmer air above the vineyards with the colder air at ground level, and, where adequate water supplies are available, sprinklers to coat the vines with a protective layer of ice.

Fruity Said of a wine that has the definite and attractive aroma and flavour of fresh, ripe fruit, though not necessarily that of grapes. Almost all fine young wines are fruity, few poor ones are, and very few old ones, however good. Beaujolais has this charming quality when young, as do all the better rosés, Alsace wines, almost all German wines, a number of red and white wines from northern Italy, and many California Zinfandels, Chenin Blancs, and Johannisberg Rieslings, among many others.

Fuder Traditional oak cask of Germany's Moselle region, with a capacity of 1,000 litres (about 111 cases); now that few German wines are still stored in wood, the *fuder* is primarily a measure of trade.

Fuissé A township west of Mâcon, in southern Burgundy, whose wines are entitled to the appellation Pouilly-Fuissé.

Full A wine-taster's term, related to body, applied to mouth-filling wines that are likely to be comparatively high in alcohol; a Châteauneuf-du-Pape is fuller than a delicate Moselle.

Fumé Blanc A name devised by Robert Mondavi in the late 1960s to market a crisp, dry Sauvignon Blanc at a time when most California wines labelled Sauvignon Blanc were semisweet; it is derived from Blanc Fumé, the name used for Sauvignon Blanc in the village of Pouilly-sur-Loire, whose wines go to market as Pouilly-Fumé.

Furmint A celebrated white-wine grape of Hungary, long the princi-

pal variety used to make the legendary Tokay, and susceptible to the beneficial effects of *Botrytis cinerea*, the "noble
rot" that creates the shrivelled Aszu berries; in recent years,
however, wines made from the Hárslevelü variety have been
blended with Furmint to make Tokay. Furmint is also
planted in other parts of Hungary, where it produces a full-
bodied dry wine. Furmint bears no relation to Tokay d'Alsace or to the Tocai of northeast Italy, but it is considered
identical to the Sipon of Yugoslavia.

Fürst   German for "prince", as in Furst von Metternich.

Fût   French for "barrel".

❦ G

Gabiano   A new DOC established in 1984 for a long-lived red wine
produced from the Barbera grape in a small zone north of
Asti, in Italy's Piedmont region.

Gaffelière, Château La   A *premier grand cru classé* of Saint-Emilion, known
as La Gaffelière-Naudes until 1964, and owned by the Malet
Roquefort family for more than 300 years; its 54 acres of
vineyards, situated just below those of Château Ausone,
produce about 9,000 cases a year of a supple red wine whose
quality has been improving in recent years. The 40-acre
Château Tertre-Daugay, a *grand cru classé*, is now under the
same ownership.

Gaillac   Red and white wines produced around the town of this
name, on the Tarn River, some 30 miles northeast of Toulouse, in southwestern France. The white, often semisweet,
is made primarily from the native Mauzac grape; such other
indigenous varieties as Oudenc and L'En de L'El are also
cultivated, as are Sauvignon Blanc and Sémillon. Much of the
white wine is transformed into sparkling wine, either by the
méthode champenoise or by the *méthode gallaçoise*, in which
the wines are bottled before the first fermentation is complete; the Gaillac sparkling wines may be dry or semisweet,
fully sparkling or *pétillant*. The red wines are made from
such native varieties as Duras and Brocol, as well as Gamay,
Syrah, and Merlot.

Galestro   A name adopted by a group of Chianti producers for a light, dry white wine from central Tuscany made primarily from Trebbiano and Malvasia grapes, plus other varieties that may include Pinot Bianco, Chardonnay, and Vernaccia. The self-imposed requirements are that Galestro must be fermented slowly at a low temperature to retain its fruit and freshness, and that it contain no more than 10.5 percent alcohol. Galestro is the name of the friable grey rock found in many Tuscan vineyards.

Gallisation The adding of water and sugar to grape juice before fermentation – the first dilutes and reduces the acidity of the finished wine, the second increases its alcoholic content; it differs from chaptalization in that water, as well as sugar, is added, which, of course, increases the volume of wine produced. This practice, first proposed by a Doctor Gall, is more often referred to as amelioration; it is outlawed in most wine-producing countries, although it is permitted in New York and certain other eastern states, where native grapes are not only low in sugar but high in acid.

Gallo Nero Italian for "black rooster", this refers to the famous neck seal depicting a black rooster on a gold ground used by members of the *consorzio* of the Chianti Classico zone for wines that conform to certain self-imposed quality requirements.

Gamay An excellent red-wine grape, grown to the virtual exclusion of all other varieties in the Beaujolais district of France, where it produces light red wines noted for their charm, fruit and lively acidity. Elsewhere in Burgundy the grape does less well and cannot legally be planted in the better vineyards, where Pinot Noir's supremacy remains unchallenged; wines made from both varieties, crushed and vinified together, may be sold as Bourgogne Passe-tout-grains. Gamay is also cultivated along the Loire and shows up in such wines as Gamay de Touraine and Anjou Gamay. In California, it was long believed that the variety known as Gamay Beaujolais was the true grape of the French district, but it has now been identified as a clone of Pinot Noir and its wines may be sold under either name. Also, a number of ampelographers now believe that the California variety known as Gamay or Napa Gamay is actually the less distinguished Valdiguié of southern France. There were more than 4,000 acres of each of these two varieties planted in the mid-1970s, much of that in Monterey, but that has since diminished to about 1,500 acres of each; if properly vinified, however, each variety is capable of producing appealing light red wines.

Gamay Beaujolais *See* Gamay

Gambellara An Italian white wine from a DOC zone adjacent to that of Soave, in the Veneto region; as for Soave, the wine is made primarily from the Garganega grape. Most of the district's production consists of dry wine, but a small amount of sweet Recioto is also made, as well as a minuscule amount of Vin Santo.

Gard A French *département* extending from the lower Rhône Valley well into what is called the Midi and considered a part of the region known as Languedoc-Roussillon; its 200,000 acres of vineyards produce about 70 million cases a year, 98 percent of it red and rosé made from Grenache, Carignan, and Cinsault. Most of this is rather ordinary, of course, but the Gard includes the village of Tavel, famous for its rosé, the nearby village of Lirac, and part of the Côtes-du-Rhône district, as well as the less-distinguished appellations Costières du Gard and Clairette de Bellegarde.

Garda The largest and one of the most beautiful of the Italian lakes, noted for its mild climate; its northern tip extends into what was, prior to 1918, Austrian territory, and the low hills round its wide southern end are largely covered with vineyards, as is the area west of the lake. These produce quite a collection of different wines, red, white and rosé, all of which, oddly enough, seem to have a certain family resemblance – they are all low in alcohol, and therefore easy to drink; they are delightfully fresh and fruity when young, and improve practically not at all with age; they are, in other words, wonderfully good carafe wines, among the best such wines in the world. Most of them are drunk up, gratefully and promptly, by the northern Italians themselves, and their Swiss neighbours, with the enthusiastic help of a good many thirsty tourists. The best of the reds is Bardolino; the village called Garda, incidentally, adjoins Bardolino, and its wines are entitled to this name. Two appealing whites produced at the southern end of the lake are Lugana and Bianco di Custoza. Reds and rosês, the latter called Chiaretto, are produced west of the lake, in the province of Brescia, and entitled to the appellation Riviera del Garda Bresciano.

Garganega An Italian white-wine grape widely planted in the Veneto, where it is the principal variety used in the popular Soave and in the similar, but less familiar, Gambellara, it is also used to a lesser extent in Bianco di Custoza.

Garnacha The most extensively planted wine grape in Spain, found in Rioja, Penedès, and many other regions; it is known as Grenache in France and California. It is a high-yielding variety whose full-bodied red wines are a useful component in blends; it is also used as the base for some sweet, fortified wines. Garnacha Blanca, a white-wine variety, is less frequently seen.

Garonne The largest river of southwestern France, rising in the Spanish Pyrenées near Luchon and flowing by way of Toulouse to Bordeaux, just north of which it is joined by the Dordogne, to form the wide estuary of the Gironde. It is navigable as far as Bordeaux, and the vineyards of Sauternes, Barsac, Cérons, Loupiac, Sainte-Croix-du-Mont, and part of Graves overlook its valley.

Garrafeira Portuguese for "wine cellar", but as used on a red-wine label it indicates a wine that has been aged in wood for at least two years and for an additional year in bottle; in practice, wines so labelled, which include some of Portugal's finest, are aged even longer. White wines so labelled have been aged for at least six months in wood and six months in bottle.

Gattinara A fine Italian red wine made primarily from the Nebbiolo grape in a small district northwest of Milan in the Piedmont region. The best examples are full-bodied, elegant, and long-lived, but few achieve the same depth and complexity as do the two classic Nebbiolo-based wines Barolo and Barbaresco, produced 50 miles south of the village of Gattinara. About 225 acres of vineyards in the DOC zone yield 40,000 to 50,000 cases a year; up to 10 percent of Bonarda may be added to Nebbiolo (whose local name is Spanna), and the wine must be aged for four years, two of them in wood.

Gavi A dry white wine, one of Italy's best, made from the Cortese grape around the little town of Gavi, in southeastern Piedmont, about 30 miles north of Genoa. This pale, fresh wine, noted for its lively acidity, was granted DOC status in 1974 as Gavi or Cortese di Gavi, and has become increasingly known since then; production has increased from about 40,000 cases a year in 1975 to more than 400,000 cases today. Gavi dei Gavi is not a special appellation, but a proprietary name created by one winery, and now prohibited by Common Market regulations. Wines labelled Gavi di Gavi come from the commune of Gavi itself (there are four adjoining communes also entitled to the DOC Gavi), but are not necessarily better than those simply labelled Gavi. Gavi is considered the best of the Cortese wines; others are sold simply as Cortese del Piemonte or with another DOC name, Cortese dell'Alto Monferrato.

Le Gay, Château A 20-acre vineyard in the Pomerol district under the same ownership as the smaller and perhaps more distinctive Château Lafleur.

Gay-Lussac A French wine chemist who, in 1810, formulated the equation for the fermentation of sugar into alcohol and carbon-dioxide gas; his name is also synonymous with a scale that measures the percent of alcohol by volume – 14 G.L. = 14 percent by volume.

Gazéifié French for "artificial carbonation", that is, making a sparkling wine by the injection of carbon dioxide.

Gazin, Château One of the biggest vineyards in the Pomerol district whose 57 acres produce about 10,000 cases a year.

Gebiet German for "region", or "district", as in Anbaugebiet.

Gebruder German for "brothers".

Geisenheim An important wine-producing village in Germany's Rheingau region, with more than 1,000 acres of vineyards, almost entirely Riesling. In great years the Geisenheimers are of absolutely top quality, with great fruit and breed; the best vineyards include Rothenberg, Mauerchen, Fuchsberg, and Mönchspfad. Geisenheim is also famous for its school of oenology and viticulture, a centre of research and training known throughout the world.

Gemeinde A German word meaning "village", or "community"; a

Gemeinde name always precedes that of an individual vineyard (Einzellage) or collective site (Grosslage), as in Wehlener Sonnenuhr or Piesporter Michelsberg.

Généreux   A French tasting term applied to a big full-bodied warming wine.

Generic   Properly speaking, this refers to a wine name, such as White Table Wine or Vintage Red, or a designation of category, such as rosé or sparkling wine, unrelated to the wine's origin or the grape variety from which it is made. But in the United States the term *generic*, or *semigeneric*, also refers to such names as Chablis, Sauterne, Burgundy, Rhine Wine, Sherry, Port, and Champagne when used to label American wines. They are names that were in wide general use and, to some extent, in the public domain before today's strict rules regarding appellations of origin went into effect, and it is an unquestioned fact that wines from New York, Ohio, and California (not to mention Australia, Chile, and other countries) were being sold with these names well over a hundred years ago. In most cases no fraud was intended, and a wine was simply given the existing name that seemed to fit it best. All this is now highly displeasing to the European countries whose names have been usurped to market wines that, in most cases, bear little relation to the original. The U.S. government has so far refused to renounce the use of these place names on the grounds that it would be unfair to American vintners to deprive them of names that now have substantial trade value. As a compromise, the number of such semigeneric names is limited and will not be extended, and the wines must show their origin on their labels, as California Burgundy, New York State Rhine Wine, and so on. And, of course, wines labelled with such semigeneric names cannot be exported to Europe.

Geranium   A descriptive term applied to a wine whose disagreeable smell is reminiscent of geraniums; it is caused by the improper use of sorbic acid.

Germany   Despite the wholly merited and centuries-old fame of its Rhine wines and Moselles, Germany cannot really be described as either a major wine-producing or a true wine-drinking country. Its vineyard acreage is about one tenth that of France, and the average German drinks less than a third as much wine as the average Italian, and barely half as much as the sober Swiss. Nevertheless, experts agree that the finest white wines of Germany are of astonishing quality, among the very best in the world, and that even the sound, less expensive wines have their special character and charm; they are light, refreshing, easy to drink, fruity, fragrant, most agreeable, and deservedly popular. All German wines of any real consequence are white – red wines, usually pale in colour and often semisweet – account for less than 15 percent of the total. With rare exceptions the white wines of Germany are low in alcohol – 8 to 11 percent is the normal range – and they usually contain a trace or more of pleasing sweetness that is, in turn, balanced by a fruity acidity that gives German wines distinction and appeal. Those ranked as the best and, in any case, the rarest and most expensive, are very sweet indeed. Almost all German wines are shipped in tall, slender bottles – brown for Rhine wines, green for Moselles; some are marketed in stumpy, flat-sided flagons called Bocksbeutel. Of course, it must be kept in mind that in Germany, as in all other wine-producing lands, there is more mediocre and common wine than good, but the average of quality is quite high.

The German vineyards have increased from 165,000 acres in the mid-1960s to nearly 250,000 acres today, and annual production, too, has increased from an average of 85 million cases in the 1970s to about 115 million in the 1980s. Grapes do not ripen fully every year in Germany's cool and uncertain climate – the vineyards are among the most northerly in the world – and the size of the crop varies enormously: 170 million cases were produced in 1982, only 57 million in 1985. In many districts, grapes can be grown commercially only on south-facing hillsides along river valleys, and relatively few varieties can be successfully cultivated. Fortunately, many of them yield superior white wine, none more so than the Riesling, which produces almost all of Germany's finest wines. This variety accounts for only 20 percent of the total acreage, however; Müller-Thurgau represents 25 percent, Sylvaner about 10 percent. Other white varieties include Gewürztraminer, Ruländer (Pinot Gris), Weissburgunder (Pinot Blanc), and Gutedel (Chasselas). In addition, a number of new varieties that ripen more easily than Riesling have been developed in Germany, and such grapes as Kerner, Bacchus, Faberrebe, Huxelrebe, Optima, Ortega, and Ehrenfelser, which did not exist in the vineyards twenty

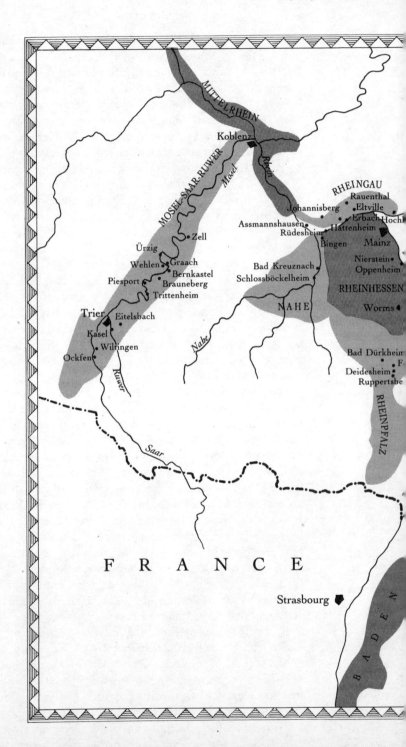

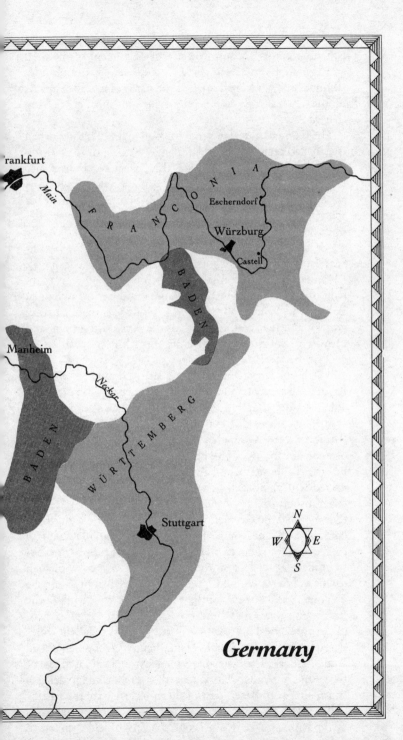

Frankfurt

Main

F R A N C O N I A

Escherndorf

Würzburg

Castell

BADEN

Manheim

Neckar

BADEN

W Ü R T T E M B E R G

Stuttgart

N
W E
S

Germany

years ago, plus the more established Morio-Muskat and Scheurebe, now account for almost 25 percent of the total acreage. Red varieties include Portugieser, Spätburgunder (Pinot Noir), and Trollinger. If the name of a grape appears on the label, at least 85 percent of the wine must come from that variety.

The German wine laws that took effect in 1971 established four broad regions whose wines may be sold only as *Tafelwein* or "table wine". (In 1982, these were subdivided into fifteen Landwein districts, similar to the French *vin de pays* appellations, but not widely used.) Eleven Anbaugebiete, or specified regions, were also established, and one or another of these appellations will be found on the labels of virtually all German wines. They are the Rheingau and the Mosel-Saar-Ruwer (which produce most of the fine Rieslings); Rheinhessen and the Rheinpfalz (which account for about half of all German wines); the Nahe; Franken, or Franconia, Baden, and Württemberg (which produce somewhat drier wines); and the small districts of the Ahr, Mittelrhein, and Hessische Bergstrasse (which accounts for less than 2 percent of the total).

All the German vineyards are situated along the Rhine River or its many tributaries, but there are six Anbaugebiete situated along the Rhine itself. The Rheingau, acknowledged as the best, faces due south along a 20-mile stretch of the Rhine between Wiesbaden and Bingen; it includes such celebrated wine towns as Hochheim, Rauenthal, Eltville, Johannisberg, Rüdesheim, and Assmannshausen (best known for its red wines), as well as such famous vineyards as Scholss Johannisberg, Schloss Vollrads, and Steinberg. Rheinhessen, the largest of the German wine regions, is on the west or left bank of the Rhine, south of the Rheingau, from Mainz down to Worms; it produces much of the world's supply of Liebfraumilch, as well as more individualized wines from such towns as Nierstein and Oppenheim. The Rheinpfalz, or the Palatinate, still farther south, is also on the west bank of the Rhine, and extends as far as the French border; it, too, produces a great deal of Liebfraumilch, as well as excellent wines from the towns of Forst, Deidesheim, Wachinheim, and Ruppertsberg. The extensive Baden district is situated east of the Rhine, and most of its vineyards stretch from Heidelberg south almost to Basel; part of the vineyards face the Rheinpfalz, part face Alsace across the Rhine. The Mittelrhein is in the Rhine gorge, from Bingen, past Koblenz, almost to

Bonn; and Hessische Bergstrasse is just north of Baden.

The Rhine's most important tributary in terms of water, but even more so in terms of wine, is the Moselle (spelled Mosel in German). The wines produced here are fully equal to the best of the Rhine, but in a different style – lighter, more delicate, higher in acid and lower in alcohol, compared to the somewhat riper and more opulent wines of the best Rhine sites. The best-known wine villages include Piesport, Brauneberg, Bernkastel, Wehlen, Graach, and Urzig. The Moselle, in turn, has its tributaries, the Saar and Ruwer, hardly less distinguished; this entire region, which extends from below Trier to Koblenz, where the Moselle joins the Rhine, is known as Mosel-Saar-Ruwer, and its wines are so labelled. The Nahe region takes its name from the river that joins the Rhine at Bingen, directly opposite Rüdesheim; it produces many wines of high quality some miles upstream, to the southwest, around Bad Kreuznach and Schlossböck-elheim. Franken (Franconia in English) is Germany's east-ernmost region: the Main, before joining the Rhine near Mainz, cuts its winding way through the hills of Franconia, whose most famous wines come from Würzburg and a half dozen other villages nearby; the quality wines are shipped in the stumpy flagon called Bocksbeutel. The Ahr, along the river of that name, is the second smallest of the eleven dis-tricts, and the northernmost; it produces more red wine than white. Württemberg, spread out along the Neckar River and its small tributaries, lies to the east of the Rhine below Fran-ken; this region, whose principal city is Stuttgart, also has extensive red-wine vineyards.

Within the eleven regions there are about 2,600 Einzella-gen, or individual vineyards, reduced from more than 25,000 by the 1971 law; with very few exceptions, the minimum size of an Einzellage is 5 hectares (12.5 acres). Vineyard names appear on a label preceded by their village of origin (which takes the possessive *er*), as Rauenthaler Baiken, Piesporter Treppchen, Forster Jesuitengarten. But between the regional names and that of individual vineyards are two other categories: Bereiche and Grosslagen. Bereich means "district"; there are more than thirty such designations within the eleven Anbaugebieten, and they can be rather ex-tensive; Bereich Johannisberg includes the entire Rheingau, Bereich Bernkastel encompasses about 60 villages of the middle Moselle, and Bereich Nierstein includes about 25,000 acres within Rheinhessen. A Grosslage is a combination of Einzellagen, or individual vineyards; there are about 150 Grosslagen with an average size of more than 1,500 acres. Although grouping a number of adjoining vineyards together into one Grosslage (whose name may be more familiar, or easier to remember, than that of the individual vineyards it encompasses) may be of help to producer and consumer alike, the problem is that such wines are labelled exactly the same way as those from individual vineyards – Rauenthaler Steinmächer, Piesporter Michelsberg, and Forster Mariengarten – with no indication that these are collective sites. Because there are so many village and vineyard names in Germany, and because almost all of the finest wines, from the best estates, are produced in limited quantities, most German wines are marketed with regional names, such as Bereich Bernkastel, Bereich Nierstein, Piesporter Michelsberg, Zeller Schwarze Katz, and Niersteiner Gutes Domtal. The best-known regional wine is, of course, Liebfraumilch, almost all of which comes from Rheinhessen and Rheinpfalz; Moseltaler, the equivalent wine from the Moselle, was introduced as an appellation in 1986.

German wines are not ranked by vineyard, but by the ripeness of the grapes at the time of harvest, as measured by their natural sugar content on the Oechsle scale. The lowest requirements are those for Tafelwein, which usually accounts for less than 10 percent of the crop. Wines that achieve somewhat higher minimum requirements – which vary from one region to another, and from one grape variety to another – are entitled to be labelled Qualitätswein bestimmter Anbaugebiete usually shortened to Qualitätswein or QbA. Those that achieve an even higher natural sugar content may be marketed as Qualitätswein mit Prädikat, or quality wine with special attributes. These attributes, which are further indications of natural sugar content, and which must appear on the label, are Kabinett, Spätlese (late picking), Auslese (selected picking), Beerenauslese (selected berry picking), Trockenbeerenauslese (selected picking of dried, or shrivelled, berries), and Eiswein (ice wine). Thus, a Riesling from the Rheingau must achieve 57 degrees Oechsle to be labelled Qualitätswein (which would produce a wine with about 7 percent alcohol), 73 degrees for the Prädikat designation Kabinett (the equivalent of about 17 percent sugar, with a potential alcohol content of 9.5 percent), 85 degrees for Spätlese (20 percent sugar, 11.4 percent potential alcohol), and so on; the minimum requirements are slightly lower for the Moselle, where the climate is somewhat cooler. (Qualitätswein and Tafelwein may be chaptalized, Qualitätswein mit Prädikat may not; today, most German wines, including Spätlesen and many Auslesen, are fermented until dry, then sweetened before bottling with *Süssreserve*, which is unfermented grape juice.) The rare, honeyed, intensely sweet Beerenauslese and Trockenbeerenauslese wines, usually made from grapes affected by *Botrytis cinerea* (the same "noble rot" that affect the wines of France's Sauternes region), and much prized by connoisseurs, are produced in only one or two vintages a decade, and then only in very limited quantities. Auslese wines, too, are produced only a few times a decade, and rarely account for more than 3 percent of the crop. Thus, a special vineyard in Germany may theoretically produce eight different levels of quality, based on ripeness and sugar content, from Tafelwein to Trockenbeerenauslese; in practice, only two or three categories would be produced in a given vintage. Germany's unusual classification system quickly reveals the wide variation in quality from one vintage to the next: in 1985 and 1989 nearly half the crop consisted of Prädikat wines, with much of it of Spätlese and Auslese quality; Prädikat wines amounted to only 5 percent in 1984 and only 15 percent in 1986, virtually all of it Kabinett.

The sweetest German wines are difficult to match with food and are more appropriately consumed on their own, after a meal. The Qualitätswein (which includes Liebfraumilch and the regional appellations) are more appealing with meals or for casual sipping, as are such Prädikat wines as the medium-dry Kabinett and the riper, medium sweet Spätlese. In fact, there has been a marked increase in the production of Trocken (dry) and Halbtrocken (half dry) wines since the mid-1970s. These dry wines, which contain no more than 1.8 percent sugar, and which are meant to be consumed with meals, account for as much as 35 percent of the Qualitätswein crop in some vintages; popular in Germany, they are less frequently seen in export markets, where a variety of dry white wines is widely available.

The labels of all quality wines bear an A.P. number, which indicates that the wine has been officially tasted and analyzed. The term *Erzeugerabfüllung*, the equivalent of "estate bottled", appears on most of the better German wines; the term may also be used by co-operative cellars, however, so the name of the estate or producer is perhaps a more important guide to quality. Germany has more than 300 co-operative cellars, and they now account for about a third of the crop; they are especially important in Baden, Württemberg, and Franken. The Germans also produce and consume a great deal of sparkling wine, called Sekt; Deutscher Sekt must be made entirely with wine from German vineyards, but a wine labelled simply Sekt will almost certainly contain wine from other Common Market countries, usually France or Italy.

Geropiga   A very sweet port, used for blending, made by stopping fermentation while the must still retains most of its grape sugar.

Gevrey-Chambertin   A world-famous wine-producing village, eight miles south of Dijon, in Burgundy's Côte d'Or region, whose red wines are among the finest in France. The 1,460 acres of vineyards situated within the commune produce, on average, a total of nearly 200,000 cases of wine, more than any other village of the Côte d'Or. Most of this is entitled only to the village appellation Gevrey-Chambertin and is so labelled; such wines can be very good, but they do not come from the best vineyards. Even better are wines from the *premier cru* vineyards, notably Clos Saint-Jacques and Les Varoilles, as well as Les Cazetiers and Combe au Moine. The very best wines of Gevrey-Chambertin come from the vineyards designated as *grands crus*; remarkably enough, there are nine such appellations in this village, out of a total of only twenty-four *grands crus* producing red wine in the entire Côte d'Or. The most famous is Chambertin (whose name was appended to that of the village in the nineteenth century) and the adjoining Chambertin-Clos de Bèze; the others are Chapelle-Chambertin, Charmes-Chambertin, Griotte-Chambertin, Latricières-Chambertin, Mazis-Chambertin, Mazoyères-Chambertin (whose wines may be labelled Charmes-Chambertin, and almost always are), and Ruchottes-Chambertin. At their best, these are among the very greatest red wines of Burgundy and, indeed, of the world.

Gewürztraminer   An excellent and unusual grape that produces distinctive white wines with a pungent, perfumed aroma and a rich, even oily texture; the name, formerly applied to a selection of Traminer (*gewürz* means "spicy"), has now replaced Traminer in most wine regions. The grape is usually associated with Alsace, where it produces a dry, flavourful wine, but it is also cultivated in Germany, Austria, and northern Italy; in fact, the grape is thought to have derived its name from the village of Tramin, in what is now the Alto Adige district. In California, plantings increased from 400 acres in the mid-1960s to more than 4,500 acres in the mid 1980s, and have since been reduced to about 2,000 acres, most of those in Sonoma, Monterey, and Santa Barbara counties. The varietal aroma of many California examples is somewhat muted, by comparison to those from Alsace, and they are usually bottled with a touch of sweetness to offset the natural bitterness of the grape; however, excellent examples have also been made in both a dry style and in a rich, honeyed, late-harvest style.

Ghemme A fine Italian red wine produced in a 140-acre DOC zone adjoining Gattinara in the Piedmont region; Nebbiolo, the principal grape, may be blended with Vespolina and Bonarda.

Gigondas An appellation created in 1971 for red wines produced round the village of that name, situated a few miles northeast of Châteauneuf-du-Pape, in the southern Rhône region of France. The sturdy, dependable wines are made primarily from Grenache (which cannot exceed 65 percent of the total) and lesser amounts of Cinsault, Syrah, and Mourvèdre; annual production generally varies from 350,000 to 400,000 cases.

Girasol An octagonal frame first used in the Penedès region of Spain to prepare wines for disgorging, an essential step in the production of *méthode champenoise* wines. The traditional technique or *rémuage*, or riddling, involves the manipulation by hand of every bottle until it is upside down, with all the sediment resting against the temporary cork. With a *girasol*, about 500 bottles can be manipulated together, providing a quicker, more efficient, and less expensive way to perform this step. This labour-saving technique has been adopted by many firms in France's Champagne region (where a similar device is usually referred to as a *gyropalette*), and in other countries as well; the latest models are automated and computerized.

Gironde From the point of view of fine wine, perhaps the most important *département* of France, since almost the entire Bordeaux wine region lies within its borders. The *département* takes its name from the river, or tidal estuary, formed by the Garonne and Dordogne rivers, which meet north of the city of Bordeaux. Most of the better Médoc vineyards overlook the Gironde, as do those of Bourg and Blaye.

Giscours, Château A Third Classed Growth of Margaux, in the Médoc district, whose reputation has been considerably revived in recent years by the Tari family, which acquired the 900-acre property in 1952, when there were only 9 acres of vineyard; today there are 200 acres of vines – as well as a large artificial lake that has improved the drainage of the vineyard and which also moderates its temperature – producing more than 25,000 cases of a rich, generous, and complex wine.

Givry One of the good, if less familiar, wine-producing communes of Burgundy, situated in the Côte Chalonnaise; about 50,000 cases a year are produced of red wine, from Pinot Noir, and about a tenth as much white, from Chardonnay.

Glasses Proper glasses play an important role in the evaluation and appreciation of wine. From a taster's standpoint, the best glasses are stemmed, made of thin, clear crystal, slightly curved in at the rim, and large: 6 ounces should be considered a minimum capacity, 8 or 10 ounces preferable. This is not a matter of mere fancy or fashion, for fine wines taste better in such glasses: the wine's colour can be seen and judged; the capacity is such that the glass need be filled only a third or a half, thus permitting the wine to be swirled to release its bouquet; and the shape of the glass serves as a sort of chimney, concentrating the wine's bouquet. A number of wine districts – the Moselle, Vouvray, Anjou, and Jerez – have their special regional glass, and still other shapes are traditional in other regions. All such glasses can, and often do, provide amusement and interest to the hobbyist and the specialist, but most consumers will find that a set of all-purpose glasses in an 8- to 12-ounce capacity will serve virtually all their needs as well or better than a variety of shapes. Such a glass comes in two basic shapes – the U-shape and the sphere, the latter similar in shape to an orange whose top third has been cut off. If you have glasses in more than one size, and if red and white wines are served at the same meal, it is traditional to serve the red in the larger glass. The major exception to the use of all-purpose glasses is champagne, whose bubbles are quickly dissipated if served in a round-bottomed glass (even more so in a shallow, wide-bottomed "champagne" glass); to maintain a single, steady stream of bubbles, sparkling wines are best presented in an elongated V-shaped flute or in a tulip-shaped glass that narrows where the bowl joins the stem.

Glögg   A traditional Swedish cold-weather drink, a special type of hot spiced wine; aquavit or brandy is usually added just before serving, in cups or glasses containing a few almonds and raisins.

Gloria, Château   A well-known vineyard in Saint-Julien, in the Médoc district, whose 110 acres were assembled beginning in the 1940s by Henri Martin, longtime mayor of the village of Saint-Julien; it produces about 20,000 cases a year of a deservedly popular wine whose quality rivals that of some of the classed growths. A part of the crop is marketed with the second labels Châteaux Haut-Beychevelle-Gloria and Peymartin.

Glycerol   One of the many products of alcoholic fermentation (and also known as glycerine); a colourless and slippery liquid whose sweet taste imparts smoothness to wine. Although the viscosity and richness of certain wines has long been attributed to glycerol, or glycerine, it is now believed that this ingredient is present in too small a quantity to have any important effect on a wine's taste or texture.

Golden Chasselas   *See* Palomino

Gordo Blanco   The name used in Australia for Muscat of Alexandria.

Gouleyant   A French term used informally for light agreeable wines that are easy to drink.

Goût   French for "taste", used, with a descriptive word, for wines that have an unusual flavour. Thus *goût de bois* means "woody", *goût de bouchon* means "corky", and *goût de terroir* refers to the special, earthy taste of certain wines, especially those grown on heavy soils.

Governo   The name given to an Italian vinification technique (also known as *governo alla toscana*) widely used in the past in the production of Chianti. Traditionally, about 10 percent of the grapes harvested were put aside to dry and shrivel until November or December, then crushed; the sugar-rich must was then added to the already fermented wine, which caused a second fermentation. Wines subjected to the *governo* process were softer, lower in acid, somewhat higher in alcohol and body, and often retained a slight, refreshing sparkle. Theoretically, the technique was limited to wines meant to be consumed young, but it was actually used for fine wines as well because, in addition to increasing alcohol and body, *governo* induced malolactic fermentation at a time when this acid-reducing process was not yet understood or controlled. Today, the use of dried grapes is virtually nonexistent; when a Chianti producer says he uses the *governo* process, he is referring to commercial grape concentrate, which is added during the primary fermentation to enrich lighter wines and to increase their alcoholic content.

Graach   A famous little town on the right bank of the Moselle, between Bernkastel and Wehlen, whose 240 acres of vineyards form part of the same incomparable steep hillside as those of its even more illustrious neighbours. The Graacher wines are admirable – sprightly and fragrant, perhaps a bit lighter and less powerful than the Wehleners, but of equal distinction. The best plots are Himmelreich, Domprobst, and the Josephshöf, a 15-acre vineyard that is part of the von Kesselstatt estate, and whose wines, once labelled simply Josephshöfer, are now labelled Graach Josephshöfer.

Graf   German for "count", as in Graf Matuschka-Greiffenclau.

Grafting   A viticultural technique by which a scion of budwood (the part of the vine that produces grapes), is attached to a rootstock. When the phylloxera louse destroyed most of the world's vineyards in the late nineteenth century, the most effective solution to this epidemic was to graft European *vinifera* scions to phylloxera-resistant native American rootstocks, and this practice has continued, with few exceptions to the present day. Vines can be field-grafted in the vineyard, or bench-grafted in a greenhouse or nursery. *See* T-Budding.

Gran Reserva   A Spanish term that may be used for red wines that have been aged for a minimum of five years, at least two of which must be in wood; whites and rosés so labelled must be aged at least four years, of which no less than six months in wood.

Grand Cru French for "great growth", in the sense of great vineyard. The phrase has a specific meaning in Burgundy where it refers to the thirty finest vineyards of the Côte d'Or, including Chambertin, Musigny, and Montrachet, and also to the top seven vineyards of Chablis. There are, in addition, nearly twenty villages in Champagne, including Avize, Ay, Cramant, and Sillery, whose vineyards are rated 100 percent, and which are referred to as *grands crus*. And in the Alsace region, too, more than two dozen vineyards have been officially classified as *grands crus*.

Grand Cru Classé French for "great classed growth", with specific reference to the great classified vineyards of Bordeaux (*cru* is here synonymous with "vineyard"). The phrase is found on the labels of classified wines of the Médoc, Graves, Saint-Emilion, and Sauternes.

Grand Ordinaire *See* Bourgogne Grand Ordinaire

Grand Vin Literally, in French, "great wine", but the term has not been legally defined and is rather freely used.

Grand-Puy Ducasse, Château A Fifth Classed Growth of Pauillac, in the Médoc district, whose reputation for dependable wines has been considerably improved since 1978, when it was acquired by the Borie family of Château Ducru-Beaucaillou; its 115 acres produce about 20,000 cases a year of rich, concentrated, well-structured wine, some of which is marketed under the second label Lacoste-Borie. *Puy* is Gascon for "hill".

Grande Marque A French term that may be translated as "great brand" and that is used informally to describe the best firms of France's Champagne region. Although the term is not officially defined, there is a Syndicat des Grandes Marques, established a century ago, with about two dozen members; these include most, but not all, of the best-known firms, plus several smaller firms whose wines are rarely seen outside France.

Grande Rue, La An extraordinary little 3.5-acre vineyard forming what is almost a corridor (or street, as its name would indicate) from east to west through the very kernel of the best vineyard land of Vosne-Romanée; La Romanée and Romanée Conti adjoin it to the north, La Tâche to the south. The vineyard, the red wines of which can be among the best of Burgundy, was elevated to *grand cru* status in 1988.

Grands Echézeaux A celebrated *grand cru* vineyard situated just above Clos de Vougeot along Burgundy's Côte d'Or. Its 23 acres produce about 3,000 cases a year of a classic red Burgundy, at its best fuller, richer, and more distinguished than that from the adjoining Echézeaux vineyard.

Grange Hermitage Perhaps Australia's most famous red wine, created by Max Schubert, then senior winemaker for the Penfolds firm, in 1952; it was originally made entirely from the Syrah grape (known in Australia as both Shiraz and Hermitage) grown in vineyards near Adelaide (one of which is known as the Grange) and aged for twelve to eighteen months in new American oak barrels. This richly textured, complex, and long-lived wine is now made from grapes from different districts in South Australia and may contain a small proportion of Cabernet Sauvignon.

Granvas A Spanish term for sparkling wines made by the Charmat, or bulk process; those made by the *méthode champenoise* are labelled *cava*.

Grape In all probability (leaving out of consideration the original apple of the Garden of Eden) the first fruit cultivated by man. Grape seeds resembling those of our present-day wine grapes have been found in Egyptian tombs and in the remains of lake dwellings dating from the Bronze Age, more than 5,000 years ago. Noah is said to have planted the first vineyard, but the arts of vine-dressing and winemaking are far older than the beginnings of recorded history. If wine is traditionally associated with grapes, rather than with another fruit, it is because grapes contain a higher proportion of fermentable sugar than other fruits and because the skins of ripe grapes are naturally covered with the yeasts that cause fermentation.

All grapes belong to the genus *Vitis*; there are some forty species, all native to the temperate zone. The most important of these, by an immense margin, is *Vitis vinifera*, the wine bearer, which, apart from some native American species and recent hybrids, is the only species grown commercially to any extent in the world. There are, of course, an almost limitless number of varieties of *vinifera* – botanists and ampelographers have recognized and classified several thousand – and at least several hundred have recognizable characteristics and are cultivated. These are propagated by plant cuttings, or by grafting, for they do not remain true to type if grown from seed; grapes grown from seed are called seedlings, and it is usually impossible to determine their precise ancestry, except in experimental vineyards and under controlled conditions. Different varieties have their special uses and advantages: some give particularly good table grapes, others produce the best raisins; some are extremely productive but give common wine; others, shy bearers, yield the best wine; some will do well under almost any conditions, others require a specific sort of soil and climate. Only about twenty varieties, and certainly fewer than forty, yield outstanding wine today.

Grapey A wine should taste like wine, not like fresh grapes, but certain grape varieties always seem to impart their special flavour to the wines made from them. Concord is an obvious example, pronounced in flavour and lacking in subtlety; another, less intense but no less distinctive, is Muscat, whose richly scented wines can be quite appealing.

Gras A French term for soft, full wines.

Grave del Friuli An extensive DOC zone in northeast Italy, in the Friuli-Venezia Giulia region, which takes its name from the gravelly soil found there; it is the biggest district in the region, and its annual production of 2 million cases accounts for more than half the DOC wines made in all of Friuli. Wines from a dozen different grapes are marketed under their varietal names; although Merlot is the most important in terms of volume, Grave del Friuli is best known for crisp, elegant whites made from Chardonnay, Pinot Bianco, Pinot Grigio, Tocai Friulano, and Sauvignon.

La Grave Trigant de Boisset, Château A vineyard in the Pomerol district, once owned by Trigant de Boisset, and acquired in 1971 by Christian Moueix, whose family is co-owner of Château

Pétrus; the property has since been expanded to 20 acres and produces about 3,500 cases of a supple, well-structured wine.

Graves   An important district in France's Bordeaux region, on the west bank of the Garonne River, largely west and south of the city of Bordeaux; Graves means "gravel", and this is the only *Appellation Contrôlée* of France that takes its name from the *terrior*, or "soil". The district, which is about 35 miles long and seven miles wide, actually begins where the Médoc ends, just north of Bordeaux, and its southern end encloses the districts of Sauternes and Cérons. Nearly 8,000 acres of vineyards produce about 1.7 million cases of red and white wine; throughout the 1960s, twice as much white Graves was made as red, but in the mid-1970s red-wine production began to exceed white, and today reds account for about 60 percent of the total. The name is still associated primarily with white wines because a great deal of white wine has been sold with the regional appellations Graves or Graves Supérieures, whereas most of the reds are marketed with the name of individual vineyards, or châteaux, on whose labels the appellation is less visible. In 1987 the northern part of the Graves discrict, which includes all of the top châteaux, was granted its own appellation, Pessac-Léognan. The red wines of Graves are made primarily from Cabernet Sauvignon, Cabernet Franc, and Merlot, and resemble the wines of the Médoc, although they are perhaps softer and riper and have a more pronounced bouquet. The white wines are made from Sémillon and Sauvignon Blanc, the former contributing body and richness, the latter freshness and acidity; a number of producers have increased the proportion of Sauvignon Blanc to create crisp, dry wines. The appellation Graves now applies to dry wines only; semidry wines are labelled Graves Supérieures.

The red and white wines of Graves were classified in 1953 and again in 1959. Unlike the classifications of the Médoc and Saint-Emilion, the one for Graves did not rank the châteaux, but simply listed the best red and white wines alphabetically as *grands crus classés*. The most famous Graves vineyard is Château Haut-Brion, which was already so famous in the nineteenth century that it was ranked as a *premier grand cru classé* in the 1855 classification. Other top châteaux include La Mission Haut-Brion, Domaine de Chevalier, Pape Clément, and Carbonnieux. (A complete listing will be found on page 543.)

Graves de Vayres A small secondary district in Bordeaux, enclosed by the Entre-Deux-Mers district, on the left bank of the Dordogne River, not far from Saint-Emilion; the dry white wines are passable, the reds less good.

Great Great wines do not come along every day, and the term should be reserved for those extraordinary ones that are head and shoulders above the rest – certainly less than 1 percent of the world's production. A great wine, almost always from a top vineyard and a fine vintage, should have no flaws, perfect balance, character, complexity, and real distinction.

Grechetto An Italian white-wine grape found primarily in Umbria, where it is a component of Orvieto and Torgiano.

Greco di Tufo A distinctive, dry white wine from a small DOC zone east of Naples, in Campania; it is made from the indigenous Greco grape cultivated round the village of Tufo, which gets its name, in turn, from the *tufa*, or volcanic soil of the district.

Greece In no ancient civilization, so far as we can judge, did wine play such a major role as in that of Greece; in the art and literature that have come down to us, the vine, the grape, and wine are omnipresent, perhaps even more so than in the Bible. Clearly, they were a familiar part of everyday living, and were even the basis of a religious cult, that of Dionysus. Today, with an annual production of about 60 million cases and a per capita consumption of 60 bottles, Greece may still be considered an important producer and consumer of wine, but the quality of its wines do not merit the attention lavished on them by Homer, 2,700 years ago. About 20 percent of the country's production consists of Retsina, a dry white wine flavoured with pine resin during fermentation; some consumers find its distinctive taste complementary to the oil-based cuisine of Greece, others compare its taste to turpentine. Retsina is made primarily from Savatiano, the most widely planted white-wine variety of Greece. The Rhoditis grape, which is used to make white wines in the Patras region, also gives its name to light red and rosé wines (which may also be labelled Roditis or Roditys). Kokkineli is a light red or rosé wine, made from the Rhoditis grape, which may be resinated. Mavrodaphne, a sweet red wine with about 15 percent alcohol, is also well known, as is the excellent Muscat produced on the island of Samos. More than two dozen appellations of origin have been established for Greek wines, among them such reds as Naoussa and Nemea, but most of the Greek wines found outside that country are marketed with such proprietary names as Demestica, Castel Danielis, Santa Helena, Hymettus, and Pendeli.

Green   A wine-taster's term applied primarily to wines made from unripe grapes, which have a green-leaf smell and a raw taste marked by excess acidity; this is not necessarily a matter of age, although young wines are more often green than older ones.

Green Hungarian   A productive white-wine grape of uncertain origin, grown to a limited extent in California, where there are about 200 acres in production; it gives a pale, agreeable, but neutral wine perhaps less charming and original than its name.

Green Valley   A small viticultural area in Sonoma, within the larger Russian River Valley appellation. Situated south of Forestville and the Russian River, this cool district, with about 1,000 acres of vineyards, is best known for its Chardonnay and Pinot Noir, much of which is used to make fine sparkling wines; wineries include Iron Horse and Domaine Laurier. There is also a Green Valley viticultural area in Solano County, about ten miles east of Napa's Carneros region; Chardonnay and Sauvignon Blanc are the most widely planted varieties, and Chateau de Leu its best-known winery.

Grêle   *See* Hail

Grenache   A productive red-wine grape widely planted in southern France, where it gives a full-bodied, somewhat alcoholic wine that tends to age relatively quickly; it is the principal variety in the red wines of Châteauneuf-du-Pape and the dry rosés of Tavel, as well as in the sweet, tawny wines of Banyuls. It is an important variety in Spain, especially in Rioja and Navarre, where it is known as Garnacha. The acreage of Grenache in California has diminished from 20,000 acres to 13,000, almost all of them in the Central

Valley; the grape can be vinified to produce the popular Grenache Rosé and also to make red table wines and tawny port. There are extensive plantings in Australia, but, as in California, these are being replaced with other varieties.

Grenouilles One of the seven *grand cru* vineyards of Chablis, and the smallest; its 24 acres are situated between Vaudésir and Valmur.

Grey Riesling A misnamed and mediocre white-wine grape planted in California; it is not a Riesling, but rather a lesser French grape known as Chaucé Gris or, more properly, as Trousseau Gris. There are fewer than 800 acres planted in California, most of them in Monterey and the Livermore Valley; the wine, sometimes labelled Grey Riesling, is mild, soft and neutral.

Grey Rot A mould that attacks grapes and causes deterioration of the fruit, and may also impart a disagreeable taste to the wine made from affected grapes; it is, in fact, *Botrytis cinerea*, known as "noble rot" when it attacks ripe grapes under certain favourable climatic conditions, but as grey or common rot when it destroys the fruit.

Greysac, Château A well-known *cru bourgeois* of the Médoc whose 150 acres produce about 30,000 cases a year of a dependable and attractive wine.

Grifi A proprietary red wine produced by Avignonesi in Montepulciano, in Tuscany; this long-lived wine is made primarily from a local clone of Sangiovese known as Prugnolo Gentile plus a small proportion of Cabernet.

Grignolino An Italian red-wine grape cultivated around the villages of Asti and Casale Monferrato in the Piedmont region. When genuine and of good quality, Grignolino is an interesting and unusual wine, light-bodied, delicate, with a hint of orange in its colour, and at its best within a year or two of the harvest; many examples, however, are faded, thin, and sharp. There are about 50 acres of Grignolino in northern California, where it produces light red and rosé wines.

Grillet *See* Château-Grillet

Griotte-Chambertin A *grand cru* vineyard in the Burgundy village of

Gevrey-Chambertin, less frequently encountered than its two illustrious neighbours, Clos de Bèze and Chapelle-Chambertin, perhaps because its 7 acres produce only 800 cases or so of nevertheless excellent red wine.

Grip A wine-taster's term applied to a distinctive red wine with an attractive combination of tannin, rich texture, and forceful character; the opposite of bland and neutral.

Groppello An Italian red-wine grape cultivated west of Lake Garda, in Italy's Lombardy region, where it produces attactive red and rosé wines; it is the principal variety used in the DOC Riviera del Garda Bresciano.

Gros Plant The name given to the Folle Blanche grape around the city of Nantes, near the mouth of the Loire, in an extensive region whose boundaries are similar to those for the better-known Muscadet. The light, fresh, tart white wine made from this variety is entitled to the VDQS Gros Plant du Pays Nantais, whose annual production of 2.5 to 3 million cases makes it the single biggest VDQS appellation of France.

Groslot A productive red-wine grape of passable quality widely grown in France's Loire Valley, especially in the Anjou district, where it is used to make the semisweet Rosé d'Anjou; also known as Grolleau.

Grosslage German for "large vineyard"; under the 1971 wine laws, a Grosslage is defined as a collective site that encompasses a number of Einzellagen, or individual vineyards, whose geography, soil, and exposure produce wines of similar quality and character. Thus, the wines of every vineyard in Germany – with a few exceptions – may be marketed with the name of the individual site or with that of a Grosslage (assuming the wines of that vintage achieve Qualitätswein status; Tafelwein may not be sold with a vineyard name). The commercial advantage of using a Grosslage name is that it may be more familiar to the public than that of the many Einzellagen it includes, but the size of Grosslagen varies enormously, from 125 to more than 5,000 acres, and from just a few Einzellagen to more than 75. As is the case with individual vineyard names, the name of a Grosslage is preceded by that of a village, as Niersteiner Gutes Domtal, Piesporter Michelsberg, Johannisberger Erntebringer, and

Wiltinger Scharzberg. Unfortunately, this can be confusing to the consumer, since there is nothing on the label to indicate whether the name is that of an Einzellage or a Grosslage. Thus, Bernkasteler Graben, is an individual vineyard in the village of Bernkastel; Bernkasteler Badstube is a Grosslage that includes just a few top sites within Bernkastel, only 125 acres in all; but Bernkasteler Kurfürstlay is a Grosslage that encompasses 4,000 acres of vineyards in ten villages. There are more than 150 Grosslagen in Germany's eleven Anbaugebiete, or specified wine regions, and many of their names will be found on page 553.

Gruaud-Larose, Château A Second Classed Growth of Saint-Julien, in the Médoc district, owned in the eighteenth century by Gruaud and then by his son-in-law, Larose; the property was later split up and then reunited in the 1930s by Jean Cordier, who also acquired the neighbouring Château Talbot. The 200-acre vineyard, one of the largest in the Médoc, produces about 35,000 cases a year of a fruity, supple, and deservedly popular wine; the second label is Sarget de Gruaud-Larose.

Grumello A small DOC zone within the Valtellina district in northern Italy, in the Lombardy region, producing fine red wines from the Nebbiolo grape.

Grüner Veltliner A white-wine grape grown almost exclusively in Austria, where it accounts for a third of that country's total acreage. It produces pale, light-bodied, refreshing wines best consumed young.

Guenoc Valley A viticultural area in the southern part of Lake County, near the Napa County border, whose 275 acres of vineyards are owned by the Guenoc Winery.

Guiraud, Château A classed growth of the Sauternes district, whose 175 acres produce, in an abundant vintage, as much as 9,000 cases of an excellent sweet wine. The vineyard is unusual in that nearly half the acreage is made up of Sauvignon Blanc, the rest Sémillon, plus 2 percent Muscadelle, whereas in most Sauternes vineyards Sémillon accounts for about 80 percent of the total. The property, which was acquired by the Narby family of Canada in 1981 and extensively renovated, also produces about 4,000 cases a year of a dry white wine, labelled "G", made entirely from Sauvignon Blanc.

Gumpoldskirchen Certainly the best-known wine-producing town of Austria and, with those situated along the Danube – Dürnstein, Loiben, Krems, and Langenlois – among the best. Its vineyards, only a dozen miles south of Vienna, produce fruity, full-bodied white wines that may be dry or semidry. Gumpoldskirchner is traditionally made from Rotgipfler and Zierfandler grapes, and if few can be described as remarkable, most are fresh, clean, and attractive.

Guntersblum A vineyard town in Germany's Rheinhessen region, with nearly 900 acres of vineyards, producing wines of good but not distinguished quality; most of it is marketed with the Grosslage Oppenheimer Krötenbrunnen.

Gutedel The German name for the productive but undistinguished Chasselas, and something of an exaggeration, since the white wine it yields is a long way from *edel* ("noble") and by no means always *gut* ("good"); it is the principal variety of the Markgräflerland district in southern Baden.

Gypsum *See* Plastering

Gyropalette A large, metal container in the form of a cube that holds about 500 bottles and whose use simplifies and shortens the process of riddling, an essential step in the production of *méthode champenoise* sparkling wines; the containers can be manipulated by hand,or, increasingly, by a computerized programme.

❧ H

Haardt A chain of hills in Germany's Rheinpfalz, or Palatinate, region, their lower slopes covered with vineyards that have made this district's fame. Overlooking the wide, fertile Rhine Valley, like a northern prolongation of the French Vosges, these extend from Schweigen, on the French frontier, northward for nearly 50 miles. All of the finer Pfalz wines come from the central portion, the Mittelhardt, which embraces such famous wine towns as Deidesheim, Forst, Ruppertsberg, Wachenheim, and Bad Dürkheim.

Hail Like frost, one of the major natural hazards of a vineyard-owner's life. Hail storms are by no means infrequent in most wine-producing countries, and if heavy they can be nothing short of catastrophic; an entire crop is often destroyed in a matter of minutes, and the vines so gravely damaged that the following year's vintage is also affected. Even light hail can take its toll during the ripening season, for the bruised berries give a wine that has what the French call a *goût de grêle*, or "taste of hail", readily recognizable by an expert as a faint overtone of rot in an otherwise sound wine.

Halbstück The traditional cask of Germany's Rheingau region, holding 600 litres, (about 66 cases).

Halbtrocken German for "half-dry", this term may be used only for wines that contain no more than 18 grams of sugar per litre (1.8 percent). *See* Trocken.

Hallgarten An important wine-producing village in Germany's Rheingau with some 500 acres of vines. Like Rauenthal and Kiedrich, this is an upland village, set well back from the river, and its best vineyards – Schönhell, Würzgarten, Hendelberg, and Jungfer – are only about a stone's throw from the famous Steinberg. The Hallgartner wines, especially in good years, are forthright and sturdy, often the fullest bodied of the whole Rheingau.

Hanteillan, Château A recently renovated *cru bourgeois* in the commune of Cissac entitled to the appellation Haut-Médoc; its 200 acres produce about 35,000 cases.

Haraszthy, Agoston Often called the father of California viticulture, Haraszthy was a talented, impetuous Hungarian count who changed his title into the more democratic colonel when he emigrated to America. He founded a town in Wisconsin and gave it his name (later changed to Sauk City), moved west, was the first sheriff of San Diego, and a member of the state assembly. In the 1850s he moved north to Sonoma, planted vineyards, and founded the Buena Vista winery. In 1861 he was officially sent to Europe by the governor of California and returned with cuttings of some 300 different grape varieties, thereby considerably advancing the California wine industry; the report of this trip, which he wrote on his return to Buena Vista, is a minor masterpiece, readable, informative, overflowing with the colonel's unquenchable optimism and enthusiasm. Soon thereafter he was struck by a series of misfortunes – financial difficulties, problems brought on by the Civil War, phylloxera in his vineyard, a disastrous fire – and went to Nicaragua in an effort to recoup his fortunes through the distillation of rum. There, in 1869, he disappeared; according to legend, he fell into a river infested with alligators.

Hard A wine-taster's term meaning austere, without charm or suppleness, and in the case of red wines, often tannic and astringent. Many excellent wines, however, are hard in their youth and come around splendidly with time; hardness, unless accompanied by the greenness of unripe grapes, is not necessarily a fault, but can be an indicator of probable long life. Red wines such as the great *crus* of the Médoc and many California Cabernet Sauvignons are hard in their youth, and such white wines as Chablis and those from the Saar are often hard and austere as well.

Harmonious A term applied to a well-balanced wine; when bouquet and flavour are in harmony, a wine may be considered very good of its type, whatever its price category.

Haro A little city on the upper Ebro River, in Spain, and the centre of the Rioja wine trade. During the final decades of the last century, when the phylloxera had devastated Bordeaux but had not yet crossed the Pyrenees into Spain, over a hundred French families settled in Haro. Many of the town's *bodegas* and much of its viticultural tradition and wine-making methods date from those briefly prosperous days.

Harsh In a wine, harshness is hardness carried to an extreme; occasionally, particularly in red wines, and provided other qualities are present, this will disappear in time.

Hárslevelü A white-wine grape grown in Hungary (its name means "lime leaf"), where it is blended with Furmint to make Tokay; it is also marketed as a varietal wine, as in Debröi Hárslevelü, from the Debrö district.

Hattenheim A charming old village in Germany's Rheingau region, producing outstanding wines. Its 565 acres of vineyards include the celebrated Steinberg in its entirety and a portion of the Marcobrunn, although neither is sold with the Hattenheimer name – the first is labelled with the vineyard name alone, the second is marketed as Erbacher Marcobrunn. Other distinguished sites, giving somewhat lighter wines, almost equally remarkable but more delicate, include Nussbrunnen, Wisselbrunnen, Mannberg, Engelsmannberg, and Schützenhaus.

Haut French word meaning "high" or, in certain combinations, "upper", "higher", or "top"; a number of French regions are divided into Haut and Bas ("low" or "lower"), and Haut rarely implies superior quality, only higher altitude. It is true tha the Haut-Médoc produces finer wines than the adjoining region formerly known as Bas-Médoc, but Bas-Armagnac produces far better brandy than does Haut-Armagnac, and the wines of the Côte de Beaune are more acclaimed than those of the Hautes-Côte de Beaune.

Haut-Bages-Averous, Château A small vineyard in Pauillac, in the Médoc district; in practice, however, the name is used to market the second wine of Château Lynch-Bages.

Haut-Bages Libéral, Château A Fifth Classed Growth of Pauillac, in the Médoc district, recently acquired by the owners of Château Chasse-Spleen; its 60 acres of vines produce about 10,000 cases a year.

Haut-Bages Monpelou, Château A *cru bourgeois* in Pauillac, in the Médoc, once part of Château Duhart-Milon; its 35 acres produce about 5,000 cases.

Haut-Bailly, Château A *grand cru classé* of the Graves district of Bordeaux, producing about 12,000 cases a year of excellent, supple, but long-lived red wine; part of the crop may be sold under the second label La Parde de Haut-Bailly.

Haut-Batailley, Château A Fifth Classed Growth of Pauillac, in the Médoc district, part of the larger Château Batailley until 1942, when this section was acquired by the family who owns Château Ducru-Beaucaillou; its 50 acres produce about 10,000 cases a year of a stylish and dependable wine.

Haut-Brion, Château The most celebrated vineyard of the Graves district, producing one of the very greatest red wines of Bordeaux, and officially ranked as a *premier grand cru classé*, or first growth, in the classification of 1855, on a par with Châteaux

Lafite, Latour, and Margaux; the wine is noted particularly for its elegance and finesse, combined with an underlying structure that enables the best vintages to improve for decades. The vineyard is situated just outside the city limits of Bordeaux, in the commune of Pessac, and consists of 110 acres, all but seven producing red wine from a combination of about 75 percent Cabernet Sauvignon and Cabernet Franc, and 25 percent Merlot; average annual production is about 13,000 cases of red wine, although recent vintages have varied from 8,000 cases in 1977 to 19,000 cases in 1982. In addition, 1,000 cases or less of a rare and exceptional dry white Graves are made from approximately equal parts of Sémillon and Sauvignon Blanc. The vineyard was already famous in the sixteenth century, when it was owned by the Pontac family; it merited a vist by Thomas Jefferson in 1787; and was owned for a few years by the statesman Talleyrand. Haut-Brion was acquired by the American financier Clarence Dillon in 1935, and is now under the direction of his granddaughter, the Duchesse de Mouchy (the former Joan Dillon). The family purchased the adjoining Château La Mission Haut-Brion in 1983.

Haut-Marbuzet, Château A *cru bourgeois exceptionnel* of Saint-Estèphe, in the Haut-Médoc, whose 200-odd acres produce about 20,000 cases; the second label is Château MacCarthy Moula.

Haut-Médoc The southern and far better part of the large Médoc district, extending from the northern edge of the city of Bordeaux to just beyond Saint-Estèphe; all of the *crus classés*, or classed growths, that have made the Médoc's fame are in this area, and a wine labelled Haut-Médoc is likely to be better than one labelled simply Médoc, which comes from the lowland area farther north. Note, however, that more than half of the wines produced in the Haut-Médoc section are marketed with one of six communal appellations – Margaux, Saint-Julien, Pauillac, Saint-Estèphe, Moulis, or Listrac – and wines labelled with the first four in particular are likely to be better than those labelled with the broader appellation Haut-Médoc. *See* Médoc.

Haut-Poitou A district around Poitiers, about 60 miles southwest of Tours, whose wines, once entitled to the VDQS Vins du Haut-Poitou are now AOC Haut-Poitou. Although two thirds of the annual production of 400,000 to 600,000 cases is red and rosé, it is the light, crisp, dry white wines made from the Sauvignon Blanc grape that are the best known; attractive wines are also made from several other varieties, including Gamay, Cabernet Franc, Pinot Noir, Chardonnay, and Chenin Blanc.

Hautes Côtes de Beaune *See* Bourgogne-Hautes Côtes de Beaune (and Bourgogne-Hautes Côtes de Nuits)

Hautvillers A village overlooking the Marne River in France's Champagne region; it was at the Abbey of Hautvillers that Dom Pérignon conducted his celebrated experiments. *See* Dom Pérignon.

Hazy Said of a wine that is possibly clear, but certainly not brilliant; this is usually the first step on the road to cloudiness, and a glass of hazy wine should be approached with some caution. *See*, however, Sediment.

Heat Summation *See* Degree-Days

Heavy Full-bodied, but lacking balance or distinction; an unfavourable term, but less severe than coarse.

Hectare A metric measure of a surface equivalent to 10,000 square metres, or 2.471 acres. Vineyard area in Europe is commonly expressed in hectares, and yield in hectolitres per hectare.

Hectolitre A metric measure of volume equivalent to 100 litres or 26.42 U.S. gallons, 22.03 British Imperial gallons. Wine production figures in Europe are given in hectolitres (or, colloquially, hectos), and yield is expressed in hectolitres per hectare. A hectolitre is equal to 133 bottles of 75 centilitres each, or 11 cases; thus a yield of 45 hectos per hectare amounts to 495 cases per hectare, or 200 cases per acre.

Hérault A French *département* on the Mediterranean, approximately halfway between Marseilles and the Spanish border, and part of what is known as the Languedoc-Roussillon or, more informally, as the Midi. The Hérault contains 320,000 acres of vineyards and produces an average of 120 million cases of wine a year, which represents about 15 percent of the total French crop; 95 percent of this is red, from such prolific varieties as Carignan, Grenache, and Cinsault, as well as

Syrah and Mourvèdre. Much of this is quite ordinary, although such appellations as Minervois, Saint-Chinian, and Faugères are found here, as well as the sweet Muscat de Frontignan. Béziers, Sète, and Montpellier are the main centres of the wine trade. *See* Languedoc-Roussillon.

Herbaceous   A distinctive odour associated with certain grape varieties, notably Sauvignon Blanc, and sometimes described as grassy; it is typical and desirable up to a point, but can be unattractive if too pronounced. Cabernet Sauvignon, too, may display this aroma, especially when grown in cool climates.

Hermitage   A deservedly famous wine of the northern Rhône Valley, produced on a single steep, spectacular, terraced hillside some 50 miles south of Lyon, near the town of Tain l'Hermitage. The 325 acres of vineyards, planted on soil that is primarily granite and facing due south, yield about 25,000 to 40,000 cases a year of red wine, made from the Syrah grape; and 15,000 to 18,000 cases of white, made almost entirely from Marsanne until the mid-1970s, when a number of growers began to replant Roussanne. White Hermitage is a dry, full-bodied, pale-gold wine that is capable of aging for a decade, although many connoisseurs prefer to drink it within two years of the harvest. Even though a third of the Hermitage crop is white, the red is decidedly better and, in favourable years, one of the truly great wines of France – deep coloured, richly-textured, and long-lived. In his famous *Notes on a Cellar-Book*, George Saintsbury described an 1846 Hermitage drunk in 1886 as "the *manliest* French wine I have ever drunk", and that epithet has been associated with Hermitage ever since. (He also wrote, "If you want delicacy, you don't go to the Rhône.") It is probable that the vineyard existed in Roman days, when its wine was known as *vin de Tain*; the legend most often told about the origin of the name Hermitage concerns Gaspard de Sterimberg, a knight who arrived in the region in the early thirteenth century after fighting in the religious wars in southern France, built a chapel on the hill, and became a hermit. Officially, there are eighteen *quartiers*, or named sites, on the Hermitage hillside, with names such as Less Bessards, and Le Méal, but they rarely appear on labels; most of what seem to be vineyard names on Hermitage labels are actually proprietary brand names created by growers and shippers, although the wines are no less good for that.

Hessische Bergstrasse The smallest of the eleven Anbaugebiete, or specified wine regions, of Germany; its 950 acres of vineyards, half of them planted with Riesling, produce about 300,000 cases a year. The region, situated east of the Rhine extends from Heidelberg north to Darmstadt, and faces parts of Rheinhessen and the Rheinpfalz. Co-operative cellars account for about 90 percent of the crop, almost all of which is consumed locally.

Heurigen The name given in Austria to fresh young wines and also to the cafés and taverns in which they are sold; the best-known *Heurigen* are produced and quaffed in the suburbs of Vienna. The tradition that permits a grower to sell his own wine directly to consumers originated in the late eighteenth century, when a producer would hang a bough or wreath outside his establishment to alert passersby that new wine was for sale. Today, some *Heurigen* are open all year round, others for only a few weeks in the spring and summer. A tavern proprietor can obtain permission to sell wines other than his own, and the "new wine" may actually be more than a year old, since a wine can be sold as *Heurige* until November of the year following the vintage.

Hippocras A wine drink popular in medieval times, flavoured with cinnamon, ginger, other spices, and sugar or honey; an ancestor of liqueurs and cordials.

Hochgewächs The literal translation of this German term is "high growth", but in the sense of superior wine; its use is limited to wines in the Qualitätswein, or QbA, category made entirely from Riesling grapes that are somewhat riper than the minimum requirements, and which pass a tasting test more stringent than for other Qualitätswein.

Hochheim An important wine-producng town in Germany, properly considered part of the Rheingau, although it overlooks the Main River rather than the Rhine and is separated from the rest of the Rheingau by at least ten miles of farmland and the city of Wiesbaden. There are about 600 acres under vines, and the better vineyards, such as Domdechaney, Kirchenstück, Stein, Hölle, and Königin Victoriaberg (named in honour of Queen Victoria) give wines that have the unmistakable Rheingau stamp of character and breed, though perhaps somewhat gentler and softer. The Grosslage is

Hochheimer Daubhaus.

Hock The British term for Rhine wine, as claret refers to red Bordeaux; many wine lists in England list German wines under the heading Hocks and Moselles. The term derives from the town of Hochheim, in the Rheingau.

Hogshead A common name for a barrel of varying capacity.

Hollow A taster's term applied to a wine that may make an immediate and positive impression, but that lacks middle body; the initial flavour is not sustained.

Honey A natural sugar available long before cane or beet sugar, and used for sweetening wines; when diluted with water and fermented, honey becomes mead.

Hospices de Beaune A charitable institution in the Burgundian town of Beaune that is the beneficiary of what is perhaps the most famous wine auction in the world, which takes place every year on the third Sunday in November. The Hospices de Beaune consists of the Hôtel-Dieu, a charity hospital founded in 1443 by Nicolas Rolin and his wife, Guigone de Salins, that is one of the most beautiful buildings in Europe; and the Hospices de la Charité, founded in the seventeenth century. Over the years the Hospices de Beaune has been bequeathed a great deal of land, including holdings in many of the best vineyards in the Côte de Beaune (plus 3.7 acres in Mazis-Chambertin, in the Côte de Nuits, acquired in 1977); the vineyards constitute the principal endowment of the Hospices, and much of its revenue comes from the sale of its wines. The prices achieved at the auction, a picturesque affair that is the central event of a three-day weekend known as Les Trois Glorieuses, tend to affect the prices of all Burgundies for the vintage in question, although it is understood that the auction prices, which benefit charity, are often exaggerated.

The Hospices owns about 135 acres of vineyards that produce an average of 15,000 cases a year, although the amount put up for auction has varied from none in the disastrous 1968 vintage to more than 17,000 cases in the abundant 1983 and 1986 vintages; red wines account for 85 to 90 percent of the total. At one time, the wines were identified by the name of the *vigneron* who tended the vines; in 1899 the wines were named after the major benefactors of the Hospices, some of whom bequeathed gifts other than vines. Their names are joined to that of a *cuvée*, most of which consist of wines from several vineyards within a particular appellation. For example, Corton, Cuvée Charlotte Dumay is made up of wines from Les Renardes, Les Bressandes, and Clos du Roi; Beaune, Cuvée Nicolas Rolin consists of Les Cents Vignes, Les Gréves, and En Genet. The wines are vinified by the Hospices, but they are aged and bottled by those who purchase them at the auction; thus, if four pièces (a Burgundian barrel holding 228 litres, or about 25 cases) of a particular *cuvée* were sold to four different merchants, the wines bottled by each one would differ somewhat. A complete list of the *cuvées* and appellations of the wines produced by Hospices Beaune will be found of page 549, as well as (merely as an indication) the quantity auctioned off in the excellent and expensive 1985 vintage. The total revenue for the 1985 auction was 24.8 million francs (compared to 13.8 million in 1983, 18.8 million in 1986, and 14.4 million in 1987). It should be added that a little Eau-de-Vie de Marc, distilled from the residue of grape skins, or *marc*, of the preceding vintage, is also sold at the same auction.

Hospices de Nuits A charitable foundation in Nuits-Saint-Georges, in Burgundy; like the far more famous Hospices de Beaune, it has endowments in the form of vineyards, in this case about 22 acres of *premiers crus*, all in Nuits-Saint-Georges. The wines, many of high quality, are auctioned off in the spring following the vintage.

Hotte A French backpack made of cane, wood, metal, or plastic into which pickers dump their hand-carried baskets during the vintage. The *hotte* carrier then climbs up and tips his grapes into the vehicle that will carry a large load to the presses.

Howell Mountain A small viticultural area within the Napa Valley appellation limited to vineyards above 1,400 feet on Howell Mountain, northeast of St. Helena; about 400 acres of vineyards are planted, primarily with Zinfandel and Cabernet Sauvignon, as well as Chardonnay. Dunn Vineyards and Domaines Woltner are situated there.

Hudson River Region The oldest commercial viticultural district in New

York State, whose first winery was established in 1839. The current renaissance of this region, which includes both banks of the Hudson River, is credited to Mark Miller, who planted vines in the 1950s and produced his first wines at Benmarl, about 75 miles north of New York City, in 1971. There are now more than twenty wineries in the Hudson River Region; most of them produce wines from French-American hybrids, especially Seyval Blanc, and a few cultivate European *vinifera* varieties as well. Some of the better-known wineries include Clinton Vineyards, Cascade Mountain, Eaton Vineyards, and Millbrook.

Hungary   Although this country is perhaps best known for Tokay, a scarce, sweet dessert wine, its annual production of 50 to 60 million cases include quite a range of red and white table wines from several districts and grape varieties. The most widely planted varieties are the indigenous red Kadarka and the Welschriesling, better known in Hungary as Olasz Riesling. Other white grapes include Ezerjó, Furmint, Hárslevelü, Kéknyelü, Leányka, and Szürkebarát (Pinot Gris); among the reds are Kékfrankos (Gamay) and Médoc Noir (Merlot). Hungary's most famous red wine is Egri Bikavér, from the Eger district, halfway between Budapest and Tokay, in the northeast part of the country. This wine, whose name means "bull's blood", was traditionally full-bodied and long-lived, but is now likely to be somewhat lighter in style; once made primarily from the Kadarka grape, it is now produced from Kékfrankos plus several other varieties that may include Pinot Noir, Merlot, Cabernet Sauvignon, and Gamay. Eger also produces a great deal of white wine including Egri Leányka. Most of Hungary's everyday wines come from the Great Plain in the centre of the country, and many of the finer wines come from the north shore of Lake Balaton, Europe's biggest lake; the overall appellation for the latter is Balatoni (Hungarian appellations take the possessive "i"), but the best-known wines come from vineyards near Mount Badacsony, and these include Badacsonyi Kéknyelü and Badacsonyi Szürkebarát. The village of Sopron, in the northwest corner of the country, is known for Soproni Kékfrankos, and some of the other names that may be encountered outside the country include such white wines as Móri Ezerjó and Debröi Hárslevelü, and such reds as Villányi Burgundi (made from Pinot Noir) and Szekszárdi Vörös.

Hunter Valley First planted in the 1820s, this is the oldest wine region in Australia, and perhaps the most famous; it is situated about 100 miles northwest of Sydney, in the state of New South Wales. The region was long famous for its Shiraz (the Syrah of the northern Rhône, also known locally as Hermitage) and Sémillon (sometimes labelled Hunter River Riesling in the past). In 1967, there were only 800 acres of vineyard and six firms in the Hunter Valley; Chardonnay and Cabernet Sauvignon were extensively planted in the late 1960s and early 1970s, as was Sauvignon Blanc, and by the late 1970s there were 13,000 acres of vineyard. Much of this, planted in unsuitable areas, was abandoned, and there are now about 7,000 acres of vineyard, with Shiraz and Sémillon accounting for half the total; outside Australia, however, the region is perhaps better known for its Chardonnay, Cabernet Sauvignon, and Sauvignon Blanc. In the late 1960s and early 1970s, a number of new vineyards and wineries were established in a region known as the Upper Hunter, about 60 miles up the Hunter River from the original vineyards, now often referred to as the Lower Hunter. The best-known wineries of the latter district include Brokenwood, Hungerford Hill, Lake's Folly, McWilliam's, the Rothbury Estate, Tyrrell's, and Wyndham Estate; Rosemount Estate is the leading winery of the Upper Hunter.

Huxelrebe One of the new German grape varieties, planted for the most part in Rheinhessen and Rheinpfalz, which ripens well even in cooler years; it produces neutral white wines useful for blending but can also make sweet, late-harvest wines.

Hybrid In viticulture, the result of a cross of two grape varieties. Botanically, the idea is a fairly new one, less than two centuries old; applied to the grape, it is wholly revolutionary, since the wine-bearing vine has been almost entirely propagated by cuttings rather than seeds since the dawn of human history. The term *hybrid* includes both true hybrids (cross-pollination of more than one species, as *vinifera* × *rotundifolia; or vinifera* × *labrusca*) and crosses (cross-pollination in the same species, as *vinifera* × *vinifera*, also known as métis). Most hybrids and crosses are an attempt to combine the best qualities of two quite different parent vines, or to produce an offspring able to contend with some special problem, such as phylloxera, mildew, winter cold, or a short growing season, without compromising its quality.

Considering the fact that there is hardly such a thing as a pure strain of grape, or one surely able to transmit its specific qualities to its seedlings, this is a monumental problem; it often takes literally thousands of crosses to come up with one that is commercially successfully, and about fifteen years are needed to determine whether a particular cross can consistently produce sound wine. It is surprising that so much definite progress has been made, but there is no doubt that a number of the newer varieties, known as French-American hybrids, are capable of giving better wine in the eastern United States than any of the original native varieties. A number of successful crosses, or métis, have also been developed in California and Germany, in response to specific local conditions, such as the hot climate of California's Central Valley and Germany's short growing season. In some instances, however, hybrids and crosses have a bad tendency to claim the name of their more illustrious parent, however few of its characteristics they may possess; as a result, wines are often presented to a somewhat confused public under names that sound familiar, but to which the wines have no well-authenticated right. Other new crosses cultivated in California include Flora, Carnelian, and Centurion and, in Germany, Bacchus, Optima, Ortega, and Ehrenfelser; the best known of all German crosses is Müller-Thurgau, created more than a century ago and now that country's most widely planted variety. *See* French-American Hybrids.

Hydrogen Sulphide *See* Rotten-Egg Flavour

 I

Ice Bucket   Except in restaurants, ice buckets, (also known as wine buckets and wine coolers) seem to be used less and less in this day of electric refrigeration; this is to be regretted, for white wines, rosés, and sparkling wines are far better served in a bucket. Pre-chilling in the refrigerator, however useful, does not provide the same service, since chilled wines lose their freshness, sprightliness, and charm as they warm up during a meal, and the last glass rarely tastes as good, or as refreshing, as the first. (Note, however, that insulated bottle containers are now available that maintain the desired temperature as the bottle is consumed, and which are less bulky than an ice bucket.) A wine that has not been put in the refrigerator for the requisite two or three hours can be chilled in an ice bucket in only fifteen minutes or so. For maximum efficiency, the bucket should be filled with ice and water; ice alone does not chill as quickly, and makes it more difficult to reinsert the bottle into the bucket after it has been opened (a point that many restaurateurs seem not to have grasped). Also, resting a bottle on top of the ice in a bucket (another common practice in restaurants) is useless, since only that part of the bottle actually in contact with ice will be chilled, or remain so. Unfortunately, many ice buckets are poorly designed and are not tall enough to accommodate an entire bottle, especially the ones used for German and Alsace wines; since the wine visible above the ice and water will never be chilled, and to avoid pouring out a glass or two of warm wine, it is an acceptable procedure to put a bottle neck-down in the bucket for a few minutes before the capsule is cut away and the cork drawn.

Ice Wine *See* Eiswein

Idaho Vineyards were planted in the early 1970s in southwest Idaho, at elevations of 2,500 feet or more, along the Snake River Valley, between Boise and Caldwell, not far from the Oregon border; the first wines were produced by the Ste. Chapelle winery in 1976, and several other wineries were established in the early 1980s. Riesling and Chardonnay are the most widely planted varieties; Chenin Blanc, Gewürztraminer, Pinot Noir, and Cabernet Sauvignon are also grown.

Imbottigliato Italian for "bottled" *imbottigliato all'origine* is the equivalent of estate bottled.

Imperial An oversize bottle, equal to eight normal bottles, occasionally used in the Bordeaux region.

Inferno A small DOC zone within the Valtellina district, in Italy's Lombardy region, not far from the Swiss border; fine red wines are produced from the Nebbiolo grape.

Ingelheim A picturesque and historic little town in the northern part of Germany's Rheinhessen region, facing Johannisberg across the Rhine. Charlemagne had a castle there, but today the village is better known for its light red wines produced from the Spätburgunder grape.

Insignia   A propietary red wine produced by the Joseph Phelps winery in California's Napa Valley; this firm, long-lived wine is a blend of selected lots of Cabernet Sauvignon, Merlot and Cabernet Franc whose proportions vary from year to year.

Iphofen   One of the better wine-producing villages of Germany's Franken, or Franconia, region; its best vineyards are Julius-Echter-Berg, Kalb, and Kronsberg.

Irancy   Pleasant, inconsequential red and rosé wines produced around the village of that name, some ten miles southwest of Chablis, in northern Burgundy. Entitled to the AOC Bourgogne-Irancy since 1977, the wines are made primarily from Pinot Noir, which results in a fresh and delightful *vin de pays*; a certain amount of the less distinguished César grape is still cultivated in this district, and may be used as well.

Irouléguy   An appellation for dry reds and rosés produced along the foothills of the Pyrenées, along the Spanish border, southeast of Bayonne and Biarritz, in the Basque country of France.

Isabella   An old, heavy-flavoured Eastern grape, an inferior predecessor of the Concord, now fortunately little used for wine, although Isabella Rosé is still produced in the Finger Lakes.

Ischia   An island in the Bay of Naples, popular with tourists, that produces attractive red and white wines.

Isonzo   A DOC zone in the Friuli region, in northeast Italy, producing a range of varietal wines; Merlot and Tocai Friulano are the most important, followed by Cabernet, Pinot Bianco, and Pinot Grigio.

Israel   Wine has been made in what is now Israel since the beginning of recorded history, but that country's wine industry originated only a century ago. In 1882, with the financial backing of Baron Edmond de Rothschild, vines were planted and a winery constructed at Rishon-le-Zion, southeast of Tel Aviv; most of the real progress in winemaking, however, dates from 1948, when Israel became an independent state. This small land may therefore be considered both the oldest and the youngest wine-producing country. There are now about 16,000 acres planted with wine grapes, producing about 2 million cases a year. As recently as the 1950s, 90 percent of Israel's wines were sweet and fortified; today, dry and semidry table wines account for 80 percent of the total. At one time Carignan, Grenache, and Alicante Bouschet accounted for most of the plantings, along with such white varieties as Sémillon, Muscat of Alexandria, and Clairette (Ugni Blanc); today there are new planting of Petite Sirah and Cabernet Sauvignon and, among the white varieties, Emerald Riesling, French Colombard, Chenin Blanc, and Sauvignon Blanc. The principal vineyard regions include Samson, southeast of Tel Aviv, which encompasses the Dan district; Shomron, which includes the Sharon district, and the cooler Galil district, north of the Sea of Galilee, where Cabernet Sauvignon and Sauvignon Blanc were planted in the mid-1970s. As a result of new plantings (brought in from California), a great demand for dry wines, and improved technology in the wineries, Israel now produces a range of crisp, distinctive whites and flavourful dry reds, notably those from Sauvignon Blanc and Cabernet Sauvignon. Israeli wines are labelled with varietal names and proprietary names; since the country subscribes to the Madrid convention, European place names such as Champagne, Sauternes, and Port no longer appear on labels. There are about a dozen wineries in Israel, the most important of which is Carmel; this co-operative, founded in 1905 as the Société Cooperative Vigneronne des Grandes Caves, with wineries at Rishon-le-Zion and Zichron Ya'akov, accounts for about three quarters of the country's production. Yarden, in the Galil district, has become known for its Sauvignon Blanc and Cabernet Sauvignon.

Issan, Château d' A Third Classed Growth of Margaux belonging to the Cruse family, this is one of the oldest vineyards in the Médoc, and the early seventeenth-century château is surrounded by a moat; its 80 acres of vines produce about 12,000 cases a year of an elegant and stylish wine.

Italy The volume and diversity of this country's wines are such that it must be ranked first among the wine-producing nations of the world. Vineyards are planted in every one of the country's 20 regions, and in most years Italy produces the equivalent of 800 to 900 million cases, which accounts for 20 to 25 percent of total world production. Italy also leads the world in exports, with 30 to 40 percent of the total; much of this is inexpensive wine shipped in bulk to provide the everyday needs of other countries, or to add body and alcohol to the weaker wine with which it is blended, but an increasing amount consists of fine wines whose quality is finally being recognized by an international market. Growing conditions in Italy vary from the cool Alpine regions in the north to the warm, fertile plains of the south and Sicily, but Italy's mountainous terrain – the Apennines traverse the country from north to south – provides hillsides where vines can be cultivated at higher, cooler altitudes in almost every region. In the past, much of Italy's vineyard acreage was categorized as *coltura promiscua*, or "promiscuous cultivation"; that is, vines were mixed in with wheat, olive trees, and other crops so that each farm provided all of its owners

needs, including wine. Even today, about a quarter of Italy's 4 million acres of vineyards are planted in this way, an indication of the extent to which wine plays a part in the everyday life of its people. Italy's extraordinary range of wines is made from many of the familiar grape varieties found in France and Germany, as well as from an extensive assortment of native varieties. The former include such red-wine grapes as Cabernet (both Franc and Sauvignon), Merlot, and Pinot Nero (Pinot Noir), and such whites as Chardonnay, Müller-Thurgau, Pino Bianco (Pinot Blanc), Pinot Grigio (Pinot Gris), Riesling Renano (Rhine Riesling), Sauvignon, and Sylvaner. Native red-wine grapes include Aglianico, Barbera, Dolcetto, Freisa, Grignolino, Lambrusco, Nebbiolo, Raboso, Refosco, Sangiovese, Schiava, and Teroldego; among the white-wine grapes are Albana, Cortese, Fiano, Graganega, Greco, Malvasia, Moscato, Picolit, Pigato, Prosecco, Tocai Friulano, Trebbiano, Verdicchio, Verduzzo, and Vernaccia.

This partial listing of the grape varieties used in Italy,

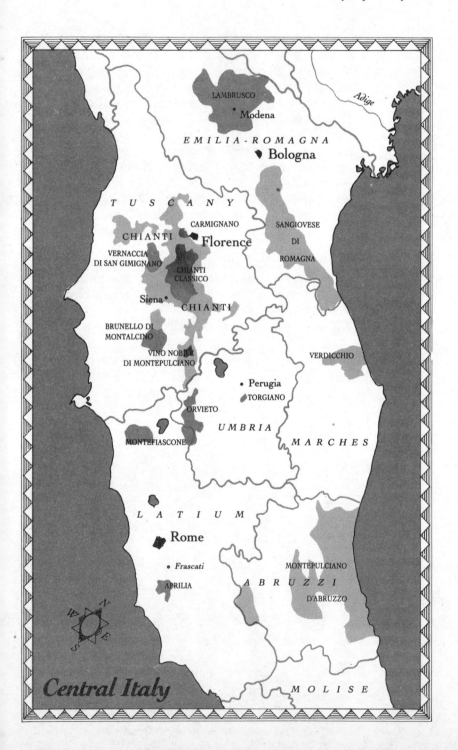

Central Italy

combined with that country's tremendous number of wine-producing districts and villages, and the tendency of many producers to go about things in their own idiosyncratic ways, suggests why, in the past, consumers may have been discouraged from exploring Italian wines beyond the most familiar labels of Chianti, Soave, Valpolicella, and, perhaps, Orvieto and Verdicchio. The wine scene in Italy has changed considerably in the past twenty years, however. To begin with, the *Denominazione di Origine Controllata*, or DOC laws (described more fully under their own entry), were established in the mid-1960s, and they resulted in more clearly defined standards, improved quality, and clearer labelling. As in the past, almost all Italian wines are labelled with either their place of origin – Barbaresco, Barolo, Chianti, Gavi, Orvieto, Soave, Valpolicella – or the grape variety from which they are made; in the case of DOC varietal wines, however, the variety must be coupled with that of a delimited production zone, as Aglianico del Vulture, Barbera d'Alba, Cabernet di Pramaggiore, Merlot del Piave, Pinot Grigio dell'Alto Adige, Verdicchio dei Castelli di Jesi, Vernaccia di San Gimignano. In effect, all DOC wines have a geographic base, even those with fantasy names, such as Est! Est!! Est!!! di Montefiascone and Lacryma Christi del Vesuvio, and non-DOC varietal wines, too, must now have at least a general geographic appellation, such as Nebbiolo del Piemonte or Pinot Bianco di Puglia. Since the early 1980s, six DOC wines have been elevated to the higher category *Denominazione di Origine Controllata e Garantita*, or DOCG. There are, in addition, a number of proprietary wines that do not qualify for DOC and must therefore be labelled *vino da tavola*, but which are nevertheless among the finest produced in Italy; these include Tignanello, Sassicaia, Grifi, Fiorano, Torcolato, Vintage Tunina, and several others.

The improved quality and increasing reputation of Italian wines also owes much to changes in viticulture and vinification. Earlier picking and temperature-controlled fermentation have resulted in a shift away from dull, heavy, wood-aged, and occasionally oxidized white wines to clean, pale, crisp wines with lively acidity that are bottled early to retain their fruit and delicacy. Similarly, many producers whose red wines were traditionally aged in wood for several years have reduced the amount of oak aging and are making wines that have more fruit and vigour, and a more supple texture than the faded, somewhat dried-out reds of the past. In addition, a number of winemakers have planted such classic varieties as Chardonnay and Cabernet Sauvignon in districts where these grapes were not previously cultivated.

The finest Italian wines, and some of the most obscure, range in style from light, fruity, elegant reds and whites from such districts as Friuli, Alto Adige, Trentino, Piave, and Oltrepò Pavese to such impressive, long-lived reds as Amarone, Barolo, Barbaresco, Brunello di Montalcino, Taurasi, Valtellina, and Vino Nobile di Montepulciano. Italy also produces many sparkling wines, the most famous of which is the sweet, Moscato-based Asti Spumante; attractive dry and medium-dry sparkling wines are made from the Prosecco grape in the Veneto region; and excellent Brut *spumanti*, dry sparkling wines, are also being made in increasing quantities from such varieties as Chardonnay, Pinot Bianco, Pinot Grigio, and Pinot Nero, many of them by the classic *methode champenoise*. The range of dessert wines from Italy includes Marsala, from Sicily; a number of rich, luscious wines made from Malvasia and Moscato grapes; and the rare and unusual Picolit. All of the wines and grape varieties mentioned above have their own entries, as do most of the DOC wines listed on page 557.

J

Jacquère The principal white-wine grape of the Savoie region of eastern France, where it produces fresh, light dry wines entitled to the appellation Vin de Savoie.

Jahrgang German for "vintage-year".

Jasnières A small district about 25 miles north of Tours in the Côteaux du Loir (a tributary of the Loire) on the northern edge of the French province of Touraine; about 10,000 cases are made of an interesting dry white wine, from the Chenin Blanc grape.

Jefferson, Thomas Author of the Declaration of Independence, sometime ambassador to France, and third president of the United States, who wrote, "No nation is drunken where wine is cheap and none sober where the dearness of wine substitutes ardent spirits as the common beverage."

Jerez de la Frontera An attractive and prosperous city in southern Spain, on the main road from Seville to Cadiz, in Andalusia; it is the birthplace of sherry, whose name is derived from Jerez. The city's full name dates back to the fourteenth century, and refers to the fact that Jerez was once on the frontier that separated the Christians and the Moors.

Jeroboam   An oversize wine bottle, holding six ordinary bottles, in which red Bordeaux of great years are sometimes laid away. The jeroboam is also used for the wines of Champagne, where it equals four bottles, but here the wine, except by some particularly fastidious firms, undergoes its second fermentation in regular bottles and is then transferred to jeroboams just prior to shipment.

Johannisberg   A world-famous little village in the heart of Germany's Rheingau region. It is the home of the famous Schloss Johannisberg vineyard and lends its name not only to the familiar Grosslage Johannisberger Erntebringer, but also to the regional appellation Bereich Johannisberg, which encompasses the whole of the Rheingau. and whose quality is invariably below that of estate-bottled wines from specific vineyards. There are, in fact, only 200 acres of true Johannisbergers, and these are of exceptional quality, with grace, breed, and bouquet. Among the individual vineyards within Johannisberg are Hölle, Vogelsang, Klaus, and Goldatzel.

Johannisberg, Schloss   See Schloss Johannisberg

Johannisberg Riesling   The name usually given to the true Riesling of Germany in California and other American states (it may also be labelled White Riesling) to differentiate it from other varieties that are not Rieslings at all; the names Riesling and Franken Riesling refer to Sylvaner, Grey Riesling is Chaucé Gris, and Emerald Riesling is a cross that gives wine of lesser quality. *See* Riesling.

Johnson, Samuel   British author and lexicographer, quoted by his biographer, James Boswell, as saying "Wine gives great pleasure and every pleasure is of itself a good." He also said, "Claret is for boys, port is for men, but he who aspires to be a hero must drink brandy." The remark is often quoted by brandy producers, but Johnson was simply pointing out that brandy, having the most alcohol, would cause drunkenness more quickly. He also said of claret "a man would be drowned by it before it makes him drunk", and dismissed a light Italian wine as "wine only to the eye ... it neither pleases the taste, nor exhilarates the spirits."

Josephshöfer An excellent 15-acre vineyard at Graach, in the Moselle, which has been part of the von Kesselstatt estate for over a century; both the steeply terraced vines and the picturesque buildings at their foot belonged to the Monastery of St. Martin until 1802, when they were secularized and given their present name. Although in the township of Graach, the Josephshöf directly adjoins Wehlen, and its wine, made entirely from Riesling, is generally more like a Wehlener than a Graacher, comparatively rich and full-bodied rather than delicate and charming; formerly labelled simply Josephshöfer, it now goes to market as Graach Josephshöfer.

Journal An old Burgundian measure of area, about a third of a hectare, or five sixths of an acre.

Jug Wine A commonly used American term for inexpensive wines sold in large bottles, such as magnums (1.5 litres) and jeroboams (3 litres).

Juliénas An important district in the northern part of France's Beaujolais region whose distinctive wines are relatively sturdy and often need a year or more to develop their potential.

Jura A mountain range, *département*, and wine-growing district in eastern France, not far from the Swiss border. The vineyards, which run roughly parallel to Burgundy's Côte d'Or, extend along the Jura foothills from the town of Arbois southward for some 50 miles, in the old French province of Franche-Comté. Neither in quality nor quantity are the wines of much consequence – total production, more than half of it white, varies from 600,000 to 900,000 cases – but the very diversity of the Jura wines makes them rather interesting. The rosé wine of Arbois is probably the best known, and the only one likely to be found outside of France; the others include a white wine called L'Etoile; a distinct oddity, Château-Châlon, which might be called a French version of unfortified sherry; a small quantity of *vin de paille*; and some fairly good reds and whites marketed under the appellations Arbois or Côtes du Jura.

Jurade de Saint-Emilion A fraternal organization formed in 1948 to celebrate and promote the wines of the Saint-Emilion district of Bordeaux. The original Jurade was a governing body that was first granted certain political powers in 1199; the current group, made up primarily of vineyard owners, is known for its convivial banquets and for the colourful costumes worn by its members on official occasions.

Jurançon An appellation for white wines, celebrated in history and legend, produced on the Pyrenées foothills south and west of Pau, in southwest France. A favourite wine of Henry IV (who was born in Pau), Jurançon is made from grape varieties unknown in other districts – Petit Manseng, Gros Manseng, and Courbu – and has a special, spicy bouquet and flavour that some local enthusiasts have compared to the scent of carnations and the taste of cinnamon or cloves. The sweeter version – made, like Sauternes, from grapes affected by *pourriture noble* – is rich and long-lived, but most producers now make Jurançon as a dry wine; average production is about 300,000 cases.

❦ K

Kabinett One of the six designations for Qualitätswein mit Prädikat (QmP), it is usually the driest and least expensive QmP wine from a given vineyard and producer in any vintage when such wines are made. Since 1971, it has replaced the term *Cabinet* which was used unofficially by many producers to indicate special lots of wine; a wine may now be labelled Kabinett only if it has been made from juice that contains certain minimum amounts of natural grape sugar at the time of harvest – about 16 or 17 percent – with a potential alcohol content of 8.5 to 9.5 percent. Although not necessarily dry – the bottled wine is likely to contain about 2 percent sugar – Kabinett wines are light, elegant, and relatively low in alcohol.

Kadarka The most widely planted red-wine grape of Hungary, producing deep-coloured, full-bodied, tannic wines; it is one of the varieties used to make the famous Egri Bikavér, and is also encountered in a number of wines that combine the grape name with a regional appellation, such as Szekszárdi Kadarka and Villányi Kadarka. The grape is known as Gamza in Bulgaria.

Kaiserstuhl-Tuniberg An important Bereich in the southern part of Germany's Baden region. The Kaiserstuhl section derives its name – which means "the emperor's seat" – from a flat-topped hill of volcanic tufa that rises out of the fertile Rhine Valley between Freiburg and the French city of Colmar; more than three quarters of its vineyards are planted with Müller-Thurgau, Spätburgunder (Pinot Noir), and Ruländer (Pinot Gris), the last producing the most distinctive wines. The Tuniberg section is situated nearby, closer to Freiburg.

Kallstadt One of the better wine-producing villages of Germany's Rheinpfalz region, north of Bad Dürkheim, with more than 1,000 acres of vines, including a fairly high percentage of Riesling. The Grosslage Kallstadter Kobnert includes seven other villages, but the best vineyards in Kallstadt are Kronenberg, Steinacker, Annaberg, and one with the unusual name of Saumagen, or "sow's belly".

Kalterersee *See* Caldaro

Kanzem A celebrated wine-producing village on the Saar, in Germany, whose 140 acres of vineyards are planted almost entirely with Riesling. In great years its wines are close in quality to those of the neighbouring villages of Wiltingen and Ockfen, and there can hardly be higher praise; the best vineyard sites are Sonnenberg and Altenberg.

Karthäuserhofberg A celebrated vineyard on the Ruwer, in Germany. *See* Eitelsbach.

Kasel The most important vineyard town of the Ruwer, a tributary of the Moselle, producing pale, light, delicate Rieslings of great bouquet and charm; its best-known vineyards are Nies'chen, Kehrnagel, Hitzlay, and Herrenberg.

Kéknyelü A white-wine grape of Hungary whose name means "blue-stalked"; what little plantings remain are in the Badacsony district, and the wine is marketed as Badacsonyi Kéknyelü.

Keller The German word for "cellar"; thus, *Kellerarbeit* means "cellar work", *Kellermeister* means 'cellar master".

Kerner One of the new German grape varieties, a cross of Trollinger and Riesling, which produces light, flowery wines with balancing acidity reminiscent of Riesling; more than 17,000 acres have been planted since the 1970s, most of them in Rheinhessen and the Rheinpfalz.

Kesselstatt, Reichsgraf von A famous estate with extensive vineyards on the Moselle, Saar, and Ruwer, including all of the 15-acre Josephshöf in Graach and 15 acres of the Scharzhofberg in Wiltingen; the 150-acre estate was acquired by the Reh family in 1978, and has since been expanded to 200 acres, almost all of it planted with Riesling.

Kiedrich A little vineyard town in Germany's Rheingau region, set back in the hills between Rauenthal and Hallgarten, which produces excellent wines – fruity, racy, and spicy – that deserve to be better known abroad. Its 420 acres of vines include the vineyards Wasseros, Grafenberg, Sandgrub, and Klosterberg.

Kinheim A small, secondary vineyard town on the Moselle, near Traben-Trarbach.

Kir A combination of white wine and crème de cassis, a sweet blackcurrant liqueur; this popular aperitif originated in Burgundy and is named after Canon Felix Kir, a former mayor of Dijon. Kir Royale is made with champagne or sparkling wine, Cardinale is made with red wine.

Kirwan, Château A Third Classed Growth of Margaux, in the Médoc district, owned by an Irishman named Kirwan in the late eighteenth century, and since 1925 by the Bordeaux firm Schröder & Schÿler; its 75 acres of vines produce 12,000 to 16,000 cases a year of a wine noted for its elegance and finesse.

Klevner The name (also spelled Clevener) sometimes used in France's Alsace region for the Pinot Blanc grape, or for a blend of Pinot Blanc and Auxerrois; the name is also used in Switzerland, around Zurich, for a red wine made from Pinot Noir.

Kloster Eberbach An ancient Gothic monastery in the Rheingau village of Hattenheim, founded by the Augustinian monks in 1116 but almost immediately taken over by the Cistercians, under the direction of the same remarkable man who created the Clos de Vougeot on a bare, Burgundian hillside, the wine-loving St. Bernard-de-Clairvaux. Here, as in Burgundy, the Cistercians constructed a wall that still stands around their superb vineyard, the Steinberg, and within a century after its foundation, Kloster Eberbach had become the principal centre of German viticulture and the German wine trade, with a branch in Cologne and a fleet of wine ships on the Rhine. Fortunately, although the monastery was secularized in 1803 and eventually became the propery of the Hessian State, most of what the Cistercians created has been preserved; the old buildings, with their great vaulted rooms and venerable wine presses, are intact and were actually in service well into this century. Wine auctions, tastings, and ceremonial dinners are held here, and the whole establishment, which is now the home of the German Wine Academy, is of the greatest interest to anyone who likes wine and has a taste for history.

Knights Valley A small viticultural area east of Healdsburg, in northern Sonoma, that adjoins the Chalk Hill and Alexander Valley districts; Cabernet Sauvignon and Sauvignon Blanc have been successfully cultivated there, notably by Beringer.

Knipperlé A mediocre white-wine grape, once widely planted in Alsace and rarely seen today.

Kosher Wine Wine made under rabbinical supervision, and so labelled; the exact requirements vary somewhat from one country to another, and may include flash pasteurization at 176 degrees F. for a few seconds; the prohibition of all animal-derived products in the winemaking process; and that only sabbath-observant Jews may handle the wine and winery equipment from the time the grapes are brought in to the time the wine is bottled. Kosher wines may be red or white, dry or sweet, but in the recent past, most were sweet red wines, including the popular examples made in New York State from Concord grapes, which are still much in demand by non-Jews who like sweet, heavy wines. Today, a wide range of dry and distinctive red, white, and rosé wines from Israel, California, France, and Italy is available to those who drink kosher wines.

Kreuznach *See* Bad Kreuznach

Kröv A pretty little town on the Moselle, near Traben-Trarbach, whose vines yield an unexceptional wine that has nevertheless achieved fame and popularity as a result of the odd name and comic label with which it is sold: Nacktarsch means "naked behind", and the label invariably shows a small boy with his trousers down being spanked. Kröver Nacktarsch is now a Grosslage name that encompasses about 840 acres around the village itself.

❧ L

La Ina A proprietary brand of fino sherry produced by the Pedro Domecq firm.

La Lagune, Château A Third Classed Growth situated in the commune of Ludon, just a few miles south of Margaux, and entitled to the appellation Haut-Médoc; of the classed growths of the Médoc, it is the one closest to the city of Bordeaux. The property had less than 1 acre of vines when it was purchased in the 1950s by Georges Brunet, who planted 100 acres, installed modern vinification equipment, and then sold the vineyard to the owner of Ayala champagne in 1961. (Brunet went on to buy and renovate Château Vignelaure in Provence.) The estate now consists of about 135 acres of vineyard producing an average of 25,000 cases a year of an excellent wine – ripe, richly textured, and stylish.

La Tâche One of the very great red-wine vineyards of Burgundy, situated in the commune of Vosne-Romanée, in the Côte de Nuits. Its 14.9 acres are entirely owned by the Domaine de la Romanée-Conti. Although *tâche* is generally translated as "stain", the vineyard is thought to derive its name from another use of *la tâche*, as "the task", a reference to an old Burgundian system whereby a vineyard owner would give a worker part of the crop in return for his labour. Until the early 1930s, La Tâche consisted of only 3.5 acres that adjoined Les Gaudichots; when the owners of the latter vineyard acquired La Tâche, they began to market the wines of both vineyards as La Tâche, thus considerably expanding its production. La Tâche now produces an average of 1,800 cases a year, although production may vary from none (in 1968) to a maximum of 2,685 cases. The wine is velvety and full-bodied, with quite an extraordinary bouquet and depth of flavour.

Labégorce Zédé, Château A *cru bourgeois* in Margaux, in the Médoc district, whose 65 acres produce about 10,000 cases a year. There is also a Château Labégorce nearby, whose vineyard is slightly larger, but whose wines are perhaps less well known.

Labels Although we now take wine labels for granted, the first paper labels date from around 1850 and were not in common usage until some time later. In the late seventeenth century, the contents of glass bottles were identified by leather or wooden tags; still later, glass decanters were hung with silver wine labels, called bottle tickets, which are now much prized by collectors. And even in the late nineteenth century, many fine Bordeaux could be identified only by the branded cork, which displayed the name of the château and the vintage year.

Labrusca One of the principal species native to North America, *Vitis labrusca* was first identified in the eighteenth century. (Other native species include *Vitis riparia*, *Vitis rupestris*, and *Vitis aestivalis*.) The Concord grape is the best known, and most widely planted *labrusca*, and Catawba and Delaware are derived from *labrusca* as well. The wines made from such grape varieties are marked by a pungent, grapey aroma often described as "foxy".

Lacryma Christi del Vesuvio For many years Lacrima Christi (as it was then spelled) was one of the best-known white wines of Italy; it was by no means distinguished, but the unusual name, which means, of course, "tears of Christ", accounted for the wine's popularity. Finally, in 1983, the DOC Vesuvio was established for red, white, and rosé wines produced along the lower slopes of Mount Vesuvius, near Naples, and the best of these wines are entitled to the more stringent DOC Lacryma Christi del Vesuvio. Production is much smaller than in the past, now that geographical limits have been defined, but quality has improved considerably.

Ladoix-Serrigny The northernmost commune of Burgundy's Côte de Beaune; some of its wines are entitled to the appellations Aloxe-Corton Premier Cru, Corton, or Corton-Charlemagne, and most of the rest goes to market at Côte de Beaune-Villages.

Lafaurie-Peyraguey, Château A classed growth of the Sauternes district whose 50 acres of vineyard, planted almost entirely with Sémillon, produce about 5,000 cases a year of sweet wine. About 20 acres of the original property, known simply as Château Peyraguey, were separated from the main vineyard in the late nineteenth century, and this section is known as Clos Haut-Peyraguey.

Lafite-Rothschild, Château A First Growth of Pauillac, in the Médoc district of Bordeaux, and perhaps the most famous vineyard in the world. The property was already well known in the eighteenth century, when it was owned by the Ségur family, who also owned Châteaux Calon and Latour; in the famous Bordeaux classification of 1855, Lafite was ranked first, and in 1868 the vineyard was purchased by Baron James de Rothschild for more than 4 million gold francs. There are about 215 acres under vines, with Cabernet Sauvignon accounting for two thirds of the total, Cabernet Franc and Petit Verdot for 15 percent, and Merlot for about 17 percent; the proportion of Merlot actually in the wine, however, varies from 10 to 25 percent, depending on growing conditions. Total annual production has varied from 16,000 to 45,000 cases, but in recent vintages 25 to 50 percent has been set aside, and the quantity bottled as Lafite-Rothschild averages around 23,000 cases of a wine noted for its elegance, finesse, and subtlety, but with enough structure to assure a long life; indeed, wines from such vintages as 1858, 1864, 1865, 1870, and 1875 have proved to be in remarkable condition, and the cellars at Lafite contain bottles dating back to 1797. Although Lafite has maintained its reputation as the world's finest red wine for more than 200 years, many connoisseurs would agree that the vineyard went through a decline in the 1960s and early 1970s; since the 1975 vintage, however, the wines are again in the very top rank. For many years wines from younger vines, and those not up to the standards of the Lafite label, were marketed under the second label Carruades de Château Lafite-Rothschild, a name derived from a particular plot that was purchased in 1845 from what was then Château Mouton d'Armailhacq; this label was discontinued after the 1967 vintage, but another second label, Moulin des Carruades, was initiated with the 1974 vintage. With the 1985 vintage the Carruades de Lafite Rothschild label was reinstated. The branch of the Rothschild family that owns Lafite also owns Château

Duhart-Milon as well as a majority interest in Château Rieussec, in Sauternes and Château l'Evangile in Pomerol.

Lafleur, Château One of the finest vineyards in the Pomerol district, situated next to Château Pétrus, and under the same ownership as Château Le Gay; its 10 acres produce not much more than 1,000 cases a year of a rich, supple, and intense wine.

Lafon-Rochet, Château A Fourth Classed Growth of Saint-Estèphe, in the Médoc district, purchased in 1961 by Guy Tesseron, who later acquired Châteaux Pontet-Canet and Malescasse; its 100 acres produce about 20,000 cases a year of a sturdy, well-structured wine.

Lagar A large, square, shallow stone or cement trough used for treading sherry grapes (with special hobnailed shoes) in Jerez and port grapes (with bare feet) in the upper Douro. *See* Treading.

Lage The German term for a vineyard site, similar to a *cru* in Bordeaux and a *climat* in Burgundy; the plural is *Lagen*. *See* Einzellage and Grosslage.

Lago di Caldaro *See* Caldaro

Lagrange, Château A Third Classed Growth of Saint-Julien, in the Médoc district, adjoining Château Gruaud-Larose; it was acquired in 1983 by the Japanese firm Suntory, which has renovated the property and doubled the size of the vineyard to 280 acres, making it perhaps the biggest of all the classed growths; a second label, Les Fiefs de Lagrange, was introduced with the 1983 vintage. There is also a Château Lagrange in Pomerol producing about 3,500 cases a year.

Lagrein An Italian red-wine grape cultivated primarily in the Alto Adige region, around the city of Bolzano; it produces a full-bodied red wine marketed as Lagrein Dunkel and even greater quantities of a rosé sold as Lagrein Kretzer. Lagrein may also be blended with Schiava, to a limited extent, in the production of Santa Maddalena and Caldaro.

Lake County Situated north of Napa County and east of Sonoma and Mendocino counties, and part of the North Coast appellation, Lake County had nearly forty wineries at the end of the nineteenth century, none after Prohibition. There were fewer than 300 bearing acres in 1972, about 2,600 acres today; Cabernet Sauvignon and Sauvignon Blanc account for about half the crop and are the most successful varieties; the rest consists mostly of Zinfandel, Chardonnay, Chenin Blanc, and Johannisberg Riesling. Most of the acreage is planted on hillsides at the southern end of Clear Lake, the biggest lake in California; vineyards are also planted in Guenoc Valley, in the southern part of the county. Kendall-Jackson, Konocti, and Guenoc are the best-known wineries.

Lalande-Borie, Château A 45-acre vineyard in the commune of Saint-Julien, in the Médoc, created in the early 1970s by the owner of Château Ducru-Beaucaillou from a parcel of land that was previously part of Château Lagrange; about 8,000 cases a year are produced.

Lalande-de-Pomerol A secondary Bordeaux district that adjoins Pomerol to the north and that now incorporates the wines formerly sold as Néac. It produces 300,000 to 400,000 cases of red wine a year, about as much as does Pomerol, although the wines are less fine than those of its more illustrious neighbour.

Lamarque, Château de One of the larger *crus bourgeois*, situated about halfway between Saint-Julien and Margaux and entitled to the appellation Haut-Médoc; the property, which contains the only medieval castle still remaining in the Médoc, produces about 25,000 cases a year.

Lambrusco An unusual and very popular red wine produced from the grape of that name around Modena, west of Bologna, in Italy's Emilia-Romagna region. Lambrusco, which is almost always *frizzante*, or lightly sparkling, is made in two basic styles, dry and semisweet. The dry version is preferred in the region itself, where its brisk, refreshing taste complements the rich local food. The sweeter version, whose sparkle is produced by the Charmat process of bulk fermentation, and which contains only 8 percent or so alcohol and about 7 percent sugar, has become extremely popular in the United States since the early 1970s, led by the success of the Riunite brand. Lambrusco has accounted for as much as two thirds of all the wines shipped from Italy to the U.S., but today the lightly sparkling, semisweet white and rosé wines marketed by the same firms that produce Lambrusco outsell the red wine. Although most of the more than 20 million cases of Lambrusco produced is non-DOC, there are four DOC zones for this wine, the best known of which are Lambrusco di Sorbara, north of Modena, and Lambrusco Reggiano, west of that city; the two appellations account for 1 to 1.5 million cases a year each.

Lamothe, Château　A classed growth of Sauternes that has been divided into two parts, both of whose wines are marketed as Château Lamothe; the two properties together amount to almost 50 acres, producing about 4,000 cases a year.

Landwein　A quality level established in 1982, within Germany's much broader Deutscher Tafelwein category, to draw attention to wines with certain regional characteristics, and similar to France's *vin de pays* category; Landwein may not contain more than 1.8 percent of sweetness, and therefore falls into the Trocken or Halbtrocken category. There are 15 Landwein appellations within the four main Deutscher Tafelwein regions, and each incorporates the word *Landwein* in its name, as Pfalzer Landwein, Frankischer Landwein, and Landwein der Mosel.

Lanessan, Château　A well-known vineyard situated just south of Saint-Julien and entitled to the appellation Haut-Médoc; its 100 acres produce about 17,000 cases a year of a relatively sturdy, generous wine.

Langhorne Creek　A small Australian wine district located about 40 miles southeast of Adelaide, in South Australia, best known for its fine, intensely flavoured red wines; Shiraz and Cabernet Sauvignon are the most important varieties, and Merlot has been planted as well.

Langoa Barton, Château　A Third Classed Growth of Saint-Julien, in the Médoc district, acquired in 1821 by Hugh Barton, who soon afterwards purchased what is now Château Léoville Barton; its 40 acres produce about 7,000 cases a year of a rich, complex, and elegant wine.

Languedoc　An ancient French province that extends along the Mediterranean from the Rhône River to beyond Narbonne and consists of the *départements* of Hérault, Aude, and Gard; most of France's *vin ordinaire* is produced here. *See* Languedoc-Roussillon.

Languedoc-Roussillon   A vast region along the Mediterranean coast of France that corresponds to what is often referred to as the Midi, and is made up of the four *départements* of Gard, Hérault, Aude, and Pyrenées-Orientales; over 900,000 acres of vineyards produce about 300 million cases of wine, about 40 percent of the total French crop. More than 90 percent of this is red, produced from such high-yielding varieties as Carignan, Grenache, and Cinsault, as well as Syrah and Mourvèdre, and most of it is common stuff that goes to market as *vin ordinaire*. There are, however, a number of *vins de pays* from delimited regions, and several *Appellation Contrôlée* wines, including Collioure, Corbières, Costières du Gard, Coteaux du Languedoc, Côtes du Rousillon, Faugères, Fitou, Minervois, and Saint-Chinian among the reds (although some of the appellations also include limited quantities of white wine), and the white-wine appellations Clairette du Languedoc and Clairette de Bellegarde. This region is also the home of the sweet, fortified *vins doux naturels*, including Banyuls, Maury, and the Muscat-based wines of Frontignan, Lunel, and Rivesaltes.

Langwerth von Simmern   *See* Simmern, Langwerth von

Larose-Trintaudon, Château   A *cru bourgeois* in Saint-Laurent, a commune just west of Saint-Julien, in the Haut-Médoc; the vineyard has been extensively replanted and is now one of the largest in Bordeaux, with more than 400 acres producing about 85,000 cases a year of an appealing and dependable wine.

Larrivet Haut-Brion, Château   A vineyard in the Graves district producing about 7,000 cases of wine, almost all of it red; it is situated some miles south of Château Haut-Brion itself and is unrelated to that famous property.

Lascombes, Château   A Second Classed Growth of Margaux, in the Médoc district, purchased in 1952 by an American group led by the late Alexis Lichine, who increased the vineyard from 48 to 190 acres; the property was sold to an English firm in 1971 and now consists of 250 acres producing about 40,000 cases a year, some of which may be sold under the second label Château Segonnes. (Chevalier Lascombes is a proprietary brand name; wines so labelled do not come from Château Lascombes.)

Late Bottled Vintage Port A type of port that has become increasingly popular, and which is defined as the port of a specific vintage that is bottled after being aged in wood for a minimum of four years and a maximum of six years; the year of bottling must appear on the label, as must the phrase *Late Bottled Vintage* or the letters LBV, to avoid confusion with true vintage port. This type of port, which has replaced what was known as Crusted Port, was created in response to a demand by restaurateurs and consumers for a vintage-dated port that could be consumed when it was bottled, without further aging, and which did not need to be decanted. It is, in effect, a fine, vigorous ruby with some of the character of a vintage port. Most of the firms that market LBV ports produce them in years other than those that they declare for their vintage ports.

Late Harvest A term used in California and elsewhere to denote wines made from especially ripe grapes or, in many instances, from grapes affected by *Botrytis cinerea*, the so-called noble rot that produces the great sweet wines of Sauternes and Germany. A very few *botrytis*-affected wines were made in California in the late 1960s, but it was in the early 1970s that such wines began to be produced on a consistent basis. Because such foreign words as *Spätlese* and *Auslese* were not permitted on American wine labels, a system of labelling was established based on the sugar content of the grapes, as in Germany. Wines labelled Late Harvest, equivalent to a German Auslese, are made from grapes with a minimum of 24 degrees Brix (that is, with approximately 24 percent sugar); the minimum for Select Late Harvest, equivalent to Beerenauslese, is 28 degrees Brix; and the minimum for Special Select Late Harvest, equivalent to Trockenbeerenauslese, is 35 degrees Brix. The labels of such wines, the best of which are characterized by a sweet, concentrated, luscious, and honeyed taste, indicate both the sugar content of the grapes at harvest and the residual sugar in the bottled wine; Select Late Harvest wines often contain 15 to 20 percent sugar, Special Select Late Harvest may contain 20 to 25 percent sugar. Johannisberg Riesling is the grape most often used for such wines, although Late Harvest wines are also made from Gewürztraminer, Sémillon, Sauvignon Blanc, Chenin Blanc, and even Chardonnay. The term *Early Harvest* is used by a number of wineries for light, crisp wines that are made from grapes picked with a maximum of 20 degrees Brix.

Latisana A small DOC zone in the Friuli region, in northeast Italy, producing a range of varietal wines, of which Merlot and Cabernet are the most important.

Latium An Italian region, whose capital is Rome, known primarily for its white wines. Made from a combination of Malvasia and Trebbiano, these include the agreeable wines of the Castelli Romani, or Alban Hills, southeast of Rome, such as Frascati, Marino, Colli Albani, and Colli Lanuvini. Other DOC wines from this region – whose name in Italian is Lazio – include the familiar Est! Est!! Est!!! di Monte-fiascone and the red and white wines of Aprilia.

Latour, Château A First Growth of Pauillac, in the Médoc district of Bor-deaux; this world-famous vineyard is properly ranked as one of the four best of the Médoc, along with Châteaux Lafite-Rothschild, Margaux, and Mouton-Rothschild. The tower from which the property derives its name was built in the early seventeenth century, and later in that century the estate came into the hands of the Ségur family, owners of what is now Château Calon-Ségur, as well as Lafite; in 1962, three quarters of the shares of Latour were acquired by two British firms – the Pearson Group and Harveys of Bristol for a little less than £1 million; in 1989 Allied Lyons, the parent company of Harveys, acquired the Pearson and other shares, thus increasing their holding of Latour to over 90 percent. (For the purposes of this transaction, the entire property was valued at £110 million.) The estate's 150 acres of vines are planted 75 percent with Cabernet Sauvignon, 10 percent Merlot, and the rest Cabernet Franc and Petit Verdot. The amount of wine marketed as Château Latour – all of it from the 125-acre plot that adjoins Château Léoville Las Cases on the border of Pauillac and Saint-Julien – averages 23,000 cases a year and has varied in recent vintages from 13,000 in 1980 and 14,000 in 1981 to 27,000 in 1983 and 24,000 in 1985. The wines are characterized by a deep colour and a power-ful, concentrated, and complex taste, and are noted for being one of the longest-lived of all the wines of Bordeaux. Wines from the other 25 acres (made up of three parcels replanted in the 1960s) are marketed as Les Forts de Latour, which also includes wines from the principal vineyard that do not meet the château's standards; about a third of the total crop is so labelled. The château label actually reads Grand Vin de Château Latour, a reference to the fact that the property was producing both a *grand vin* and a second wine as early as 1800. The label Les Forts de Latour was first used for the 1966 vintage, released for sale in 1972, and these second wines are traditionally put on the market only when they are considered mature, usually six years after the vintage.

There are dozens of châteaux in the Bordeaux region whose names include the words *La Tour*, and the most important are listed under Tour; they should not, of course, be confused with the great Château Latour of Pauillac.

Latour à Pomerol, Château One of the finest vineyards of Pomerol, its 20 acres produce about 3,500 cases a year of richly textured, concentrated, and long-lived red wine.

Latricières-Chambertin A distinguished Burgundy vineyard, in the village of Gevrey-Chambertin, that adjoins Chambertin on the south and shares the same exposure and practically the same soil; the 18 acres of this *grand cru* produce about 2,700 cases a year of an outstanding red wine, perhaps less powerful but no less elegant and distinguished than that of Chambertin and Clos de Bèze.

Laudun A village northwest of Avignon whose red, white, and rosé wines are entitled to the superior appellation Côtes-du-Rhône-Villages; Laudun is unusual among Rhône villages in that it is particularly known for its white wines.

Lauretan A vineyard in the Premières Côtes de Bordeaux owned by the Cordier firm whose wines were originally marketed as Château Lauretan; in recent years, however, the name (without the designation "château") has become a proprietary brand for red and white Bordeaux from various sources.

Lavaux A district of impressive terraced vineyards along the northern shore of Lake Geneva, between Lausanne and Montreux, in the canton of Vaud; it produces, from the Chasselas grape, some of the best white wines of Switzerland, many of which go to market with the name of their village of origin, such as Saint-Saphorin and Vevey.

Lavilledieu A VDQS for reds and rosés produced along the Garonne River, northwest of Toulouse.

Laville Haut-Brion, Château An excellent *grand cru classé* of the Graves district, producing 1,000 to 2,000 cases a year of white wine from Sémillon and Sauvignon Blanc. The vineyard was created out of the southern part of Château La Tour Haut-Brion in the 1920s, and since that vineyard and the adjoining, and more celebrated, Château La Mission Haut-Brion are under the same ownership, Laville Haut-Brion is generally considered as the white wine of La Mission Haut-Brion, although it comes from a separate 15-acre plot.

Layon A little river in the Anjou region, a tributary of the Loire, famous for its white wines. *See* Coteaux du Layon.

Lazio *See* Latium

LBV *See* Late Bottled Vintage Port

Leányka A Hungarian grape variety whose name means "young girl"; it produces an agreeable white wine usually marketed as semisweet. The grape is known as Fetească in Romania.

Lebanon *See* Musar, Château

Lees The heavy, coarse sediment that young wines throw in barrel, tank, or vat as a result of fermentation, aging, or storage. These are left behind when the wine is racked, or transferred from one container to another, and this process is generally repeated two or three times before the wine is bottled. *See* Sur Lie.

Legs After being swirled in a glass, the wine adhering to the inside surface slowly descends, forming legs (also known as tears). Although many oenophiles believe that the thickness and rate of descent of these legs are an indication of a wine's viscosity and glycerol content, this effect really has more to do with a wine's alcohol content and is not a useful guide to its quality.

Léognan A commune in the northern part of the Graves district whose wines are entitled to the new appellation Pessac-Léognan.

Léon Millot   A French-American hybrid, known officially as Kuhlmann 1942, producing good red wines and related to the more widely planted Maréchal Foch.

Léoville Barton, Château   A Second Classed Growth of Saint-Julien, in the Médoc district, originally part of the much larger Léoville estate and acquired in 1826 by Hugh Barton (who already owned what is now Château Langoa Barton); his great-great-grandson, Ronald Barton, administered the two vineyards for nearly sixty years until his death in 1986, when they came under the direction of Ronald's nephew, Anthony Barton – thus, these two vineyards and Château Mouton-Rothschild are the only classed growths that are still owned by the same family as at the time of the 1855 classification. There are now 110 acres of vineyards producing about 20,000 cases of an elegant, supple wine with great breed and finesse.

Léoville Las Cases, Château   A Second Classed Growth of Saint-Julien, in the Médoc, the principal part of the large domain known as Léoville in the early eighteenth century, and later owned by the Marquis de Las Cases; a quarter of the domain was sold to Hugh Barton in 1826, and a few years later a part of what was left passed to the Baron de Poyferré – whence the names of the three adjoining Léoville vineyards. (The name on the label is actually Grand Vin de Léoville du Marquis de Las Cases.) Under the direction of the Delon family, Léoville Las Cases now has 230 acres of vineyard (part of which adjoins Château Latour in Pauillac) that produce about 25,000 cases a year of an exceptional wine, perhaps the richest of all the Saint-Juliens, noted for its combination of power and finesse, firmness and elegance; another 12,000 to 18,000 cases or so are marketed under the second label Clos du Marquis.

Léoville Poyferré, Château   A Second Classed Growth of Saint-Julien, in the Médoc, originally part of the extensive Léoville estate; its 150 acres of vines produce about 24,000 cases a year of a wine that has not always kept pace with the other two Léoville vineyards, but several recent vintages have been promising.

Lessona   A fine Italian red wine produced in very limited quantities from a 12-acre DOC zone just west of Gattinara, in the Piedmont region; Nebbiolo, the principal grape, may be blended with Vespolina and Bonarda.

Lestage, Château A well-known *cru bourgeois* in the commune of Listrac, in the Haut-Médoc, whose 135 acres produce about 25,000 cases a year of a dependable wine.

Lexia A name used in Australia for Muscat of Alexandria.

Liebfraumilch One of the most universally known of all wine names, this German word simply means "milk of the Blessed Mother". It was originally used for the wines from the vineyards around the Liebfrauenkirche, a church in Worms, in the Rheinhessen region. The name was eventually used for any wine from the Rhine, often the cheapest and poorest of all. In 1971 Liebfraumilch was defined as a Qualitätswein, with certain minimum quality standards, and since 1983 the wine must come from one of four specific regions, whose name must appear on the label. In practice, about half of all Liebfraumilch comes from Rheinhessen, and almost all the rest from the Rheinpfalz, although a little comes from the Nahe and even less from the Rheingau. The wine must have a minimum of 18 grams of residual sugar, may not bear such Prädikat designations as Spätlese and Auslese, and may be made only from Riesling, Müller-Thurgau, Sylvaner, and, since 1985, Kerner; little Riesling is actually used. In some vintages this mild, simple white wine accounts for as much as 20 percent of the Qualitätswein crop, and for many years Liebfraumilch has represented more than 50 percent of total German exports.

Lieser A little wine town near Bernkastel, on the Moselle, whose wines are good, but not of top quality, being somewhat heavier than those of Bernkastel and Graach.

Lieu-dit In French, a place name that has no precise official meaning, other than one based purely on tradition and local usage; in Burgundy, a *lieu-dit* is pretty much synonymous with *climat* and *cru* and refers to a specific vineyard site.

Light As used by a wine taster, it is the opposite of full-bodied and also of heavy, and as such can be complimentary; light wines may have finesse, fruit, and charm, but only in rare instances can they be called great.

Liguria An Italian region that extends along the Mediterranean from the French border to the northwest corner of Tuscany; its capital is Genoa, and its coastline, also known as the Italian Riviera, includes such resorts as San Remo, Portofino, and La Spezia. The region is best known for the white Cinqueterre and the red Dolceacqua, both DOC; some excellent white wines are also made from the Pigato and Vermentino varieties, especially in the southwestern part of Liguria, in a new DOC zone known as Riviera Liguria del Ponente.

Limousin A forest in central France, east of the Charente, near Limoges, from which it derives its name. Its oak is used for aging cognac and Burgundies and was the first French oak to be widely used by California winemakers; because Limousin imparts relatively pronounced oak flavours, however, many Californians now prefer the more subtle contribution of Nevers, Alliers, and Tronçais oak.

Limoux *See* Blanquette de Limoux

Limpid A term applied to wines whose appearance is absolutely clear and star bright.

Lipari The largest of a group of small islands off the north coast of Sicily; according to Greek mythology, the home of Aeolus, god of the winds. Several of the islands, especially Salina, produce a famous golden dessert wine made from the Malvasia grape and entitled to the DOC Malvasia delle Lipari.

Liqueur In common, conventional usage, a sweet, flavoured after-dinner drink based on spirits; synonymous with cordial. When applied, somewhat confusingly, to whisky or brandy, it means, rather vaguely and unofficially, one of particularly fine quality, although, of course, not sweet. As far as wine is concerned, however, the word has other and specific meanings. In the Champagne region, *liqueur de tirage* is the solution of sugar in wine that is added, with a yeast culture, to the still wine before bottling, to bring about a second fermentation in the bottle; *liqueur d'expédition* is a similar syrup added to an already sparkling wine at the time of disgorging to determine its relative sweetness. (*See* Dosage.)
   When used in connection with naturally sweet dessert

wines, such as those of Sauternes and Anjou, *liqueur* refers to the sweetness, in the form of unfermented grape sugar, left in the finished wine. What is called a *vin de liqueur*, however, is almost always a specially made sweet fortified wine to which wine spirits have been added; it is similar to what are known as *vins doux naturels*.

Liquoreux A French term used to describe a sweet, luscious white wine, such as Sauternes, that has retained, without being fortified, a good deal of natural grape sugar.

Liquoroso An Italian term that indicates a wine relatively high in alcohol – 17 to 20 percent – almost always a sweet dessert wine that has been fortified with grape spirits; examples of wines that may be produced in a *liquoroso* version include Malvasia delle Lipari and Moscato di Pantelleria.

Lirac A village immediately north of Tavel, in the lower Rhône Valley, producing about 200,000 cases a year of red and rosé wines made primarily from the Grenache grape, plus lesser amounts of Cinsault, Syrah, and Mourvèdre; a few thousand cases of white are also produced. Although long known for its attractive, dry rosés, similar to those of Tavel, Lirac now produces more red than rosé.

Lison-Pramaggiore A new DOC zone in the Veneto, east of Piave, that encompasses the districts producing Tocai di Lison and Cabernet di Pramaggiore. Although Cabernet, Tocai and Merlot are the principal varieties produced in this DOC region, other varieties include Pinot Grigio, Chardonnay, Refosco and Verduzzo.

Listrac A village in the Médoc district of Bordeaux, a few miles northwest of Margaux, producing a good deal of sturdy red wine; 1,300 acres of vineyards produce about 300,000 cases a year. There is a large co-operative cellar in Listrac, but most of the wines come from *crus bourgeois*, including Châteaux Fourcas-Hosten, Fourcas-Dupré, Clarke, and Lestage.

Litre A metric measure of volume equivalent to 33.8 ounces, or .22 of a gallon. *See* Bottle.

Livermore Valley A viticultural area in California's Alameda County, about 40 miles southeast of San Francisco, near the town of

Livermore; the Livermore Valley, 15 miles long and 10 miles wide, has long been recognized as one of the best wine districts in the state. Robert Livermore first planted a vineyard there in the 1840s, and Wente and Concannon, the region's best-known wineries, were established in 1883. There were 7,000 acres of grapes by the turn of the century, and nearly 15,000 acres just before Prohibition, but the combination of Prohibition and land development reduced the acreage to 1,100 in the late 1950s. Today, there are 1,800 acres of vineyards planted in the rolling, gravelly soil of this district, which is best known for its white wines: Chardonnay, Sauvignon Blanc, Sémillon, and Grey Riesling are the most widely planted white varieties, Cabernet Sauvignon is the leading red grape.

Loché *See* Pouilly-Loché

Lodge A ground-level warehouse in Vila Nova de Gaia, in northern Portugal, for the storage of port; the same as *chai* in

The Loire

Bordeaux and *bodega* in Jerez.

Lodi A viticultural area around the city of that name in the northern, and somewhat cooler, part of the San Joaquin Valley; Chenin Blanc, French Colombard, Sauvignon Blanc, and Cabernet Sauvignon are planted in Lodi, but the district is best known for Zinfandel and, in fact, accounts for 40 percent of California's total Zinfandel crop.

Logroño A city, and province, on the Ebro River in northern Spain; most of the celebrated Rioja district is in the province of Logroño, although the city is less important than Haro as a centre of the wine trade.

Loir A tributary of France's Loire River, which it joins near Angers; it gives its name to the AOC Coteaux du Loir, situated north of Tours, and its best-known wine is Jasnières.

Loire The longest and one of the most beautiful rivers of France,

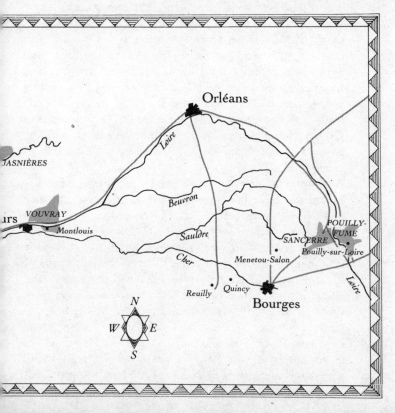

which traverses – in the course of its 600-mile journey from its source, west of Lyons, to the Atlantic, near Nantes – a whole series of different provinces and viticultural areas. Its wines, sometimes collectively called *Vins de la Loire*, include a most diverse and interesting collection of reds, whites, and rosés ranging in quality from ordinary to great. There are more than forty *Appellations Contrôlées* along the Loire, producing an average of 22 million cases a year, slightly more than 10 percent of all the AOC wines of France; white wines usually account for about two thirds of the total. The wines of the Loire can be grouped into five principal geographical regions: the Pays Nantais, at the mouth of the river, best known for Muscadet; Anjou, famous for its Rosé d'Anjou and for a somewhat better rosé labelled Cabernet d'Anjou, as well as for a number of white wines made from Chenin Blanc (known locally as Pineau de la Loire), including the dry Savennières and the sweeter wines of Bonnezeaux and Quarts de Chaume, from the Coteaux du Layon; Saumur, which produces dry white wines and a great deal of sparkling wine from Chenin Blanc, and reds from Cabernet Franc, the best known of which is labelled Saumur-Champigny; the Touraine, where agreeable red wines are produced from Gamay and whites from Sauvignon Blanc, and which also includes the famous villages of Vouvray and Montlouis, whose white wines are made from Chenin Blanc; and, farther up the Loire, Sancerre and Pouilly-Fumé are made from Sauvignon Blanc, as are the less familiar wines of Quincy, Reuilly, and Ménetou-Salon. All of these Loire wines, and others, will be found listed in this volume.

Lombardy   An important region of northern Italy, whose capital is Milan; about 25 million cases are produced a year, of which 20 percent or so qualify for DOC. There are three principal wine areas within Lombardy: the Valtellina Valley to the north, near the Swiss border, known for its fine reds made from the Nebbiolo grape; the Oltrepò Pavese, south of Pavia, where Barbera is the most widely planted grape, and which is also known for fine sparkling wines made from Pinot Bianco, Pinot Grigio, and Pinot Nero; and the province of Brescia, west of Lake Garda, where such wines as Franciacorta, Lugana, and Riviera del Garda Bresciano are made. Lombardy also has its share of more obscure DOC wines, including the red and white Valcalepio, produced north and east of Bergamo; Botticino, a red based on

Barbera, from a district east of Brescia; and the red, white, and rosé wines of the Colli Morenici Mantovani del Garda district, just south of Lake Garda, in the province of Mantua.

Long Island The newest viticultural area of New York State, situated on eastern Long Island, about 85 miles from New York City. The first vineyard was planted in 1973 on a former potato farm by Alex and Louisa Hargrave, who made their first wines at Hargrave Vineyard in 1975. There are now about 1,200 acres of vineyards, virtually all planted with European *vinifera* varieties such as Chardonnay, Sauvignon Blanc, Johannisberg Riesling, Gewürztraminer, Cabernet Sauvignon, Merlot, and Pinot Noir. Most of the vineyards and wineries are in the viticultural area known as the North Fork of Long Island, but there is also some acreage in the South Fork, entitled to the appellation The Hamptons. Some of the better-known wineries include Bridgehampton, Hargrave, Lenz and Pindar.

Lorch A town on the Rhine that is officially a part of the Rheingau, although it is actually in the Rhine gorge, north of Assmannshausen. The best Rieslings can be quite good, although perhaps closer in style to those of the Mittelrhein than the Rheingau. The Grosslage is Rüdesheimer Burgweg, and individual vineyards include Schlossberg, Krone, and Pfaffenwies.

Loudenne, Château A well-known *cru bourgeois* in the northern Médoc, in the village of Saint-Yzans, under British ownership since 1875; its 125 acres of vines produce about 20,000 cases a year of an attractive Médoc and about 4,000 cases of a distinctive white wine entitled only to the appellation Bordeaux.

Loupiac A village on the right bank of the Garonne, directly opposite Barsac, in the Bordeaux region; the sweet white wines of Loupiac and its adjoining appellation, Sainte-Croix-du-Mont, are similar in style to those of Sauternes, though less well known.

La Louvière, Château A well-known vineyard in the Graves district of Bordeaux, situated between Châteaux Carbonnieux and Haut-Bailly; it is one of the biggest Graves properties, and its 115 acres produce about 20,000 cases, three quarters of it red.

Lubéron *See* Côtes du Lubéron

Lugana A very agreeable dry white wine produced around the village of this name, at the southern end of Lake Garda, in Italy's Lombardy region; made from the Trebbiano di Lugana grape, it is similar to the best wines of Soave, produced a few miles to the east.

Lugny A village in the Mâcon region of southern Burgundy known for its fine dry white wines, made from the Chardonnay grape, which sometimes go to market as Mâcon-Lugny.

Luna dei Feldi A proprietary white wine produced by Santa Margherita from the Feldi vineyard on the border of Trentino and Alto-Adige, in a district known as Roveré della Luna; first produced in 1983, this crisp, stylish wine is made primarily from Chardonnay plus Müller-Thurgau and Traminer.

Lunel A village northeast of Montpellier, near the Mediterranean coast of France, producing a sweet white wine from the Muscat grape entitled to the appellation Muscat de Lunel; production of this *vin doux naturel* is about 75,000 cases a year.

Lussac-Saint-Emilion The appellation for the red wines produced in the commune of Lussac, northeast of Saint-Emilion itself; the best wines are full, supple, and usually moderately priced.

Luxembourg The thirsty citizens of the Grand Duchy of Luxembourg are among the most dedicated of Europe's wine drinkers – per capita consumption is more than 80 bottles a year. Most of that is imported, but the country has 3,000 acres of vineyards along a 25-mile stretch of the Moselle River that forms the boundary with Germany, a few miles upriver from Trier. The light and fruity wines of Luxembourg, all white, are made from such German grapes as Riesling, Traminer, Ruländer (Pinot Gris), and Müller-Thurgau (known locally as Rivaner); some agreeable sparkling wines are also produced.

Lynch-Bages, Château A Fifth Classed Growth of Pauillac, in the Médoc, owned for more than fifty years by the Cazes family (who also own Château Les Ormes de Pez in Saint-Estèphe); situated on what is known as the Bages plateau (which also includes Châteaux Croizet-Bages and Haut-Bages Libéral), the property belonged to the Irishman Thomas Lynch in the eighteenth century. Its 200 acres of vines produce an average of 30,000 cases of a deep-coloured, generous, and richly textured wine that has for many years been considered one of the finest of the Médoc, on a par with the second growths; another 7,000 cases or so are marketed under the second label Château Haut-Bages-Averous.

Lynch-Moussas, Château   A Fifth Classed Growth of Pauillac, in the Médoc district, acquired in 1970 by the proprietors of the adjoining Château Batailley, and extensively renovated and expanded; its 100 acres produce about 15,000 cases a year.

❧ M

Macabeo   Widely planted in northern Spain, this grape accounts for almost all the white wine produced in Rioja, where it is known as Viura; this variety is also found in southern France.

Maceration   See Cuvaison

Mâcon   An important town on the Saône River in southern Burgundy that has given its name to an extensive region, the Mâconnais, and to red, white, and rosé wines entitled to the appellations Mâcon, Mâcon-Supérieur, and Mâcon-Villages. The region is best known for its dry, fresh, palatable and moderately priced white wines, made from the Chardonnay grape, most of which are marketed as Mâcon-Villages; the best known of these villages are Lugny, Viré, and Prissé, whose names often appear on labels. Most of the red wines, which are made from the Gamay grape, go to market as Mâcon Supérieur; they are pleasant, sound wines that are, nevertheless, less fruity and attractive than good Beaujolais. Pinot Noir is also planted in this region and may be sold as Bourgogne Rouge; wines made from both Pinot Noir and Gamay are entitled to the appellation Bourgogne-Passe-tout-grains.

Mâconnais   A large region in southern Burgundy, north and east of the town of Mâcon, in the *département* of the Saône-et-Loire. Known primarily for white wines made from the Chardonnay grape, the region includes the appellations Mâcon, Mâcon-Supérieur, Mâcon-Villages, Pouilly-Fuissé, Pouilly-

Vinzelles, Pouilly-Loché, and Saint-Véran. Curiously enough, two villages that have given their names to grape varieties – Chardonnay and Chasselas – are situated in the Mâconnais.

Mâcon-Villages An appellation for better-quality white wines of the Mâcon region, which must come from specified communes.

Madeira A Portuguese island in the Atlantic Ocean, 400 miles off the coast of Morocco, that has been producing wines since the fifteenth century. Oddly enough, the distinctive wines for which the island became famous first achieved what might be called an international reputation because of the favour they enjoyed in America in colonial days, and the British taste for Madeira dates from the War of Independence, when returning British officers spoke enthusiastically of the wines they had tasted in America. Not only was Madeira the preferred wine in America in the late eighteenth and early nineteenth centuries, but it played a role in early American history as well. In 1768, for example – five years before the more famous Boston Tea Party – there was a riot on the Boston docks when British customs officials tried to impose duties on a shipment of Madeira. Madeira was used to toast the signing of the Declaration of Independence and, in 1789, the inauguration of George Washington.

Today, Madeira may well be the most neglected of the world's fine wines, and it is possible that more of this wine is now used in the kitchen than on the dining table. Madeira is, with port and sherry, one of the three great fortified wines, that is, wines whose alcohol content has been increased to 18 to 20 percent. Madeira's taste is unique, however. Although the various styles, usually labelled Sercial, Verdelho, Rainwater, Boal (or Bual), and Malmsey, range from off-dry to quite sweet, they are all characterized by a pungent tang attributed to the volcanic soil of the island, a relatively high acidity that prevents even the sweetest examples from being cloying, and by an unusual burnt, caramel-like flavour, the result of the special way the wine is made.

The wine we know as Madeira first began to achieve its present style in the mid-eighteenth century, when British merchants who had established themselves in Funchal, now the island's capital, started to add distilled spirits to the wine as a way of preserving it during the long sea voyage to the Americas. In time, the merchants noted that the heat and movement of a voyage improved the wine and transformed its taste, and that the wines that had travelled the most tasted the best. In the early 1800s the merchants began to simulate the effect of sea voyages by baking the wines in *estufas*, or hot rooms, and a variation of that technique is used today. The wines destined to become Madeira, most of which have been fermented until dry, are put into large, glass-lined cement tanks that contain heating coils, and baked at around 120 degrees F. for a minimum of three months, which affects the wine as long sea voyages did 200 years ago. This treatment, which would ruin any other wine, transforms the product of the steep, terraced vineyards of Madeira into the special wine we know, with its unusual burnt flavour. After baking, the wines are fortified with neutral spirits, aged in casks for a minimum of three years, and sweetened according to the style desired. Wines labelled Reserve must be aged a minimum of five years in cask, Special Reserve, ten years. Most Madeira is labelled with the name of a grape variety: Sercial (which is bottled with 2 or 3 percent sugar) is the driest and is usually served chilled, as an aperitif; Verdelho is a bit fuller; Boal, or Bual (with 8 or 9 percent sugar), is richer, and distinctly sweet; and Malmsey (with 10 to 14 percent sugar) is the sweetest of all, quite full-bodied, but it still retains the burnt flavour and acidity that sets it apart from, say, cream sherry. Boal and Malmsey complement many desserts, and can also be served on their own after dinner. There is one other basic style of Madeira, labelled with the generic name Rainwater; this popular blend is a medium-dry wine similar to Verdelho.

The decline in Madeira's reputation since the mid-nineteenth century is the result of two natural calamities, and these, in turn, have created an unusual marketing problem for the island and its wines. In the 1850s the vineyards of Madeira were severely afflicted by oidium, or powdery mildew. Then, in the 1870s, the vineyards were destroyed by phylloxera, the vine louse that attacks the roots. When the vineyards were eventually reconstituted – by grafting European vines to phylloxera-resistant American roots – many growers switched to the more prolific Tinta Negra Mole variety rather than replanting with the four classic Madeira varieties, Sercial, Verdelho, Boal, and Malmsey. As a result, for most of this century the wine marketed as Madeira was made almost entirely from a single variety, Tinta Negra Mole, and the varietal names used on labels were no more than an indication of style and relative sweetness. This curious aspect of Madeira labelling became a serious one when Portugal entered the Common Market, in 1986, since one of its regulations is that a wine labelled with the name of a specific variety must contain at least 85 percent of that grape. New plantings of the classic varieties have been established in recent years, and the wines now contain more of the variety listed on the label than in the past; trying to attribute specific varietal characteristics to these wines, however, would be a mistake. Not only has nomenclature become more standardized, but many of the old, once-famous export houses have come together and tend to draw their wines from jointly held stocks. Thus, such leading brands of Madeira as Blandy's, Cossart Gordon, Leacock, Rutherford & Miles, and Welsh Brothers are now produced and bottled by one firm, the Madeira Wine Company.

Madeira has the reputation of being the longest-lived of all wines, and there are, in addition to the usual range, some expensive vintage-dated wines to be found going back to the nineteenth century. These old bottles are quite fascinating – the special qualities of Madeira are concentrated as the wines age, and provide a remarkably intense and pungent taste. (New laws have been established for vintage-dated Madeiras produced today; they must come entirely from the vintage and variety named on the bottle, and must be aged a minimum of twenty years in cask and two in bottle.) Occasionally, old vintage-dated Madeiras with the word *solera* on them are offered for sale; these, however, are blends that have been continually refreshed with younger wines, so it is unlikely that they bear any relation to the year on the bottles.

Maderized A term applied to a wine, especially a white or rosé, which is past its prime, has become oxidized, and has acquired an aroma and flavour reminiscent of Madeira; it is anything but a favourable epithet. The terms *maderized* and *oxidized* are often used interchangeably, but stricly speaking a maderized wine is one that has acquired its special character through a combination of heat plus exposure to air (which is the way Madeira is produced), whereas the term *oxidized* does not imply that the wine has been stored in a warm place.

Madiran An appellation for red wines produced in a district along the Adour River, about 25 miles north of Pau, in southwest

France. The wines, which must contain between 40 and 60 percent of the native Tannat grape, are sturdy, tannic, even harsh; producers also cultivate Cabernet Franc (known locally as Bouchy) and Cabernet Sauvignon to make a more balanced wine. The district was granted AOC status in 1948, when there were little more than 100 acres of vineyards; today, more than 2,500 acres produce 400,000 to 600,000 cases a year. The white wines made from this district are marketed as Pacherenc du Vic-Bilh.

Magdelaine, Château One of the *premiers grands crus classés* of Saint-Emilion, directly adjoining Belair; its 27 acres, planted primarily with Merlot, produce an average of 4,500 cases of fine red wines that combine suppleness and finesse.

Magence, Château One of the best of the lesser-known vineyards of the Graves district of Bordeaux, whose 75 acres produce about 15,000 cases a year of attractive red and white wines.

Magnol, Château A *cru bourgeois* entitled to the appellation Haut-Médoc, owned by the Bordeaux *négoçiant* Barton & Guestier; formerly called Château du Dehez, it is situated in Blanquefort, near the border of the Médoc and Graves, and its 42 acres produce about 6,000 cases.

Magnum A large bottle, the equivalent of two normal bottles, with a capacity of 1.5 litres or 50.7 ounces. Since wines, red wines especially, tend to develop and age more slowly in large bottles than in small, red Bordeaux and Burgundies of great years are often bottled in magnums for laying away. Champagne, too, is available in magnums, and such wines have been fermented in the larger bottle, not transferred from a normal bottle. Of course, many inexpensive, so-called jug wines are marketed in magnums as well, but that is for purposes of price and convenience, not longevity.

Maigre A French term applied to a wine that is thin, weak, and deficient in body.

Main A river that flows through Germany's Franken, or Franconia, region, passes below the Rheingau village of Hochheim, and joins the Rhine at Mainz.

Maître de Chai French for "cellar master"; the term is most often used in the châteaux of Bordeaux, where the *maître de chai*, who is in charge of all cellar operations, reports to the proprietor or, at some of the larger vineyards, to a *régisseur*, or "estate manager".

Málaga A fortified wine, usually sweet, produced around the city of that name, along the Mediterranean coast, in Spain's Andalusia region. The vineyards are situated in the mountains behind the city, hence its eighteenth-century name of Mountain, a word found on silver decanter tags of that time. There are two districts that produce Málaga, the smaller planted with Pedro Ximénez grapes, the larger, with Moscatel; annual production varies from 350,000 cases to 1 million. Although Málaga may be a light, dry wine, it is better known as one that is dark brown in colour and quite sweet in taste.

The Malaga grape of California, also known as White Malaga, is a table grape, and has no connection whatsoever with Málaga wine; about 1,800 acres are planted in the San Joaquin Valley.

Malartic-Lagravière, Château A *grand cru classé* of the Graves district of Bordeaux, producing about 8,000 cases a year of sound red wine and 1,000 cases of a dry white made from Sauvignon Blanc.

Malbec A red-wine grape cultivated in Bordeaux, where it is also known as Cot or Pressac and where it plays a relatively small role compared to that of Cabernet Sauvignon, Merlot, and Cabernet Franc. It is, however, the principal variety in the Cahors district, where it is known as Auxerrois, and where it is capable of producing firm, well-structured wines as well as lighter, more supple ones. Malbec is also extensively planted in Argentina.

Malescasse, Château A *cru bourgeois* situated in the village of Lamarque, a few miles north of Margaux, and entitled to the appellation Haut-Médoc; it was acquired by an American group in the early 1970s and now belongs to the Tesseron family, owners of Châteaux Pontet-Canet and Lafon-Rochet. Its 75 acres produce about 13,000 cases a year.

Malescot Saint-Exupéry, Château A Third Classed Growth of Margaux, in the Médoc, whose owners have included Simon Malescot in the late seventeenth century and, more than a century later, the great-grandfather of the writer Antoine de Saint-Exupéry; its 80 acres produce about 14,000 cases a year of a wine known for its finesse and subtlety.

Malle, Château de A classed growth of the Sauternes district, owned by the same family since the sixteenth century and renowned for its seventeenth-century château as well as for its elegant sweet wines; the 60 acres of vineyard produce about 5,000 cases a year, plus a dry white wine labelled Chevalier de Malle.

Malleret, Château A *cru bourgeois* situated not far from the city of Bordeaux and entitled to the appellation Haut-Médoc; the impressive 1,000-acre estate has 150 acres of vines producing about 25,000 cases a year of a deservedly popular wine.

Malmsey A white-wine grape said to be identical to Malvasia, once widely planted on the island of Madeira; the name is now used to describe the sweetest style of Madeira.

Malolactic Fermentation A secondary fermentation that takes place in many table wines; its effect is to transform malic acid, which is the acid of many fruits, especially apples, into the milder lactic acid, the acid of milk, thus making the wine less harsh, less tart, and more supple. Formerly thought to be a continuation of the original alcoholic fermentation, brought about in the spring following the harvest by the change of season, it is now known to be a bacterial fermentation that can be induced shortly after the original fermentation by the addition of specially propagated lactic-acid bacteria. Most red wines undergo malolactic fermentation, but few whites, since crisp, lively acidity is an important part of their appeal; white Burgundies are one notable exception, as are a number of California Chardonnays, as malolactic fermentation may add richness and complexity to these wines.

Malvasia An ancient and famous white-wine grape (a red variant exists but is far less important) originally from Greece and the Aegean Islands, transplanted to most other Mediterranean countries, to the island of Madeira, to California, and elsewhere. The wines it produces may be dry or sweet; the latter, when fortified in the traditional way, can be very luscious, with an intense bouquet, heavy in body, golden in colour but turning deep amber with age, and long-lived. The most famous version is probably the one produced on Madeira, where the grape is known by its English name, Malmsey (although there is actually very little acreage left of this variety, and the name is now used primarily to describe a sweet style of Madeira). A number of sweet Malvasia wines are produced in Italy, the best known of which comes from a little archipelago of islands off the north coast of Sicily, and sold as Malvasia delle Lipari, after the most important island of this group. When the name *Malvasia* appears on an Italian label, the wine is likely to be sweet, but the grape is widely planted in that country, especially in Tuscany, Umbria, and around Rome. Frascati and Orvieto are two examples of dry white wines made from a combination of Malvasia and Trebbiano. There are more than 2,000 acres of Malvasia Bianco planted in California, most of it in the San Joaquin Valley, where it is usually blended with other varieties to make fortified wines.

Malvoisie   French for Malvasia, a superior dessert-wine grape widely planted in the Côtes du Roussillon region of the *département* of Pyrenées-Orientales; there, in conjunction with Muscat, Grenache, and other varieties, it yields the sweet, amber, fortified wines known as *vins doux naturels*.

Mancha, La   An extensive area south of Madrid on Spain's central plateau; its 1.7 million acres of vineyards produce 170 to 200 million cases a year, about half of the country's total crop. The white Airén grape accounts for 90 percent of the plantings and produces relatively neutral, low-acid, high-alcohol wines. The inner *Denominación de Origen* Mancha consists of about 375,000 acres, but only 8 million cases or so are marketed with the *Denominación*. In recent years a number of producers have begun picking their white grapes earlier to retain acidity, fermenting them at lower temperatures to retain fruit, and bottling them without wood aging to preserve their freshness. The most famous district within La Mancha is Valdepeñas, known for its light red wines.

Manzanilla   A special type of sherry made on the edge of the sherry region, in southern Spain, in the village of Sanlucar de Barrameda, situated about ten miles west of Jerez de la Frontera. Technically a kind of fino, manzanilla is a very pale, almost painfully dry wine, with a taste that is appetizing, faintly bitter, almost salty. Some connoisseurs claim that the wine's special tang is due to the sea wind that blows off the Atlantic, but it is likely that the wine owes its taste to the more humid atmosphere of Sanlucar; if a young manzanilla is taken to Jerez to mature, it will take on the characteristics of a traditional fino. The wine, which contains 16 to 17 percent alcohol, accounts for less than 3 percent of the total sherry crop.

Maranges   A new appellation in Burgundy's Côte d'Or that encompasses the wines from the villages of Cheilly-les-Maranges, Dezize-les-Maranges, and Sampigny-les-Maranges, all previously marketed as Côte de Beaune-Villages.

Marbuzet, Château de   A small vineyard in Saint-Estèphe, in the Médoc, graced by a Louis XIV château; in practice, the label is used for the second wine of Château Cos d'Estournel. Château Haut-Marbuzet, also in Saint-Estèphe, is a separate property.

Marc   Grape pressings, the mass of skins and seeds left in the press after the wine – or, in the case of white-wine grapes, the juice – has been extracted; known in English as pomace. The brandy distilled from the pressings is called *eau-de-vie de marc* (*grappa* in Italy). In the Champagne region, the word has a different and special meaning; a *marc* is 4,000 kilograms of grapes, the load that one of the traditional presses can handle at one time.

Marches   A region in central Italy – Marche in Italian – along the Adriatic Sea, whose most famous wine is Verdicchio dei Castelli di Jesi, a crisp, dry white marketed in a distinctive amphora bottle. Other wines from this region include Verdicchio di Matelica and two attractive reds, Rosso Piceno and Rosso Cònero.

Marcobrunn   A celebrated 13-acre vineyard in Germany's Rheingau region. It takes its name from the Marcobrunnen, a spring feeding an attractive little fountain of red sandstone that marks the boundary between the villages of Erbach and Hattenheim. About half the vines are in each village, although the fountain is in Erbach, and a local poet has written "Let Erbach keep the water, Give Hattenheim the wine." Since the new laws of 1971, all the wines from this vineyard must be sold as Erbacher Marcobrunn. Particularly outstanding in dry years, the best Marcobrunners are remarkable wines – fruity, racy, and well-balanced, they have truly astonishing bouquet and breed.

Maréchal Foch A French-American hybrid developed in Alsace and known officially as Kuhlmann 1882; related to Léon Millot, and sometimes known simply as Foch, it produces good red wines and is planted in the eastern United States.

Margaret River A new district in Western Australia, about 200 miles south of Perth, first planted in the late 1960s. The wines produced in this cool climate from a range of varieties that include Chardonnay, Sauvignon Blanc, Sémillon, Rhine Riesling, Cabernet Sauvignon, and Shiraz have been impressive, and have quickly established this district as one of the most promising in Australia. Its wineries include Cape Mentelle, Cullen's Willyabrup, Leeuwin Estate, Moss Wood, and Vasse Felix.

Margaux One of the best sections of the Médoc district of Bordeaux, producing red wines remarkable for their bouquet, silky texture, elegance, and breed. The appellation now includes, in addition to the township of Margaux proper, the neighbouring communes of Cantenac, Soussans, Arsac, and Labarde; 2,800 acres of vineyards produce about 500,000 cases a year. The finest wines of Margaux come from individual vineyards, of course; Château Margaux is the most famous, and there are more than twenty other *crus classés*, or classed growths, including Châteaux Palmer, Durfort-Vivens, Giscours, Brane-Cantenac, Lascombes, and Prieuré-Lichine.

Margaux, Château A First Growth of Margaux, in the Médoc district of Bordeaux, and one of the finest and most famous vineyards in the world. As long ago as 1788, Thomas Jefferson, writing from Paris about the 1784 vintage, stated that "according to the taste of this country and of England there cannot be a bottle of better Bordeaux produced in France." The 650-acre estate, dominated by a beautiful neo-Palladian château built in the early nineteenth century, and owned for many years by the Ginestet family, was acquired by André Mentzelopoulos in early 1977; since his death in 1980, the property has been under the direction of his widow, Laura, and her daughter Corinne. Although the château produced a number of disappointing wines in the 1960s and 1970s, the 1978 and 1979 vintages were both considered among the very best of Bordeaux, and the vineyard has now fully reclaimed its place among the First Growths. There are 185 acres planted with 75 percent Cabernet Sauvignon, 20 percent Merlot, and the rest Cabernet Franc and Petit Verdot; an average of 22,000 cases a year is bottled as Château Margaux (recent vintages have varied from 15,000 to 29,000 cases), and the wine – supple, elegant, richly textured, complex, and long-lived – is exceptional. That part of the total crop that is not up to the château's standards is set aside and bottled under a second label, Pavillon Rouge du Château Margaux. There are, in addition, 30 acres planted entirely with Sauvignon Blanc and producing 4,000 to 5,000 cases a year of a distinctive white wine – entitled only to the appellation Bordeaux – marketed under the name Pavillon Blanc du Château Margaux.

Marino An Italian dry white wine produced around the village of that name in the Castelli Romani, the hillsides southeast of Rome; as with all the whites of this district, Marino is made from a combination of Malvasia and Trebbiano grapes.

Markgräflerland An extensive German wine district situated along the Rhine, in the southern part of the Baden region; it produces mild, agreeable white wines made primarily from the Gutedel, or Chasselas, grape.

Marque A French word that simply means "brand"; *marque deposée* means "registered trademark". A *vin de marque* is a wine sold under a trade name rather than a regional or vineyard name; it can be anything and come from anywhere.

Marquis d'Alesme Becker, Château A Third Classed Growth of Margaux, in the Médoc, owned by the same family as Château Malescot Saint-Exupéry, and until 1979 both wines were vinified at Malescot; production is about 4,000 cases a year.

Marquis de Terme, Château A Fourth Classed Growth of Margaux, in the Médoc; its 75 acres produce about 15,000 cases a year.

Marsala The best-known fortified wine of Italy; it has 17 to 19 percent alcohol, is amber to brown in colour, is increasingly made in a drier style, but is still more often sweet. The wine, which takes its name from the city of Marsala in western Sicily, where it is produced, was developed in the late eighteenth century by John Woodhouse, an English merchant, who realized that by fortifying the local wine he would be able to create a less expensive substitute for the sherries and ports that were then at the height of their popularity in England. Marsala achieved its greatest success in the mid-nineteenth century; today, most people know the wine, if they know it at all, as an ingredient in *zabaglione*, and the decline in sales of this wine has been such that a few years ago producers began to market Marsala flavoured with eggs, almond, and fruit flavours in an attempt to find new consumers.

Marsala is produced from Catarratto, Grillo, and Inzolia grapes; as is the case with sherry, the base wines are fermented out completely until they are dry, and then fortified with high-proof spirits. The least expensive style, labelled *Fine*, is made by adding concentrated must for sweetness and *mosto cotto*, or "cooked must" (juice that has been reduced by a third and caramelized), which provides colour and a special flavour. Marsala *Superiore*, a category that includes most of the wines that are exported, is also made with *mosto cotto*, but may be sweetened with *sifone*, grape juice whose fermentation has been stopped by the addition of spirits; *sifone*, which is identical to the French *mistelle*, provides a more subtle, and expensive, form of sweetening than does concentrated must. Marsala *Superiore*, which must be aged a minimum of two years in cask, may be marketed as dry (which is not quite dry) or sweet, in which case it must have a minimum of 10 percent sugar. The finest Marsala, called *Vergine*, has nothing added to it at all (except enough spirits to bring its alcohol content to at least 18 percent), and is aged for a minimum of five years in cask; the result is a completely dry, rather austere wine suitable as an aperitif.

Marsannay A village a few miles south of Dijon, in Burgundy, known for its appealing rosés and light red wines, all made from the Pinot Noir grape; the appellation for the red was Bourgogne Marsannay-la-Côte, and for the rosé, Bourgogne Marsannay-la-Côte Rosé, although the former was often found simply as Pinot Noir de Marsannay, and the latter as Rosé de Marsannay. New legislation in 1987 established the name Marsannay as the appellation for all wines produced in this village; it is the first village appellation established in the Côte d'Or since the 1930s, and the only one that encompasses red, white, and rosé wines.

Marsanne A white-wine grape found in the northern Rhône, where it produces the white versions of such appellations as Hermitage, Crozes-Hermitage, and Saint-Joseph; the wines are likely to be rather full-bodied, perhaps even heavy.

Martha's Vineyard A celebrated 40-acre Cabernet Sauvignon vineyard situated south of Oakville on the western side of Napa Valley; the rich, elegant, and long-lived wines from this vineyard, whose distinctive taste is most often characterized as minty, have been produced by Heitz Cellars and bottled with the vineyard name in every vintage since 1966 (with the exception of 1971). The original 12-acre plot, planted in 1960 and acquired in 1962 by Tom May and his wife, Martha (after whom the vineyard is named), originally produced about 1,000 cases a year. Another 28 acres were planted in the late 1960s, half with Cabernet Sauvignon and half with Johannisberg Riesling; the 14 acres of Riesling were converted to Cabernet Sauvignon in 1982, and the vineyard now produces 4,000 to 5,000 cases a year.

Master of Wine A title conferred by the Institute of Masters of Wine, a British organization created in 1953; in 25 years more than 500 members of the British wine trade have applied for membership, but by 1989 only 141 had passed the four-day examination that takes place every May. The exam includes blind tastings (usually of 36 wines) and written essays on viticulture, vinification, wine laws, and marketing, as well as one final essay that tests the literacy and imagination of the applicant, rather than his or her factual knowledge. Most of those who apply for membership have first passed an advanced two-year diploma course run by the London-based Wine and Spirit Education Trust, and then supplement this with trade experience before undertaking the intensive four-month course taught by Masters of Wine. Until recently, applicants had to be British citizens, at least 25 years old, and with five years' experience in the British wine trade. The institute is now open to non-British citizens of any age who have been making a living from wine for at least five years (and is thus open to journalists). Members of the Institute may put the initials M. W. after their names.

Mataro *See* Mourvèdre

Maury A small AOC district northwest of Perpignan in the Roussillon region of France; it produces a sweet, fortified *vin* *doux naturel* made primarily from the Grenache grape.

Mavrodaphne One of the best-known red grapes of Greece, producing full-bodied wines which are usually transformed into sweet, fortified, port-like wines with 15 or 16 percent alcohol.

Maximin Grünhäus A famous 81-acre vineyard, near the hamlet of Mertesdorf in Germany's Ruwer district, which produces, although only in good years, white wines of the very highest class. The vineyard, which has belonged to the von Schubert family for more than a century, and which is planted almost entirely with Riesling, has traditionally been divided into three plots whose names appear on the label as Maximin Grünhäuser Herrenberg, Abtsberg, and Bruderberg.

May Wine Originally a German speciality; a sweetened, light white wine flavoured with woodruff, an aromatic herb. It is traditionally served well chilled, in a bowl, with strawberries floating in it.

Mayacamas Mountains A range of wooded hills, of volcanic origin, running north to south and separating the Napa and Sonoma valleys, in northern California. A number of vineyards and wineries are situated along this range, and on such specific peaks as Spring Mountain and Mount Veeder; perhaps the best known is Mayacamas Vineyards, established in the early 1940s, whose 50 acres produce rich, intense, long-lived Cabernet Sauvignon and Chardonnay.

Mazis-Chambertin A *grand cru* vineyard in the Burgundy village of Gevrey-Chambertin whose 23 acres directly adjoin Clos de Bèze; about 3,000 cases a year are produced of a firm, slow-maturing red wine of unmistakable class, not far from Chambertin itself in quality.

Mazoyères-Chambertin *See* Charmes-Chambertin

McDowell Valley A viticultural area southeast of Ukiah, in Mendocino County; about 700 acres are planted, half of which belong to the area's only winery, McDowell Valley Vineyards.

McLaren Vale A small wine district in Australia, about 25 miles south of Adelaide, in the Southern Vales region. New vineyards and a number of small wineries were established there in the early

1970s, and the district has become especially known for its Shiraz and Cabernet Sauvignon. More recently, very good Chardonnays, Rhine Rieslings, and Sauvignon Blancs have come from this area. Hardy's is the major producer; others include Château Reynella, Pirramimma, Seaview, and Wirra Wirra.

Mead   Honey wine, made by fermenting honey and water; known since ancient times, it was probably the first of the many wines described as "nectar of the gods".

Médoc   A long, narrow strip of land, world-famous for its red wines, extending some 50 miles north of Bordeaux, between six and ten miles wide, bounded on the west by the dunes and pine forest along the Atlantic, and on the east by the Gironde estuary. Much of the district consists of gently rolling, gravelly hills, and the best vineyards overlook or are near the estuary. The entire Médoc encompasses about 26,000 acres of vineyards, and their average production generally varies from 4 to 7 million cases a year. This is a red-wine appellation exclusively, and the few whites produced in the Médoc are entitled only to the appellation Bordeaux or Bordeaux Supérieur.

Wines labelled simply Médoc almost invariably come from the less fine northern part of the district, with its heavier clay soils, which begins just past Saint-Seurin-de-Cadourne; formerly called the Bas-Médoc, this section produces a little less than a third of the total crop of the Médoc district, and the wines, while never great, are generally well-balanced and of good quality. The Haut-Médoc, which includes the rest of this district, produces wines of a far higher class. (*Haut* and *Bas* are simply geographical references – the Bas-Médoc is farther downstream and at a lower elevation than the Haut-Médoc – but as it happens, the latter does produce better wines.) Although many wines are labelled with the appellation Haut-Médoc, the best carry the names of one of the four celebrated villages or communes that are situated within the Haut-Médoc – Margaux, Saint-Julien, Pauillac, and Saint-Estèphe; wines from the less familiar communes of Moulis and Listrac are also likely to be so labelled. The Médoc is planted primarily with Cabernet Sauvignon, Cabernet Franc, and Merlot, plus lesser amounts of Petit Verdot and Malbec; because this district has a higher proportion of Cabernet than does any other, the wines are firmer, more tannic when young, and longer-lived than other red Bordeaux, and many connoisseurs would add that the best Médocs have more finesse and subtlety as well. (Confusingly, although there is a real distinction between the wines of the northern Médoc and those from the Haut-Médoc section, the entire district is usually referred to, in conversation and in print, as "the Médoc"). The finest wines of the Médoc come from specific châteaux, or vineyards, and the very best of them are included in the famous Classification of 1855; all of these *crus classés*, or "classed growths", are in the Haut-Médoc. In fact, well over half of the greatest Bordeaux châteaux – including Lafite-Rothschild, Latour, Margaux, Mouton-Rothschild, Cos d'Estournel, Léoville Las Cases, Ducru-Beaucaillou, Palmer, and many others – are in the Haut-Médoc. There are, in addition, more than a hundred vineyards known as *crus bourgeois*, and many of these, too, are very good and often good value as well; about two thirds of the *crus bourgeois* are in the Haut-Médoc, the rest are in the northern part of the district and entitled only to the appellation Médoc. A listing of these *crus* will be found beginning on page 539.

Melon A white-wine grape whose full name is Melon de Bourgogne, but better known as Muscadet, and extensively planted in the region around Nantes, near the mouth of the Loire. This variety may also be used in Bourgogne Grand Ordinaire, but although the grape was brought to the Loire from Burgundy in the seventeenth century, it has virtually disappeared from Burgundy itself.

Mendocino The northernmost of the California counties entitled to the appellation North Coast; most of the vineyards are situated in the Ukiah Valley, north and south of that town, along a ten-mile stretch of the Russian River, which continues south into Sonoma County. In the 1960s, most of the county's acreage consisted of Carignane, Zinfandel, and French Colombard, and these three varieties still account for a third of the crop. Chardonnay, Cabernet Sauvignon, and Sauvignon Blanc, which amounted to fewer than 40 acres in 1964, now account for 4,000 of the area's 11,000 acres of vineyards; other varieties include Pinot Noir, Gamay Beaujolais, Chenin Blanc, and Johannisberg Riesling. The Ukiah Valley (which includes the 60-acre Cole Ranch viticultural area) extends north to the Redwood Valley and south to the Sanel

Valley, near Hopland. Vineyards have also been established in the cooler, more northerly Potter Valley and in the McDowell Valley, southeast of Ukiah. The Anderson Valley, an especially cool viticultural area to the west of Ukiah, is known for Gewürztraminer and Johannisberg Riesling, and for *méthode champenoise* sparkling wines made from Chardonnay and Pinot Noir. There are about thirty wineries in Mendocino, the best known of which are Parducci and Fetzer.

Mendoza The largest wine-producing province in Argentina, along the foothills of the Andes, about 600 miles west of Buenos Aires.

Menetou-Salon A village southwest of Sancerre, in France's Loire Valley, that produces interesting and attractive dry white wines from Sauvignon Blanc, and red and rosé wines from Pinot Noir; total production is about 70,000 cases a year, more than half of it white.

Mercaptans Compounds formed by the reduction of hydrogen sulphide; their presence, a sign of poor winemaking, is revealed by a rotten, stagnant odour.

Mercurey A wine-producing commune in Burgundy, about 15 miles south of Beaune, whose red wines are the best, and best known, of the Côte Chalonnaise (which is, in fact, sometimes called the Région de Mercurey); made entirely from Pinot Noir, they are comparable to a sound, pleasant red Burgundy of the Côte de Beaune. Total production of Mercurey amounts to over 200,000 cases a year, 95 percent of it red; the limited amount of white is made from Chardonnay.

Meritage A name selected by an association of American vintners to describe an expanding category of wines blended from the traditional Bordeaux grape varieties; the reds may be made from Cabernet Sauvignon, Cabernet Franc, Merlot, Malbec, and Petit Verdot, the whites from Sauvignon Blanc and Sémillon. Because a varietal wine, such as Cabernet Sauvignon or Sauvignon Blanc, must contain at least 75 percent of the variety named on the label, producers who prefer to blend in more than 25 percent of complementary varieties (as is traditionally done in Bordeaux) must label such wines with a proprietary name rather than a varietal name. The name Meritage (which rhymes with heritage) was chosen to be used by wineries, retailers, and restaurateurs to describe this group of deluxe, nonvarietal red and white wines; so far, it has not been widely accepted within the American wine trade.

Merlot   A distinguished red-wine grape, as important as Cabernet Sauvignon and Cabernet Franc in the Bordeaux region, where it contributes softness, fruit, suppleness, and charm to many famous wines that would otherwise be less attractive. Because it is so widely planted in that part of Bordeaux that includes Saint-Emilion, Pomerol, Bourg, and Blaye, Merlot accounts for half the total acreage of red grapes in Bordeaux, almost twice that of Cabernet Sauvignon. Merlot ripens earlier than Cabernet, produces grapes with more sugar, and yields wines that are less tannic and astringent, and sooner ready to drink – if shorter-lived – than Cabernets. The variety accounts for 10 to 30 percent of the acreage in most of the best vineyards of the Médoc (where Cabernet Sauvignon is the dominant grape), but is the principal variety in Saint-Emilion and Pomerol, where it makes up 50 to 80 percent of most top properties (with Cabernet Franc accounting for most of the rest). In California, acreage of Merlot has increased dramatically from fewer than 100 in the mid-1960s to 5,500, most of that in Napa and Sonoma. The grape was originally planted to provide wines that would lighten the intensity of Cabernet Sauvignon, but many wineries now bottle Merlot as a varietal wine, often blending in some Cabernet to add structure. In northern Italy, Merlot is by far the most important variety in the Friuli region (where it produces 10 to 15 million cases a year), and is widely planted in the Piave district of Veneto and in Trentino. Merlot is also extensively planted in eastern Europe, in Bulgaria and Romania.

Mesland   A village between Blois and Amboise, in the Touraine region of France's Loire Valley, producing red, rosé, and a little white wine, all marketed with the appellation Touraine-Mesland.

Mesnil-sur-Oger, Le   One of the top wine villages in the Côtes de Blancs district of the Champagne region; its vineyards, rated 100 percent, are planted entirely with Chardonnay.

Metallic   A term used to describe an acrid, unpleasant taste, not unlike greenness, that wines sometimes acquire through contact with metal.

Méthode Champenoise The French term for making sparkling wines by the classic method, first perfected in the Champagne region, of bottling a *cuvée*, or blend, of still wines with a measured amount of sugar and yeast, thereby inducing a second fermentation in the bottle. One result of this fermentation is carbon-dioxide gas, which is trapped in the bottle and dissolved in the wine, creating the sparkle; another byproduct is sediment, which must eventually be disgorged. *Méthode champenoise* wines are marketed in the bottle in which the second fermentation occurred; sparkling wines made by the transfer method may not be labelled *méthode champenoise*. Bottle-fermented sparkling wines are produced in several regions of France apart from Champagne (and those entitled to *Appellation Contrôlée* status must be aged in bottle a minimum of nine months), as well as in Spain and the United States, and to a lesser extent, in Italy and Germany. Many of these wines are labelled, quite properly, *Méthode Champenoise*, but this phrase will no longer be permitted within the Common Market after 1992; Spanish wines produced by this method may be labelled *Cava*, and the Italian equivalent is *Metodo Classico*.

Méthode Rurale *See* Rural Method

Methuselah An oversize champagne bottle holding the equivalent of eight ordinary bottles, or about 203 ounces; also spelled methusalem.

Métis Cross-pollination in the same species, as *vinifera* x *vinifera*, also known as a cross. *See* Cross, Hybrid.

Metodo Classico An Italian term used for sparkling wines made by the classic *méthode champenoise*; an increasing amount of fine, dry sparkling wines are made in this way from Chardonnay, Pinot Bianco, Pinot Grigio, and Pinot Nero grapes by producers in Trentino-Alto Adige, Oltrepò Pavese, and Franciacorta, as well as by firms in Tuscany and Piedmont using grapes from those regions.

Metric *See* Bottle, Hectare, Hectolitre

Meunier *See* Pinot Meunier

Meursault   An ancient wine-producing village of Burgundy's Côte de
Beaune; its average annual production of 150,000 cases of
white wine (plus a few thousand cases of red) is second in
volume only to Gevrey-Chambertin among the villages of
the Côte d'Or. There are no *grand cru* vineyards in Meursault, but the *premiers crus* Les Perrières, Les Genevrières,
and Les Charmes are justly acclaimed, and their names
usually appear on labels hyphenated with that of Meursault,
as Meursault-Perrières, Meursault-Genevrières, and Meur-
sault-Charmes. Les Poruzot and Les Gouttes d'Or are also
well-known *premier cru* vineyards. The northernmost
vineyard of Meursault is Les Santenots, which adjoins Volnay; red wines from that part of the Santenots vineyard
planted with Pinot Noir are sold as Volnay-Santenots, the
whites as Meursault-Santenots. The hamlet of Blagny also
adjoins Meursault; its reds are sold as Blagny, its whites as
Meursault-Blagny. Green-gold in colour, full-bodied but
racy and well-balanced, dry but not austerely so, the wines
of Meursault are remarkable white Burgundies and fully
merit their fame. Although wines labelled simply Meursault
often have real distinction, those from the *premier cru*
vineyards are usually considerably better and are among the
very finest of France's dry white wines.

Mexico   As might be expected, America's southern neighbour has a
climate poorly suited to the growing of wine grapes, since a
good part of the country is actually in the Tropic Zone, and
even its northernmost corner, near San Diego, is as far south
as Egypt. Most of the vineyards produce table grapes, but
wine varieties are nevertheless grown in many provinces of
Mexico, particularly in Baja California and in some of the
higher central states, where the prevailing weather is somewhat cooler as a result of the altitude. Traditional European
vinifera varieties have been introduced in recent years, as
well as modern wine-making techniques, but even so 90 percent of Mexico's wines are distilled into brandy; annual per
capita consumption is about a third of a bottle of wine, compared to nearly 50 bottles of beer.

Meyney, Château   A well-known *cru bourgeois exceptionnel* of Saint-
Estèphe, in the Médoc, part of the Cordier domain; its 125
acres produce about 25,000 cases a year of firm, dependable
wine.

Microclimate   A term that refers to the combination of soil – gravel, chalk, clay – and such factors as altitude, angle of slope, drainage, and orientation towards the sun; their influences on quality have been recognized, if not fully understood, for more than 2,000 years. Assuming that a given district is planted with the most suitable grape varieties, a particular plot or vineyard with just the right microclimate will produce extraordinary wines, while adjacent vineyards that are higher or lower, or around the curve of a hill, or with a different soil composition (which affects drainage and water retention) cannot produce wines of the same quality.

Midi A French word that means both "12 noon" and "the South" – an *accent du Midi* is a French southern accent. Midi is a rather more specific term when applied to wine: the Rhône Valley is excluded, as are Provence and the Côte d'Azur. A *vin du Midi* is commonly understood to mean an ordinary table wine produced along the Mediterranean coast of France, in the *départements* of Gard, Hérault, Aude, and Pyrénées-Orientales, between Nîmes, Carcassonne, and the Spanish border. This vast region is now referred to as Languedoc-Roussillon.

Mildew A grave malady of the vine caused by fungus; it appears in two related types, downy mildew and powdery mildew, the latter also known as oidium. Of American origin, mildew was introduced into Europe accidentally about the middle of the nineteenth century, and produced damage almost as serious as did phylloxera, which arrived a few years later. Within limits, it can now be controlled through the use of powdered sulphur or copper sulphate sprays.

Millésime French for "vintage"; a wine that is *millésimé* is one marked with its vintage.

Minervois One of the best of the not particularly distinguished red wines of the Languedoc-Roussillon region of France, also known as the Midi. Full-bodied and often agreeable, the wine is made from Carignan, Grenache, and Cinsault in a district just northeast of Carcassonne that extends into two *départements*, Hérault and Aude. Annual production amounts to 2 to 2.5 million cases of red, plus very limited amounts of white and rosé; Minervois was elevated from VDQS to *Appellation Contrôlée* in 1985.

Mireval A village on the Mediterranean coast of France known for its sweet white wine made from the Muscat grape and marketed as Muscat de Mireval; the wine is officially classed as a *vin doux naturel.*

Mis en bouteille French for "bottled". *See* Château Bottled and Estate Bottled.

Mission The first of the European *vinifera* vines to reach California, this red-wine grape of only fair quality at best was brought in during the last half of the eighteenth century by Franciscan monks and planted around their missions – whence, presumably, its name; although unquestionably of European origin, it has never been fully identified and is thought to be the same grape as the Criolla of Argentina and the Pais of Chile. It gives a poor table wine and is more likely to be used for white wine than red. Probably the most widely planted grape in California until the 1870s, acreage decreased to 6,000 in the mid-1970s and has since declined to fewer than 2,000 acres, all in the Central Valley and southern California.

La Mission Haut-Brion, Château A *grand cru classé* of the Graves district, situated just across the road from Château Haut-Brion, a few miles outside the city of Bordeaux. The vineyard produces an exceptional red wine that combines power and finesse, elegance and longevity, and which is second only to that of its illustrious neighbour; indeed, for many years now it has commanded a price higher than any of the *crus classés* of the Médoc, with the exception of the first growths. The vineyard is actually made up of two parts: the original property, which consists of 47 acres, and the adjoining 25-acre vineyard, La Tour Haut-Brion, acquired in the 1920s. About 15 acres of La Tour Haut-Brion were then uprooted and planted with Sémillon and Sauvignon Blanc to produce a dry white wine, which is marketed as Château Laville Haut-Brion. In recent years, the wines from the rest of the property, planted with approximately two thirds Cabernet and one third Merlot, were vinified together; the best lots were marketed as La Mission Haut-Brion, and La Tour Haut-Brion became a second label for the combined vineyards. In 1983, the entire property was purchased by the owners of Château Haut-Brion, who decided to re-establish the original boundaries of La Mission Haut-Brion (whose annual production is now about 10,000 cases) and La Tour

Haut-Brion (about 2,000 cases) and to vinify and bottle the wines separately, while continuing to produce the white wines of Laville Haut-Brion (1,000 to 2,000 cases).

Mistelle Grape juice to which sufficient alcohol is added to prevent fermentation; it is always sweet and is used in wine-based aperitifs, notably vermouth.

Mittelheim A small village situated between Oestrich and Winkel in Germany's Rheingau region, most of whose wines are marketed with the Grosslagen Winkeler Honigberg and Johannisberger Erntebringer.

Mittelmosel The central and finest section of Germany's Moselle River, which winds it way downstream, or northeast, from just past Trier to Zell and includes such classic wine villages as Trittenheim, Piesport, Brauneberg, Bernkastel, Graach, Wehlen, Zeltingen, and Urzig. This district, known for its exceptional Rieslings, corresponds pretty closely to the Bereich Bernkastel.

Mittelrhein The third smallest of the eleven Anbaugebiete, or specified wine regions, of Germany, it consists of a narrow ribbon of vineyards that stretches along the Rhine from just north of Bingen and the Rheingau past Koblenz and almost to Bonn. About 1,800 acres of vineyards, 75 percent of them planted with Riesling, produce an average of 600,000 cases a year, virtually all of it white. This ancient and stunningly picturesque part of Germany produces less than 1 percent of that country's total output, and very little is exported.

Moelleux A French tasting term applied to wines, usually white, that are not necessarily sweet, but certainly not bone dry; the term, derived from the French word for "marrow", suggests a rich, lush quality, and mellow is a poor, imprecise English equivalent.

Monastrell Widely planted in Spain, especially in the Alicante region as well as in Rioja and Penedès, this grape is second in acreage only to Garnacha, or Grenache, among that country's red varieties; it produces a light, agreeable if undistinguished wine.

Monbazillac An appellation for semisweet white wines produced in an extensive district near the town of Bergerac, in the Dordogne region, just east of Bordeaux; the wines are made primarily from Sémillon and Sauvignon Blanc, and production varies from 400,000 to 600,000 cases a year.

Monbousquet, Château A well-known estate in Saint-Emilion whose history goes back to the sixteenth century, acquired in the 1940s by the Querre family, who completely replanted the vineyards; its 75 acres produce about 15,000 cases a year of an appealing, dependable, and deservedly popular *grand cru* wine.

Robert Mondavi Winery A famous Napa Valley winery created in 1966 by the dynamic Robert Mondavi, known for his experimental and innovative attitude; he was among the first to ferment white wines at low temperatures and to age wines in small French oak barrels. The winery is particularly known for its Cabernet Sauvignon, Chardonnay, and Sauvignon Blanc (which is labelled Fumé Blanc, a name created by Mondavi in the late 1960s); these wines are also marketed in Reserve bottlings, as is Pinot Noir. The winery also produces Chenin Blanc, Johannisberg Riesling, and a sweet Muscat wine labelled Moscato d'Oro. Moderately priced varietal wines – including Cabernet Sauvignon, Sauvignon Blanc, White Zinfandel, and Gamay Rosé – are produced in a separate winery near Lodi, in the Central Valley. Robert Mondavi entered into a joint venture with the late Baron Philippe de Rothschild of Château Mouton-Rothschild to produce a Napa Valley Cabernet-based wine called Opus One, first made in 1979.

Mondeuse A superior if not outstanding French red-wine grape, grown in the Savoie and the upper Rhône Valley, east of Lyons, where it gives a rather fruity wine of definite character; this variety is known as Refosco in Italy.

Monopole A term sometimes used on French wine labels in connection with a brand name to indicate sole ownership, or monopoly, of the name; it is in no sense related to the wine's origin or its quality.

Montagne-Saint-Emilion An important appellation for red wines produced in the commune of Montagne, northeast of the village of Saint-Emilion itself; the name may also be used for wines once labelled Parsac-Saint-Emilion and Saint-Georges-Saint-Emilion (although the latter appellation is still used as well), and total production may exceed 700,000 cases a year. These soft, supple red wines are of good quality, and if they lack the distinction and velvety softness of the best Saint-Emilions, they are correspondingly less expensive.

Montagny A village in the Côte Chalonnaise, in Burgundy, that produces attractive white wines; made from the Chardonnay grape, they are dry, fresh, and attractive white Burgundies and deserve to be better known.

Montalcino A village 30 miles southeast of Siena, in Tuscany, best known for its long-lived red DOCG wine Brunello di Montalcino; two DOC wines – Rosso di Montalcino and Moscadello di Montalcino – are also produced in the Montalcino zone, which lies within the large Chianti Colli Senesi district.

Montefiascone *See* Est! Est!! Est!!! di Montefiascone

Montepulciano *See* Vino Nobile di Montepulciano

Montepulciano d'Abruzzo A red DOC wine produced primarily from the Montepulciano grape in the Abruzzi region (Abruzzo in Italian) on hillside vineyards not far from the Adriatic Sea; a rosé, labelled Cerasuolo, is also made. This wine should not be confused with Vino Nobile di Montepulciano, a red wine produced from the Sangiovese grape around the village of Montepulciano, in Tuscany.

Monterey A county south of San Francisco famous for the lettuce, artichokes, strawberries, and other produce grown in the Salinas Valley, celebrated in the novels of John Steinbeck and now also known for its wines. As recently as 1959 there were fewer than 30 acres of grapes in Monterey; in the early 1960s the Wente, Mirassou, and Paul Masson wineries planted extensively in this region, and, when others followed, the vineyards eventually increased to a peak of 35,000 acres in the early 1980s before settling down to the current level of about 28,000 acres. Most of the vineyards in Monterey are situated in the Salinas Valley, between the Santa Lucia Mountains on the west and the Gavilan Mountains on the east. Water for irrigation is supplied by wells drilled into the

Salinas River, which runs underground for most of the year, and the vineyards are cooled by ocean breezes, which create a particularly long, slow growing season. More than two thirds of the vineyards planted in the 1970s consisted of red varieties, some of which, as it turned out, did not ripen fully in this cool climate, especially in the upper part of the valley nearest the ocean. Many vineyards were replanted, others uprooted, and some, planted with less desirable grapes such as French Colombard, Grey Riesling, and Sylvaner, were abandoned; the acreage of such red-wine grapes as Gamay, Gamay Beaujolais, Merlot, Petite Sirah, and Zinfandel was considerably reduced, and today white wines account for nearly three quarters of the Monterey crop. Chardonnay and Chenin Blanc are the principal varieties, followed by Johannisberg Riesling and Cabernet Sauvignon; there are extensive plantings of Sauvignon Blanc, Pinot Noir, Gewürztraminer, Pinot Blanc, and Zinfandel. The Arroyo Seco viticultural area, along a protected canyon west of Greenfield, is known for Johannisberg Riesling, Chardonnay, Sauvignon Blanc, and Cabernet Sauvignon; the Carmel Valley is a small viticultural area west of the Salinas Valley and the Santa Lucia Mountains. Because much of the acreage in Monterey was planted by wineries in other regions, or by farming companies that sell their grapes, there are relatively few wineries in the county; Jekel Vineyards and the Monterey Vineyard are the best known. Chalone is situated on a benchland of the Gavilan Mountains, east of the Salinas Valley, at an elevation of 1,800 feet.

Monthélie   A tiny village situated between Volnay and Meursault, on Burgundy's Côte de Beaune. Its red wines, usually labelled Monthélie or Monthélie-Côte de Beaune, are among the best of the lesser-known Burgundies, similar in style to Volnay, and often good value. About 35,000 cases of red wine are produced in an average year, plus a few hundred cases of white.

Montilla   An excellent, unusual, and all too little-known Spanish wine produced in a district of arid, chalky hills, around the villages of Montilla and Moriles, between Córdoba and Málaga. The wine, whose official *Denominación de Origen* is Montilla-Moriles, is similar to sherry (in fact, *amontillado* means "in the style of Montilla"), and in the past much of its production was sent to Jerez, only 100 miles away, where it was blended with sherry and marketed as such. The region was finally granted its own appellation in 1945, and since 1960 its wines may no longer be blended with those of Jerez. The principal differences between Montilla and sherry are that the former is made almost entirely from the Pedro Ximénez grape, rather than the Palomino of Jerez, and that Montilla, which usually attains a natural alcohol content of 14 to 16 percent, is not always fortified. The region's 45,000 acres produce 6 to 10 million cases of wine that is still fermented in *tinajas*, huge earthenware jars shaped like Roman amphoras that hold about 50 or 60 hectolitres (about 1,300 to 1,600 gallons). The best wines come from the chalky soil known as *albero*, similar to the *albariza* soil of Jerez. As is the practice for sherry, the wines of Montilla are classified as fino, amontillado, and oloroso (although those terms may not be used on labels in some export markets) and aged by the solera system of fractional blending. The best and best-known wines of Montilla are the dry, crisp finos, which are lighter in alcohol than an equivalent sherry and can be more delicate and perhaps easier to drink, since they have not been fortified; they are served chilled both as an aperitif and as a table wine, especially with *mariscos*, or shellfish. The amontillado, oloroso, and cream versions are likely to be fortified to 18 percent or so of alcohol.

Montlouis A village almost directly across the Loire River from Vouvray, in the Touraine region of France; its dry and semidry white wines, made, like Vouvray, from the Chenin Blanc grape, were legally sold as Vouvray until 1938 and are of a similar quality today, although perhaps lighter and less concentrated. Production averages close to 200,000 cases a year, and a quarter to a half of the crop is transformed into *mousseux*, or sparkling wine.

Montrachet An extraordinary 20-acre *grand cru* vineyard in the Côte de Beaune district of Burgundy's Côte d'Or, producing the most celebrated and expensive dry white wine of France. Half the vineyard lies within the communal limits of Puligny-Montrachet, half in Chassagne-Montrachet; both villages have appended its name to their own, and the name has also been incorporated into those of several adjoining *grand cru* vineyards – Bâtard-Montrachet, Chevalier-Montrachet, Bienvenues-Bâtard-Montrachet, and Criots-Bâtard-Montrachet. Its wine, like all fine white Burgundies, is made entirely from the Chardonnay grape. The vineyard, which is divided among seventeen owners, has an average annual production of about 3,000 cases, although production has varied, in recent vintages, from 2,000 to 5,700 cases. The name is said to come from the Latin *Mons rachicensis*, which became Mont-Rachat, or "Bald Hill", and the barren hilltop behind the stony vineyards is covered with thin scrub and almost "bald", even today. The vineyard itself is probably the most valuable agricultural land in France, despite its small yield per acre, and its wine, rivalled in Burgundy only by that of its immediate neighbours, is wholly remarkable. Pale gold in colour, with a hint of green, it has tremendous bouquet, flavour, and class; dry, but with an underlying trace of luscious softness, especially in good years, it is, as someone has said, "not so much a wine as an experience". For map, *see* Puligny-Montrachet.

Montravel A vineyard district situated east of Bordeaux, on the north bank of the Dordogne River, near the town of Bergerac; about 300,000 cases a year are produced of dry white wines marketed as Montravel and semisweet wines entitled to the appellations Haut-Montravel or Côtes de Montravel, depending on the exact zone from which each comes.

Montrose, Château A Second Classed Growth of Saint-Estèphe, in the Médoc, owned by the Charmolüe family since 1896; its 168 acres produce about 25,000 cases a year, although production in recent years has varied from 14,000 to 32,000 cases, some of which is marketed under the second label La Dame de Montrose. The deep-coloured, intense, slow-maturing wine is one of the firmest of the Médoc and one of the finest.

Morey-Saint-Denis A Burgundian village in the Côte de Nuits district of the Côte d'Or whose 675 acres of vineyards produce a number of red wines of the very highest class, firm, sturdy, and long-lived. Despite the quality of its wines, the village name is not as well known as others along the Côte d'Or, partly because Morey is situated between the better-known villages of Gevrey-Chambertin and Chambolle-Musigny, and also because its top wines are marketed with the names of the *grand cru* vineyards from which they come – Clos Saint-Denis (whose name was appended to that of the village in 1927), Clos de la Roche, Clos de Tart, Clos des Lambrays, and a small part of Bonnes Mares. Wines labelled Morey-

Saint-Denis – on average, fewer than 30,000 cases a year – may be of a less exalted status than the *grands crus*, but are excellent nevertheless and often surpass those of Gevrey-Chambertin. About 300 cases of white wine are also produced, from the Mont-Luisants vineyard.

Morgon One of the best and yet least typical wines of France's Beaujolais region, produced in a district whose principal village is Villié-Morgon. It is less fruity than many other Beaujolais *crus*, longer-lived than most, and often displays a distinctive cherrylike aroma and flavour attributed to the special soil of this district, known as *roche pourrie*, that is, friable, or decomposed rock. Local experts use the phrase "*il morgonne*" to describe typical examples of this wine, or others that have taken on the characteristics of a Morgon.

Morio-Muscat A new German variety created by Peter Morio, which, despite its name, does not contain Muscat; it is a cross of Sylvaner and Weissburgunder, or Pinot Blanc, and produces white wines with a pronounced bouquet that makes them useful for blending with neutral wines.

Morocco A former French protectorate in North Africa whose vineyards were established by French settlers in the 1920s and 1930s; wine production has diminished considerably since the country achieved independence in 1956, but efforts have been made to improve quality. Because the Moslem population is prohibited from drinking alcoholic beverages, most of the wines are consumed by tourists or exported in bulk. The current annual production of about 4 million cases consists primarily of red wines and rosés made from Cinsault, Carignan, Grenache, and Alicante-Bouschet; the country's best red wines come from the region around Meknès and Fez.

Moscadello di Montalcino A sweet, aromatic, and lightly sparkling Muscat-based white wine from the Montalcino district of Tuscany. Although praised in the late seventeenth century as the best wine of the area, it virtually disappeared in this century until new plantings were established in the late 1970s; the wine was granted DOC status in 1985.

Moscatel de Setúbal A famous Portuguese wine made in limited quantities from Muscat of Alexandria around the town of Setúbal, southeast of Lisbon; this intense, fortified, amber-coloured wine is surprisingly long-lived, and twenty- or thirty-year-old examples are not uncommon.

Moscato The Italian name for Muscat, a variety of grape, or family of grapes (for there are literally dozens of subvarieties), cultivated in many parts of Italy. They produce wines that may be still or sparkling, lightly sweet or intensely sweet, low in alcohol or fortified to 20 percent; all are aromatic, with a pronounced musky, grapey bouquet and flavour. Perhaps the best known is Moscato di Canelli, which takes its name from a village near Asti, in the Piedmont region, where it produces the pale, sweet, low-alcohol wines used to make Italy's most famous sparkling wine, Asti Spumante. A number of very sweet DOC wines are produced in Apulia (Moscato di Trani), Sardinia (Moscato di Cagliari, Moscato di Sorso-Sennori), and Sicily (Moscato di Noto, Moscato di Siracusa). Perhaps the most famous of the dessert Muscats is Moscato di Pantelleria, made from a variety of the Muscat family called Zibibbo on the island of Pantelleria, between Sicily and Tunisia. As is the case with many sweet wines, it may be produced in a naturally sweet version, in a *passito* version from shrivelled grapes, and as a fortified *liquoroso*. The Moscato Giallo, or yellow Muscat, produces attractive sweet wines in the Trentino-Alto Adige region, and production of the sweet, lightly sparkling Moscadello di Montalcino has been revived in southern Tuscany.

Moscato d'Asti A sweet, white, lightly sparkling DOC wine made from Moscato di Canelli grapes in the Piedmont region of Italy; it contains only 5 or 6 percent alcohol and about 10 percent residual sugar; most of the crop is transformed into the fully sparkling Asti Spumante.

Mosel The German spelling of Moselle.

Moselle The Moselle River rises in France, skirts Luxembourg, and then winds for nearly a hundred miles down one of the most beautiful valleys of western Germany, from Trier to Koblenz, where it joins the Rhine. There are a few vineyards along its banks in France, and even more in Luxembourg, but those of real consequence and international fame are all in Germany (where the river is spelled Mosel). The official name for the Anbaugebiet, or specified wine region, that includes the Moselle is Mosel-Saar-Ruwer, the latter being two of the Moselle's small tributaries. The region's 31,000 acres of vineyards produce an average of 15 million cases of wine, all of it white, which amounts to about 15 percent of the total German crop; growing conditions are so uncertain, however, that in recent years the Mosel-Saar-Ruwer harvest has varied from 6 to 25 million cases. Riesling, which accounted for 80 percent of the acreage in the mid-1960s, now accounts for 55 percent, but it is this grape that is responsible for the region's finest wines; about a quarter of the vineyards are planted with Müller-Thurgau, and Elbling and Kerner represent another 15 percent. Approximately at the latitude of Winnipeg, these are among the northernmost commercial vineyards in the world; the best are planted on unimaginably steep hillsides, in slate soil. Thin, tart, even acid in poor vintage years, Moselle Rieslings at their best are perhaps the most delicate, fragrant, and distinguished of all white wines. They rarely exceed 11 percent alcohol and often have substantially less; pale, flowery, spicy, with great breed, they are like no other wines on earth, combining ripeness and varying degrees of sweetness with a balancing acidity that gives them a unique, piquant style. Even in those favourable vintages that produce a wide range of Spätlese and Auslese wines, those from the Moselle and its tributaries are always lighter and more delicate than those from the Rhine.

The Mosel-Saar-Ruwer region is divided into four districts: Bereich Zell/Mosel is the northernmost part, from Koblenz to Zell; Bereich Bernkastel, which accounts for about 60 percent of the crop, includes what is sometimes called the Mittelmosel, and encompasses more than 60 villages along the most favoured part of the Moselle, from just beyond Zell upstream to an area past Trittenheim; Bereich Saar-Ruwer includes the vineyards along those two rivers, and Bereich Obermosel, or Upper Moselle, is the southernmost district. The best-known Grosslagen of the Mosel-Saar-Ruwer are Zeller Schwarze Katz, Piesporter Michelsberg, Bernkasteler Badstube, Bernkasteler Kurfürstlay, Kröver Nacktarsch, and Wiltinger Scharzberg. The very best wines of the region are almost always estate bottlings from individual vineyards situated in such renowned villages as Trittenheim, Piesport, Brauneberg, Bernkastel, Graach, Wehlen, Zeltingen, Urzig, and Erden along the Moselle; Serrig, Ockfen, Ayl, and Wiltingen along the Saar; and, from the Ruwer, Avelsbach, Kasel, and Eitelsbach. A complete list of the region's villages and their best vineyards will be found on page 555.

Moselle, Vins de Curiously enough, this is a VDQS appellation for a few thousand cases of light red and white wines produced along the Moselle, near Metz, in northeast France.

Mosel-Saar-Ruwer The official name of one of the eleven Anbaugebiete, or specified wine regions, of Germany; this is the designation that appears on the labels of wines produced along the Moselle and its two tributaries, the Saar and the Ruwer. The region is divided into four Bereiche (Zell/Mosel, Bernkastel, Saar-Ruwer, and Obermosel), 19 Grosslagen, and a record number of more than 500 Einzellagen. *See* Moselle, Ruwer, Saar.

Moseltaler A new regional appellation, introduced in 1986, for Qualitätswein from the Mosel-Saar-Ruwer region; the wine, the Moselle equivalent of the Rhine's Liebfraumilch, may be made from Riesling, Müller-Thurgau, Elbling, or Kerner grapes, and must contain between 1.5 and 3 percent sugar balanced by a minimum acidity of 0.7 percent.

Mou A French tasting term meaning soft, flat, and lacking in character; it may be applied to a white wine with insufficient acidity, or to a red without enough tannin.

Mouldy Having the unpleasant odour and flavour that mould imparts to grapes and the wines made from them. This is far more likely to be present in red wines than in white, since mould attacks the skins first and, in the making of red wine, the skins are fermented with the juice. It is usually brought on by warm, humid weather during the ripening season and is practically identical with rot.

Moulin des Carruades *See* Lafite-Rothschild, Château.

Moulin-à-Vent Generally ranked as the finest wine of France's Beaujolais region and almost always the most expensive, Moulin-à-Vent is also by a considerable margin the longest-lived. The vineyards, partly in the commune of Romanèche-Thorins and partly in Chénas, cover the slopes of a round hill crowned with an ancient *moulin-à-vent*, or "windmill", from which the wine derives its name. A Moulin-à-Vent of a good year can almost be classified as a great wine; deep-coloured, sturdy, rather high in alcohol, it is mouth-filling and, at the same time, has undeniable breed and class.

Moulis A village in the Médoc district of Bordeaux, situated a few miles northwest of Margaux, whose 1,200 acres of vineyards produce about 200,000 cases of red wine a year, much of it good, dependable, and moderately priced. Most of the wines come from *crus bourgeois*, including Châteaux Chasse-Spleen, Poujeaux-Thiel, and Dutruch-Grand-Poujeaux.

Mount Barker A promising new cool-climate district in Western Australia, about 240 miles southeast of Perth, usually linked with the adjoining Frankland River district. The first wines were produced in the early 1970s from Chardonnay, Sémillon, Rhine Riesling, Cabernet Sauvignon, and other top varieties; Plantagenet is the best-known winery.

Mourvèdre A French red-wine grape grown in southern France, where it is often used to add colour and sturdiness to such wines as Côtes-du-Rhône, Côtes de Provence, and even Châteauneuf-du-Pape; it is the principal variety used for the red wines of Bandol. This grape is known as Mataro in California, where plantings have dwindled to fewer than 500 acres, and in Australia, too, the acreage of Mataro is being reduced.

Mousse The French term for "foam", the "head" that forms on a glass of champagne or, for that matter, of beer.

Mousseux A word applied to all French sparkling wines, no matter how produced, with the exception of those from the Champagne region, which are considered in a class apart. There are about twenty *vins mousseux* that are entitled to *Appellation Contrôlée* status, among them Clairette de Die, Gaillac, Blanquette de Limoux, Saint-Péray, Seyssel, Saumur, Touraine, Vouvray, Montlouis, and the more recent appellations Crémant de Bourgogne, Crémant de Loire, and Crémant d'Alsace. Almost all of the AOC *mousseux* are made by the *méthode champenoise*, one or two by the *méthode rurale*, or "rural method"; all must be aged in bottle at least nine months.

Mousy A wine-taster's term for a disagreeable smell and taste produced by bacterial infection.

Moût   French for "must" – unfermented or fermenting grape juice.

Mouton Baronne Philippe, Château   A Fifth Classed Growth of Pauillac, in the Médoc, acquired in 1933 by Baron Philippe de Rothschild of Château Mouton-Rothschild, who changed its name from Mouton d'Armailhacq to Mouton Baron Philippe in 1956; beginning with the 1975 vintage, the label was changed to Mouton Baronne Philippe, in honour of the baron's late wife, who will also be remembered by the wine museum that she created at Mouton-Rothschild. The 130-acre vineyard produces about 23,000 cases a year.

Mouton-Rothschild, Château   A First Growth of Pauillac, in the Médoc district of Bordeaux, and one of the most famous vineyards in the world. It was purchased in 1853 by Baron Nathaniel de Rothschild and ranked as the first of the second growths in the famous 1855 classification, a judgement that was never fully accepted by the new owners. In 1922, Baron Philippe de Rothschild, who died in 1988 at the age of 85, took over direction of the château and began a long struggle to revise the classification; for many years the wines of Mouton brought prices as high or higher than the First Growths, and finally, in 1973, the vineyard was officially accorded First Growth status by the French minister of agriculture. The 175 acres of vines are planted 85 percent with Cabernet Sauvignon, the rest with Cabernet Franc and Merlot, and they produce 20,000 to 30,000 cases a year of a rich, ripe, generously flavoured wine that is, at its best, among the most powerful and impressive of Bordeaux. A superb small museum of art objects related to wine, collected over the years by Baron Philippe and his wife, Pauline, was installed on the estate in 1962. For almost every vintage since 1946, Baron Philippe invited a different artist to contribute a work to be reproduced along the top of the Mouton label; those who have agreed, in exchange for wine, include Jean Cocteau, Marie Laurencin, Salvador Dali, Henry Moore, Georges Braque, Marc Chagall, Robert Motherwell, and Andy Warhol. Exceptions to this charming custom are the label for the 1953 vintage, which commemorated the centenary of Rothschild ownership; the 1973 label, which incorporates a 1959 gouache by Picasso from the museum's collection, reproduced in honour of Mouton's elevation to a First Growth and in homage to the artist, who died in 1973; and the 1977 label, which commemorates the visit of the Queen Mother to the château. Baron Philippe also acquired Châteaux Mouton d'Armailhacq (now Mouton Baronne Philippe) and Clerc Milon and created a proprietary brand of red and white Bordeaux labelled Mouton-Cadet.

Moutonne, La Once a proprietary name used to market Chablis from various vineyards, La Moutonne now refers specifically to a 5.8-acre vineyard that straddles the two *grands crus* Vaudésir and Les Preuses; its wines may be labelled Chablis Grand Cru, but it is not itself a *grand cru* appellation.

Mudgee A small district in the Australian state of New South Wales, west of the better-known Hunter Valley and about 160 miles north-west of Sydney; wine has been made here since 1858, and Chardonnay was first planted as long ago as the 1930s. The cool climate of these vineyards, situated at an elevation of about 1,500 feet, has been successful for Chardonnay and for intensely flavoured Cabernet Sauvignon and Merlot; the wineries include Huntington Estate and Montrose.

Muid An old and far from specific French term for a small cask or large barrel whose capacity varied from one district to another, from 274 to 685 litres.

Mulled Wine Red wine to which sugar, lemon peel, and such spices as nutmeg, cloves, and cinnamon are added; the mixture is heated and served hot.

Müller-Thurgau The most widely grown grape in Germany, whose 59,000 acres account for a quarter of total plantings; it is a cross of Riesling and Sylvaner, although in recent years some scientists have suggested it may be a cross of Riesling and Riesling. It was created at the Geisenheim institute in 1882 by Dr. Hermann Müller-Thurgau (who added Thurgau, the Swiss canton where he was born, to his name), was planted experimentally in Germany in the 1920s, and supplanted Sylvaner as the most popular variety in the 1970s. Most of the acreage is in Baden, Rheinhessen, and Rheinpfalz, and the pleasant, neutral white wines, which can be low in acid and a bit dull, are widely used in inexpensive blends and in Liebfraumilch. The grape is known as Riesling-Sylvaner in Switzerland and also in New Zealand, where it is the most widely planted variety; it is known as Rizlingszilvani in Hungary and as Rivaner in Luxembourg.

Munson, T. V. An American hybridizer from Denison, Texas, who discovered, identified, and classified many species of grapes; during the phylloxera epidemic in the late nineteenth century, he provided many of the rootstocks for the replanting of France's devastated vineyards.

Musar, Château The most distinguished wine of Lebanon, and perhaps the finest wine of the Middle East, Château Musar comes from 320 acres of vineyards in the Bekaa Valley, 40 miles south of Beirut, planted primarily with Cabernet Sauvignon and Cinsault, plus lesser amounts of Syrah, Merlot, and Pinot Noir. Out of a total production of 50,000 to 60,000 cases, about a third are bottled as Château Musar, the rest as Cuvée Musar; Château Musar usually contains between 50 and 75 percent Cabernet Sauvignon and the wine tends to be firm, tannic, and long-lived. The winery, situated 15 miles north of Beirut, was founded in the 1930s by Gaston Hochar and, since 1959, has been under the direction of his son, Serge.

Muscadelle A white-wine grape grown in the Bordeaux region, especially where sweet wines are produced; interplanted with Sémillon and Sauvignon Blanc, in a proportion of no more than 5 or 10 percent, it contributes an agreeable aroma to such wines as Sauternes and Barsac, although some Sauternes vineyards have only 1 or 2 percent, others none at all. This grape is also used to make the rich, sweet, fortified Australian wines known as liqueur Tokays, and it is likely that the variety known in California as Sauvignon Vert is actually Muscadelle.

Muscadet A light, dry white wine produced around the old Breton capital, Nantes, in the lower Loire Valley of France. The grape from which it comes is also known locally as Muscadet, although its true name is Melon de Bourgogne, and as such it was brought from Burgundy to the Loire Valley in the seventeenth century; of little consequence or quality when grown elsewhere, the grape yields, in this particular district, a small, fresh, pale, agreeable, early maturing wine, dry but generally not green or acid, with good fruit and, in the opinion of local experts, a faint trace of muskiness, from which the name Muscadet is derived. Muscadet was the first appellation of France for which a maximum alcohol content was established – 12 percent – to ensure the wine's light-bodied delicacy. Once regarded as little more than a *vin du pays*, an inexpensive wine to be consumed locally, it has achieved a particular success in Paris and in export markets as well; current production often amounts to 6 to 8 million cases a year. There are, in addition to the basic Muscadet appellation, two others – Sèvre-et-Maine, from extensive vineyards that fan out to the east of Nantes, and Coteaux de la Loire, up the river to the northeast. Although Muscadet de Sèvre-et-Maine is considered the best of the three, that appellation now accounts for 70 to 85 percent of the crop, so the distinction is perhaps less important than it is sometimes made out to be. The phrase *sur lie* was traditionally applied to Muscadet that was bottled directly from the container in which it was fermented, without first being racked, or trans-ferred, away from the lees, or spent yeast cells; this gave the wine an extra measure of freshness and crisp flavour. Today, legislation permits any wine bottled before June of the year following the harvest to be labelled *sur lie*, and about three quarters of the crop is so marketed, although only a few pro-ducers continue to make these wines in the authentic manner.

Muscadine The name used to describe a number of varieties in the native American family of vines known, because of its round leaves, as *Vitis rotundifolia*; the varieties include Scupper-nong, Dixie, Carlos, and Magnolia. Wine from the Musca-dine family has been made in the Carolinas, Florida, and the Gulf states for several centuries, and at one time a single vine on Roanoke Island covered two acres of pergola and yielded 2,000 gallons of wine a year. Muscadine wine has a pro-nounced and special flavour, and its juice requires the addi-tion of a considerable amount of sugar to become wine at all; the result could more properly be described as a sort of sweet, light cordial than as a normal wine.

Muscat A table, raisin, and wine grape, of which literally scores of subvarieties exist, ranging in colour from pale yellow to blue-black, in yield from prolific to shy-bearing, in quality from excellent to poor, in style from pale, delicate, fruity, and low in alcohol to dark amber, rich, sweet, and fortified; all, to a varying degree, have the special, characteristic, unmistakable, perfumed and musklike Muscat odour and flavour, both as fresh grapes and as wine. Muscats of one sort or another are widely planted in Italy, southern France, Spain, Portugal, Greece, Tunisia, and on almost all of the Mediterranean islands, notably Sardinia, Sicily, Elba, Pantelleria, Cyprus, and the whole Aegean archipelago; also in Alsace, the Tyrol, and Hungary; and, of course, in California and Australia. A catalogue of the various sorts of Muscat would be of more interest to a botanist than to a wine drinker, but there is general agreement that the finest variety is the one known as Muscat Blanc à Petits Grains or Muscat de Frontignan, which produces wines as different as Muscat de Beaumes-de-Venise from the southern Rhône; Asti Spumante and Moscato d'Asti from Italy's Piedmont region, where it is known as Moscato di Canelli; the dark, fortified liqueur Muscats of Australia, where the variety is called Brown Muscat; and attractive sweet wines in California, where it is known as Muscat Blanc or Muscat Canelli. The Muscat of Alexandria, more extensively planted but less highly regarded, nevertheless produces such famous wines as France's Muscat de Rivesaltes, Italy's Moscato di Pantelleria, and Portugal's Moscatel de Setúbal. In Australia it is known as Gordo Blanco and produces a great deal of neutral white wine, as well as some elegant, delicate wines labelled Lexia, but in California, the Muscat of Alexandria is classified as a raisin grape. Muscat Ottonel is planted in Alsace, where it is made into a light, dry wine; and in California, Orange Muscat is made into a sweet, fortified, dessert wine.

Muscat de Beaumes-de-Venise A sweet, fortified white wine produced from Muscat grapes round the village of Beaumes-de-Venise, situated a few miles northeast of Châteauneuf-du-Pape, in the southern Rhône Valley. This appealing dessert wine, characterized by an intense bouquet, is known as a *vin doux naturel*, although it is made by adding neutral grape spirits to stop fermentation; the resulting wine must have a minimum of 15 percent alcohol and at least 11 percent residual sugar. Production amounts to 80,000 to 100,000 cases a year.

Musigny One of the very greatest red Burgundies, produced in a 26-acre vineyard situated directly above and behind Clos de Vougeot, in the commune of Chambolle-Musigny. The vineyard is split up among a dozen owners, and their combined total production averages 3,000 cases a year. In delicacy, distinction, and that indefinable combination of qualities often called breed, the finest examples of Musigny are unsurpassed by any other red wine of the Côte d'Or, and equalled by few. Lighter and more elegant than Chambertin, it belongs in the same noble and incomparable class. The vineyard also produces a very small amount of an excellent dry white wine known as Musigny Blanc; production, which has ranged from 45 to 220 cases in recent years, averages about 100 cases.

Must Grape juice or crushed grapes ready to be fermented into wine, or in the process of fermenting into wine.

Musty A disagreeable odour and flavour caused by improperly cleaned casks; it is related to mouldy, but comes from different conditions.

Muté Unfermented grape juice; fermentation is inhibited by sterile filtration of the juice to remove yeasts, by storing the juice at a very low temperature, or by the addition of sulphur dioxide. Muté, which retains all of the natural sugar in the grapes, is widely used in the production of aperitifs, and is also used for blending, to give sweetness and body to wines that need both.

Myrat, Château A classed growth of the Sauternes district, in the commune of Barsac; the vineyard was uprooted in 1976.

❧ N

Nackenheim One of the best wine-producing towns of Germany's Rheinhessen region – perhaps second in quality only to Nierstein – whose vineyards directly overlook the Rhine south of Mainz. The hillside soil, the colour of brick, gives wines, both from Riesling and Sylvaner, of exceptional fruit, bouquet, and breed; the best vineyard sites are Rothenberg and Englesberg.

Nacktarsch *See* Kröv

Nahe One of the eleven Anbaugebiete, or specified wine regions, of Germany, situated along both sides of the Nahe River, which joins the Rhine at Bingen. The region's 11,400 acres of vineyards produce an average of 4.5 million cases of wine, 98 percent of it white. Müller-Thurgau accounts for nearly 30 percent of the vines, Riesling for about 20 percent, and Sylvaner for 14 percent, but it is the wines made from Riesling that have established the Nahe's reputation for fine, racy wines that deserve to be better known; some resemble Moselles, others display the body and ripeness found in the adjoining Rheinhessen region. The Nahe is divided into Bereich Kreuznach and Bereich Schloss Böckelheim, and the best-known wine villages are Bad Kreuznach, Schlossböckelheim, Niederhausen, and Rüdesheim. The latter gives its name to the most familiar Grosslage of the region, Rüdesheimer Rosengarten, whose wines are often confused with those produced in the Rheingau village of the same name. Fine Nahe estates include those of August E. Anheuser, Paul Anheuser, Reichsgraf von Plettenberg, Hans Crusius, and the Nahe State Domain.

Nairac, Château A classed growth in the Sauternes district, in the commune of Barsac; its 40 acres, planted 90 percent with Sémillon, produce about 2,000 cases a year.

Napa The most celebrated wine county in California, whose principal appellation, Napa Valley, has long been associated with many of America's finest wines. The lower end of the county, south of the town of Napa (which is about 40 miles northeast of San Francisco), is on tidewater and touches San Pablo Bay; the vineyards extend north for about 30 miles from the cool Carneros region nearest the bay, past Napa, Yountville, Oakville, and St. Helena to Calistoga, at the foot of Mount St. Helena. The valley is bisected by Highway 29, and many of Napa's wineries are situated along this road; a number of other wineries are found along the Silverado Trail, described by Robert Louis Stevenson a century ago, which parallels the highway to the east. The Mayacamas Mountains form Napa's western border and separate it from Sonoma County; Lake County is to the north.

The first wines were made in Napa (the Indian word for "plenty") by George C. Yount in 1844; Charles Krug established the first commercial winery in 1861 and was followed by Jacob Schram at Schramsberg in 1862, the Beringer brothers in 1876, Gustave Niebaum at Inglenook Vineyards in 1879, and Georges de Latour at Beaulieu Vineyard in 1900, which indicates this area's long history of winemaking. By

1880 more than a million cases of wine were being produced in Napa by about 140 wineries, but phylloxera and Prohibition reduced to a handful the number of wineries that managed to stay in existence through the 1930s. In the mid-1960s there were perhaps fifteen wineries in Napa, and fewer than 10,000 acres of vines; Petite Sirah was the most widely planted variety, and there were only 850 acres of Cabernet Sauvignon, 325 of Sauvignon Blanc, and 225 of Chardonnay. Today, there are more than 150 wineries in Napa and more than 32,000 acres planted, with Cabernet Sauvignon and Chadonnay accounting for nearly half the total; Merlot, Pinot Noir, Sauvignon Blanc, and Johannisberg Riesling amount to more than 8,000 acres, with Zinfandel and Chenin Blanc making up most of the rest. Despite its fame, however, Napa accounts for only 5 percent of all the wine grapes harvested in California and produces the equivalent of about 6 million cases of wine.

The Napa Valley viticultural area was officially defined to encompass almost the whole county, including not only the Napa River watershed, but also Chiles, Pope, Wooden, and Gordon valleys; at least 85 percent of a wine labelled Napa Valley must come from this appellation. The small Howell Mountain viticultural area, which consists of hillside vineyards on the eastern side of Napa Valley, is best known for Cabernet Sauvignon; the extensive Carneros viticultural area, at the cool southern end of the valley, has achieved a reputation for Chardonnay and Pinot Noir. Other districts within the Napa Valley appellation that have become known to connoisseurs include hillside vineyards in the Mayacamas Mountains, and on such peaks as Mount Veeder and Spring Mountain; the Stag's Leap district, east of Yountville and the Silverado Trail, famous for its Cabernet Sauvignon; and a three-mile stretch from Rutherford to Oakville, sometimes referred to as the Rutherford Bench, which contains some of Napa's finest Cabernet Sauvignon vineyards.

The Napa Valley has the greatest concentration of well-known wineries of any California region; here are just a few of the established names, listed by the varietal wine for which each is particularly known. Excellent Cabernet Sauvignon is produced by Beaulieu Vineyard, Caymus, Clos Du Val, Château Montelena, Freemark Abbey, Heitz, Inglenook, Louis Martini, Mayacamas, Robert Mondavi, Shafer, Stag's Leap Wine Cellars, and Sterling. Wineries known for Chardonnay include Beringer, Grgich Hills,

Raymond, and Trefethen; distinctive Zinfandels are produced by Burgess and Clos Du Val; Johannisberg Riesling by Joseph Phelps and Smith-Madrone; Sauvignon Blanc by Cakebread, Robert Mondavi, Robert Pepi, and Sterling; and Merlot by Duckhorn and Rutherford Hill. Acacia and Saintsbury are known for Pinot Noir, and fine sparkling wines are made by Domaine Chandon, Domaine Mumm, Hanns Kornell, and Schramsberg.

Native American Grapes A term used to describe grapes from vine species native to the New World. The wine grape species *Vitis vinifera*, which originated in the Middle East and thence spread to Europe, was subsequently transported to all the other major wine-growing areas of the world. In the United States and Canada, however, many native species of grapes have been interbred with each other and with the imported *vinifera* species; from the resultant crosses, some manmade, others natural, a number of grape varieties have been selected for winemaking. There are four major native American species: *Vitis labrusca*, whose best-known grape is the widely planted Concord, noted for its musky, or foxy flavour; *Vitis rotundifolia*, the muscadine grape, which flourishes in the south; *Vitis aestivalis*, whose best-known variety is Cynthiana, is widely used in hybridization for its vigour and resistance to disease; and *Vitis riparia*, which is particularly resistant to phylloxera.

Nature A French term for a wine to which nothing has been added, that is, in its natural state; when seen on the label of sparkling wines other than champagne, it usually means a wine without *dosage*, or sweetening, or very little, and thus drier than a Brut. Also, until 1974, the term *Vin Nature de la Champagne* was used for still, nonsparkling wines from the Champagne region; these wines are now called Coteaux Champenois.

Navarre An extensive region that adjoins the better-known Rioja district in northern Spain; its capital is Pamplona. Garnacha (Grenache) is the principal grape cultivated, but there are increased plantings of Tempranillo, which produces sturdier, longer-lived reds. Navarre (Navarra in Spanish) has been particularly successful with its rosés, which account for half the region's production.

Néac *See* Lalande-de-Pomerol

Nebbiolo One of the two outstanding indigenous red-wine grapes of Italy – the other is Tuscany's Sangiovese – and one of the world's best. Its name comes from *nebbia*, or "fog", because it ripens best and gives its finest wines in districts where there is a good deal of morning fog during the harvest, notably in the hills of Piedmont, where it produces Barolo, Barbaresco, Gattinara, and a number of other fine, if lesser-known wines. A shy bearer, at its best on steep hillsides, it yields full-bodied, sturdy wines, fairly high in alcohol and tannin, with a richer texture and more acidity than the classic wines of Bordeaux and Burgundy, and almost always requiring a good deal of age; when mature, these have real distinction and great class. Despite the fame and quality of its best wines, however, Nebbiolo accounts for less than 3 percent of the vineyards of Piedmont. In addition to the wines cited, Nebbiolo is planted in the Roeri hills north of Alba, where its wines are entitled to the DOC Nebbiolo d'Alba or to the new DOC Roero. Nebbiolo delle Langhe is a new appellation for declassified wines from the vineyards of Barolo and Barbaresco; in addition, much of the Nebbiolo crop is sold without any DOC name simply as Nebbiolo del Piemonte. Around the village of Gattinara, about 50 miles north of Barolo and Barbaresco, Nebbiolo is known by the local name Spanna, and so labelled as a varietal wine. Clonal variations of Nebbiolo within Piedmont include Michet and Lampia. Nebbiolo is widely planted in Lombardy's Valtellina district, where it is known as Chiavennasca. There are about 300 acres of Nebbiolo planted in California's Central Valley.

Nebuchadnezzar The name given to a giant champagne bottle holding the equivalent of 20 ordinary bottles, or 507 ounces; unwieldy and ridiculous when full, it makes a conversation piece when empty.

Négociant French for "shipper", an important link in the chain between winemaker and consumer. A traditional *négociant* buys wine soon after it is made, matures it in his cellars, bottles it when ready, and ships it in proper condition. In some areas, notably Champagne and Alsace, the *négociant* buys grapes from local growers and makes the wine in his own cellars, and this practice now occurs in other regions as well.

Nenin, Château One of the biggest vineyards in the Pomerol district, whose

70 acres produce as much as 12,000 cases a year of soft, generous wine.

Nerveux A French tasting term applied to wines that are lively and well-balanced, with a well-defined character; sometimes foolishly translated as "nervous", the word properly refers to wines that are both fine and vigorous.

Neuchâtel Perhaps the best-known, although a long way from the best, white wine of Switzerland, produced from the Chasselas grape along the northern shore of Lake Neuchâtel, fewer than 20 miles from the French border; the wine is fresh, pale, and agreeable. Pinot Noir is also planted and produces light red wines as well as a pale rosé known as *oeil de perdrix*, or "partridge eye"; the best examples come from the village of Cortaillod.

Neumagen Proudly claiming to be the oldest wine town in Germany, perhaps with some justification, Neumagen is situated on the Moselle between Trittenheim and Dhron, within the Grosslage Piesporter Michelsberg. Its wines, hardly of the first rank, are fresh, light, and charming; Rosengärtchen is considered its best vineyard.

Neustadt A substantial and prosperous little city in Germany's Rheinpfalz, or Palatinate; it produces no wines of much consequence, but is an important centre of the trade.

Neutral A taster's term applied to a wine without flaws that nevertheless lacks a distinctive character; acceptable but of little interest.

New York State Although New York is second to California in total wine production, and although the four labels that were to dominate the state's wine industry for most of this century – Gold Seal, Great Western, Taylor, and Widmer's – were established in the late nineteenth century, it is only in the past dozen years or so that New York State wines have been taken seriously by connoisseurs. The reason has more to do with the grape varieties cultivated in the state than with technology or vinification, for New York is unusual in that its wines are made from native American varieties, French-American hybrids, and European *vinifera* varieties. Until the 1940s, virtually all of the state's vineyards were planted with the native varieties that could withstand New York's cold winters and humid, disease-producing summers. Even today, 60 percent of the state's 38,000 acres consist of Concord grapes, most of it planted in the Chautauqua region, southwest of Buffalo, along Lake Erie; the Concord crop is used primarily for juice, and much of the rest for wine coolers or kosher wines. (In recent years, only one third to one half of the total New York grape crop has been crushed for wine, whose production has varied from 11 to 16 million cases.) Other native varieties, such as Catawba, Niagara, Delaware, and Elvira, account for another 20 percent of the total plantings, and these, too, are less widely used for wine than in the past, although there is still a large market for the sweet, pungent, grapey wines that they produce. (Native grapes are also used for some New York State sparkling wines and for such fortified wines as sherry and port.) In the 1940s, a few growers began to cultivate such French-American hybrids as Baco Noir, DeChaunac, Chelois, Maréchal Foch, and Aurora, which had originally been created by French viticulturalists at the time of the phylloxera epidemic to combine the taste qualities of *vinifera* varieties with the sturdiness and disease-resistant qualities of native American varieties. More recently, such hybrids as Seyval Blanc, Ravat, Cayuga, and Ventura have been planted as well; Aurora and Seyval Blanc now account for about half the 5,000 acres planted with hybrid varieties. It has long been believed that *vinifera* grapes could not withstand the cold New York winters, but in the 1950s, Dr. Konstantin Frank, who had successfully grown *vinifera* grapes in the Ukraine, was encouraged by Charles Fournier of Gold Seal to graft *vinifera* varieties to native rootstocks in the Finger Lakes region, and the first New York State Chardonnay and Johannisberg Riesling wines were made in 1961. Today, there are more than 2,000 acres of *vinifera* varieties in New York; Chardonnay accounts for about half of this, much of the rest is Johannisberg Riesling, and other varieties include Sauvignon Blanc, Gewürztraminer, Cabernet Sauvignon, Merlot and Pinot Noir.

The major catalyst for changes in the style and quality of New York State wines occurred in 1976 with the passage of the Farm Winery Act, which permitted wineries with an annual production of no more than 50,000 U.S. gallons (about 21,000 cases) to sell their wines directly to consumers. This made it easier for enthusiasts to start their own wineries

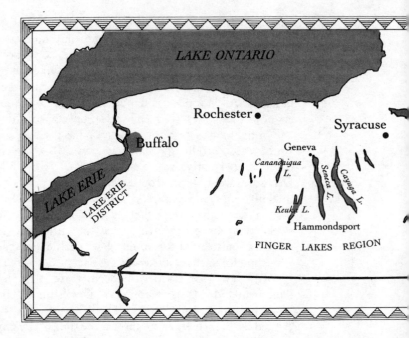

and encouraged grape growers to produce wines from their
own grapes. Of the 80-plus wineries in New York, more
than 70 have been established since 1976, and although they
account for less than 10 percent of total wine sales, most of
them concentrate on French-American hybrids, especially
Seyval Blanc, and increasingly on the *vinifera* varieties that
have drawn attention to New York State wines.

The principal wine-producing region of New York is still
the Finger Lakes, which gets its name from several elongated
lakes that resemble an imprint made by the fingers of a giant
hand; its 40-odd wineries produce 80 to 90 percent of the
state's wines. Although major wineries were established in
the nineteenth century along the shores of Keuka and
Canandaigua lakes, most of the new wineries have been
created along the shores of Seneca and Cayuga lakes. There
are more than 20 wineries in the Hudson River region,
which begins about 60 miles north of New York City; most
specialize in French-American hybrids, a few produce *vinifera* wines. The Lake Erie region (which includes the extensive Chautauqua district) is the major source of Concord
grapes, but a few wineries are now producing hybrid and
vinifera wines. New York's newest wine district is on the
eastern end of Long Island, about 100 miles east of New

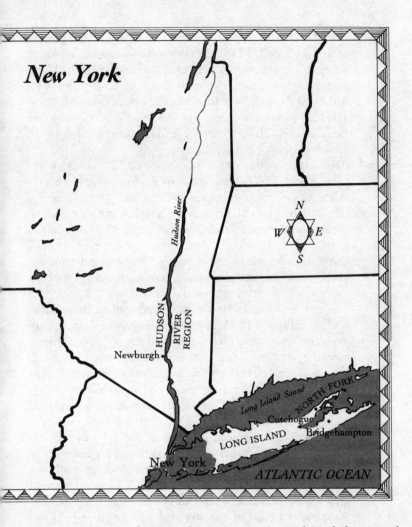

New York

Hudson River

N
W *E*
S

HUDSON RIVER REGION

Newburgh

Long Island Sound NORTH FORK

Cutchogue Bridgehampton

LONG ISLAND

New York

ATLANTIC OCEAN

York City, where 1,000 acres are planted almost exclusively with *vinifera* varieties; most of the acreage is on the North Fork of Long Island, where the first vineyards were planted in 1973, but there are also vineyards along the South Fork, in a viticultural area known as The Hamptons. New York State wines are marketed with such generic names as Chablis, Burgundy, Rhine Wine, and Sauterne; with proprietary names such as Lake Roselle and Lake Country White; and with such varietal names as Pink Catawba, Niagara, Seyval Blanc, Aurora, Chardonnay, and Sauvignon Blanc. At least 75 percent of a varietally named wine must come from the named grape, with the exception of those made from the intensely flavoured native American varieties, for which the minimum requirement is only 51 percent. At least 75 percent of a wine labelled New York State must come from that state, and a minimum of 85 percent of a wine labelled with such defined viticultural areas as Finger Lakes Region, Hudson River Region, Lake Erie, North Fork of Long Island, or The Hamptons must come from the named appellation. *See* Finger Lakes, Hudson River Region, Long Island.

New Zealand   In just a few years this country, made up of two islands situated about 1,200 miles southeast of Australia, has established an enviable reputation for its wines – first for crisp, elegant Sauvignon Blanc, then for balanced and subtle Chardonnay, and more recently for its Cabernet Sauvignon and Cabernet-Merlot blends. Although winemaking goes back more than 150 years, the modern New Zealand wine industry really began about fifteen years ago, and a number of today's best wineries produced their first wines in the 1980s. The first New Zealand vineyard was planted north of Auckland in 1819 and, in 1832, James Busby, who had already pioneered commercial winemaking in Australia, established vineyards in New Zealand as well. Many others followed, but disease and phylloxera put an end to this industry by the 1880s; then, in the 1890s, families who had arrived from Dalmatia established a number of vineyards around Auckland producing wine for local consumption. By 1960, the vineyards did not exceed 1,000 acres, and most of this was planted with such hybrid varieties as Baco 22A and Albany Surprise. In 1970, hybrids still accounted for more than a third of the acreage, but by the early 1980s there were about 15,000 acres of vines, almost all of European *vinifera* varieties; about a third of this was Müller-Thurgau, which was easy to grow and produced a high yield. Much of the Müller-Thurgau acreage has since been uprooted, and in 1990 there were 12,000 acres of vines. Although Müller-Thurgau still accounts for about one quarter of the total (its light, pleasant, semisweet wines are often marketed as Riesling-Sylvaner), there are extensive plantings of such classic white varieties as Chardonnay and Sauvignon Blanc, as well as increasing acreage of Rhine Riesling, Sémillon, Gewürztraminer, and Chenin Blanc. The most widely planted red is Cabernet Sauvignon, and there is also Merlot, Pinot Noir, and Pinotage (the latter a cross of Pinot Noir and Cinsault). Annual production is about 4 million cases, more than 75 percent of that white wines.

The two islands extend for about 1,000 miles from north to south, but most of the vineyard sites share a temperate maritime climate and a long, relatively cool growing season that results in wines with good fruit flavours, elegance, complexity, and crisp acidity. Much of the country suffers from rain in autumn, during the harvest, but many of the coastal vineyards are protected to some extent by mountain ranges. Wine production began on the North Island around Auckland, but acreage there has diminished considerably in recent years, although a number of leading firms are still situated in this district. There are extensive vineyards around Gisborne, on the east coast of the island; Müller-Thurgau, used for inexpensive blends, is the most widely planted variety, but Chardonnay and Gewürztraminer have been successful in this district. The Hawkes Bay district, south of Gisborne, produces many of the country's best wines, and has made a particular reputation for its Cabernet Sauvignon, rich Chardonnays, and Gewürztraminer. The newest district on the North Island is Wairarapa, or Martinborough, near Wellington, at the southern end of the island. The cool climate of this region, first planted in 1979, seems to favour Chardonnay and Pinot Noir.

The most acclaimed district on the South Island is Marlborough, near the town of Blenheim, whose vineyards were established in 1973 by the Montana firm. The early success of Marlborough Sauvignon Blanc, in particular, did much to establish New Zealand's reputation as a first-class wine producer. Chardonnay and Rhine Riesling are also planted there, as is Cabernet Sauvignon, whose wines are somewhat lighter than those from Hawkes Bay. The quality of Marlborough wines is such that it may overtake Gisborne and Hawkes Bay as the country's most extensively planted region. The small Canterbury district, with its cool climate, is becoming known for Rhine Riesling and Pinot Noir.

Two major firms, Montana (which acquired Penfolds) and Corbans (which acquired Cooks and McWilliams), account for more than 85 percent of the country's wine sales, but there are dozens of small and medium-sized firms that have made a name for themselves both locally and in export markets. Among them are Babich, Cloudy Bay, Delegat's, Hunter, Kumeu River, Morton Estate, Matua Valley, Nobilo's, Selaks, Te Mata, and Villa Maria.

Niagara A native American white-wine grape variety widely planted in the eastern United States, producing wines with a pungent, grapey *labrusca* aroma; it has achieved popularity as a sweet, aromatic varietal white wine.

Niederhausen　One of the best wine-producing villages of Germany's Nahe region, situated just downstream from the better-known village of Schlossböckelheim; its best vineyards are Hermannshöhle and Hermannsberg.

Nierstein　One of the very great names in German wine, and easily the foremost wine town of the Rheinhessen region – first in celebrity, first by far in vineyard acreage, and first in quality as well. Its vines overlook the Rhine south of Mainz and produce mostly good-quality wines, with little of it superb. The best are made from the Riesling grape, and so designated on the label; the finest vineyards include Hipping, Orbel, Pettenthal, Bildstock, Paterberg, Hölle, Olberg, and Kranzberg. The name of an Einzellage, or vineyard site, is especially important on a bottle of Niersteiner because the village name is also used for Bereich Nierstein, which may be used for a third of all the wines produced in Rheinhessen, the equivalent of 8 to 12 million cases a year (although much of this actually goes to market as Liebfraumilch); in addition, the popular Grosslage name Niersteiner Gutes Domtal may be used for wines from fifteen villages around Nierstein. The vineyards of Nierstein itself are divided among three Grosslagen – Niersteiner Spiegelberg, Niersteiner Rehbach, and Niersteiner Auflangen – and many top estates market their wines with these names, as well as with those of individual vineyards.

Noble　A word used, with considerable justification, of certain grape varieties, vineyards, and wines that seem to possess an inherent and permanent superiority over their fellows and their neighbours. A noble variety is one capable of giving outstanding wine under proper conditions, and better-than-average wine almost wherever planted, within reason. A noble vineyard yields wine of some distinction, even in lesser years. A noble wine is one that will be recognized as remarkable, even by a novice.

Noble Rot　*See* Botrytis Cinerea

North Coast　An extensive viticultural area in California that encompasses the grape-growing districts of five counties north of San Francisco; Napa, Sonoma, Mendocino, Lake, and Solano. Previously, the appellation also included the coastal counties between San Francisco and Los Angeles, but most of these are now part of the Central Coast viticultural area.

Northern Sonoma An extensive viticultural area that encompasses virtually all the vineyards of northern Sonoma County, including the Alexander Valley, the Russian River Valley, Chalk Hill, Green Valley, Knights Valley, and Dry Creek Valley. The appellation excludes the Sonoma Valley in the southern part of the county.

Nose A wine-taster's term for bouquet or aroma; it is a neutral word – like *taste* – and bears no connotation of superior quality.

Nostrano The name originally given by the growers of Ticino, in the Italian-speaking part of Switzerland, to the European *vinifera* vine, as opposed to what is called *Americano*, which refers to the native American vines planted in this region after phylloxera; the word literally means "ours". Nostrano is now the name with which the lesser red wines of this region go to market, while wines made from the widely planted Merlot grape are labelled as such.

Nouveau French for "new", and originally applied to any wine less than a year old. The term has taken on a different meaning in connection with certain wines, notably Beaujolais Nouveau, which refers to a wine released for sale as early as mid-November, only weeks after the harvest. *Nouveau* wines are now produced in other parts of France, in the United States, and in Italy (where they are labelled *novello*). Such wines, almost always red, are light, fruity, appealing, and short-lived; they have become popular with consumers, and certainly with producers, who are able to market such wines before the end of the year in which they were harvested.

Novello *See* Vino Novello

Nu French for "naked"; a price quoted *nu* means without cask or bottles.

Nuits-Saint-Georges A celebrated Burgundian town (whose inhabitants are known as Nuitons) on the Côte de Nuits, to which it has given its name. About 100,000 cases a year are produced of admirable reds that, while rarely of the very topmost class of red Burgundies, are generous, sturdy, well-balanced and long-lived; in certain years, those from the less-good vineyards often have a characteristic *goût de terroir*, or earthy flavour. Of the 785 acres whose wines may be marketed as Nuits-Saint-Georges or Nuits-Saint-Georges Premier Cru (there are no *grands crus* in Nuits), about 130 acres are situated in the adjoining village of Prémeaux. Among the most celebrated *premiers crus* of Nuits are Les Pruliers, Les Saint-Georges, Les Cailles, Les Vaucrains, and, from the commune of Prémeaux, Clos Arlot, Clos des Corvées, Les Perdrix, and the 23-acre Clos de la Maréchale, owned by Domaine Faiveley. Château Gris, long associated with the Lupé-Cholet firm, is a 7-acre plot within the *premier cru* Les Crots; Clos des Porrets, a 9-acre plot within the *premier cru* Les Poirets, is owned by Domaine Gouges, which also produces about 250 cases a year of an unusual white wine from the Perrière vineyard. The name *Nuits* on a label, followed by the term *Premier Cru* or the name of a specific vineyard, has exactly the same standing as Nuits-Saint-Georges; the two names are interchangeable.

Nutty A taster's term applied to wines with a bouquet reminiscent of walnuts or hazelnuts; most often applied to sherries, especially amontillado.

 O

Oak The one wood in which wine can almost always be counted on to improve, oak is used for such small and medium-sized containers as barrels, casks, butts, pipes, and the like; chestnut and redwood are acceptable substitutes, but far less good, especially for red wines. All of the fine red wines of the world, a number of excellent white wines, and most fortified wines owe part of their quality and taste to the oak in which they have been aged. Nearly every wine-producing district has its special and cherished source of supply, and a few French names in particular have become familiar even to consumers: Limousin comes from a forest near Limoges, east of the Cognac region; Nevers comes from the region around that town, in the Nièvre *département*, in central

France; the adjoining *département* of Allier is also known for its oak, as is the forest of Tronçais, within Allier. American oak, which imparts more oak flavour and a slightly sweeter taste than does French oak, is also widely used. Small oak barrels are used by the leading producers of Bordeaux, Burgundy, California, Australia, Spain, and increasingly Italy, many of whom age all or part of their wine in new oak, which imparts even more flavour and tannin. Oak adds complex nuances to both red and white wines, as well as a toasty quality whose intensity depends on the extent to which the inside of the barrel was charred when assembled by the cooper. (In fact, the cooper's contribution to the characteristics of the finished barrel is almost as important as the source of the oak.) If kept too long in oak, however, a wine's varietal or regional character may be overwhelmed, and it will taste more of wood than of wine. *See* Barrel Aging.

Oaky A taster's term for a wine that retains the distinctive bouquet and taste of the oak barrel in which it has been aged; oak aging adds an element of complexity and interest to many red and white wines, but if the oaky element is too pronounced, it overwhelms the fruit and character of the wine itself.

Obermosel A Bereich situated, as its name suggests, along the upper Moselle, upriver (that is, southwest) of Trier, the Saar, and the Ruwer.

Ockfen One of the very great white-wine villages of the world, situated between Saarburg and Wiltingen, along Germany's Saar River. There are some 250 acres of Riesling planted on one incredibly steep, slate hillside, and in favourable years the wines, unsurpassed by those of any other German or French vineyard, are light, almost steely, elegant, and with a bouquet that can only be called incomparable; in lesser vintages the wines are hard, green, and acid. The best-known vineyard is the 128-acre Bockstein.

Oechsle The German and Swiss equivalent of Brix, a way to measure the sugar content of the must, or grape juice, before fermentation, which gives a fairly accurate indication of the potential alcohol content of the resulting wine; it is based on the difference between the specific gravity, or density, of must and that of water. The Oechsle scale, created by C. F. Oechsle in the early nineteenth century, is now used to determine the official quality levels of German wines, which are based on the ripeness of the grapes at the time of harvest, as expressed by the proportion of sugar in the juice. Thus, a Riesling Qualitätswein from the Rheinpfalz must have a minimum of 60 Oechsle degrees, the equivalent of 15 percent of natural grape sugar, with a potential alcohol content of 7.5 percent; a Riesling Spätlese from the Moselle must have a minimum of 76 Oechsle degrees, and a Riesling Beerenauslese from the Rheingau must have at least 125 Oechsle degrees. Of course, not all of the sugar in the juice is converted into alcohol, so the Beerenauslese would not end up as a dry wine of 17.7 percent alcohol, but as a very sweet wine of perhaps 7 or 8 percent alcohol.

Oeil de Perdrix   French for "patridge eye", and used to describe the colour of certain wines, made from black grapes, whose appearance is a combination of very pale pink and bronze. The old term has its charm, but few wines are now produced with this colour, and almost none so labelled.

Oenology   The whole science of wine production, from the harvest and vinification to bottling; the name is derived from Oeneus, the legendary Greek god of Calydon and originally a wine god. An oenologist is a professional who is skilled in the production of wine, and should not be confused with an oenophile, derived from the Greek for "lover of wine", and which refers to someone who enjoys wine. Also spelled enology, enologist, and enophile.

Oenothèque   French for "wine library"; a collection of bottled wines for display, reference, and tasting.

Oestrich   With 1,100 acres under vines, this is probably the largest wine-producing village in Germany's Rheingau region; its best vineyards are Schloss Reichhartshausen, whose name appears on a label without that of the village, and Lenchen, Doosberg, and Klosterberg.

Off   Perhaps the broadest and least specific term of disapprobation that can be applied to a wine. Basically, it means abnormal; an offtaste is one that the wine should not have, for whatever reason and from whatever cause. It may be a fault that will soon correct itself, or it may be a permanent flaw, but *off* should not be used of a wine, however poor, that is simply coarse, thin, or earthy.

Ohio In pre-Civil War days and, in fact, until the first transcontinental railway was completed, Ohio was by far America's most important wine-producing state. The earliest vineyards were planted by German settlers east and west of Cincinnati, where the steep hills overlooking the swift Ohio River recalled the landscape of the Rhine and inspired the most optimistic prophecies concerning the district's viticultural future. Nicholas Longworth, who first planted Catawba grapes in the 1820s, which he used to make both still and sparkling wines, established a business that was national in scope. Somewhat later, grapes began to be planted on a fairly large scale along the southern shore of Lake Erie, west of Cleveland, especially around Sandusky and on the Lake Erie islands. Oidium and black rot destroyed most of the vineyards around Cincinnati in the late nineteenth century, and Prohibition considerably reduced the volume of wine produced along the Lake Erie shore. Today, there are fewer than 3,000 acres of vineyards, most of them situated in the Lake Erie district, in the northeast corner of the state, and planted, for the most part with such native grapes as Concord, Catawba, and Niagara. French-American hybrids, especially Vidal and Seyval Blanc, account for about a third of the acreage, and a limited amount of such *vinifera* varieties as Johannisberg Riesling and Chardonnay are also planted, much of this on Isle St. George, near Sandusky. Meier's Wine Cellars is by far the biggest producer in the state; others include Chalet DeBonne, Grand River, and Markko Vineyard.

Oidium A fungus, probably of American origin, which attacks the fruit, leaves, shoots, and tendrils of the vine; also called powdery mildew. It caused enormous damage in European vineyards when it first appeared there, in the mid-nineteenth century, and is still troublesome, although it can now be prevented by dusting or spraying with sulphur.

Olivier, Château A popular *grand cru classé* vineyard in the Graves district of Bordeaux; its 90 acres produce about 20,000 cases, of which the better-known white wine accounts for somewhat more than half the total.

Oloroso   One of the two basic types of Spanish sherry (the other being fino); the word means "fragrant", and fine, old olorosos do, in fact, possess an intense and recognizable bouquet. Darker and fuller-bodied than finos, and higher in alcohol (with 18 to 21 percent), olorosos are matured without the *flor* yeasts that give finos their special character. Although olorosos, like all sherries, are completely dry while they mature in cask, few are shipped in their natural state; most are sweetened and marketed as cream sherries.

Oltrepò Pavese   An extensive district in Italy's Lombardy region, south of the Po River, in the province of Pavia. Barbera is the most widely planted grape here and forms the base not only of Barbera dell'Oltrepò Pavese, but of the basic red of the region, Rosso dell'Oltrepò Pavese. A variety called Bonarda, which is actually the Croatina in this part of Italy, is also extensively cultivated, as are Moscato, Riesling Renano, and Riesling Italico. Oltrepò Pavese is also known for the fine sparkling wines produced from Pinot Bianco, Pinot Grigio, Pinot Nero, and, increasingly, Chardonnay.

Onctueux   A French tasting term whose literal meaning is "unctuous", but used most often to describe rich, sweet, full-bodied white wines of good quality, such as the great Sauternes; also used, less frequently, for fat, fleshy, red wines.

Oporto   The second-largest city of Portugal, on the Douro River not far from its mouth, it has given its name to what is perhaps the most famous of all dessert wines – port; all the port shippers, however, are located across the Douro in the town of Vila Nova de Gaia.

Oppenheim   An important wine-producing town, directly south of Nierstein, in Germany's Rheinhessen region. The vineyards lie mostly south of the village on gently sloping soil that falls away toward Dienheim and the flat plain in the direction of Worms. Although many of the Oppenheimers are made from Riesling, and are of good class, they are generally below the Niersteiners in quality, softer, and with less breed. The better sites include Herrenberg and Sackträger; the principal Grosslage is Oppenheimer Krötenbrunnen.

Optima   A new German variety introduced in the 1970s, a cross that includes Sylvaner, Riesling, and Müller-Thurgau; the grape ripens more consistently than does Riesling, and its white wines are useful for blending.

Opus One   The proprietary name for a red wine produced in the Napa Valley in a joint venture between California's Robert Mondavi and the late Baron Philippe de Rothschild, proprietor of Château Mouton-Rothschild in Bordeaux. The wine, first produced in 1979 (both the 1979 and 1980 vintages were released for sale in 1984), is made up of about 80 percent Cabernet Sauvignon plus varying amounts of Merlot and Cabernet Franc.

Ordinaire   French for "common" or "ordinary"; as applied to wine, one of unknown or unstated origin, sold simply as *vin rouge*, *vin blanc*, or *vin rosé*, perhaps with a proprietary brand name. It would be safe to say that fully half of the total French wine crop can be described as *ordinaire*, and the same would be true of most major wine-producing countries.

Ordinary   A rather loose term in English, and never legally defined; usually applied to inexpensive, undistinguished table wine without special character.

Oregon   Best known for its excellent Pinot Noir wines, this state has achieved its reputation for quality in a relatively short time. Although vineyards were extensively planted throughout the state in the nineteenth century, Prohibition almost wiped out Oregon's wine industry, and until the 1970s the state's best-known wines were those made from fruits and berries. In 1961 Richard Sommer, who was mainly interested in Riesling, planted a vineyard in the Umpqua Valley, near Roseburg, about 180 miles south of Portland; two years later he produced his first wines at Hillcrest Vineyard. Then in 1966 David Lett, whose goal was to make fine Pinot Noir, planted a few acres in the Willamette Valley, the first *vinifera* grapes planted in that region since Prohibition. In 1970, when Lett first produced wines at the Eyrie Vineyards, there were only seven wineries in Oregon and fewer than 100 acres of vineyard; today, there are more than 70 wineries and about 5,000 acres. Most of the state's wineries are in the Willamette Valley, within a 50-mile radius south and west of Portland; other vineyards and wineries are located in the Umpqua Valley, in the Rogue River and Applegate Valley regions near the California border, and in the eastern part of the state. Pinot Noir is the most widely planted grape in Oregon, followed by Chardonnay and Riesling (which in Oregon is called White Riesling, not Johannisberg Riesling), and these three varieties account for two thirds of the total; Pinot Gris, Gewürztraminer, and Müller-Thurgau are also cultivated, and a few wineries produce Cabernet Sauvignon, Merlot, and Sauvignon Blanc. The choice of early-ripening grapes was dictated by growing conditions – most of the vineyards are in the western part of the state, between the Coast Range and the Cascade Mountains, where the climate is cooler, wetter, and more variable than in California or even Washington, most of whose vineyards are in an irrigated desert east of the Cascades. Winemaking in Oregon is on a relatively small scale; most wineries produce fewer that 10,000 cases a year, and only a few – Knudsen Erath, Tualatin, Sokol Blosser, Hinman, and Oak Knoll – produce more than 20,000 cases. Oregon's labelling regulations are perhaps the strictest in the country: all of the grapes must come from the geographical area designated on the label, such as Oregon, Willamette Valley, or Umpqua Valley; varietally labelled wines must contain at least 90 percent of the variety named on the label (except for Cabernet Sauvignon, which may be blended with up to 25 percent of such complementary grapes as Merlot and Cabernet Franc); and generic names such as Burgundy and Chablis are not permitted. Oregon wineries in addition to those already cited include Adelsheim, Amity, Elk Cove, and Ponzi. For map, *see* Washington.

Organoleptic When applied to the evaluation or judgement of wines, it means what can be determined or perceived by the senses – taste, smell, and sight – rather than by physical or chemical analysis, as in a laboratory. An expert's organoleptic examination will generally give a far better and more exact idea of a wine's marketability, quality, and value than the tests of a laboratory technician, however competent. Technical analysis is of particular importance and value to a winemaker, however.

Originalabfüllung Before 1971 the most widely used of several German terms meaning "estate bottled". It was a guarantee of authenticity, when followed by the producer's name, and almost never abused. Furthermore, only unsugared, unchaptalized *Naturwein* could be so labelled, and all great

German wines carried this designation, or one of its equivalents, on their labels. In 1971 the term was replaced by Erzeugerabfüllung, which also means "estate bottled", but which may be used for chaptalized Qualitätswein as well as unchaptalized Qualitätswein mit Prädikat. Both individual estates and co-operative cellars may label their wines with this designation.

Orléannais A small wine-producing district around the city of Orleans, about 70 miles south of Paris. Most of the vineyards, important and celebrated in the past, have disappeared, but about 450 acres, planted primarily with Pinot Meunier (known locally as Gris Meunier), are entitled to the VDQS Vins de l'Orléannais. Production consists almost entirely of light reds and rosés, some of them quite pleasant; the rest is history and legend.

Les Ormes de Pez, Château A *cru bourgeois* in Saint-Estèphe, in the Médoc, under the same ownership as Château Lynch-Bages; its 75 acres of vines produce 12,000 to 15,000 cases a year.

Ortega One of the new German grape varieties, a cross of Müller-Thurgau and Siegerrebe; the grape ripens well and produces white wines with a slight Muscat aroma that are useful for blending.

Ortsteil A German word meaning part of a community, as in a suburb or section, that is independent and self-contained. Under the 1971 wine laws, several famous vineyards were classified as Ortseile, and were granted the right to continue using their own names on their labels without any reference to the town or village in which they are actually located. The most famous vineyards with such status are Schloss Johannisberg, Schloss Vollrads, and the Steinberg, all in the Rheingau; and the Scharzhofberg, on the Saar.

Orvieto A famous Italian white wine produced around the hilltop village of Orvieto, situated about two thirds of the way from Florence to Rome, in Italy's Umbria region. The wine, made primarily from a clone of the Trebbiano grape known as Procanico, plus Grechetto and Verdello, was traditionally bottled as *abboccato*, or semisweet; today, most Orvieto is *secco*, or dry, and much of that is clean but neutral. The Orvieto zone is quite extensive – annual production can be as much as 1.4 million cases; the best examples come from the inner *classico* zone, and are so labelled.

Ouillage *See* Ullage

Ouvrée An old Burgundian measure of area, equal to 0.0428 hectare, or about one tenth of an acre.

Overripe A wine-taster's term applied to a dry red or white wine made from overripe grapes – in a warm region or in an especially hot year – and having an almost raisiny smell and taste; the wine, which is likely to be high in alcohol as well, is usually overpowering and unbalanced.

Oxidized Said of a wine, especially a white wine, which has had too much contact with the air, has lost its freshness and perhaps darkened in colour, and is on the way to becoming maderized. Such wines never recover, and should either be drunk immediately or thrown away.

❧ P

Pacherenc du Vic-Bilh A curious white wine that may be dry or sweet, somewhat comparable to that of Jurançon, produced north of Pau, in southwest France. Its odd name comes from the local dialect, in which Pacherenc, or *pachet-en-renc*, means "pickets in rank", these vineyards having been the first in this part of France to be planted in the modern fashion, with the vines in regular rows and a picket, or prop, for each vine; Vic-Bilh is the name of a small, hilly district around the village of Portet, south of the Adour River. The wines are made from a combination of such native grapes as Manseng and Courbu and the traditional Bordeaux varieties Sauvignon Blanc and Sémillon; annual production is about 30,000 cases, considerably less than for Madiran, a red-wine appellation whose boundaries are the same as for Pacherenc du Vic-Bilh.

Padthaway A new district in the southeast part of South Australia, previously referred to as Keppoch. The first vines were planted there in the early 1960s, when all the available vineyard land in the more famous Coonawarra district, about 50 miles away, had been cultivated; whereas Coonawarra is known for its outstanding red wine, Padthaway has been especially successful for such white wines as Rhine Riesling and Chardonnay.

Paille *See* Vin de Paille

Palatinate *See* Rheinpfalz

Palette An appellation for red, white, and rosé wines made in a small zone just east of Aix-en-Provence, in southern France, where it enjoys a certain local fame; annual production averages 6,000 cases, and almost all of this comes from one property, Château Simone.

Palmer, Château A Third Classed Growth of Margaux, in the Médoc, extensively renovated and replanted by the group that purchased it in 1938, and which now consists of members of the Sichel and Mahler-Besse families; its 100 acres of vines, which include 40 percent Merlot (an unusually large proportion for the Médoc), produce an average of 15,000 cases a year, although recent vintages have varied from 7,000 to 20,000 cases. The wine of Palmer – generous and supple, elegant and complex – is one of the finest of Bordeaux and has long been sold at prices higher than those of the second growths; a second wine, first bottled in the 1983 vintage, is labelled Réserve du Général, a reference to General Palmer, who owned the vineyard in the early nineteenth century.

Palo Cortado A comparatively rare, intermediate classification of Spanish sherry, technically a light oloroso, it also has some of the elegance and bouquet of an amontillado.

Palomino The principal variety grown around Jerez de la Frontera, in southern Spain, where it accounts for more than 90 percent of the acreage, and where it achieves its greatest success as the grape used to make sherry. It is also grown in Australia, South Africa, and in California's San Joaquin Valley, where it is known as Golden Chasselas.

Palus A French word whose original meaning was "swamp" or "marsh", and which is now used in the Bordeaux region to describe the areas of alluvial soil along the riverbanks. Little such land is planted with vineyards, and most of the *palus* are specifically excluded from the delimited *Appellation*

Contrôlée zones; vines on such soil are usually very productive but never yield wines of any quality.

Pape Clément, Château An excellent and ancient vineyard in the Graves district of Bordeaux, now a *grand cru classé*; in the early thirteenth century it was owned by the bishop of Bordeaux, who later became Pope Clément V, hence its name. The vineyard produces some 15,000 cases of fine red wine, one of the best of Graves.

Paso Robles An extensive viticultural area in the northern part of San Luis Obispo County – defined by the Santa Lucia Mountains on the west and Monterey County on the north – most of whose vineyards are situated east of the town of Paso Robles and in the somewhat warm climate around the town of Shandon; Cabernet Sauvignon and Zinfandel are particularly successful. York Mountain is a small district within the Paso Robles appellation.

Passé A French tasting term applied to a wine that is too old, past its prime, on the decline.

Passe-tout-grains *See* Bourgogne Passe-tout-grains

Passito An Italian wine made from grapes that have been partially dried or raisined by placing the bunches in cool, well-ventilated rooms for several weeks after they are picked, which increases the proportion of sugar in the juice and affects the flavour of the resulting wine as well. The technique is almost always used to produce sweet dessert wines, usually from Moscato and Malvasia grapes, but the rich juice may also be fermented out completely to produce a dry wine, as is occasionally the case with Vin Santo and always the case with the dry red Recioto della Valpolicella Amarone.

Pasteur, Louis An eminent French scientist who first determined the true nature of the fermentation that produces wine, and the cause and cure of many of wine's maladies. He gave his name to the celebrated Institut Pasteur in Paris (founded in 1888, seven years before his death), and to the process of pasteurization, which he developed in the 1860s. He once stated that "wine is the most hygienic and healthful of beverages".

Pasteurization The process of sterilizing wines and other liquids by heating them (usually to 130 degrees for an hour or so, or to between 170 degrees and 180 degrees for one or two minutes) so that the micro-organisms they contain are destroyed, thus rendering the wine microbiologically stable. There is nothing illegal about pasteurization, and it is still used for common table or dessert wines destined for early consumption; it does cut short the development and aging potential of fine wines, however, which are rarely pasteurized. Very fine membrane filters, which remove bacteria without affecting the taste of the wine, have increasingly replaced pasteurization in wineries throughout the world.

Patache d'Aux, Château A well-known *cru bourgeois* in the commune of Bégadan, entitled to the appellation Médoc; its 90 acres produce about 18,000 cases a year of a sound and dependable wine.

Patrimonio An *Appellation Contrôlée* for relatively sturdy and full-bodied red, white, and rosé wines produced near the northern end of the island of Corsica; about 100,000 cases a year are made and, as Corsica is a part of France, these wines are occasionally found in restaurants in Marseilles and along the French Riviera.

Pauillac A celebrated little town in the Médoc district of Bordeaux whose 2,400 acres of vineyards produce 500,000 cases or more in abundant vintages. Perhaps the most remarkable red-wine village in France (its only rival is Vosne-Romanée), it encompasses some of the greatest vineyards in the world, including Châteaux Lafite-Rothschild, Latour, Mouton-Rothschild, the two Pichons, Lynch-Bages, and many others. In good years, the wines of Pauillac are classic clarets in every sense of the word – subtle but distinctive, elegant but long-lived, combining breed and power.

Paulée A meal celebrating the end of the vintage; nowadays the only one left is the Paulée de Meursault, a convivial Burgundian lunch that takes place every November on the Monday following the previous day's wine auction at the Hospices de Beaune.

Pavie, Château A *premier grand cru classé* of Saint-Emilion whose 90 acres of vines, producing about 14,000 cases a year of excellent, generous red wines, make it one of the biggest vineyards in the district; the proprietors also own Château La Clusière, which is enclosed within Pavie, and Château Pavie-Decesse, which adjoins it.

Pays *See* Vin de Pays, Vin du Pays

Pécharmant A fresh and attractive little red wine produced just outside the town of Bergerac, in the Dordogne region of France; it is made from Merlot and Cabernet, the same grape varieties as in the adjoining region of Bordeaux, whose wines Pécharmant resembles.

Pédesclaux, Château A Fifth Classed Growth of Pauillac, in the Médoc; its 50 acres produce some 8,000 cases a year.

Pedicel The botanical name for the short stem that connects the individual grape to the bunch of which it is a part.

Pedro Ximénez A Spanish grape variety widely planted in the Montilla district and, to a lesser extent, in the Málaga and sherry regions. In Montilla, where it predominates, it gives a fine, dry wine, somewhat fuller-bodied and higher in natural alcohol than that which the Palomino grape yields around Jerez de la Frontera, and often sold in a lightly fortified state with only 15 or 16 percent alcohol. In Málaga and the sherry region it is vinified quite differently to produce a very sweet, fortified blending wine often referred to as P.X. The grape is also widely planted in Argentina and Australia, where it produces neutral white wines.

Peduncle The botanical term for the stalk by which a bunch of grapes is attached to the vine.

Pelure d'Oignon French for "onion skin"; with respect to wine, the special russet-brown or tawny tinge that certain red wines acquire as they grow old. The term is also applied to any light red or rosé that has this colour.

Penedès A district west of Barcelona that stretches along the Mediterranean coast of Spain almost to Tarragona, and back into the hills; its capital is Vilafranca del Penedès. A little more than half of its 60,000 acres of vineyards are now entitled to the *Denominación de Origen* Penedès, whose annual production is 18 to 20 million cases; two thirds of that is white, much of it transformed into sparkling wine. In fact, Penedès produces nine out of ten bottles of Spanish sparkling wine, and most of that is entitled to be labelled *cava*, indicating that it has been made by the classic *méthode champenoise*. (Sparkling wine production, which is centred round the town of San Sadurni de Noya, is described more fully under Cava.) The principal red grapes grown in Penedès are Garnacha, Cariñena, Tempranillo (known locally as Ull de Llebre, "eye of the hare"), and Monastrell; the whites include Xarello, Macabeo (the Viura of Rioja), and Parellada. There are, in addition, almost 2,000 acres of Cabernet Sauvignon and another 1,200 acres of other nontraditional varieties, including Chardonnay, Chenin Blanc, Gewürztraminer, and Pinot Noir. The region is divided into three zones: Bajo Penedès, along the coast, is the hottest, and produces full-bodied reds; Medio Penedès, situated on the hills, accounts for more than half the total crop, most of it whites made from Xarello and Macebeo and used for sparkling wines; and Alto Penedès, which has the highest elevation and coolest climate, is planted primarily with Parellada. Once known primarily for its pleasant but undistinguished table wines, the reds of Penedès now rank with the best Rioja and the whites are generally superior, which is to say that these wines are among the best of Spain. Much of this transformation is due to the innovative Torres firm, which introduced new grape varieties to the region and pioneered such vinification techniques as temperature-controlled fermentation. Other noteworthy estates include that of Jean Léon, who produces Cabernet Sauvignon and Chardonnay, and Masía Bach, best known for its sweet white dessert wine, Extrísimo Bach.

Perelada A small wine-producing town on the Spanish side of the Pyrenées, within the *Denominación de Origen* Ampurdán-Costa Brava, known for its popular rosé and sparkling wine; the latter was the subject of a celebrated legal controversy in the late 1950s. Shipped to London as Perelada Spanish Champagne, its use of the name was challenged in the British courts by the French *Institut National des Appellations d'Origine,* which eventually emerged victorious and thereby confirmed the exclusive right, under British law, of French champagne producers to the name champagne.

Perfume A loosely used tasting term that properly means fragrance or aroma, the qualities that a young wine possesses and that come from the grape, rather than bouquet, which a wine acquires as it matures.

Le Pergole Torte A proprietary red wine produced at the Monte Vertine estate in Tuscany's Chianti Classico district; first produced in 1977, this richly textured wine is made entirely from the Sangiovese grape.

Periquita A Portuguese red-wine grape producing sturdy, tannic wines, capable of aging; widely planted in the southern part of the country.

Perlant A French term meaning a wine very slightly sparkling (less so than *crémant* or *pétillant*), and always naturally so; the German equivalent is *spritzig*.

Perlwein A German term for a slightly sparkling wine that may be fresh, agreeable, and inexpensive, but one that should not be confused with the finer, fully sparkling wines known as *Sekt*.

Pernand-Vergelesses A small village in Burgundy's Côte de Beaune, just behind Aloxe-Corton. Some of its vineyards lie within the appellations Corton and Corton-Charlemagne, but what goes to market as Pernand-Vergelesses – about 30,000 cases of red, and a few thousand cases of white – can nevertheless be very good, and has the advantage of being less celebrated, and therefore less expensive, than wines from the best-known villages. The reds have the better reputation, especially those from the *premier cru* Ile des Vergelesses.

Persistence The lingering and pleasant taste that remains after a wine is swallowed; good wines always have length and aftertaste, their flavour remaining up to half a minute for the greatest sweet wines. The number of seconds of persistence is known as the caudalie.

Pessac-Léognan A new *Appellation Contrôlée* established in 1987 for red and white wines from ten communes in the northern part of the Graves district of Bordeaux whose wines are generally recognized as superior to those produced farther south; the most important of these communes, in addition to Pessac and Léognan, are Talence, Cadaujac, Martillac, and

Villenave d'Ornon. The appellation accounts for a quarter of the vineyard acreage in the Graves district and encompasses 55 châteaux, including all of the *crus classés* of Graves; annual production is 450,000 to 500,000 cases, 80 percent of it red. For the two or three years before this appellation was established, several châteaux labelled their wines as Graves-Pessac or Graves-Léognan; those using the appellation Pessac-Léognan must also display the phrase *Cru Classé de Graves* or *Grand Vin de Graves* on their labels.

Pétillant A French term meaning "slightly sparkling", or "crackling", as *frizzante* in Italian and *perlwein* in German. Such wines may not have a pressure in excess of 2 atmospheres (4 atmospheres is the minimum for wines classified as *mousseux*, or "sparkling"), and many of the French ones have far less pressure, including those produced in such AOC districts along the Loire as Vouvray, Saumur, Anjou, and Touraine. The sparkle must be natural, the result of bottling the wines before their fermentation is complete, while they still contain residual grape sugar (compared to champagne and *mousseux*, whose sparkle is induced by adding sugar and yeast to still, dry wines), but it is by no means accidental, and is the planned result of special methods of vinification. Wines labelled *pétillant*, which may not be marketed in champagne bottles, nor packaged to look like champagne, are often agreeable, fresh, and charming, but not widely exported.

Petit French for "little", or "small", and when applied to wine, more unfavourable than its English equivalent. A *petit vin* is a "small wine", low in alcohol, deficient in body, of no real consequence.

Petit Chablis An agreeable, rather short-lived white wine, pale, dry, and refreshing, made from the Chardonnay grape in 300 acres of the Chablis district where the soil is less chalky and the exposure less good than for wines labelled Chablis; production amounts to about 6 percent of the total Chablis crop. It is, as its name indicates, a small Chablis, interesting only in good vintages, and not often exported.

Petit Château A French term that has one meaning in Bordeaux, another among wine merchants and consumers. To a Bordelais, a *petit château* is a lesser property of no particular standing entitled only to such a basic appellation as Bordeaux, Bordeaux Supérieur, or Côtes de Bourg. Consumers tend to apply the term to any moderately priced château-bottled wine, including *crus bourgeois* of the Médoc or *grands crus* of Saint-Emilion; that is, the use of this term is based more on price than on appellation of origin.

Petit Verdot   A superior red-wine grape grown in Bordeaux in limited quantities, which produces full-bodied, deep-coloured wines, high in tannin; despite its contribution to the usual Bordeaux blend of Cabernet and Merlot, Petit Verdot is declining in importance because in many years it fails to ripen and cannot be harvested.

Petit-Village, Château   One of the best-known vineyards in the Pomerol district, situated near Vieux Château Certan and La Conseillante, and, until recently, under the same ownership as Château Cos d'Estournel in the Médoc; its 27 acres, planted 80 percent with Merlot and 10 percent each of Cabernet Franc and Cabernet Sauvignon, produce about 5,000 cases a year of fine, richly textured red wine.

Petite Sirah   The name given in California to a red-wine grape that was presumed to be the Syrah of the northern Rhône Valley in France, but which has now been identified as Durif, a less-distinguished variety introduced into southern France a century ago, but no longer grown there. By the mid-1970s, plantings in California had increased to 13,000 acres; but have since diminished to 3,500 acres, divided between Napa, Sonoma, Monterey, and the Central Valley. The deep-coloured, full-bodied, rather tannic and harsh wines it produces have long been used for blending with lighter red wines, but a number of wineries market Petite Sirah on its own as a varietal wine; the best examples have an intriguing peppery or spicy aroma and are capable of improving with bottle age.

Pétrus, Château   The finest and most famous vineyard of Pomerol, a district in France's Bordeaux region, and now ranked – unofficially, to be sure – on a par with the first growths of the Médoc. The 28-acre vineyard (which includes 12 contiguous acres acquired from Château Gazin in 1969) produces 4,000 to 4,500 cases in an abundant year, and a combination of quality, scarcity, and glamour has made Pétrus the most sought-after and expensive red wine of Bordeaux. Situated on a part of the Pomerol plateau that is especially rich in clay, the vineyard is planted 95 percent with Merlot and 5 percent with Cabernet Franc, although in most years the wines made from the latter variety are not used in the final blend. Pétrus is thus the only great wine of Bordeaux made entirely from Merlot, and its rich, powerful, opulent, even exotic taste is much admired by connoisseurs. Pétrus began to establish its present reputation in the 1950s under the guidance of Jean-Pierre Moueix, a noted Bordeaux *négoçiant*, or shipper, who has been half-owner of the property since 1964.

Pez, Château de An excellent vineyard in Saint-Estèphe, in the Médoc, first planted in the mid-eighteenth century; its 62 acres produce about 13,000 cases a year of a rich, concentrated, and aromatic wine that often rivals some of the classed growths.

Pfalz *See* Rheinpfalz

pH An indication of a wine's acidity expressed by the number of hydrogen ions it contains and sometimes referred to as its real acidity; in practice, some acids are more intense than others, so that wines with the same fixed acidity or total acidity might have a quite different pH, which indicates the *intensity* of the wine's acidity. Confusingly enough, pH is a reverse measure of a wine's acidity, so the lower the pH of a wine, the more intense its acid. Thus a wine with a pH of 2.8 would taste disagreeably tart, one with a pH of 3.9 would taste neutral and flat. Although perhaps esoteric to the consumer, pH is very important to the winemaker, because a wine with a low pH has greater bacterial stability, a brighter colour, more aroma, is less sensitive to oxidation, and has a better aging potential than one with a higher pH, which is more likely to spoil.

Phélan Ségur, Château A well-known *cru bourgeois exceptionnel* of Saint-Estèphe, in the Médoc, purchased in 1985 by Xavier Gardinier, whose family previously owned the Lanson and Pommery champagne firms. Its 175 acres of vineyards produce about 35,000 cases a year, as well as a second wine, introduced with the 1986 vintage, under the name Frank Phélan, in honour of the Irishman who combined Château Ségur and Clos de Gamarey in the nineteenth century to create the present estate. The wines from the 1983 vintage were recalled and the 1984 and 1985 vintages were never released because they were marred by a pronounced vegetal aroma, attributed to a chemical sprayed on the vines by the previous owner.

Phylloxera   An insect, or plant louse, which is, of all the enemies of the vine, perhaps the most devastating, whence its Latin name, *Phylloxera vastatrix*. It apparently has always existed in the eastern part of the United States, but the native American vines are resistant to it, largely on account of their heavier and tougher roots. Phylloxera was accidentally introduced into Europe around 1860, on vine cuttings brought over for experimental purposes. *Vitis vinifera*, the species from which almost all the world's good wines are made, is especially vulnerable to its attack, and within two decades phylloxera destroyed virtually all the vineyards of France and, soon after, those of other wine-producing countries as well, eventually reaching as far as Russia, South Africa, Australia, and New Zealand. Countless remedies and preventive measures were proposed and attempted, including chemical sprays and flooding the vineyards, but none had any lasting success. Finally, native American vine stocks were brought over, and the European vines were grafted on to these phylloxera-resistant roots. Many varieties of American vines, and innumerable crosses of these, have been planted, including *Vitis riparia, Vitis rupestris*, and *Vitis berlandieri*, and practically all European wines now come from vines grafted onto American roots. In California, too, phylloxera crossed the Rockies and laid waste the vineyards in the 1880s, and the *Vitis vinifera* vines were grafted on to American rootstocks imported from Europe, where the most resistant crosses had already been developed. At this time, it seems that the insect is less dangerous, and may no longer exist in its winged, most infectious form. In fact, some the of new acreage in California, situated in places where vineyards did not previously exist, and where, therefore, there is no infestation in the soil, has been planted with ungrafted *vinifera* vines. In the mid-1980s, however, phylloxera was discovered in vineyards in Napa and Monterey.

Piave   A large DOC zone northeast of Venice that extends on either side of the Piave River, and whose range of wines is marketed with varietal names. Merlot is the most widely planted grape, with an annual production in excess of a million cases, and a great deal of wine is made from the native white Verduzzo grape as well; other varietal wines include Cabernet, Pinot Bianco, Pinot Grigio, and the native red Raboso.

Pichet A French term for a small jug or pitcher of earthenware or wood, often used in restaurants for serving wine at table.

Pichon-Longueville, Château A Second Classed Growth of Pauillac, in the Médoc, whose vineyard directly adjoins that of Château Latour; the property was divided in the mid-nineteenth century, part of it going to the Baron de Pichon-Longueville, the rest to his three sisters, one of whom was the Comtesse de Lalande. The vineyard, sometimes referred to as Pichon-Longueville-Baron or Pichon-Baron, came under new ownership in 1987; the vineyard was expanded to 135 acres, and a second label, Les Tourelles de Longueville, has been introduced.

Pichon-Longueville Comtesse de Lalande, Château A Second Classed Growth of Pauillac, in the Médoc, whose vineyards adjoin those of the Château Pichon-Longueville; the two vineyards formed a single estate until 1850, when they were divided between the Baron de Pichon-Longueville and his three sisters, one of whom was the Comtesse de Lalande – the wines are often referred to as Pichon-Baron and Pichon-Lalande. A part of the vineyard's 150 acres is actually in Saint-Julien, and that circumstance, as well as the relatively high proportion of Merlot vines, make the wine more supple and fleshy than most Pauillacs, without losing anything in the way of structure and elegance. Since 1978 the property has been under the direction of May-Eliane de Lancquesaing (whose father, Edouard Miailhe, purchased the vineyard in 1926), and the wines are now considered among the very best of the Médoc; production is about 26,000 cases a year, and part of the crop may be marketed under the second label Réserve de la Comtesse.

Picking Boxes Instead of the picturesque wicker baskets generally used in Europe at vintage time, American growers more often use wooden boxes, or lugs; these can be stacked on trailers or dumped into gondolas for transportation to the winery.

Picolit A rare and unusual Italian white-wine grape found in the northeast corner of that country, in the Friuli region. At its best, it can produce, from partially dried grapes, sweet, luscious dessert wines with 14 or 15 percent alcohol whose reputation is almost legendary; very little is made, however, and it is likely that much of what is now marketed as Picolit is blended with wines from the Verduzzo grape.

Picpoul A white-wine grape variety cultivated, to a limited extent, in the southern Rhône region of France and also in the Languedoc region, where the light, dry VDQS Picpoul de Pinet is produced east of Sète. Also: Picpoule is the local name for the Folle Blanche grape in the Armagnac region.

Pièce French for the oak barrel in which the wines of Burgundy's Côte d'Or district are traditionally aged and stored; it contains 228 litres, the equivalent of 50 imperial gallons or 25 cases; and is almost the same size as the *barrique* of Bordeaux. In the Beaujolais region, a *pièce* contains only 216 litres, and in the Mâcon region, 215.

Pied French for "foot", but in wine parlance it is one of several words for a single vine, *cep* and *souche* being two others.

Piedmont A major wine-producing region of Italy situated in the northwestern part of the country, at the foot of the Alpine chain that separates Italy from France and Switzerland. (The Italian name Piemonte means "foot of the mountain".) The region's 230,000 acres of vineyards produce 40 to 50 million cases of wine a year, of which about 20 percent is of DOC status; there are, in fact, more than three dozen DOC zones in Piedmont, as well as two DOCG appellations, Barolo and Barbaresco. Turin is the capital of Piedmont and of Italy's flourishing vermouth trade, and the region's most popular wine is Asti Spumante, made from the Moscato di Canelli grape; Piedmont's reputation for quality, however, is based on such outstanding red wines as Barolo, Barbaresco, and Gattinara, made from the Nebbiolo grape, which is also the primary variety used for Boca, Carema, Fara, Ghemme, Roero, and, of course, Nebbiolo d'Alba and Nebbiolo delle Langhe. Despite the fame of its wines, however, Nebbiolo, also known as Spanna in the region around Gattinara, amounts to less than 3 percent of the total acreage. Many excellent wines are made from Barbera, which accounts for more than half the acreage in Piedmont, and from Dolcetto, which accounts for about 15 percent of the total. Other red grapes found in Piedmont include Freisa and Grignolino, whose names appear on labels, as well as Bonarda, Vespolina, and Croatina. Plantings of white grapes other than Moscato di Canelli are limited in this region, but they include the distinctive Cortese, used to make Gavi, and such unusual varieties as Arneis, Erbaluce, and Favorita. In addition, the classic French varieties Chardonnay and Cabernet Sauvignon have recently been introduced to this region. Because it is traditional in Piedmont to plant different grape varieties in the same district and even on the same hillside, each at the altitude and exposure most suited to its ripening cycle, many of the region's DOCs are based on different varietal names coupled with a specific delimited zone, such as Barbera d'Alba and Dolcetto d'Alba, or Barbera d'Asti, Dolcetto d'Asti, and Freisa d'Asti. A complete list of the DOC appellations of Piedmont will be found on page 557.

Pierre-à-Fusil French for "gunflint"; when applied to wine, most often to Chablis, it refers to a special odour that recalls the smell of flint struck with steel.

Piesport One of the smallest but, deservedly, one of the most famous wine-producing villages situated along Germany's Moselle River. Its steep, rocky vineyards produce wines that, at their best, have few equals – wonderfully delicate, fragrant, and fruity, with an incomparable piquancy. The village's best-known vineyards are the 300-acre Goldtröpfchen, which faces due south, and the 600-acre Treppchen, on the opposite side of the river; Falkenberg and Günterslay are also renowned. Piesporter Michelsberg, however, is a Grosslage name that may be used for wines produced well beyond Piesport itself.

Pigato An Italian white-wine grape cultivated in the Liguria region; it produces attractive, full-bodied dry wines.

Pinard French slang originated by soldiers in World War I for inexpensive red wine.

Pineau de la Loire A name sometimes used along the Loire Valley for the Chenin Blanc grape.

Pineau des Charentes A sweet aperitif produced in the Cognac region of France, which is situated in the *départements* of Charente and Charente-Maritime; it is made by adding young cognac to unfermented grape juice. The resulting product, which combines the fruitiness and sweetness of the juice with the taste of cognac, contains 16 to 22 percent alcohol and 12 to 15 percent residual sugar.

Pinot Blanc This variety is considered a true Pinot, derived from Pinot Noir (and therefore unrelated to Chardonnay, which is not a member of the Pinot family); it produces attractive dry white wines with perhaps less flavour than Chardonnay and not quite as aromatic as Pinot Gris. Pinot Blanc is planted in Alsace; in Germany and Austria, where it is known as Weissburgunder; and in northern Italy, where it is known as Pinot Bianco, although much of those plantings turned out to be Chardonnay and are now marketed as such. There are 2,000 acres planted in California, half of that in Monterey; with some exceptions, the wines lack the weight and texture of Chardonnay, but their relatively high acidity makes them suitable for sparkling wine.

Pinot Grigio The Italian name for Pinot Gris, a white-wine grape extensively planted in the northern part of that country; at its best the dry wines it produces are crisp and assertive, with a refreshing bite, but many examples of the popular wine are bland, weak, and neutral. Much of the crop is marketed simply as Pinot Grigio delle Venezie, but it is entitled to DOC as a varietal wine in a number of districts, including Collio and Grave del Friuli in the Friuli region; Alto Adige, where it may be marketed under its German name, Ruländer, and in Oltrepò Pavese.

Pinot Gris An authentic member of the Pinot family that evolved from Pinot Noir; its grapes are a sort of greyish-rose when ripe and yield full-bodied white wines that can sometimes achieve considerable distinction. It has been known as Tokay d'Alsace in Alsace; as Ruländer in Germany, where most of whose plantings are in the Baden region; and as Pinot Grigio in Italy, where good examples are fresh and crisp. There are also limited, but successful, plantings of Pinot Gris in Oregon.

Pinot Meunier A French grape variety related to Pinot Noir, but less distinguished; it derives its name from the fact that the underside of its leaves are powdery white, as if covered with flour, and *meunier* is the French word for "miller". Although not often discussed, it is the most widely planted grape in France's Champagne region, where it accounts for 40 percent of the acreage. It contributes fruit when blended with Chardonnay and Pinot Noir, but does not age well, and is therefore less often used for the finest bottlings.

Pinot Noir A distinguished and celebrated grape variety that produces all the great red Burgundies, from Beaune, Pommard, and Volnay to Chambertin, Corton, Musigny, and Romanée-Conti; it is even more extensively planted in the Champagne region, where it accounts for about a third of the acreage and where it is vinified as a *blanc de noirs* to produce white wines; it is also planted in other areas of France and throughout the world, although not always with the success it is capable of achieving in the Côte d'Or district of Burgundy. Pinot Noir is a fragile grape, not as reliable as Cabernet Sauvignon, and produces fine wines only in certain wine districts, and then not every year. Even in Burgundy, the use of more productive clones of Pinot Noir, combined with certain vinification techniques, often results in relatively light wines. At their best, however, wines made from Pinot Noir have a subtlety, complexity, elegance, and finesse unmatched by any other wine, and it is the search for those elusive qualities that has encouraged winemakers in other parts of the world to cultivate this difficult grape. Apart from the Champagne region, where Pinot Noir adds body to a blend that includes Chardonnay and Pinot Meunier, it also produces rosés in Alsace and rosés and fragrant reds in Sancerre. The grape is less successful in Germany, where it is known as Spätburgunder; although it is that country's leading red grape, the wines it produces tend to be pale, even weak, and are often slightly sweetened. Pinot Nero, as the grape is known in Italy, is found in the northeast, where it produces agreeable, light wines, and also in the Oltrepò Pavese region, where it is most often used for sparkling wines. In California, where plantings increased from 500 acres in 1959 to more than 10,000 fifteen years later, and have since diminished to about 9,000, most producers admit that it has been the least successful of the classic grape varieties grown in that state. More recently, however, better clonal selection and greater focus on the particular microclimate suitable for Pinot Noir have led to more plantings in such cool districts as Carneros, the Russian River Valley, the Anderson Valley, and the Edna Valley, where the grapes may be used for fine varietal wines or for *méthode champenoise* sparkling wines. Pinot Noir is the most widely planted grape in Oregon and has achieved particular success there, especially in the Willamette Valley.

Pinot St. George The name of a red-wine grape cultivated to a very limited extent in California; it is not a member of the Pinot family and has been identified as the Negrette of southwest France.

Pinotage A red-wine grape grown extensively in South Africa, where is produces a medium-bodied wine; first developed in 1925, it was not widely planted until the 1960s. Pinotage is a cross of Pinot Noir and Cinsault, the latter known as Hermitage in South Africa, whence its name.

Pipe A large barrel, customarily of oak and rather sharply tapered towards the ends, traditionally associated with port, and used by the shippers of northern Portugal to mature and ship that wine. A pipe has a capacity of 522.5 litres, or 116 gallons, which amounts to about 58 cases or 700 bottles. The standard Medeira pipe contains 418 litres.

Piquant A Wine-taster's term used of a fresh, almost tart white wine, characterized by its lively acidity; a fine Riesling from the Moselle might be so described.

Piqué Said of a wine that has begun to go sour, with more than a trace of acetic acid in its makeup.

Piquette A derisive term applied to any poor, thin, acid wine; it properly refers to a low-alcohol beverage made by adding water to *marc*, or grape pressings, and refermenting the result.

Plastering The addition of calcium sulphate, or gypsum, to grapes before fermentation to increase the total acidity of the resulting wine, and to improve its colour and clarity; this was once normal practice in the making of sherry and certain other wines. Curiously enough, the term *plastering* is also used to indicate the procedure that results in the opposite effect – the addition of substances such as neutral potassium tartrate or precipitated calcium carbonate to reduce the acidity of grapes grown in northern wine regions.

Plein French for "full"; the term is applied to wines with body, character, and perhaps richness. When colloquially applied to people, it means inebriated.

Plince, Château A vineyard in the Pomerol district, under the same ownership as Clos l'Eglise, producing about 3,500 cases a year.

Podere An Italian term often used in Tuscany to describe a small farm; its use implies, but does not guarantee, estate bottling.

Pointe The French word for the indentation, or push-up, in the bottom of most wine bottles, especially those used for champagne; derived from the English *punt*, although few dictionaries define the word in this sense. A bottle of sparkling wine *mise sur pointe* is one placed neck-down and stacked vertically, with the cork of each bottle in the punt of the bottle below; this occurs after *rémuage* and before disgorging, so all the sediment is resting against the cork. This system of stacking for additional aging is also called *mise en masse*.

La Pointe, Château One of the biggest and best-known vineyards in the Pomerol district, its 50 acres produce as much as 8,000 to 10,000 cases a year of wines that are perhaps lighter and less concentrated than those of some of its neighbours.

Pomace The mass of skins, seeds, pulp, and stems left in the fermenting vat or wine press after the wine or juice has been drawn off; called *marc* in French.

Pomerol The smallest of the fine wine districts of Bordeaux, producing rich, round, generously flavoured red wines; its most famous vineyard is Château Pétrus. The 1,800 acres of vineyards in Pomerol, which is situated about 25 miles east of the city of Bordeaux, produce between 250,000 and 400,000 cases a year, only 1 percent or so of all red Bordeaux, but the château-bottled wines of this district are now among the most expensive of the entire region. The wines were little known in the nineteenth century, when the great châteaux of the Médoc were already famous, and in fact Pomerol was considered a part of the adjoining, and considerably larger, Saint-Emilion district until 1923; it was only in the 1960s that the châteaux of Pomerol, led by Pétrus, began to establish their present reputation. The finest vineyards, situated on a plateau made up for the most part of clay and gravel, are planted primarily with Merlot and Cabernet Franc grapes, since Cabernet Sauvignon does not ripen properly when planted in clay soils. The combination of soil and grape varieties results in wines that are fleshier and more supple than those of the Médoc, sooner ready to drink, and perhaps not as long-lived.

Most of the Pomerol vineyards are quite small. Château Nenin, La Pointe, Gazin, and de Sales, which have more than 50 acres each, are the biggest, but most properties are considerably smaller, and several produce fewer than 3,000 cases a year, which makes their wines both expensive and difficult to obtain. Furthermore, Pomerol is the only one of the major Bordeaux districts whose wines have never been classified, so there is no established reference to guide the consumer. Pétrus stands apart, of course, as the finest wine of Pomerol; if pressed for an informal ranking, many connoisseurs would list Trotanoy, L'Evangile, La Conseillante, Lafleur, Certan-de-May, La Fleur-Pétrus, Petit Village, Vieux Château Certan, Latour à Pomerol, and Clos L'Eglise. A more complete listing of Pomerol châteaux will be found on page 544.

Pomino   A small zone situated about 20 miles east of Florence, within the largest Chianti Rufina district of Tuscany, Pomino was granted DOC status in 1983. The zone, most of whose vineyards are owned by the Frescobaldi firm, is best known for its flavourful dry white wine made primarily from Pinot Bianco, with Chardonnay, Trebbiano, and Pinot Grigio; the red is made from Sangiovese, Cabernet Sauvignon, Merlot, and Pinot Noir.

Pommard   One of the best known and most popular of all red Burgundies, especially in English-speaking countries, whose name has often been abused in the past by unscrupulous merchants; even today, the name Pommard alone on a label is not a sure sign of quality, and informed consumers look for bottles bearing the name of one of the better vineyards. The village of Pommard, in the Côte de Beaune district of the Côte d'Or, is bounded by Beaune itself on the north and Volnay to the south; its 835 acres produce about 110,000 cases a year. Wines from the best vineyards and top producers are not only dependable, but fine – firm, well-structured, and with considerable breed. The two outstanding *premier cru* vineyards of Pommard are Les Rugiens, which adjoins Volnay and gives a rather full-bodied, concentrated wine;

and Les Epenots (also spelled Epeneaux), which adjoins
Beaune and is remarkable for its finesse and class. Wines
from these two vineyards are often labelled Pommard-Epe-
nots or Pommard-Rugiens. Other fine *premiers crus* include
Clos Blanc, Les Arvelets, Les Chaponnières, Les Pézerolles,
La Platière, and Clos de la Commaraine. Two *cuvées* of the
Hospices de Beaune, Dames de la Charité and Billardet,
come from Pommard and bring high prices.

Pontac-Monplaisir, Château A lesser-known vineyard in the Graves district of Bordeaux, whose 35 acres produce about 7,500 cases
a year of very attractive red and white wines.

Pontet-Canet, Château A Fifth Classed Growth of Pauillac, in the Médoc,
owned by the Cruse family for more than a century until
1975, when it was acquired by Guy Tesseron, proprietor of
Château Lafon-Rochet and Malescasse; its 185 acres of vines
produce about 30,000 cases a year.

Porron A Spanish glass or ceramic wine vessel with two spouts, a
wide, funnel-like one for filling the container and to use as a
handle, and a narrow, pointed one to provide a thin stream
of wine that is meant to go directly from the spout to the
mouth of the drinker.

Port A sweet, red, fortified wine, probably the most famous and
certainly the most admired of the trio of fortified wines traditionally served with dessert or after a meal (the other two
being the sweet versions of sherry and Madeira). The name
properly refers to a wine produced in northern Portugal in a
delimited district along the Douro River that begins about
60 miles east of Oporto and continues 50 miles to the
Spanish frontier. About 68,000 acres of vineyards are
planted with more than forty red and white grape varieties,
the best known of which are Tinta Roriz, Tinta Francisca,
Tinta Cão, Touriga Nacional, Touriga Francesca, Mourisco,
and the white Malvasia. The average annual wine crop of the
Douro is about 15 million cases, but much of this consists of
robust red table wines that are not transformed into port; the
amount of port produced varies from 7 to 9 million cases a
year. The red grapes are crushed and begin to ferment in the
usual way, but after only 36 to 48 hours the fermenting must,
which now has about 6 percent alcohol and about 10 percent
unfermented grape sugar, is run off into containers holding

aguardente, neutral wine spirits with 77 percent alcohol, the traditional ratio being 440 litres of must to 110 litres of spirits. The spirits stop fermentation, and the result is a naturally sweet, fortified wine that, when bottled, contains 19 to 21 percent alcohol and about 9 or 10 percent residual sugar. The young wine is transported from the vineyards of the upper Douro to the lodges, or warehouses, of the many port firms situated in Vila Nova de Gaia, which faces the city of Oporto near the mouth of the Douro. The wines are aged in wooden casks called pipes, which vary somewhat in size; the traditional shipping pipe contains 534 litres, or approximately 710 bottles.

There are two basic styles of port – wood aged and vintage ports. (White port, which accounts for about 10 percent of sales, is made like red port, but from white grapes, and fermentation is permitted to continue longer when a shipper wants to produce a relatively dry version to be marketed as an aperitif). Wood-aged ports are further divided into two broad categories – ruby and tawny – although those words do not always appear on port labels. Ruby port is a young, fruity, and flavourful dark-red wine that is generally aged in wood for only three or four years, if that; tawny port, as its name implies, is lighter in colour, with a brownish tinge, and is softer and more subdued in taste. It takes eight to ten years of wood aging to produce a true tawny, so inexpensive tawnies are made either by adding white port to red, or by vinifying the wines in such a way that they are lighter and softer to begin with. Ruby and tawny ports are blended from many different years to maintain a continuity of style, and are ready to drink when bottled. Vintage ports, which are produced only three or four times in a decade, are made entirely from the grapes of a single harvest, are bottled after only two years in wood, and require another ten to twenty years in bottle to achieve maturity. Despite their fame, vintage ports account for less than 3 percent of the total production of port. Vintage ports are usually blended from a number of different vineyards along the Douro, but in recent years several firms have begun to produce vintage ports from individual *quintas*, or estates; single-*quinta* vintage ports, as these wines are referred to, are usually made in years other than the ones used for traditional vintage ports. Late Bottled Vintage ports, also known as LBV, are wines from a single harvest that must be aged at least four years in wood, but no more than six years; they are, in effect fine ruby ports, and are ready to drink when bottled. Crusted port, not often seen any more, is a nonvintage blend of two or three years bottled after about four years in wood; it, too, is a fine ruby, but it throws a deposit, or crust, in the bottle, hence its name. There are a number of old vintage-dated ports on the market that are not true vintage ports (which have to be bottled within two years or so of the vintage named); these, known as ports with the date of the harvest (and sometimes referred to as ports of the vintage, or *colheita* ports), must be aged in wood at least seven years, and the date of bottling must appear on the label. These are simply vintage-dated tawny ports that can be drunk when bottled, and are very different in style from the more vigorous and firmly structured vintage ports, which mature in bottle for thirty years or more. Finally, there is a category known as ports with an indication of age, which may be labelled ten, twenty, thirty, or forty years old; these, too, are wood-aged tawny ports, and the age indicated represents an average, not a minimum. *See* Vintage Port, Late Bottled Vintage Port.

The word *port* is used in a number of non-European countries, including the United States, Australia, and South Africa, to describe sweet, fortified wines similar in style to the wine produced in northern Portugal, and these may be made anywhere, out of any grapes. As it happens, a few small California wineries produce limited amounts of California port of excellent quality.

Porto The official designation for all ports shipped to the United States; this ruling was adopted by the Portuguese government in 1968 in an attempt to distinguish between the authentic product of northern Portugal and the imitations labelled "port" produced in California, New York State, and elsewhere. Many firms continue to use the word *port*, but all must show either Porto or Vinho do Porto somewhere on the label. This ruling does not apply to ports shipped to England, nor to those bottled in England and shipped to the United States. Despite this ruling, the term *porto* has never caught on in America, and consumers continue to refer to these wines as port.

Portugal When it comes to wine, most people tend to think of Portugal in terms of its two famous fortified wines, port and Madeira, and a few popular labels of rosé. Actually, port and Madeira account for less than 10 percent of Portugal's total

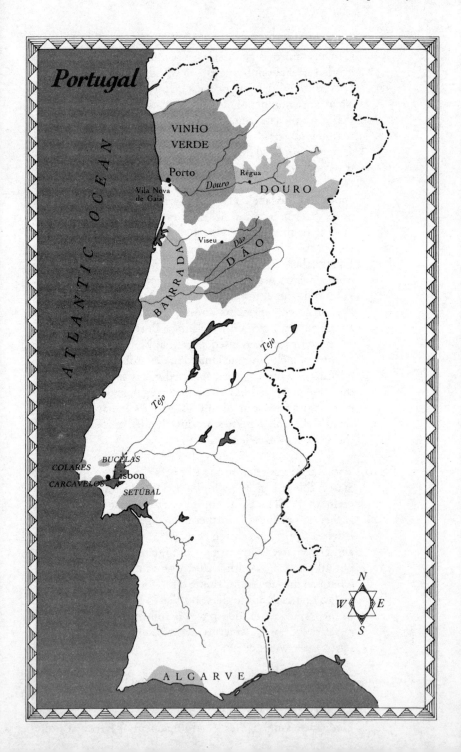

crop of 90 to 110 million cases, and those wines, as well as most of the rosés, are primarily for the export market. What the Portuguese themselves prefer, and consume in abundance, are the red and white table wines that make up most of the production of that country's 900,000 acres of vineyards; the per capita consumption of wine in Portugal averages about 75 bottles a year, five times as much as in the United Kingdom. The country's most interesting table wines are probably its sturdy, tannic reds, perhaps lacking finesse, but often good value; the introduction of modern vinification techniques has also resulted in many more good, dry white wines than in the recent past. But with the exception of the fortified wines and such well-known table wines as Vinho Verde and Dão, most of the country's best-selling wines are labelled with proprietary brands rather than an appellation of origin, and there has not been the same relation between a wine and its place of origin as in France, Italy, or Germany, or with a particular grape variety as in California. For most of this century, there were only six defined regions in Portugal whose table wines could be labelled with the phrase Região Demarcada: Vinho Verde, Dão, and the four rather obscure appellations Colares, Carcavelos, Bucelas, and Moscatel de Setúbal. In 1979, Bairrada and Algarve were added to the list, and since then the Douro district, best known for port, has been recognized as a demarcated region for table wines; others are likely to follow. Vinho Verde, produced in the northwest corner of the country, means "green wine", but only in the sense that it is young, fresh, and lively; actually, more red than white is made, but it is the light, crisp white that is more often encountered outside the country. The Dão region, in north-central Portugal, is best known for its full-bodied reds, although dry whites are also made. The four other long-established appellations are all situated within 15 or 20 miles of Lisbon and are produced in very limited quantities: Colares is a sturdy red made along the Atlantic coast; Carcavelos is a sweet, fortified white from vineyards near the resort town of Estoril; Bucelas is a full-bodied dry white; and Moscatel de Setúbal is a sweet, long-lived wine made from Muscat of Alexandria around the village of Setúbal. The Algarve region, along the southern coast of Portugal, has not yet achieved much of a reputation for its wines, but Bairrada, situated north of Lisbon between Dão and the Atlantic, produces a great deal of sturdy, tannic reds, plus a small amount of dry white wine. Interesting table wines, mostly red, are also being produced along the Douro, only half of whose wines are transformed into port; in Beira, a district between the Douro and Dão that includes Pinhel and Lafões; in Alentejo, an extensive region east of Lisbon that stretches from central Portugal down to the Algarve; in Estremadura, north of Lisbon along the Atlantic coast; and in the adjoining district of Ribatejo. Among the best known of Portugal's proprietary wines are Periquita, Camarate, and Serradayres; Barca Velha and Ferreirinha Reserva Especial are produced in the Douro in limited quantities; Quinta da Côtto comes from an estate along the Douro; and Quinta da Bacalhôa from an estate near Lisbon planted with Cabernet Sauvignon and Merlot. Some of the terms found on Portuguese labels include *garrafeira*, which indicates a special selection that has been given additional aging in wood and in bottle; *reserva*, similar but perhaps less distinguished; *casta*, which means "grape variety"; *colheita*, or "vintage"; *adega*, or "cellar"; and *quinta*, which refers to a particular vineyard, or estate, as do *casa* and *palácio*.

Portugieser   A red-wine grape that, despite its name, has no connection to Portugal; it is the most widely planted red grape in Austria, and second only to Spätburgunder among Germany's red varieties. The wine is usually light in colour and likely to be slightly sweet.

Pot   A small, heavy bottle holding 50 centilitres – two thirds of a normal bottle, or about 16 ounces – in which young Beaujolais is often served in the region and in nearby Lyons; it is still the custom in some cafés there for the owner to offer a free *pot* to clients who manage to consume "a metre of Beaujolais", that is, a dozen *pots* lined up in a row.

Potensac, Château   A *cru bourgeois* in the northern Médoc, under the same ownership as Château Léoville Las Cases, producing more than 20,000 cases a year of a generous, well-structured wine.

Pouget, Château   A Fourth Classed Growth of Margaux, in the Médoc, under the same ownership as Château Boyd-Cantenac; its 25 acres produce about 4,000 cases a year.

Pouilly-Fuissé   An excellent dry white wine made from the Chardonnay grape in four small communes just west of Mâcon, in southern Burgundy. Pouilly itself is a hamlet in the commune of

Solutré; the three other communes are Fuissé, Chaintré, and Vergisson. At its best, the wine is dry, green-gold, racy, and fruity, with good balance and fine bouquet – perhaps not a great wine, but very nearly one – although unlikely to improve beyond the age of three. Despite its comparatively limited production – which varies from 250,000 to 500,000 cases – Pouilly-Fuissé has become especially popular in the United States, where even undistinguished examples often sell for two or three times the price of Mâcon-Villages from neighbouring vineyards.

Pouilly-Fumé An excellent dry white wine from France's Loire Valley, produced around the village of Pouilly-sur-Loire. Made entirely from the Sauvignon Blanc grape, known locally as Blanc-Fumé, the wine was previously labelled Blanc-Fumé de Pouilly-sur-Loire and is still occasionally labelled Pouilly-Blanc-Fumé; it is pale, racy, fruity, with a lively acidity and a distinctive grassy or herbaceous taste. The wine has acquired a well-merited popularity in recent years, and production has increased dramatically from about 20,000 cases in the 1950s to 400,000 today. The wine labelled simply Pouilly-sur-Loire is made from the lesser Chasselas grape.

Pouilly-Loché An attractive dry white wine made, in limited quantities, from the Chardonnay grape in the village of Loché, which adjoins but is not part of the Puilly-Fuissé production zone; wines from Loché may, however, be sold with the better known appellation Pouilly-Vinzelles.

Pouilly-sur-Loire A small town on the Loire River, not far from Nevers, in central France, whose vineyards are planted with two varieties, Sauvignon Blanc and Chasselas. The former is known locally as Blanc-Fumé, and its popular and distinctive wines are marketed as Pouilly-Fumé. The dry white wines made from Chasselas are sold simply as Pouilly-sur-Loire; they are fresh, agreeable carafe wines at best, short-lived and without character.

Pouilly-Vinzelles An excellent dry white wine made, in limited quantities, from the Chardonnay grape in the village of Vinzelles, near Mâcon. Vinzelles adjoins the Pouilly-Fuissé district, and its wines, while possibly a little lighter and shorter-lived, are very like those of its considerably more famous neighbour. The similar wines from the adjoining village of Loché may be sold as Pouilly-Loché or Pouilly-Vinzelles; the two appellations together account for only 25,000 to 40,000 cases annually, less than a tenth that of Pouilly-Fuissé.

Poujeaux, Château A *cru bourgeois exceptionnel* in the commune of Moulis, in the central Médoc, owned by the Theil family; it produces about 20,000 cases a year of a sturdy, soundly made, and dependable wine. *Poujeaux* is old French for "high place", and several neighbouring properties incorporate this word into their names, including Châteaux Dutruch Grand Poujeaux, Gressier Grand Poujeaux, Branas Grand Poujeaux, and Franquet Grand Poujeaux.

Pourriture Noble *See* Botrytis Cinerea

Powerful A term used for wines, usually red, that are assertive in aroma and flavour and have a definite character.

Prädikat *See* Qualitätswein mit Prädikat

Pramaggiore A DOC zone for red wines made from Merlot and Cabernet situated in the eastern part of Italy's Veneto region; the boundaries, which are almost identical to those for the white Tocai di Lison, actually extend partly into the adjoining Friuli-Venezia Giulia region. The wines marketed as Merlot di Pramaggiore account for about three quarters of the total, Cabernet di Pramaggiore for the rest. This district has now been incorporated into the new DOC Lison-Pramaggiore.

Précoce A French term meaning "precocious", or "early maturing", applied both to grape varieties and to wines. Most varieties grown in cool, northern districts are *précoces*, for otherwise they would not ripen, and their number includes most of the very best. On the other hand, a *vin précoce*, one soon ready and gaining little if aged, is, however agreeable and charming, rarely much more than that.

Predicato Loosely defined as "special qualification", this Italian term is used for a category created by a number of producers in Tuscany for nontraditional red and white wines; there are four kinds of Predicato wines, each based on different grape varieties. Predicato del Muschio is made primarily from Chardonnay and Pinot Bianco; Predicato del Selvante, primarily from Sauvignon Blanc; Predicato di Biturica must contain at least 30 percent Cabernet Sauvignon, with most of the rest Sangiovese; and Predicato di Cardisco is based on Sangiovese, but may not contain Cabernet Sauvignon. The wines must come from vineyards situated at least 150 metres above sea level and, in fact, the labels of these wines also bear the phrase *Colli della Toscana Centrale*, or "hills of central Tuscany".

Prémeaux A village in Burgundy that adjoins Nuits-Saint-Georges on the south; its admirable red wines are entitled to the appellation Nuits-Saint-Georges and are always marketed as such.

Premier Cru French for "first growth"; *cru* is synonymous with "vineyard", and the term has a specific, but different, meaning in Bordeaux and Burgundy. In Bordeaux the terms refers to just a handful of top vineyards, some of which were classified in 1855, others more recently. In the Côte d'Or and Chablis districts of Burgundy, *premier cru* vineyards are among the best, but not as exceptional as those entitled to the higher appellation *grand cru*. *See* Cru Classé, First Growth.

Premières Côtes de Bordeaux An extensive district in the Bordeaux region, stretching about 35 miles along the hilly right bank of the Garonne River from just north of the city of Bordeaux down almost to opposite Langon; the 12,000 acres of vineyards, which face Graves, Cérons, and Sauternes across the Garonne, produce about a million cases a year, more than two thirds of it red. The pleasant, sound reds are marketed as Premières Côtes de Bordeaux, and the same appellation is used for the slightly sweet white wines; whites that are completely dry are sold as Bordeaux or Bordeaux Supérieur. In addition, whites produced in the southern part of the district that have at least 1.8 percent sugar may be sold as Cadillac, which takes its name from a village just north of Loupiac and Sainte-Croix-du-Mont, whose sweet wines are marketed under their own names.

Press An instrument of many diverse forms used since time immemorial to extract juice from grapes, either before fermentation, to make white wines, or after, in the production of red wines. The major considerations in the design of various presses have been the yield of juice per ton of grapes, the quality of the juice, speed of extraction and cost. A number of modern presses, including some that use pneumatic pressure and expanding rubber bags, are able to to extract liquid with a comparatively gentle pressure, which results in more delicate wines.

Press Wine That fraction of a fermented red wine that is extracted from the mass of skins and pulp by pressure, as contrasted with free-run wine that drains off without pressure. Press wine, which accounts for 15 percent or so of the total, is particularly rich in tannin and extracts derived from the skins; if it is bitter and astringent, it will be kept apart from the free-run wine, but if not, it is often blended back to add character and structure. In the production of white wines, the grapes are pressed before fermentation and, here again, the richer, but less delicate press juice may be added back to the free-run juice.

Preuses One of the best of the seven *grand cru* vineyards of Chablis, whose 27 acres are situated between Bourgros and Vaudésir; its wines, often hard when young, develop slowly and generally acquire a very special and attractive bouquet and flavour reminiscent of hazelnuts.

Prieuré-Lichine, Château A Fourth Classed Growth of Margaux, in the village of Cantenac, originally a Benedictine priory known as Prieuré-Cantenac; in 1951 it was purchased by the late Alexis Lichine, who renovated the cellars and the house and gradually expanded the vineyard from 27 to 155 acres. The château, which acquired its present name in 1953, now produces about 25,000 cases a year of a deservedly popular wine noted for its finesse and elegance; the second label is Château de Clairefont.

Primeur A French term applied to wines consumed soon after the harvest; in the case of Beaujolais, *nouveau* and *primeur* are interchangeable and refer to wines released for sale on the third Thursday of November. In the wine trade, buying wines such as fine Bordeaux *en primeur* means while they are still maturing in barrel.

Primitivo A red-wine grape cultivated in Italy's Apulia region that produces intensely flavoured wines with 14 percent or more alcohol as well as sweet dessert wines. It is now thought to be identical to the Zinfandel grape of California, although some ampelographers believe the Primitivo originated outside

Italy.

Priorato A small district within the larger Tarragona zone situated southwest of Barcelona along the Mediterranean coast of Spain; best known for its rich, sweet fortified red wines, made primarily from the Garnacha grape, the district also produces full-flavoured red table wines.

Prohibition The "noble experiment" that prohibited the commercial production or sale of any intoxicating beverage in the United States; it lasted almost fourteen years, from January 1920 to December 1933. The cost of enforcing it can never be determined, but it has been estimated that, to the government alone, the cost approximated $1 billion a year, including loss in federal, state, county, and municipal revenues; and it is estimated that the American people spent $36 billion for bootleg and smuggled liquor during those years. Actually, home winemaking was permitted, with the curious result that wine consumption in America was twice as high during Prohibition as before. Home winemakers preferred thick-skinned varieties that could be shipped east without damage, however, and the better varieties were uprooted from California vineyards and replaced with high-yield, thick-skinned ones. This transformation of California's vineyards, and the severe reduction in the total number of wineries (some of which continued to make sacramental wines), adversely affected the California wine industry for many years after Repeal.

Proof A system of measuring and expressing alcoholic content, used for spirits rather than wine. There are two scales: in Great Britain, proof spirit contains 57.06 percent alcohol by volume; thus, a Scotch whisky sold in England and labelled 70 proof contains 40 percent alcohol; if exported to America, it would be labelled 80 proof because, according to the scale used in the United States, proof is the double of alchoholic content by volume; thus, an 86 proof whisky contains 43 percent alcohol by volume, and a 100 proof vodka contains 50 percent alcohol.

Proprietary Name A name or brand created by a producer for his exclusive use; a proprietary name is often better known to consumers than that of the producer or the wine's place of origin. Examples include Blue Nun, Mouton Cadet, Bristol

Cream, Lake Country White, Partager, and Black Tower; although most such names are created for moderately priced wines, some producers use proprietary names for their finest wines – Opus One, Tignanello.

Prosecco An Italian white-wine grape cultivated in the Veneto region and best known as the principal variety for the DOC Prosecco di Conegliano-Valdobbiadene, produced in a zone about 35 miles north of Venice, in the province of Treviso. This crisp, attractive wine can be still, *frizzante*, lightly sparkling, or *spumante*, fully sparkling, and each of the three versions may be dry or *amabile*; a small proportion of Verdiso grapes may be used, and for the sparkling version, up to 25 percent of Pinot Bianco and Pinto Grigio may be used as well. Annual production is now close to a million cases, and the sparkling wines in particular have developed an excellent reputation. Wines from a small district near Valdobbiadene may be marketed as Cartizze or Superiore di Cartizze.

Provence Historically and traditionally, an ancient province of France where Provençal, a separate language and by no means just a dialect, was spoken and, to some extent, still is; Aix-en-Provence was its capital, and the region became part of France in 1487. As far as wine is concerned, the boundaries have been somewhat differently defined; the vineyards, which stretch west from Aix-en-Provence and Marseilles to the environs of Nice and Cannes, lie mostly within the *départements* of Bouches-du-Rhône and Var. More than 40 million cases are produced annually, of which about 9 million cases are entitled to *Appellation Contrôlée* status; the AOC Côtes de Provence accounts for most of this, and other appellations are Coteaux d'Aix-en-Provence, Coteaux des Baux, Bandol, Bellet, Cassis, and Palette.

Provignage An ancient method of propagating vines by burying an entire vine when it was old and then letting a shoot from it grow roots and become a new vine. This haphazard system, once used throughout France, was discontinued after phylloxera, and new techniques have permitted the creation of orderly, well-spaced vinyards.

Prüm An important wine family of Germany's Moselle region, with branches in the adjoining villages of Wehlen and Bernkastel. The best-known estate is that of Joh. Jos. Prüm, whose most famous wine comes from its portion of the Wehlener Sonnenuhr vineyard; fine wines are also made by S. A. Prüm Erben and Dr. Zach. Bergweiler-Prüm Erben (*Erben* means "heirs").

Pruning A complex agricultural science, of concern to vineyardists and vine-dressers since the time of Noah, by which vines are cut back – in almost all cases during their dormant season – so as to form and train them systematically with some specific end in view. This goal may be increased production, higher quality, greater facility of machine-harvesting, a longer life for the vine itself, or any combination of these and many other desired results. Literally thousands of books have been written on the subject over a period of more than twenty centuries, and a capsule condensation of them is impossible; however, a few generalizations may be of interest to the wine drinker. Within certain limits imposed by soil, climate, and rainfall or irrigation, almost any grape variety can be pruned to produce twice or even five times its minimum. Nevertheless, the few grape varieties that can properly be described as great, surely less than twenty, almost always give better wine if carefully pruned to maintain an optimum balance between fruit production and vegetative growth, providing, of course, that they are planted in districts suited to them. The commoner grape varieties, on the other hand, do not yield markedly better wine when pruned to produce less per acre. There are, in addition, many intermediate varieties that yield wines best drunk young, such as Sylvaner, Gamay, and Grenache, which gain nothing and even lose quality if their production is too restricted. *See* Yield.

Puglia *See* Apulia

Puisseguin-Saint-Emilion An appellation for red wines produced in a district that is west of Saint-Emilion itself; about 400,000 cases are produced in abundant vintages, much of it soft and light, and often of good value.

Puligny-Montrachet A village on the Côte de Beaune, in Burgundy, which produces some of the finest dry white wines of France. The two *grand cru* vineyards Chevalier-Montrachet and Bienvenues-Bâtard-Montrachet are entirely situated within this commune, and the *grands crus* Montrachet and Bâtard-Montrachet straddle the boundary between Puligny-

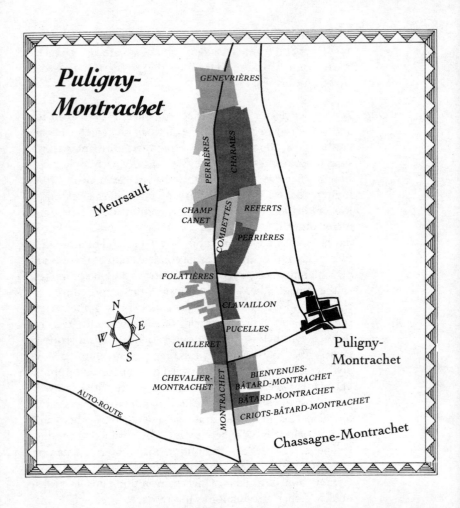

Puligny-Montrachet

GENEVRIÈRES

PERRIÈRES

CHARMES

Meursault

CHAMP CANET

COMBETTES

REFERTS

PERRIÈRES

FOLATIÈRES

CLAVAILLON

N
W E
S

PUCELLES

CAILLERET

Puligny-Montrachet

CHEVALIER-MONTRACHET

BIENVENUES-BÂTARD-MONTRACHET

BÂTARD-MONTRACHET

MONTRACHET

CRIOTS-BÂTARD-MONTRACHET

AUTO-ROUTE

Chassagne-Montrachet

Montrachet and the neighbouring village of Chassagne-Montrachet (both of which have affixed the name of the famous Montrachet vineyard to their own, to the confusion of many consumers). Wines from *grands crus* are labelled with the vineyard name alone, without reference to the village or origin, but white Burgundies that carry the name Puligny-Montrachet alone or, better yet, in conjunction with that of a *premier cru*, have great breed and class and would rank as extraordinary in any other district. Among the best of the *premiers crus* are Le Champ Canet, Clavaillon, Les Folatières, Le Cailleret, Les Pucelles, Les Referts, and Les Combettes. Annual production of Puligny-Montrachet averages about 90,000 cases, which includes 3,000 cases or so of an infrequently encountered red wine.

Pulp The fleshy and juicy part of the grape.

Punt The indentation, or push-up, in the bottom of a wine or champagne bottle.

Pupitre The two-sided rack, whose shape resembles the letter A, used in the production of champagne and other bottle-fermented sparkling wines. The rack, known in English as a riddling rack or an A-frame, is perforated with sixty holes on each side in which bottles are placed neck first and manipulated, a technique known as *rémuage*, or riddling. In many sparkling-wine firms, *pupitres* have been replaced by automatic riddling machines.

Puttonyos The Hungarian term for the baskets or hods used during the harvest in the Tokay district to gather the overripe berries affected by *Botrytis cinerea*, which are used to make the sweet, Aszú-style of wine. The number of *puttonyos* added to each cask of normal wine, usually between three and five, is indicated on the label, as Tokaji Aszú 5 Puttonyos; naturally, the more *puttonyos*, the sweeter, richer, and more expensive the wine. *See* Tokay.

PX *See* Pedro Ximénez

 Q

QbA *See* Qualitätswein

QmP *See* Qualitätswein mit Prädikat

Qualitätswein German for "quality wine", a legally defined category established by the 1971 German wine laws; its official name is Qualitätswein bestimmter Anbaugebiete ("quality wine from specified regions"), sometimes abbreviated to QbA. A wine labelled Qualitätswein must be made from grapes with a certain minimum amount of natural grape sugar (although chaptalization is permitted), and must come from one of the eleven Anbaugebiete, or specified wine regions – such as Rheingau, Rheinhessen, or Mosel-Saar-Ruwer – whose name must appear on the label. QbA wines may be labelled with only a regional name, or with that of a Bereich, Grosslage, or Einzellage, and they may be estate bottled.

(Prior to 1971, German regulations did not permit wines that were chaptalized to be labelled as estate bottled, even if they were.) Qualitätswein, and the higher-quality category Qualitätswein mit Prädikat, account for an average of 95 percent of the German wine crop, although the percentage may vary from 85 percent to 98 percent, depending on the vintage. See page 552 for additional Qualitätswein statistics.

Qualitätswein mit Prädikat The designation, established by the 1971 laws, for the highest category of German wines; it may be translated as "quality wine with special attributes", or "with distinction", and is often abbreviated as QmP. The labels of such wines must carry, in addition to this phrase, one of six specific terms – *Kabinett, Spätlese, Auslese, Beerenauslese, Eiswein,* or *Trockenbeerenauslese.* The regulations for QmP wines are more stringent than those for Qualitätswein; although the label must indicate which one of the eleven Anbaugebiete, or specified wine regions, the wine comes from, a QmP wine may not come from an area larger than a Bereich and is more likely to be from a Grosslage or Einzellage, and estate bottled. QmP wines may not be chaptalized, and the proportion of natural sugar in the juice, known in Germay as the Oechsle degree, determines the specific designation, or Prädikat, to which each wine is entitled (and in the case of Eiswein, the wine must be made from frozen grapes). Thus, a Riesling Spätlese from the Mosel-Saar-Ruwer must have a minimum Oechsle degree of 76, equivalent to 17 percent sugar and 10 percent potential alcohol; the minimum Oechsle degree for a Riesling Auslese from the Rheingau is 100, equivalent to 23 percent sugar and 13.8 percent potential alcohol. On the average, about 30 percent of the German crop is entitled to QmP status, although this has varied in recent years from 7 to 60 percent, depending on the quality of the vintage. To take a more specific, and extreme example, 69 percent of the 1983 Rheingau crop was entitled to be sold as Qualitätswein mit Prädikat, but only 2 percent in 1984. See page 552 for additional QmP statistics.

Quarto Vecchio An estate situated south of Padua in Italy's Veneto region known for its fine red wine produced from Cabernet and Merlot.

Quarts de Chaume A celebrated appellation in the Coteaux du Layon district, situated within the large Anjou region of France's

Loire Valley. The vineyard, designated a *grand cru* in 1954, consists of 120 acres of Chenin Blanc, and produces scarcely 10,000 cases a year of one of the finest of the rich, golden, fruity wines for which the Loire is famous, and similar in style to those produced nearby at Bonnezeaux.

Quatourze A village near Narbonne, along the Mediterranean coast of France, whose sturdy red wines, similar in style to those of the adjoining Corbières and Fitou districts, are entitled to the regional appellation Coteaux du Languedoc, but are more often marketed as Quatourze.

Queue An old French measure of volume; in Burgundy, it is equivalent to two *pièces* of 228 litres each.

Quincy A pleasant dry white wine from the village of this name, on the River Cher, not far from Bourges, in central France. Considered a wine of the Loire Valley (the Cher being a tributary of the Loire), and made entirely from the Sauvignon Blanc grape, Quincy is similar to Sancerre and Pouilly-Fumé; average annual production is about 50,000 cases.

Quinta A Portuguese term for a farm or, when seen on a wine label, a vineyard estate; similar in meaning to that of a château in Bordeaux. A number of red and white table wines come from specific *quintas*, as do a few ports.

❧ R

Rabaud-Promis, Château A classed growth of the Sauternes district, the larger part of what was originally Château Rabaud (the other part is now known as Château Sigalas Rabaud); its 70 acres of vineyard produce about 4,000 cases a year.

Raboso An Italian red-wine grape indigenous to parts of the Veneto region, especially the province of Treviso; the austere, tannic wine it produces has been granted DOC status in Piave.

Racking The drawing off of clear young wine from one vat, cask, or barrel to another, leaving the lees and sediment behind; its main purpose is to clarify the wine. Essential in winemaking, racking – called *soutirage* in French, *Abstich* in German, *travaso* in Italian – normally results in a loss of 2 or 3 percent of the wine's volume. The process also aerates the wine, and this oxidation contributes to its evolution, especially in the case of such tannic red wines as Bordeaux and California Cabernet Sauvignon. All well-made wines, except certain delicate whites, are racked at least twice, and some four times, before bottling.

Rahoul, Château An excellent, if less familiar, vineyard in the Graves district of Bordeaux, whose 35 acres produce about 6,000 cases a year of an attractive red wine and 1,000 cases of a distinctive white made from Sémillon.

Rainwater An odd name for a style of Madeira. There are several versions of the origins of this curious name, which began to appear on price lists in the late eighteenth century; today Rainwater is used generically for a medium-dry wine similar in style to Verdelho.

Rancio The special flavour that certain wines, especially sweet, fortified ones, acquire as they are aged in wood, akin to maderization, but in this case desirable. Madeira itself, like tawny port and some Marsala, has this characteristic taste, but it is perhaps most pronounced in the aperitif wines of southern France, such as Banyuls.

Randersacker One of the better wine-producing villages of Germany's Franken, or Franconia, region; its wines are shipped in Bocksbeutel, the traditional flagon of the area. Its individual vineyards are Pfülben, Marsberg, Teufelskeller, Sonnenstuhl, and Dabug.

Rasteau A village northeast of Avignon, within the Rhône district, whose sturdy red wines are entitled to the appellation Côtes-du-Rhône-Villages; the village is better known for a sweet, fortified red wine made from the Grenache grape and similar in style to a light port.

Ratafia A sweet, fruity aperitif made in the Champagne region and elsewhere by the addition of brandy to unfermented grape juice; it is similar to Pineau des Charentes.

Rauenthal A small village in Germany's Rheingau region, set back in the Taunus hills behind Eltville. Its better vineyards – Baiken, Gehrn, Langenstück, Wülfen, Rothenberg, and

Nonnenberg – constitute some of the most valuable agricultural land in Germany and produce distinguished wines known for their spiciness, fruit, and breed; in good vintages they are truly incomparable. Note that Rauenthaler Steinmächer is a Grosslage, and wines so labelled may not even come from Rauenthal itself; and those that do are, in any case, never among the best wines from this village.

Rausan-Ségla, Château A Second Classed Growth of Margaux, in the Médoc, extensively renovated by its British owners; its 100-odd acres of vines produce about 17,000 cases a year of a wine that has shown a marked improvement in the 1980s. The second label is Château Lamouroux.

Rauzan-Gassies, Château A Second Classed Growth of Margaux, in the Médoc, once part of the same estate as Château Rausan-Ségla; its 75 acres produce about 10,000 cases a year.

Ravat The French hybridizer J. F. Ravat created a number of successful crosses of native American and *vinifera* vines in the late nineteenth century, including Ravat Noir (the popular name for Ravat 262), which gives a light, fruity red wine, and Ravat Blanc (Ravat 6), a superior white-wine grape. In recent years, however, it is the Ravat 51, more commonly known as Vignoles, that has become more widely planted, especially in New York; it produces grapes that are high in acidity, yet susceptible to *Botrytis cinerea*, and its white wines range from off-dry to sweet and honeyed.

Ravello A memorably beautiful little town on the Amalfi coast in southern Italy, not far from Naples. Its upland vineyards produce a small amount of red, white, and especially rosé wine of good but not remarkable quality; some of it is exported and much of that consumed, no doubt, by those who find it a nostalgic reminder of hours or days spent in this enchanting place.

Raymond-Lafon, Château A property in the Sauternes district of Bordeaux that was acquired in 1972 by Pierre Meslier, for many years the *régisseur* of Château d'Yquem; the vineyard, expanded to nearly 50 acres, produces about 2,000 cases a year of an excellent, concentrated sweet wine.

Rayne-Vigneau, Château A classed growth of the Sauternes district whose

165 acres produce about 16,000 cases of sweet wine, as well as a certain amount of dry white wine marketed as Rayne-Vigneau Sec.

Rebe   German for "vine", as in such grape varieties as Faberrebe and Scheurebe.

Recioto   An Italian term used for an unusual sweet wine produced in the Veneto region from grapes grown in the Soave or Valpolicella DOC zones. These special wines, which are marketed as Recioto di Soave and Recioto della Valpolicella, are produced by taking especially ripe bunches of grapes and spreading them on trays or hanging them from hooks for two or three months after the harvest in cool, well-ventilated rooms until they are partially shrivelled and dehydrated, thus concentrating the proportion of sugar in the juice. The resulting wines are rich and sweet; some producers also make a sparkling Recioto. The most famous version of this type of wine, however, is Recioto della Valpolicella Amarone, which is dry.

Récolte   French for "harvest" or "crop"; a grower who estate-bottles his wines might refer to himself as a *récoltant* or *propriétaire-récoltant* on his label.

Red Wine   A wine made from red (or blue, purple or black) grapes, most of which have no red colour in the juice; the wine's colour comes from the inside of the grape skin during fermentation. Pink and rosé wines, made from red grapes, are kept light by being separated from the skins when the desired hue is attained.

Refosco   An Italian red-wine grape found in the Friuli region, in the northeast corner of that country; considered to be the same as the Mondeuse of France, it produces sturdy reds with an enthusiastic local following.

Regaleali   An estate in Sicily, situated at an altitude of about 1,800 feet, with nearly 500 acres of vineyards producing red, white, and rosé wines. Starting in the 1960s, the vineyards were revitalized and expanded by its owners, the Tasca d'Almerita family, whose wines are now considered among the best of the island.

Regional   A wine that takes its name from a district or region rather than from a specific town or vineyard; it is generally a blend. Wines labelled Anjou, Médoc, Côte de Beaune-Villages, Sonoma Red, and Napa Valley White are regional wines.

Régnié A village in the Beaujolais region situated between the *crus* of Morgon and Brouilly; its distinctive and appealing red wines, previously entitled to the appellation Beaujolais-Villages, were elevated to the AOC Régnié in 1988, making it the tenth Beaujolais *cru*.

Rehoboam A large bottle, occasionally used in the Champagne region, that holds the equivalent of six regular bottles.

Reichsgraf German for "count", as in Reichsgraf von Kesselstatt.

Rémuage *See* Riddling

Repeal The 21st Amendment, passed on 5 December 1933, which repealed the 18th Amendment, the one that instituted Prohibition in America in 1920.

Reserva A Spanish term that may be used for red wines that have been aged for at least three years, at least one of which must be in wood; whites and rosés so labelled must be at least two years old and must have spent a minimum of six months in wood.

Reserve A word often seen on labels, especially of California wines, either by itself or as part of such phrases as Private Reserve, Special Reserve, Proprietor's Reserve, and the like. It has no legal meaning, and the producer is free to use the phrase in any way. In France, *réserve* has no legal meaning, either. The Italian Riserva and the Spanish Reserva are legally defined, however, and indicate wines that are aged longer in wood (or in a combination of wood and bottle) than regular bottlings; such wines are usually selected from special lots that merit additional aging and are often produced only in the best vintages. In California and elsewhere in the United States, reserve bottlings almost always consist of wines that are considered by their producer to be finer and longer-lived than the regular bottling of the same variety, and are sold at a higher price. (A few producers, however, use the reserve designation for their cheapest wines.) Cabernet Sauvignon is the variety most often seen as a reserve wine, but many wineries market special bottlings of Chardonnay, Sauvignon Blanc, and Pinot Noir. Depending on the winery, a reserve Cabernet may be the same wine as the regular bottling, but with more barrel age; it may consist of distinctive lots that are aged separately; it may simply be a selection, made just before bottling, of the top 5 or 10 percent of the available wines; or it may be a wine from selected vineyards that is vinified and aged differently from the regular bottling.

Retsina A dry white Greek wine, made primarily from the Savatiano grape and flavoured with pine resin, which probably derives from an ancient custom of sealing wine amphoras with pitch. The wine, which is also produced in a rosé version called Kokkineli, is an acquired taste; some consumers find its distinctive and pungent taste an excellent match with the rich, oil-based cuisine of Greece, others find its turpentinelike flavour too strange to enjoy.

Reuilly A village near Quincy, not far from the Cher River, in the upper Loire Valley of France; crisp, dry white wines, similar in style to those of Sancerre, are produced from the Sauvignon Blanc grape, and light reds and rosés from Pinot Noir, all in limited quantities.

Rhein The German name for the Rhine River

Rheingau A German region whose white wines are considered by most experts to be among the greatest in the world. The principal section of the Rheingau covers the foothills of the Taunus Mountains, west of Wiesbaden and more or less opposite Mainz and Bingen, and overlooks an extraordinary stretch of the Rhine, which here, on its way north from Switzerland to the North Sea, makes a great bend and runs slightly south of west for over 20 miles. The vineyards, strung out along the right, or north, bank of the river, therefore have the most ideal exposure, nearly due south, and also benefit from the warmth reflected off the Rhine. Legally, the wines of Hochheim, east of the Rheingau proper, and overlooking the Main, are Rheingau wines, as are also those of Assmannshausen and Lorch, on the steep slopes of the Rhine gorge to the north.

Few, if any, of the world's great vineyard districts can compare with the Rheingau when it comes to the average quality of their wines. There is, of course, a wide variation between the wines of a poor vintage and those of a great year, as well as among those of any given harvest, but, in general, Rheingaus are characterized by a ripe, full-bodied style; they are richer and more concentrated than those of the Moselle, and possess a steeliness and balancing acidity that sets them apart from those of the Rheinpfalz and Rheinhessen. The big wines of the best years – Auslesen and Beerenauslesen – are exceptionally rich and opulent, long-lived, and rather slow to mature.

The Rheingau, one of the eleven Anbaugebiete of Germany, has an average production of 2.3 million cases, although the crop has varied in recent years from about 1.7 million to as much as 4.4 million cases; this represents only 3 percent of Germany's total production. There are 6,700 acres of vineyards, 80 percent of which are planted with Riesling; Müller-Thurgau and Spätburgunder (Pinot Noir) account for about 11 percent. Only one Bereich, or regional appellation – Bereich Johannisberg – encompasses all of the Rheingau, whose wine villages include, in addition to the three mentioned above, Rauenthal, Eltville, Kiedrich, Erbach, Hattenheim, Hallgarten, Oestrich, Mittelheim, Winkel, Johannisberg, Geisenheim, and Rüdesheim. (Although 95 percent of the Rheingau wines are white, the region is also known for the light reds produced in Assmannshausen from Spätburgunder grapes). There are ten Grosslagen, the best known of which are Johannisberger Erntebringer, Rauenthaler Steinmächer, Hattenheimer Deutelsberg, and Rüdesheimer Burgweg. The Rheingau has nearly 125 Einzellagen, or individual vineyards, and these include some of the finest and most famous in all of Germany. Among them are three whose names may appear alone on a label, without that of the specific village in which each is situated – Schloss Johannisberg, Schloss Vollrads, and Steinberg. Other fine vineyards include Rauenthaler Baiken, Erbacher Marcobrunn, Johannisberger Klaus, Winkeler Hasensprung, and Rüdesheimer Berg Schlossberg. Although there are more than 2,000 growers in the Rheingau, less than a quarter bottle their own wines, and even fewer have extensive vineyard holdings. The latter include some of the most celebrated producers of all, among them the Staatsweingüter, or State Domain, which is the proprietor of the Steinberg vineyard and also of Kloster Eberbach, a twelfth-century Cistercian abbey; other top estates are Schloss Schönborn, Schloss Reinhartshausen, Schloss

Groenesteyn, Langwerth von Simmern, Baron von Brentano, and Wegeler-Deinhard.

Rheinhessen The largest of the eleven Anbaugebiete, or specified wine regions, of Germany, whose 62,000 acres of vineyards account for about 20 percent of that country's total crop – an average of 26 million cases or so, as much as 40 million cases in some years. The region is bounded on the east and north by the Rhine, on the south by the Rheinpfalz, and on the west by the Nahe. Müller-Thurgau accounts for a quarter of the plantings, Sylvaner and Scheurebe for another quarter, and such new, earlier-ripening varieties as Bacchus, Faberrebe, and Kerner for more than 20 percent. (Although 95 percent of Rheinhessen wines are white, the village of Ingelheim has achieved a reputation for its light reds made from Portugieser and Spätburgunder.) Riesling amounts to only 6 percent of the total acreage, but there are 3,500 acres planted, mostly in the adjoining villages of Nierstein, Oppenheim, and Nackenheim (in a district known as the Rheinterrasse because of its excellent location overlooking the Rhine), and also in the village of Bingen. Although wine is produced in about 160 villages (amusingly enough, 120 of these have names that end in *heim*, or "home"), all of the truly superior wines come from just a few villages situated along the Rhine, from Worms north to Mainz, and then west to Bingen; the fertile, rolling country away from the river is known for large quantities of mild, pleasant whites – more than half of the wines marketed as Liebfraumilch come from the Rheinhessen. The best Rheinhessen Rieslings, however, are another story – if they lack the concentration and raciness of the finest Rheingau Rieslings, they have great fruit and fragrance, and a ripe, lush quality that is very appealing, the result of a comparatively warmer climate; in fact, Rheinhessen usually produces a much higher proportion of Prädikat wine than does the Rheingau, including distinguished and opulent Spätlesen and Auslesen from Sylvaner and Scheurebe. Rheinhessen has three Bereiche – Bereich Nierstein, which includes about a third of the entire region; Bereich Bingen; and the less important Bereich Wonnegau, around Worms. Of its 24 Grosslagen, the most famous by far is Niersteiner Gutes Domtal, which encompasses more than a dozen villages – not including Nierstein, ironically enough – set back from the Rhine. The finest wines of this region are estate-bottled Rieslings from such individual sites as Niersteiner Hipping, Niersteiner Orbel, Niersteiner Pettenthal, Niersteiner Olberg, Nackenheimer Engelsberg, Oppenheimer Herrenberg, and Binger Scharlachberg; in addition, many top producers around Nierstein market their wines with the Grosslagen Niersteiner Auflangen, Niersteiner Rehbach, and Niersteiner Spiegelberg.

Rheinpfalz One of Germany's eleven Anbaugebiete, or specified wine regions, and in most years first in production; its 56,000 acres account for slightly more than a quarter of the total German wine crop, an average of 28 million cases. Known in medieval days as "the wine cellar of the Holy Roman Empire", the Pfalz, also called the Palatinate, is bounded on the east by the Rhine, on the south by France's Alsace-Lorraine region, and on the north by Rheinhessen. The vineyards are not actually situated on the Rhine, but extend along the lower slopes of a chain of hills called the Haardt, a sort of lesser northern prolongation of Alsace's Vosges Mountains, and over a good portion of the fertile plain that extends eastward towards the Rhine, opposite Mannheim and Karlsruhe. Müller-Thurgau is the most widely planted grape, accounting for about 20 percent of the total; Riesling plantings amount to only 14 percent, but the area is so large that this amounts to more than 8,000 acres, even more than in the Rheingau. Kerner and Sylvaner make up another 10 percent each (plantings of the latter variety have declined from 40 percent of the total in the mid-1960s), and Scheurebe and Morio-Muskat are also well represented. Red varieties, primarily Portugieser, account for 10 percent of the acreage.

There are two Bereiche in the Rheinpfalz – the southern half, known as Südliche Weinstrasse, produces a great deal of sound wine from a number of different varieties, especially the newer ones, but most of this is consumed locally; the northern Bereich Mittelhaardt/Deutsche Weinstrasse includes all the villages and famous estates that have made Pfalz wines famous. These are situated in a small central section known as the Mittelhaardt, between Neustadt and Bad Dürkheim; four especially favoured villages – Wachenheim, Forst, Deidesheim, and Ruppertsberg – produce wine of the highest class, primarily from Riesling. Bad Dürkheim, Kallstadt, and Königsbach can be ranked not too far behind. Although there are a few individual vineyards in the Pfalz that have achieved particular acclaim, such as Forster Jesuitengarten, Forster Kirchenstück, Deidesheimer Paradiesgarten, and Wachenheimer Gerümpel, many of the finest estate-bottled wines are sold under two well-known Grosslagen, Forster Mariengarten and Deidesheimer Hofstück. Bassermann-Jordan, von Buhl, and Bürklin-Wolf are the best-known Pfalz producers. The wines of the Palatinate have a special character of their own; the lesser ones display a *Bodengeschmack*, or taste of heavy soil, but the Rieslings from the better vineyards are truly of the highest quality – rounder, riper, and fuller-bodied than the Rheingaus, but hardly inferior to them. They have considerable bouquet and breed and complement food better than most German wines. The Beerenauslesen and Trockenbeerenauslesen of great vintages are much sought after and bring astronomic prices.

Rheinterrasse German for "Rhine terrace", this refers to a particularly well-situated strip of vineyards overlooking the Rhine in the eastern part of Rheinhessen. The district, once called the Rheinfront, extends from Mettenheim north to Bodenheim, but the best vineyards are in the villages of Nierstein, Nackenheim, and Oppenheim; the wines, especially those made from Riesling, are characterized by ripeness, fruit, and elegance.

Rhenish An old British term for wines of the Rhine, now largely replaced by Hock.

Rhine Riesling The name by which the true Riesling of Germany is known in Australia and New Zealand; the grape is known as Rheinriesling in Austria and Riesling Renano in Italy.

Rhône One of the great rivers of Western Europe, rising in Switzerland, traversing Lake Geneva, and emptying into the Mediterranean west of Marseilles. Vineyards are cultivated along its banks throughout much of its length, and a great variety of different wines is produced – those of the Valais, the Vaud, Lavaux, and La Côte in Switzerland; Seyssel, between Geneva and Lyons; and all those known as Rhône wines, from south of Lyons past Avignon, including Hermitage, Côte Rôtie, Châteauneuf-du-Pape, and Tavel. *See* Côtes-du-Rhône.

Ribeiro A district in the Galicia region, in northwest Spain, producing red and white wines low in alcohol and high in acid, similar to the *vinhos verdes* made across the border in Portugal.

Ribera del Duero A district in northern Spain, east of Valladolid, along the Duero River (which becomes the Douro in Portugal); light, fresh rosés and fine, oak-aged reds are made there, primarily from the Tinta del Pais grape, similar to the Tempranillo of Rioja. The Vega Sicilia estate, whose red wines are among the most famous of Spain, is located there, as is the Alejandro Fernandez winery, which produces Pesquera.

Ribolla A native Italian white-wine grape cultivated in Friuli; the pleasant dry wine it produces, sometimes labelled Ribolla Gialla ("yellow Ribolla"), owes at least some of its interest to scarcity, although, crisp, lively examples are made in the Collio district.

Rice Wine Since it is made from grain, rice wine could be considered a kind of beer, although it usually contains 12 to 15 percent alcohol. It is a speciality in the Far East, especially in Japan, where it is called saké.

Riceys A curious, almost forgotten little district in the southern part of France's Champagne region, in the *département* of the Aube, which produces a nonsparkling rosé from Pinot Noir; only 3,000 cases a year are produced of this pleasant wine, which is entitled to the appellation Rosé de Riceys.

Richebourg One of the very great red-wine vineyards of Burgundy, situated in the village of Vosne-Romanée, in the Côte de Nuits. Its 19.75 acres, which produce about 2,500 cases a year, are bounded on the south by Romanée-Conti and La Romanée, and on the east by Romanée-Saint-Vivant; its wine is generally somewhat sturdier and fuller, with deeper colour, than that of its illustrious neighbours. The vineyard has nearly a dozen owners, the best-known of which is the Domaine de la Romanée-Conti.

Riddling One of the essential operations in producing sparkling wines by the *méthode champenoise* of individual bottle fermentation; known in France as *rémuage*. The second fermentation that creates the bubbles also produces sediment, which must be disgorged; riddling consists of shaking and turning each bottle in a special A-shaped rack, known as a *pupitre*, over a period of several weeks, until the bottle is resting upside down and all the sediment is lodged against the cork. This manual operation has been largely replaced by the use of large metal containers, known in France as *gyropalettes* and in Spain as *girasols*, in which 500 or more bottles can be manipulated at a time, and the process shortened to ten days or fewer. *See* Calcium Alginate Beads.

Riesling One of the very greatest of white-wine grapes, apparently a native of Germany's Rhine Valley, where it may have been grown since Roman days, certainly since the fifteenth century; no evidence exists to show that it originated elsewhere, or that it is identical to the Sercial of Madeira or the Pedro Ximénez of Spain, as is sometimes claimed. In modern times it has been transplanted into many other countries and has almost always yielded superior wine, especially if grown in relatively cool districts. Riesling is certainly the classic grape variety of Germany, where it accounts for only 20 percent of the total acreage but is cultivated in all of the best sites of the Rheingau and the Moselle and is also planted in the top vineyards of Rheinhessen and the Rheinpfalz. The grape is able to retain its acidity as it ripens, and its wines are characterized by a flowery, fragrant aroma and a distinctive fruity acidity; they range in style from the light, delicate wines of the Moselle and its tributaries, the Saar and Ruwer, to the fuller, riper wines of the Rheingau. When affected by *Botrytis cinerea*, the grapes produce rich, honeyed, concentrated wines labelled Auslese, Beerenauslese, and Trockenbeerenauslese, although the last two are especially rare. The Riesling grape is widely planted in Alsace, where local connoisseurs rate it above the more perfumed Gewürztraminer, and where it produces dry, flavourful wines with more body and alcohol than those from Germany. The grape has been cultivated to a certain extent in northern Italy, where its light, crisp wines are known as Rheinriesling in Alto Adige, and Riesling Renano in other parts of the country. (Wines labelled simply as Riesling are made from the lesser Riesling Italico.) In California, where the grape is known as Johannisberg Riesling or White Riesling, plantings increased from 600 acres in the mid-1960s to more than 11,000 acres in the mid-1980s, and now amount to fewer than 6,000 acres, most of it in Monterey, Santa Barbara, Napa, and Sonoma; the California bottlings have evolved from rather dry, austere wines to a more delicate and aromatic style with a touch of sweetness balanced by lively acidity. Since the early 1970s, a number of California wine-makers have consistently and successfully produced late-harvest, *Botrytis*-infected Rieslings that rival the finest sweet wines of Germany. Riesling is the most widely planted grape in Washington, where it accounts for a quarter of the acreage, and is second only to Pinot Noir in the cool climate of Oregon; Riesling has also been successfully cultivated in New York. And Rhine Riesling, as the grape is known in Australia, is the second most widely planted white-wine variety in that country, with more than 9,000 acres in production. Australian winemakers, especially in the Barossa Valley, produce a dry, steely, full-bodied, and distinctive style of Riesling; its reputation has suffered, however, as a result of the current fashion for Chardonnay. Unfortunately, there are wines sold throughout the world as Riesling that are not made from that noble variety. In California, a wine labelled simply Riesling may come from Sylvaner (also known as Franken Riesling), Grey Riesling (which is actually Chaucé Gris), or Emerald Riesling. The Welschriesling of central Europe is really the lesser Italian Riesling, also known as Riesling Italico, and no relation to the true Riesling; and in Australia, wines labelled Hunter River Riesling are actually made from Sémillon, and those marketed as Clare Riesling are made from the Crouchen of France.

Rieussec, Château A classed growth in the Sauternes district whose 135 acres produce about 8,500 cases of an excellent, balanced sweet wine, as well as a dry wine labelled "R". In 1984, the branch of the Rothschild family that owns Chateau Lafite-Rothschild and several other properties acquired a major interest in Rieussec.

Rioja The most famous table-wine district of Spain, and generally considered the best, especially for its reds (although the Penedès region is now producing excellent wines as well). It takes its name from the Rio Oja, a small tributary of the Ebro River, which it joins on the edge of the Basque country, near Pamplona, not very far from the western Pyrenées and the French border. This is high, cold, upland country, and the bare hills north and south of the valley are often white with snow as late as April; the average altitude of the vineyards is well over 1,500 feet. The red wines are therefore anything but fiery and full-bodied, as they have sometimes been described, and on the whole are lighter, lower in alcohol, softer, and more polished than most Spanish wines, and bear a certain superficial resemblance to the wines of Bordeaux.

This kinship – more marked in the red wines than in the whites – is not altogether accidental; when phylloxera began to devastate the Bordeaux vineyards in the 1880s, several hundred French families from Bordeaux moved 250 miles south into the still-uninfected Ebro Valley and settled in Haro and Logroño, the main centres of the Rioja wine trade even today, bringing with them their skills and traditional methods of winemaking. Although most of the French eventually moved back to Bordeaux when those vineyards were replanted (and when phylloxera struck Rioja), their nineteenth-century techniques were still in use through the 1960s – long maceration of the skins with the fermenting must, wood aging the reds for three to five years, liberally sulphuring the whites and aging them in wood for one or two years. The finest Riojas have long been among the best values in mature red wines, but many reds and most whites have been less esteemed. In recent years, the faded, austere, woody reds and the dull, oxidized, sometimes acrid whites have to a large extent been replaced by wines made in a more contemporary style, with less skin contact during fermentation, less wood aging for the reds and none at all for certain whites, the latter fermented at lower temperatures than in the past.

There are about 110,000 acres of vineyards in the Rioja district, producing between 11 and 15 million cases a year, 80 percent of it red, the rest white and rosé. The principal red grapes are Tempranillo, which accounts for about half the plantings, Garnacha (Grenache), Graciano, and Mazuela; Viura is the most important white grape (and is now often used by itself to make crisp, fresh wines), the others are Garnacha Blanca and Malvasia. The district is divided into three parts: Rioja Alta, planted mostly with Tempranillo, produces the best wines; the wines of Rioja Alavesa are almost as good, and these two areas include about 80 percent of the total acreage; Rioja Baja makes up the rest, and its wines, made almost entirely from Garnacha, have more body and alcohol, but are less fine. The *Denominación de Origen* Rioja, first established in 1926 and refined in 1976, is the only one used for the wines of this extensive district; there are no inner zones or individual vineyards. The wines are marketed with proprietary brand names, such as Banda Azul, Añares,

Monte Real, Viña Pomal, Viña Real, and Viña Tondonia, each of which represents a particular style of wine. (*Viña* means "vineyard", but the names do not refer to specific sites.) Most of the Rioja *bodegas*, or firms, use several proprietary brands, each representing a somewhat different style of wine. The emphasis on style, rather than on vintage and vineyard, reflects the fact that Rioja is a wine blended from three or four complementary grape varieties and, for the most part, from at least two of the three inner zones. Perhaps the most significant difference between the many bottlings is based on age: styles range from light reds without wood aging, labelled *sin crianza*, to those with some wood aging, labelled *con crianza* or *vino de crianza*, to the specially aged Riojas labelled Reserva or Gran Reserva. In keeping with the trend toward less wood aging, the minimum requirements for such wines have been lowered; a Reserva must be aged a minimum of three years, of which at least one in 225-litre oak barrels, a Gran Reserva must be aged a minimum of five years, at least two of which in oak barrels. These wines, the finest a *bodega* has to offer, are specially selected lots from the best vintages, and many firms continue to age such wines in wood and in bottle for more than the current minimums; it is not unusual for a winery to age its best Gran Reserva for four or five years in oak and as many more in bottle before releasing it for sale. Because of the traditional emphasis on blending, house styles, and long wood aging, specific vintage years were not always reliable; new regulations established in anticipation of Spain's entry into the Common Market specify that at least 85 percent of a wine must come from the year on the label. Although co-operative cellars produce more than half the wines of Rioja, most of the exports are in the hands of about fifty *bodegas* of a certain minimum size; according to self-imposed regulations, Rioja may be exported only by firms that have a storage capacity of at least 7,500 hectolitres and whose cellars contain a minimum of five hundred 225-litre oak barrels of maturing wine.

Riparia The most widespread species of native American vines, *Vitis riparia* is particularly resistant to phylloxera and widely used for breeding rootstocks.

Ripasso An Italian word that refers to a technique used by some producers in Valpolicella to produce richer, fuller wines. After the specially dried grapes used to make Amarone are crushed and fermented in vats, the wine is drawn off the skins and put into casks, usually in February or March. A part of the regular Valpolicella crop (which was fermented into wine in the normal way 3 or 4 months earlier) is then transferred to the vats and remains in contact with the residue of skins for 10 or 15 days, acquiring additional colour, flavour, and tannin; in effect, the wine is enriched by being passed over the skins (hence, *ripasso*). Two wines made in this way are Campo Fiorin of Masi and Catullo of Bertani.

Ripeau Château One of the better-known *grands crus classés* of Saint-Emilion, whose 37 acres produce about 6,500 cases a year of agreeable red wine.

Riserva Italian for "reserve"; DOC and DOCG wines entitled to note this distinction on their labels have been aged for a longer period than regular bottlings, although the extra aging need not necessarily take place in wood. The requirements for a Riserva are often three years of aging, as for Chianti Riserva, but they vary – Barbaresco Riserva must be aged for a total of four years, Barolo Riserva and Brunello di Montalcino Riserva, for five. It is generally assumed that the wines selected for extra aging in order to qualify for Riserva status are the best a producer has to offer.

Rivaner Another name for the Müller-Thurgau grape in Luxembourg and parts of Germany.

Rivesaltes A town north of Perpignan in the French *département* of Pyrenées-Orientales. It has given its name to a district comprising over a dozen townships and producing some 4 to 6 million cases a year of fortified dessert wines, about a fifth of it called Muscat de Rivesaltes, and the rest, principally from Grenache and Malvoisie grapes, sold simply as Rivesaltes. The latter must contain a minimum of 15 percent alcohol and is somewhat comparable to Banyuls, although generally less fine.

Riviera del Garda Bresciano An extensive DOC district west of Lake Garda in the province of Brescia, in Italy's Lombardy region; attractive, light-bodied red and Chiaretto, or rosé, wines are produced, primarily from the local Groppello grape, plus Sangiovese, Barbera, and Marzemino.

Rkatsiteli A white-wine grape extensively planted in Russia and Bulgaria, and possibly the second most widely planted white grape in the world, after the Airén of Spain; curiously enough, a few acres were cultivated until recently in California's Livermore Valley, and two acres were planted in New York's Finger Lakes region by the late Konstantin Frank.

Robe A French term that refers to a wine's colour and appearance.

Robust A term applied to a wine that is sound, sturdy, and full-bodied, but not necessarily fine.

Roche aux Moines A famous Loire vineyard in the district of Savennières, in France's Anjou region, which produces a dry white wine from Chenin Blanc grapes. Its 50 acres are divided between the Château de Chamboreau and the Joly family (proprietors also of the neighbouring Coulée de Serrant vineyard).

Roero A new Italian DOC for sturdy, dry red wines produced from the Nebbiolo grape (plus 2 to 5 percent of the white Arneis) in the Roeri hills north of Alba, in the Piedmont region; the boundaries of this district are contained within those established for the DOC Nebbiolo d'Alba, and many wines may therefore be marketed with either appellation.

Romanée, La A tiny *grand cru* vineyard, just two acres in size, producing about 300 cases a year of one of the rarest of red Burgundies, although not always one of the very finest. Long the property of the Liger-Belair family, it is in the township of Vosne-Romanée and situated just above the Romanée-Conti vineyard, on the Côte de Nuits. Because every *grand cru* vineyard of Burgundy has its own *Appellation Contrôlée*, La Romanée (and not, as is often stated, Château-Grillet, in the northern Rhône) is the smallest vineyard in France with its own appellation.

Romanée-Conti A *grand cru* vineyard in the village of Vosne-Romanée, in the Côte de Nuits, that produces what is perhaps the most celebrated of all red Burgundies, and often fully worthy of its extraordinary reputation. The vineyard, which takes its name from the Prince de Conti, its owner from 1760 to 1795, consists of only 4.5 acres and produces an average of 600 cases a year, although the amount bottled varies from none (in 1968) to a maximum of 802 cases. Wines continued to be produced from old, ungrafted, prephylloxera vines until 1945; the vineyard was then replanted in 1946 with vines (Pinot Noir, needless to say) grafted on to American rootstocks, and produced its first postwar vintage in 1952. The vineyard is owned by the Domaine de la Romanée-Conti, whose codirectors are Aubert de Villaine, a direct descendant of J-M Duvault-Blochet, who acquired the vineyard in 1869, and Lalou Bize-Leroy, whose father bought half of Romanée-Conti from one of Duvault-Blochet's heirs in 1942. The Domaine de la Romanée-Conti, the most famous single estate of the Côte d'Or, consists of Romanée-Conti and La Tâche in their entirety, 8.7 acres of Richebourg, 8.7 of Grands-Echézeaux, and 11 of Echézeaux, as well as 1.3 acres of the famous Montrachet vineyard (acquired in 1964, and enough to make a scant 200 cases a year); and, since 1966, the Domaine has been vinifying, bottling, and marketing the wines from the 13 acres of Romanée-Saint-Vivant that belonged to Général Marey-Monge. The Domaine's total annual production is about 10,000 cases. The wines suffered a certain loss of prestige among many connoisseurs during the 1960s and early 1970s, but recent vintages have once again justified their reputation as exceptional, distinctive, and long-lived Burgundies. They are among the most expensive wines of the region, and in most vintages Romanée-Conti itself is likely to be the most expensive wine of France. For map, *see* Vosne-Romanée.

Romanée-Saint-Vivant   An admirable Burgundian *grand cru* vineyard, directly adjoining Romanée-Conti and Richebourg, in the village of Vosne-Romanée. It takes its name from the Priory of Saint-Vivant, having been conveyed as a gift to its monks in 1232, and remained their property until the French Revolution. Its 23 acres, which produce about 2,500 cases a year, are now divided among several owners, among them the heirs of Général Marey-Monge (whose wines are vinified and bottled by the Domaine de la Romanée-Conti) and the firm of Louis Latour, which owns a part of the vineyard known as Les Quatre Journaux. One of the finest of all red Burgundies, full, soft, and elegant, it has the incomparable distinction of all the Romanée *grands crus*, and there are few better wines in France.

Romania   Although relatively few of its wines are exported, Romania's 600,000 acres of vineyards and annual production of 90 million cases make it one of Europe's major producers. Wines are made from such familiar varieties as Cabernet Sauvignon, Merlot, Pinot Noir, Chardonnay, Traminer, Pinot Gris, and Welschriesling (the lesser Italian Riesling), as well as from such native grapes as Fetească (the Leányka of Hungary) and Grasă (which may be related to Furmint). Romania's principal wine regions include Tîrnăve, or Tarnave, in Transylvania, north of the Carpathian Mountains, known particularly for its white wines; the Dealul Mare region, north of Bucharest, which includes the Valea Călugărească district, known for its reds; Dobrugda (or Dobrudja), in the southeast corner of the country, best known for the sweet Muscat wines from the Murfatler district; and Cotnari, in the northwest, which gives its name to a sweet white wine made from grapes affected by *Botrytis cinerea*.

Römer   A traditional German wine glass with a long stem, usually green and a round bowl of 7- or 8-ounce capacity; also spelled roemer.

Romer, Château   A classed growth in the Sauternes district that was split into two parts; the larger section was acquired by the Hayot family, who eventually leased the smaller section as well. Today, the wines from both parts of the 35-acre vineyard are vinified together, and the approximately 4,000 cases produced are sold under the name Château Romer du Hayot.

Rosato   Italian for "rosé". Pink wines are made throughout Italy, from the north, where the Lagrein grape produces wines marketed as Lagrein Rosato or Lagrein Kretzer, to the south, where rosés are produced at Ravello, south of Naples, and Castel del Monte, in Apulia. Light rosés produced around Lake Garda are known as Chiaretto, and a number of darker rosés are marketed as Cerasuolo, which means "cherry-coloured".

Rosé   The French word for "pink", now pretty much part of the English language. A true *vin rosé* is by no means a blend of red and white wines; indeed, this is prohibited in France (except for rosé champagne) and some other countries. It is made from black grapes whose skins are left in contact with the fermenting juice just long enough to extract the desired amount of colour. (The juice of almost all black grapes is clear; the colour of red wine is extracted from the skins during fermentation.) The grapes are then pressed and the now-pink juice continues to ferment and is vinified as if it were a white wine. Rosés are produced in almost all wine-growing countries from a wide variety of grapes. Many of the resulting wines are simple, semisweet, and undistin-guished; others, made from such varieties as Pinot Noir, Cabernet Sauvignon, Cabernet Franc, and Zinfandel, can be distinctive and flavourful. Whatever their qualities, rosés should be served chilled and drunk young. *See* Blanc de Noirs.

Rosé d'Anjou A French semisweet pink wine produced along the Loire, in the Anjou region, from such grapes as Groslot, Gamay, and Cot (the local name for Malbec); production can be as high as 2.5 or 3 million cases, making this the biggest AOC of the region.

Rosé de Loire An appellation established in 1974 for relatively dry rosés pro-duced in France's Loire Valley from a combination of several grape varieties, with a minimum of 30 percent Caber-net Franc; production averages around 300,000 cases, most of it from the Anjou region, although Saumur and Touraine are also included within this appellation.

Roses Flowers in the vineyard are weeds to the *vigneron* – except for roses. These are often grown, not for decorative pur-poses, but because they are extremely susceptible to oidium, and therefore indicate when preventive spraying is required.

Rosette An appellation for white wines produced near the city of Bergerac in the Dordogne region of southwest France.

Rossese An Italian red-wine grape cultivated in the Liguria region, where it produces the DOC Dolceacqua, also known as Rossese di Dolceacqua.

Rosso Italian for "red", and *vino rosso* is "red wine"; the word appears as part of several DOC names, including Rosso Cònero, Rosso di Montalcino, and Rosso Piceno. The term has been given a somewhat different meaning in California, and a few wineries still use the name Vino Rosso to market inexpensive red table wines that are not altogether dry.

Rosso Cònero A dry red wine produced along the Adriatic coast, just south of Ancona, in Italy's Marches region; the wine is made primarily from the Montepulciano grape, although Sangiovese is permitted up to 15 percent.

Rosso di Montalcino A DOC established in 1983 for wines from the same grape and vineyards that produce Brunello di Montalcino, in Italy's Tuscany region, but which need not be aged in wood and may be sold a year after the harvest; it enables producers to market a less-expensive and lighter-bodied alternative to the austere and powerful Brunello di Montalcino, which must be aged a minimum of four years, of which three and a half in wood.

Rosso Piceno A dry red wine produced in an extensive DOC zone around Ancona, along the Adriatic coast, in Italy's Marches region; the traditional mix of varieties is 60 percent Sangiovese, 40 percent Montepulciano.

Rotten-Egg Flavour This is the definite, unmistakable odour of hydrogen sulphide; it is entirely harmless, extremely disagreeable, inexcusable in wine, and fortunately very infrequent. It may result from the action of yeast on sulphur that has been sprayed on the grapes before the harvest, from failing to rack, or aerate, wines sufficiently as they age, or from other causes.

Rotundifolia A Muscadine vine, *Vitis rotundifolia* is a native American species that flourishes in the southern part of the United States; its most famous grape variety is Scuppernong.

Rotwein German for "red wine".

Rouge French for "red", as in *vin rouge*.

Rouget, Château A vineyard in the Pomerol district whose 45 acres, planted with more Cabernet than Merlot, produce about 7,000 cases a year of a wine that is perhaps more tannic and less supple than those of its neighbours.

Rough A term applied to a wine that is astringent, harsh, and full of tannin; some rough wines may soften with time, but the word is not usually used of fine wines, even when young.

Round A term used to describe a well-balanced, complete wine, without a major defect; it could never be applied to a poor wine, but it does not necessarily mean fine or great.

Roussanne   A white-wine grape cultivated in the northern Rhône Valley, where it may be used in the white versions of Hermitage, Crozes-Hermitage, Saint-Joseph, and Châteauneuf-du-Pape; in practice, this variety has been almost entirely replaced by the sturdier and more productive Marsanne, whose wines tend to be heavier and less elegant than those made from Roussanne.

Roussette   Another name for the Altesse grape, which produces fresh, light-bodied, dry white wines in the Savoie region of eastern France, where they are entitled to the appellation Roussette de Savoie; this grape should not be confused with the Roussanne of the Rhône Valley.

Roussillon   An extensive vineyard area within the *département* of the Pyrénées-Orientales, which adjoins Spain along the Mediterranean coast, in France's Languedoc-Roussillon region, also known as the Midi; its principal city is Perpignan. An annual production of about 20 million cases makes Roussillon one of the major wine-producing regions of France; most of this is *vin ordinaire*, a certain amount falls into the *vin de pays* category, but about a third is entitled to AOC status. This includes the large Côtes du Roussillon and Côtes du Roussillon-Villages appellations, the small AOC Collioure, and a number of sweet fortified wines known as *vins doux naturels*, among them Banyuls, Rivesaltes, Côtes d'Agly, Maury, and Muscat de Rivesaltes.

Rubesco   A proprietary name for a fine red wine, entitled to the DOC Torgiano, produced by Lungarotti in that zone, situated just south of Perugia, in Italy's Umbria region. Made primarily from Sangiovese, plus about a third Canaiolo, Rubesco is considered one of Italy's finest red wines, especially the Riserva bottling.

Rubino di Cantavenna   A dry red Italian DOC wine produced primarily from Barbera grapes in a small district north of Asti in the Piedmont region.

Rubired   A cross developed in California and planted in the Central Valley; like Royalty, a similar variety, Rubired is a *tenturier*, a red grape that gives red juice instead of white, and is therefore useful for adding colour to red-wine blends.

Ruby Cabernet A red-wine grape variety developed in California, a cross of Cabernet Sauvignon and Carignane, which was meant to combine the quality of the former with the productivity of the latter; in practice, the grape produces an agreeable red wine with perhaps less Cabernet character than was anticipated, and plantings have diminished from 17,000 acres in the early 1970s to less than half that, virtually all in the Central Valley.

Ruby Port A young, fruity port that has been aged in wood only three years or so and bottled while it still retains its deep red colour and vigorous taste. Not all such ports are so labelled, as many shippers prefer to market their young ports with a proprietary name.

Ruchottes-Chambertin A less familiar *grand cru* vineyard in the Burgundy village of Gevrey-Chambertin; its eight acres, which adjoin the *grand cru* Mazis-Chambertin, produce only 1,000 cases or so of an excellent red wine.

Rüdesheim A picturesque and celebrated little town of the Rheingau region of Germany, directly facing Bingen and the mouth of the Nahe across the wide Rhine. It is a major tourist centre, and its two main streets, squeezed in between the river and the steep vineyards behind, are crowded all summer long, and no less so during the vintage-festival season. The 800 acres of vineyards produce Rieslings that can be outstanding, especially in poor or fair years, when they are often the best of the whole Rheingau; in great vintages, however, they are sometimes too heavy and too high in alcohol. Their good qualities, like their faults, can be attributed to the steepness of the rocky terraced vineyards, which are gravely affected by drought in hot summers, especially on what is called the Rüdesheimer Berg. These carry the word *Berg* as parts of their names, as in the three vineyards Rüdesheimer Berg Schlossberg, Berg Roseneck, and Berg Rottland; other Rüdesheimer vineyards (not from the Berg) are Drachenstein, Rosengarten, Klosterberg, Kirchenpfad, and Bischofsberg.

Rüdesheim is also a small vineyard town of no great distinction along the Nahe, whose wines, made primarily from

Müller-Thurgau and Sylvaner, are often confused by the unwary with those of the great Rheingau slope described above. The labels of these wines should carry the designation Nahe, whereas those of the more acclaimed Rüdesheim will be labelled Rheingau. Rüdesheimer Rosengarten, a Grosslage, is the most frequently seen label from this part of the Nahe.

Rueda One of the good, lesser-known dry white wines of northern Spain, produced round the town of that name, southwest of Valladolid. Since the 1970s, new plantings of the native Verdejo grape, and some of Viura, and the introduction of modern vinification techniques, has resulted in an increasing production of crisp, light-bodied white wines. In 1980, the *Denominación de Origen* Rueda was established; wines so labelled must contain a minimum of 25 percent Verdejo, those labelled Rueda Superiore must contain 60 percent of that grape. These wines account for about 85 percent of the district's 1 million cases; the rest consists of the traditional *vinos generosos* – wood-aged, sherry-like wines with a minimum of 14 percent alcohol made from the widely planted Palomino grape.

Ruländer *See* Pinot Gris

Rully A small town in Burgundy, just south of the Côte de Beaune, in the Côte Chalonnaise; its average annual production of 65,000 cases is almost equally divided between dry, fruity, and very palatable red and white wines, the former made from Pinot Noir, the latter from Chardonnay.

Ruppertsberg One of the best wine-producing towns of Germany's Rheinpfalz, or Palatinate. Its wines are perhaps slightly less distinguished than those of Forst and Deidesheim, but they are nevertheless remarkable – full-bodied, ripe, and rich – and the finest Rieslings, from the best estates, are great wines in every sense of the word. These come from such vineyards as Hoheburg, Gaisböhl, Reiterpfad, Spiess, and Nussbien, all of which are part of the Grosslage Deidesheimer Hofstück.

Rural Method An ancient and difficult way of making sparkling wines by bottling the fermenting must before fermentation is complete, thus trapping a light sparkle in the bottle; since fermentation produces sediment as well as carbon-dioxide gas, such wines are bound to be cloudy. A few French sparkling wines are still produced in this way in Gaillac and Limoux (Vin de Blanquette, not Blanquette de Limoux), and one version of Clairette de Die is made by a variation of the *méthode rurale* that involves filtering the must before bottling and, after fermentation has continued in the bottle, emptying the bottles under pressure, filtering the sparkling wine, and rebottling it.

Russia More than 3 million acres of vineyards produce about 370 million cases of wine a year, which makes Russia the third biggest wine producer in the world, surpassed only by Italy and France. Most of the country's vineyards have been planted in the past 40 years as the government has attempted to promote wine as an alternative to vodka. Russia's production consists, for the most part, of sweet, fortified wines in the style of port and sherry, and much of the rest is made up of semisweet table wines and sparkling wines. The principal wine regions of Russia are Moldavia, west of Odessa; the Ukraine, which includes Crimea; Georgia; the republic of Russia, an extensive region that lies between the Ukraine and Georgia; and to the east, the republics of Azerbaijan and Armenia. Wines are produced primarily from indigenous grape varieties and from varieties associated with eastern Europe, such as Feteasca and Rkatsiteli; such traditional European varieties as Chardonnay, Cabernet Sauvignon, Sauvignon Blanc, and Riesling are also cultivated. Russia imports considerably more wine than it exports, and its wines are infrequently encountered outside the country.

Russian River Valley Like many California rivers, the Russian River is a not-too-impressive stream that nevertheless includes Mendocino County and the northern half of Sonoma County in its basin. It runs north-south for most of its course, which includes the Ukiah Valley in Mendocino and the Alexander Valley in northern Sonoma, then cuts abruptly west to the Pacific, some 50 miles north of San Francisco. The Russian River Valley viticultural area, however, is limited to that part of the river's course from Healdsburg west to Guerneville, plus an extensive region east and south of the river, about 10,000 acres of vineyards in all. This area, which has a particularly cool climate, is noted for fine sparkling wines produced from Chardonnay and Pinot Noir, as well as for a range of still wines made from Chardonnay and Pinot Noir, Sauvignon Blanc, Gewürztraminer, and, from somewhat warmer zones, Cabernet Sauvignon and Zinfandel. The smaller Green Valley and Chalk Hill viticultural areas are included within the Russian River Valley appellation. Sonoma-Cutrer, Iron Horse, De Loach, Mark West, Domaine Laurier, Dehlinger, and Korbel are situated there.

Rutherford Bench A name increasingly used, albeit unofficially, for a three-mile section of the Napa Valley, from just north of Rutherford to just south of Oakville, which contains some of the area's finest Cabernet Sauvignon vineyards; their deep, well-drained soils produce wines that are especially rich and long-lived. Included in this district are Martha's Vineyard and Bella Oaks (whose wines are produced by Heitz Cellars), Bosché (produced by Freemark Abbey), and vineyards belonging to Beaulieu Vineyard, Inglenook, Robert Mondavi, Far Niente, Pine Ridge, and Joseph Phelps, among others.

Ruwer A small tributary of the Moselle, which it joins some four miles east of Trier, looking much more like a trout stream than a famous river. Its wines are legally Moselles, and their labels carry the regional designation Mosel-Saar-Ruwer; there are fewer than 500 acres of vineyards in the whole valley, virtually all Riesling, planted on preposterously steep, black-slate, south-facing hillsides. Thin and tart in lesser years, Ruwer wines can nevertheless achieve greatness in fine vintages and are very close in quality and character to those of the Saar – delicate, elegant, flowery, and racy. Two estates, each dominating a tiny village, are internationally known – the Karthäuserhofberg in Eitelsbach and Maximin Grünhaus in Mertesdorf. Very good, somewhat lighter wines are made in the villages of Kasel, Avelsbach, and Waldrach.

❦ S

Saar A small river in Germany, a tributary of the Moselle which it joins at Konz, just west of Trier; it rises in the Saar Basin, famous for its heavy industry, then, farther downstream, near the frontier of France and Luxembourg, runs through a steep valley no less famous for its wines. Legally these are Moselles, and their labels carry the designation Mosel-Saar-Ruwer; nevertheless, they have a special character of their own, being austere, almost steely, very pale, low in alcohol, and remarkable for their bouquet. Made primarily from the Riesling grape in one of the coldest wine-growing areas of the world, they are tart and green in all except good vintage years, and are often converted into *Sekt*, or sparkling wine; but when growing conditions are right, Saar wines are altogether extraordinary, fully the equals of any other white wines on earth. The leading wine-producing towns are Ayl, Kanzem, Oberemmel, Ockfen, Saarburg, Serrig, and Wiltingen; all of the Saar vineyards, nearly 4,000 acres in all, are included in the single Grosslage Wiltinger Scharzberg, *not* to be confused with the Scharzhofberg vineyard, considered the best single site in the Saar district.

Saar-Ruwer A Bereich, one of four in the Mosel-Saar-Ruwer region, that includes all the vineyards in the Saar and Ruwer districts, about 4,300 acres in all; the Bereich has two Grosslagen, Kaseler Römerlay for Ruwer wines, and Wiltinger Scharzberg for wines from the Saar.

Saccharomyces The principal yeasts of wine fermentation.

Sack A term used in Elizabethan England for a sweet, fortified wine, most often sherry, although there are references to Málaga sack and Canary sack as well. The word derives from the Spanish *sacar*, one of whose meanings is a wine destined for export. Dry Sack is a proprietary brand name for a medium-sweet sherry.

Sacramental Wine Mass wine or altar wine, made in accordance with the strict church regulations governing purity, naturalness, and alcohol content.

Saint-Amour The northernmost of the important wine-producing communes of France's Beaujolais region, and officially ranked as one of the ten best; the wine is popular, perhaps because of its romantic name, but on the whole it deserves its rank and its fame: it is a fruity, supple red wine, soon ready.

Saint-Aubin A small wine-producing village on Burgundy's Côte de Beaune, situated behind Chassagne-Montrachet and

Puligny-Montrachet; it produces an average of 30,000 cases a year – two thirds red – and both the red and white wines are charming and agreeable, if somewhat lighter than those of its more famous neighbours.

Saint-Bris   *See* Sauvignon de Saint-Bris

Saint-Chinian   A red wine produced near Béziers, in the Hérault *département* of southern France, and similar in style to those from the neighbouring, and somewhat-better-known vineyards of Faugères; the wine was elevated from VDQS to *Appellation Contrôlée* in 1982.

Saint-Emilion   An ancient and wonderfully picturesque little town, rich in ruins and medieval buildings, set on the edge of an escarpment overlooking the Dordogne Valley, some 25 miles east of Bordeaux. It was already famous for its wines in the fourth century, and today its 12,000 acres of vineyards produce more than 3 million cases of red wine in abundant vintages; although the Médoc district produces more than twice as much wine, it is marketed with several different appellations (Médoc, Pauillac, Margaux, etc.), and consequently, more fine wine is sold with the appellation Saint-Emilion than any other in the Bordeaux region. Most of the best vineyards are in the township of Saint-Emilion itself, but seven adjoining communes are also entitled to the appellation. The producers also make a distinction between the steep, chalky slopes of the escarpment itself, known as the Côtes, and the high, gravelly plateau that is contiguous to the Pomerol district and is known as Graves-Saint-Emilion; Châteaux Cheval Blanc and Figeac are the best vineyards of the Graves-Saint-Emilion (which is *not* an appellation), and almost all the other top vineyards are in the Côtes. Because Cabernet Sauvignon, the classic grape of the Médoc region, does not always ripen in the cooler clay soils of Saint-Emilion, its vineyards are planted primarily with Merlot and Cabernet Franc (known locally as Bouchet), and with lesser amounts of Malbec (known locally as Pressac); Cabernet Sauvignon is planted in those parts of the district that have gravelly soils (notably, of course, Graves-Saint-Emilion). The preponderance of Merlot results in warm, generous wines that are naturally softer and more supple than those of the Médoc, and quicker to mature; the greatest wines, of course, are among the very best of Bordeaux, and long-lived as well.

The top vineyards of Saint-Emilion were first classified in 1955 (and again in 1969 and 1985 – a current list will be found on page 542), but the categories are somewhat different from those of the more famous 1855 classification of the wines of the Médoc. The top dozen châteaux of Saint-Emilion (reduced to eleven in 1985) are all called *premiers grands crus classés*, whereas there are only four such wines in the Médoc; in practice, only Châteaux Ausone and Cheval Blanc are considered on a par with the *premiers crus*, or first growths, of the Médoc, and the others are equal in quality to the best of the *crus classés*, or classed growths. There is also a second category of Saint-Emilion vineyards that may call themselves *grands crus classés*, and this group now includes 63 châteaux. Only a few of these are equal to the *crus classés* of the Médoc, and many are no better than the *crus bourgeois*. Finally, a third category was established of wines known as *grands crus*; this is not a classification at all, and permission to label a wine *grand cru* is granted on a year-by-year basis after the wines are sampled by a local commission. In a good vintage, 200 châteaux may achieve *grand cru* status, and these vineyards account for about a third of the total Saint-Emilion crop.

In addition to the basic and extensive appellation Saint-Emilion, there are four so-called satellite appellations from adjoining communes whose wines may be marketed with the name Saint-Emilion added to their own: Montagne-Saint-Emilion (which includes the wines formerly sold as Parsac-Saint-Emilion), Saint-Georges-Saint-Emilion (whose wines may also be sold as Montagne-Saint-Emilion), Lussac-Saint-Emilion, and Puisseguin-Saint-Emilion; the wines formerly entitled to the appellation Sables-Saint-Emilion are now sold as Saint-Emilion. These communes produce more than 1.5 million cases of wine, much of it sound, agreeable, and often good value.

In the Cognac region of France, Saint-Emilion is the local name for the Ugni Blanc grape, which now accounts for virtually all of the wine produced for distillation; the grape is productive, resistant to disease, and yields exactly what is required – a wine low in alcohol and high in acid.

Saint-Estèphe The northernmost of the major wine-producing townships of the Haut-Médoc district of Bordeaux, directly adjoining Pauillac; its 2,700 acres of vineyards produce about 500,000 to 700,000 cases a year of sturdy, full-bodied, firm, and long-lived red wines that are generally the slowest-maturing of all the Médocs. There are five classed growths in Saint-Estèphe – Châteaux Cos d'Estournel, Montrose, Calon-Ségur, Lafon-Rochet, and Cos Labory – and a great many other vineyards as well; some of the best of these châteaux are de Pez, de Marbuzet, Meyney, Phélan-Ségur, and Les Ormes de Pez.

Saint-Georges-Saint-Emilion One of the satellite appellations of Saint-Emilion, from the adjoining commune of Saint-Georges; its agreeable red wines may be sold under this name or as Montagne-Saint-Emilion.

Saint-Joseph An appellation of the northern Rhône Valley, created in 1956, for red and white wines produced in a district that extends for 35 miles on the west bank of the river, across from Hermitage. The red wine, which accounts for 90 percent of the total of nearly 200,000 cases, is made from the Syrah grape; it is an agreeable wine, lighter and more accessible than those from Hermitage or Cornas.

Saint-Julien A township in the very heart of the Médoc district of Bordeaux whose 1,900 acres of vineyards produce as much as 500,000 cases in abundant years. The excellent and dependable red wines of Saint-Julien, which have been called the perfect claret, are a little fuller than those of Margaux, softer and more supple than the Saint-Estèphes, and quicker to mature than Pauillacs. Eleven of its vineyards are classed growths, including Châteaux Ducru-Beaucaillou, Beychevelle, the three Léovilles, Gruaud Larose, and Talbot.

Saint-Laurent A township just west of Saint-Julien whose wines are entitled to the appellation Haut-Médoc; it is the home of three classed growths, Châteaux La Tour Carnet, Belgrave, and Camensac.

Saint Macaire A small district in the Bordeaux region, about 35 miles southeast of the city of Bordeaux, within the larger Entre-Deux-Mers district; it produces about 30,000 cases a year of semi-sweet white wines entitled to the appellation Côtes de Bordeaux-Saint Macaire.

Saint-Nicholas-de-Bourgueil A distinctive red wine made around the village of that name, in the Touraine region of the Loire Valley, from the Cabernet Franc grape, and similar in its fruity, agreeable, and berry-like style to the wines of Bourgueil and Chinon.

Saint-Péray A white wine of the northern Rhône Valley, produced around the village of that name, opposite Valence, on the west bank of the river. The light, agreeable dry wine is made primarily from the Marsanne grape, with some Roussanne; about 20,000 cases are produced, and more than three quarters of that is transformed into a sparkling wine that is one of the better *vins mousseux* of France.

Saint-Pierre, Château A Fourth Classed Growth of Saint-Julien, in the Médoc, which had for many years been divided into two parts – Saint-Pierre-Sevaistre and Saint-Pierre-Bontemps; Henri Martin, owner of Château Gloria, gradually reassembled most of the original domain over many years, and in 1982 he made his first vintage as the owner of the reconstituted property, which produces about 8,000 cases a year of a fine, elegant wine.

Saint-Pourçain A VDQS for wines from a district around the village of Saint-Pourçain-sur-Sioule, about 20 miles northwest of Vichy, in central France, in the Allier *départment*, best known for its oak forests; the Sioule River joins the Allier, itself a tributary of the Loire. About three quarters of the annual production of 200,000 cases consists of agreeable reds and rosés made primarily from the Gamay grape; the crisp, dry white wine is made from Tresallier (the local name for the Sacy grape), Sauvignon Blanc, and others.

Saint-Romain A picturesque wine-producing village behind Meursault and Auxey-Duresses, on Burgundy's Côte de Beaune; its 330 acres produce about 25,000 cases a year, almost equally divided between red and white wines, both agreeable.

Saint-Saphorin A village along the northern shore of Lake Geneva, in the Lavaux district of the canton of Vaud, producing an attractive white wine, pale and dry, from the Chasselas grape (known locally as Dorin).

Saint-Saturnin A village in the Hérault *département* of southern France whose red and rosé wines are entitled to the regional appellation Coteaux du Languedoc, but which are more often marketed as Saint-Chinian.

Saint-Seurin-de-Cadourne An important wine-producing commune just north of Saint-Estèphe whose wines are entitled to the appellation Haut-Médoc; Châteaux Coufran, Verdignan, and Sociando-Mallet are among the *crus bourgeois* located there.

Saint-Véran An appellation, created in 1971, for white wines produced near Mâcon in southern Burgundy. Actually, it rectifies an injustice originally done to a number of villages that directly adjoin the delimited zone of Pouilly-Fuissé and that make, from the same Chardonnay grape, wines scarcely less good. Saint-Véran comprises six villages (one of which is Saint-Vérand, so spelled) adjoining Pouilly-Fuissé to the south and previously entitled to the appellation Beaujolais Blanc, and two villages on the north formerly entitled to the appellation Mâcon Blanc; average production is now 250,000 cases or more.

Saint Vincent One of the patron saints of vine growers, particularly in Burgundy, where his holiday is observed at the end of January.

Sainte-Croix-du-Mont A hilly and picturesque little district some 20 miles southeast of the city of Bordeaux, on the right bank of the Garonne, facing Sauternes and Barsac; it produces, as does the adjoining and smaller Loupiac district, fruity, golden, sweet white wines somewhat comparable to Sauternes.

Sainte-Foy-Bordeaux A small district in the Bordeaux region that adjoins Entre-Deux-Mers to the northeast; its semisweet white wines are passably good, somewhat like Monbazillac produced nearby in the Bergerac region.

Saké A Japanese rice wine usually served warm in tiny cups; because of its grain base, it is sometimes considered a beer.

Sales, Château de The biggest vineyard in the Pomerol district of Bordeaux, and owned by the same family since the mid-sixteenth century; its 115 acres produce a total of 15,000 to 20,000 cases a year of an elegant, supple wine, some of which is marketed under the second label Château Chantalouette.

Salmanazar An oversize bottle occasionally used in the Champagne region, equivalent to twelve regular bottles.

Sampigny-les-Maranges A village south of Santenay, at the extreme southern end of Burgundy's Côte d'Or, whose small production of red wine was marketed as Côte de Beaune-Villages. It is now entitled to the appellation Maranges.

San Benito A county south of San Francisco and separated from Monterey County by the Gavilan Mountain range; almost all of the region's 4,500 acres of hillside vineyards were planted by the Almadén winery, starting in the 1950s. The county contains three viticultural areas: Paicines, east of the San Benito River; Cienega Valley, west of the river; and Lime Kiln, a small district within the Cienega Valley. The Calera winery, known for its Pinot Noir, is situated in this county.

San Luis Obispo A county situated between Monterey and Santa Barbara within California's Central Coast appellation, about halfway between San Francisco and Los Angeles. Grapevines were first planted in 1797 by Franciscan missionaries, and a number of wineries were established in the late nineteenth century, but most of the vineyards in the county are of recent origin – there were only 400 acres in 1966; today, more than 7,000 acres have been planted. The principal varieties cultivated are Chardonnay, Cabernet Sauvignon, Zinfandel, Sauvignon Blanc, and Chenin Blanc. Most of the county's acreage is in the Paso Robles viticultural area, a relatively warm district most of whose vineyards are planted east of the town of Paso Robles, and around the towns of Shandon and Templeton. The cooler Edna Valley, south of the city of San Luis Obispo, is noted for its Chardonnay, Pinot Noir, and Sauvignon Blanc, as is the small Arroyo Grande Valley district near the Santa Barbara border. Edna Valley Vineyards, Meridian, Corbett Canyon, and Maison Deutz, established by the French Champagne firm, are some of the best-known wineries.

Sancerre One of the most popular dry white wines of France, produced around the village of that name, in the Loire Valley, about 120 miles south of Paris. Made from the Sauvignon Blanc grape, it has a fresh, lively acidity and an assertive, herbaceous taste with hints of blackcurrant; not surprisingly, it resembles the wines of Pouilly-Fumé, produced from the same grape only a few miles away on the opposite bank of the Loire. The best examples come, not from the township of Sancerre, but from surrounding villages, of which Bué, Chavignol, and Verdigny are especially noteworthy. In the past thirty years, Sancerre has become a great favourite in Parisian restaurants and export markets as well, and production has increased from about 70,000 cases in the 1950s to more than 900,000 cases today. Although the village of Sancerre is best known for its white wine, about 200,000 cases a year are produced from the Pinot Noir grape; the wine, which varies in colour from rosé to light red, is light-bodied and very agreeable.

Sangiovese   An excellent Italian red wine grape that is, with the Nebbiolo of Piedmont, one of that country's two finest native red varieties. The dominant grape of Tuscany, it is the principal variety in Chianti, Vino Nobile di Montepulciano, and Carmignano; and a variant of Sangiovese known as Brunello is the only variety permitted for the powerful Brunello di Montalcino. In addition, a number of Tuscan producers now make sturdy non-DOC reds from Sangiovese alone and market them with various proprietary names. Sangiovese can produce light, fresh, early maturing red wines, such as the youthful versions of Chianti, and can also be cultivated and vinified to produce some of Italy's longest-lived wines, notably Brunello. The grape is found in other parts of Italy as well, including Umbria, where it is used for Torgiano; near Bologna, where it produces Sangiovese di Romagna; near Rome, as Sangiovese di Aprilia; and in the Marches region along the Adriatic, where it is blended with Montepulciano to produce Rosso Piceno and Rosso Cònero.

Sangria   A refreshing sort of wine punch, popular in Spain in warm weather; its usual ingredients are red wine, slices of lemon and orange, sugar, and sometimes soda water. Many bottled Sangrias are now shipped from Spain, both red and white.

Sangue di Giuda   A red wine, likely to be *frizzante* and *amabile*, lightly sparkling and semisweet, produced in the Oltrepò Pavese district of Italy's Lombardy region; the name means "blood of Judas".

Sanlúcar de Barrameda   *See* Manzanilla

Santa Barbara   A county south of San Luis Obispo, and part of California's extensive Central Coast appellation. There were fewer than 100 acres of grapes in the mid-1960s, but new vineyards were established beginning in the early 1970s, and more than 9,000 acres are now planted, about three quarters with white-wine grapes. Almost all of these are in the cool Santa Maria Valley, near the San Luis Obispo border; in the Santa Ynez Valley, 20 miles to the south; and in the more recently planted Los Alamos Valley, situated between the two. Chardonnay, Johannisberg Riesling, Gewürztraminer, and Chenin Blanc are the most widely planted white varieties, along with Sauvignon Blanc; Cabernet Sauvignon and Pinot Noir are the principal red grapes.

Santa Clara A valley and county in the southern end of San Francisco Bay that takes its name from the old Spanish mission in what is now the town of Santa Clara, near San José. Almadén, Paul Masson, and Mirassou were first established in this area, and not so long ago most of the valley floor was planted with walnuts and prune orchards, and many of the foothills to the east and west were covered with vineyards. Most of these have been replaced by housing developments, and the region is now better known for the microchips produced in Silicon Valley than for grapes. Vineyards, which amounted to 2,000 acres in the late 1950s, have been reduced to 1,000 acres, and most of the vineyards and wineries are in the southern part of the county, around Gilroy and to the west of that town, in the Hecker Pass area.

Santa Cruz A county that lies along the Pacific, some 50 to 80 miles south of San Francisco and directly west of Santa Clara, with fewer than 200 acres of vineyards. It gives its name, however, to the Santa Cruz Mountains viticultural area, which lies along the border of Santa Cruz and Santa Clara counties, and also includes a part of San Mateo. The vineyards produce rich, intense wines, but there is so little acreage in this district that most of the wineries situated in the Santa Cruz Mountains also use grapes from other regions; the best-known wineries are Ridge, David Bruce, Bonny Doon, and Roudon-Smith.

Santa Maddalena An Italian DOC from the Alto Adige region, and one of its best reds – fresh, soft, fruity, appetizing, rather light in colour, but with adequate body and good balance. It is produced on the hillsides above the town of Bolzano, principally from the Schiava grape, and is quite as well known and fully as popular in Switzerland and Austria, where it is marketed as St. Magdalener, as in Italy itself.

Santa Maria Valley A viticultural area in Santa Barbara county, near the San Luis Obispo border, situated between the Santa Lucia Mountains and the San Luis Range; its cool maritime climate has made it especially suitable for Chardonnay and Pinot Noir, some of which is transformed into sparkling wine; Sauvignon Blanc, Johannisberg Riesling, and Gewürztraminer also grow well, as do Cabernet Sauvignon and Merlot in the warmer part of the valley, inland from the ocean, along the Tepusquet Mesa.

Santa Ynez Valley An L-shaped viticultural area in southern Santa Barbara county, about 20 miles south of the Santa Maria Valley, which extends from the town of Santa Ynez west to Solvang, and then north past Los Olivos. The region's 1,500 acres of vineyards are planted primarily with Chardonnay, Cabernet Sauvignon, and Sauvignon Blanc, and some wineries have achieved success with Johannisberg Riesling and Pinot Noir; principal wineries include Firestone, Zaca Mesa, Sanford, and Brander.

Santenay The southernmost village of the Côte d'Or, in Burgundy, producing about 12,000 cases a year of attractive red wines that resemble somewhat those of the adjoining commune of Chassagne-Montrachet, being rather full and soft, yet with a good deal of tannin and, occasionally, an earthy taste. The best of the *premier cru* vineyards are Les Gravières, Clos de Tavannes, and La Comme; their wines, less expensive than more famous Burgundies, are often excellent value. About 2,000 cases of white wine are produced as well, less distinguished than the red.

Saône A French river that parallels Burgundy's Côte d'Or and then flows along the eastern edge of the Mâconnais and Beaujolais regions before joining the Rhône River at Lyon.

Sardinia A large island off the west coast of Italy producing about 25 million cases a year, much of it quite ordinary and rather high in alcohol, although a number of light, fresh, appealing wines are now being made in addition to the more traditional full-bodied reds and wood-aged, sherry-like whites.

Vineyards are planted throughout the island, but most of Sardinia's wines come from the provinces of Cagliari and Oristano and are made by co-operative cellars; local grape varieties include the red Cannonau, Monica, and Giró, and the white Nuragus, Torbato, Vermentino, and Vernaccia. The principal DOC is the pale, neutral Nuragus di Cagliari; others are the light red Monica di Sardegna, the distinctive, sherry-like Vernaccia di Oristano, and a number of excellent sweet wines made from Malvasia and Moscato grapes, among them Malvasia di Cagliari and Moscato di Sorso-Sennori. Two successful crisp, dry white wines produced by modern vinification methods are Torbato di Alghero and Vermentino di Alghero from Sella & Mosca, the island's most innovative firm, which also makes an unusual sweet red fortified wine labelled Anghelu Ruju.

Sassella A small DOC zone within the Valtellina district in Italy's Lombardy region producing fine red wines from the Nebbiolo grape.

Sassicaia An excellent, almost legendary Italian red wine produced by Tenuta San Guido near Bolgheri, along the coast of Tuscany. The vineyard, planted primarily with Cabernet Sauvignon and about 10 percent of Cabernet Franc, now yields 8,000 to 10,000 cases a year of a firm, well-structured Bordeaux style of wine. The wines were first produced in the early 1950s, but it was not until the early 1970s that Sassicaia was offered to the public by the Antinori firm.

Saumur A major wine-producing area along the south bank of the Loire River, in France; although technically part of the province of Anjou, most of its wines resemble rather more those of the adjoining province of Touraine. Saumur itself is an attractive river town, with an old château and a famed cavalry school; its best vineyards are south and southeast of the town and planted almost exclusively with Chenin Blanc and Cabernet Franc grapes. Total AOC production of the Saumur district varies from 1.5 to 3 million cases, but much of this is transformed into sparkling wine, most of it by the *méthode champenoise*, and marketed as Saumur *mousseux* or Crémant de Loire. (Although Chenin Blanc is the base for the sparkling wines, some producers blend in 20 to 30 percent of Cabernet Franc, which, vinified to make a white wine, is actually softer and rounder than the more austere and acid wines made from Chenin Blanc.) The white wines are drier than those from neighbouring Anjou; the rosés are entitled to the AOC Cabernet de Saumur. The best red wines of the region, made entirely from Cabernet Franc, have the appellation Saumur-Champigny; they can be surprisingly fine, somewhere between a light Saint-Emilion and a Chinon in character.

Saussignac A minor appellation for the semisweet white wines produced near the town of Bergerac, in the Dordogne region of France.

Sauternes A celebrated district in France's Bordeaux region, known for its exceptional, sweet white wines. The officially delimited Sauternes zone, situated about 30 miles southeast of the city of Bordeaux, is comprised of five townships or communes – Preignac, Bommes, Fargues, Barsac, and Sauternes itself. The 5,000 acres of vineyards in the Sauternes district usually produce 450,000 to 500,000 cases a year (which amounts to about 1 percent of the entire Bordeaux crop), but a third of this goes to market as Barsac, whose producers may call their wines either Barsac or Sauternes. The vineyards are planted primarily with Sémillon, which makes up about 80 percent of the total, and Sauvignon Blanc, which contributes bouquet and acidity, plus a limited amount of Muscadelle. The grapes are picked late – after the harvest for red and dry white wines – when they are not only ripe but overripe, and ideally when the grapes have been partially shrivelled and their juice further concentrated by the action of *Botrytis cinerea*, a beneficial mould also known as *pourriture noble*, or "noble rot". When the juice, which now contains a high proportion of sugar, is fermented, not all of the sugar ferments into alcohol, and the result is a naturally sweet wine with about 14 percent alcohol and 5 to 8 percent residual sugar. As a result of *botrytis*, a fine Sauternes is not simply sweet, but also honeyed, concentrated and complex. The climatic conditions that cause *botrytis* do not occur every year, however, and affect only grapes that have been left on the vine beyond the normal harvest dates. Consequently, the finest Sauternes and Barsacs are produced only in the best vintages, and almost invariably come from the best vineyards, or châteaux, whose proprietors are willing to wait for *botrytis* to occur, and to send their harvesters into the vineyards not just once, but several times to pick only those bunches affected by *botrytis*. Regional bottlings, those labelled simply Sauternes or Barsac, rarely have the intensity of flavour for which these wines are famous. (The terms *Haut-Sauternes* and *Haut-Barsac*, occasionally seen on labels, have no official meaning.) The leading vineyard of Sauternes is Château d'Yquem, one of the most famous and expensive wines in the world, and officially classified as a *premier cru*, or first growth; other top châteaux include Suduiraut, Climens, Coutet, Guiraud, and Rieussec. (The wines of Sauternes were classified in 1855, along with those of the Médoc, and a listing will be found on page 541.)

There is no such thing as a dry Sauternes from France, but most producers in Sauternes and Barsac also produce a dry white wine, primarily from Sauvignon Blanc grapes, so that even when climatic conditions do not permit them to produce a sweet, botrytised wine, they still have wine to sell; such wines may be labelled only as Bordeaux or Bordeaux Supérieur. In the United States and a few other non-European countries, the name Sauterne (usually spelled without the final "s") is used for inexpensive white wines that may be dry or semisweet, and which bear no resemblance to the French original; in fact, some American producers have been known to bottle the same wine as Chablis and Sauterne. Those who do make *botrytis*-infected wines, known in America as late-harvest wines, almost always label them with the name of the grape variety from which each is made.

Sauvignon Blanc A popular white-wine grape, extensively planted in Bordeaux and along the Loire, in California, and increasingly in Australia and New Zealand. It produces wines noted for their grassy, or herbaceous, aroma and lively, even aggressive, acidity. Despite its traditional association with Bordeaux, it accounts for less than 10 percent of the white-wine vineyards of the region (Sémillon makes up half that acreage), but it adds aroma and acidity to the Sémillon-based wines of Sauternes; is the major component in many Graves, which are usually bolstered by the richer, longer-lived Sémillon; and is increasingly vinified separately and marketed as a varietal wine with a Bordeaux appellation. Sauvignon Blanc is used exclusively for the wines of Sancerre and Pouilly-Fumé (where the grape is known locally as Blanc Fumé), and for such wines as Quincy, Menetou-Salon, Sauvignon de Touraine, and Sauvignon de Saint-Bris. It is planted to some extent in northeast Italy, although not as frequently encountered as Pinot Grigio and Chardonnay. In California, Sauvignon Blanc plantings have increased from fewer than 1,000 acres in 1970 to 15,000 acres, about a third of that in Napa and Sonoma; excellent wines are also produced in the Livermore Valley, Lake County, and the Santa Ynez Valley. Throughout the 1960s, California Sauvignon Blanc was usually marketed as a semisweet wine, and some examples were even labelled Sauterne; then, in the late 1960s, Robert Mondavi produced a crisp, dry Sauvignon Blanc that he labelled Fumé Blanc, to evoke the wines of the Loire, and the variety has achieved a success second only to Chardonnay. Some California bottlings are assertive and grassy, others enriched by oak aging, and many are now made softer and more complex by blending in Sémillon, as in Bordeaux; there is no longer a clear stylistic distinction between wines labelled Sauvignon Blanc and Fumé Blanc. Australia and particularly New Zealand have produced excellent Sauvignon Blancs, although plantings are still relatively limited.

Sauvignon de Saint-Bris A crisp, lively white wine made from the Sauvignon Blanc grape in the village of Saint-Bris-le-Vineux, situated a few miles from Chablis, in northern Burgundy; the wine achieved VDQS status in 1974.

Sauvignon Vert A white-wine grape grown in limited quantities in California; unrelated to Sauvignon Blanc, it is probably the Muscadelle of Bordeaux.

Savagnin A distinguished white-wine grape grown in the Jura district of France, where it produces the unusual Château-Châlon; it is also used, along with Chardonnay, for such white wines as Côtes du Jura and Arbois.

Savennières An attractive little village some ten miles southwest of Angers, producing, from the Chenin Blanc grape, the finest dry white wines of the Coteaux de la Loire, in the Anjou region of France; the average production of this appellation, whose two most famous vineyards are Coulée de Serrant and Roche aux Moines, is about 22,000 cases a year.

Savigny-les-Beaune A little Burgundian village situated between Beaune and Aloxe-Corton in the Côte de Beaune; although not as well known as its neighbours, Savigny-les-Beaune's average annual production of 120,000 cases of red wine is about as much as is made in Beaune and Pommard. The wines are light, supple, fruity, and early maturing; never great but always agreeable, they are among the best and most dependable of the lesser red Burgundies. The *premier cru* vineyards include Les Vergelesses, Les Lavières, Les Marconnets, La Dominode, and Les Jarrons. A few thousand cases of attractive white wines are also made.

Savoie A district in eastern France, in the *départements* of Savoie and Haute-Savoie, whose scattered vineyards are situated near Lake Geneva, Aix-les-Bains, and Chambéry. About a million cases a year are entitled to the regional appellation Vin de Savoie – three quarters of this consists of crisp, light, dry white wines produced primarily from the Jacquère grape, plus some Altesse (known locally as Roussette); the light reds are made from Gamay and Mondeuse. The best-known appellations of the Savoie are Crépy and Seyssel; Roussette de Savoie is another regional appellation, and all three apply to white wines only.

Scharzhofberg One of the greatest white-wine vineyards of the world, consisting of 67 acres planted almost entirely with Riesling on an exceedingly steep, slate hillside in Wiltingen, on the Saar, in Germany. The Scharzhof is an old manor house that has belonged for several generations to the Egon Müller family, which owns the largest and best part of the vineyard. The wine is labelled simply Scharzhofberger, without reference to the village of Wiltingen (although that produced by the Hohe Domkirche, another important proprietor, is labelled Dom Scharzhofberger). Light, but with great depth of flavour, austere and yet fragrant and flowery, fresh and yet satisfying, the Scharzhofbergers of great years are not far from perfection. Note that the wine from this vineyard should not be confused with Wiltinger Scharzberg, a Grosslage that takes in the entire Saar district.

Schaumwein The lowest category of German sparkling wines, which accounts for about 10 percent of that country's sparkling-wine production; the better wines are known as Qualitätsschaumwein or, more popularly, as *Sekt*.

Scheurebe A German variety created by Georg Scheu in 1916 (*rebe* means "grape"), a cross of Sylvaner and Riesling; there were fewer than 1,000 acres in Germany as recently as the 1960s, but plantings have increased to 11,000 acres, mostly in Rheinhessen and the Rheinpfalz. The white wines, which retain a lively acidity, have a pungent bouquet reminiscent of blackcurrants; sweet, late-harvest wines can also be made from this grape, which is susceptible to *Botrytis cinerea*.

Schiava An interesting red-wine grape native to Italy's Alto Adige region, where it accounts for two thirds of the area under cultivation; generally trained on high pergolas, it gives wines that are rather light in colour, low in tannin, fresh, fragrant, and early maturing. Schiava, called Vernatsch by the German-speaking population of that region, is the principal variety in such wines as Santa Maddalena (St. Magdalener in German), Caldaro, or Lago di Caldaro (Kalterersee), and several other light-red and rosé wines produced in Alto Adige and the adjoining Trentino region.

Schillerwein A pink wine that is a speciality of the German region of Württemberg, and rarely exported; traditionally, it is made by fermenting red and white grapes together. Its name has nothing to do with the poet Schiller, but comes from the German verb *schillern*, which means "shimmer".

Schloss German for "castle"; when used for wine it is the equivalent of the French château, and means the property, its vineyards, and its wine. In some cases, notably Schloss Johannisberg and Schloss Vollrads, the term refers to a single vineyard; in many other instances, such as Schloss Schönborn and Schloss Groenesteyn, it refers to an estate comprised of several different vineyards. The word *Schloss* is also incorporated into a number of individual vineyards, such as Zeltinger Schlossberg, and regional names, such as Bereich Schloss Böckelheim.

Schloss Eltz A famous estate in Germany's Rheingau region whose 98 acres include vineyards in Eltville, Kiedrich, Rauenthal, and Rüdesheim. Although the present Count Eltz still owns the Schloss, or castle, the vineyards are now the property of the government, and since 1981 the wines have been made by the Langwerth von Simmern estate and marketed under the latter's name.

Schloss Groenesteyn An important estate in Germany's Rheingau region with 80 acres of vineyards situated in the villages of Kiedrich and Rüdesheim. Since 1640 the estate, which dates from the fourteenth century, has been in the hands of the Barons von Ritter zu Groenesteyn.

Schloss Johannisberg Germany's most famous vineyard, whose 87 acres are spectacularly situated on one of the steepest hillsides of the Rheingau region. In 1100 a Benedictine abbey was constructed on the site and dedicated to St. John the Baptist; since then the hill has been known as Johannisberg. Vines were planted at that time, but it was not until the early eighteenth century that Riesling was first planted there, and thus introduced into the Rheingau. The association of this classic variety with Johannisberg is such that the true Riesling is known as Johannisberg Riesling in California and as Johannisberger in Switzerland. When church properties were secularized in 1803, the estate passed to Prince William of Orange; the Congress of Vienna later ceded it to the emperor of Austria, and he bestowed it on Prince Clemens von Metternich in 1816. For many years the wines from this noble estate were marketed with two different labels – one reproduced the Metternich coat of arms, the other, used for better wines, bore a colour engraving of the Schloss and its vineyard. For a brief period in the early 1980s, the estate adopted a gold label depicting the castle for its Prädikat wines, and marketed its Qualitätswein under the name Domäne Clemens; starting with the 1985 vintage, all the wines have been sold with the same basic label. As in the past, different-coloured capsules are used to denote the various quality categories, such as Kabinett, Spätlese, and Auslese, but these simply conform to the appropriate designations on the label. An average of 25,000 cases a year are marketed as Schloss Johannisberg, but this varies enormously – 32,000 cases in 1982, only 5,000 in 1984. Schloss Johannisberg is one of the few German vineyards whose name may appear alone on the label, without reference to the village in which it is situated. Although the present Prince von Metternich is still involved, the property is now controlled by a group that also owns the 175-acre G. H. von Mumm estate, also in Johannisberg. Fürst von Metternich is the brand name of a *Sekt*, or sparkling wine, produced by the same group.

Schloss Reichartshausen A 7.5-acre vineyard in Germany's Rheingau region, near the town of Oestrich. Although most of the vineyard actually lies within the Einzellage Oestricher Doosberg, it has been classified as one of the few vineyards entitled to be labelled with its own name alone, without reference to that of a village (as is also the case with Schloss Vollrads and Schloss Johannisberg); it is owned by the Balthasar Ress firm.

Schloss Reinhartshausen A celebrated German wine estate in the heart of the Rheingau, between Erbach and Hattenheim, whose 168 acres of vineyard belonged to the princes of Prussia, collateral descendants of Kaiser Wilhelm, until 1987. Most of the estate's vineyards lie in Erbach (including a part of Marcobrunn) and Hattenheim, and there are also sites in Kiedrich, Rauenthal, and Rüdesheim; the two vineyards Erbacher Rheinhell and Hattenheimer Rheingarten are actually situated on the island of Mariannenau, on the Rhine. The Schloss itself, actually a large mansion, is now a hotel.

Schloss Schönborn This celebrated estate in Germany's Rheingau region has been owned by the same family since the mid-fourteenth century and gradually expanded to its present size of 185 acres. The vineyards of this extensive property, the biggest in private hands in the Rheingau, are situated in ten villages – Hattenheim, Erbach, Rauenthal, Hallgarten, Oestrich, Winkel, Johannisberg, Geisenheim, Rüdesheim, and Hochheim.

Schloss Vollrads The largest and one of the most famous vineyard estates of the Rheingau, situated above the village of Winkel and east of Schloss Johannisberg. The central tower dates from the early fourteenth century, when the Greiffenclau family first moved there, and the spendid castle was built in the seventeenth century. Sales of wine from Schloss Vollrads, whose 120 acres are now planted almost exclusively with Riesling, were first recorded in the early thirteenth century, and today these fine, elegant wines are among the most sought after of Germany. The present owner, Count Erwein Matuschka-Greiffenclau, has made a particular speciality of the drier Trocken and Halbtrocken wines in an effort to integrate his wines as part of fine dining, and in many recent vintages as much as 80 percent of his production consists of these wines. The Schloss Vollrads wines, which may be labelled with the name of the vineyard alone, without reference to the village of Winkel, are decorated with different-coloured capsules for the various quality categories – green for Qualitätswein, blue for Kabinett, pink for Spätlese, white for Auslese, and gold for Beerenauslese and Trockenbeerenauslese. For the first four categories, two gold bands on the capsule indicate that the wine is finer, richer, and sweeter than one without that distinction, and for the Qualitätswein, Kabinett, and Spätlese categories, two silver bands indicate that the wine is a drier Trocken or Halbtrocken. Since 1979 Count Matuschka-Greiffenclau has leased the Fürst Löwenstein vineyards, whose 45 acres are in the nearby village of Hallgarten; the wines are vinified and bottled at Schloss Vollrads.

Schlossböckelheim One of the top wine-producing villages in Germany's Nahe region, situated upstream and southwest of Bad Kreuznach; its top vineyards include the 35-acre Kupfergrube, owned primarily by the State Domain of Nahe, and Felsenberg. Confusingly, the village also gives its name to the Bereich Schloss Böckelheim (usually spelled as two words), which encompasses the southern part of the Nahe region, as well as to the Grosslage Schlossböckelheimer Burgweg, which includes the wines produced in nine villages.

Schramsberg A Napa Valley winery originally established in the nineteenth century and revived in 1965 by Jack Davies, who was the first to specialize in *méthode champenoise* sparkling wines made primarily from Chardonnay and Pinot Noir, as in France's Champagne region. The winery's selection of distinctive and complex sparkling wines includes Blanc de Blancs, Blanc de Noirs, a Reserve bottling that is aged for four years, a rosé labelled Cuvée de Pinot, and Crémant, a semisweet wine made primarily from the Flora grape.

Schwarze Katz *See* Zell

Scuppernong One of the Muscadine grapes, originally wild, now cultivated to some extent in the southeast United States; wine has been made from its grapes since early colonial days. It is not a proper wine grape, however, and the result – pungent, aromatic, sweet, and unusual – is not to everyone's taste.

Sec French for "dry"; with respect to wine, the opposite of sweet. A notable exception is in the case of champagne, where a wine labelled Sec is anything but dry and, with 1.7 to

3.5 percent sugar, considerably sweeter than one labelled Brut or Extra Dry. Sweet champagne has been considered unfashionable for well over a century, and even those who prefer it seem to accept it more readily when it comes to them disguised as its opposite.

Secco An Italian word meaning "dry"; when applied to wine, the opposite of *abboccato, amabile,* or *dolce.*

Séché A French term applied to wines that have lost their freshness and fruit, usually through excessive aging in barrel; its literal meaning is "dried", although withered is perhaps a more accurate translation.

Seco Spanish for "dry"

Sediment The deposit that most red wines tend to throw as they age in bottle; it is as natural a part of an old wine as the shell is part of an egg. It should not be confused with cloudiness, haziness, or lack of clarity, any of which often indicate that a wine is not fit to drink. Sediment is not a defect in any sense; it is a sign of bottle age, and a fine red wine that claims to be old and has no trace of any sediment may well be regarded with suspicion. The sediment, which sometimes forms a mask or crust along the inside of the bottle, is composed primarily of tannins and colour pigments that combine and precipitate out of solution; it is for this reason that red wines become lighter in colour and less harsh in taste as they age. Sediment should settle fairly rapidly if a bottle is disturbed, and such wines should always be decanted to separate the harmless but bitter-tasting sediment from the wine. Sediment can occur in white wines, too, usually in the form of colourless crystals of potassium bitartrate, or cream of tartar, which is the base of baking powder; these are precipitated by cold and, while tasteless and harmless, are admittedly unattractive in a wine glass. The crystals are occasionally found sticking to the bottom of the cork of both red and white wines that are bottled young, and are sometimes mistakenly thought to be sugar crystals.

Seedling Almost all vines are propagated from cuttings that are planted in a nursery and take root. A seedling, on the other hand, comes directly from a grape seed, and except under controlled conditions, its precise ancestry can hardly be known.

Seeweine The name given to a collection of rather unimportant wines produced along the northern, or German, shore of Lake Constance (known in German as the Bodensee). These include several whites made from Müller-Thurgau and Ruländer (Pinot Gris), and the locally famous Weissherbst, a pale rosé made from Spätburgunder (Pinot Noir).

Seibel The French hybridizer Albert Seibel created a number of new varieties in the late nineteenth century, among them the French-American hybrids now known as Aurora, Cascade, Chancellor, Chelois, and DeChaunac.

Sekt The German term for sparkling wine, and more widely used than the official term Qualitätsschaumwein; nearly 25 million cases a year of *Sekt* are produced in Germany, about 90 percent of it by the Charmat method. Sparkling wines labelled simply *Sekt* are made from base wines that invariably include neutral white wines from other Common Market countries, notably Italy and France; sparkling wines made entirely from grapes grown in Germany may be labelled *Deutscher Sekt*. Some German sparkling wines are made from Riesling, and so labelled; and a small proportion, labelled Deutscher Sekt bA, comes entirely from one or another of Germany's eleven Anbaugebiete, or specified wine regions. *Sekt* tends to be fruitier and not quite as dry as the sparkling wines made in France and Spain. Leading producers – and their brands – include Deinhard Lila Imperial, Henkell Trocken, Kupferberg Gold, Söhnlein Rheingold, and Fürst von Metternich.

Sélection de Grains Nobles This designation, officially established in 1983, is used in France's Alsace region for sweet, honeyed wines produced in very limited quantities in the best vintages from grapes affected by *Botrytis cinerea*. Only wines made from one of the top four Alsace varieties are eligible, and only if the juice contains a minimum natural sugar content equal to that of a German Beerenauslese – 27.9 percent for Gewürztraminer and Pinot Gris, 25.6 percent for Riesling and Muscat d'Alsace. Production of these special wines has increased from 8,500 cases in 1983 to 37,000 cases in 1988 and 100,000 cases in the excellent 1989 vintage; even so, the last figure represents less than 1 percent of the total Alsace crop.

Sémillon An excellent white-wine grape, widely grown in southwestern France, to some extent in California, and extensively in Australia and Chile. It usually gives its best results when blended with another variety, especially Sauvignon Blanc; alone, the wine has definite character and considerable class, but is often low in acid and may lack freshness and fruit. Sémillon is the principal variety in Sauternes, where it is susceptible to *Botrytis cinerea*, which shrivels the grapes and results in rich, honeyed, sweet wines. It is also an important component of Graves and Bordeaux Blanc, with Sauvignon Blanc adding aroma and lively acidity, as it does in Sauternes. There are nearly 2,500 acres of Sémillon in California, where it is most often used as a blending wine to soften Sauvignon Blanc; a few producers also market Sémillon on its own as a varietal wine. In Washington, curiously enough, Sémillon takes on some of the grassiness and acidity more often associated with Sauvignon Blanc. Sémillon is widely planted in Australia, where it is third to Chardonnay and to Rhine Riesling among the leading white wine varieties; some of that country's most famous wines are the richly textured, long-lived Sémillons from the Hunter Valley (where the wine has long been called Hunter River Riesling). A number of Australian producers now blend their Sémillon with Chardonnay, which contributes freshness and acidity, as Sauvignon Blanc does in Bordeaux. The vineyards of Chile are extensively planted with Sémillon, although few wines go to market as such; much of what was once shipped as Chilean Riesling or Rhine Wine was actually made primarily from Sémillon.

Sénéjac, Château A well-known vineyard in the Haut-Médoc district producing about 7,000 cases a year of sound, dependable wine.

Sercial The driest style of Madeira, usually served chilled as an aperitif.

Serpette The French name for a special pruning knife with a sharp, hooked tip, used for light pruning and for picking grapes at vintage time.

Serrig One of the highest and coldest villages along the Saar River, in Germany. Its 200 acres of vineyards yield a few Riesling wines of fine quality, but only in exceptionally good vintages; in most years the wines – tart, pale, and low in alcohol

– are used for *Sekt*, or sparkling wine.

Serving So much pretentious etiquette, not to say ritual, has come to surround the service of wine that many eager potential wine drinkers become frightened and discouraged at the start. Rules do exist, of course, but the most useful ones are based on common sense, and it is safe to say that any person of taste would discover these for himself or herself in the course of a month of daily wine drinking. Thus, the host (or, in a restaurant, whichever person selected the wine) is served first so that he or she can sniff or taste the wine and be sure that it is good before it is offered to the others. White wines and rosés are chilled for the simple reason that ninety-nine people out of a hundred find them more refreshing and agreeable when so served. When several wines are served at a meal, which is not often these days, the proper sequence may pose a problem, but here, too, common sense will help: a less good wine should precede a better one, a lighter wine should precede a richer, fuller one (in both instances, to avoid anti-climax); a dry white wine is served before a red, just as a light appetizer or fish course precedes the more flavourful meat course; and sweet wines belong at the end of the meal, not the beginning, just as do chocolate cake and strawberry tart. One so-called rule that has been considerably amended in recent years is white with fish and white meat, red with red meat and cheese. The combination of innovative cuisines that freely mix ingredients and a more casual attitude about wine has resulted in a more flexible and experimental approach to matching wine and food. Much additional information on this subject will be found elsewhere in this volume. *See* Breathing, Corkscrew, Cradle, Chambrer, Decanting, Glasses, Ice Bucket, Temperature, and the discussion of food and wine on page 521.

Set A vineyardist refers to the crop in prospect, once the vine's flowering is over and the grape berries have begun to form, as the set.

Settling *See* Débourbage

Setúbal *See* Moscatel de Setúbal

Sève French for "sap"; as applied to wine, it means vigour and character.

Sèvre-et-Maine An extensive district that spreads out east of Nantes, in the lower Loire Valley, in which 70 to 85 percent of the Muscadet crop is produced. Such wines are entitled to the appellation Muscadet de Sèvre-et-Maine to differentiate them from the perhaps less-good wines labelled simply Muscadet or Muscadet des Coteaux de la Loire, the latter produced farther up the Loire.

Seyssel An interesting white wine, pale, fresh, light, and dry, produced around the little town of this name on the Rhône River, in the Savoie region of eastern France, from the Altesse grape (known locally as Roussette); about a third of the annual production of 35,000 cases is transformed into an excellent *mousseux*, or sparkling wine, from a blend that usually includes the local Molette grape.

Seyval Blanc A French-American hybrid created by the French hybridizer Seyve-Villard and widely planted in the United States; although second to Aurora in acreage among all hybrid varieties, it is increasingly marketed as a varietal wine. The grape produces a fresh, crisp white wine that reminds some consumers of a mild Sauvignon Blanc; a number of producers use oak aging to make a richer, longer-lived wine.

Sfursat An unusual red wine, also known as Sforzato, made from the Nebbiolo grape in the Valtellina district of Italy's Lombardy region. After the harvest, specially selected bunches are spread out indoors for several weeks to dehydrate before being crushed; the resulting wine, which must have a minimum of 14.5 percent alcohol, is a dry, sturdy, full-bodied red similar in style to the Amarone of Valpolicella.

Shenandoah Valley A viticultural area in California's Amador County, about 40 miles east of Sacramento, known primarily for its intensely flavoured Zinfandels; Sauvignon Blanc, Cabernet Sauvignon, and Chardonnay are also planted. This district, which includes almost all of the grape acreage in Amador County, is actually a collection of hills and valleys, and some of its vineyards are planted at an elevation of 1,200 feet. The Shenandoah Valley appellation may also be used for a viticultural area in Virginia.

Sherry Originally and correctly, a fortified wine from a delimited district in southern Spain, around the city of Jerez de la

Frontera, in the region of Andalusia; the wine ranges in style from pale gold and bone dry to dark brown and quite sweet. Sherry is an anglicized version of Jerez, and is known in France as Xérès; in fact, the official *Denominación de Origen* for this region is Jerez-Xérès-Sherry. The sherry vineyards, which encompass about 46,000 acres and produce about 15 million cases of wine a year, lie mostly north, west, and southwest of the town of Jerez, within a triangle formed by Jerez, Sanlúcar de Barrameda, and Puerto de Santa Maria; the traditional best districts, or *pagos* (the names of which almost never appear on sherry labels) are Macharnudo, Carrascal, Añina, Balbaina, and Los Tercios. The geographical location of the vineyards is less important to the quality of the wines than the type of soil in which the vines are grown. The best and least productive is known as *albariza*, a hard white soil containing a large proportion of chalk, which gives wines of exceptional bouquet and finesse; *barro*, or clay, is browner in colour, more fertile, and yields larger crops of generally fuller-bodied wine; and *arena*, or sand, gives the highest yield of all, but the wines have much less substance and character. The principal grape variety is Palomino, which accounts for about 90 percent of the plantings; the Pedro Ximénez grape gives an admirable, sweet, heavy wine used in blending; and the Moscatel grape still produces a limited amount of sweet blending wines.

The *vendimia*, or harvest, usually takes place in mid-September and is eminently worth seeing – there are numerous *fiestas*, and the whole operation is very picturesque. In the past, the grapes were brought to the press houses on donkey-back, sorted by hand, and set out on straw mats to dry for a few hours in the sun (a technique still used for Pedro Ximénez grapes); they were then placed in *lagares*, shallow stone troughs, and trodden by workers wearing special cleated boots. Once the free-run juice was drawn off, the pomace was stacked, wound round with bands of esparto grass, and pressed. Today, of course, modern equipment is used to transport, crush, and press the grapes, which are fermented in large temperature-controlled tanks. All sherry begins as a clean, neutral, dry white wine, and the finished wine owes most of its character and a good deal of its quality to the way it is matured after fermentation is complete.

The traditional way of producing sherry until the 1970s was to put all the wines into 630-litre *botas*, or butts, which were not completely filled; the deliberate exposure of the wine to air was the first step in the production of sherry. After a few months, the wines were classified, barrel by barrel, into one of two broad categories – finos and olorosos. Those wines that developed *flor*, a white film of yeast cells that floats on the surface of the wine, were classed as finos and were lightly fortified to about 15.5 percent alcohol; those that did not develop *flor* were classed as olorosos and fortified to 18 percent or so, which prevents spoilage and also prevents *flor* from developing at a later time. Today, the separation of wines into finos and olorosos takes place when the wines are pressed: the light, delicate wines produced from the first pressing will be transformed into finos; the fuller-bodied wines from subsequent pressings will be used for olorosos. When these wines are transferred into barrels, a few months after the vintage, the potential olorosos are fortified and put into barrels that are completely filled; the lighter wines selected to be finos are put into incompletely filled barrels, as in the past, so that *flor* can develop. (*Flor* can now be successfully induced by storing the potential finos in special *bodegas* whose temperature and humidity are carefully controlled. Even in the past, although there was always some uncertainty as to whether or not a particular barrel would develop *flor*, it was not quite so mysterious and unpredictable as it was sometimes made out to be: the sherry producers knew that the soil and location of a vineyard, the age of the vines, whether the grapes are picked early or late, and certain vinification techniques all played a role in the eventual development of *flor*.) *Flor*, which means "flower", is indigenous to the sherry region, the nearby Montilla region, and the Château-Châlon district of France's Jura region. Essential in the production of fine dry sherry – *flor* prevents oxidation while adding complexity to the wine – it is a sort of white film that may take on the appearance of cottage cheese or may become a thin, pebbly white crust on the wine's surface; it has an odd, rather agreeable, appetizing odour that has been compared to the smell of fresh warm bread, and wines on which it has worked have an altogether special character and flavour. Finos are light, elegant wines with a fine bouquet, and the best of them are considered exceptionally fine aperitif wines. As finos age, some are reclassified as amontillados; these are fortified to 17 percent alcohol to inhibit *flor*, and in time become darker and richer, and develop a nutty taste. Finos that are matured in the *bodegas*, or warehouses, of Sanlúcar de Barrameda, near the Atlantic, develop into manzanillas, austerely dry sherries characterized by a special tang. Olorosos are fuller-bodied, heavier wines, with less bouquet than finos; they form the basis of the popular cream sherries.

Within a year or so of the harvest, each barrel is assigned to a particular *criadera*, or nursery, which in turn feeds a specific *solera*, the system by which wines of the same type and quality but of different ages are fractionally and progressively blended as they mature, thus maintaining a continuity of style year after year. A *solera* can be visualized as, say, six rows of barrels stacked one above the other; when wines from the lowest row are drawn out – perhaps a quarter or a third of the contents of each barrel – they are replaced by slightly younger wines from the next row; those from the second row are replaced by wines from the third row, and so on back to the *criadera*, which contains the youngest wines of all. Thus, at each stage the younger wines "refresh" the older ones, which in turn "educate" the younger ones, and the final wine of a *solera* consists of small fractions of wines of anywhere from half-a-dozen to fifty or more different vintages. The *solera* system is much more complicated in practice, and not as schematic; each row, called a scale, may consist of hundreds of barrels, and the scales are not necessarily piled up one upon the other, but stored in several different *bodegas*; the wines drawn from the lowest scale may be used as the youngest wines of another, older *solera*; and, in some cases, a third of the contents of a *solera* may be drawn off four or five times a year without affecting its style and quality. The word *solera* is derived from the Spanish *suelo*, which means "floor" and, technically speaking, only the lowest scale, containing the oldest wines, is actually the *solera*; however, the term is generally used to refer to the entire collection of barrels back to the *criadera*.

The sherries that are put on the market are almost never wines drawn from the final stage of any single *solera* – they are blends of these blends, finished, where appropriate, by the addition of sweetening and colouring wines. The best finos are completely dry (inexpensive brands are often slightly sweetened) and lightly fortified to 16 or 17 percent alcohol before bottling. Amontillados and olorosos are also completely dry as they age in their respective *soleras*, but rarely marketed as such; amontillados are usually darker-coloured, medium-dry sherries; and cream sherries, almost

all of which are made from olorosos, are sweetened to 12 to
14 percent sugar with Pedro Ximénez, *mistela* (sweet, fortified Palomino grape juice), or concentrated grape juice, and
fortified to about 19 percent alcohol. Since sherry is a
blended wine, and more often than not a blend of blends, it
follows that there are at least as many sherries of any given
type as there are shippers. Cream sherries and most finos are
so labelled, but many medium-sweet amontillados are not;
in any case, most of the sherry business is based on proprietary brands such as Bristol Cream, Dry Sack, Tio Pepe, and
La Ina. Dry sherries should be kept in the refrigerator and
served chilled, like any white wine, and all sherries are best
enjoyed in a proper wine glass, rather than the small,
v-shaped glass that has unfortunately become associated
with this wine.

Wines called sherry have been produced in other
countries, especially Australia, South Africa, and the United
States, for well over a hundred years. A small percentage of
these, made, blended, and aged as sherry is in Spain, and
using some variation of the *flor* process, are surprisingly
good. But much of what is produced in the United States is
made from neutral white wines that are baked at high temperatures (a technique actually used to produce Madeira),
sweetened with grape concentrate, fortified with high-proof
spirits, and marketed with only a year or two of age.

Shiraz The Australian name for the Syrah of France's Rhône Valley, also known there as Hermitage, although the latter
usage is declining to conform to Common Market requirements. (Hermitage is, of course, the name of a famous
French vineyard.) Shiraz is the most widely planted red
variety in Australia and produces a great deal of sound red
wine, the best examples of which are full-bodied, well-
structured, and capable of aging; in fact, Grange Hermitage,
a wine made by Penfolds from Shiraz, is perhaps Australia's
most famous and expensive wine, and one of the longest-
lived. Many winemakers also use Shiraz to soften the tannic
austerity of Cabernet Sauvignon, as Merlot does in Bordeaux and California, and some of Australia's most popular
red wines are Cabernet-Shiraz blends.

Short A taster's term applied to a wine lacking persistence, or
length of flavour; a good wine is never short and should have
some echoes of taste after it is swallowed.

Shot Berries   Small, seedless berries sometimes found in a bunch of otherwise normal wine grapes; these are the result of incomplete pollination at the time of flowering, a problem called *millerandage* in French.

Sicily   The largest island in the Mediterranean, whose annual production of 100 to 130 million cases regularly places it among the top three regions of Italy in volume. Historically, its most famous wine is the fortified, amber-coloured Marsala, which may be dry or sweet. In the past, Sicily's heavy, high-alcohol table wines were shipped in bulk to northern Italy and other countries, where they were blended with wines lacking body and alcohol. In recent years, new vineyards have been planted on cooler mountain slopes, rather than in the hot plains, and winemaking has been vastly improved by the use of new techniques and modern equipment, especially in the co-operative cellars that account for 80 percent of the island's production. The result is that many of Sicily's table wines, most of which are white, are now clean, fresh, and light-bodied. Corvo, a proprietary brand for red and white wines produced near Casteldaccia, is a particularly successful example of this transformation; the wines from the Regaleali estate have also re-established themselves. Neither is a DOC wine and, in fact, most of the DOC zones of Sicily produce limited quantities of sweet dessert wines. The best-known are Moscato di Pantelleria, from an island between Sicily and Tunisia, and Malvasia delle Lipari, from a group of islands north of Sicily. Other DOC wines, all of them dry, include Alcamo, or Bianco d'Alcamo, a white wine from vineyards around that village, in the western part of the island; Etna, which encompasses red, rosé, and a very small amount of white produced on the lower slopes of Mount Etna; and Faro, a red wine from the northeastern tip of the island. The principal grape varieties cultivated in Sicily for its dry table wines are Inzolia, Catarratto, and some Trebbiano for the whites and, for the reds, Nerello Mascalese, Perricone, and Nero d'Avola.

Sick   A sick wine is a bad wine, almost always cloudy, usually with a bouquet that is odd, unfamiliar, and unpleasant, and a flavour that is definitely off. Fortunately, very few such wines ever reach the consumer.

Sierra Foothills   A California viticultural area, southeast of Sacramento, that extends along the western foothills of the Sierra Nevada Mountains and includes parts of eight counties, of which the most important are Amador, El Dorado, and Calaveras. Site of the 1849 Gold Rush, the region has seen a revival of interest in vineyards since the late 1960s; Zinfandel accounts for two thirds of the region's crop, which also includes Sauvignon Blanc, Chardonnay, Chenin Blanc, and Cabernet Sauvignon.

Sigalas Rabaud, Château A classed growth in the Sauternes district, the smaller part of what was originally Château Rabaud (the other part is now known as Château Rabaud-Promis); its 35 acres produce about 3,000 cases a year of an elegant and stylish sweet wine.

Silky A term applied to wines that are notably smooth and fine-textured.

Simard, Château A well-known vineyard in Saint-Emilion producing about 7,000 cases a year of a popular and dependable *grand cru* wine.

Simmern, Langwerth von A celebrated 110-acre estate in the Rheingau whose wines are among the very best of that region, and whose richly decorated label is one of the most famous in Germany. The estate, owned by the barons Langwerth von Simmern since the fifteenth century, includes vineyards in Eltville, Rauenthal, Erbach, and Hattenheim.

Sion An interesting and picturesque little town, capital of the Swiss canton of Valais, set down in the high, rocky, narrow upper valley of the Rhône, not far from its source, in southwestern Switzerland. The wines produced around Sion – that is, the wines of the Valais – include fresh, light dry whites made from the Chasselas grape (known locally as Fendant); attractive reds known as Dôle, made from Pinot Noir and Gamay; and the white Johannisberg, which may be made from Riesling or Sylvaner.

Siran, Château A well-known vineyard in Margaux, in the Médoc, whose 60 acres produce about 9,000 cases of a rich, elegant wine.

Sitges A village along the Mediterranean coast of Spain, south of Barcelona, in the Penedès region; its once-famous sweet dessert wines, made from Malvasia and Moscatel grapes, are rarely seen today.

Sizzano A dry red Italian DOC wine produced from Nebbiolo, Vespolina, and Bonarda grapes in a small district near Gattinara, in the Piedmont region.

Skin The peel or outer covering of the grape; in some English-speaking countries, skins are more commonly called hulls or husks.

Skin Contact A technique sometimes used in the production of white wines whereby the grapes are crushed and the juice kept in contact with the skins for two to twenty-four hours, depending on the grape variety and the stylistic preferences of the winemaker. Unlike red wines, which are fermented with the grape skins, white wines are fermented away from the skins, so this initial skin contact permits the increased extraction of flavour, aroma, tannin, and other elements that affect the character and balance of the resulting wine. Many winemakers prefer to vinify white wines without skin contact to produce lighter, more delicate wines.

Small A taster's term applied to a wine without much consequence or distinction, let alone body and power, but possibly very agreeable and enjoyable all the same.

Smith Haut Lafitte, Château One of the biggest of the *grands crus classés* of the Graves district of Bordeaux, whose 135 acres produce about 27,000 cases a year, almost all of it red. The white Graves is unusual in that it is made entirely from Sauvignon Blanc; the red is made primarily from Cabernet Sauvignon. *La fitte*, incidently, means "hill", and the property, which was owned by George Smith in the eighteenth century, has no connection with the more famous Lafite in the Médoc.

Soapy A taster's term used to describe wines that are disagreeably flat, low in acid, and unappetizing.

Soave Italy's most famous dry white wine, produced a few miles northeast of Verona, on the southernmost foothills of the Alps. The 5 to 6 million cases produced annually make Soave Italy's most important white DOC, and second only to Chianti. The principal grape variety is Garganega, plus a certain amount of Trebbiano. The wood-aged, faded, and occasionally oxidized bottlings of the past have largely given way to wines that are pale straw in colour, dry without being acid and, at their best, light, clean, and fresh. Soave can be a most agreeable wine, though hardly a great one. The best wines are likely to come from the inner *classico* zone, and are so labelled. Soave means "suave", of course, but the name most likely derives from Suavia, the name of an area near Verona settled in the sixth century.

Sociando-Mallet, Château   A *cru bourgeois* situated just north of Saint-Estèphe and entitled to the appellation Haut-Médoc; its 75 acres of vines produce about 15,000 cases a year of a rich, firm, and distinctive wine whose reputation has increased in recent years.

Société Civile   A French estate company that owns and manages vineyard and winemaking operations (or other farming operations); most Bordeaux châteaux, for example, are owned by a Société Civile, a sort of corporation, rather than by an individual, as in Burgundy.

Soft   A wine-taster's term, generally favourable, although not always so. A soft wine is neither harsh nor green, but possibly mild and dull; all wines should have some softness, but if they have too much they may be flat or even common.

Solera   An ingenious system of fractional blending used to produce certain fortified wines, Spanish sherries above all; the object is to maintain a consistent style and quality year after year, and this is accomplished by adding younger wines to older ones at progressive stages of maturation. (The operation of a *solera* is described in the entry for Sherry.) Occasionally a sherry or Madeira is labelled with the term *solera* and a vintage year; the latter simply indicates when the *solera* was begun, and it would be a mistake to assume that the bottle contains any wine from the year indicated. In recent years, a number of producers of sherry-style wines in California, Australia, and elsewhere have set up *soleras* in the Spanish pattern, with beneficial effects on the quality of their wines.

Solid   A term applied to a wine that is sound and firm and that has the ability to last and improve with age.

Solutré   One of the four communes in the Mâcon region whose wines are entitled to the appellation Pouilly-Fuissé; the rock of Solutré, an extraordinary butte rising directly behind the village, is a famous landmark, visible for miles, and appears on many Pouilly-Fuissé labels.

Sommelier The French term for "wine waiter"; in many restaurants in France, the *sommelier* is also in charge of cellar work and, in the dining room, is responsible for all beverages, alcoholic and not. The traditional uniform includes a chain worn around the neck holding a *tastevin*, or shallow tasting cup, and sometimes an apron; today, many *sommeliers* eschew this paraphernalia and can often be identified by the emblem of a grape bunch sewn to their lapels.

Sonoma One of the most important wine-producing counties of California, situated north of San Francisco, between the Pacific and the Mayacamas Mountains, which separate Sonoma and Napa counties; Mendocino is to the north. Franciscan missionaries planted vines near the town of Sonoma in the 1820s, and those were the first vineyards established north of San Francisco. General Mariano Vallejo of Mexico acquired the vineyards in the 1830s, and Agoston Haraszthy, often referred to as the father of California viticulture, arrived in the 1850s and soon introduced a number of *vinifera* varieties from cuttings he had brought back from Europe. Sonoma became a major source of California wines in the nineteenth century, but its importance was considerably reduced by Prohibition, and it was not until the early 1970s that its reputation for fine wines was re-established. As recently as the mid-1960s, there were fewer than 10,000 acres of vineyards in Sonoma, and most of that consisted of such red varieties as Zinfandel, Carignane, Petite Sirah, and Alicante Bouschet, with only 300 acres of Cabernet Sauvignon; French Colombard and Palomino were the most widely planted white varieties, with Chardonnay accounting for only 50 acres. Most of the existing wineries produced inexpensive jug wines, very few produced varietal wines, and several continued to sell wines in bulk to other wineries rather than bottling and marketing them under their own names. Today, there are 32,000 acres in Sonoma, including 10,000 of Chardonnay and more than 6,000 of Cabernet Sauvignon, and those two varieties, plus Pinot Noir, Sauvignon Blanc, Johannisberg Riesling, Gewürztraminer, and Merlot make up two thirds of the total. The number of wineries has increased from about two dozen in the early 1970s to more than 100.

The vineyards of Sonoma, which are closer to the ocean and its maritime breezes than those of Napa, are relatively cool overall, but the county has an astonishingly wide diversity of climates and soils; unlike Napa, many of whose wineries are situated along a 15-mile strip, those of Sonoma are found in several different districts, most of which have been established as distinct viticultural areas. As a result, Sonoma does not present a single name to consumers, as does the Napa Valley, and Sonoma's geography is more difficult to grasp, but the quality of its wines is evident, and its appellations are becoming increasingly familiar to wine drinkers. In the southern part of the county, the Sonoma Valley extends from San Pablo Bay north almost to Santa Rosa, and includes part of the Carneros district and the small Sonoma Mountain area. The northern part of the county owes much of its climatic conditions to the Russian River, which flows south from Mendocino through the Alexander Valley and then, near Healdsburg, turns west toward the Pacific; the area around this west-flowing section of the river has been defined as the Russian River Valley. The Green Valley and Chalk Hill districts are contained within the Russian River Valley area, Knights Valley is just to the east, and the Dry Creek Valley runs parallel to the Alexander Valley. The extensive area known as Northern Sonoma includes most of the vineyards in the county except for those in Sonoma Valley, and the Sonoma Coast appellation includes about a third of the county's vineyards. Additional information about each of Sonoma County's viticultural areas will be found elsewhere in this volume.

Sonoma Coast An extensive viticultural area that encompasses nearly a third of the vineyards in California's Sonoma County, specifically those in the cooler parts of the county; the appellation includes the Russian River Valley, Green Valley, Chalk Hill, and the Bennett Valley and Carneros districts of Sonoma Valley.

Sonoma Mountain A small viticultural area within the larger Sonoma Valley appellation, situated above the town of Glen Ellen on the eastern face of Sonoma Mountain, opposite the Mayacamas Mountains. The area, which is best known for Cabernet Sauvignon, contains about 600 acres of vineyards; the Laurel

Glen winery is located there.

Sonoma Valley A viticultural area in southern Sonoma County that extends for about 20 miles from Santa Rosa south past Kenwood, Glen Ellen, and Sonoma to San Pablo Bay; most of the area lies between the Sonoma Mountains and the Mayacamas Mountains, which form the boundary between Sonoma and Napa counties. Sonoma Valley, also known as the Valley of the Moon, is best known for Cabernet Sauvignon and Sauvignon Blanc; the appellation also includes the small Sonoma Mountain viticultural area, known for Cabernet Sauvignon, and part of the large Carneros region, famous for Pinot Noir and Chardonnay. Among the wineries situated in this area are Buena Vista, Carmenet, Chateau St. Jean, Hacienda, Hanzell, Gundlach-Bundschu, Grand Cru, Kenwood, Laurel Glen, Matanzas Creek, and Sebastiani.

Sophisticated When applied to wines, this term means adulterated, usually by the addition of illegal substances that are meant to make the wine seem better than it really is.

Sorí In the dialect of Italy's Piedmont region, this refers to a hill or slope with a southern exposure, which presumably results in riper grapes and finer wines; the term is occasionally found on labels of Barolo and Barbaresco, as Sorí Tildin, Sorí San Lorenzo.

Souche A French word for "grape stock", or "vine"; others are *cep* and *pied*. When wines are sold before the grapes are picked, as occurred in Bordeaux in the 1950s, the sale is *sur souche*.

Sound A taster's term for a wine that is, as the French say, *franc de goût* – clean, well made, without defects; it is, of course, the least one should expect of any wine.

Souple French for "supple"; applied to wines that are not too high in tannin or acid, smooth, agreeable, ready to drink.

Sour In the realm of wine, the opposite of sweet is dry, not sour, and a wine with too much natural acidity is described as tart or acid, not as sour. A sour wine is one that is spoiled, well on its way to becoming vinegar, and not fit to drink.

Soutard, Château A *grand cru classé* of Saint-Emilion whose 50-odd acres of vineyards produce about 10,000 cases a year of a generous, well-structured red wine that deserves to be better known.

South Africa The first vineyards were planted in the mid-seventeenth century by Dutch settlers, but only recently have modern winemaking techniques and plantings of classic European varieties begun to transform the country's wine scene. Once best known for its well-made fortified wines in the style of port and sherry, South Africa is now gaining a reputation for its range of red and white table wines and sparkling wines; the German influence that resulted in light, fruity, semi-sweet white wines in the early 1970s is giving way to the French and California influence, with its emphasis on dry, oak-aged wines. About 100,000 acres are planted, virtually all of them around Cape Town, in the southwest corner of the country, and they produce the equivalent of 100 million cases of wine; in most recent years, however, about half the wine crop has been distilled. Steen, which is the local name for Chenin Blanc, is the most widely planted variety and accounts for one quarter of the total acreage; other traditional white-wine varieties include Palomino, Clairette Blanche, Muscat of Alexandria (known as Hanepoot), and Sémillon (known as green grape). There are new plantings of Chardonnay (many of which turned out to be the Auxerrois of Alsace), Sauvignon Blanc, Gewûrztraminer, and Rhine Riesling (the grape known as Paarl Riesling is the Crouchen of France). Cinsault is the most widely planted red-wine grape, but Cabernet Sauvignon is considered to produce the country's finest reds; other varieties include Pinotage, a cross of Pinot Noir and Cinsault (which is known locally as Hermitage, hence the name), and new plantings of Pinot Noir, Shiraz, Merlot, and Cabernet Franc. Generic names, such as Chablis and Burgundy, are not widely used in South Africa, whose wines are most often labelled with proprietary names – such as Lieberstein, Autumn Harvest, Fonternelle, Rubicon, and Baronne – or with varietal names; a varietal wine must contain at least 75 percent of the named variety. Appellation laws, known as Wines of Origin, were established in 1973; the best-known districts are Paarl and Stellenbosch, both of which lie within the larger Coastal District appellation. The Cooperative Wine Growers' Association, known as KWV, oversees the entire South African wine industry and also markets a range of wines and brandies; other major firms are Oude Meester and the Stellenbosch Farmers'

Winery, or SFW. About 80 percent of the country's wines are made by co-operative cellars, the rest by farmers and about 70 major estates, among them Boschendal, Hamilton Russell, Meerlust, Twee Jonge Gezellen, and Groot Constantia (which once produced a legendary sweet, fortified Muscat known as Constantia, said to be a favourite of Napoleon.) The Nederburg estate, which produces a famous late-harvest, *botrytis*-infected Chenin Blanc called Edelkeur, is also the site of an annual auction of South African wines first conducted in 1974.

Southern Vales A region south of Adelaide, in the state of South Australia, which includes the districts of McLaren Vale and Reynella.

Soutirage A French word for the process of drawing off wine from one tank or barrel to another, leaving the sediment or lees behind. *See* Racking.

Spain Although this country has the largest extent of vineyards of any country in the world, over 4 million acres in all, its prevailingly arid climate and the advanced age of many of its vines results in an average yield per acre that is far lower than in France or Italy; the total production of Spanish wines is only half that of France or Italy, but it amounts, nevertheless, to a very respectable 330 to 440 million cases a year. Sherry is Spain's best-known and most celebrated wine, but it accounts for only 4 percent of the total crop and is no more the typical wine of Spain than champagne is of France; in fact, many Spaniards have never tasted it. Spain's production consists, for the most part, of common table wine, *vino corriente*, consumed locally, but several of its wines have achieved international acclaim.

The hot climate typical of most of Spain's vineyard regions results in many full-bodied reds that are relatively high in alcohol, such as those from Alicante, Cariñena, Priorato, and Tarragona; and neutral, low-acid whites such as those from the vast central plateau of La Mancha (whose most famous wine village is Valdepeñas, known for its pale, light-bodied reds). In recent years, however, there have been new plantings at higher altitudes; a number of innovative firms have introduced new vinification techniques, including temperature-controlled fermentation; and many producers – especially in the famous Rioja region – are reducing the time their red wines spend in wood, and eliminating wood-aging entirely for certain whites. In addition, a number of producers, notably Torres and Jean Léon in the Penedès region and the Raimat estate in Lérida, have planted such classic French varieties as Chardonnay and Cabernet Sauvignon. The result of all these changes is that Spain is now producing a considerably greater quantity of attractive table wines, notably the reds and whites of Rioja and Penedès, the reds of Ribera del Duero, the crisp whites of Rueda, and the dry rosés of Navarre. There are, of course, many firms in Rioja and elsewhere that continue to produce wines in the traditional way, many of them excellent; perhaps the most famous such estate is Vega Sicilia, near Valladolid. (The 850

co-operative cellars in Spain, with their 200,000 members, account for half of the country's total wine production; although some of them have adopted modern winemaking techniques, many of them are not yet equipped to produce wines in keeping with contemporary tastes.)

Another factor that has improved the overall quality of Spain's wines is the creation of appellation of origin laws, known as *Denominación de Origen*, for many districts; these are similar to the *Appellation Contrôlée* laws of France and the *Denominazione di Origine Controllata* laws of Italy. The first appellation laws were established for Rioja in 1926 and for Jerez, the home of sherry, in 1933; two dozen additional districts were defined in the mid-1970s, and a number of others have been added since then. (A complete listing will be found on page 563.) Most of Spain's 30-odd *Denominación* wines, from Alella and Alicante to Valdeorras and Yecla, are better known within the country than in export markets, but the wines of Rioja, Penedès, Navarre, Ribera del Duero, Rueda, and Valdepeñas are becoming more familiar to consumers; sherry continues to be the most widely exported Spanish wine. In addition to sherry, aperitif and dessert wines are also made in Montilla, Málaga, and to some extent in the Priorato and Tarragona districts. Spain has also achieved particular success with its *espumosos*, or sparkling wines; almost all of them are made in Penedès, and most of those are made by the *méthode champenoise*, known in Spain as *cava*, and described under that entry.

Spanna The local name for the Nebbiolo grape in the Novara-Vercelli hills, around the village of Gattinara, in Italy's Piedmont region. The name is said to derive from the viticultural practice of training the grapes in a long, low span – *a spanna* in Italian – for better exposure to the sun. Spanna is the primary variety used in such fine red wines as Gattinara, Boca, Fara, and Ghemme, and is also marketed under its own name as a non-DOC varietal wine whose quality ranges from excellent to ordinary.

Spätburgunder The German name for Pinot Noir, that country's most widely planted red grape, most of it grown in the Baden region.

Spätlese A German term meaning "late picking", and one of the special designations within the category Qualitätswein mit Prädikat. A wine labelled Spätlese must be made from grapes that were picked at least a week after the start of the harvest for that particular grape variety, and from juice that contains a specified minimum percentage of natural grape sugar – about 18 to 20 percent – depending on the variety and the region. Such grapes are somewhat riper than the average, and a Spätlese wine is therefore richer, fuller-bodied, and somewhat sweeter than a wine labelled simply Qualitätswein or one labelled Kabinett. Although the bottled wine usually contains 2.5 to 5 percent sugar (balanced by the wine's natural acidity, of course), some producers prefer to market Spätlesen that contain less than 2 percent sugar; a Spätlese labelled Trocken would contain less than 1 percent sugar. The amount of Spätlesen produced varies enormously from one vintage to another, and from region to region. In the Mosel-Saar-Ruwer, for example, 31 percent of the 1983 crop was of Spätlese quality, none in 1984, and 8 percent in 1985; in the Rheinhessen, the proportion of Spätlesen varied from 58 percent in 1979 to 7 percent in 1982 to only 2 percent in 1984.

Special Natural Wine A category of U.S.-produced wine, which may be made from grapes or such other fruits as apples and pears, to which natural flavours are added; these may be fortified, such as Thunderbird and Wild Irish Rose, or relatively low in alcohol, such as Boone's Farm. In the mid-1970s, when low-alcohol wines were especially popular (they were also known as pop wines and refreshment wines), this category accounted for almost 20 percent of the total American wine market; today, sales amount to only 5 percent or so. *See* Wine Cooler.

Spicy Said of a wine with a pronounced and special natural aroma, on the whole agreeable; Gewürztraminer is an obvious example, but there are others, among them certain Rhône wines characterized by a spicy and peppery bouquet.

Spiritueux The French word for "spirits"; thus, a restaurant sells *vins et spiritueux*. Applied to wine, the word means high in alcohol.

Spitzen German for "peak", an indication of outstanding quality, as in the terms *Spitzenwein*, an "exceptional wine", and *Spitzenjahr*, an "exceptional vintage".

Split A quarter-bottle of wine or champagne, containing about 6 ounces.

Spoiled Said of an unsound wine, which can be the result of various causes, among them poor vinification and improper storage in barrel or bottle.

Spraying The treating of vines with liquid insecticides or fungicides; an essential and laborious part of the vine-grower's summer work in all countries.

Spritz A light sparkle, just enough to give a prickling sensation on the tongue, and very pleasant in simple young white wines and rosés; it may be the natural result of a second fermentation in the bottle, or of special bottling techniques by which a little carbon dioxide is added to give a wine freshness. *Spritzig* in German, *frizzante* in Italian, *pétillant* in French.

Spritzer A refreshing and thirst-quenching drink traditionally made from one third Rhine wine and two thirds soda water, but the term is now generally used to mean a combination of any wine and soda.

Spumante Italian for "foaming" or "sparkling" (plural *spumanti*), applied to wines that are fully sparkling, rather than *frizzante*, lightly sparkling. The best known is the sweet Asti Spumante, from Piedmont; also popular are the *spumanti* made from the Prosecco grape in the Veneto region. In addition, an increasing amount of dry, or Brut, *spumanti* is being produced from such traditional sparkling wine grapes as Chardonnay, Pinot Bianco (Pinot Blanc), Pinot Grigio (Pinot Gris), and Pinot Nero (Pinot Noir) in such regions as Trentino-Alto Adige, the Veneto, Oltrepò Pavese, and Franciacorta. Many of these are made by the classic *méthode champenoise* and may be so labelled, or with the equivalent Italian phrase *metodo classico*.

Staatsweingüter German for "state domain". The most famous, which belongs to the Hessian State, is headquartered in Eltville, in the Rheingau region, and its 482 acres of vineyards make it the largest wine producer in Germany. About 400 acres are situated in the Rheingau, the rest in the Hessische Bergstrasse region, and the seven estates that make up the domain include vineyards in the villages of Hochheim, Rauenthal, Hattenheim, Rüdesheim, and Assmannshausen (where red wines are made from Spätburgunder), as well as the entire Steinberg vineyard. The domain, whose familiar white label depicts a stylized black and gold eagle, also owns the twelfth-century Kloster Eberbach monastery.

Stabilizing The various treatments, of varying severity, to which wines may be subjected before bottling so that they may withstand, as far as possible, exposure to heat, cold, and light without losing their clarity and balance; these treatments include the use of sulphur dioxide, cold stabilization, fining, filtering, and even pasteurization.

Stags Leap District Officially defined as a viticultural area in 1989, the Stags Leap District, in California's Napa Valley, stretches for two miles on either side of the Silverado Trail, about five miles north of the city of Napa. The district, which has become famous for its supple and refined Cabernet Sauvignon, encompasses 2,700 acres, of which about half are planted, primarily with Cabernet Sauvignon, Merlot, Cabernet Franc, and Chardonnay. Among the wineries situated there are Stag's Leap Wine Cellars, Clos Du Val, Pine Ridge, Shafer, Silverado, and Steltzner Vineyards.

Stake A light post or picket, either of wood or metal, used to support a vine or, in some instances, the wire on which the vine is trained.

Steely A taster's term for a wine that is hard, austere, even tart, without being harsh or green; sometimes said of Chablis and certain wines from the Rhine.

Steen The name by which Chenin Blanc is known in South Africa; this variety now accounts for almost a third of that country's total vineyard acreage.

Steinberg A celebrated and historic 79-acre vineyard situated near the village of Hattenheim in Germany's Rheingau region. It was created, and the wall around it constructed, in the twelfth century by monks of the same Cistercian order as those responsible for its sister domain, Burgundy's Clos de Vougeot. The vineyard, together with the adjoining monastery, Kloster Eberbach, was eventually taken over by the Hessian

State, and is now part of the Staatsweingüt in Eltville; the wines are labelled simply Steinberger, without reference to the village of Hattenheim. The vineyard is 95 percent Riesling, but a number of experimental varieties are planted as well, so one should look for the word Riesling on the label. At their best, Steinbergers have full body, authority, great class, power, and depth of flavour, sometimes at the expense of subtlety and charm.

Steinwein A name that was loosely given to wines from the German region of Franken, or Franconia; that is, to wines shipped in the traditional flat-sided Bocksbeutel. The 1971 German wine law made this name obsolete, and only wines from the 210-acre Stein vineyard in Würzburg may use this name, as Würzburger Stein.

Stemmer A machine, called an *égrappoir* in French, for separating the newly picked grapes from their stems, prior to crushing and fermentation. The stems contain bitter, astringent elements, so destemming produces wines that are softer and more delicate; destemming grapes also has the practical advantage of reducing their volume in the press or fermentation vat by 30 percent. Certain varieties that are low in tannin, however, notably Pinot Noir, are sometimes fermented with part of their stems added back.

Stemmy The harsh, green, disagreeable flavour that wines sometimes acquire if fermented with the stems, or stalks.

Still Nonsparkling; a wine that contains no perceptible amount of carbon dioxide.

Storage *See* Cellar

Straw Wine *See* Vin de Paille

Stück A large German cask that contains 1,200 litres, the equivalent of about 133 cases of wine.

Stuck Wine When fermentation accidentally stops while there is still fermentable sugar in the must, this is known as a stuck fermentation; it may be caused by excessively high temperatures, which kill the yeasts that are necessary to convert sugar into alcohol. This situation, although solvable, is undesirable and dangerous; it occurs, for example, when the temperature at the time of the harvest is unseasonably warm, and when the winemaker does not have the means to control the temperature of the fermentation vats. It may also occur at the start of fermentation if the juice does not contain enough nutrients for the yeasts to function.

Sturdy A wine-taster's term for a solid, substantial wine.

Suau, Château A classed growth in the Sauternes district, in the commune of Barsac; its 17 acres produce about 1,500 cases a year.

Südliche Weinstrasse A Bereich that encompasses the southern half of Germany's Rheinpfalz, or Palatinate, the part south of the city of Neustadt. It has become the source of large quantities of sound wines from a number of different grape varieties, including several of the newer ones, but the wines are not often seen outside Germany.

Südtirol South Tyrol, the German name for the Alto Adige province, the northernmost in Italy, and used on labels of wines destined for German-speaking markets; thus Pinot Bianco dell'Alto Adige would become Südtiroler Weissburgunder.

Suduiraut, Château A splendid château and famous classed-growth vineyard in the Sauternes district; the entire estate consists of 500 acres, of which about 200 are devoted to vineyards, planted 95 percent with Sémillon. Annual production varies from fewer than 4,000 cases to 10,000 (no wine at all was bottled in 1972, 1973, and 1977), and at its best the wines are noted for a luscious, elegant, and stylish character that places them among the very finest of Sauternes.

Sugaring The adding of sugar (but not water) to must, or fermenting juice, to increase the alcoholic degree of the wine. *See* Chaptalization.

Sulphur An element properly and widely used in many phases of grape growing and winemaking; sulphur dioxide (SO_2) is the gas produced when sulphur is burned. Dusted or sprayed on the vines, sulphur is an efficient safeguard against many of the diseases, fungi, and pests to which grapes are subject; in the cellar, it is a standard sterilizing agent, and empty casks and barrels are treated with sulphites (the derivative of sulphur most often used in the winery) to eliminate harmful bacteria. At harvest time, sulphites are often added to the juice or must to prevent browning and to inhibit the natural yeasts; the must is then innoculated with specially selected yeast cultures to obtain a more controlled fermentation. Sulphites may also be used to stop the fermentation of certain semisweet white wines while they still retain some residual sugar and, because sulphur is an antioxidant and prevents microbial spoilage, sulphites are used to protect wines in the cellar and during bottling. There is nothing objectionable about the use of sulphur, providing it is not too obvious in the taste of the finished wine. The presence of an excessive amount of free SO_2 in wine (bound, or fixed, SO_2 has no odour) is noted by a slight prickling sensation in the nose, an odd, pasty impression on the tip of the tongue, and an acrid, biting sensation in the throat. E.C. regulations permit 160 parts per million of sulphites in dry red wines and 210 ppm in dry white wines, but good quality wines are usually well below this level.

Superiore Italian for "superior". Wines so labelled must have a slightly higher minimum alcohol content than regular bottlings (that is, they must be made from somewhat riper grapes), and they must undergo a minimum amount of aging before being marketed; this may vary from a few months for some white wines to a year or more for certain reds.

Supple A term that describes an attribute of quality wines – smooth and drinkable, yet with character and backbone.

Sur Lie French for "on the lees", a deposit which is a byproduct of fermentation made up primarily of dead yeast cells, and which affects the taste of wine by the process of autolysis. Winemakers in France, California, and elsewhere deliberately leave certain still white wines *sur lie* for a few months after fermentation to add complexity, and the time that a bottle-fermented sparkling wine spends *sur lie* before being disgorged (the process by which the lees are expelled from the bottle) is considered an important factor in its eventual quality. The term has a specific meaning in France's Muscadet region, where a young wine bottled *sur lie*, without first having been separated from the lees, will taste fresher and perhaps slightly *pétillant*. By law, however, a Muscadet may be labelled *sur lie* even if it has first been transported from the cellar where it was made to that of a *négoçiant*, or shipper, before being bottled, as long as the move occurs before mid-February and bottling takes place before mid-June of the year following the harvest.

Surdo A Portuguese term for unfermented grape juice to which alcohol has been added; identical to *mistelle*, it is used to sweeten the wines of Madeira.

Süssreserve German for "sweet reserve", this term refers to unfermented grape juice, rich in natural sugar, which is stored under pressure and eventually added to wines just before bottling to increase their sweetness. The use of this technique began in the mid-1950s and is now used for most German wines up to, and often including, Auslesen. The primary advantage of using Süssreserve is that the winemaker does not have to stop fermentation when just the right amount of residual sugar is left in the wine; he can ferment all his wines until they are completely dry (except, of course, the very sweet Beerenauslesen, Trockenbeerenauslesen, and Eiswein), and then, at the time of bottling, add just the proportion of sweetness he thinks appropriate to each wine. The other advantage of this technique is that much less sulphur is used than if wines have to be stabilized while they still retain residual sugar. The use of Süssreserve makes it easier to produce moderately priced wines that are sweet and appealing, but some connoisseurs believe that its use for the finest bottles results in wines that are not as complex and long-lived as in the past. Süssreserve, which may amount to as much as 15 percent of the finished wine, must come from the same quality category and district as the wine to which it is added, although not necessarily from the same grape variety.

Swan Valley One of Australia's oldest wine regions, established in the 1840s near Perth, in Western Australia; long known for its fortified wines, the region is now producing attractive table wines as well, with some wineries obtaining their grapes from cooler regions to the south and north. Wineries include Evans and Tate, Houghton's, and Sandalford.

Sweet One of the four basic tastes, the others being salt, sour, and bitter. Most of the world's table wines are dry, but a number of very popular ones are not, as are a few dessert wines of the highest class. A wine's sugar content is easily determined by laboratory analysis, but a consumer's reaction to its presence is more subjective and based to some extent on the balance between sugar and acid; in any case, sweetness is not of itself a fault or a virtue – this depends on the character of the wine. Sweetness in a table wine or fortified wine may be wholly natural, partly natural, or not natural at all. In wines made from overripe grapes, such as Sauternes and late-harvest Rieslings, the sweetness comes entirely from the grapes, whose juice contains so much sugar that not all of it can be fermented out. In many slightly sweet table wines, the sweetness also comes entirely from the grapes, but remains in the wine because fermentation has been deliberately arrested by the addition of sulphur, centrifuging, or filtering; in the case of port, a great deal of natural grape sugar is retained in the wine by stopping the fermentation through the addition of neutral wine spirits. Cream sherries and certain other sweet fortified wines are produced by adding heavy, sweet wine or concentrated grape juice to dry wines before they are bottled. Similarly, a number of inexpensive red, white, and rosé table wines are slightly sweetened by the addition of concentrate or unfermented juice just before bottling, to make them more appealing to consumers who prefer semidry wines.

Switzerland Despite her 35,000 acres of vineyards, producing about 11 million cases of wine, Switzerland imports almost twice as much wines as she makes, most of this light red wine from France and Italy; per capita consumption is 60 bottles a year. There are vineyards in over a dozen different cantons, but most of the country's wines are produced in the two French-speaking cantons of Valais and Vaud. The Valais extends along the upper valley of the Rhône River, which here runs parallel to the Italian border, and is best known for light white wines made from the Chasselas grape, here called Fendant; Pinot Noir and Gamay are also grown in the Valais and combined to make a light red wine called Dôle. Some Valais wines also take on the name of the canton's principal city, as Fendant de Sion or Dôle de Sion. The Vaud encompasses all the vineyards situated along the shore of the Lake of Geneva (also known as Lac Léman); again, the principal grape is Chasselas, whose local name is Dorin. Within the Vaud, the vineyards between Geneva and Lausanne are known as La Côte; those between Lausanne and Montreux are called Lavaux and include the wine villages of Vevey and Saint-

Saphorin; Chablais, which includes the villages of Aigle and Yvorne, is situated between Montreux and Martigny, at the southern end of the Valais region. Some of the best wines of the Vaud come from the village of Dézaley, near Lausanne, and are so labelled. Neuchâtel is a well-known white wine made from Chasselas – which accounts for more than half the Swiss vineyards – along the northern shore of Lake Neuchâtel; this district is also planted with Pinot Noir, which makes light red wines and pale rosés, the latter called *oeil de perdrix*, "partridge eye". Ticino, the Italian-speaking region around the lakes of Locarno and Lugano, is best known for its attractive red wines made from Merlot, and labelled Merlot del Ticino. The German-speaking cantons around Zurich are planted with such varieties as Pinot Noir, Müller-Thurgau, and Riesling. On the whole, Swiss wines are never great, and few of them can even be called outstanding, but they are always well made, generally light, fresh, and appealing; most of them are bottled within months of the harvest, and few improve with age.

Swizzle Stick A fiendish implement for undoing in a minute the time, effort, and expense of making wines sparkle; those who don't like bubbles should drink still wines.

Sylvaner A rather productive, good-quality white-wine grape widely planted in Germany, where it is spelled Silvaner; it is also called Osterreicher in the Rheingau, perhaps in reference to its Austrian origins. Sylvaner gives a lighter, softer, shorter-lived wine than the more distinguished Riesling, and plantings in Germany are now less than half of what they were twenty years ago, as Müller-Thurgau and the newer varieties have increased their share; most of the German acreage is in Rheinhessen, Rheinpfalz, and Franken, where the variety is also called Franken Riesling. Sylvaner yields a fresh, fruity, and agreeable wine in Alsace, in northern Italy, and in Switzerland, where it is sometimes known as Johannisberger. Plantings have decreased to fewer than 300 acres in California, where Sylvaner produces a pleasant, semidry wine; unfortunately, it is entitled to the name Riesling, and may also be marketed as Monterey Riesling or Sonoma Riesling. (The true Riesling is known in California as Johannisberg Riesling or White Riesling.) In Germany, Sylvaner has often been successfully crossed with Riesling to produce such varieties as Müller-Thurgau, Scheurebe, and

Ehrenfelser.

Symphony A cross of Grenache Gris and Muscat of Alexandria developed in California; the biggest planting of Symphony is at Chateau De Baun in Sonoma County, which harvested its first crop of this variety in 1984 and markets a range of wines that vary from the semidry Overture to the sweet, late-harvest Finale.

Syrah An excellent red-wine grape cultivated in the northern Rhône Valley of France, where it produces Côte Rôtie and the red wines of Hermitage, Crozes-Hermitage, and Saint-Joseph, and is also a small but important component of Châteauneuf-du-Pape and Côtes-du-Rhône. It gives a deep-coloured, slow-maturing, long-lived wine, rich in tannin, with a distinctive and memorable bouquet often reminiscent of spice or black pepper. Syrah is increasingly planted in the Midi and Provence, where it adds structure, body, and longevity to the wines with which it is blended. The Petite Sirah of California is actually the less distinguished Durif of southern France, but there are about 200 acres of true Syrah planted, mostly in Napa and Mendocino. Syrah is the most widely planted red grape of Australia, where it is known as Shiraz or Hermitage; many of the Australian examples are sound reds, some are outstanding. *See* Shiraz.

Szamorodni A term used in Hungary to indicate a style of Tokay that may be dry or semisweet, depending on the proportion of overripe Aszú grapes in the blend, which will vary from year to year; the term means "as it comes" or "as is", and the wines are labelled Tokaji Szamorodni Edes (sweet) or Száraz (dry).

Szürkebarát The name – which means "grey friar" – by which Pinot Gris is known in Hungary; this variety is grown in the Badacsony region near Lake Balaton.

 T

T-Budding A relatively new technique for converting an individual vine from one variety to another; the mature vine is cut off above the ground, and the bud of a new variety is attached to the remaining vine in a T-shaped incision. The vine will produce a partial crop the following year and a full crop in the second year, whereas a newly planted vine would need three years or more to achieve full production. This technique has been widely used in California to convert vineyards relatively quickly from one variety to another as dictated by the needs of the market or, more importantly, by a better understanding of which varieties are best suited to specific sites.

Table Wine This term commonly refers to red, white, or pink wines that are naturally fermented; that contain, for the most part, 10 to 14 percent alcohol; and that are consumed primarily with meals. According to U.S. federal regulations, a table wine is defined as one that contains at least 7 percent alcohol and less than 14 percent, and such wines may be labelled Table Wine, without an indication of their exact alcohol content. In the E.C. a table wine – *vin de table, vino da tavola, Tafelwein* – is specifically defined as one that does not have a quality designation, such as *Appellation Contrôlée*, DOC or Qualitätswein; it is a simple wine of no geographical appellation and is subject to few, if any, production limitations.

Tâche, La *See* La Tâche

Tafelwein German for "table wine". *See* Deutscher Tafelwein.

Taillan, Château du A well-known *cru bourgeois*, owned by the Cruse family, situated just a few miles from the city of Bordeaux; its 50 acres of vines produce a red wine entitled to the appellation Haut-Médoc and a white Bordeaux marketed as La Dame Blanche.

Taille A term used in France's Champagne region. A traditional load of 4,000 kilos of grapes produces the equivalent of thirteen barrels of 205 litres of juice; the first 2,050 litres of juice (the equivalent of 10 barrels) are known as the *vin de cuvée*, the next 410 litres are the *première taille*, and the last 205 litres of juice are known as the *deuxième taille*. The *tailles* are less fine, and less expensive, than the *vin de cuvée*, and most firms do not use them in their best champagnes.

Taillefer, Château A well-known vineyard in the Pomerol district whose 50 acres produce about 10,000 cases a year.

Talbot, Château A Fourth Classed Growth of Saint-Julien, in the Médoc, acquired in 1918 by the Cordier family, owners of Châteaux Gruaud-Larose and Meyney in the Médoc, Clos des Jacobins in Saint-Emilion, and Lafaurie-Peyraguey in Sauternes; John Talbot, the Earl of Shrewsbury, was governor of the region that includes Bordeaux until his death in 1453, but it is unlikely that he was ever the proprietor of the estate that now bears his name. The 250-acre vineyard, one of the largest in all of Bordeaux, produces about 45,000 cases a year of a supple, elegant, and justifiably popular wine; since 1979 the name Connetable Talbot has been used for the second wine. There are about a dozen acres planted with Sémillon and Sauvignon Blanc producing a white wine labelled Caillou Blanc du Château Talbot.

Tank A large container used for fermentation or storage of wine. If made of wood, it is usually in the form of an upright cylinder; if made of stainless steel, it may be an upright or horizontal cylinder; if made of concrete – usually lined with glass tile or epoxy, a synthetic resin – it is generally cubical.

Tannin Technically, a group of organic compounds, known as phenolic compounds, that exist in the bark, wood, roots, seeds, and stems of many plants. The tannins present in many red wines are extracted from the grape skins and seeds – and, if not previously removed, the stems – during fermentation; the longer the skins are left in contact with the fermenting must, the greater the extraction of tannins (and of colouring matter, another phenolic compound). Tannin is also picked up from wood by red and white wines stored in oak barrels, especially new oak barrels. Tannin imparts structure, flavour, texture, and complexity to a wine, and, since it is an antioxidant, also enables a wine to age; it is an important component of such long-lived red wines as Bordeaux, California Cabernet Sauvignon, and Barolo. To the taste, tannin is astringent and makes the mouth pucker (it is the dominant taste of strong tea); its presence makes young red wines hard, firm, even harsh, but as wines age some tannin and colouring matter will precipitate as sediment, which is why older red wines are both softer to the taste and lighter in colour. The presence of tannin is not in itself a guarantee of quality or longevity; it must be balanced by adequate fruit and acidity to form an overall impression of harmony.

Tappit-hen An old Scottish term for an oversize drinking vessel; also, a large bottle holding three normal wine bottles.

Tarragona A city and province southwest of Barcelona on the Mediterranean coast of Spain perhaps best known for sweet, fortified red wines once marketed as Tarragona port. Today, the
region continues to produce rich reds that are high in alcohol
and body, much of it used for blending with lighter wines
from other regions, but is becoming increasingly known for
its appealing dry white wines and rosés.

Tarry A wine-taster's term used for certain full-bodied red wines,
notably Barolo and Barbaresco; this attribute, known in
French as *goût de goudron*, is far from disagreeable and is
also one of the characteristics acquired with bottle age by a
number of fine red wines made from very ripe grapes.

Tart Some wine tasters apply this word to a wine high in acid, but
not necessarily unpleasant; others consider it a pejorative
term that describes a disagreeably sharp wine.

Tartar Tartaric acid is the principal acid of wine; some of this is invariably thrown off in the form of crystals of potassium
bitartrate, or cream of tartar, as the wine ages. These harmless and tasteless crystals sometimes show up in bottled
wine, either as loose flakes or attached to the bottom of the
cork, where they are often mistakenly identified as sugar
crystals.

Tastevin A shallow, saucer-shaped wine-taster's cup with dimpled
bottom and sides, usually of silver, still widely used in Burgundy cellars for sampling young wines out of the barrel.
The *tastevin* is obviously easier to carry around than a glass,
and its dimpled sides refract the light, making it possible to
evaluate the colour and clarity of a young wine even in the
dim light of a cellar. It is part of a *sommelier*'s traditional
equipment, attached to a silver chain that is worn around the
neck, and has also given its name to the Chevaliers du Tastevin, a Burgundian fraternity.

Tastevinage A system of labelling certain Burgundy wines that have been
approved, in a blind tasting, by a committee of the
Chevaliers du Tastevin; in recent years, about half the wines
submitted have been approved. These wines may carry a
special, rather elaborate Tastevin label on which the

shipper's name also appears; it is an indication, but by no means a guarantee, of superior quality.

Tasting Wine tasting is both a simple and enjoyable activity, and also an extremely complex art, or science, or skill; it may quite properly be described as any of these, or a combination of all three. There exist quite definite standards as to what can be called quality or superiority in wine, and when experts evaluate wines they are likely to achieve a far higher level of agreement than do music, art, or literary critics. Yet taste and smell are in general the beggars among our five senses, for they have no accurate written language, no permanent record, and no past. There are two approaches to tasting wine: one is that of the casual wine drinker seeking enjoyment, whose main concern is whether or not he or she likes a particular wine; the palate of such a consumer is the final arbiter, and there is not, nor should there be, any appeal from this decision – a wine is good if it tastes good. The second approach, which is more critical, and which attempts to evaluate a wine's character and quality, involves at least a certain amount of knowledge, and those with wide experience and a well-developed taste memory are likely to be more successful at this task.

Nevertheless, those who want to develop the ability to taste wines – and thus to obtain even more pleasure from them – can do so by adopting the approach of serious tasters, who begin by taking a moment to concentrate on the wine in their glass, noting where it comes from and the vintage, evaluating the wine, and then placing it in the context of other wines from the same region or made from the same grape variety. First they tip the glass, preferably against a white cloth, to evaluate its appearance and its colour, which indicates how the wine is aging; white wines become darker as they age, red wines lose their colour, and both red and white wines eventually acquire a brownish hue. Tasters then swirl the glass to release its aroma or bouquet; the sense of smell is more accurate and evocative than that of taste, and in any event, much of what we think of as taste is actually revealed by our sense of smell. Finally, the wine is tasted; some tasters chew the wine in their mouths for a moment to intensify the wine's taste by putting it in contact with all the taste buds; others whistle in – that is draw air into their mouths – to direct the aroma or bouquet to the nasal passages, thus utilizing both the senses of smell and taste. There are actually only four tastes: salt, which is rarely discernable in wines; sour, represented in wine by its acidity, which contributes liveliness, especially in white wines; sweet, found in many popular whites and rosés, fewer reds, and, of course, in such dessert wines as port and Sauternes; and bitter, which is usually considered a flaw in table wines. Many young red wines contain tannin, which is sometimes described as bitter, but is most often experienced as a puckerish, astringent tactile sensation. A taster also notices other tactile sensations, such as the sparkle of champagne, or a wine's temperature, especially if it is served too warm or too cold. Weight and texture are also important tactile elements, and these may vary from a light-bodied, simple, almost watery white to a richly textured, full-bodied, and mouth-filling red; a wine's weight and texture are especially important when trying to match it with food. And to evaluate a wine's overall quality, a taster pays particular attention to its balance, the extent to which all its component parts, including fruit, acidity, tannin, alcohol, and body, are in harmony; and to its length, a combination of intensity of flavour and persistence on the palate.

Taking a moment or two to jot down a few words about a wine in a notebook or on a card helps a taster to clarify his or her impressions and makes the wine easier to recall. Professionals have their own jargon, or cant, and although the terms they use often appear bizarre or pretentious, or even ridiculous to those unfamiliar with them, they can be considerably more precise than the language of music critics (a lyric tone, a warm voice) or that of painting (vibrant, sincere, well-organized). Here are a few of the terms used by professional tasters; all will be found in this volume, defined as accurately as seems possible. (A number of French tasting terms are also included from *apre* and *capiteux* to *velouté* and *vivace*.) *See*, especially, Acid, Aroma, Bouquet, Colour, Sweet, and Tannin.

Acetic	Elegant	Light	Short
Acid	Empty	Lively	Sick
Aftertaste	Extract	Maderized	Silky
Aromatic	Faded	Mature	Small
Astringent	Fat	Mellow	Soapy
Austere	Feeble	Mercaptans	Soft
Balanced	Fine	Metallic	Solid
Big	Finesse	Mild	Sound
Bitter	Firm	Mouldy	Sour
Body	Flabby	Mousy	Spicy
Bouquet	Flat	Neutral	Spoiled
Brilliant	Flinty	Noble	Spritz
Butyric	Flowery	Nutty	Steely
Character	Foxy	Oaky	Stemmy
Clean	Fragrant	Off	Sturdy
Cloudy	Fresh	Ordinary	Subtle
Cloying	Fruity	Overripe	Sulphur
Coarse	Full	Oxidized	Supple
Colour	Gassy	Perfume	Sweet
Common	Geranium	Piquant	Tannic
Complex	Great	Pleasant	Tart
Cooked	Green	Poor	Thin
Corky	Grip	Powerful	Velvety
Crisp	Hard	Rancio	Vinous
Delicate	Harmonious	Rich	Withered
Distinguished	Harsh	Ripe	Woody
Dry	Hazy	Robust	Yeasty
Dull	Heavy	Rotten Egg	Young
Dumb	Herbaceous	Rough	
Earthy	Hollow	Round	

Taurasi An exceptional DOC red wine, one of Italy's finest, produced about 30 miles east of Naples, around the village of Taurasi, in Campania. This long-lived wine is made primarily from the Aglianico grape (Mastroberadino, the leading producer of the district, uses this grape exclusively), and must be aged a minimum of three years, one of them in wood; annual production is about 25,000 cases.

Tavel The most famous rosé of France, and probably the oldest, since it was said to have been a favourite of François I and was praised by the poet Ronsard. It comes from vineyards around the village of Tavel, a few miles northwest of Avignon, and is made primarily from the Grenache grape, which cannot exceed 60 percent of the total, with Cinsault accounting for most of the rest; annual production often amounts to 400,000 cases, about half of it from a large, modern co-operative cellar. The wine, always dry, has a distinctive pink-orange colour, more flavour and bouquet than other rosés of the Rhône, and good examples combine character with an agreeable suppleness; the wine is at its best within two years of the harvest.

Tawny Port   A mature, wood-aged port that has lost its deep-red colour, acquired an amber tinge, and which tastes softer, rounder, and more subdued than a ruby port. Inexpensive tawny ports, which may be only three or four years old, are made by adding white port to red, or by vinifying the wine so that it is lighter in colour and softer in taste to begin with. True tawny ports have been aged in wood for at least eight to ten years, and fine, delicate tawnies that have matured in wood for twenty years or more are among the most distinguished and prized of all ports.

Tears   *See* Legs

Temecula   A California viticultural area north of San Diego first planted with fine wine grapes in the late 1960s; the principal varieties in this region, also known as Rancho California, are Chardonnay, Chenin Blanc, and Sauvignon Blanc, and its best-known winery is Callaway.

Temperature   Wines, especially fine wines, are strikingly affected by the temperature at which they are served; a white wine too warm seems lifeless, flat, and dull; a red wine too cold seems numbed, almost entirely lacking in bouquet, and often astringent as well. This is not a matter of etiquette, but of fact. On the other hand, the specific temperature sometimes suggested for various wines are not very practical: it is almost impossible, even for someone with a temperature-controlled cellar, to serve one wine at 52 degrees, another at 60 degrees, and a third at 68 degrees; and, in any event, once a wine is poured, it begins to warm up in the glass. A few basic guidelines can be useful, however. Whites and rosés, which owe most of their appeal to their freshness and fruit, are served chilled; this can be accomplished in two or three hours in the refrigerator, or in 20 minutes in a tall bucket filled with ice and water. The ice bucket has the added advantage, important in warm weather, of keeping the wine cool throughout the meal. Light reds, such as Beaujolais and Valpolicella, usually taste better cool, say 60 degrees or so; this can be accomplished in an hour in the refrigerator, or with a bucket that contains more water than ice. (Note that a refrigerator will chill a bottle of wine about 10 degrees in an hour, so more time may be needed during the summer months, when room temperature may be higher.) Most fine reds are served at room temperature, about 68 degrees or so; indeed, great red wines, especially old ones, are at their best at 65 to 68 degrees. A red wine served too warm – as all too many are – will not only taste flabby, but also have an alcoholic bite. If there is no cool area where a red wine can be placed for an hour to two before the meal, the bottle may be placed in a container of cool water. Note that cold intensifies the taste of bitterness, so that if a fine red that contains tannin, such as Bordeaux, California Cabernet Sauvignon, or Barolo, is chilled, rather than slightly cooled, it will taste disagreeably harsh. Experience, and a little experimentation, will soon determine the temperature at which you prefer to drink whites, rosés, and light reds, and will also enable you to decide whether it pays to take the trouble to adjust the temperature of fine red wines.

Tempranillo A native Spanish red-wine grape widely planted in Rioja, in Penedès (where it is called Ull de Llebre), and in Valdepeñas (where it is called Cencibel); it produces deep-coloured, well-balanced wines.

Tendre French for "tender"; applied to wines that are young, light, charming, and easy to drink.

Tenuta An Italian term that means "holding", more specifically a property; traditionally used to describe an estate that produces and bottles its own wines.

Terlano An Italian white wine produced primarily from Pinot Bianco and Chardonnay in the Alto Adige region. Although the DOC Terlano (Terlaner in German) may also be coupled with that of a varietal name, such as Müller-Thurgau or Sauvignon, there is actually very little planted in the zone other than the two varieties that make up the basic appellation.

Termeno A village south of Bolzano in Italy's Alto Adige province; called Tramin in German and, according to tradition, the original home of the Traminer grape.

Terne French for "dull"; when applied to wine, it means one that lacks brilliance of colour, as well as liveliness and character.

Teroldego Rotaliano An unusual Italian red wine from Trentino; made
from the Teroldego grape in the gravelly plain north of
Trento known as Campo Rotaliano, the wine has, at its best,
more character and interest than most of the rather light reds
produced in the Trentino-Alto Adige region.

Terroir French for "soil" or "earth", used in a very special sense in
the phrase *goût de terroir* or "taste of the soil". Certain
wines produced on heavy soils have a characteristic, persistent, and sometimes unpleasant earthy flavour; the German
equivalent is *Bodenton* or *Bodengeschmack*. The word *terroir* is also used in an extended sense to describe the soil together with the associated climatic conditions of a district or
a vineyard; the English equivalent might be microclimate.

Tertre, Château du A Fifth Classed Growth of Margaux, in the Médoc,
under the same direction as Château Calon-Ségur; its 120
acres produce about 16,000 cases a year.

Tête de Cuvée A term once used to denote the best vineyards of Burgundy,
many of which are now classified as *grands crus*; also used
unofficially in the Champagne region to designate a firm's
finest bottling.

Texas In 1975 the state had one winery and only 25 acres of
vineyard; a dozen years later there were more than 20 wineries and 4,500 acres of vineyard. The earliest plantings included native American varieties and such French-American
hybrids as Vidal Blanc, Chambourcin, and Chancellor, but
most of the pioneers of the new Texas wine industry soon
focused their efforts on traditional European *vinifera* varieties, which now account for 90 percent of the total; acreage
includes Chardonnay, Sauvignon Blanc, Johannisberg Riesling, Cabernet Sauvignon, Chenin Blanc, Gewürztraminer,
and French Colombard, as well as Muscat Canelli, Ruby
Cabernet, and Emerald Riesling. The state's four principal
wine-producing regions (and their best-known wineries) are
the High Plains near Lubbock (Llano Estacado and Pheasant
Ridge); the area west and north of Dallas/Fort Worth
(Chateau Montgolfier); west Texas, near Fort Stockton
(Domaine Cordier); and the hill country around Austin
(Fall Creek Vineyards).

Thanisch, Wwe, Dr. H. A renowned 32-acre estate in the village of Bernkastel, on the Moselle, where the Thanisch family first settled in the seventeenth century. The estate owns vineyards in several villages, including Brauneberg and Graach, but its most famous wine comes from the Bernkasteler Doctor vineyard, of which it owns 4.5 acres. In 1988, the estate was divided into two equal parts, and the crop from each half is vinified separately; one wine is still labelled Thanisch, the other Thanisch Müller-Berggräf.

Thief A pointed tube of glass or metal used for taking samples of wine through the bunghole of a barrel; called a *pipette* in French.

Thin A term applied to a wine deficient in body, one that is poor and watery.

Thompson Seedless The most widely planted grape in California, whose 260,000 acres account for nearly 40 percent of all the vineyards in the state; officially classified as a raisin grape, it is known as a three-way grape because it may be used for raisins, table grapes, or wine. Although its use for wine has diminished over the past fifteen years, it still makes up about 20 percent of the total white-wine harvest; it gives a neutral wine used in blends of inexpensive jug wines and sparkling wines, but it is too nondescript to be marketed on its own. This grape accounts for more than a quarter of the vineyards of Australia, where it is known as Sultana; there, too, part of the crop is used to make white wine for inexpensive blends.

Thouarsais A VDQS for red, white and rosé wines produced around the city of Thouars, south of Saumur and the Loire.

Ticino An Italian-speaking canton of Switzerland, south of the Alps, around Lake Lugano, producing, for the most part, red wines. The best of these – and in favourable years about the best red of Switzerland – is made from the Merlot grape and marketed as Merlot del Ticino.

Tignanello The proprietary name of one of Italy's most famous red wines – well-structured and long-lived – created by the Antinori firm. The wine, which comes from Tuscany's Chianti district, was first produced in 1971 entirely from red grapes, primarily Sangiovese, as an alternative to Chianti, which then had to have a minimum of 10 percent white grapes. Tignanello was made again in 1975, this time with a proportion of Cabernet Sauvignon, and has been made in almost every vintage since 1977, usually with 20 percent of Cabernet Sauvignon; average production is about 15,000 cases. The tremendous and fully merited success of this wine has encouraged other Chianti producers to make similar full-flavoured reds, some entirely from Sangiovese, others from a combination of Sangiovese and Cabernet Sauvignon. Antinori later created Solaia, a blend of Cabernet Sauvignon and 10 percent Sangiovese.

Tinaja   The Spanish word for the immense earthenware amphoras in which the wines of Montilla and La Mancha have traditionally been fermented; these are gradually being replaced by even larger cement cylinders.

Tinta   The name given in Portugal to a family of red-wine grapes, all producing deep-coloured, full-bodied red wine, most used for port, but some for table wines; these include Tinta Cão, Tinta Barroca, and Tinta Francisca. The varieties known as Tinta Madeira and Tinta Souzão are grown to a limited extent in California's Central Valley.

Tinto   In Spanish, a *vino tinto* is a "red wine".

Tio Pepe   A proprietary name for a fino sherry produced by the Gonzalez Byass firm.

Tirage   French for the process of bottling; a *tireuse* is a bottling machine. In the Champagne region, it refers to the bottling of the still wine with a mixture of sugar and yeast – known as *liqueur de tirage* – which will cause a second fermentation in the bottle.

Tischwein   German for "table wine", but usually applied to wines of no particular quality; similar to the French term *vin ordinaire*. *See* Deutscher Tafelwein.

Tocai   An Italian white-wine grape widely cultivated in the northeast part of that country. No relation to the Tokay of Hungary (which is made primarily from the Furmint grape), the indigenous Tocai makes some of Italy's finest whites, noted for their finesse, elegance, and dry, almost bitter finish. It is the most extensively planted white-wine grape in the Friuli district, where it is known as Tocai Friulano, and a clonal variant, Tocai Italico, is also found in the Veneto, where it produces Tocai di Lison and Tocai del Piave.

Tocai di Lison An Italian dry white wine produced in the eastern Veneto, in the new DOC zone Lison-Pramaggiore.

Tokay One of the most famous and, at its best, one of the finest sweet white wines of the world. The best has never been inexpensive or easy to find, and this has been more than ever the case since World War II, now that the former royal, princely, and even papal reserves are presumably consumed by deserving commissars. All true Tokay comes from a small district along the foothills of the Carpathian Mountains, in northeastern Hungary, called Tokaj-Hegyalja; although the wine and the region are commonly referred to as Tokay, the wine's name appears as Tokaji on labels. The wine is made primarily from the Furmint grape, with a proportion of Hárslevelü, grown on volcanic soil in Tokay and nearly thirty nearby villages. Wines labelled simply Tokaji Furmint are dry and full-bodied. Those marketed as Tokaji Szamorodni may be dry or semisweet, depending on the proportion of overripe Aszú berries in the blend, which varies from year to year; *Szamorodni* means "as it comes". The wine that has created Tokay's reputation, however, is labelled Tokaji Aszú and is made from grapes affected by *Botrytis cinerea*, the same "noble rot" that produces the sweet wines of Sauternes and Germany. The traditional method of making Aszú wines is to mash up the botrytised grapes in a *puttony*, a basket holding about 25 litres, and then add this to a cask holding about 140 litres of dry wine; the more *puttonyos* added to the dry wine, the sweeter the resulting Tokaji Aszú. Most of the wines put on the market contain three to five *puttonyos*, and are so labelled, although today's winemaking practices may no longer involve the use of the traditional *puttony*. A Tokaji Aszú of five *puttonyos* contains about 12 percent residual sugar and, like all Aszú wines, is relatively high in acidity; it has an intense, caramel-like taste, but less fruit than most other *botrytis* wines because it is aged in cask for five to seven years. The wines once marketed in distinctive 50-centilitre bottles (about seventeen ounces), are now sold in half-bottles. Even rarer are the Aszú with six *puttonyos*; the sweeter Aszú Essencia, equivalent to a Trockenbeerenauslese, but aged in cask for ten years; and the special wine known simply as Essencia, made from the very richest juice, which barely ferments to about 3 percent alcohol, and which is especially high in sugar. Bottlings of Essencia from the eighteenth and nineteenth centuries occasionally show up at wine auctions; the version produced today is used primarily to sweeten and intensify the other grades of Tokay Aszú.

Also: Tokay d'Alsace is another name for Pinot Gris in the Alsace region of France and is unrelated to Hungarian Tokay or to the Furmint grape. The rich, sweet, fortified wines of Australia known as liqueur Tokays are made from the Muscadelle grape. Tokay is also the name of a California table grape, sometimes called Flame Tokay, grown in the San Joaquin Valley; part of the crop is used to make wine, which is distilled into brandy.

Tokay d'Alsace　A name traditionally given to the Pinot Gris in Alsace, although it bears no relation to the Tokay of Hungary. Most Alsace producers are now labelling wines made from Pinot Gris with that name; in any case, Common Market regulations now specify that even if such a wine is labelled Tokay d'Alsace, the name Pinot Gris must also appear.

Tonne　French for a large cask, or tun, of indefinite size.

Tonneau　A traditional measure of trade in the Bordeaux region, equivalent to four *barriques*. In the past, this was understood to mean 96 cases of wine, but since the late 1970s a *tonneau* represents 100 cases of 12 bottles each. For some years, however, virtually all the top châteaux have been marketing their wines at a price per bottle, rather than by the *tonneau*, even when the wines are still maturing in barrel.

Topping　The refilling of casks or barrels of young wine to ensure that there is no ullage, or air space, between the wine and the bung, or stopper; topping, an essential part of good cellar work, is necessary because of the evaporation that occurs in the barrel.

Torbato　An Italian white-wine grape grown in Sardinia, where it produces light, fresh wines, especially those marketed as Torbato di Alghero.

Torcolato　A proprietary white wine produced by Maculan in the

Breganze district of the Veneto; this sweet, honeyed wine is made by the *passito* technique from Vespaiolo, Tocai, and Garganega grapes that are spread out on trays in well-ventilated rooms for three or four months until they shrivel; the resulting wine, which is barrel-aged for a year, has 13 or 14 percent alcohol and 7 to 10 percent of residual sugar.

Torgiano A DOC zone situated a few miles south of Perugia, in Italy's Umbria region. Although its red and white wines are entitled to the appellation Torgiano, the wines are more familiar to consumers under the proprietary names Rubesco (for the red) and Torre di Giano (for the white) created by Lungarotti, the district's leading producer. The red is made primarily from the Sangiovese grape, plus Canaiolo, the white from Trebbiano plus Grechetto. Lungarotti produces about 80,000 cases of each and has achieved a particular reputation for Rubesco, especially the Riserva, considered one of Italy's finest reds.

Torre Quarto An estate in Italy's Apulia region, owned by the Cirillo-Farrusi family, which produces red, white and rosé wines; the red, made from Malbec and local varieties, is the best known.

La Tour Blanche, Château A well-known classed growth of the Sauternes district, donated to the French government at the beginning of the century and now operated as a school of viticulture and oenology; its 65 acres produce about 6,000 cases a year of wines perhaps lighter and less concentrated than others of its class.

La Tour Carnet, Château A Fourth Classed Growth situated in the commune of Saint-Laurent, just west of Saint-Julien, and entitled to the appellation Haut-Médoc (as are the two adjoining classed growths, Châteaux Belgrave and Camensac); its 75 acres of vineyard, completely replanted since the early 1960s, produce about 14,000 cases a year.

La Tour de By, Château A deservedly popular *cru bourgeois* entitled to the appellation Médoc; its 150 acres produce about 30,000 cases a year of a dependable, well-balanced wine.

La Tour de Mons, Château A *cru bourgeois* in Margaux, in the Médoc, producing about 13,000 cases a year of a distinctive and relatively long-lived wine.

La Tour Haut-Brion, Château A well-known *grand cru classé* of the Graves district that has long been under the same ownership as the adjoining, and more celebrated, Château La Mission Haut-Brion. The La Tour Haut-Brion vineyard consists of 10 acres with a potential annual production of about 2,000 cases. For many years, however, the red wines from the two vineyards have been vinified together, and the La Tour Haut-Brion name has been used as a second label for the wines of La Mission Haut-Brion; on average, about 40 percent of the crop has been sold as La Tour Haut-Brion. In 1983, both properties (and the white-wine vineyard Laville Haut-Brion) were acquired by the owners of Château Haut-Brion, who vinify and bottle La Tour Haut-Brion separately.

La Tour Martillac, Château A well-known *grand cru classé* of the Graves district of Bordeaux, producing about 10,000 cases a year of red wine and 2,000 cases of white; part of the crop may be marketed with the second label Château La Grave Martillac.

Touraine An old and extremely beautiful French province in the Loire Valley consisting of the modern French *départements* of Indre-et-Loire and Loir-et-Cher, with some vineyards in Indre and Sarthe; its chief city is Tours, and the area makes up most of what has come to be called the château country of France. The total production of *Appellation Contrôlée* wines amounts to 6 to 7 million cases in abundant vintages, a little more than half of it red and rosé; the best-known names are Vouvray and Montlouis (both white wines made from Chenin Blanc, and both sometimes sparkling), and Chinon, Bourgueil, and Saint-Nicholas-de-Bourgueil (all three red wines made from Cabernet Franc); other appellations are Coteaux du Loir and Jasnières. A great deal of light, pleasant red, white and rosé wines (the whites made from Chenin Blanc or Sauvignon Blanc, the reds and rosés from Gamay, plus Cabernet Franc and Groslot) are marketed under the regional appellation Touraine and, increasingly with such varietal names as Sauvignon de Touraine, Gamay de Touraine, and Cabernet de Touraine; limited amounts of wine from three specific districts are entitled to the appellations Touraine-Amboise, Touraine-Azay-le-Rideau, and Touraine-Mesland. Little of what is labelled Touraine is exported; most of it is drunk up within a year or two of the harvest by the fortunate inhabitants of this garden of France, and by thirsty tourists.

Touriga The name given in Portugal to a family of red-wine grapes planted in the Douro region, all producing deep-coloured, full-bodied wines used primarily for port; these include Touriga Nacional and Touriga Francesca.

Traben-Trarbach Twin towns on the Moselle, downstream from Bernkastel and Wehlen, but still part of that classic district of great white wine known as the Mittelmosel. Traben is on the left bank of the river, Trarbach on the right; between them, they have some 500 acres of vineyards, the best sites being Schlossenberg, Hühnerberg, and Ungsberg.

Traisen A wine-producing village along the Nahe River, just upstream from Bad Kreuznach, situated near the steep cliff known as the Rotenfels; its best vineyards, planted with Riesling, are Rotenfels and Bastei.

Traminer A name still used in some wine regions for the grape variety more commonly known as Gewürztraminer.

Transfer Method A technique used in the production of sparkling wines that is less expensive than the classic *méthode champenoise*. The second fermentation that produces the bubbles takes place in individual bottles, but the time-consuming steps of riddling and disgorging are eliminated by emptying the sparkling wines, and their sediment, into large tanks under pressure, filtering the wines, adding the appropriate *dosage*, and then rebottling the wines. The transfer method, which is not permitted in France's Champagne region, is widely used elsewhere in France and in the United States. Wines produced in this way may be labelled "Fermented in the bottle", but not "Fermented in this bottle".

Traube German for "grape"; *Traubensaft* is "grape juice".

Treading A technique formerly used in the sherry region of Spain and the port region of northern Portugal whereby teams of workers would tread the grapes for several hours at a time in shallow stone or cement *lagares*. The Spanish treaders wore special hobnailed boots that crushed the grapes without crushing the seeds, which impart a bitter taste to the resulting wine; the Portuguese were barefoot. The purpose of treading was not, as some people imagine, to press the juice out of the grapes (which could be done much more effectively with even a primitive press), but to accelerate the start of fermentation and to extract colour and flavour from the skins. This is particularly important in the production of port, whose sweetness comes from stopping fermentation after only two or three days, when the must still retains much of the natural grape sugar; constant treading permitted the maximum extraction of colour and tannin in a minimum amount of time. The shortage of labour in the late 1950s and early 1960s resulted in the adoption of modern vinification equipment that could achieve the same result, and treading is rarely practiced today, although a very few firms continue to use this technique for the grapes from their best vineyards.

Trebbiano   A good but not especially distinguished Italian white-wine grape that produces rather neutral wines, and whose 300,000-plus acres account for more than 10 percent of Italy's vineyards. It is extensively cultivated in Tuscany, where, blended with Malvasia, it is used for most of that region's many white wines; it is also the principal variety in Orvieto and a component of Frascati and Soave; and it is widely planted in Emilia-Romagna. Trebbiano is known in France as Ugni Blanc and in California as Saint-Emilion.

Trebbiano d'Abruzzo   A simple white DOC wine produced from the Trebbiano grape in the Abbruzzi region (Abruzzo in Italian).

Trentino   A district in northern Italy, around the city of Trento, now coupled with the adjoining district of Alto Adige to form the Trentino-Alto Adige region. Wine production is almost entirely confined to the deep, narrow valley of the Adige River and the lower slopes of the 7,000-foot peaks that form the valley walls. Many of Trentino's lively and appealing wines are marketed with varietal names, which include Cabernet, Chardonnay, Merlot, Moscato, Müller-Thurgau, Pinot Bianco, Pinot Grigio, Riesling, and Traminer, as well as the indigenous red Lagrein and the unusual white Nosiola. These names may be coupled with that of the basic DOC of the region, Trentino. Teroldego Rotaliano is a fine red, sturdy and complex, produced from the native Teroldego grape in a district north of Trento known as Campo Rotaliano; Casteller is a simple light red or rosé produced from

Schiava, Merlot, and Lambrusco grapes. An increasing part of Trentino's production of Chardonnay, Pinot Bianco, and Pinot Nero is being used to make fine sparkling wines, many of them by the *méthode champenoise*.

Tre Venezie *See* Venezie

Trentino-Alto Adige The northernmost region of Italy, made up of two provinces: Alto Adige to the north, whose capital is Bolzano, and Trentino, whose capital is Trento. As a result of cool climate, extensive hillside vineyards, modern technology, and a wide range of fine grape varieties, more than half of Trentino-Alto Adige's annual production of 12 to 16 million cases is of DOC quality, the highest proportion of any region in Italy. About 80 percent of the DOC wines are red, and most of that is from the native Schiava grape, but a diverse collection of light, fruity red and white wines with lively acidity are produced from such well-known varieties as Chardonnay, Pinot Bianco, Pinot Grigio, Sauvignon, Traminer, Cabernet, Merlot, and Pinot Nero, as well as from such native red grapes as Lagrein, Marzemino, and Teroldego. Many of these are marketed as varietal wines whose names are coupled with those of the appropriate DOC production zones. In addition, an increasing part of the wines made from Chardonnay, Pinot Bianco, and Pinot Nero are being transferred into sparkling wines, many of them by the *méthode champenoise*. *See* Alto Adige, Trentino.

Triage *See* Epluchage

Tricastin *See* Coteaux du Tricastin

Trie A French term that means "sorting" or "selection" and that describes a special, expensive method of harvesting grapes by repeated partial pickings of only the very ripest bunches or individual grapes. Almost all the wines made from grapes affected by *Botrytis cinerea* are harvested in this way, including the great sweet wines of Sauternes, where a conscientious vineyard owner will send his pickers out for several *tries* before the harvest is over.

Trier The principal city of Germany's Moselle Valley, not far from the border of Luxembourg; it was already an important city in Roman days, and its Roman monuments and ruins are still impressive. Many of the leading producers of wines from the Moselle, and its tributaries, the Saar and the Ruwer, have their cellars in Trier, and most of the great annual auctions at which fine Moselles are sold take place there. There are nearly 1,000 acres of vineyards within the city limits, which now include the vineyards of the adjoining village of Avelsbach.

Trittenheim One of the good, but hardly great, wine-producing villages along the Moselle, in Germany; its light, engaging, and attractive wines come from such individual vineyard sites as Apotheke and Altärchen, which lie within the Grosslage Piesporter Michelsberg.

Trocken German for "dry"; the term has an official meaning and may be applied only to wines with no more than 9 grams of sugar per litre (0.9 percent), although many examples actually contain even less. Since the late 1970s, both Trocken and Halbtrocken (half-dry) wines have become increasingly popular in Germany, since they are more appropriate with meals than that country's more traditional, semisweet white wines. In some recent vintages as much as 30 percent of the Qualitätswein crop has been vinified to make Trocken and Halbtrocken wines, and a number of major estates in the Rheinpfalz, Rheingau, Mosel-Saar-Ruwer, and other regions now transform more than half their production into these drier styles. Most of these wines are Qualitätswein, but some producers also make Prädikat wines entitled to the Kabinett, Spätlese, and even Auslese designations by fermenting the wines until they are dry, or nearly so; such bottlings have correspondingly more body and flavour. In general, Trocken and Halbtrocken wines have been less successful in the United States and other export markets, where there is a much greater choice of traditional dry white wines; of the two, many consumers prefer the slightly sweeter, rounder Halbtrocken to the more austere, lighter-bodied Trocken.

Trockenbeerenauslese A term applied to the sweetest and most expensive of all German wines, it is one of the designations within the category Qualitätswein mit Prädikat. Literally, the word means a wine made from a "special selection" (Auslese) of individual "grapes" (Beeren) that have been left on the vine until so shrivelled that they are practically "dry" (Trocken).

A wine labelled Trockenbeerenauslese must be made from grapes with a minimum of 150 degrees Oechsle, the equivalent of 35 percent natural grape sugar, which represents a potential alcohol content of 21.5 percent. Actually, the wines may have as little as 5.5 percent alcohol when bottled, and contain 15 to 20 percent or more of residual, or unfermented, sugar. TBAs, as these wines are sometimes referred to are produced very rarely – some Rheingau estates for example, have made such wines only three or four times in 30 years – and in exceedingly limited quantities, perhaps just a few hundred bottles in all. The finest examples are made from Riesling grapes that have been affected by *Botrytis cinerea*, known as *Edelfäule* in Germany, but TBAs have also been made in very dry years from raisined grapes, even though *botrytis* did not occur. Nor are the grapes for these wines necessarily the last ones picked; in a year heavily affected by *botrytis*, such as 1976, some growers actually picked the grapes for TBA before those for Spätlese and Auslese. The wines themselves are wholly remarkable – concentrated, intense, luscious, long-lived, and fabulously expensive.

Trois Glorieuses, Les A three-part weekend celebration held every year in Burgundy around the wine auction at the Hospices de Beaune, which takes place on the third Sunday in November; it is preceded by an enormous banquet on Saturday night hosted by the Chevaliers du Tastevin at Clos de Vougeot, and followed on Monday by an informal lunch, the Paulée de Meursault.

Trollinger The name used in Germany for the red-wine grape known in Italy's Trentino-Alto Adige region as Schiava or Vernatsch; virtually all of Germany's acreage is in the Württemberg region.

Tronquoy Lalande, Château A *cru bourgeois* in Saint-Estèphe, in the Médoc; its 40 acres produce about 8,000 cases.

Troplong-Mondot, Château A *grand cru classé* of Saint-Emilion whose 70-odd acres of vineyard produce about 14,000 cases a year of well-structured, relatively long-lived red wine.

Trotanoy, Château One of the very finest vineyards of the Pomerol district of Bordeaux owned since 1953 by Jean-Pierre Moueix, co-owner of Château Pétrus, and considered by many connoisseurs to be second in quality only to Pétrus itself; its 20 acres, planted 85 percent with Merlot, produce between 1,800 and 3,500 cases a year of a substantial, concentrated, long-lived, and truly outstanding wine.

Trottevieille, Château A *premier grand cru classé* of Saint-Emilion whose 25 acres of vineyards produce about 5,000 cases of red wine a year.

Troublé A French word applied to a wine that is hazy or cloudy, one that has lost its clear appearance.

Tuilé A French term used to describe red wines whose colour has evolved into a red-orange hue resembling that of a brick or, more literally, roof tile; it is generally the mark of a wine that has begun to grow old and is likely to be short-lived.

Tun A very large cask used for wine storage; perhaps the most famous example is the Heidelberg tun, built in the mid-eighteenth century, with a capacity of 220,000 litres, or almost 300,000 bottles.

Tunisia The vineyards of this North African country were originally established by the French in the late nineteenth century and then completely replanted after the outbreak of phylloxera in the 1930s. Current production consists primarily of red wines and rosés made form Alicante-Bouschet, Carignan, and Cinsault; the country is also known for its Muscat wines, which vary from light, dry table wines to sweet, fortified dessert wines.

Turà A name created by a group of producers in Italy's Veneto region for a light-bodied, low-alcohol, lightly sparkling dry white wine made from a blend of several grape varieties.

Tursan A VDQS for red, white, and rosé wines produced in the Landes *département,* south of Bordeaux, in southwest France; the indigenous Baroque is the principal grape for the white wines, Tannat for the reds.

Tuscany A region in central Italy whose capital is Florence and whose most famous wine is Chianti. Annual production in Tuscany varies from 45 to 60 million cases, of which about a third is DOC and DOCG; although there are about two dozen DOC zones in the region, the extent of the Chianti vineyards is such that they account for almost all of the DOC and DOCG wines produced. The principal red-wine grape of Tuscany is Sangiovese, which is the primary variety not only for Chianti, but also for Vino Nobile di Montepulciano and Carmignano; and a variant of Sangiovese known as Brunello is the only grape permitted for the famous Brunello di Montalcino. A certain amount of Cabernet Sauvignon is also planted in Tuscany, where it may be blended with Sangiovese, as in Carmignano and the proprietary brands Tignanello and Grifi, or with Cabernet Franc, as in the proprietary wines Sassicaia and Solaia. The principal white varieties of Tuscany are Trebbiano and Malvasia, which were until recently an important, and controversial, component of Chianti; they are now used primarily for the many Tuscan whites produced under various names by Chianti firms. Such whites as Galestro, Bianco della Lega, and the DOCs Bianco della Val d'Arbia, Bianco di Pitigliano, and Bianco Vergine della Valdichiana are based on Trebbiano blended with Malvasia or other varieties. Vernaccia di San Gimignano, from the Vernaccia grape, is the one major Tuscan white not based on the Trebbiano and Malvasia. A small amount of Rosé di Bolgheri is produced around that village, southeast of Livorno.

❧ U

Ugni Blanc A productive white-wine grape, better-known as the Trebbiano of Italy, and one of the most widely planted grapes in the world. Ugni Blanc is known as Saint-Emilion in the Cognac region of France, where it has almost entirely replaced Folle Blanche and Colombard as the base wine for that famous brandy, and is also extensively planted in the Armagnac region and in southern France, especially in Provence; it is also grown in the Central Valley of California, where it is known as Saint-Emilion. The wines range from low-alcohol, high-acid wines suitable for distillation to agreeable, if neutral, table wines with a touch of crisp acidity.

Ull de Llebre Catalán for "eye of the hare"; the name by which the

Tempranillo grape is known in the Penedès region.

Ullage The empty space above the liquid in an incompletely filled wine cask; the amount that it lacks of being full. It is important that casks or barrels be kept full to avoid spoilage, and this is done by topping at regular intervals; the French term for this indispensable cellar work is *ouillage*.

Umbria A region in central Italy whose capital is Perugia; its most famous wine is the white produced round the hilltop village of Orvieto. Other DOC zones are Torgiano, whose red is better known under the proprietary name Rubesco, and Colli Altotiberini, Colli del Trasimeno, Colli Perugini, and Montefalco. Chardonnay and Cabernet Sauvignon have been planted near Torgiano, around the village of Miranduolo, and a certain amount of Vin Santo is made in Umbria, as in adjoining Tuscany, and is likely to be *amabile*, slightly sweet.

Umpqua Valley A viticultural area in Oregon, near Roseburg, about 180 miles south of Portland, where the state's first *vinifera* vineyard since Prohibition was planted in 1961. Although most of Oregon's vineyards have since been established in the Willamette Valley, a number of wineries producing such varietal wines as White Riesling, Chardonnay, Pinot Noir, and Cabernet Sauvignon are situated in the somewhat warmer and less rainy Umpqua Valley, including the Hillcrest Vineyard and the Henry Winery.

Urzig A tiny village on the Moselle whose steeply terraced vineyards are made up primarily of brick-red soil, rather than the prevailing black slate of the region; its wines have a rather special spicy character, and, indeed, the name of its best-known vineyard is Würzgarten, or "spice garden".

Usé French for "worn out", and having a similar meaning when applied to wine; a tired wine, on the decline and definitely past its prime.

United States With a total wine production that has varied in recent years from 180 to 240 million cases – slightly more than a quarter as much as France or Italy – America usually ranks fifth or sixth in the world. As consumers, however, Americans rank nearly thirtieth, with a per capita consumption of about eleven bottles a year, compared to nearly a hundred in France and Italy, and more than sixty in Argentina, Luxembourg and Switzerland. Nevertheless total consumption has increased almost fourfold in the past twenty-five years, and table wines, which once accounted for less than 20 percent of the total (which was made up primarily of inexpensive port, sherry, and muscatel), now amount to three quarters of the wines consumed. About 90 percent of the wines made in America come from California, but wine is now produced in more than forty states, and of the 1,300 wineries in the United States about half are outside California. New York is second to California in the amount of wine produced, but most of that is made from native grapes and French-American hybrids, with European *Vitis vinifera* grapes accounting for only 2,000 acres. There are about 11,000 acres of *vinifera* grapes in Washington, about 5,000 acres in Oregon, and significant new plantings in Idaho, Texas, and Virginia; entries for these states, plus Ohio, which was once America's premier wine producer, will be found elsewhere in this volume.

While almost all the vineyards and wineries outside California are of relatively recent origin, a number of states have a long history of winemaking. Nicholas Longworth first produced Catawba wines in Ohio in the 1820s; the Brotherhood Winery in New York State has been in operation since 1839; Wisconsin's Wollersheim Winery traces its origins back to 1857; the Renault Winery in New Jersey dates back to 1864; Bardenheimer's Wine Cellars was established in Missouri in 1873; and two Arkansas wineries, Post and Wiederkehr, were founded in 1880. Today, a number of American wineries continue to produce wines from such native grapes as Concord, Catawba, Delaware, and, in the south, Muscadine and Scuppernong; many cultivate French-American hybrids such as Seyval Blanc, Vidal, Vignoles, Aurora, Baco Noir, Chelois, Léon Millot, and Maréchal Foch; and most of the wineries founded in the past dozen years produce at least some wines from *vinifera* grapes, especially Chardonnay, Johannisberg Riesling, and Cabernet Sauvignon. It is not unusual for wineries east of the Rockies to make wines from both native grapes and French-American hybrids, or from hybrids and *vinifera*; some make wine from all three. It should perhaps be added that many wineries throughout the country buy California wine in bulk to blend with their locally-produced wine. In addition, a number of wineries specialize in fruit wines; these range from pineapple wine made in Hawaii to blueberry wine from Maine to the full range of fruit wines produced in Oregon. There are more than forty officially recognized appellations of origin, called viticultural areas, outside California; these include such familiar names as New York's Finger Lakes and Hudson River Region, Washington's Yakima Valley and Columbia Valley, and Oregon's Willamette Valley, as well as appellations less frequently encountered, such as Augusta in Missouri, Catoctin in Maryland, Fennville and Leelanau Peninsula in Michigan, and the North Fork of Long Island. Wineries now exist in states where wine production was considered unlikely, such as Arizona, Colorado, Florida, Iowa, New Mexico, Oklahoma, and Tennessee. Other wine-producing states (and some of their most interesting wineries) include Connecticut (Haight Vineyards, Crosswoods Vineyards), Georgia (Chateau Elan), Maryland (Boordy Vineyards, Byrd Vineyards, Montbray Wine Cellars), Massachusetts (Chicama Vineyards, Commonwealth Winery), Michigan (Boskydel Vineyard, Château Grand Travers, Fenn Valley Vineyards, Tabor Hill Winery), Minnesota (Alexis Bailly Vineyard), Missouri (Mount Pleasant Vineyard, Stone Hill Winery), New Jersey (Tewksbury Wine Cellars), North Carolina (Biltmore Estate), Pennsylvania (Allegro Vineyard, Chaddsford Winery), Rhode Island (Sakonnet Vineyards), and South Carolina (Truluck Vineyards).

 V

Vacqueyras   A village northeast of Avignon and Châteauneuf-du-Pape whose wines have been entitled to the superior appellation Côtes-du-Rhône-Villages; the fame of the sturdy red wines of Vacqueyras is such that they have recently been granted their own AOC, and the name may now appear alone on a label as for Gigondas.

Valais   A Swiss canton producing most of that country's best red wines and some of the more interesting whites. The extensive vineyards are strung along the rocky, enormously impressive upper valley of the Rhône, separated from Italy by the highest peaks of the Alps, from near Martigny, at the foot of Mont Blanc, past Sion, Sierre, and Visp. Among the finer Valais wines are the reds known as Dôle; dry white wines made from Chasselas (known there as Fendant); Johannisberger, which may be either Riesling or Sylvaner; and the white Ermitage (the local name for the Marsanne of France).

Valdadige An Italian DOC for undistinguished red and white wines produced in an area that extends from north of Bolzano down past Trento and almost to Verona; about a dozen varieties are permitted for the *bianco*, almost as many for the *rosso*.

Valdepeñas A district within the large La Mancha area in central Spain known primarily for its light red wines. The 70,000 acres entitled to the *Denominación de Origen* Valdepeñas, which produce about 7 to 10 million cases annually, are planted 90 percent with the white Airén grape and the rest with the red Cencibel (identical to the Tempranillo of Rioja). Curiously enough, most of the wines made in this district are light reds known as *clarete*; the juice of Cencibel is so dark in colour that even a small proportion blended with white Airén wines is enough to achieve the desired colour. The light red, generally better than the rather golden, low-acid white, has considerably more fruit and charm, as well as a refreshing lightness and lack of astringency; it can be served chilled and is best drunk young.

Valdepeñas is also the name of a red-wine grape cultivated in California's San Joaquin Valley, where about 700 acres are planted; it is certainly of Spanish origin, but almost certainly not the Cencibel.

Valençay A VDQS for red, white and rosé wines produced southeast of Tours, near the Loire River.

Valgella A small DOC zone within the Valtellina district, in Italy's Lombardy region, producing fine red wines from the Nebbiolo grape.

Val d'Aosta Italy's smallest region, situated in the northwest corner of the country, and best known for the ski resort at Courmayeur. Total wine production amounts to 300,000 to 400,000 cases a year, of which only 6,000 cases or so come from the region's two traditional DOC zones, Donnaz and Enfer d'Arvier, both known for their fine red wines. A number of other unusual and rarely seen wines are produced in Valle d'Aosta, including two crisp, dry whites made from the Blanc de Valdigne grape near the villages of Morgex and La Salle, and labelled Blanc de Morgex and Blanc de La Salle. In 1986, the appellation Valle d'Aosta was established as a DOC which encompasses nearly all of this region's vineyards.

Valle Isarco A DOC zone along the Isarco River, northeast of Bolzano, in the Alto Adige region; several distinctive varietal white wines are produced in this small district (called Eisacktaler in German), including Sylvaner, Müller-Thurgau, and Riesling.

Valmur One of the seven *grand cru* vineyards of Chablis, whose 33 acres are situated between Grenouilles and Les Clos.

Valpantena A valley within the Valpolicella district, near Verona, whose name occasionally appears on labels, as Valpolicella-Valpantena.

Valpolicella One of Italy's most famous red wines, fragrant, fruity, rather light in alcohol and body, but most agreeable if consumed young. Four million cases or more are produced annually from a district above Verona that lies between Bardolino and Soave and the name of which means "valley of many cellars"; the grapes, as for the lighter-bodied Bardolino, are Corvina Veronese, Rondinella, Molinara, and Negrara. The best wines are likely to come from the inner *classico* zone, and are so labelled; wines from the Valpantena Valley just north of Verona may be marketed as Valpolicella-Valpantena. In favourable years, a part of the Valpolicella crop is set aside and treated specially to produce the sweet Recioto della Valpolicella and the dry Recioto della Valpolicella Amarone.

Valtellina A DOC district in northern Italy, near the Swiss border, in the Lombardy region, whose red wines are among the country's best. Most of the vineyards are situated north of the Adda River on steep, south-facing, terraced hillsides; the producing grape, known as Chiavennasca, is the famous Nebbiolo of Piedmont, and here again gives wines of remarkable class, although in a somewhat lighter and leaner style, as a result of the high elevation of the vineyards. The basic appellation Valtellina need be made with only 70 percent Nebbiolo; Valtellina Superiore must contain 95 percent of that grape and must be aged a minimum of two years, one of them in wood. The 1,200 acres entitled to the latter DOC are, in turn, divided into four smalller zones which are, extending from west to east along this Alpine valley, Sassella, Grumello, Inferno, and Valgella, and so labelled. They are interesting and unusual wines, sturdy and well-knit; almost unattractively firm when young, they develop slowly and well in bottle, and are long-lived. A special wine called Sfursat, or Sforzato, is made from grapes that have been carefully selected during the harvest and then spread out to dry indoors for some weeks before being crushed; the resulting wine, a sturdy red with a minimum of 14.5 percent alcohol, is similar to the Amarone of Valpolicella.

Var A French *département* along the Mediterranean, between Marseilles and Cannes, whose principal city is Toulon; its vineyards produce a surprising amount of wine, mostly rosés and reds, including most of the AOC Côtes de Provence and all of the VDQS Coteaux Varois, as well as the small appellation of Bandol.

Varietal Wine A wine that takes its name from the grape variety from which it is primarily, or entirely, made. Varietal names are used in regions where a number of different varieties are cultivated, so that the name of the grape is a more useful indication of a wine's taste than its place of origin. California wines provide the best-known examples of this type of labelling, and hundreds of wineries market wines with such varietal names as Cabernet Sauvignon, Chardonnay, Sauvignon Blanc, Zinfandel, Chenin Blanc, and so on. Wines from many other states also bear varietal names, such as Pinot Noir from Oregon, Sémillon from Washington, Chenin Blanc from Texas, and Chardonnay, Seyval Blanc, and Catawba from New York.

Most European wines are labelled with the names of the districts or villages from which they come, but the grape varieties grown are specifically designated by tradition and by law, and are implicit in the wine's appellation of origin: Beaujolais is made from the Gamay grape, Sancerre from Sauvignon Blanc, Barolo from Nebbiolo, and so on. However, wherever a number of varieties are grown in the same region, varietal names are used to identify the wines:

Riesling and Gewüztraminer from France's Alsace region; Dolcetto, Pinot Grigio, Verdicchio, and Lambrusco from Italy; Riesling, Sylvaner, and Müller-Thurgau from Germany. Non-European varietal wines include Shiraz, Sémillon, and Chardonnay from Australia and Cabernet Sauvignon from Chile. Often the varietal name is combined with that of a region, such as Napa Valley Cabernet Sauvignon, Brunello di Montalcino, Fendant du Valais, and Hunter Valler Sémillon. The minimum varietal content required by law varies: 75 percent in California, 80 percent in Australia, 85 percent in Germany, and 100 percent in Alsace. Note that "varietal" refers to a system of labelling, not the grape itself, which is properly called a variety. The term *varietal wine* does not indicate superior quality, and the phrase *varietal grapes* is redundant, since all grapes belong to some variety.

Vat A large container of wood, cement, or metal, sometimes open at the top, used for fermenting, storing, and blending wine.

Vaucluse A French *département* in the lower Rhône Valley whose principal city is Avignon and whose wines include Châteauneuf-du-Pape, Gigondas, Muscat de Beaumes-de-Venise, Côtes du Ventoux, Côtes du Lubéron, and part of the Côtes-du-Rhône.

Vaud A canton in Switzerland which, with the adjoining canton of Valais, produces most of that country's wines; the Vaud produces white wines almost exclusively, and almost all of those are fresh, dry, light wines made from the Chasselas grape (known locally as Dorin). Light red wines made from Pinot Noir and Gamay, and similar to the Dôle of the Valais, are known as Savagnin. The most important districts of the Vaud are La Côte, which extends along the northern shore of Lake Geneva from just past Geneva to Lausanne; Lavaux, which continues from Lausanne to Montreux, and includes the wine villages of Vevey and Saint-Saphorin; and Chablais, which extends from the eastern tip of the Lake of Geneva along the Rhône almost to Martigny, and which includes the villages of Aigle and Yvorne.

Vaudésir One of the best of the seven *grand cru* vineyards of Chablis, whose 40 acres are situated between Les Preuses and Grenouilles.

VDQS or Vins Délimités de Qualité Supérieure A category of French wines created in 1949 that includes many of excellent quality that are nevertheless not entitled to *Appellation Contrôlée* status. They are, however, strictly controlled by the French government as to delimited production zones, permitted grape varieties, and yield per acre. Their labels carry a special stamp with the initials VDQS and the words *Label de Garantie*. In one way, the regulations concerning VDQS wines were originally stricter than those for AOC wines in that the former must be approved by a tasting panel before being granted the *label*; only in the past few years have tasting panels been established, region by region, for AOC wines, More than 20 VDQS wines have been elevated to AOC, among them Cahors, Corbières, Coteaux d'Aix-en-Provence, Coteaux du Languedoc, Côtes de Buzet, Côtes du Lubéron, Côtes de Provence, Côtes du Ventoux, Haut-Poitou, and Minervois. There are now about 35 VDQS districts, and they account for 9 million cases or so of wine, about 60 percent of it red and rosé; in the early 1980s, before several of the major red-wine districts were elevated to AOC, the VDQS category accounted for 25 million cases, 85 percent of it red and rosé. Some of the better-known VDQS names are Gros Plant du Pays Nantais, Saint-Pourçain, Sauvignon de Saint-Bris. A complete list will be found on page 536.

Vecchio Italian for "old", this term may be used on the labels of certain Italian wines, notably Chianti, that are at least two years old.

Vega Sicilia A famous Spanish estate situated about 130 miles northwest of Madrid at Valbuena, on the Duero River, east of Valladolid; it produces rare, interesting, and expensive red wines of near-legendary status that few people have tasted. Its 300 acres of vineyards, planted with 60 percent Tinto Fino (similar to the Tempranillo of Rioja), 20 percent Cabernet Sauvignon, and 10 percent each of Merlot and Malbec, produce an average of 16,000 cases a year, although abundant vintages have achieved 25,000 cases. Two red wines are made, of which the most famous is Vega Sicilia Unico, aged in a combination of small barrels and large casks for 6 to 8 years; remarkably, some older vintages have been aged for 15 or even 20 years before being bottled. Despite this extended period of wood aging, the wines are by no means faded or dried out, but rich, substantial, and well-structured. Production of Unico has varied from 2,000 cases to 8,000 cases a year, with an average of about 5,000 cases. The second wine, called Valbueno, accounts for the rest of the estate's production; depending on the quality of the vintage, it is bottled after approximately 15 months or three years of wood aging. The owners of Vega Sicilia (the name is a combination of the word for riverbank and a reference to Saint Cecilia) have also planted 125 acres of white varieties – two thirds Sauvignon Blanc and one third Viura – near Escoril, 120 miles from the original estate.

Velouté French for "velvety" and applied to wines that are notably mature, finely textured, and agreeably soft.

Veltliner *See* Grüner Veltliner

Vendange French for "grape harvest", or "vintage", but the word is never used in the sense of the vintage year of a particular wine, which would be *année* or *millésime*. Equivalent terms are *vendemmia* in Italian and *vendimia* in Spanish, and these too are applied to the harvest itself, not to the vintage year on a wine label.

Vendange Tardive This term, which means "late harvest", is used in France's Alsace region for certain wines produced in limited quantities (less than 1 percent of the crop in the excellent 1983 vintage). Given official sanction in 1983, the designation may be used only for wines made from grapes that have achieved a minimum natural sugar content equal to that of a German Auslese – 24.3 percent for Gewürztraminer and Pinot Gris, 22 percent for Riesling and Muscat d'Alsace. Because they are fermented out until they are dry or almost dry, however, Alsace Vendange Tardive wines are relatively rich, full-bodied and flavourful. Although production of these wines amounted to more than 225,000 cases in the excellent 1989 vintage, that still represents less than 2 percent of the total Alsace crop.

Vendimia Spanish for "vintage", or "harvest"

Venegazzù An estate, originally owned by the Loredan Gasparini family, situated in what is now the Montello e Colline Asolani DOC zone of Italy's Veneto region; its best-known wines are Riserva della Casa, a red made from Cabernet Sauvignon, Cabernet Franc, Merlot, and Malbec; a varietal Cabernet Sauvignon; and a white sparkling wine made from Prosecco.

Venencia An instrument used in the sherry region of Spain to take samples of wine through the bunghole of a cask. In its simplest form, it is a strip of bamboo with one cylindrical section left intact at the lower end, so as to form a little cup. This was largely replaced by a silver cup attached to a pliable whalebone rod, and today a *venencia* is likely to consist of a stainless-steel cup attached to a plastic handle. An expert *bodeguero* in Jerez can use his *venencia* with extraordinary grace and skill to pour sherry from the cup, raised above his head, into a small glass held at his waist.

Veneto An extensive region in northeast Italy that stretches from Lake Garda to the Adriatic and whose principal cities are Venice and Verona. Total wine production is 90 to 130 million cases a year, of which 16 to 20 million cases qualify for DOC; this amounts to about 20 percent of all the DOC wines of Italy. The Veneto's most famous wines are the three produced near Verona – Soave, Valpolicella, and Bardolino. In addition, a diverse and often excellent range of wines is made throughout this region, many of which are marketed with varietal names. These include attractive reds from the widely planted Merlot grape, as well as from Cabernet Franc, Cabernet Sauvignon, Pinot Nero, and the native Raboso; whites are made from Pinot Bianco, Pinot Grigio, and the native Verduzzo, Tocai Italico, and Prosecco, the latter usually transformed into *frizzante* and fully sparkling *spumante*. Whites similar to Soave include Bianco di Custoza and Gambellera; other DOCs include Tocai di Lison, the Merlot and Cabernet made in the Pramaggiore district (now known as Lison-Pramaggiore), and varietal wines from Breganze, Colli Berici, Colli Euganei, and Piave. Two well-known estates are situated in the Veneto – Venegazzù and Quarto Vecchio.

Venezie An Italian term, interchangeable with Tre Venezie, used to describe the three contiguous regions of Trentino-Alto Adige, Veneto, and Friuli-Venezia Giulia; sometimes seen on the labels of non-DOC varietal wines, as in Pinot Grigio delle Venezie.

Vente Sur Souches French for "sale on the vine", this refers to the commercial practice, once prevalent in the Bordeaux region, whereby a vineyard proprietor sold part of his crop to local *négociants*, or shippers, in the early summer before the harvest, long before anything was known of its quality. This speculation on the part of the shippers was made possible by the proprietors' need for cash to get through the coming harvest; the vineyard owners suffered financially from this practice in 1959 and again in 1961, and such sales have not taken place since.

Ventoux *See* Côtes du Ventoux

Veraison The French term for the stage in the ripening process when the grapes change colour; this occurs after flowering but before the grapes attain their full sugar content and are ready to be harvested.

Verbesco A name created by a number of producers in Italy's Piedmont region for a light, dry white wine made primarily from Barbera vinified as a *blanc de noirs*.

Verdelho Once one of the classic white-wine grape varieties on the island of Madeira; the name is now used to describe a medium-dry style of wine.

Verdicchio An Italian white-wine grape cultivated in the Marches region, along the Adriatic Sea; the best-known Verdicchio comes from the DOC zone Castelli di Jesi, situated in the foothills of the Apennines, about 20 miles west of Ancona, around the town of Jesi. Verdicchio dei Castelli di Jesi (which can include up to 20 percent of Trebbiano and Malvasia) is a pale, light-bodied, fresh, crisp wine that owes part of its reputation to the unusual amphora bottle in which it is marketed; its success is such that production now often exceeds 1.5 million cases. Verdicchio di Matelica is a smaller DOC zone southwest of Jesi whose production is less than a tenth that of Castelli di Jesi; the wine is fuller-bodied and perhaps longer-lived than that of its more famous and more easily found neighbour.

Verdignan, Château A well-known *cru bourgeois* of the Haut-Médoc that produces about 25,000 cases a year; it is under the same direction as Château Coufran.

Verduzzo A native Italian white-wine grape found primarily in the Friuli region, where it produces wines that may be dry or *amabile*, semisweet. The best of the sweet wines, known as Verduzzo di Ramandolo, is produced in the northern part of the Colli Orientali del Friuli zone. Verduzzo is also marketed as a varietal wine from the Piave district in the Veneto.

Vereinigte Hospitien A charitable hospital in Trier, on the Moselle, whose endowments include extensive vineyard holdings in such villages as Piesport, Bernkastel, Graach, and Zeltingen on the Moselle, and Serrig and Wiltingen on the Saar.

Verjus A French word that refers to the juice of unripe grapes, high in acid.

Vermentino An Italian grape that produces what is probably the best white wine of the Italian Riviera, in the Liguria region – fresh, pale, tart, excellent with seafood; one of the grapes used to make the DOC Cinqueterre, it is even better on its own, as a varietal wine. Vermentino is also cultivated in Sardinia, where its style varies from the light, clean, crisp Vermentino di Alghero to the heavier, more alcoholic Vermentino di Gallura.

Vermouth A popular kind of flavoured wine used principally as an aperitif and as an ingredient in cocktails; it consists of a neutral white wine flavoured with various herbs, plants , fruits, and spices, and fortified to a minimum of 16 percent alcohol by the addition of grape spirits. Traditionally, the principal aromatic agent in vermouth has been flowers of the shrub *Artemisia absinthium*, also known as wormwood; in fact, vermouth derives from *Wermut*, the German for "wormwood". There are two basic types: dry vermouth is pale in colour and contains 2 to 4 percent sugar; sweet vermouth is dark (the colour comes from caramel) and sweet, with a minimum of 14 percent sugar. The two types are sometimes referred to as French and Italian, respectively, both types are made in each of those countries, and in many others as well, including the United States; locally produced vermouth, about 90 percent of it from California, now accounts for more than half the vermouth consumed in the United States.

Vernaccia di Oristano An unusual, deliberately oxidized, sherry-like wine produced north of the city of Oristano on the island of

Sardinia. Relatively high in natural alcohol – 15 or 16 percent is not unusual – the wines are aged in wood for a minimum of two years (three for Superiore, four for Riserva); its taste ranges from dry to sweet, but the fruity, appealing, slightly austere dry version is considered the best. It is unlikely that the Vernaccia grape of Sardinia is related to the variety of the same name cultivated round San Gimignano in Tuscany.

Vernaccia di San Gimignano A dry white wine produced in Italy's Tuscany region, on the slopes and plains below the historic hill town of San Gimignano, about 30 miles south of Florence. The traditional robust, wood-aged style of these wines, the first in Italy to achieve DOC status, have been transformed in recent years by a number of producers who prefer pale, fresh, crisp wines with less alcohol and more fruit. About 300,000 cases are produced annually, and some firms have begun to make sparkling Vernaccia as well. Wines labelled Vernaccia are produced in other parts of Italy, but few are made from the Tuscan grape; the best-known is Vernaccia di Oristano from Sardinia.

Vernatsch The German name, widely used in Italy's Alto Adige province, for the native Schiava grape.

Vert French for "green" and applied to wines that are tart and high in acid.

Verwaltung German for "administrative estate", as in Verwaltung Staatsweingüter.

Vesuvio An Italian DOC established in 1983 for red, white, and rosé wines produced at the foot of Mount Vesuvio, near Naples. The better wines from this district are entitled to the DOC Lacryma Christi del Vesuvio.

Vidal Blanc A French-American hybrid descended from Ugni Blanc, producing attractive white wines that may be crisp and dry or semisweet; some sweet, luscious ice wines have also been made from frozen grapes.

VIDE The acronym for Vitivinicoltori Italiani d'Eccellenza, an association, established in 1978, of about three dozen Italian producers, all of whom market only estate-bottled wines. The members of this group have established standards for themselves stricter than those imposed by DOC and DOCG laws, and only those wines that have been approved by an independent tasting panel may wear the VIDE neck label.

Vieux French for "old" and about as loosely used as in English; the feminine form is *vieille*.

Vieux Château Certan One of the best-known and most acclaimed vineyards of the Pomerol district; its 33 acres produce 7,000 cases or so in an abundant vintage. The vineyard, situated on soil that is comparatively gravelly, is planted with less Merlot and more Cabernet Franc and Cabernet Sauvignon than is usual in Pomerol, and the excellent wines (marketed with a distinctive pink capsule) often display more tannic structure and less suppleness than those of its neighbours.

Vif A French term applied to a young wine that is fresh and light, with lively acidity.

Vigne A French word for "vine"; others are *cep* and *souche*.

Vignelaure, Château Perhaps the best-known estate in the AOC Coteaux d'Aix-en-Provence, its 135 acres produce about 25,000 cases of an attractive, well-structured red wine made from a blend – unusual for the region – of 60 percent Cabernet Sauvignon, 30 percent Syrah, and 10 percent Grenache.

Vigneron French for a vineyardist, someone who tends vines, whether for his own account or not.

Vignoble A French word that can refer to a single vineyard or to all the vineyards of a given district.

Vignoles *See* Ravat

Vila Nova de Gaia A town directly opposite Oporto, on the Douro River, in northern Portugal; the lodges, or warehouses, of all the port shippers are located in this picturesque old town.

Villard Blanc A French-American hybrid created by the French hybridizer Seyve-Villard (who also developed the better-known Seyval Blanc); this variety, suited to warmer areas, is still widely planted in southern France.

Vin The French word for "wine", legally defined in France, as in the United States, as a beverage made by the partial or complete fermentation of the juice of fresh grapes.

Vin de l'Année French for "wine of the year" and used to describe any wine that is less than a year old.

Vin Blanc French for "white wine"

Vin Bourru A French term for a young, unfinished wine just drawn from the fermentation vat; the wine, still gassy and perhaps slightly sweet, is sometimes consumed in this state in France and in a number of other wine-producing countries.

Vin Cuit A French term for a wine that has been heated before fermentation so as to increase its eventual alcohol and sweetness; the term is also used by tasters to describe a red wine made from overripe grapes, as in a very hot year, and marked by a somewhat sweet and raisiny taste.

Vin Doux Naturel A category of sweet, fortified red and white wines produced in France, primarily along the Mediterranean Coast; between 5 and 6 million cases are produced annually, two thirds of it white. The grapes must be harvested with a minimum sugar content of 25.2 percent, between 5 and 10 percent of neutral high-proof spirits are added to the fermenting must to stop fermentation, and the finished wine must have a minimum alcohol content of 15 percent. The category gets its somewhat misleading name not because the wines are made naturally – they are, in fact, fortified just like port – but because they are naturally sweet; that is, the residual sugar of 10 or 12 percent comes from the grapes. The red wines, which become tawny when they have aged, are made primarily from Grenache grapes, and include Banyuls, Maury, Rasteau, and Rivesaltes; a considerably greater quantity of white Rivesaltes is also made from Malvoisie. The best-known VDN wines, however, are those made from the Muscat grape, and include Muscat de Beaumes-de-Venise, Muscat de Frontignan, Muscat de Lunel, Muscat de Mireval, and Muscat de Rivesaltes. The requirements for the category *vins de liqueur* are similar to those for VDN, and many of the appellations listed above qualify for both.

Vin Fin A loosely used French term meaning, in general, a wine of superior quality; it is not legally defined, although at one time the wines now known as Côte de Nuits-Villages were called Vins Fins de la Côte de Nuits.

Vin de Garde   A French term that refers to a wine worth keeping, one that will improve with age.

Vin Gris   A French term used to describe very pale rosé wines, especially those made from the Pinot Noir grape in Burgundy and Alsace; some of these are practically white, with a slight pink or bronze tinge.

Vin Jaune   An odd, special "yellow wine" produced in the Jura district of France, especially round Château-Châlon, from the Savagnin grape; it is similar in character to a very light Spanish sherry.

Vin de Liqueur   Most often, a sweet wine obtained by adding alcohol to the must before fermentation is complete, thus preserving the sweetness of the natural grape sugar; the term also applies, however, if the alcohol is added before fermentation or after fermentation is complete.

Vin Mousseux   *See* Mousseux

Vin Nouveau   *See* Nouveau

Vin Ordinaire   *See* Ordinaire

Vin de Paille   An unusual white wine produced in the Jura district of France, similar to Italian Vin Santo, made from grapes that have been spread on mats of straw (*paille*) or hung from hooks in well-ventilated rooms for several weeks until they are dehydrated. The resulting wine, produced in very limited quantities, is rich, golden, and sweet.

Vin de Pays   The third category of French wines, after *Appellation Contrôlée* and VDQS. Established in 1973, this category includes what might be called country wines of some distinction that come from specific regions, and for which permitted grape varieties and maximum yields per acre have been established; the creation of this category and its regional appellations has encouraged growers in these areas to improve the quality of their wines. Some of the regional boundaries are rather extensive: Vin de Pays du Jardin de France encompasses all of the Loire vineyards, Vin de Pays d'Oc includes most of southern France and the Mediterranean coast; other names conform to *départements*, such as Côtes du Tarn and Coteaux de l'Ardèche; and there are about 100 smaller *vin de pays* districts, most of them in the Aude, Gard, and Hérault *départements* of the Languedoc region. Production, almost all of it red, amounts to 10 million cases a year, more than 10 percent of the total French crop. Not to be confused with *vin du pays*.

Vin du Pays A French term that means "wine of the country" or, more often, "wine of the region"; that is, the local wine, whatever that may be. The term has no legal meaning, as does *vin de pays*, and the wine referred to may be ordinary or excellent.

Vin de Presse *See* Press Wine

Vin Rosé *See* Rosé

Vin Santo An Italian white wine produced principally in Tuscany from Trebbiano and Malvasia grapes that have been specially dehydrated by leaving the bunches on trays or hooks in well-ventilated rooms for three or four months after the harvest. The concentrated juice, especially rich in sugar, is then fermented in small barrels that are not completely filled, and that are sealed up for two or three years. The result is a richly textured golden wine with 14 to 16 percent alcohol that usually contains some residual sugar, with an intense, slightly oxidized taste reminiscent of sherry; sometimes fermentation continues in the sealed barrel until the wine is dry, but most Vin Santo is sweet. This unusual wine is also produced in Umbria and, to a limited extent, in Trentino and the Veneto.

Vin de Table The lowest category of French wines, not unlike *vin ordinaire*; although such wines have no geographical appellation of origin and can be a blend of wines from anywhere in France, they are generally inexpensive, their quality has improved in the past decade, and many of them are good values.

Vin d'Une Nuit A French term for an inexpensive, light red wine that has been left to ferment on its skins for twenty-four hours or less, and that therefore has little colour and tannin; it is, for all practical purposes, a dark rosé, and identical with a *vin de café* or a *vin de vingt-quatre heures*.

Viné A French word meaning "fortified"; wines to which brandy or, more often, high-proof grape spirits have been added are called *vins vinés*. This is sometimes done to strengthen inexpensive wines exported in bulk.

Vineux A French term applied to a substantial, well-structured wine, probably high in alcohol, but not disagreeably so.

Vineyard A plantation of grapevines

Vineyard Site The rather clumsy English equivalent of the French *climat* or *cru*, meaning a specifically named plot of vines.

Vinho Verde Portuguese for "green wine", this is the odd name given to the sprightly, light-bodied red and white wines – which are green only in the sense of being fresh and youthful – produced in the northwest corner of the country, between the Douro and Minho rivers, the latter forming the border with Spain. The rather harsh red is something of an acquired taste, but the pale, crisp, dry white, most examples of which contain less than 10 percent alcohol, is an agreeable wine that retains a refreshing *pétillance*, or light sparkle; many examples bottled for export, however, are slightly sweet. The vines are traditionally grown high above the ground, on pergolas, and harvesters need a ladder to pick the grapes; increasingly, new vineyards are planted along the ground. A number of grape varieties are used to make the white wines, including Avesso in the Amarante district, Loureiro and Trajudura around Braga, and Alvarinho in the northern village of Monçao; the last rather fuller-bodied than typical Vinho Verde, are considered the finest wines of all.

Viniculture A general term covering the whole science and business of growing wine grapes, making wine and aging it, and preparing wine for market.

Vinifera By all odds the most important of the 40-odd species that make up the genus *vitis*. Appropriately named "the wine bearer", *Vitis vinifera*, which originated in Transcaucasia in prehistoric times, is responsible for virtually all of the world's wines (the rest are made from hybrids and from a number of native American varieties). There are more than a thousand varieties of *vinifera* – black, purple, blue, red, pink, amber, yellow, green – of which the most famous include Cabernet Sauvignon, Pinot Noir, Zinfandel, Nebbiolo, Chardonnay, Riesling, Sauvignon Blanc, Sémillon, Chenin Blanc, and Grenache.

Vinification   Properly speaking, this refers to the process of transforming grape juice into wine.

Vino Corriente   The Spanish equivalent of the French *vin ordinaire*; the young, inexpensive, relatively common wine produced for current consumption.

Vino de Mesa   Spanish for "table wine".

Vino Nobile di Montepulciano   A fine red wine from southern Tuscany, produced around the picturesque old hill town of that name, about 35 miles southeast of Siena. The wine, which was granted DOCG status in 1983, derives its name from the time when it was reserved for the tables of the nobility; today, about 225,000 cases are produced annually from 1,600 acres of hillside vineyards. The wine is made primarily from a variant of Sangiovese known locally as Prugnolo Gentile, plus Canaiolo and a certain amount of white Trebbiano and Malvasia; the formula differs from that used for Chianti in that a small amount of the red Mammolo, which adds a flowery bouquet, may also be used. The Vino Nobile zone actually lies within the Chianti Colli Senesi district, and many examples of this wine are really indistinguishable from Chianti; the best examples, however, are sturdy, long-lived wines, powerful, intense, and distinctive. The wine must be aged a minimum of two years in cask, a Riserva an additional year.

Vino Novello   Italian for "new wine", a term applied to light, fruity wines, usually red, bottled and marketed within weeks of the harvest; these wines are similar in style to the *vins nouveaux* of France, of which Beaujolais Nouveau is the best-known example. In Italy, this type of wine was first produced in the mid-1970s, and some of the best-known versions are San Giocondo of Antinori, based on Sangiovese; Vinòt of Gaja, based on Nebbiolo; and Santa Costanza of Villa Banfi, based on Brunello.

Vino da Pasto An Italian term used informally for table wine, as distinguished from aperitif and dessert wines. In Spanish, *vino de pasto*.

Vino da Tavola Italian for "table wine", the basic and least distinguished category of wine, equivalent to *vin de table* in France and *Tafelwein* in Germany. Wines so labelled in Italy, however, include some of that country's finest wines, from producers who found the DOC laws too confining and who therefore created innovative wines that are marketed with proprietary names. Tignanello and Sassicaia are probably the best known; other examples are Anghelu Ruju, Fiorano, Grifi, Luna dei Feldi, Le Pergole Torte, Torcolato, and Vintage Tunina.

Vinous A term applied to a wine that is clean, acceptable, and without flaws, but without character or personality.

Vintage This refers to the annual grape harvest and to the wine made from those grapes; thus, every year is a vintage year and all wines are vintage wines unless they are blended from two or more years – their vintage is the year they were produced. Actually, the concept of vintage years is a relatively recent one. For most of the past two thousand years, wine was served from a jug or squat flagon filled from a barrel. Wines from the most recent year were considered better, and cost more, than older wines, which were likely to be spoiled. The distinction between vintages, and the possibility of aging wines, first occurred in the late eighteenth century, with the dual development of the binnable bottle – one that could be stored on its side – and the cork stopper that could protect the wine from air. The squat bottle evolved into the tall, cylindrical bottle that we associate with Bordeaux and port in the 1770s. The first vintage-dated port was probably made in 1775 and, in 1787, Thomas Jefferson could write from Bordeaux that he had bought wines from "the vintage of 1784, the only very fine one since the year 1779".

The frequently used term *vintage wine* to denote excellence is actually meaningless, since every wine, good or bad, is made from grapes harvested in a specific year. In the case of port and champagne, most of which are blended from wines of several years, however, a vintage year does indicate one good enough to bottle on its own; eventually, in the popular mind, vintage year came to have the meaning of good year, although it can have no such connotation except with regard to those two wines. For all the attention lavished on vintages, most of the wines sold are inexpensive wines, nonvintage blends that are meant to be palatable and agreeable. There is no need for these moderately priced bottles and magnums to carry a vintage, but the lack of a year on the label does prevent the consumer from knowing just how old such wines are; there are undoubtedly a great many cheap but faded wines displayed on retail shelves. Many of the wines that do carry a vintage date, and all of those that do not, are best consumed young, within a year of the harvest, so the vintage is more useful as a guide to the wine's age than to its quality. This applies to virtually all rosés, most white wines, and many light reds, all of which are noted primarily for their fruit and charm, and have nothing to gain by aging in bottle. It is certain that most of these wines are drunk too late rather than too early. Many of the very finest wines, those at the top of the quality pyramid, are grown in poor soil and in marginal climatic regions where the grapes do not ripen fully every year. These include the wines of Bordeaux, Burgundy, Champagne, the Rhine and Moselle, and the top reds of Italy. Vines are often planted in cool areas with uncertain growing conditions so that when everything does come together, the wines display a finesse and elegance that is difficult to achieve in warmer regions where grapes ripen more consistently.

Not long ago, we were told that every year was a good one in California, which also implied that they were all alike. Although vintage variations are less extreme in California (and Australia) than in most of Europe, we now know that some vintages are more successful than others, and that distinctions can be made between different districts, as well as between different grape varieties within each district.

One traditional source of information about vintages is, of course, a vintage chart, whose numerical ratings of different wines are useful in a general way. It is often pointed out that some properties make a good wine in an off-year, while others may turn out a mediocre bottling in a good year, but that point of view is more useful to a wine merchant than a consumer: no château in Bordeaux produced a better wine in 1977 than in 1978 or 1979, and only a poorly managed one produced a better wine in 1980 or 1984 than in 1982, 1983, or

1985. Similarly, it is unlikely that many estates in Germany made a better 1984 than 1983 or 1985. Another popular notion is that lesser years provide the opportunity to buy famous names from Bordeaux, Burgundy, and other top wine regions at lower prices. But why buy a merely acceptable example of what is supposed to be a great wine? The wine will disappoint, and thus be overpriced. It is better to pay more and get everything the vineyard has to offer. In fairness, though, a fine wine from a top year may need eight or ten years to mature, whereas the same wine from a lighter vintage will be ready sooner; but, of course, the latter will never be as great. If you want the best, you must wait – or pay the premium for a mature wine.

Vintage Port The most famous, expensive, and long-lived style of port, produced from selected lots of wine of a single year, and bottled after only two years of aging in wooden casks. Unlike ruby and tawny ports, which are blends of several vintages that are aged in wood until they are ready to drink, vintage ports must be aged (the bottles lying on their sides, of course) for ten or twenty years before they are considered mature enough to be consumed. There are no official vintage years for port, and every shipper is free to declare a vintage whenever he thinks his wines merit the distinction, which usually occurs only three or four times in a decade. Recent vintages that were declared by twenty or more shippers include 1985, 1983, 1982, 1980, 1977, 1975, 1970, 1966, 1963, and 1960, but a few firms also chose to produce a vintage port in 1972, 1967 and 1962. A shipper traditionally declares a vintage in the second spring after the harvest, so that he has two consecutive vintages to compare before making his decision. In 1984, for example, a number of firms declared 1982 as a vintage year, other firms waited a year and declared 1983 instead. For all its fame, vintage port accounts for less than 3 percent of all the port made. There are about a dozen well-known firms that produce most of what there is of vintage port, and most will set aside only 200 or 300 pipes each from a given vintage, the equivalent of 12,000 to 18,000 cases; thus the total mount of vintage port produced by the leading firms in a generally declared year might be no more than 200,000 to 300,000 cases out of a total port crop of 7 to 9 million cases. Since 1974, all vintage ports must be bottled in Portugal; previously many were bottled in England. Because vintage port represents specially selected lots of wine from the very best vintages, it is one of the most dependable of fine wines, and one of the longest-lived; fifty-year-old bottles in excellent condition are by no means unusual, although they will certainly be expensive. Vintage ports throw a heavy deposit as they age and must always be decanted. There are two other types of port that also display a vintage date on their labels. Late Bottled Vintage ports are bottled four to six years after the harvest and are ready to drink when bottled. Those known as ports with the date of harvest must be aged in wood for a minimum of seven years, but are usually wood-aged considerably longer; they are, in effect, vintage-dated tawny ports. A true vintage port will always display the words *Vintage Port* or *Vintage Porto* on its label. A list of recent port vintages declared by the leading shippers will be found on page 562.

Vintage Tunina A proprietary white wine produced by Jermann in the Collio district of the Friuli-Venezia Giulia region; first made in 1973, this crisp, elegant wine is composed primarily of Chardonnay and Sauvignon Blanc plus varying amounts of such local varieties as Ribolla Gialla, Malvasia Istriana, and Picolit grown in Jermann's 12-acre Tunina vineyard.

Vinzelles *See* Pouilly-Vinzelles

Viognier A rare but celebrated grape of the northern Rhône Valley, in France, giving an excellent and unusual white wine whose bouquet often contains hints of peach or apricot. There are fewer than 100 acres of this variety, sometimes spelled Vionnier, almost all in the vineyards producing Château-Grillet and Condrieu; there are also a dozen acres or so planted within the Côte Rôtie vineyard, and some producers harvest and vinify a small proportion of Viognier along with Syrah to add bouquet and acidity to this sturdy red wine.

Viré A village north of Mâcon, in southern Burgundy, whose fresh dry white wines, made from Chardonnay, are among the best of the Mâconnais, as are those from the neighbouring village of Lugny; their wines are often labelled as Mâcon-Viré or Mâcon-Lugny.

Virginia The first colonists produced wine from native grapes at Jamestown in the early seventeenth century, and Thomas Jefferson tried unsuccessfully to cultivate European *vinifera* varieties in the late eighteenth century. The modern Virginia wine industry, however, dates from the early 1970s, when French-American hybrids and *vinifera* varieties were planted by Archie Smith at his Meredyth Vineyards. Today, there are more than forty wineries in Virginia, and 1,300 acres of vineyards, most of them planted along the eastern slopes of the Blue Ridge Mountains, between Middleburg and Charlottesville; the leading varieties are Chardonnay, Riesling, Cabernet Sauvignon, Seyval Blanc, Merlot, and Vidal Blanc. The best-known wineries include Ingleside Plantation, Meredyth, Montdomaine, Oakencroft, Prince Michel, and Rapidan River.

Viticulteur French for a "vine grower", generally one who cultivates his own vineyard; *vigneron* is nearly synonymous, but more often used of an employee or sharecropper.

Viticultural Area The American term for appellation of origin (the official term is American Viticultural Area), first established in 1983 by the federal government, specifically by the Bureau of Alcohol, Tobacco, & Firearms (BATF); of the 90-plus viticultural areas in the United States, more than 50 are in California. A viticultural area is a delimited grape-growing region whose boundaries have been recognized and defined, based on geographical features, climate and historical precedent; it is the growers in a given area who must determine its boundaries and then petition the government for the right to use the name of the area on their labels. If the name of a viticultural area appears on a label, at least 85 percent of the wine must come from that area. Some viticultural areas are quite extensive: the Napa Valley appellation includes virtually all of Napa County, the Columbia Valley appellation includes almost all the vineyards in Washington. Some areas include only a single winery, such as Guenoc Valley, McDowell Valley, and Chalone; some, like Knights Valley, have no wineries. A number of viticultural areas encompass others within their boundaries: the Russian River Valley includes Chalk Hill and Green Valley, the Columbia Valley includes the Yakima Valley and the Walla Walla Valley. Some viticultural areas overlap county lines, such as Carneros, which extends into both Napa and Sonoma. And sometimes the same name has been approved for more than one viticultural area: there is a Green Valley in Sonoma and another in Solano, the Shenandoah Valley name may be used for a district in California'a Amador County and for another in Virginia.

The regulations concerning a viticultural area apply only to its geography, not to the quality of the fruit grown there or to the specific grape varieties best suited to its particular microclimate. It is certainly too soon to impose on American growers and winemakers the European laws of appellation, which define not only the grape varieties that may be planted in a given region, but maximum production per acre, minimum alcohol content, and, often, how long the wine must be aged in cask or bottle. In many European regions the wines must also be submitted to a tasting panel, which determines whether or not each sample has achieved a minimum quality level and if it is typical of that particular appellation; the latter requirement would be especially difficult to determine in California, where a winemaker's style often dominates that of the appellation. Although defining viticultural areas provides no guarantee of the quality or style of the wines produced, a number of areas, especially in California, have already achieved a reputation for specific varieties; the increased emphasis on appellations of origin represents a shift of focus from the technology of winemaking to viticulture, soil, and microclimate, and will encourage wineries and growers to pay greater attention to the varieties best suited to each district.

Viticulture That branch of agriculture that involves the science of grape-growing; when this extends to the production of wine as well, the proper word is *viniculture*

Vitis Grapes belong to the botanical family *Vitaceae*, and more specifically to the genus *Vitis*; of the many species of *Vitis* found throughout the world, such as *Vitis labrusca* and *Vitis rupestris*, the most important by far for wine production is *Vitis vinifera*, of which there are, in turn, thousands of varieties. *See* French-American Hybrids, Grape, Labrusca, Native American Grapes.

Viura A native Spanish white-wine grape widely cultivated in Rioja and Penedès (where it is known as Macabeo); it can produce attractive dry whites, especially if fermented at cool temperatures and bottled early to retain its fruit.

Vivace A French term usually applied to a young wine that is fresh, has lively acidity, and is likely to keep well.

Vollrads *See* Schloss Vollrads

Volnay A justly celebrated village of the Côte de Beaune, in Burgundy, situated between Pommard and Meursault. About 80,000 cases a year are produced of a red wine whose average quality is quite high, certainly above that of an average Pommard; Volnays of good vintages are among the most prepossessing of all red Burgundies, wonderfully soft and delicate, with a special velvety quality and great breed but by no means short-lived. The better *premier cru* vineyards include Clos des Ducs, Champans, Les Caillerets, Bousse d'Or, Fremiets, and Clos des Chênes; the Santenots vineyard is actually in Meursault, but its red wines are marketed as Volnay-Santenots.

Vosne-Romanée A celebrated village in the Côte de Nuits district of Burgundy's Côte d'Or, perhaps the most remarkable red-wine producing commune of all France, its only rival being Pauillac, in the Médoc district of Bordeaux. Although its total production is comparatively small, about 65,000 cases a year, Vosne-Romanée encompasses five *grand cru* vineyards whose incomparable red wines, among the glories of Burgundy, are known around the world: Romanée-Conti, La Tâche, Richebourg, La Romanée, and Romanée-Saint-Vivant, each labelled simply with the vineyard name. The *premier cru* vineyards, whose names on a label are preceded by that of Vosne-Romanée, include La Grande Rue, Les Malconsorts, Les Suchots, and Les Beaux Monts. All the wines of this commune, including those marketed simply with the village appellation, have certain characteristics in common – breed, elegance, exceptional balance; those from the best vineyards have more richness and concentration, sometimes display a spicy, almost exotic bouquet, and are, of course, longer-lived.

Vougeot A small village in Burgundy's Côte d'Or best known for its world-famous vineyard, Clos de Vougeot. The village itself has 40 acres of vineyards producing about 5,000 cases a year of an attractive red wine that may be sold as Vougeot or Vougeot Premier Cru; in addition, the Clos Blanc vineyard produces white wine that is labelled Clos Blanc de Vougeot.

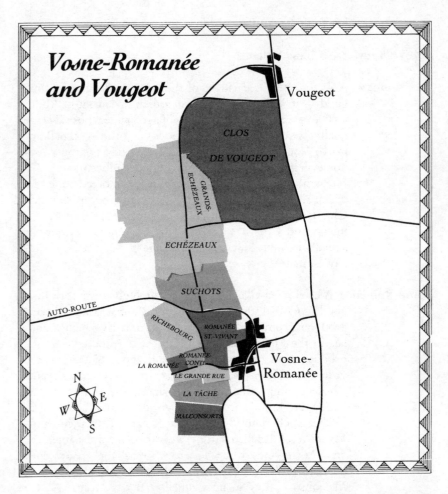

Vosne-Romanée and Vougeot

Vouvray The most famous white wine of Touraine, in the Loire Valley of France; the vineyards, planted entirely with Chenin Blanc, are situated about ten miles east of Tours, on the north bank of the Loire. A changeling among wines if there ever was one, Vouvray can be (depending on vintage conditions and cellar treatment) fruity and bone dry; soft, semidry, and *moelleux*; or rich, sweet, honeyed, and long-lived. What's more, the dry and semidry versions can be still; *pétillant*, with a slight sparkle; or *mousseux*, fully sparkling, and one of the best such wines of France. Production in recent years has often exceeded a million cases, with the *mousseux* version accounting for 20 to 60 percent of the total, depending on the style of the vintage; crisp, dry wines are more easily transformed into *mousseux* than are ripe, semisweet wines.

VQPRD A category, established by the European Common Market, whose full name is *Vins de Qualité Produits dans des Régions Déterminées*, or "quality wines produced in specific regions". Some European wines that fall into this category include the *Appellation Contrôlée* and VDQS wines of France, the Qualitätswein and Qualitätswein mit Prädikat of Germany, and the *Denominazione di Origine Controllata* (DOC) and *Denominazione di Origine Controllata e Garantita* (DOCG) of Italy. The use of the VQPRD designation on a label is optional, and most wines are labelled with the more familiar terms just cited.

Vray Croix de Gay, Château A small vineyard in the Pomerol district producing about 2,000 cases a year.

 # W

Wachenheim One of the best wine-producing towns of the German Rheinpfalz, or Palatinate, its wines are a little lighter than those of Forst and Deidesheim nearby, but of the same noble class; its best vineyards, planted with a high proportion of Riesling, include Gerümpel, Rechbächel, Böhlig, and Goldbächel.

Waldrach A wine-producing village of secondary importance along the Ruwer, near Trier, in Germany.

Walla Walla Valley A small viticultural area in southeast Washington, within the larger Columbia Valley appellation.

Walluf A little village in Germany's Rheingau whose name may be used for wines coming from the townships of Niederwalluf and Oberwalluf; in practice, most are sold with the Grosslage Rauenthaler Steinmächer.

Washington The first commercial wines made from European *vinifera* varieties since Prohibition were produced in this state in 1967 by two wineries – Associated Vintners (which changed its name to Columbia Winery in 1984), and by the firm now known as Château Ste. Michelle. Ten years later there were six wineries and about 3,000 acres of *vinifera* grapes; today,

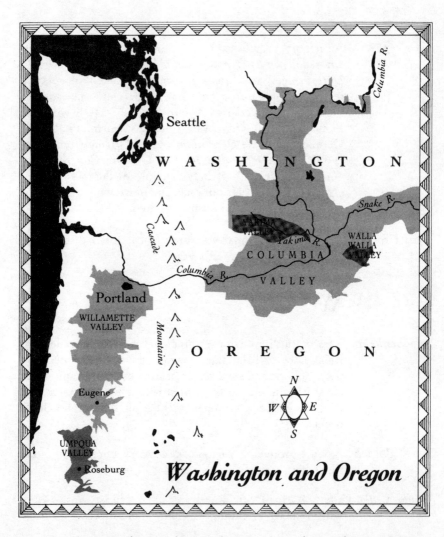

Washington and Oregon

Washington has 80-plus wineries and more than 10,000 acres of *vinifera* vineyards, the largest such planting in the United States outside California. (There are, in addition, about 20,000 acres of Concord grapes, used primarily for juice and preserves.) Although a number of wineries are situated west of the Cascade Mountains, near Seattle, virtually all of the state's vineyards are east of the Cascades, in an irrigated desert known as the Columbia River Basin. This area has a growing season marked by long sunny days and cool nights, which permits the grapes to ripen fully while retaining balancing acidity. Riesling is the most widely planted grape in Washington, followed by Chardonnay, Chenin Blanc, and Sauvignon Blanc, and white varieties, which also include Sémillon, Gewürztraminer, and Muscat Canelli account for 75 percent of the total acreage; red varieties consist mainly of Cabernet Sauvignon and Merlot. The whites are marked by intense fruit and crisp acidity, the reds by elegance and balance. Virtually all of the state's wines are marketed with varietal names, a few with proprietary names. The Columbia Valley viticultural area extends east of the Cascades, in south central Washington, and includes virtually all of the state's vineyards; the Yakima Valley, an important district about 200 miles southeast of Seattle, and the Walla Walla Valley, a small district in the southeast part of the state, are also defined viticultural areas, both within the larger Columbia Valley appellation. There are a few vineyards planted west of the Cascades, in areas sheltered from the rains that are prevalent in western Washington, and also in the southern part of the state, near the Oregon border; in addition, a few wineries have been established in the eastern part of the state, near Spokane. Chateau Ste. Michelle, the largest winery in the Pacific Northwest, accounts for more than half the state's production, other wineries include Arbor Crest, Columbia Winery, Columbia Crest (under the same ownership as Chateau Ste. Michelle), Covey Run, the Hogue Cellars, Preston and Snoqualmie.

Water The principal component of grape juice and of wine; the second most important, by volume, is the sugar in juice and the alcohol in wine. Water is also one of the three substances, the others being acid and sugar, which together or separately constitute amelioration; in the few places where the addition of water is permitted, its role is to reduce acidity.

Weeper One of the many terms employed to describe a wine bottle that has shown a tendency to leak or lose wine around its cork; this can be caused either by bad storage conditions or by an inferior cork. Although the problem can result in a spoiled bottle, appearances are often deceiving, and if there is no appreciable loss of wine, it is likely to be in good condition.

Wegeler-Deinhard The German shipping firm Deinhard, situated in Koblenz and best known for such branded wines as Hanns Cristof Liebfraumilch, Green Label Bereich Bernkastel

Riesling, and Lila Imperial Riesling Sekt is also an important
vineyard owner; as of the 1985 vintage, the estate wines of
Deinhard are marketed under the Wegeler-Deinhard name.
The firm has vineyards in the Rheingau (138 acres in the villages of Oestrich, Hallgarten, Mittleheim, Winkel, Johannisberg, Geisenheim, and Rüdesheim), the Rheinpfalz (43
acres in the villages of Ruppertsberg, Deidesheim, and
Forst); and the Moselle (34 acres primarily in Bernkastel,
Wehlen, and Graach, including a part of the famous Bernkasteler Doctor vineyard).

Wehlen A little town on the Moselle, between Bernkastel and Zeltingen, now considered by many experts to rank with Piesport and Bernkastel as the best of that small but renowned
wine district, sometimes referred to as the Mittelmosel,
which includes the river's best sites. The wines of Wehlen
were not always so well regarded, and the change has been
brought about largely through the efforts of a single
numerous family called Prüm, and especially the Joh. Jos.
Prüm branch, whose wines consistently bring some of the
highest prices at the great annual auctions in Trier, where the
best Moselles are sold. The village is on the left (here the
south) bank of the winding river, and faces the incredibly
steep, high vineyard slope in the heart of which, painted on
an almost perpendicular outcropping of slate, is the Sonnenuhr, or "sundial", which has given its name to the 120-acre
vineyard that produces Wehlen's best wine. This, in good
years, has few if any equals – flowery, well-balanced, with an
almost supernatural combination of delicacy and richness, it
is perfection itself. Other vineyard sites include Klosterberg,
Nonnenberg, Abtei, and Rosenberg.

Wein The German word for "wine".

Weinbaugebiete The term for the four basic wine regions of Germany
whose names are used in conjunction with *Deutscher Tafelwein*, or German table wine: Rhein-Mosel, Bayern, Neckar,
and Oberrhein. These are further divided into subregions
and into fifteen *Landwein* districts.

Weinberg The German word for "vineyard".

Weingut German for "vineyard estate", including the vines and the
cellar; a wine so labelled must come entirely from the estate's

own vineyards.

Weinkellerei German for "wine cellar"; its appearance on a label indicates that the wine does not necessarily come from the producer's own vineyards.

Weissburgunder The name used for the Pinot Blanc grape in Germany and Austria.

Weissherbst German for "white harvest", this term may now be applied only to rosés that are made from a single grape variety and that meet the requirements for a Qualitätswein. Although it may be produced in half-a-dozen regions, the best-known examples are made from Spätburgunder in Württemberg and in Baden, especially in the little villages strung along the northern shore of the Bodensee, or Lake Constance.

Welschriesling A widely planted white-wine grape that is not related to the true Riesling of Germany, and whose wines, which range from agreeable and fruity to neutral and dull, bear no resemblance to those made from Riesling. The grape is known as Walschriesling in Austria, as Riesling Italico in Italy, as Laski Rizling in Yugoslavia, and as Olaszriesling in Hungary.

White Pinot A name once used in California, rather misleadingly for wines made from the Chenin Blanc grape.

White Riesling The name used in Oregon, and by some producers in California and other American states, to describe the true Riesling of Germany; the name more commonly used in the United States is Johannisberg Riesling.

White Wine Any wine that is not, and has no trace of, red; the colour can vary from a pale, almost watery appearance to deep gold and even amber, yet all are considered white wines.

White Zinfandel A popular California varietal wine made from Zinfandel grapes vinified as a *blanc de noirs* to retain as little colour as possible, although in practice most examples range from pale salmon to pink. Almost unheard of in 1980, sales of White Zinfandel eventually exceeded those of such traditional varietal wines as Chardonnay and Cabernet Sauvignon and resulted in a new category known as blush wines; the Sutter

Home Winery is generally credited with establishing a market for this simple, appealing wine – almost always bottled with a little sweetness – and within a few years the number of wineries producing White Zinfandel jumped from half a dozen to more than a hundred. The grapes used for White Zinfandel are usually harvested earlier than those made into red wines so that they have less colour, less sugar (which results in wines with less alcohol), and more crisp acidity; such grapes also have relatively little flavour, so many producers blend in a proportion of wines made from such aromatic and distinctive varieties as Johannisberg Riesling, Gewürztraminer, or Muscat. *See* Blanc de Noirs, Blush Wine.

Willamette Valley   A viticultural area in western Oregon considered by many experts to be second only to Burgundy's Côte d'Or as a source of fine Pinot Noir wines; Riesling and Chardonnay are also widely planted there, and other varieties include Pinot Gris and Gewürztraminer. The Willamette Valley is situated between the Coastal Range and the Cascade Mountains, and stretches from the Columbia River, which forms the border with Washington, 120 miles south almost to the Umpqua Valley; most of its 40-odd wineries, however, are within a 50-mile radius south and west of Portland. Pinot Noir was first planted there in 1966, and the first wines made in 1970, so this region has achieved its reputation in a relatively short time. Some Willamette Valley wineries label their wines with the more specific appellations Yamhill County or Polk County, and a few include such geographical references as Dundee Hills or Chehalem Mountain.

Wiltingen   One of the most celebrated wine-producing towns of Germany, situated on the Saar River, southwest of Trier. Its 475 acres of vineyards, almost entirely planted with Riesling, cover a few incredibly steep, black-slate hillsides facing south. In poor years the wines are so light and thin that they are often used to make sparkling wine, but in the greatest vintages they display exceptional breed and class and are unsurpassed throughout Germany. The best vineyard site is the 67-acre Scharzhofberg, which many experts rank among the top white-wine vineyards in the world; its fame is such that the name may appear alone on a label, without references to Wiltingen. Other sites include Braune Kupp, Braunfels, Kupp, and Rosenberg. Note that Wiltinger Scharzberg is a Grosslage name that includes the entire Saar district.

Wine As legally defined in most countries, a beverage made from the partial or complete fermentation of the juice of fresh grapes.

Wine Bucket *See* Ice Bucket

Wine Cooler A wine-based beverage with 4 to 6 percent alcohol, most often a blend of neutral wine, water, sugar, carbon-dioxide gas, and various flavours, usually fruit; the 12-ounce bottles are sold in six-packs. First created in 1981, wine coolers increased their sales from 4,000 cases the first year to more than 50 million cases five years later, and accounted for more than 25 percent of total American wine sales; sales have diminished since then. Wine coolers are produced primarily in California and New York State, and best-selling brands include Bartles & Jaymes, California Cooler, and Sun Country Cooler. Coolers based on malt and on spirits have also been introduced, and other flavours, such as chocolate, are now used as well.

Winemaker According to American usage, the person in charge of production in a winery.

Winery The American name for the establishment where wine is made, as brewery is for beer and distillery for spirits.

Wine Taster A person, either professional or amateur, whose trained palate and specialized knowledge permit him or her to judge and evaluate wines organoleptically, that is, by tasting.

Winkel A small but important wine-producing village situated just below Johannisberg, in Germany's Rheingau region. Its best-known vineyard is Schloss Vollrads; others are Hasensprung and Jesuitengarten.

Wino The slang or colloquial term used to describe an alcoholic, generally of limited means, addicted to cheap, sweet, fortified wines.

Wintrich One of the good, lesser wine towns of Germany's Moselle, situated just up the river from Braunberg; its wines may be marketed with the Grosslage Bernkasteler Kurfürstlay.

Winzergenossenschaft The German term for a "co-operative cellar"; from *Winzer*, "wine grower", and *Genossenschaft*, "association". *Winzerverein* which also appears on wine labels, means the same thing.

Withered A taster's term applied to a wine that has lost its freshness and fruit, and most of its appeal, through overlong storage in barrel or bottle.

Woody A taster's term for a wine that has been stored too long in cask or barrel and has acquired an excessively woody aroma and flavour.

Worms A historic little city on the Rhine near the southern edge of Germany's Rheinhessen region. One of its churches, the Liebfrauenkirche, is surrounded by a 26-acre vineyard called the Liebfrauenstift, which gave its name to what is now Germany's best-known wine, Liebfraumilch. Despite its fame, however, wines from the Liebfrauenstift vineyard are not in the same class as those from such Rheinhessen villages as Nierstein and Nackenheim.

Württemberg One of the eleven Anbaugebiete, or specified wine regions, of Germany, whose principal city is Stuttgart and whose vineyards extend east and west of the Neckar River; 24,000 acres produce about 10 million cases a year. Riesling accounts for almost a quarter of the acreage, and Müller-Thurgau and Kerner for nearly 20 percent, but Württemberg is unique among the German regions in that half the vineyards are planted with red varieties; the indigenous Trollinger is the most important, followed by Müllerrebe, or Pinot Meunier. Co-operative cellars account for about 80 percent of the crop of this region, one of whose specialities is Schillerwein, a pink wine traditionally made by fermenting red and white grapes together. The local inhabitants, known as Swabians, are great consumers of their own produce, both liquid and solid, and as a result little of their wine is exported.

Würzburg The capital and principal town of the German province of Franken, or Franconia, in Bavaria, and no less famous for its beer than its wine, both called Würzburger. There are 500 acres of vineyards, largely planted with Sylvaner and Riesling, on the rocky slopes overlooking the Main River; Stein is the best-known vineyard, and the others are Innere Leiste, Abtsleite, Kirchberg, Pfaffenberg, Schlossberg, and Stein/ Harfe.

 X

Xérès An old name for the town of Jerez de la Frontera, in southern Spain, and for its wine, which we call sherry; the word is still used to describe sherry in France and, in fact, the official name for the sherry district its Jerez-Xérès-Sherry.

Y

Yakima Valley A widely acclaimed viticultural area in Washington, east of the Cascade Mountains, and about 200 miles southeast of Seattle; the district, which extends from the eastern foothills of the Cascades east to the Tri-Cities area, is situated within the larger Columbia Valley appellation.

Yarra Valley A small district on the outskirts of Melbourne, capital of the Australian state of Victoria, known primarily for Cabernet Sauvignon, Merlot, Pinot Noir, and Chardonnay.

Yeasts Unicellular micro-organisms, some of which (primarily *Saccharomyces ellipsoideus* also called *cerevisiae*) bring about fermentation in grape juice by secreting numerous enzymes that turn it into wine; a drop of fermenting must may contain more than 5 million yeasts. It was Pasteur who determined, in 1857, that fermentation was caused by yeasts, which are also essential to the production of such diverse products as bread, beer, and soy sauce. There exist many selections or cultures of yeasts, each with its particular characteristics – some work at lower temperatures, some create a more rapid fermentation, others are resistant to alcohol; in most modern wineries; the yeast cultures are chosen with great care, especially since there are some that are responsible for various sorts of wine spoilage.

Yeasty A wine-taster's term applied, most often, to young wines in barrel or tank that still have the odour of fermentation, or of lees, which are composed primarily of spent yeast cells. This is not a grave fault, and it usually disappears when the wine has been racked from one container to another, leaving the lees behind. A few white wines are actually bottled *sur lie*, that is, right off the lees, so as to retain this special aroma, which some connoisseurs of Muscadet and Swiss wines consider a virtue. In most bottled wines, however, a yeasty smell is considered a flaw. Champagnes, which are aged on the lees for an extended period, sometimes have a bouquet reminiscent of freshly baked bread that some consumers describe as yeasty, but the champagne producers themselves, who use the term more literally, consider a yeasty smell undesirable.

Yield As far as wine is concerned, this refers to the production of a given extent of vines, expressed as tons per acre in California and Australia, and as hectolitres per hectare in Europe. It is on the basis of yield that the relative productivity of different grape varieties can be compared, and also that of different regions or vineyards, although pruning, irrigation, and general vineyard practices are also factors, as are such natural calamities as frost, poor flowering, and hail. It is generally accepted that low yields are a prerequisite for superior wines, and that high yields dilute the quality of the wines produced, which have less concentration and intensity of flavour. Indeed, many of the world's fine wine regions have poor soils that produce limited amounts of wine, and yield per acre or hectare is one of the basic elements in any comparative rating of superior vineyards and their wines. Nevertheless, improved techniques of viticulture – better control of vineyard diseases, using healthier clones of specific grape varieties – have permitted growers in some regions to achieve higher yields without loss of quality. For example, several Bordeaux vintages in the 1980s produced excellent wines at yields that were nearly double those of the 1960s. In California, too, changed viticultural practices have permitted some growers to achieve greater yields with no loss of quality. And in Germany's Rhine and Moselle districts, yields of 100 hectolitres per hecare, or 450 cases per acre, are not unusual. One of the premises about yield and quality is that a given surface of vines, say an acre, can produce only a certain quantity of fine wine. But the traditional California vineyard contains 450 vines per acre, whereas many top French vineyards contain 4,000, yet their yields for specific grape varieties are about equal, which has led to increased experiments in vine spacing. There is no question that excessive yields within a given region diminish the quality of the wines produced, but there may be more flexibility than was previously assumed. (To compare European and California yields, note that a ton of grapes – which produces 60 to 65 cases of wine – equals about 15 hectolitres per hectare; thus 60 hectolitres per hectare is about equal to 4 tons per acre, or about 260 cases per acre.)

Yonne The northernmost of the French *départements* that make up the old province of Burgundy. Its best-known wine by far is Chablis, but there are a few others of fair quality, such as Sauvignon de Saint-Bris and Irancy.

Young So far as wine is concerned, this is not always a matter of months or years. A four-year-old California Cabernet Sauvignon or fine red Bordeaux may still be young, and a six-year-old vintage port is still an infant; on the other hand, a three-year-old Muscadet, Beaujolais, or rosé is likely to be middle-aged, if not senile. Properly speaking, a wine described as young is one not yet at its peak, vigorous, and still improving.

Yquem, Château d' The incomparable *grand premier cru* of the Sauternes district, and the only wine to be accorded this exalted rank in the famous 1855 classification of the wines of Bordeaux. (Even the top châteaux of the Médoc, such as Lafite and Latour, were classed simply as *premiers crus*.) It is one of the most famous vineyards in the world, and perhaps the most valuable as well of all those producing white wines, its only rival being Montrachet. The estate, graced by a superb fifteenth-century château, has been owned by the Lur-Saluces family sine 1785; Comte Alexandre du Lur-Saluces inherited the property from his uncle, Marquis Bertrand de Lur-Saluces, in 1968. In the mid-nineteenth century, the Grand Duke Constantine of Russia (brother of the czar) paid the then staggering price of 20,000 gold francs for four barrels of the 1847 vintage, and Yquem has been, since then, one of the most consistently expensive of all wines. There are 250 acres of vineyards, of which only 200 produce wine at any given time, the rest being made up of young vines in a re-planting cycle; Sémillon accounts for 80 percent of the acreage, Sauvignon Blanc for the rest. The grapes are harvested in successive *tries*, or selective pickings, as the *Botrytis cinerea* reaches its peak, and the resulting wine is sweet, luscious, almost creamy, with extraordinary fruit and breed. Ideally, the wine, which spends three and a half years in new oak barrels, contains about 14 percent alcohol and 100 grams per litre, or 10 percent, of residual sugar, although this will vary from year to year. Great vintages of Château d'Yquem are truly fabulous, the *ne plus ultra* of dessert wines (and well-matched with foie gras or Roquefort cheese as well), but even those of lesser years are often remarkable, less rich and concentrated, but with classic distinction and finesse. Production of this exceptional wine, or rather the quantity bottled under the château name, varies enormously – about 10,000 cases were made in such abundant vintages as 1967 and 1975; only 2,000 cases in 1977, 1,000 cases in 1978, and 4,000 cases in 1979; and none at all in 1972 and 1974. (By comparison, a 200-acre vineyard in the Médoc might well produce 30,000 to 40,000 cases of red wine almost every year.) The estate also produces, on an occasional basis, a dry, but rich and complex white wine made from approximately equal parts of Sémillon and Sauvignon Blanc, which is entitled only to the appellation Bordeaux; first made in 1959, it is labelled simply "Y" (pronounced, in the French manner, ee-greck). Here again production varies enormously: 1,000 caes of "Y" in 1980, none at all in the four vintages from 1981 to 1984, 7,500 cases in 1985, and only 250 cases in 1986.

Yugoslavia With an annual production of about 70 million cases, this country is one of the major wine producers of central Europe; its extensive range of red, white and rosé wines are made, for the most part, by half a dozen co-operative cellars. The vineyards of Yugoslavia, most of which are situated in Slovenia and Croatia, are planted with such traditional white varieties as Sauvignon Blanc, Traminer, Rhine Riesling, and Welschriesling (known there as both Graševina and Laski Riesling), and with such native varieties as Sipon and Plavac. Red grapes include Cabernet Sauvignon, Merlot, Pinot Noir, Gamay and such native grapes as Prokupac and Mali Plavac. The better-known appellations include the villages of Lutomer and Maribor in the north; Istria and Dalmatia along the Adriatic coast; and Fruška Gora. Yugoslavian wines may be labelled with the name of the grape, of a district, or with a combination of both, as Cabernet of Istria and Lutomer Riesling.

Yvorne One of the better white wines of Switzerland, made around the village of that name from the Chasselas grape (known locally as Dorin) in the Chablais district southeast of Lake Geneva.

Z

Zell A little vineyard town in the lower Moselle Valley, well outside the district of superior wine, and presumably the original source of Zeller Schwarze Katz; the wine, which was for many years a common, commercial Moselle blend, doubtless owes its popularity to its odd name – Schwarze Katz means "black cat", and the familiar cat is always present on the label. Under the 1971 German wine law, Zeller Schwarze Katz became a Grosslage, and production of this wine is now limited to about 1,000 acres of vineyards situated around Zell. The village also gives its name to the Bereich Zell/Mosel, one of four in the Mosel-Saar-Ruwer region; it extends from Zell down to Koblenz, where the Moselle joins the Rhine.

Zeltingen One of the very best wine villages of the Moselle, whose 440 acres of vineyards – virtually all Riesling – form part of the same high, incredibly steep, black-slate valley wall as those of Wehlen, Graach, and Bernkastel, and have an admirable southwestern exposure. Its wines, with those of Brauneberg, are about the fullest-bodied of the fine Moselles; the top vineyard sites are Sonnenuhr (part of which is in Zeltingen), Schlossberg, Himmelreich, and Deutschherrenberg.

Zinfandel The most widely planted red-wine grape in California, whose more than 33,000 acres account for about 20 percent of the state's red-grape vineyards. Although virtually all the world's plantings are in California, it is a *vinifera* grape transplanted from Europe whose exact origins are still somewhat uncertain, although persuasive evidence suggests it is identical to the Primitivo of southeast Italy. Its wine, unlike that of almost all other widely planted grapes, such as Grenache, Carignane, and Barbera, has a definite and easily recognizable varietal character most often described as spicy, berry-like, or brambly. The grape lends itself to a number of wine styles, from light and fruity, in the Beaujolais style, to medium-bodied, with more character and structure, to ripe, rich, tannic, intensely flavoured, and long-lived; a few producers have made late-harvest, port-like Zinfandels, and many others have made appealing and distinctive rosés. By the early 1980s, Zinfandel had lost some of its popularity, partly because the diversity of styles confused many consumers, partly because of the ascendance of Cabernet Sauvignon as *the* California red wine. By the mid-1980s, however, the phenomenon of White Zinfandel had taken hold – the grape was vinified to produce pale salmon or light pink wines that were simple, slightly sweet, and immensely popular. Many producers continue to make traditional red Zinfandels that display intensity of flavour without being overpowering; Sonoma's Dry Creek Valley is noted for its Zinfandels, as are Amador's Shenandoah Valley, the Paso Robles area of San Luis Obispo, and parts of the Napa Valley. The grape is widely planted in the Central Valley, especially in the Lodi district, which accounts for about 40 percent of the Zinfandel crop.

Zwicker *See* Edelzwicker

Zymase The name used for the numerous enzymes secreted by yeast; it is these enzymes, rather than the yeast itself, which cause fermentation, thereby converting grape sugar into alcohol and carbon dioxide.

Appendices

Wine and Food

Millions of people drink wine daily, wherever wine is made, in the temperate zones of both hemispheres. This is mostly the inexpensive product of their own local vineyards, and as much a part of their ordinary diet as all the rest – meat, fish, vegetables, fruit, and bread. Such wines are staples and, apart from the general principle of moderation, they should be drunk exactly as one wishes to drink them: there are no rules.

Wines of superior class are another matter. They are the result of a special effort on the part of the producer, who has planted selected grape varieties on particular sites where they are likely to yield better wine. Such wines should be treated with the same respect and care that have gone into their production. No hard-and-fast rules govern their service, but the comments that follow reflect the accumulated experience and preference of a good many knowledgeable wine drinkers. (Additional information about the service of wine will be found elsewhere in this volume, under Breathing, Chambrer, Corkscrews, Cradle, Decant, Ice Bucket, and Temperature.)

Matching wine and food is not quite as easy as "red with meat, white with fish and fowl", especially today. The number and variety of wines now available are much greater than even a decade ago, and the innovations that have taken place in the kitchen make the choice of an appropriate wine even more of an adventure than before. The emphasis on fresh, flavourful ingredients; a freer use of such distinctive herbs and spices as green peppercorns, coriander, mint, and ginger; the oriental influence in the combination of meat and fish on the same plate; the use of such fruits as lime, blackcurrants, and orange peel as garnish or ingredient; and the different textures provided by vegetables – some undercooked, some combined into purées – are just a few of the new approaches in the preparation of food that call for a re-examination of the traditional guidelines for selecting wines.

Suggesting specific wine and food combinations – Saint-Emilion with lamb, Médoc with beef, Zinfandel with barbecued chicken, Barbaresco with veal – is likely to be more inhibiting than helpful, however, and it may be more useful to examine the effects that food and wine have on each other. Once you recognize how taste, weight, and texture interact, you'll find it much easier to choose a wine to accompany a particular dish and to avoid common pitfalls.

To begin with, consider the tastes found in wine – sweetness, acidity and bitterness. Sweetness, which is present in a number of white wines and rosés and in a very few reds, often adds weight and body to an otherwise simple wine and enables it to stand up to some rich foods and seasoned dishes. (Cold diminishes the taste of sweetness, by the way, so chilling a wine that seems too sweet to you, such as an inexpensive white or red, will make it taste drier.)

Acidity gives wine a certain liveliness – just as a zest of lemon does to a drink, or a squeeze of lemon does to fish. Too much acidity, as in a wine made from unripe grapes, is disagreeable, but wines – especially whites – lacking sufficient acidity tend to taste flat and dull. It's the lively acidity present in many wines that makes them such suitable partners to most foods – the richness of the dish determines just how crisp a wine would best accompany it.

Some red wines, such as Bordeaux, Chianti, Rioja, and California Cabernet Sauvignon, have a slightly astringent or puckerish taste – similar to that of strong tea – that comes from the tannin extracted from the grape skins during fermentation and from the oak barrels in which some wines are aged. The puckerish taste of some young reds may overwhelm certain dishes, but other foods are complemented by a relatively assertive wine.

In addition to these three basic tastes, you should also be aware of a wine's body or weight. Just as there is a readily discernible difference between skimmed milk and cream, so there is between light, delicate wines and big, robust, mouth-filling ones. A wine's weight is one of the key factors in determining whether or not it will complement a particular dish. Some people also consider a wine's texture – some wines are light and simple, others rich and chewy – when matching it with foods whose textures are as different as beef, veal, and fish.

With these elements in mind, it's much easier to understand how certain foods affect wines and to predict suitable combinations. A dish may complement a particular wine by matching it in taste, weight, or texture; it may emphasize its qualities by providing a contrasting taste or texture; or it may distort its taste entirely.

A classic, if infrequently encountered, example of complementary tastes is Sauternes and *foie gras*. Here, the richness of Sauternes, a honeyed, luscious dessert wine, is matched by the rich texture of the *foie gras*. In the Sauternes district of France, however, this unique wine is often served with Roquefort cheese – the salty, tangy taste of the cheese providing a striking contrast to the rich, sweet wine and underscoring its taste. But serving a Sauternes with a chocolate mousse, cream-filled pastry, or any other sweet desert is usually a mistake, because the sweetness of the dessert diminishes the wine's sweetness. Poached fruit, such as pears or peaches, would complement the wine more successfully and, of course Sauternes, or any other sweet wines, can be served *as* the dessert, without the distraction of food.

A more obvious example of a dish that distorts the taste of wine is a salad with a vinegar-based dressing. The intense acidity of the vinegar has the effect of reducing the taste of acid in any wine served with it – that is, whatever acidity is present in the wine is suppressed on the palate by the stronger acidity in the dressing. The result of drinking wine with dishes that contain vinegar is that, rather than tasting too acid or vinegary, as is commonly supposed, most wines taste flat or flabby. The same general effect occurs if lemon juice is substituted for vinegar in a dressing, or if a dish contains such high-acid fruits as orange or grapefruit.

The simplest solution is not to drink wine with salad courses, which is why it may be unwise to serve cheese and salad on the same plate if you plan to accompany the cheese with an interesting bottle. If you do serve a dish that contains vinegar or another high-acid ingredient as a main course, then choose a white wine that is both assertive and high in acid, such as Sancerre, to compensate.

Mayonnaise, an oil-based sauce, has the opposite effect of vinegar's and will usually increase the acid taste in wine; this is more of a problem with reds, which may become disagreeably tart, than whites. Poached eggs, the basis of several brunch dishes, tend to dull and diminish the taste of any wine served with them, although most omelettes are a good foil for wine – the type of wine depending on the omelette's filling.

Anything sweet, such as a fruit sauce, will make wine taste slightly bitter by comparison. Rich food, such as a cream-based dish or even a chestnut or vegetable purée, may make a light wine taste a bit thin by comparison. This means that the choice of vegetable purées, sauces, and accompanying dishes must be taken into account when choosing wine. Incidentally, this also explains why serving champagne with a rich, sweet dessert usually diminishes this light, delicate wine and makes it taste thin and bitter.

The use of spices – peppercorns, for example – requires a wine with enough flavour and intensity to stand up to them. Very spicy foods, such as chillies, curries, and certain Chinese dishes simply overwhelm wine, not because of their taste, but because the hot, burning sensation they provoke makes it virtually impossible to perceive more subtle tastes. Those who insist on wine rather than beer may want to try an assertive white wine, such as Sancerre or Gewürztraminer, or a slightly sweet one, such as any number of California Chenin Blancs and Rieslings, although if a dish is very spicy even those wines will seem flavourless. In that case, it's best to treat the wine as a refreshing beverage, as you would beer, and simply drink an inexpensive white wine served very cold – its temperature will be its most distinctive feature.

These examples suggest some of the problems to be aware of. But just as some combinations diminish or distort a wine, others improve a wine by modifying its taste. One of the most common examples is based on the effect of protein on tannin. A strong cup of tea tastes rather bitter, but when milk is added, the tea tastes softer – that's because the protein in milk combines with, and softens, the tannin in tea. Similarly, the protein in beef, chicken, or cheese, for example, softens the tannin in such red wines as young Bordeaux, Chianti, and California Cabernet Sauvignon. Thus, many red wines that seem a bit harsh or puckerish when tasted without food are more attractive when drunk with a meal.

Another example is that of a medium-sweet white wine that some people might not enjoy on its own, but which may be just right with a rich cream sauce, which diminishes the wine's sweetness. And while a pungent wine with a pronounced flavour may not be the best choice as an aperitif, it would be appropriate with a seasoned dish, which will mute its assertiveness.

When selecting a wine, remember that the main ingredient in a dish – beef, chicken, fish – is often a less important guide to selecting an appropriate wine than the other ingredients with which it is prepared. A simply grilled fish, for example, calls for a dry white wine – the weight or acidity of the wine depending, in turn, on whether the fish is lean or oily. The same fish, baked with a rich cream sauce, might better be accompanied by a fuller-flavoured white. And if the fish is sautéed in oil and garlic, the assertiveness of the wine is more important than its weight. Add tomatoes to the last dish, or a layer of cheese to the baked fish, and there are those who would choose a cool, light-bodied red wine.

A simple rack of lamb is an excellent foil for a mature and well-balanced red wine. If the lamb were to be served with a rich sauce, however, the wine would then have to be fuller-bodied and perhaps younger and more tannic as well. If the sauce also contained peppercorns, then the wine would have to be vigorous and intense enough to stand up to their spiciness. Veal and pasta, too, are dishes that can be prepared in dozens of ways, each of them calling for a somewhat different style of wine, from a light-bodied white to a robust red.

The combination of wine and cheese, considered an ideal match, deserves a few words. There's no doubt that a wedge of cheese and a young, vigorous red show each other off, especially as the protein in cheese will subdue some of the tannic harshness of the wine. If the wine is complex or mature, however, many cheeses are more likely to diminish the wine than to enhance it. A ripe, pungent Brie, a tangy goat cheese, a richly textured triple crème such as Explorateur, Boursin, or St. André, and a strong blue cheese such as Roquefort are all, in their different ways, relatively assertive. The selection of an appropriate cheese may not be so important if the wine is uncomplicated and flavourful, but at many formal or wine-oriented dinners, the best and oldest wine is served last, with the cheese tray. Rather than overwhelm the mature, subtle, and delicate wine that has the place of honour, it may be best to sacrifice a complete cheese tray and choose instead a mild cheese, such as an old Gouda, that will show off the wine rather than clash with it. If, on the other hand, you prefer to end a meal with a varied selection of cheeses, serve a vigorous, tannic red or a pungent white.

Although the food being served is usually the principal consideration when choosing wine, variables that are not directly related to taste sometimes play an important role as well. For example, white wine has become so fashionable in this country that many people are prepared to drink white with everything. In many parts of France, on the other hand, the vogue is to drink red with everything – even fish.

More relevant factors than fashion that affect which wine people choose are season and temperature. Most people would choose red wine with beef, but if the beef is cold and served outdoors on a warm summer day, a chilled white wine might seem more suitable. Just as many people switch from hot tea to iced tea during the summer, so many prefer chilled whites and rosés, or cool, light-bodied reds when it's warm – the wine's temperature, weight, and refreshing quality become more important than its complexity and subtlety of flavour.

World Wine Production and Consumption

	1986 Production per 1,000 Cases	1988 Per Capita Consumption in Bottles (75 cl.)
Total: All Countries	3,632,156	—
Italy	844,778	96
France	805,431	98
Spain	377,350	63
Russia	376,970	12
United States	208,417	11
Argentina	204,281	74
Germany	110,682	34
*Romania	95,700	57
*South Africa	91,454	13
Portugal	88,693	72
Yugoslavia	61,831	35
Hungary	48,587	29
Greece	47,762	40
Australia	44,285	28
Bulgaria	38,500	20
Chile	36,300	47
Brazil	25,135	2
Austria	24,530	45
Switzerland	13,805	64
Algeria	10,692	2
Czechoslovakia	10,373	15
*Uruguay	8,250	37
Cyprus	7,315	17
*Canada	5,170	13
New Zealand	5,170	17
Japan	5,654	1
Morocco	4,994	2
Tunisia	4,422	6
*Turkey	4,290	0.5
Israel	2,090	5
Luxembourg	1,760	77
*Mexico	1,617	—
*Peru	990	1
*Lebanon	550	—
*Madagascar	550	—
*Bolivia	220	—
Great Britain	88	15
Poland		4
Belgium		28
Holland		18
Sweden		16
Denmark		33
Finland		7
Norway		7
Ireland		5

All figures are as reported to the Office International du Vin in Paris by the various governments. * Indicates estimates based on reports from previous years.

Note that per capita consumption figures are for 1988, but production figures are for the 1986 harvest, which is closer to the average for the past ten years than the small 1988 crop. For example, in 1988 Italy produced only 680 million cases, France 632 million, Spain 236 million, and Portugal 42 million. Although worldwide vineyard acreage has decreased in the past decade, production has remained the same; in France and Italy, where vineyard acreage has decreased about 20 percent, average production has actually increased as a result of improved viticultural techniques. Wine consumption, however, has decreased significantly since 1976 in a number of traditional wine-consuming countries, including Italy (whose per capita consumption in 1976 was 143 bottles), France (135 bottles), Spain (94 bottles), and Argentina (113 bottles).

France

Production of Appellation Contrôlée Wines: 1986

The following tables are official French production figures supplied by the Institut des Appellations d'Origine Contrôlée (INAO). Note that 1986 was a copious vintage and produced an above average crop of AOC wines in almost all French districts; in fact, AOC wines accounted for 29 percent of the total French harvest. The 1987 and 1988 crops were similar in size – about 230 million cases each – but because the total French crop was relatively small in 1988, AOC wines represented nearly 35 percent of that harvest. Although the figures for red wines and rosés are combined, only a few appellations are made up entirely or primarily of rosés: Rosé d'Anjou, Cabernet d'Anjou, Tavel, and Côtes de Provence are the best known.

	White	Cases Red and Rosé
Bordeaux		
Bordeaux	7,120,421	19,605,223
Bordeaux Côtes de Castillon		206,591
Bordeaux Côtes de Francs	2,442	14,201
Bordeaux Supérieur Côtes de Francs		138,600
Bordeaux Supérieur	75,361	5,680,169
Bordeaux Supérieur Côtes de Castillon		1,465,233
Bordeaux Haut Benauge	36,586	
Bordeaux Clairet		64,350
Bordeaux Rosé		163,350
Bordeaux Mousseux	275	4,950
Blaye or Blayais	118,283	4,950
Côtes de Blaye	112,178	
Premières Côtes de Blaye	8,536	1,965,205
Bourg or Côtes de Bourg	34,144	2,381,016
Entre-Deux-Mers	2,149,763	
Côtes de Bordeaux St-Macaire	18,293	
Graves de Vayres	162,184	168,300
Premières Côtes de Bordeaux	353,617	1,217,733
Ste Foy-Bordeaux	53,350	46,112
Médoc		
Médoc		2,430,516
Haut-Médoc		2,029,566
Listrac		333,611
Margaux		697,972
Moulis		272,261
Pauillac		653,422
Saint-Estèphe		782,122
Saint-Julien		460,361
Saint-Emilion, Pomerol, and the Right Bank		
Saint-Emilion		3,356,507
Lussac-Saint-Emilion		777,172
Montagne-Saint-Emilion		930,622
Puisseguin-Saint-Emilion		450,461

	Cases	
	White	*Red and Rosé*
St. Georges-Saint-Emilion		113,850
Pomerol		475,211
Lalande de Pomerol		564,311
Canon-Fronsac		207,900
Fronsac		534,611
Sauternes, Graves, and others		
Barsac	165,836	
Sauternes	363,374	
Graves	557,260	1,004,872
Graves Supérieures	317,042	
Graves Pessac-Léognan	107,305	450,461
Cérons		29,260
Cadillac	17,963	
Loupiac	115,841	
Sainte-Croix-du-Mont	199,990	
Bordeaux Total	12,119,294	49,654,825
Grand Total	61,774,119	
The Southwest		
Dordogne		
Bergerac	982,080	2,602,743
Saussignac	17,644	
Côtes de Bergerac		330,539
Côtes de Bergerac Moelleux	418,418	
Côtes de Montravel	56,298	
Haut Montravel	3,938	
Montravel	334,279	
Monbazillac	627,374	
Pécharmant		139,788
Rosette	14,916	
Béarn		
Béarn	4,114	109,615
Irouléguy		42,878
Jurançon	341,506	
Madiran		595,881
Pacherenc de Vic-Bilh	35,816	
Other Southwest		
Cahors		2,015,717
Buzet	11,935	827,838
Côtes de Duras	365,475	476,971
Côtes du Frontonnais		868,186
Gaillac	434,555	592,273
Blanquette de Limoux	499,389	
Southwest Total	4,147,737	8,602,429
Grand Total	12,750,166	
Burgundy		
Bourgogne	213,243	1,668,623
Bourgogne Irancy		42,229
Bourgogne Aligoté	872,344	
Bourgogne Passe-tout-Grains		1,026,113

	White	Cases Red and Rosé
Bourgogne Grand Ordinaire	31,196	170,907
Crémant de Bourgogne	99,000	18,205
Total	1,216,424	2,926,077
Chablis		
Chablis Grand Cru	59,246	
Chablis Premier Cru	442,068	
Chablis	882,321	
Petit Chablis	80,597	
Total	1,464,232	
Côte de Nuits		
Chambolle Musigny		78,870
Côte de Nuits-Villages	902	97,944
Fixin	682	37,015
Gevrey-Chambertin		201,124
Morey-Saint-Denis	341	42,625
Nuits-Saint-Georges	220	153,285
Vougeot	1,243	6,358
Vosne-Romanée		88,979
Marsannay		26,543
Bourgogne-Hautes Côte de Nuits	20,977	205,975
Total	24,365	938,718
Côte de Nuits: Grands Crus		
Bonnes Mares		5,984
Chambertin		5,987
Chambertin Clos de Bèze		9,350
Chapelle-Chambertin		2,618
Charmes-Chambertin		13,453
Clos de Lambrays		3,740
Clos de la Roche		8,228
Clos Saint-Denis		2,992
Clos de Tart		3,366
Clos de Vougeot		22,055
Echézeaux		15,697
Grands Echézeaux		3,363
Griotte-Chambertin		1,122
La Tâche		1,781
Latricières-Chambertin		3,366
Mazis-Chambertin		4,114
Musigny	110	4,477
Richebourg		3,366
La Romanée		374
Romanée-Conti		527
Romanée-Saint-Vivant		2,618
Ruchottes-Chambertin		1,496
Total	110	120,074
Côte de Beaune		
Aloxe-Corton	231	65,879
Auxey-Duresses	15,532	56,078
Beaune	1,364	196,713
Blagny	1,815	1,870
Chassagne-Montrachet	85,393	96,987
Cheilly-Les-Maranges		20,603

	White	Cases Red and Rosé
Dezize-Les-Maranges		1,595
Chorey-Les-Beaune	231	80,773
Côte de Beaune	1,815	26,169
Côte de Beaune-Villages	528	92,224
Ladoix	2,266	40,370
Ladoix Premier Cru		5,236
Meursault	221,848	14,971
Monthélie	1,133	59,444
Pernand-Vergelesses	1,100	42,614
Pommard		151,844
Puligny-Montrachet	130,636	4,114
Saint-Aubin	20,405	38,511
Saint-Romain	16,665	25,047
Sampigny-Les-Maranges		1,991
Santenay	3,487	182,017
Savigny	6,468	180,554
Volnay		97,944
Bourgogne-Hautes Côtes de Beaune	11,330	271,249
Total	**532,147**	**1,754,797**
Côte de Beaune: Grands Crus		
Corton	572	40,843
Corton-Charlemagne	17,457	
Bâtard-Montrachet	6,688	
Bienvenues-Bâtard-Montrachet	2,376	
Criots-Bâtard-Montrachet	902	
Chevalier-Montrachet	3,509	
Montrachet	2,728	
Total	**34,232**	**40,843**
Côte Chalonnaise		
Givry	8,250	88,418
Mercurey	19,976	335,951
Montagny	72,138	
Rully	73,733	68,783
Total	**174,097**	**493,152**
Mâconnais		
Mâcon	4,895	57,354
Mâcon Supérieur	145,497	682,726
Mâcon-Villages	1,461,119	1,199
Pouilly-Fuissé	460,031	
Pouilly-Loché	13,761	
Pouilly-Vinzelles	30,261	
Saint-Véran	269,907	
Total	**2,385,471**	**741,279**
Beaujolais		
Beaujolais	66,429	7,054,377
Beaujolais-Supérieur	6,116	126,192
Beaujolais-Villages	25,982	4,084,762
Brouilly		777,238
Chénas		168,036
Chiroubles		227,689

	White	Cases Red and Rosé
Côte de Brouilly		189,739
Fleurie		508,552
Juliénas		375,650
Morgon		691,691
Moulin-a-Vent		418,891
Saint-Amour		187,660
Total	98,527	14,810,477
Coteaux du Lyonnais	5,104	148,984
Burgundy Total	5,934,419	21,972,841
Grand Total	27,907,660	

Loire Valley

Muscadet
Muscadet	2,012,912	
Muscadet des Coteaux de la Loire	236,016	
Muscadet de Sèvre-et-Maine	5,316,630	

Anjou-Saumur
Anjou	860,860	1,127,456
Anjou Gamay		6,083
Anjou Mousseux	53,218	16,588
Rosé d'Anjou		1,161,611
Cabernet d'Anjou		1,070,058
Anjou Coteaux de la Loire	17,446	
Savennières	28,171	
Coteaux du Layon	559,383	
Bonnezeaux	19,701	
Quarts de Chaume	9,801	
Coteaux de L'Aubance	22,352	
Cabernet de Saumur		29,546
Saumur Champigny		417,351
Coteaux de Saumur	1,529	
Rosé de Loire		223,960
Saumur	338,976	251,966
Saumur Mousseux	874,005	63,173
Crémant de Loire	101,277	13,750

Touraine
Touraine	1,141,217	1,542,431
Touraine-Amboise	39,193	85,371
Touraine Azay-le-Rideau	14,597	12,276
Touraine-Mesland	17,468	105,094
Touraine Mousseux	27,951	9,108
Bourgueil		673,915
Saint-Nicholas-de-Bourgueil		428,098
Chinon	4,917	757,570
Vouvray	612,370	
Vouvray Mousseux	403,854	
Montlouis	172,964	
Montlouis Mousseux	45,595	

Sarthe
Coteaux du Loir	4,279	10,835
Jasnières	13,211	

	Cases	
	White	*Red and Rosé*
Central Loire		
Pouilly-Fumé	429,396	
Pouilly-Sur-Loire	44,484	
Quincy	49,566	
Menetou-Salon	40,821	32,087
Reuilly	10,835	8,415
Sancerre	965,514	241,208
Loire Valley Total	14,490,509	8,287,950
Grand Total	22,778,459	
Rhône Valley		
Côtes-du-Rhône	485,199	21,500,094
Côtes-du-Rhône-Villages	45,529	2,386,571
Château-Grillet	1,001	
Châteauneuf-du-Pape	51,678	1,172,358
Condrieu	9,834	
Cornas		31,438
Côte Rôtie		41,833
Crozes-Hermitage	43,934	452,771
Hermitage	12,914	34,826
Gigondas		413,842
Lirac	9,141	214,742
Saint-Joseph	16,797	176,055
Saint-Péray	30,679	
Tavel		421,773
Total	706,706	26,846,303
Other Rhône		
Clairette de Die	636,658	
Chatillon-en-Diois	9,317	21,054
Coteaux du Triscatin	9,658	946,286
Côtes du Ventoux	31,251	2,796,002
Rhône Valley Total	1,397,990	30,609,645
Grand Total	32,007,635	
Provence		
Côtes de Provence	482,614	7,075,002
Bandol	16,566	362,175
Bellet	4,158	7,909
Cassis	49,632	20,757
Palette	1,782	4,917
Coteaux d'Aix-en-Provence	98,230	1,426,326
Coteaux des Baux-en-Provence	1,969	140,646
Alsace		
Alsace	1,166,154	729,300
Alsace Grand Cru	239,547	
Crémant d'Alsace	501,314	14,135
Champagne		
Champagne	21,260,019	261,052
Coteaux Champenois	3,751	5,401
Rosé des Riceys		3,135

	Cases	
	White	Red and Rosé
Other Regions		
Franche-Comté		
Arbois	171,424	253,231
Château-Chalon	17,380	
Etoile	29,843	
Côtes du Jura	289,234	83,556
Savoie		
Vin de Savoie	737,990	333,465
Roussette de Savoie	47,553	
Crépy	37,686	
Seyssel	25,575	
Seyssel Mousseux	8,437	
Corsica		
Vin de Corse	77,044	815,144
Languedoc-Roussillon		
Côtes du Roussillon	114,180	3,355,803
Fitou		883,377
Collioure		72,435
Clairette du Languedoc	102,190	
Clairette de Bellegarde	32,582	
Faugères		598,620
Saint-Chinian		739,563
Minervois	68,508	2,778,534
Corbières	286,385	6,991,347
Coteaux du Languedoc	192,236	3,227,697
Costières du Gard	61,380	2,002,418
Total	957,660	22,216,766
Vins Doux Naturels		
Banyuls Grand Cru		89,760
Banyuls		446,072
Grand Roussillon	330	4,158
Maury		423,588
Muscat de Beaumes-de-Venise	104,082	
Muscat de Frontignan	243,518	
Muscat de Lunel	86,856	
Muscat de Mireval	71,313	
Muscat de Rivesaltes	1,221,121	
Muscat de Saint-Jean de Minervois	29,909	
Rasteau	8,173	1,683
Rivesaltes	3,246,562	863,489
Total	4,768,346	2,072,268
Languedoc-Roussillon Total	5,726,006	24,289,034
Grand Total	30,015,040	
Total Appellation Contrôlée	79,473,273	153,380,980
Grand Total	232,854,253	

Vins Délimités de Qualité Supérieure: 1986

Because many VDQS wines have been promoted to *Appellation Contrôlée* in recent years (most recently Côtes de Lubéron in 1988 and Haut Poitou in 1989), the VDQS crop now represents only 1 percent of the total French harvest.

	In Cases	
Appellation VDQS	White	Red and Rosé
Alsace		
Côtes de Toul	726	42,218
Vin de Moselle	5,423	3,322
Burgundy		
Sauvignon de Saint-Bris	40,227	
Côtes Roannaises		53,955
Côtes du Forez		82,324
Franche-Comté & Savoie		
Vins du Bugey	112,420	68,706
Roussette du Bugey	7,744	
Rhône Valley		
Côtes du Vivarais	13,497	387,365
Côtes du Lubéron	230,670	1,155,407
Provence		
Coteaux de Pierrevert	10,362	101,607
Coteaux Varois		531,960
Languedoc		
Cabardès		163,460
Côtes de la Malepère		111,958
Southwest		
Tursan	61,182	89,144
Côtes de St Mont	19,371	254,914
Vin de Lavilledieu		22,440
Vin de Marcillac		39,050
Vin d'Entraygues	1,837	3,146
Vin d'Estaing	495	2,948
Côtes du Brulhois		111,606
Côtes du Marmandais	21,593	703,043
Loire Valley		
Gros Plant du Pays Nantais	2,664,486	
Coteaux d'Ancenis	1,628	261,030
Fiefs Vendéens	36,762	188,144
Vin du Haut-Poitou	147,422	245,487
Vins du Thouarsais	7,733	7,106
Valençay	10,285	56,705
Cheverny	66,726	88,847
Coteaux du Vendomois	5,566	47,113
Vin de l'Orleannais	5,236	84,568
Coteaux du Giennois	6,853	46,255
Châteaumeillant		33,374
Côtes d'Auvergne	132	224,092
Saint-Pourçain	56,408	260,040
Total	3,534,784	5,471,334
Grand Total VDQS		9,006,118

Bordeaux
Classification of 1855 for the Médoc

Vineyard	Commune	Approximate Cases per Year
First Growths – Premiers Crus		
Château Lafite-Rothschild	Pauillac	23,000
Château Latour	Pauillac	23,000
Château Margaux	Margaux	22,000
Château Mouton-Rothschild*	Pauillac	22,000
Château Haut-Brion	Pessac (Graves)	13,000
Second Growths – Deuxièmes Crus		
Château Rausan-Ségla	Margaux	15,000
Château Rauzan-Gassies	Margaux	10,000
Château Léoville Las Cases	Saint-Julien	25,000
Château Léoville Poyferré	Saint-Julien	24,000
Château Léoville Barton	Saint-Julien	18,000
Château Durfort-Vivens	Margaux	8,000
Château Gruaud-Larose	Saint-Julien	35,000
Château Lascombes	Margaux	40,000
Château Brane-Cantenac	Cantenac-Margaux	32,000
Château Pichon-Longueville-Baron	Pauillac	16,000
Château Pichon Longueville Comtesse de Lalande	Pauillac	26,000
Château Ducru-Beaucaillou	Saint-Julien	20,000
Château Cos d'Estournel	Saint-Estèphe	25,000
Château Montrose	Saint-Estèphe	25,000
Third Growths – Troisièmes Crus		
Château Kirwan	Cantenac-Margaux	14,000
Château d'Issan	Cantenac-Margaux	12,000
Château Lagrange	Saint-Julien	30,000
Château Langoa Barton	Saint-Julien	6,000
Château Giscours	Labarde-Margaux	25,000
Château Malescot Saint Exupéry	Margaux	14,000
Château Cantenac-Brown	Cantenac-Margaux	22,000
Château Boyd-Cantenac	Margaux	8,000
Château Palmer	Cantenac-Margaux	15,000
Château La Lagune	Ludon	25,000
Château Desmirail	Margaux	8,000
Château Calon-Ségur	Saint-Estèphe	18,000
Château Ferrière	Margaux	1,500
Château Marquis d'Alesme Becker	Margaux	4,000

*Reclassified as a First Growth in 1973

Fourth Growths – Quatrièmes Crus

Château Saint-Pierre	Saint-Julien	8,000
Château Talbot	Saint-Julien	45,000
Château Branaire-Ducru	Saint-Julien	20,000
Château Duhart-Milon-Rothschild	Pauillac	20,000
Château Pouget	Cantenac-Margaux	3,500
Château La Tour Carnet	Saint-Laurent	14,000
Château Lafon-Rochet	Saint-Estèphe	20,000
Château Beychevelle	Saint-Julien	25,000
Château Prieuré-Lichine	Cantenac-Margaux	25,000
Château Marquis de Terme	Margaux	15,000

Fifth Growths – Cinquièmes Crus

Château Pontet-Canet	Pauillac	30,000
Château Batailley	Pauillac	25,000
Château Haut-Batailley	Pauillac	10,000
Château Grand-Puy-Lacoste	Pauillac	20,000
Château Grand-Puy-Ducasse	Pauillac	18,000
Château Lynch-Bages	Pauillac	30,000
Château Lynch-Moussas	Pauillac	15,000
Château Dauzac	Labarde	22,000
Château Mouton-Baronne-Philippe	Pauillac	23,000
Château du Tertre	Arsac	16,000
Château Haut-Bages Libéral	Pauillac	10,000
Château Pédesclaux	Pauillac	7,500
Château Belgrave	Saint-Laurent	23,000
Château Camensac	Saint-Laurent	30,000
Château Cos Labory	Saint-Estèphe	7,000
Château Clerc-Milon	Pauillac	12,000
Château Croizet Bages	Pauillac	10,000
Château Cantemerle	Macau	20,000

Crus Bourgeois of the Médoc

A discussion of this list, which is the revision published in 1978, will be found under Cru Bourgeois. Note that a few excellent Médoc properties – among them Châteaux d'Angludet, Gloria, Lanessan, de Pez, Siran, and La Tour de Mons – do not belong to the Syndicat des Crus Bourgeois and are therefore not included on its list. Note also that a number of châteaux joined the *cru bourgeois* association after 1978 and are not on this list, including Châteaux Clarke, Lestage Simon, Malescasse, Maucaillou, and Terrey-Gros-Cailloux.

Grands Crus Bourgeois Exceptionnel

Château d'Agassac	Ludon
Château Andron Blanquet	Saint-Estèphe
Château Beausite	Saint-Estèphe
Château Capbern	Saint-Estèphe
Château Caronne Sainte-Gemme	Saint-Laurent
Château Chasse-Spleen	Moulis
Château Cissac	Cissac
Château Citran	Avensan
Château Le Crock	Saint-Estèphe
Château Dutruch-Grand-Poujeau	Moulis
Château Fourcas Dupré	Listrac
Château Fourcas Hosten	Listrac
Château Du Glana	Saint-Julien
Château Haut-Marbuzet	Saint-Estèphe
Château Marbuzet	Saint-Estèphe
Château Meyney	Saint-Estèphe
Château Phélan-Segur	Saint-Estèphe
Château Poujeaux	Moulis

Grands Crus Bourgeois

Château Beaumont	Cussac
Château Bel-Orme	Saint-Seurin-de-Cadourne
Château Brillette	Moulis
Château La Cardonne	Blaignan
Château Colombier Monpelou	Pauillac
Château Coufran	Saint-Seurin-de-Cadourne
Château Coutelin-Merville	Saint-Estèphe
Château Duplessis-Hauchecorne	Moulis
Château Fontesteau	Saint-Sauveur
Château La Fleur Milon	Pauillac
Château Greysac	Bégadan
Château Hanteillan	Cissac
Château Lafon	Listrac
Château Lamarque	Lamarque
Château Lamothe	Cissac
Château Laujac	Bégadan
Château Liversan	Saint-Sauveur
Château Loudenne	Saint-Yzans
Château MacCarthy	Saint-Estèphe
Château Malleret	Le Pian
Château Morin	Saint-Estèphe
Château Moulin à Vent	Moulis
Château Le Meynieu	Vertheuil
Château Martinens	Margaux
Château Les Ormes Sorbet	Couquèques
Château Les Ormes de Pez	Saint-Estèphe

Château Patache d'Aux	Bégadan
Château Paveil de Luze	Soussans
Château Peyrabon	Saint-Sauveur
Château Pontoise Cabarrus	Saint-Seurin-de-Cadourne
Château Potensac	Potensac
Château La Rose Trintaudon	Saint-Laurent
Château Reysson	Vertheuil
Château Ségur	Parempuyre
Château Sigognac	Saint-Yzans
Château Sociando Mallet	Saint-Seurin-de-Cadourne
Château du Taillan	Le Taillan
Château La Tour de By	Bégadan
Château La Tour du Haut-Moulin	Cussac
Château Tronquoy Lalande	Saint-Estèphe
Château Verdignan	Saint-Seurin-de-Cadourne

Crus Bourgeois

Château Aney	Cussac
Château Balac	Saint-Laurent-de-Médoc
Château Bellerive	Valeyrac
Château Belle Rose	Pauillac
Château la Bécade	Listrac
Château Bonneau	Saint-Seurin-de-Cadourne
Château le Bosq	Saint-Christoly
Château le Breuil	Cissac
Château la Bridane	Saint-Julien
Château de By	Bégadan
Château Castéra	Cissac
Château Chambert-Marbuzet	Saint-Estèphe
Château Cap Léon Veyrin	Listrac
Château Carcannieux	Queyrac
Château Clare	Bégadan
Château la Closerie	Moulis
Château Duplessis-Fabre	Moulis
Château Fonréaud	Listrac
Château Fonpiqueyre	Saint-Sauveur
Château Fort de Vauban	Cussac
Château la France	Blaignan
Château Gallais Bellevue	Potensac
Château Grand Duroc Milon	Pauillac
Château Grand-Moulin	Saint-Seurin-de-Cadourne
Château Haut-Bages Monpelou	Pauillac
Château Haut-Canteloup	Couquèques
Château Haut-Garin	Bégadan
Château Haut-Padarnac	Pauillac
Château Houbanon	Prignac
Château Hourtin-Ducasse	Saint-Sauveur
Château de Labat	Saint-Laurent
Château Lamothe Bergeron	Cussac
Château Landon	Bégadan
Château Lassalle	Potensac
Château Lartigue de Brochon	Saint-Seurin-de-Cadourne
Château le Landat	Cissac
Château Lestage	Listrac
Château MacCarthy Moula	Saint-Estèphe
Château Monthil	Bégadan
Château Moulin Rouge	Cussac

Château Panigon	Civrac
Château Pibran	Pauillac
Château Plantey de la Croix	Saint-Seurin-de-Cadourne
Château Pontet	Blaignan
Château Ramage la Batisse	Saint-Sauveur
Château la Roque de By	Bégadan
Château Saint-Bonnet	Saint-Christoly
Domaine de la Rose Maréchale	Saint-Seurin-de-Cadourne
Château Saransot	Listrac
Château Soudars	Avensan
Château Tayac	Soussans
Château la Tour Blanche	Saint-Christoly
Château la Tour du Mirail	Cissac
Château la Tour Haut-Caussan	Blaignan
Château la Tour Saint-Bonnet	Saint-Christoly
Château la Tour Saint-Joseph	Cissac
Domaine des Tourelles	Blaignan
Château Vieux Robin	Bégadan

Sauternes and Barsac
The Classification of 1855

		Approximate Cases per Year
Great First Growth – Grand Premier Cru		
Château d'Yquem	Sauternes	7,000
First Growths – Premiers Crus		
Château La Tour Blanche	Bommes	5,000
Château Lafaurie-Peyraguey	Bommes	4,000
Clos Haut-Peyraguey	Bommes	2,000
Château de Rayne-Vigneau	Bommes	12,000
Château Suduiraut	Preignac	8,000
Château Coutet	Barsac	8,000
Château Climens	Barsac	5,000
Château Guiraud	Sauternes	8,000
Château Rieussec	Fargues	8,500
Château Rabaud-Promis	Bommes	8,000
Château Sigalas Rabaud	Bommes	4,000
Second Growths – Deuxièmes Crus		
Château Myrat*	Barsac	—
Château Doisy Daëne	Barsac	3,000
Château Doisy-Dubroca	Barsac	500
Château Doisy-Védrines	Barsac	5,000
Château D'Arche	Sauternes	8,000
Château Filhot	Sauternes	10,000
Château Broustet	Barsac	2,000
Château Nairac	Barsac	2,000
Château Caillou	Barsac	3,500
Château Suau	Barsac	1,500
Château de Malle	Preignac	4,000
Château Romer	Fargues	4,000
Château Lamothe	Sauternes	1,800

*The vineyard was uprooted in 1976.

Saint-Emilion
The Revised Classification of 1985

The wines of Saint-Emilion were first classified in 1955, and the classification was revised in 1969 and again in 1985. It should be noted that Château Ausone and Château Cheval Blanc are generally considered in a category apart, although they share the designation *premier grand cru classé* with nine other vineyards.

Approximate Cases per Year

First Great Classed Growths – Premiers Grands Crus Classés

Château Ausone	2,500
Château Cheval Blanc	13,000
Château Beauséjour (Duffau-Lagarrosse)	2,500
Château Belair	5,000
Château Canon	7,500
Clos Fourtet	7,000
Château Figeac	14,000
Château La Gaffelière	9,000
Château Magdelaine	4,500
Château Pavie	14,000
Château Trottevieille	5,000

Great Classed Growths – Grands Crus Classés

Château L'Angelus
Château L'Arrosée
Château Balestard La Tonnelle
Château Beau-Séjour-Bécot
Château Bellevue
Château Bergat
Château Berliquet
Château Cadet-Piola
Château Canon La Gaffelière
Château Cap de Mourlin
Château Le Chatelet
Château Chauvin
Clos de Jacobins
Clos la Madeleine
Clos de l'Oratoire
Clos Saint Martin
Château La Clotte
Château Corbin
Château Corbin-Michotte
Château La Clusière
Château Couvent des Jacobins
Château Croque-Michotte
Château Curé-Bon la Madeleine
Château Dassault
Château La Dominique
Château Faurie de Souchard
Château Fonplegade
Château Fonroque
Château Franc-Mayne
Château Grand-Barrail-Lamarzelle-
  Figeac
Château Grand-Corbin
Château Grand-Corbin-Despagne

Château Grand-Mayne
Château Grand-Pontet
Château Guadet-Saint-Julien
Château Haut Corbin
Château Haut Sarpe
Château Laniote
Château Larcis-Ducasse
Château Lamarzelle
Château Larmande
Château Laroze
Château Matras
Château Mauvezin
Château Moulin-du-Cadet
Château Pavie-Decesse
Château Pavie-Macquin
Château Pavillon-Cadet
Château Petit-Faurie de Soutard
Château Le Prieuré
Château Ripeau
Château Sansonnet
Château Saint-Georges Côte-Pavie
Château La Serre
Château Soutard
Château Tertre-Daugay
Château La Tour du Pin-Figeac
Château La Tour du Pin-Figeac
  (Moueix)
Château La Tour-Figeac
Château Trimoulet
Château Troplong-Mondot
Château Villemaurine
Château Yon-Figeac

Graves

The châteaux of the Graves district (neglected except for Château Haut-Brion in the classification of 1855) were officially rated by the Institut National des Appellations d'Origine in 1953, and this classification was revised in 1959 to include a listing of white wines as well. (Château Haut-Brion is not included in the white-wine classification by request of the owner.) The listing is alphabetical by commune and by château.

		Approximate Cases per Year
Classified Wines (Red) – Crus Classés (Rouges)		
Château Bouscaut	Cadaujac	20,000
Château Haut-Bailly	Léognan	12,000
Château Carbonnieux	Léognan	15,000
Domaine de Chevalier	Léognan	4,000
Château Fieuzal	Léognan	10,000
Château Olivier	Léognan	9,000
Château Malartic-Lagravière	Léognan	7,000
Château La Tour-Martillac	Martillac	10,000
Château Smith Haut Lafitte	Martillac	24,000
Château Haut-Brion	Pessac	13,000
Château Pape Clément	Pessac	15,000
Château La Mission Haut-Brion	Talence	10,000
Château La Tour Haut-Brion	Talence	2,000
Classified Wines (White) – Crus Classés (Blancs)		
Château Bouscaut	Cadaujac	4,000
Château Carbonnieux	Léognan	15,000
Domaine de Chevalier	Léognan	1,500
Château Malartic-Lagravière	Léognan	1,000
Château Olivier	Léognan	12,000
Château Latour-Martillac	Martillac	2,000
Château Laville Haut-Brion	Talence	2,000
Château Couhins	Villenave-d'Ornon	1,500
Château Couhins-Lurton	Villenave-d'Ornon	1,500

Pomerol

The wines of Pomerol, the smallest of the great Bordeaux districts, have never been classified. What follows is an alphabetical list of the best-known properties, divided into two groups; most experts would agree that the châteaux in the first group represent the best wines of Pomerol. Château Pétrus is considered to be in a class by itself.

	Approximate Cases per Year
Château Pétrus	4,000
Château Certan-de-May	2,000
Château La Conseillante	5,000
Château l'Evangile	6,000
Château La Fleur-Pétrus	3,000
Château Lafleur	1,500
Château Latour à Pomerol	3,500
Château Petit Village	5,000
Château Trotanoy	3,000
Vieux Château Certan	7,000
Château Beauregard	5,000
Château Le Bon Pasteur	2,500
Château Certan Giraud	2,000
Château Clinet	4,000
Clos L'Eglise	2,500
Clos René	5,000
Château La Croix de Gay	6,000
Château L'Eglise Clinet	2,000
Château Gazin	10,000
Château Le Gay	2,000
Château La Grave Trigant de Boisset	3,500
Château La Pointe	9,000
Château Lagrange	3,500
Château Nenin	12,000
Château Rouget	7,000
Château de Sales	18,000

Burgundy
Vineyards of the Côte d'Or

The vineyards of Burgundy can never be classified with anything like the precision of the Bordeaux châteaux, where every major vineyard has a single owner and a single name. On the Côte d'Or, most of the named vineyards are divided among different growers; some sixty producers, for example, own vines in the Clos de Vougeot vineyard, and even the small Montrachet vineyard has nearly twenty owners. Nevertheless, a careful survey and classification, no less official and no less thorough than the famous Classification of 1855 in Bordeaux, was published in 1861. This eventually served as the basis of the *Appellation Contrôlée* regulations established in the 1930s and, as a result, only the wines from certain specific vineyards may legally be called *Grand Cru* or *Premier Cru*. The list that follows includes all of the *grands crus* of the Côte d'Or (shown in SMALL CAPS) and most of the *premiers crus* that one is likely to find on labels.

Red Wines

Commune	Leading Vineyards	Acres
Côte de Nuits		
Fixin (551 acres)	Clos de la Perrière	16.1
	Clos du Chapitre	11.8
	Les Arvelets	8.2
	Les Hervelets	10.8
Gevrey-Chambertin (1,462 acres)	CHAMBERTIN	31.8
	CLOS DE BÈZE	38.0
	LATRICIÈRES-CHAMBERTIN	18.1
	MAZIS-CHAMBERTIN	22.5
	CHARMES-CHAMBERTIN	76.1
	GRIOTTE-CHAMBERTIN	6.7
	RUCHOTTES-CHAMBERTIN	8.2
	CHAPELLE-CHAMBERTIN	13.6
	Clos Saint Jacques	16.5
	Les Varoilles	14.8
	Combe au Moine	11.8
	Les Cazetiers	24.8
Morey-Saint-Denis (674 acres)	BONNES MARES	3.8
	CLOS DE TART	18.6
	CLOS DE LA ROCHE	41.7
	CLOS SAINT-DENIS	16.2
	CLOS DES LAMBRAYS	21.8
	Clos Bussière	6.4
Chambolle-Musigny (551 acres)	MUSIGNY	26.3
	BONNES MARES	33.4
	Les Amoureuses	13.2
	Les Charmes	23.0
	Combe d'Orveau	5.9
	Les Cras	8.5
Vougeot (170 acres)	CLOS DE VOUGEOT	125.0
	Vougeot	28.8
Flagey-Échézeaux (252 acres)	GRANDS ÉCHÉZEAUX	22.6
	LES ÉCHÉZEAUX	93.1

Commune	Leading Vineyards	Acres
Vosne-Romanée (519 acres)	ROMANÉE-CONTI	4.5
	LA TÂCHE	14.9
	ROMANÉE SAINT-VIVANT	23.6
	RICHEBOURG	19.8
	LA ROMANÉE	2.1
	LA GRANDE RUE	3.5
	Les Gaudichots	2.9
	Aux Malconsorts	14.7
	Les Suchots	32.1
	Les Beaux-Monts	10.6
	Aux Brulées	11.1
	Clos des Réas	5.3
Nuits Saint-George (1,386 acres,	Les Saint-Georges	18.6
including Prémeaux)	Les Cailles	9.4
	Clos des Corvées	16.3
	Les Vaucrains	15.0
	Les Pruliers	18.8
	Les Porrets	17.5
	Aux Thorey	12.3
	Aux Boudots	15.8
	Aux Cras	7.7
	Aux Murgers	12.1
	La Richemone	4.9
	La Perrière	6.1
	Aux Perdrix	8.3
	Clos des Argilières	10.4
	Clos Arlot	13.4
	Clos de la Maréchale	23.6
Côte de Beaune		
Aloxe-Corton (605 acres)	LE CORTON	28.8
	CORTON BRESSANDES*	42.9
	CORTON CLOS DU ROI*	26.4
	CORTON RENARDES*	35.3
	CORTON PERRIÈRES*	23.6
	CORTON MARÉCHAUDES*	11.0
	CORTON LES POUGETS*	24.6
	Les Chaillots	11.4
	Les Fournières	13.8
	Les Valozières	16.3
Pernand-Vergelesses (869 acres)	Ile des Vergelesses	23.0
	Les Vergelesses	44.0
Savigny Les Beaune (1,344 acres)	Les Vergelesses	42.0
	Les Lavières	43.7
	Les Marconnets	20.5
Beaune (1,618 acres)	Grèves	77.3
	Fèves	10.9
	Bressandes	42.0
	Clos des Mouches	61.4
	Les Cent-Vignes	57.6
	Aux Cras	12.5
	Champimonts	41.0
	Boucherottes	21.1
	Marconnets	23.2

*All of the wines whose names are preceded by Corton come from specific plots in the extensive *grand cru* vineyard of Corton and may also be labelled simply as Le Corton.

Commune	Leading Vineyards	Acres
	Clos de la Mousse	8.4
	Les Avaux	38.1
	Aigrots	19.9
	Clos du Roi	20.7
	Les Toussaints	16.1
	Les Teurons	37.1
Pommard (1,655 acres)	Rugiens	31.1
	Épenots	25.6
	Clos Blanc	10.6
	Pézerolles	14.6
	Petits-Epenots	48.4
	Chaponnières	7.1
	Boucherottes	4.1
	Platière	6.2
	Jarollières	7.9
	Argillières	9.0
	Arvelets	20.9
	Clos de la Commaraine	9.8
Volnay (904 acres)	Clos des Ducs	6.0
	Caillerets	29.6
	Champans	28.0
	Frémiets	16.1
	Santenots	71.6
	Les Angles	8.6
	Bousse d'Or	4.9
	Clos des Chênes	38.0
Auxey (1,235 acres)	Les Duresses	25.4
Monthélie (450 acres)	Les Champs Fulliot	19.9
Chassagne-Montrachet (1,109 acres)	La Boudriotte	44.3
	Clos St. Jean	35.5
	La Maltroie	28.7
Santenay (1,270 acres)	Les Gravières	71.6
	La Comme	53.4

White Wines

A limited amount of white wine – perhaps 1,500 cases a year – is produced in the Côte de Nuits villages of Morey Saint-Denis, Chambolle-Musigny, Vougeot, and Nuits-Saint-Georges, but the most celebrated white wines of the Côte d'Or come from the Côte de Beaune, most of them from the villages listed below.

Aloxe-Corton	CORTON-CHARLEMAGNE	178.0
Meursault (2,482 acres)	Perrières	33.3
	Genevrières	40.5
	Charmes	76.8
	Poruzots	27.9
	La Pièce-sous-le-Bois	27.8
	Blagny	57.8
	Goutte d'Or	13.8
Puligny-Montrachet (1,260 acres)	MONTRACHET (part)	9.9
	CHEVALIER-MONTRACHET	18.2
	BÂTARD-MONTRACHET (part)	14.8
	BIENVENUE-BÂTARD-MONTRACHET	9.1
	Combettes	16.6
	Chalumeaux	14.3
	Folatières	43.2
	Pucelles	16.8
	Champ-Canet	13.6
	Clavaillon	13.8
	Les Referts	13.6
Chassagne-Montrachet (1,109 acres)	MONTRACHET (part)	9.8
	BÂTARD-MONTRACHET (part)	14.4
	CRIOTS-BÂTARD-MONTRACHET	4.0
	Grandes-Ruchottes	5.2
	Les Caillerets	26.2
	Abbaye de Morgeot	21.0

Hospices de Beaune Auction: 1985

Cuvée	Appellation Contrôlée	Pièces (25 cases)
Red Wines		
Nicolas Rolin	Beaune	19
Guigone de Salins	Beaune	20
Charlotte Dumay	Corton	14
Docteur Peste	Corton	15
Dames Hospitalières	Beaune	22
Dames de la Charité	Pommard	14
Blondeau	Volnay	11
Brunet	Beaune	25
Jehan de Massol	Volnay-Santenots	13
Clos des Avaux	Beaune	20
Billardet	Pommard	15
Gauvain	Volnay-Santenots	17
Hugues et Louis Bétault	Beaune	30
Rousseau-Deslandes	Beaune	21
Général Muteau	Volnay	17
Maurice Drouhin	Beaune	30
Boillot	Auxey-Duresses	4
Arthur Girard	Savigny-les-Beaune	21
Fouquerand	Savigny-les-Beaune	25
J. Lebelin	Monthélie	14
Forneret	Savigny-les-Beaune	14
Rameau-Lamarasse	Pernand Vergelesses	7
Madeleine Collignon	Mazis-Chambertin	15
Cyrot-Chaudron	Pommard	50
Cyrot-Chaudron	Beaune	22
White Wines		
François de Salins	Corton-Charlemagne	4
de Bahèzre de Lanlay	Meursault-Charmes	18
Albert Grivault	Meursault-Charmes	5
Baudot	Meursault-Genevrières	18
Philippe le Bon	Meursault-Genevrières	9
Jehan Humblot	Meursault	12
Goureau	Meursault	7
Loppin	Meursault	6
Paul Chanson	Corton-Vergennes	2
Total		555 pièces (13,875 cases)

Total Revenue 1985

Red Wine	20,069,500 francs
White Wine	4,826,000
Eaux de Vie	86,854
	24,982,354 francs

Champagne
Cuvées Spéciales

The *cuvées spéciales* of France's Champagne region, which are also known as prestige *cuvées* and deluxe bottlings, are the most expensive wines offered by the Champagne firms. The *cuvée* of still wines is made from a special selection of the wines available to each firm, the wines are usually aged somewhat longer than the regular vintage bottling, and most firms market their *cuvées spéciales* in distinctive bottles that have been specially created for these wines. The first of these wines was Louis Roederer Cristal, originally produced for the Russian court in the 1870s; Cristal, in its unusual clear-glass bottle, was not sold commercially until the early 1950s. The first deluxe bottling offered to the public was Dom Pérignon, in the 1930s; its success was such that most Champagne firms now market a *cuvée spéciale*. The following list includes the best-known labels.

Besserat de Bellefon	*Cuvée B de B*
Billecart Salmon	*Cuvée N.F. Billecart*
Bollinger	*R.D.*
Canard-Duchêne	*Charles VII*
Charbaut	*Certificate*
Deutz & Geldermann	*Cuvée William Deutz*
Gosset	*Grand Millésime*
Heidsieck Monopole	*Diamant Bleu*
Piper Heidsieck	*Rare*
Krug	*Grande Cuvée*
Laurent Perrier	*Cuvée Grand Siècle*
Moët & Chandon	*Dom Pérignon*
Mumm	*René Lalou*
Perrier Jouët	*Belle Epoque (Fleur de Champagne* in the U.S.A.)
Pol Roger	*Cuvée Sir Winston Churchill*
Pommery	*Louise Pommery*
Louis Roederer	*Cristal*
Ruinart	*Dom Ruinart*
Taittinger	*Comtes de Champagne*
Venoge	*Champagne des Princes*
Veuve Clicquot	*La Grande Dame*

Germany

Vineyard Acreage by Variety and Region

Grape Variety	Abr	Mittel-rhein	Mosel-Saar-Ruwer	Nahe	Rhein-hessen	Rhein-pfalz	Rhein-gau	Hess. Berg-strasse	Baden	Würt-tem-berg	Franken	Total in 1985	Total in 1964
Bacchus	2	17	716	632	4,942	1,183	–	–	96	10	1,225	8,825	5
Weissburgunder	5	5	22	146	269	635	–	–	1,186	12	10	2,287	1,149
Elbling	–	–	2,885	–	–	–	–	–	22	–	2	2,910	3,070
Faberrebe	–	10	22	343	4,271	936	–	–	–	–	50	5,632	–
Guedel	15	–	–	–	2	2	–	–	3,100	2	–	3,107	2,944
Kerner	15	109	1,976	877	4,861	6,061	111	34	346	2,100	701	17,191	12
Morio-Muskat	–	2	10	126	1,213	3,888	–	–	7	–	39	6,523	2,598
Müller-Thurgau	125	210	7,287	3,122	15,144	13,533	432	178	13,802	2,332	6,308	62,471	34,864
Riesling	153	1,400	17,206	2,475	3,705	8,633	5,802	506	2,616	5,649	304	48,449	42,195
Ruländer	2	13	22	294	1,154	1,475	42	79	4,337	235	62	7,714	3,169
Scheurebe	–	13	35	798	5,923	3,495	32	22	124	20	371	10,831	845
Sylvaner	–	22	7	1,576	8,153	4,972	44	74	1,277	1,144	2,613	19,884	46,389
Gewürztraminer	–	5	5	37	311	879	37	15	733	74	99	2,196	1,074
Others	15	15	1,299	679	7,494	4,490	314	32	812	67	655	15,872	1,929
Total White Varieties	317	1,820	32,602	11,105	58,677	50,183	6,815	941	28,459	11,646	12,439	213,892	140,244
Spätburgunder	388	20	2	82	669	620	390	12	8,005	716	175	11,080	4,542
Limberger	–	–	–	–	5	–	–	–	20	1,314	–	1,339	879
Müllerrebe	–	–	–	7	18	166	–	–	210	3,189	49	3,638	798
Portugieser	269	5	2	128	2,050	4,476	23	2	96	719	91	7,862	13,148
Trollinger	–	–	–	–	7	7	–	–	7	5,402	–	5,424	4,105
Others	79	–	–	64	810	1,121	34	5	5	252	67	2,358	995
Total Red Varieties	736	25	4	281	3,559	6,390	447	19	8,343	12,214	382	31,701	24,468
Total All Varieties	1,053	1,845	32,606	11,386	62,236	56,573	7,262	960	36,802	23,860	12,821	245,593	164,712

The "other" white varieties consist mostly of the new crosses Ehrenfelser, Huxelrebe, Optima, and Ortega; virtually nonexistent in the mid-1960s, these four varieties now account for about 10,000 acres planted primarily in Rheinhessen and the Rheinpfalz. A comparison of the 1964 and 1985 figures shows that the increased plantings of other new crosses such as Bacchus, Faberrebe, Kerner, Morio-Muskat, and Scheurebe are equally dramatic. Note also the increase in Müller-Thurgau at the expense of Sylvaner. The 1988 report shows that although total vineyard acreage is the same as in 1985, there has been a slight decrease in Müller-Thurgau and Sylvaner and an increase of 2,500 acres of Riesling.

Production by Region

	Average of 1984-88 per 1,000 Cases	% of Total
Rheinhessen	21,384	23.3
Rheinpfalz	24,035	26.3
Rheingau	2,134	2.3
Mosel-Saar-Ruwer	13,607	14.8
Nahe	3,773	4.2
Baden	12,210	13.3
Franken	3,828	4.2
Württemberg	9,361	10.3
Ahr	286	0.3
Mittelrhein	605	0.7
Hessische Bergstrasse	286	0.3
Total	91.773	100.0

Although the average production for the years 1984-1988 is nearly 92 million cases, the annual German wine crop has varied in recent years from 59 million cases in 1985 to 169 million cases in 1982. Note that about half of Germany's wines are produced in two regions – Rheinhessen and the Rheinpfalz.

Production by Quality Category

German wines are classified according to the sugar content of the grapes at harvest, and this chart provides a comparison of the overall ripeness of the six vintages 1984 through 1989 as well as a breakdown of the crop in each of the eleven Anbaugebiete, or specific districts. The wines are classified by three basic quality categories – Tafelwein, Qualitätswein, and Qualitätswein mit Prädikat (which includes Kabinett, Spätlese, Auslese, and higher grades). The chart indicates, for example, that Prädikatswein accounted for 60 percent of the 1985 harvest and 54 percent of the 1988 crop, but only 7 percent in 1984 and 21 percent in 1987. More specifically, in the Rheingau region, 82 percent of the successful 1988 crop achieved Prädikatswein status, but only 2 percent in 1984.

	% of Each Category					
	1984	1985	1986	1987	1988	1989
Total Harvest						
Tafelwein	13	–	5	2	–	1
Qualitätswein	80	40	76	77	46	51
Prädikatswein	7	60	19	21	54	48
Rheinhessen						
Tafelwin	–	–	1	1	–	–
Qualitätswein	78	38	75	74	18	38
Prädikatswein	8	62	24	25	82	62
Rheinpfalz						
Tafelwein	16	–	12	3	–	1
Qualitätswein	75	47	78	79	53	48
Prädikâtswein	9	53	10	18	47	51
Rheingau						
Tafelwein	25	–	3	1	–	–
Qualitätswein	73	40	72	84	18	40
Prädikatswein	2	60	25	15	82	60

	1984	1985	% of Each Category 1986	1987	1988	1989
Mosel-Saar-Ruwer						
Tafelwein	20	—	4	4	—	1
Qualitätswein	79	63	72	88	46	59
Prädikatswein	1	37	24	8	54	40
Nahe						
Tafelwein	7	1	1	2	—	—
Qualitätswein	87	36	69	83	40	34
Prädikatswein	6	63	30	15	60	66
Mittelrhein						
Tafelwein	12	—	—	—	—	—
Qualitätswein	84	32	73	79	41	42
Prädikatswein	4	68	27	21	59	58
Ahr						
Tafelwein	5	—	2	3	—	3
Qualitätswein	94	37	85	85	50	81
Prädikatswein	1	63	12	12	50	16
Baden						
Tafelwein	15	—	10	1	1	1
Qualitätswein	75	33	79	71	60	59
Prädikatswein	10	67	11	28	39	40
Württemberg						
Tafelwein	14	—	4	1	—	1
Qualitätswein	83	27	82	60	55	60
Prädikatswein	3	73	14	39	45	39
Franken						
Tafelwein	14	—	1	1	—	1
Qualitätswein	81	14	68	85	44	80
Prädikatswein	5	86	31	14	56	19
Hessische Berg-strasse						
Tafelwein	20	—	—	—	—	—
Qualitätswein	78	15	72	77	27	38
Prädikatswein	2	85	28	23	73	62

Principle Bereiche, Grosslagen, and Einzellagen

This list of Bereiche (district appellations), Grosslagen (combined vineyard sites), and Einzellagen (individual vineyards) includes the names most likely to be encountered on labels. For each group of Einzellagen, the first column indicates the village, the second column lists the best-known vineyards situated in that village; the wines are labelled with a combination of village and vineyard names: Eltviller Sonnenberg, Erbacher Marcobrunn. (*Indicates vineyards whose names appear alone on the label.)

Rheingau

Bereich Johannisberg
Grosslagen

Johannisberger Erntebringer
Hattenheimer Deutelsberg
Hochheimer Daubhaus
Rauenthaler Steinmächer
Rüdesheimer Burgweg

Einzellagen	Eltville	Sandgrub
		Sonnenberg
		Taubenberg
	Erbach	Marcobrunn
		Steinmorgen
	Geisenheim	Rothenberg
	Hallgarten	Hendelberg
		Schönhell
	Hattenheim	Steinberg*
		Mannberg
		Nussbrunnen
		Wisselbrunnen
	Hochheim	Domdechaney
		Kirchenstück
		Königin Victoria Berg
	Johannisberg	Schloss Johannisberg*
		Hölle
		Klaus
	Kiedrich	Sandgrub
		Wasseros
	Oestrich	Schloss Reichartshausen*
		Doosberg
		Lenchen
	Rauenthal	Baiken
		Gehrn
		Rothenberg
		Wülfen
	Rüdesheim	Berg Rottland
		Berg Schlossberg
		Bischofsberg
	Winkel	Schloss Vollrads*
		Hasensprung

Rheinhessen
Bereich Nierstein
Bereich Bingen

Grosslagen	Niersteiner Gutes Domtal
	Niersteiner Auflangen
	Niersteiner Rehbach
	Niersteiner Spiegelberg
	Oppenheimer Krötenbrunnen

Einzellagen	Bingen	Scharlachberg
	Nierstein	Hipping
		Hölle
		Ölberg
		Orbel
		Pettenthal
	Oppenheim	Sackträger
		Herrenberg
		Daubhaus

Rheinpfalz

Grosslagen	Forster Mariengarten	
	Deidesheimer Hofstück	
Einzellagen	Deidesheim	Hohenmorgen
		Leinhölle
	Dürkheim	Herrenmorgen
		Spielberg
	Forst	Jesuitengarten
		Kirchenstück
		Pechstein
		Ungeheuer
	Ruppertsberg	Hoheberg
		Nussbien
	Wachenheim	Gerumpel
		Goldbächel

Nahe

Bereich Kreuznach
Bereich Schloss Böckelheim

Grosslagen	Rüdesheimer Rosengarten	
	Schlossböckelheimer Burgweg	
Einzellagen	Kreuznach	Hinkelstein
	Niederhausen	Hermannshöhle
	Schlossböckelheim	Kupfergrube
		Felsenberg

Mosel-Saar-Ruwer

Moselle
Bereich Bernkastel

Grosslagen	Piesporter Michelsberg	
	Bernkasteler Kurfürstlay	
	Bernkasteler Badstube	
	Zeller Schwarze Katz	
	Kröver Nacktarsch	
Einzellagen	Bernkastel	Bratenhöfchen
		Doctor
		Graben
		Lay
	Brauneberg	Juffer
	Erden	Prälat
		Treppchen
	Graach	Domprobst
		Himmelreich
		Josephshöfer
	Piesport	Falkenberg
		Goldtröpfchen
		Günterslay
		Treppchen
	Trittenheim	Altärchen
		Apotheke

	Ürzig	Würzgarten
	Wehlen	Nonnenberg Sonnenuhr
	Zeltingen	Himmelreich Schlossberg Sonnenuhr
Saar ***Bereich Saar-Ruwer*** Grosslage	Wiltinger Scharzberg	
Einzellagen	Ayl	Herrenberger Kupp
	Ockfen	Bockstein Geisberg Herrenberg
	Serrig	Kupp Würtzberg
	Wiltingen	Scharzhofberg* Kupp
Ruwer ***Bereich Saar-Ruwer*** Grosslage	Kaseler Römerlay	
Einzellagen	Avelsbach	Altenberg Herrenberg
	Eitelsbach	Karthäuserhofberg
	Kasel	Hitzlay Kehrnagel Nieschen
	Maximin Grünhaus	Abtsberg Bruderberg Herrenberg
	Waldrach	Krone Laurentiusberg
Franken (Franconia) Einzellagen	Castell	Hohnart Schlossberg
	Escherndorf	Berg Lump.
	Iphofen	Julius-Echter-Berg
	Randersacker	Teufelskeller
	Würzburg	Innere Leiste Schlossberg Stein

Italy

Production by Region: 1988

This chart provides a regional breakdown of all Italian wines and also of DOC (and DOCG) wines for the 1988 vintage. Note that 1988 – and 1989, too, which produced a total of only 660 million cases – are both well below the recent average of 800 million cases. The differences are due primarily to the smaller crops in Puglia and Sicily, which often produce 130 to 140 million cases each and account for a third of the total Italian harvest. The Veneto, Tuscany, and Piedmont are the main producers of DOC wines, however, and accounted for 45 percent of all DOC wines produced in 1988.

Region	Total Production Per 1,000 Cases	DOC Production in Cases	Number of DOC
Piedmont	36,315	13,130,447	36
Valle d'Aosta	363	23,650	1
Lombardy	16,865	5,219,808	13
Liguria	2,844	126,049	2
Veneto	90,173	19,333,721	14
Friuli-Venezia Giulia	19,293	4,572,997	7
Trentino-Alto Adige	12,637	7,908,241	12
Emilia-Romagna	82,893	9,530,213	12
Tuscany	36,962	11,815,683	21
Umbria	12,375	1,910,084	6
Marches	22,498	3,379,453	10
Latium	53,405	6,412,153	17
Abruzzi	35,989	4,305,598	2
Molise	4,290	23,463	2
Campania	26,255	267,630	8
Apulia	94,849	2,123,033	23
Basilicata	4,217	91,234	1
Calabria	11,803	400,631	8
Sicily	105,699	4,014,461	9
Sardinia	20,766	1,096,238	17
Total	680,493	95,684,712	219

The DOC and DOCG Wines of Italy

Piedmont

Asti Spumante
*Barbaresco
Barbera d'Alba
Barbera d'Asti
Barbera del Monferrato
*Barolo
Boca
Brachetto d'Acqui
Bramaterra
Caluso Passito
Carema
Colli Tortonesi
Cortese dell'Alto Monferrato
Dolcetto d'Acqui

Dolcetto di Ovada
Erbaluce di Caluso
Fara
Freisa d'Asti
Freisa di Chieri
Gabiano
Gattinara
Gavi or Cortese di Gavi
Ghemme
Grignolino d'Asti
Grignolini del Monferrato Casalese
Lessona
Malvasia di Casorzo d'Asti
Malvasia di Castelnuovo Don Bosco

*DOCG

Dolcetto d'Alba
Dolcetto d'Asti
Dolcetto delle Langhe Monregalesi
Dolcetto di Diano d'Alba
Dolcetto di Dogliani

Moscato d'Asti
Nebbiolo d'Alba
Roero
Rubino di Cantavenna
Sizzano

Valle d'Aosta

Valle d'Aosta (Vallée d'Aoste)

Lombardy

Botticino
Capriano del Colle
Cellatica
Colli Morenici Mantovani del
   Garda
Franciacorta
Lambrusco Mantovano
Lugana

Oltrepò Pavese
Riviera del Garda Bresciano
San Colombano
Tocai di S. Martino della Battaglia
Valcalepio
Valtellina
Valtellina Superiore

Trentino-Alto Adige

Alto Adige (Südtirol)
Caldaro or Lago di Caldaro
Casteller
Colli di Bolzano
Meranese or Meranese di Collina
Santa Maddalena

Sorni
Terlano
Teroldego Rotaliano
Trentino
Valdadige
Valle Isarco

Veneto

Bardolino
Bianco di Custoza
Breganze
Colli Berici
Colli Euganei
Gambellara
Lessini Durello
Lison-Pramaggiore

Montello e Colli Asolani
Piave or Vini del Piave
Prosecco di Conegliano-Valdobbiadene
Soave and Recioto di Soave
Tocai di Lison
Valpolicella and Recioto della Valpolicella

Friuli-Venezia Giulia

Aquileia
Carso
Collio Goriziano or Collio
Colli Orientali del Friuli

Grave del Friuli
Isonzo
Latisana

Liguria

Cinqueterre or
Cinqueterre Sciacchetrà

Rossese di Dolceacqua or Dolceacqua

Emilia-Romagna

*Albana di Romagna
Bianco di Scandiano
Colli Bolognese Monte San Pietro
   or Castelli Mediovali
Colli di Parma
Colli Piacentini
Lambrusco Grasparossa di Castelvetro

Lambrusco Reggiano
Lambrusco Salamino di S. Croce
Lambrusco di Sorbara
Montuni del Reno
Sangiovese di Romagna
Trebbiano di Romagna

*DOCG

Tuscany

Bianco della Valdinievole
Bianco di Pitigliano
Bianco Pisano Santorpé
Bianco Vergine Valdichiana
Bolgheri
*Brunello di Montalcino
Candia dei Colli Apuani
Carmignano
*Chianti
Colline Lucchesi
Elba

Montecarlo
Montescudaio
Morellino di Scansano
Moscadello di Montalcino
Parrina
Pomino
Rosso di Montalcino
Val d'Arbia
Vernaccia di San Gimignano
*Vino Nobile di Montepulciano

*DOCG

Marches

Bianchello del Metauro
Bianco dei Colli Maceratesi
Falerio dei Colli Ascolani
Lacrima di Morro
Rosso Cònero

Rosso Piceno
Sangiovese dei Colli Pesaresi
Verdicchio dei Castelli di Jesi
Verdicchio di Matelica
Vernaccia di Serrapetrona

Umbria

Colli Altotiberini
Colli del Trasimeno
Colli Perugini

Montefalco
Orvieto
Torgiano

Latium

Aleatico di Gradoli
Bianco Capena
Cerveteri
Cesanese del Piglio or Piglio
Cesanese di Affile or Affile
Cesanese di Olevano Romano or
Olevano Romano
Colli Albani

Colli Lanuvini
Cori
Est! Est!! Est!!! di Montefiascone
Frascati
Marino
Merlot di Aprilia
Montecompatri Colonna
Sangiovese di Aprilia
Trebbiano di Aprilia
Velletri
Zagarolo

Abruzzi and Molise

Biferno
Montepulciano d'Abruzzo

Pentro di Isernia
Trebbiano d'Abruzzo

Campania

Aglianico del Taburno
Capri
Fiano di Avellino
Greco de Tufo

Ischia
Solopaca
Taurasi
Vesuvio

*DOCQ

Apulia

Aleatico di Puglia
Cacc'e Mmitte di Lucera
Castel del Monte
Copertino
Gioia del Colle
Gravina
Leverano
Locorotondo
Martina or Martina Franca
Matino
Moscato di Trani

Nardo
Ortanova
Ostuni
Primitivo di Manduria
Rosso Barletta
Rosso Canosa
Rosso di Cerignola
Salice Salentino
S. Severo
Squinzano

Basilicata

Aglianico del Vulture

Calabria

Cirò
Donnici
Grecodi Bianco
Lamezia

Melissa
Pollino
Sant'Anna di Isola Capo Rizzuto
Savuto

Sicily

Alcamo or Bianco Alcamo
Cerasuolo di Vittoria
Etna
Faro
Malvasia delle Lipari

Marsala
Moscato di Noto
Moscato di Pantelleria
Moscata di Siracusa

Sardinia

Arborea
Campidano di Terralba or Terralba
Cannonau di Sardegna
Carignano del Sulcis
Girò di Cagliari
Malvasia di Bosa
Malvasia di Cagliari
Mandrolisai

Monica di Cagliari
Monica di Sardegna
Moscata di Sorso-Sennori
Nasco di Cagliari
Nuragus di Cagliari
Vermentino di Gallura
Vernaccia di Oristano

The Top Twenty DOC Wines: 1988

In terms of volume, the top twenty DOC appellations (which includes the DOCG Chianti) accounted for 62 percent of the total in 1988; in fact, just five names represented 29 percent of all DOC wines. Note that almost all of the wines entitled to the DOC Moscato d'Asti are transformed into the popular sparkling wine Asti Spumante.

	Quantity in Cases
Chianti	9,318,144
Moscato d'Asti	6,096,431
Soave	5,098,742
Valpolicella	3,827,087
Oltrepò Pavese	3,678,048
Marsala	3,538,733
Montepulciano d'Abruzzo	2,812,227
Bardolino	2,383,777
Grave del Friuli	2,226,015
Lambrusco Reggiano	2,055,416
Frascati	2,048,541
Barbera d'Asti	1,967,240
Caldaro	1,954,843
Piave	1,920,754
Verdicchio dei Castelli di Jesi	1,905,695
Prosecco di Conegliano	1,879,482
Alto Adige	1,783,782
Sangiovese di Romagna	1,716,550
Colli Piacentini	1,631,542
Valdadige	1,618,518
Total of Top 20 DOC	59,460,547
Total DOC	95,684,712

Portugal

Vintage Port

Although more than thirty firms, both British and Portuguese, market vintage ports, fewer than a dozen produce such wines on a regular basis and make wines whose quality is such that they are acquired for investment purposes. Most connoisseurs would consider the firms listed below (along with the vintages each has declared since 1945) to be among the very best producers of vintage port. Note that there has been a certain amount of amalgamation among port producers in recent years. Thus, the Symington family owns Dow, Graham, and Warre, as well as Quarles Harris and Smith Woodehouse; Croft owns Delaforce and Morgan; Cockburn owns Martinez; and Taylor Fladgate owns Fonseca.

Cockburn	1947, 1950, 1955, 1960, 1963, 1967, 1970, 1975, 1983, 1985
Croft	1945, 1950, 1955, 1960, 1963, 1966, 1970, 1975, 1977, 1982, 1985
Quinta do Noval	1945, 1947, 1950, 1955, 1958, 1960, 1963, 1966, 1967, 1970, 1975, 1978, 1982, 1985
Dow	1945, 1947, 1950, 1955, 1960, 1963, 1966, 1970, 1972, 1975, 1977, 1980, 1983, 1985
Fonseca	1945, 1948, 1955, 1957, 1960, 1963, 1966, 1970, 1975, 1977, 1980, 1983, 1985
Graham	1945, 1948, 1955, 1960, 1963, 1966, 1970, 1975, 1977, 1980, 1983, 1985
Sandeman	1945, 1947, 1950, 1955, 1957, 1958, 1960, 1962, 1963, 1966, 1967, 1970, 1975, 1977, 1980, 1982, 1985
Taylor Fladgate	1945, 1948, 1955, 1960, 1963, 1966, 1970, 1975, 1977, 1980, 1983, 1985
Warre	1945, 1947, 1950, 1955, 1958, 1960, 1963, 1966, 1970, 1975, 1977, 1980, 1983, 1985

Other familiar vintage port labels include Delaforce, Ferreira, Fonseca, Gould Campbell, Boa Vista of Offley Forrester, and Rebello Valente of Robertson's. In addition, a number of firms produce single-quinta vintage ports – that is, unblended ports from a single estate – usually in years not declared under the firm's principal label. Some of the better-known quintas (in addition to Quinta do Noval and Boa Vista) are Vargellas of Taylor Fladgate, Malvedos of Graham, Roeda of Croft, Bomfim of Dow, Corte of Delaforce, Bom Retiro of Ramos Pinto, and Foz of Calem.

Spain

Denominación de Origen Wines

Of Spain's 4 million acres of vineyards, about 30 percent are entitled to Denominación de Origen, and these produce about 40 percent of the country's total wine crop of 350 to 400 million cases. In recent years, however, only half to two thirds of the wines entitled to DO have been marketed as such, although the proportion is much higher for such well-known wines as sherry and Rioja. These figures show the acreage for each Denominación de Origen and the amount sold (not produced) with the DO name in the twelve months ending August 1988. Sherry and Rioja are clearly the most important wines in terms of volume, followed by *cavas*, or sparkling wines (primarily those from Penedès), Valdepeñas, and La Mancha.

Denominación de Origen	Acreage	Quantity in Cases Marketed as DO
Alella	805	78,474
Alicante	38,186	648,046
Almansa	11,747	559,328
Ampurdán-Costa Brava	6,434	829,125
Campo de Borja	20,686	555,563
Cariñena	53,431	3,398,681
Cava		10,697,841
Condado de Huelva	32,110	1,629,672
Costers del Segre	7,973	1,108,800
Jerez-Xérès-Sherry	47,869	14,400,947
Jumilla	83,212	13,863,443
La Mancha	274,027	5,736,038
Malaga	1,319	8,737,101
Méntrida	56,795	407,517
Montilla-Moriles	40,508	832,007
Navarra	48,400	5,232,216
Penedès	31,618	4,316,884
Priorato	4,609	6,422,482
Rias Baixas	1,852	323,620
Ribeiro	1,660	46,497
Ribera del Duero	10,127	1,382,700
Rioja	95,095	355,300
Rueda	10,305	11,047,949
Somontano	3,359	37,554
Tarragona	42,993	1,004,498
Terra Alta	13,138	1,554,905
Toro	7,324	329,769
Utiel-Requena	86,400	4,585,834
Valdeorras	3,700	3,753,431
Valdepeñas	81,473	291,511
Valencia	52,290	9,831,844
Yecla	65,995	4,945,380
Total	1,201,885	106,489,790

United States

California Vineyard Acreage by County: 1988

County	Total Wine Grapes
Alameda	1,795
Amador	1,631
Butte	139
Calaveras	176
Colusa	547
Contra Costa	735
El Dorado	496
Fresno	35,175
Glenn	1,258
Kern	29,481
Kings	1,238
Lake	2,644
Madera	38,085
Mendocino	11,829
Merced	14,472
Monterey	27,863
Napa	32,165
Placer	109
Riverside	2,650
Sacramento	3,385
San Benito	1,591
San Bernardino	1,642
San Diego	108
San Joaquin	34,661
San Luis Obispo	7,280
San Mateo	53
Santa Barbara	9,289
Santa Clara	1,088
Santa Cruz	145
Solano	1,221
Sonoma	31,555
Stanislaus	15,117
Tulane	11,999
Yolo	1,658
Yuba	352
Other Counties	242
State Total	324,054

Note that the wine grape acreage accounts for less than half of California's total vineyards, which amount to 692,000 acres. There are 269,000 acres of raisin grapes, virtually all of it Thompson Seedless, which alone represents nearly 40 percent of the state's total acreage; and table grapes, primarily Flame Seedless, Emperor, and Flame Tokay, account for 93,000 acres. Of the grape harvest transformed into wine, however, wine grapes accounted for 84 percent of the total "crush" in 1988, and for 89 percent in 1989.

California Vineyard Acreage by Variety

Red Wine Grapes	1966	1976	1988
Aleatico	227	89	20
Alicante Bouschet	5,862	3,315	2,542
Barbera	1,313	16,043	11,327
Black Malvoisie	726	301	87
Cabernet Franc	—	124	1,142
Cabernet Sauvignon	2,659	18,303	26,404
Carignane	23,959	17,793	12,295
Carnelian	—	1,591	1,345
Centurian	—	886	591
Charbono	—	43	87
Early Burgundy	560	302	208
Gamay	1,081	2,861	1,855
Gamay Beaujolais	477	2,652	1,631
Grenache	11,897	13,569	13,286
Grignolino	220	58	37
Malbec	15	47	77
Mataro	1,697	694	236
Merlot	66	1,856	3,996
Meunier	—	—	138
Mission	5,954	2,711	1,444
Muscat Hamburg	42	59	59
Petite Sirah	3,303	5,657	3,495
Petit Verdot	—	—	54
Pinot Noir	1,749	7,747	8,857
Pinot St. George	75	190	84
Royalty	1,961	1,311	912
Rubired	2,188	7,692	6,905
Ruby Cabernet	1,958	11,184	7,318
Salvador	1,729	1,309	842
St. Macaire	183	106	50
Syrah	—	31	139
Tinta Madeira	350	192	123
Valdepeñas	1,862	1,005	635
Zinfandel	17,022	22,006	30,735
Other	1,430	411	329
Total Red	91,242	142,467	139,278

White Wine Grapes	1966	1976	1988
Burger	1,817	1,302	2,613
Chardonnay	1,378	11,321	41,870
Chasselas Doré	71	9	55
Chenin Blanc	1,970	19,299	36,247
Emerald Riesling	476	2,323	1,618
Feher Szagos	467	155	54
Flora	109	358	100
Folle Blanche	183	276	64
French Colombard	5,941	24,179	66,029
Gewürztraminer	413	2,185	2,735
Gray Riesling	646	1,654	754
Green Hungarian	256	248	219
Malvasia Bianca	176	753	2,050
Muscat Blanc	263	955	1,538
Muscat Orange	—	—	73

	1966	*1976*	*1988*
Palomino	5,749	3,010	1,813
Pedro Ximénes	562	158	35
Peverella	—	409	409
Pinot Blanc	507	1,401	1,974
Sauvignon Blanc	726	3,706	14,164
Sauvignon Vert	775	315	147
Sémillon	959	2,314	2,518
St. Emilion	—	1,109	805
Sylvaner	908	1,092	297
Symphony	—	—	59
White Riesling	757	7,048	6,839
Other	143	223	176
Total White	25,252	85,878	184,776
Total All Wine Grapes	116,494	228,345	324,054

Nearly 200,000 acres of new vineyards were planted in the years 1969 to 1974, bringing the total to 322,000 acres of wine grapes; however, a significant part of the acreage planted in the 1970s was subsequently abandoned, uprooted, or replaced with different varieties, and these shifts are not always reflected in the figures. Also, the limited plantings of such varieties as Nebbiolo, Muscadelle, Aramon, and Grand Noir are not listed individually.

Note that Gamay = Napa Gamay, Muscat Blanc = Muscat Canelli, St. Emilion = Ugni Blanc, and White Riesling = Johannisberg Riesling.

French-American Hybrids

Red Hybrids

Variety	Seedling No.
*Baco Noir	Baco No. 1
Bellandais	Seibel 14596
†Cascade	Seibel 13053
Chambourcin	Joannès-Seyve 26205
†Chancellor	Seibel 7053
Chelois	Seibel 10878
Colobel	Seibel 8357
De Chaunac	Seibel 9549
Landal	Landot 244
*Léon Millot	Kuhlmann 194-2
*Maréchal Foch	Kuhlmann 188-2
*Ravat Noir	Ravat 262
Villard Noir	Seyve-Villard 18315

White Hybrids

Variety	Seedling No.
*Aurore	Seibel 5279
*Ravat Blanc	Ravat 6
*Rayon d'Or	Seibel 4986
Seyval Blanc	Seyve-Villard 5276
†Verdelet	Seibel 9110
Vidal Blanc	Vidal 256
†Vignoles	Ravat 51
Villard Blanc	Seyve-Villard 12375

*Names that arose naturally in France.
†Names coined in 1970 by the New York Finger Lakes Wine Growers Association.
Names not marked were coined by a French official body several years ago.

Native American Grapes

Variety	Predominant Species Character
Bacchus	Riparia
Campbell's Early	Labrusca
Catawba	Labrusca
Clinton	Riparia
Concord	Labrusca
Cynthiana	Aestivalis
Delaware	Aestivalis-Vinifera
Diamond	Labrusca
Diana	Labrusca
Dutchess	Aestivalis-Vinifera
Elvira	Riparia
Fredonia	Labrusca
Iona	Labrusca
Isabella	Labrusca
Ives	Labrusca
James	Rotundifolia
Lenoir	Aestivalis
Missouri Riesling	Riparia
Moore's Diamond	Labrusca
Muscadine	Rotundifolia
Niagara	Labrusca
Noah	Riparia
Norton	Aestivalis
Ontario	Labrusca
Scuppernong	Rotundifolia
Steuben	Labrusca-Vinifera
Vergennes	Labrusca

American Viticultural Areas

American viticultural areas were first established in the early 1980s; a description of this system of appellations of origin will be found under Viticultural Area. All appellations are in California unless otherwise noted.

Viticultural Area

Anderson Valley
Alexander Valley
Altus (Arkansas)
Arkansas Mountain (Arkansas)
Arroyo Seco
Augusta (Missouri)
Bell Mountain (Texas)
Ben Lomond Mountain
Carmel Valley
Carneros
Catoctin (Maryland)
Central Coast
Central Delaware Valley (Pennsylvania, New Jersey)
Chalk Hill
Chalone
Cienega Valley
Clarksburg
Clear Lake
Cole Ranch
Columbia Valley (Washington, Oregon)
Cumberland Valley (Maryland, Pennsylvania)
Dry Creek Valley
Edna Valley
El Dorado
Fennville (Michigan)
Fiddletown
Finger Lakes (NY)
Grand River Valley (Ohio)
Green Valley (Solano County)
Green Valley (Sonoma County)
Guenoc Valley
The Hamptons, Long Island (NY)
Hermann (Missouri)
Howell Mountain
Hudson River Region (NY)
Isle St. George (Ohio)
Kanawha River Valley (West Virginia)
Knights Valley
Lake Erie (NY, Pennsylvania, Ohio)
Lake Michigan Shore (Michigan)
Lancaster Valley (Pennsylvania)
Leelanau Peninsula (Michigan)
Lime Kiln Valley
Linganore (Maryland)
Livermore Valley
Lodi
Loramie Creek (Ohio)
Madera
Martha's Vineyard (Massachusetts)
McDowell Valley

Viticultural Area

Mendocino
Merritt Island
Mesilla Valley (New Mexico, Texas)
Mimbres Valley (New Mexico)
Mississippi Delta (Mississippi, Tennessee, Louisiana)
Monterey
Monticello (Virginia)
Mt. Veeder
Napa Valley
North Coast
North Fork of Long Island (NY)
Northern Sonoma
North Yuba
Ohio River Valley (Ohio, Kentucky, Indiana, West Virginia)
Ozark Mountain (Arkansas, Missouri, Oklahoma)
Pacheco Pass
Paicines
Paso Robles
Potter Valley
Rocky Knob (Virginia)
Russian River Valley
San Benito
San Lucas
San Pasqual Valley
Santa Clara Valley
Santa Cruz Mountains
Santa Maria Valley
Santa Ynez Valley
Shenandoah Valley
Shenandoah Valley (Virginia, West Virginia)
Sierra Foothills
Sonoita (Arizona)
Sonoma Coast
Sonoma Mountain
Sonoma Valley
South Coast
Southeastern New England (Connecticut, Rhode Island, Massachusetts)
Stags Leap District
Suisun Valley
Temecula
Umpqua Valley (Oregon)
Walla Walla Valley (Washington, Oregon)
Wild Horse Valley (Washington, Oregon)
Willamette Valley (Oregon)
Willow Creek (Oregon)
Yakima Valley (Washington)
York Mountain

Australia

Vineyard Acreage by Variety

This chart shows the total vineyard acreage for Australia by variety in 1988-89. Although Australia has achieved success with its Cabernet Sauvignon, Chardonnay, and Sauvignon Blanc, the traditional varieties Shiraz (the Syrah of the Rhône Valley), Rhine Riesling (the Riesling of Germany), and Sémillon are still extensively planted. Note that most of the crop of Sultana (much of which is identical to the Thompson Seedless of California) is used as raisins and table grapes, as is virtually all of the Currant and Waltham Cross harvest. (And such "other" red and white varieties as Cardinal, Flame Seedless, Purple Cornichon, Red Emperor, Calmeria, and Ohanez – which amount to about 4,000 acres – are also used as raisins and table grapes.) Muscat Gordo Blanco is the Muscat of Alexandria.

Red Grapes	Acreage	White Grapes	Acreage
Cabernet Franc	620	Chardonnay	9,423
Cabernet Sauvignon	9,598	Chenin Blanc	1,388
Currant	3,278	Colombard	1,583
Grenache	5,488	Crouchen	1,210
Malbec	558	Doradillo	2,391
Mataro	1,628	Muscadelle	983
Merlot	946	Muscat Blanc	1,208
Muscat Hamburgh	1,539	Muscat Gordo Blanco	9,499
Pinot Meunier	69	Palomino & Pedro Ximenès	3,389
Pinot Noir	2,297	Rhine Riesling	8,907
Rubired	89	Sauvignon Blanc	2,201
Shiraz	12,150	Sémillon	6,701
Other Red Grapes	2,188	Sultana	
		Thompson Seedless	24,428
Total Red Grapes	43,670	Other	14,734
		Sylvaner	314
		Traminer	1,564
		Trebbiano	3,305
		Verdelho	334
		Waltham Cross	2,653
		Other White Grapes	1,129
		Total White Grapes	98,820
		Total Grapes	142,489

Acknowledgements

A number of people were kind enough to read sections of the revised manuscript, and I would like to thank them for their time and effort: David Adelsheim, Burton Anderson, Gerald Asher, William Bolter, José Ignacio Domecq, Jr., Robert Drouhin, Lamar Elmore, Barbara Ensrud, Tom Ferrell, Pasquale Iocca, Gerard Jaboulet, Hans-Walter Kendermann, Rémi Krug, Zelma Long, Robert Mayne, David Orr, Christian Pol-Roger, Robert M. Pool, Bruno Prats, Robin Reid, Alistair Robertson, Jancis Robinson, Brian St. Pierre, Johannes Selbach, Peter Allan Sichel, Bob Thompson, Miguel Torres, James Trezise, and Manfred Völpel.